Pauline Parallels

Pauline Parallels

A COMPREHENSIVE GUIDE

Walter T. Wilson

WESTMINSTER
JOHN KNOX PRESS
LOUISVILLE · KENTUCKY

© 2009 Walter T. Wilson

First edition
Westminster John Knox Press
Louisville, Kentucky

09 10 11 12 13 14 15 16 17 18—10 9 8 7 6 5 4 3 2 1

Material quoted from *The Old Testament Pseudepigrapha,* © 1983, James H. Charlesworth, ed., and published by Yale University Press, is used with the permission of Yale University Press.

Quotations from *The Dead Sea Scrolls Translated,* 2nd ed. (Leiden: Brill; Grand Rapids: Eerdmans Press, 1996), Florentino García Martínez, ed., Wilfred G. E. Watson, trans., are used with the permission of Koninklijke Brill NV.

Quotations from the Apocrypha are from the New Revised Standard Version of the Bible and are copyright © 1989 by the Division of Christian Education of the National Council of the Churches of Christ in the U.S.A. and are used by permission.

Scripture taken from the NEW AMERICAN STANDARD BIBLE®, © Copyright 1960, 1962, 1963, 1968, 1971, 1972, 1973, 1975, 1977, 1995 by The Lockman Foundation. Used by permission. (www.Lockman.org)

Book design by Drew Stevens

Library of Congress Cataloging-in-Publication Data

Bible. N.T. Epistles of Paul English. New American Standard. Selections. 2009.
  Pauline parallels : a comprehensive guide / Walter T. Wilson.—1st ed.
    p. cm.
  ISBN 978-0-664-23120-0 (alk. paper)
  1. Bible. N.T. Epistles of Paul—Harmonies, English. I. Wilson, Walter T. II. Title.
  BS2643.W55 2009
  227'.065—dc22

                                                        2008028022

PRINTED IN THE UNITED STATES OF AMERICA

Contents

Acknowledgments

Many people have helped with the production of this book. I am especially indebted to my research assistants, Emily Hayden, Cami Koepke, Sarah Rohrer, and Shea Tuttle, for all their hard work, as well as the editorial staff at Westminster John Knox Press, especially Jon Berquist and Daniel Braden. Along the way students in my courses on Paul at Candler School of Theology also offered many helpful suggestions. To one and all, my sincere thanks.

Introduction

In 1975 Fred Francis and Paul Sampley published the first edition of *Pauline Parallels*, with a second edition appearing in 1984.[1] Based on the Revised Standard Version, the volume presents ten of the apostle's letters in canonical order and divided into paragraphs, with relevant passages from elsewhere in the Pauline corpus set alongside each paragraph for easy comparison. Given how often we find Paul addressing the same topic in two or more places, the utility of such a reference tool is obvious, making it possible to see at a glance what in a particular text is characteristic of his thought and what is distinctive. This current attempt to compile Pauline parallels builds on the success of Francis and Sampley's fine work, which has proved valuable to so many students and pastors over the years.

Features of This Volume

1. In selecting parallels for their volume, Francis and Sampley were guided primarily by considerations for the similarity of literary structure and/or form between passages. Among other things, this meant that their selections tended to be quite long and as a result incorporated material that was not always thematically pertinent to the primary text. By contrast, the inclusion of parallels for this volume is based on the similarity of specific terms, concepts, and/or images between passages. These represent the sort of cross-references familiar to students from study Bibles, commentaries, and other basic research tools.[2] The version chosen for this volume, the New American Standard Bible, is particularly well suited for the presentation of such parallels, since it is among the most literal translations available.[3]

---

1. Fred O. Francis and J. Paul Sampley, eds., *Pauline Parallels*, 2nd ed. (Philadelphia: Fortress Press, 1984).

2. Students with knowledge of Greek will also be familiar with the references provided in the outer margin of Eberhard Nestle, Erwin Nestle, Kurt Aland, et al., eds., *Novum Testamentum Graece*, 27th ed. (Stuttgart: Deutsche Bibelgesellschaft, 1993); cf. Kurt Aland and Barbara Aland, *The Text of the New Testament* (Grand Rapids: Eerdmans; Leiden: Brill, 1987), 248–49.

3. The margins of the NASB also provide an abundance of cross-references; cf. Steven M. Sheeley and Robert N. Nash, *The Bible in English Translation: An Essential Guide* (Nashville: Abingdon Press, 1997), 38–41.

2. This volume covers all thirteen New Testament letters attributed to Paul, presented in canonical order. Paragraph divisions ordinarily follow those of the NASB, though on occasion larger paragraphs (e.g., Eph. 2:11–22) have been divided and shorter paragraphs (e.g., Gal. 1:6–9, 10) have been combined.

3. The biblical parallels for each paragraph are organized into three sections: (1) parallels from the same letter as the paragraph; (2) parallels from other Pauline letters; (3) parallels from biblical texts outside the Pauline corpus. Within each section parallels are presented in canonical order. For many paragraphs a fourth section, with noncanonical parallels, is also provided. In order to conserve space, parallels from the paragraphs that immediately precede and immediately follow a given paragraph are not included. So, for example, parallels for Ephesians 2:1–10 from Ephesians 1:15–23 and 2:11–16 are not provided in the section for that paragraph (see below).

4. Key words and word forms that the paragraph has in common with the parallels are italicized in the latter.[4] Ordinarily, if the common word or word form occurs more than once in a given parallel, it is italicized either the first time it occurs or in the place where its usage most clearly approximates that in the paragraph. So, for example, among the parallels for Romans 3:21–26 is Galatians 2:16 (". . . not justified by the works of the Law but through faith in Christ Jesus, even we have *believed* in Christ Jesus, so that we may be *justified* by faith . . ."), with *believed* corresponding to "believe" in Romans 3:22, and the second instance of *justified* corresponding to the use of "justified" in Romans 3:24. Unless they are part of a longer phrase, common terms such as "God," "Christ," and "Lord" are usually not italicized.

5. The capitalization of text in the New Testament of the NASB (as, e.g., in Rom. 9:27–33) as used "to indicate Old Testament quotations or obvious references to Old Testament texts" has been retained yet with small caps changed to full caps.[5] To conserve space, poetic writings are not printed with the NASB's paragraph breaks but as a continuous text, though the capitalization of the first word of each line is retained so as to show the text's structure (e.g., Prov. 3:27: "Do not withhold good from those to whom it is due, When it is in your power to do it.").

Suggestions for Using This Volume

This study tool is meant to be employed as part of a comprehensive approach to the interpretation of Paul's letters. For a basic orientation, readers are encouraged to consult John Hayes and Carl Holladay's *Biblical Exegesis: A Beginner's Handbook*.[6] Among other things, they emphasize the importance of doing concordance

---

4. Note that this differs from the text of the NASB, where italics are used "to indicate words which are not found in the original Hebrew, Aramaic, or Greek but implied by it" (from the NASB's "Explanation of General Format").

5. See the NASB's "Explanation of General Format."

6. John H. Hayes and Carl R. Holladay, *Biblical Exegesis: A Beginner's Handbook*, 3rd ed. (Louisville, KY: Westminster John Knox Press, 2007).

work when exegeting a passage, preferably with an analytical concordance. It should be emphasized that the current volume in no way represents a substitute for such work. In addition, it is important for students to acquire a working knowledge of the entire collection of Paul's writings, their major themes, and the challenges associated with their interpretation. Among many excellent guides, mention may be made of Charles Cousar's *The Letters of Paul*.[7] Before focusing on a particular passage, it is also important to gain an overview of the letter in which it occurs. For this, relevant material from a Bible encyclopedia, such as the *Anchor Bible Dictionary*,[8] or an introductory textbook, such as Luke Johnson's *The Writings of the New Testament*,[9] will be helpful. Such sources also provide bibliographies of commentaries and other publications where more detailed information can be found. Study Bibles, such as the *New Oxford Annotated Bible*,[10] will also provide brief introductions to each text as well as annotations to each passage.

Bearing all this in mind, readers are encouraged to consider the following suggestions when using this book:

— One of the first tasks for the interpreter is to determine the boundaries of the passage under investigation, being particularly careful not to be misled by paragraph or chapter divisions. For example, a study of "the prince of the power of the air" in Ephesians 2:2 would need to take into consideration not only the material in 2:1–10, but also what Paul has just said about "power" in the immediately preceding paragraph, 1:15–23. Since parallels from adjacent paragraphs are not included in this volume (see no. 3 above), it is essential in any interpretation to cut across such textual boundaries and read one's passage within its immediate literary context.

— The first section following each paragraph contains parallels from the same letter as that paragraph. In perusing these, students will want to be attentive to how Paul may be developing a particular theme or argument over the course of the letter. A glance at the parallels for 2 Corinthians 1:3–11, for example, indicates that when he mentions the experience of affliction in 1:4 he is actually introducing a term to which he will repeatedly return later in the letter. Particular attention should be paid to parallels that contain clusters of common words. For example, among the parallels for 2 Corinthians 2:5–13 is 2 Corinthians 7:5–15, with which it shares a number of terms (sorrow, comfort, obedience, Macedonia, Titus), suggesting that the latter is in some sense a resumption or continuation of the former.

— The second section following each paragraph contains parallels from other Pauline letters. Examining these provides an opportunity to read across the different letters, comparing the different ways in which the apostle articulates

---

7. Charles B. Cousar, *The Letters of Paul* (Nashville: Abingdon Press, 1996).
8. David Noel Freedman, ed., *The Anchor Bible Dictionary*, 6 vols. (New York: Doubleday, 1992).
9. Luke Timothy Johnson, *The Writings of the New Testament: An Interpretation*, rev. ed. (Minneapolis: Fortress Press, 1999).
10. Michael D. Coogan, ed., *The New Oxford Annotated Bible*, 3rd ed. (Oxford: Oxford University Press, 2001).

the same concept or argument. Romans 8:29, for example, refers to the process of being conformed to the image of Christ, an idea that is at work in 1 Corinthians 15:49; 2 Corinthians 3:18; Philippians 3:10, 21; and Colossians 3:9–10 as well, though in each case there are certain distinct variations and emphases depending on the epistolary context.

— The third section following each paragraph contains parallels from biblical texts outside the Pauline corpus. With regard to Old Testament parallels, attention should be paid not only to obvious citations (Rom. 3:9–20 has multiple examples), but also to the possibility of more subtle allusions and echoes. The description of the *parousia* in 1 Thessalonians 4:13–18, for example, shares a number of elements (descent of the Lord, meeting, cloud, trumpet) with the theophany in Exodus 19:16–18, even if Paul does not refer to that text directly. Parallels with New Testament texts, especially Acts, are helpful in shedding light on some of the specific figures and events to which he alludes (e.g., compare 2 Cor. 11:30–33 with Acts 9:22–25). Such comparisons can also illuminate some of the places where the apostle may be utilizing traditional concepts and language. For example, comparison of the christological affirmation in Romans 1:3–4 with Acts 2:36; 13:32–33; and 1 Peter 3:18 suggests that here Paul draws on or incorporates some sort of preexisting confessional statement.

— Following many paragraphs is a fourth section with noncanonical parallels. Consideration for these texts reveals some of the ways in which Paul's thought and language participate in the broader religious and cultural trends of his time. Returning to Romans 1:3–4, comparison with 4Q174 indicates that the early Christians would not have been alone in describing a messianic figure descended from the line of David and referred to as God's Son. For those interested, a number of helpful guides to such parallels are available, including the *Hellenistic Commentary to the New Testament*.[11]

— In assessing parallels, readers should be alert to how the same word or phrase can be employed in different ways or with different connotations. For example, in Romans 7:17–18, Paul laments that sin "dwells" in him. A bit later he resorts to the same imagery, though in a contrastive way, not with reference to sin but with reference to the Spirit of God (Rom. 8:9; cf. 1 Cor. 3:16). Similarly, a glance at the parallels for 1 Timothy 1:12–17 indicates that it would not have been unusual for Paul to open a letter by giving thanks for divine grace. However, in a passage like 1 Corinthians 1:4, it is for the readers' experience of grace that he gives thanks, while in 1 Timothy it is for the grace that he has experienced himself. In this regard the 1 Timothy passage more closely resembles Galatians 1:13–16, though the autobiographical reflections in that passage manifest their own set of priorities.

---

11. M. Eugene Boring, Klaus Berger, and Carsten Colpe, eds., *Hellenistic Commentary to the New Testament* (Nashville: Abingdon Press, 1995).

— Although the italicized words can serve as an aid to identifying interconnections between texts, they hardly exhaust the possible comparisons that can be made between the parallels and the main passage. Indeed, in many instances some of the most important parallels come from texts that have no italicized words at all. This is evident, for example, in the portrayal of Christ's death as a "propitiation in His blood" in Romans 3:25. Although the term "propitiation" does not occur elsewhere in the Pauline corpus (cf. Heb. 2:17; 1 John 2:2), comparison may nevertheless be made with Romans 8:3 (which describes Christ's death as a sin offering) as well as 1 Corinthians 5:7 and Ephesians 5:2 (which describes it as a sacrifice).

— No translation, even a rigorously literal one, can always follow its source strictly and consistently. So even with the NASB, one cannot assume that a particular Greek term is always rendered with the same English term, or that a particular English term always corresponds to the same Greek term. To give just one example, we may compare Ephesians 6:22 ("I have sent him to you for this very purpose, so that you may know about us, and that he may comfort your hearts") and Colossians 4:8 ("For I have sent him to you for this very purpose, that you may know about our circumstances and that he may encourage your hearts"). In Greek the two verses are exactly the same. However, besides other differences, in the former the NASB translates the Greek verb *parakalein* as "comfort," while in the latter it is translated as "encourage." Meanwhile, in 1 Thessalonians 5:14, the term "encourage" is used to translate not *parakalein*, but an entirely different verb, *paramytheisthai*. When examining the material in this volume, then, and especially the italicized material, it is important to bear in mind that the parallels are based on the NASB and not the original text. By consulting commentaries, one may gain a clearer sense of the Greek upon which the English translation is based. Students should also be in the practice of using the NASB in conjunction with other versions, such as the NIV or NRSV.

Sources for Noncanonical Parallels

Translations for all books in the Old Testament Apocrypha are from the New Revised Standard Version (1989).

Translations for Pseudo-Phocylides' *Sentences* are from Walter T. Wilson, *The Sentences of Pseudo-Phocylides,* Commentaries on Early Jewish Literature (Berlin: de Gruyter, 2005). Translations for all other texts in the Old Testament Pseudepigrapha are from James H. Charlesworth, ed., *The Old Testament Pseudepigrapha,* 2 vols. (Garden City, NY: Doubleday, 1983–85).

Translations for the *Genesis Apocryphon* are from Joseph A. Fitzmyer, *The Genesis Apocryphon: A Commentary,* 3rd ed. (Rome: Pontifical Biblical Institute, 2004). Translations for all other Qumran texts are from Florentino García Martínez, ed., *The Dead Sea Scrolls Translated,* 2nd ed. (Leiden: Brill; Grand Rapids: Eerdmans, 1996).

Translations for the Mishnah are from Jacob Neusner, ed., *The Mishnah: A New Translation* (New Haven, CT: Yale University Press, 1988). Translations for *Targum Neofiti* are from Martin McNamara, *Targum Neofiti 1: Deuteronomy* (Collegeville, MN: Liturgical Press, 1997).

Translations for Philo's *Questions and Answers on Genesis and Exodus* are from Ralph Marcus, ed., *Philo: Supplement,* 2 vols., Loeb Classical Library (London: Heinemann; Cambridge: Harvard University Press, 1953).

Translations for texts from the Nag Hammadi Library are from James M. Robinson, ed., *The Nag Hammadi Library in English* (3rd ed.; San Francisco: Harper & Row, 1988). Translations for the *Acts of Paul and Thecla* are from J. K. Elliott, *The Apocryphal New Testament* (Oxford: Clarendon Press, 1993).

The translation of Posidonius as cited by Galen, *On the Teaching of Hippocrates and Plato,* is from *The New Testament Background,* ed. C. K. Barrett, rev. ed. (San Francisco: HarperCollins, 1987), 70.

The translation of Statutes of a Cultic Fellowship (P.Lond. 2710) is from H.-J. Klauck, *The Religious Context of Early Christianity* (Edinburgh: T. & T. Clark, 2000), 49.

The translation of the Letter to Theon (P.Oxy. 18.2190) is from E. Lobel, C. H. Roberts, and E. P. Wegener, *The Oxyrhynchus Papyri,* Part 18 (London: Egypt Exploration Society, 1941), 147–48.

The translation of Catullus's *Poems* is from D. Mulrow, *The Complete Poetry of Catullus* (Madison: University of Wisconsin Press, 2002), 56.

Unless otherwise noted, translations for all Greek and Latin authors (including Philo and Josephus) were newly prepared for this volume.

Abbreviations for Collections of Papyri and Inscriptions

BGU *Aegyptische Urkunden aus den Königlichen Museen zu Berlin, Griechische Urkunden.* 4 vols. Berlin: Weidmann, 1895–1912.

CI *Corinth: The Inscriptions.* Edited by John Harvey Kent. Vol. 8, part 3. Princeton, NJ: American School of Classical Studies at Athens, 1966.

P.Col. *Columbia Papyri.* Edited by William L. Westermann and Elizabeth S. Hasenoehrl. Greek Series. Vol. 3, *Zenon Papyri.* New York: Columbia University Press, 1934.

PGM *Papyri graecae magicae: Die griechischen Zauberpapyri.* Edited by K. Preisendanz. Berlin: Teubner, 1928. Translations are from *The Greek Magical Papyri in Translation.* Edited by Hans Dieter Betz. 2nd ed. Chicago: University of Chicago Press, 1992.

P.Lond. *Greek Papyri in the British Museum.* Edited by Frederic G. Kenyon, H. Idris Bell, and Walter E. Crum. 5 vols. London: British Museum, 1893–1917.

P.Mert. *A Descriptive Catalogue of the Greek Papyri in the Collection of Wilfred Merton.* Edited by H. Idris Bell and C. H. Roberts. Vol. 1. London: Walker, 1948.

P.Mich. *Papyri in the University of Michigan Collection.* Edited by John G. Winter. Ann Arbor: University of Michigan Press, 1936.

P.Oxy. *The Oxyrhynchus Papyri.* London: Egypt Exploration Society. Part 1, edited by Bernard P. Grenfell and Arthur S. Hunt, 1898. Part 12, edited by Bernard P. Grenfell and Arthur S. Hunt, 1916. Part 18, edited by E. Lobel, C. H. Roberts, and E. P. Wegener, 1941.

SIG *Sylloge inscriptionum graecarum.* Edited by Wilhelm Dittenberger. 4 vols. Hildesheim: Olms, 1960.

Romans

Romans 1:1–7

Paul, a bond-servant of Christ Jesus, called as an apostle, set apart for the gospel of God, ²which He promised beforehand through His prophets in the holy Scriptures, ³concerning His Son, who was born of a descendant of David according to the flesh, ⁴who was declared the Son of God with power by the resurrection from the dead, according to the Spirit of holiness, Jesus Christ our Lord, ⁵through whom we have received grace and apostleship to bring about the obedience of faith among all the Gentiles for His name's sake, ⁶among whom you also are the called of Jesus Christ; ⁷to all who are beloved of God in Rome, called as saints: Grace to you and peace from God our Father and the Lord Jesus Christ.

ROMANS PARALLELS

Romans 6:5–6

For if we have become united with Him in the likeness of His death, certainly we shall also be in the likeness of His *resurrection*, ⁶knowing this, that our old self was crucified with Him, in order that our body of sin might be done away with, so that we would no longer be slaves to sin.

Romans 9:23–24

And He did so to make known the riches of His glory upon vessels of mercy, which He prepared *beforehand* for glory, ²⁴even us, whom He also *called*, not from among Jews only, but also from among *Gentiles*.

Romans 11:13–14

But I am speaking to you who are Gentiles. Inasmuch then as I am an *apostle* of *Gentiles*, I magnify my ministry, ¹⁴if somehow I might move to jealousy my fellow countrymen and save some of them.

Romans 15:15–16

But I have written very boldly to you on some points so as to remind you again, because of the *grace* that was given me from God, ¹⁶to be a minister of Christ Jesus to *the Gentiles*, ministering as a priest *the gospel of God*, so that my offering of the Gentiles may become acceptable, sanctified by the Holy Spirit.

Romans 16:25–26

Now to Him who is able to establish you according to my *gospel* and the preaching of Jesus Christ, according to the revelation of the mystery which has been kept secret for long ages past, ²⁶but now is manifested, and by *the Scriptures* of the *prophets*, according to the commandment of the eternal God, has been made known to all the nations, leading to *obedience of faith*.

OTHER PAULINE PARALLELS

1 Corinthians 1:1–3

Paul, called as an apostle of Jesus Christ by the will of God, and Sosthenes our brother, ²To the church of God which is at Corinth, to those who have been sanctified in Christ Jesus, *saints* by *calling*, with all who in every place call on the name of our Lord Jesus Christ, their Lord and ours: ³*Grace to you and peace from God our Father and the Lord Jesus Christ.*

Galatians 1:15–16

But when God, who had *set me apart* even from my mother's womb and *called* me through His *grace*, was pleased ¹⁶to reveal

His Son in me so that I might preach Him among *the Gentiles*, I did not immediately consult with flesh and blood.

Galatians 2:7, 9
But on the contrary, seeing that I had been entrusted with *the gospel* to the uncircumcised, just as Peter had been to the circumcised . . . [9]and recognizing the *grace* that had been given to me, James and Cephas and John, who were reputed to be pillars, gave to me and Barnabas the right hand of fellowship, so that we might go to *the Gentiles* and they to the circumcised.

Philippians 1:1–2
Paul and Timothy, *bond-servants of Christ Jesus*, To all the *saints* in Christ Jesus who are in Philippi, including the overseers and deacons: [2]*Grace to you and peace from God our Father and the Lord Jesus Christ.*

Philippians 3:8, 10–11
More than that, I count all things to be loss in view of the surpassing value of knowing Christ Jesus my Lord, for whom I have suffered the loss of all things, and count them but rubbish so that I may gain Christ, . . . [10]that I may know Him and the *power* of His resurrection and the fellowship of His sufferings, being conformed to His death; [11]in order that I may attain to *the resurrection from the dead.*

1 Timothy 3:16
By common confession, great is the mystery of godliness: He who was revealed in *the flesh*, Was vindicated in *the Spirit*, Seen by angels, Proclaimed among the nations, Believed on in the world, Taken up in glory.

2 Timothy 2:8–9
Remember Jesus Christ, risen *from the dead*, *descendant of David*, according to my *gospel*, [9]for which I suffer hardship even to imprisonment as a criminal; but the word of God is not imprisoned.

Titus 1:1–4
Paul, a bond-servant of God and *an apostle* of Jesus Christ, for the *faith* of those chosen of God and the knowledge of the truth which is according to godliness, [2]in the hope of eternal life, which God, who cannot lie, *promised* long ages ago, [3]but at the proper time manifested, even His word, in the proclamation with which I was entrusted according to the commandment of God our Savior, [4]To Titus, my true child in a common faith: *Grace* and *peace from God* the *Father* and *Christ Jesus* our Savior.

OTHER BIBLICAL PARALLELS

Jeremiah 23:5
"Behold, the days are coming," declares the LORD, "When I will raise up for *David* a righteous Branch; And He will reign as king and act wisely And do justice and righteousness in the land."

Matthew 1:1
The record of the genealogy of Jesus the Messiah, the son of *David*, the son of Abraham . . .

Acts 2:36
"Therefore let all the house of Israel know for certain that God has made Him both Lord and Christ—this Jesus whom you crucified."

Acts 9:15–16
But the Lord said to him [Ananias], "Go, for he is a chosen instrument of Mine, to bear My name before *the Gentiles* and kings and the sons of Israel; [16]for I will show him how much he must suffer for My *name's sake.*"

Acts 13:2
While they were ministering to the Lord and fasting, the Holy Spirit said, "*Set apart for Me Barnabas and Saul for the work to which I have called* them."

Acts 13:32–33
"And we preach to you the good news of the *promise* made to the fathers, [33]that God has fulfilled this promise to our children in that He raised up Jesus, as it is also written in the second Psalm, 'YOU ARE MY *SON*; TODAY I HAVE BEGOTTEN YOU.'"

1 Peter 3:18
For Christ also died for sins once for all, the just for the unjust, so that He might bring us to God, having been put to death in *the flesh*, but made alive in *the spirit.*

4QFlorilegium *(4Q174) 1–3 1.11–13*

" . . . I will be a father to him and he will be a *son* to me." This (refers to the) "branch of *David*," who will arise with the Interpreter of the law who [12][will rise up] in Zi[on in] the last days, as it is written: "I will raise up the hut of David which has fallen." This (refers to) "the hut of [13]David which has fallen," who will arise to save Israel.

Romans 1:8–15

First, I thank my God through Jesus Christ for you all, because your faith is being proclaimed throughout the whole world. [9]For God, whom I serve in my spirit in the preaching of the gospel of His Son, is my witness as to how unceasingly I make mention of you, [10]always in my prayers making request, if perhaps now at last by the will of God I may succeed in coming to you. [11]For I long to see you so that I may impart some spiritual gift to you, that you may be established; [12]that is, that I may be encouraged together with you while among you, each of us by the other's faith, both yours and mine. [13]I do not want you to be unaware, brethren, that often I have planned to come to you (and have been prevented so far) so that I may obtain some fruit among you also, even as among the rest of the Gentiles. [14]I am under obligation both to Greeks and to barbarians, both to the wise and to the foolish. [15]So, for my part, I am eager to preach the gospel to you also who are in Rome.

Romans 11:13

But I am speaking to you who are *Gentiles*. Inasmuch then as I am an apostle of Gentiles, I magnify my ministry.

Romans 15:15–16

But I have written very boldly to you on some points so as to remind you again, because of the grace that was given me from God, [16]to be a minister of Christ Jesus to *the Gentiles*, ministering as a priest *the gospel* of God, so that my offering of the Gentiles may become acceptable, sanctified by the Holy Spirit.

Romans 15:20, 22–25

And thus I aspired *to preach the gospel*, not where Christ was already named, so that I would not build on another man's foundation; . . . [22]For this reason I have often been *prevented* from *coming to you*; [23]but now, with no further place for me in these regions, and since I have had for many years a *longing* to come to you [24]whenever I go to Spain—for I hope to see you in passing, and to be helped on my way there by you, when I have first enjoyed your company for a while— [25]but now, I am going to Jerusalem serving the saints.

Romans 15:30–32

Now I urge you, brethren, by our Lord Jesus Christ and by the love of the Spirit, to strive together with me in your *prayers* to God for me, [31]that I may be rescued from those who are disobedient in Judea, and that my service for Jerusalem may prove acceptable to the saints; [32]so that I may *come to you* in joy *by the will of God* and find refreshing rest in your company.

Romans 16:19

For the report of your obedience has reached to all; therefore I am rejoicing over you, but I want you to be *wise* in what is good and innocent in what is evil.

Romans 16:25

Now to Him who is able to *establish* you according to my *gospel* and the *preaching* of Jesus Christ, according to the revelation of the mystery which has been kept secret for long ages past.

1 Corinthians 1:26–27

For consider your calling, brethren, that there were not many *wise* according to the flesh, not many mighty, not many noble; [27]but God has chosen the *foolish* things of the world to shame the wise, and God has chosen the weak things of the world to shame the things which are strong.

1 Corinthians 9:16

For if I *preach the gospel*, I have nothing to boast of, for I am under compulsion; for woe is me if I do not preach the gospel.

1 Corinthians 14:12

So also you, since you are zealous of *spiritual gifts*, seek to abound for the edification of the church.

2 Corinthians 1:8

For we *do not want you to be unaware, brethren*, of our affliction which came to us in Asia, that we were burdened excessively, beyond our strength, so that we despaired even of life.

Ephesians 1:15–16

For this reason I too, having heard of the *faith* in the Lord Jesus which exists among you and your love for all the saints, [16]do not cease giving *thanks for you,* while *making mention of you in my prayers.*

Philippians 1:3–4, 8

I thank *my God* in all my remembrance of you, [4]*always* offering *prayer* with joy in my every prayer for you all. . . . [8]For *God is my witness,* how *I long* for you all with the affection of Christ Jesus.

Colossians 3:11

. . . a renewal in which there is no distinction between *Greek* and Jew, circumcised and uncircumcised, *barbarian*, Scythian, slave and freeman, but Christ is all, and in all.

1 Thessalonians 1:2, 8

We give *thanks* to *God* always *for all* of *you, making mention of you* in our *prayers*; . . . [8]For the word of the Lord has sounded forth from you, not only in Macedonia and Achaia, but also in every place your *faith* toward God has gone forth, so that we have no need to say anything.

1 Thessalonians 2:17–18

But we, brethren, having been taken away from you for a short while—in person, not in spirit—were all the more *eager* with great desire to *see* your face. [18]For we wanted *to come to you*—I, Paul, more than once—and yet Satan hindered us.

1 Thessalonians 3:2, 6

And we sent Timothy, our brother and God's fellow worker in *the gospel* of Christ, to strengthen and *encourage* you as to your *faith.* . . . [6]But now that Timothy has come to

us from you, and has brought us good news of your faith and love, and that you always think kindly of us, longing to see us just as we also *long to see you.*

1 Timothy 4:14

Do not neglect the *spiritual gift* within you, which was bestowed on you through prophetic utterance with the laying on of hands by the presbytery.

2 Timothy 1:3–4

I thank God, whom I serve with a clear conscience the way my forefathers did, as I constantly remember you *in my prayers* night and day, [4]*longing to see you,* even as I recall your tears, so that I may be filled with joy.

1 Samuel 20:12

Then Jonathan said to David, "The LORD, the *God* of Israel, be *witness*! When I have sounded out my father about this time tomorrow, or the third day, behold, if there is good feeling toward David, shall I not then send to you and make it known to you?"

Acts 19:21

Now after these things were finished, Paul purposed in the spirit to go to Jerusalem after he had passed through Macedonia and Achaia, saying, "After I have been there, I must also see *Rome.*"

Romans 1:16–17

For I am not ashamed of the gospel, for it is the power of God for salvation to everyone who believes, to the Jew first and also to the Greek. [17]For in it the righteousness of God is revealed from faith to faith; as it is written, "BUT THE RIGHTEOUS man SHALL LIVE BY FAITH."

Romans 2:9–10

There will be tribulation and distress for every soul of man who does evil, of the Jew first and also of the Greek, [10]but glory and honor and peace to everyone who does good, *to the Jew first and also to the Greek.*

Romans 3:1–2

Then what advantage has *the Jew*? Or what is the benefit of circumcision? [2]Great in every respect. First of all, that they were entrusted with the oracles of God.

Romans 3:21–22

But now apart from the Law *the righteousness of God* has been manifested, being witnessed by the Law and the Prophets, [22]even the righteousness of God through *faith* in Jesus Christ for all those who *believe*; for there is no distinction.

Romans 4:4–5

Now to the one who works, his wage is not credited as a favor, but as what is due. [5]But to the one who does not work, but *believes* in Him who justifies the ungodly, his *faith* is credited as *righteousness*.

Romans 9:30–31

What shall we say then? That Gentiles, who did not pursue righteousness, attained righteousness, even the *righteousness* which is by *faith*; [31]but Israel, pursuing a law of righteousness, did not arrive at that law.

Romans 10:10–12

For with the heart a person *believes*, resulting in *righteousness*, and with the mouth he confesses, resulting in *salvation*. [11]For the Scripture says, "WHOEVER BELIEVES IN HIM WILL NOT BE DISAPPOINTED." [12]For there is no distinction between *Jew* and *Greek*; for the same Lord is Lord of all, abounding in riches for all who call on Him.

Romans 15:15–16, 18–19

But I have written very boldly to you on some points so as to remind you again, because of the grace that was given me from God, [16]to be a minister of Christ Jesus to the Gentiles, ministering as a priest *the gospel* of God, so that my offering of the Gentiles may become acceptable, sanctified by the Holy Spirit. . . . [18]For I will not presume to speak of anything except what Christ has accomplished through me, resulting in the obedience of the Gentiles by word and deed, [19]in the *power* of signs and wonders, in the power of the Spirit; so that from Jerusalem and round about as far as Illyricum I have fully preached the gospel of Christ.

1 Corinthians 1:23–24

But we preach Christ crucified, to Jews a stumbling block and to Gentiles foolishness, [24]but to those who are the called, both *Jews* and *Greeks*, Christ *the power of God* and the wisdom of God.

2 Corinthians 5:21

He made Him who knew no sin to be sin on our behalf, so that we might become *the righteousness of God* in Him.

Galatians 3:11–12

Now that no one is justified by the Law before God is evident; for, "THE RIGHTEOUS MAN SHALL LIVE BY FAITH." [12]However, the Law is not of faith; on the contrary, "HE WHO PRACTICES THEM SHALL LIVE BY THEM."

Philippians 3:8–10

More than that, I count all things to be loss in view of the surpassing value of knowing Christ Jesus my Lord, for whom I have suffered the loss of all things, and count them but rubbish so that I may gain Christ, [9]and may be found in Him, not having a righteousness of my own derived from the Law, but that which is through faith in Christ, the *righteousness* which comes from God on the basis of *faith*, [10]that I may know Him and the *power* of His resurrection and the fellowship of His sufferings, being conformed to His death.

2 Timothy 1:12

For this reason I also suffer these things, but *I am not ashamed*; for I know whom I have *believed* and I am convinced that He is able to guard what I have entrusted to Him until that day.

Psalm 31:1

In You, O LORD, I have taken refuge; Let me never be *ashamed*; In Your *righteousness* deliver me.

Psalm 98:2

The LORD has made known His *salvation*; He has *revealed* His *righteousness* in the sight of the nations.

Isaiah 46:13

"I bring near My *righteousness*, it is not far off; And My *salvation* will not delay. And I will grant salvation in Zion, And My glory for Israel."

Habakkuk 2:4

"Behold, as for the proud one, His soul is not right within him; *But the righteous* will *live by* his *faith.*"

Luke 9:26

"For whoever is *ashamed* of Me and My words, the Son of Man will be ashamed of him when He comes in His glory, and the glory of the Father and of the holy angels."

Acts 3:12, 26

But when Peter saw this, he replied to the people, "Men of Israel, why are you amazed at this, or why do you gaze at us, as if by our own power or piety we had made him walk? . . . [26]For you *first*, God raised up His Servant and sent Him to bless you by turning every one of you from your wicked ways."

Acts 15:7, 9

After there had been much debate, Peter stood up and said to them, "Brethren, you know that in the early days God made a choice among you, that by my mouth the Gentiles would hear the word of *the gospel* and *believe.* . . . [9]and He made no distinction between us and them, cleansing their hearts by *faith.*"

Hebrews 10:36–39

For you have need of endurance, so that when you have done the will of God, you may receive what was promised. [37]FOR YET IN A VERY LITTLE WHILE, HE WHO IS COMING WILL COME, AND WILL NOT DELAY. [38]*BUT MY RIGHTEOUS* ONE *SHALL LIVE BY FAITH*; AND IF HE SHRINKS BACK, MY SOUL HAS NO PLEASURE IN HIM. [39]But we are not of those who shrink back to destruction, but of those who have faith to the preserving of the soul.

Romans 1:18–25

For the wrath of God is revealed from heaven against all ungodliness and unrighteousness of men who suppress the truth in unrighteousness, [19]because that which is known about God is evident within them; for God made it evident to them. [20]For since the creation of the world His invisible attributes, His eternal power and divine nature, have been clearly seen, being understood through what has been made, so that they are without excuse. [21]For even though they knew God, they did not honor Him as God or give thanks, but they became futile in their speculations, and their foolish heart was darkened. [22]Professing to be wise, they became fools, [23]and exchanged the glory of the incorruptible God for an image in the form of corruptible man and of birds and four-footed animals and crawling creatures. [24]Therefore God gave them over in the lusts of their hearts to impurity, so that their bodies would be dishonored among them. [25]For they exchanged the truth of God for a lie, and worshiped and served the creature rather than the Creator, who is blessed forever. Amen.

ROMANS PARALLELS

Romans 5:8–9

But God demonstrates His own love toward us, in that while we were yet sinners, Christ died for us. [9]Much more then, having now been justified by His blood, we shall be saved from *the wrath of God* through Him.

Romans 6:19

I am speaking in human terms because of the weakness of your flesh. For just as you presented your members as slaves to *impurity* and to lawlessness, resulting in further lawlessness, so now present your members as slaves to righteousness, resulting in sanctification.

Romans 13:14

But put on the Lord Jesus Christ, and make no provision for the flesh in regard to its *lusts.*

OTHER PAULINE PARALLELS

1 Corinthians 1:20

Where is the *wise* man? Where is the scribe? Where is the debater of this age? Has not God made *foolish* the wisdom of the world?

Ephesians 2:1–3

And you were dead in your trespasses and sins, [2]in which you formerly walked according to the course of this world, according to the prince of the power of the air, of the spirit that is now working in the sons of disobedience. ³Among them we too all formerly lived in the *lusts* of our flesh, indulging the desires of the flesh and of the mind, and were by nature children of *wrath*, even as the rest.

Ephesians 4:17–19
So this I say, and affirm together with the Lord, that you walk no longer just as the Gentiles also walk, in the *futility* of their mind, ¹⁸being *darkened* in their understanding, excluded from the life of God because of the ignorance that is in them, because of the hardness of their *heart*; ¹⁹and they, having become callous, have given themselves over to sensuality for the practice of every kind of *impurity* with greediness.

2 Thessalonians 2:11–12
For this reason God will send upon them a deluding influence so that they will believe what is false, ¹²in order that they all may be judged who did not believe *the truth*, but took pleasure in wickedness.

1 Timothy 1:17
Now to the King *eternal*, immortal, *invisible*, the only God, be *honor* and glory forever and ever. Amen.

Psalm 19:1–2
The heavens are telling of *the glory of God*; And their expanse is declaring the work of His hands. ²Day to day pours forth speech, And night to night reveals knowledge.

Psalm 81:11–12
"But My people did not listen to My voice, And Israel did not obey Me. ¹²So I *gave them over* to the stubbornness of their *heart*, To walk in their own devices."

Psalm 106:19–20
They made a calf in Horeb And *worshiped* a molten *image*. ²⁰Thus they *exchanged* their *glory For* the image of an ox that eats grass.

Isaiah 40:26
Lift up your eyes on high And *see* who has *created* these stars, The One who leads forth their host by number, He calls them all by name; Because of the greatness of His might and the strength of His *power*, Not one of them is missing.

Acts 14:16–17
"In the generations gone by He permitted all the nations to go their own ways; ¹⁷and yet He did not leave Himself without witness, in that He did good and gave you rains from heaven and fruitful seasons, satisfying your hearts with food and gladness."

OTHER BIBLICAL PARALLELS

Exodus 20:4–5
"You shall not make for yourself an idol, or any likeness of what is in heaven above or on the earth beneath or in the water under the earth. ⁵You shall not *worship* them or *serve* them; for I, the LORD your God, am a jealous God."

Deuteronomy 4:15–18
"So watch yourselves carefully, since you did not see any form on the day the LORD spoke to you at Horeb from the midst of the fire, ¹⁶so that you do not act corruptly and make a graven *image* for yourselves in the form of any figure, the likeness of male or female, ¹⁷the likeness of any *animal* that is on the earth, the likeness of any winged *bird* that flies in the sky, ¹⁸the likeness of anything that creeps on the ground, the likeness of any fish that is in the water below the earth."

NONCANONICAL PARALLELS

Wisdom of Solomon 13:1, 5, 10
For all people who were ignorant of God were *foolish* by nature; and they were unable from the good things that are *seen* to know the one who exists, nor did they recognize the artisan while paying heed to his works; . . . ⁵For from the greatness and beauty of *created* things comes a corresponding perception of their *Creator*. . . . ¹⁰But miserable, with their hopes set on dead things, are those who give the name "gods" to the works of human hands, gold and silver fashioned with skill, and likenesses of *animals*, or a useless stone, the work of an ancient hand.

Wisdom of Solomon 14:11–12, 27
Therefore there will be a visitation also upon the heathen idols, because, though part of what God *created*, they became an abomination, snares for human souls and a

trap for the feet of the *foolish*. [12]For the idea of making idols was the beginning of fornication, and the invention of them was the corruption of life; . . . [27]For the *worship* of idols not to be named is the beginning and cause and end of every evil.

1 Enoch *99:7–9*

(And those) who worship stones, and those who carve *images* of gold and silver and wood and clay, . . . they shall get no manner of help in them. [8]They shall become wicked on account of the folly of their *hearts*; their eyes will be blindfolded on account of the fear of their hearts. . . . [9]They shall become wicked and fearful through them, for they wrought all their deeds in falsehood and *worshiped* stone.

2 Baruch *54:17–18*

But now, turn yourselves to destruction, you *unrighteous* ones who are living now, for you will be visited suddenly, since you have once rejected the understanding of the Most High. [18]For his works have not taught you, nor has the artful work of his *creation* which has existed always persuaded you.

Romans 1:26–32

For this reason God gave them over to degrading passions; for their women exchanged the natural function for that which is unnatural, [27]and in the same way also the men abandoned the natural function of the woman and burned in their desire toward one another, men with men committing indecent acts and receiving in their own persons the due penalty of their error. [28]And just as they did not see fit to acknowledge God any longer, God gave them over to a depraved mind, to do those things which are not proper, [29]being filled with all unrighteousness, wickedness, greed, evil; full of envy, murder, strife, deceit, malice; they are gossips, [30]slanderers, haters of God, insolent, arrogant, boastful, inventors of evil, disobedient to parents, [31]without understanding, untrustworthy, unloving, unmerciful; [32]and although they know the ordinance of God, that those who practice such things are worthy of death, they not only do the same, but also give hearty approval to those who practice them.

Romans 7:5

For while we were in the flesh, the sinful *passions*, which were aroused by the Law, were at work in the members of our body to bear fruit for *death*.

Romans 12:2

And do not be conformed to this world, but be transformed by the renewing of your *mind*, so that you may prove what the will of God is, that which is good and acceptable and perfect.

Romans 13:9

For this, "YOU SHALL NOT COMMIT ADULTERY, YOU SHALL NOT *MURDER*, YOU SHALL NOT STEAL, YOU SHALL NOT COVET," and if there is any other commandment, it is summed up in this saying, "YOU SHALL LOVE YOUR NEIGHBOR AS YOURSELF."

Romans 13:13–14

Let us behave *properly* as in the day, not in carousing and drunkenness, not in sexual promiscuity and sensuality, not in *strife* and jealousy. [14]But put on the Lord Jesus Christ, and make no provision for the flesh in regard to its lusts.

1 Corinthians 6:9–10

Or do you not know that the *unrighteous* will not inherit the kingdom of God? Do not be deceived; neither fornicators, nor idolaters, nor adulterers, nor effeminate, nor homosexuals, [10]nor thieves, nor the covetous, nor drunkards, nor revilers, nor swindlers, will inherit the kingdom of God.

2 Corinthians 12:20

For I am afraid that perhaps when I come I may find you to be not what I wish and may be found by you to be not what you wish; that perhaps there will be *strife*, jealousy, angry tempers, disputes, *slanders*, *gossip*, *arrogance*, disturbances.

Galatians 5:19–21

Now the deeds of the flesh are evident, which are: immorality, impurity, sensuality, [20]idolatry, sorcery, enmities, *strife*, jealousy, outbursts of anger, disputes, dissensions, factions, [21]*envying,* drunkenness, carousing, and things like these, of which I forewarn you, just as I have forewarned you, that *those who practice such things* will not inherit the kingdom of God.

Colossians 3:5–8
Therefore consider the members of your earthly body as dead to immorality, impurity, *passion,* evil desire, and *greed,* which amounts to idolatry. [6]For it is because of these things that the wrath of God will come upon the sons of disobedience, [7]and in them you also once walked, when you were living in them. [8]But now you also, put them all aside: anger, wrath, *malice, slander,* and abusive speech from your mouth.

1 Thessalonians 4:3–5
For this is the will of God, your sanctification; that is, that you abstain from sexual immorality; [4]that each of you know how to possess his own vessel in sanctification and honor, [5]not in lustful *passion,* like the Gentiles who do not know God.

1 Timothy 1:8–10
But we know that the Law is good, if one uses it lawfully, [9]realizing the fact that law is not made for a righteous person, but for those who are lawless and rebellious, for the ungodly and sinners, for the unholy and profane, for those who kill their fathers or mothers, for *murderers* [10]and immoral men and homosexuals and kidnappers and liars and perjurers, and whatever else is contrary to sound teaching.

1 Timothy 6:3–5
If anyone advocates a different doctrine and does not agree with sound words, . . . [4]he is conceited and understands nothing; but he has a morbid interest in controversial questions and disputes about words, out of which arise *envy, strife,* abusive language, evil suspicions, [5]and constant friction between men of *depraved mind* and deprived of the truth, who suppose that godliness is a means of gain.

2 Timothy 3:2–4
For men will be lovers of self, lovers of money, *boastful, arrogant,* revilers, *disobedient to parents,* ungrateful, unholy, [3]*unloving,* irreconcilable, malicious *gossips,* without self-control, brutal, haters of good, [4]treacherous, reckless, conceited, lovers of pleasure rather than lovers of God.

OTHER BIBLICAL PARALLELS

Leviticus 18:22
"You shall not lie with a male as one lies with a female; it is an abomination."

Psalm 81:11–12
"But My people did not listen to My voice, And Israel did not obey Me. [12]So I *gave them over* to the stubbornness of their heart, To walk in their own devices."

Matthew 15:19
"For out of the heart come evil thoughts, *murders,* adulteries, fornications, thefts, false witness, *slanders.*"

NONCANONICAL PARALLELS

Wisdom of Solomon 14:22, 24–27, 30–31
Then it was not enough for them to err about the knowledge of God, but though living in great *strife* due to ignorance, they call such great evils peace. . . . [24]they no longer keep either their lives or their marriages pure, but they either treacherously kill one another, or grieve one another by adultery, [25]and all is a raging riot of blood and *murder,* theft and *deceit,* corruption, faithlessness, tumult, perjury, [26]confusion over what is good, forgetfulness of favors, defiling of souls, sexual perversion, disorder in marriages, adultery, and debauchery. [27]For the worship of idols not to be named is the beginning and cause and end of every *evil.* . . . [30]But just penalties will overtake them on two counts: because they thought wrongly about God in devoting themselves to idols, and because in deceit they swore unrighteously through contempt for holiness. [31]For it is not the power of the things by which people swear, but the just *penalty* for those who sin, that always pursues the transgression of the *unrighteous.*

Pseudo-Phocylides, Sentences *190–92*
Do not exceed *natural* sexual unions for illicit *passion;* [191]unions between males are not pleasing even to beasts. [192]Let not women mimic the sexual role of men at all.

Plato, Laws *636C*

When male and female join for procreation the resulting pleasure appears to be *natural,* but when male joins with male or female with female it is *unnatural.*

Romans 2:1–11

Therefore you have no excuse, everyone of you who passes judgment, for in that which you judge another, you condemn yourself; for you who judge practice the same things. ²And we know that the judgment of God rightly falls upon those who practice such things. ³But do you suppose this, O man, when you pass judgment on those who practice such things and do the same yourself, that you will escape the judgment of God? ⁴Or do you think lightly of the riches of His kindness and tolerance and patience, not knowing that the kindness of God leads you to repentance? ⁵But because of your stubbornness and unrepentant heart you are storing up wrath for yourself in the day of wrath and revelation of the righteous judgment of God, ⁶who WILL RENDER TO EACH PERSON ACCORDING TO HIS DEEDS: ⁷to those who by perseverance in doing good seek for glory and honor and immortality, eternal life; ⁸but to those who are selfishly ambitious and do not obey the truth, but obey unrighteousness, wrath and indignation. ⁹There will be tribulation and distress for every soul of man who does evil, of the Jew first and also of the Greek, ¹⁰but glory and honor and peace to everyone who does good, to the Jew first and also to the Greek. ¹¹For there is no partiality with God.

ROMANS PARALLELS

Romans 1:16

For I am not ashamed of the gospel, for it is the power of God for salvation to everyone who believes, to *the Jew first and also* to *the Greek.*

Romans 1:18, 20

For the *wrath* of God is revealed from heaven against all ungodliness and *unrighteousness* of men who suppress *the truth* in unrighteousness. . . . ²⁰For since the creation of the world His invisible attributes, His eternal power and divine nature, have been clearly seen, being understood through what has been made, so that they are without *excuse.*

Romans 9:22

What if God, although willing to demonstrate His *wrath* and to make His power known, endured with much *patience* vessels of wrath prepared for destruction?

Romans 11:22

Behold then the *kindness* and severity of God; to those who fell, severity, but to you, God's kindness, if you continue in His kindness; otherwise you also will be cut off.

Romans 14:1, 10

Now accept the one who is weak in faith, but not for the purpose of *passing judgment* on his opinions. . . . ¹⁰But you, why do you judge your brother? Or you again, why do you regard your brother with contempt? For we will all stand before the *judgment* seat *of God.*

OTHER PAULINE PARALLELS

1 Corinthians 4:5

Therefore do not go on *passing judgment* before the time, but wait until the Lord comes who will both bring to light the things hidden in the darkness and disclose the motives of men's hearts; and then each man's praise will come to him from God.

1 Corinthians 15:53

For this perishable must put on the imperishable, and this mortal must put on *immortality.*

Colossians 3:25

For he who does wrong will receive the consequences of the wrong which he has done, and that without *partiality.*

1 Timothy 1:15–16

It is a trustworthy statement, deserving full acceptance, that Christ Jesus came into the world to save sinners, among whom I am foremost of all. ¹⁶Yet for this reason I found mercy, so that in me as the foremost, Jesus Christ might demonstrate His perfect *patience* as an example for those who would believe in Him for *eternal life.*

OTHER BIBLICAL PARALLELS

Deuteronomy 9:6–7

"Know, then, it is not because of your righteousness that the LORD your God is giving you this good land to possess, for you are a *stubborn* people. [7]Remember, do not forget how you provoked the LORD your God to *wrath* in the wilderness; from the day that you left the land of Egypt until you arrived at this place, you have been rebellious against the LORD."

Deuteronomy 10:17
"For the LORD your God is the God of gods and the Lord of lords, the great, the mighty, and the awesome God who does *not* show *partiality* nor take a bribe."

Deuteronomy 32:34–35
"Is it not laid up in *store* with Me, Sealed up in My treasuries? [35]Vengeance is Mine, and retribution, In due time their foot will slip; For the day of their calamity is near, And the impending things are hastening upon them."

Proverbs 24:12
If you say, "See, we did not know this," Does He not consider it who weighs the hearts? And does He not know it who keeps your soul? And *will* He not *render to* man *according to his* work?

Joel 2:13
Now return to the LORD your God, For He is gracious and compassionate, Slow to anger, abounding in lovingkindness And relenting of evil.

Zephaniah 1:14–15
Near is the great day of the LORD, Near and coming very quickly; Listen, the day of the LORD! In it the warrior cries out bitterly. [15]A *day of wrath* is that day, A day of trouble and *distress*, A day of destruction and desolation, A day of darkness and gloom, A day of clouds and thick darkness.

Matthew 7:1–2
"Do not *judge* so that you will not be *judged.* [2]For in the way you judge, you will be judged; and by your standard of measure, it will be measured to you."

Acts 10:34–35
Opening his mouth, Peter said: "I most certainly understand now that God is *not* one to show *partiality,* [35]but in every nation the man who fears Him and does what is right is welcome to Him."

James 3:14, 16
But if you have bitter jealousy and *selfish ambition* in your heart, do not be arrogant and so lie against *the truth.* . . . [16]For where jealousy and selfish ambition exist, there is disorder and every evil thing.

2 Peter 3:9
The Lord is not slow about His promise, as some count slowness, but is *patient* toward you, not wishing for any to perish but for all to come to *repentance.*

Wisdom of Solomon 11:23
But you are merciful to all, for you can do all things, and you overlook people's sins, so that they may *repent.*

Sirach 18:11–12
That is why the Lord is *patient* with them and pours out his mercy upon them. [12]He sees and recognizes that their end is miserable; therefore he grants them forgiveness all the more.

Romans 2:12–16

For all who have sinned without the Law will also perish without the Law, and all who have sinned under the Law will be judged by the Law; [13]for it is not the hearers of the Law who are just before God, but the doers of the Law will be justified. [14]For when Gentiles who do not have the Law do instinctively the things of the Law, these, not having the Law, are a law to themselves, [15]in that they show the work of the Law written in their hearts, their conscience bearing witness and their thoughts alternately accusing or else defending them, [16]on the day when, according to my gospel, God will judge the secrets of men through Christ Jesus.

Romans 2:27
And he who is physically uncircumcised, if he keeps *the Law*, will he not *judge* you who though having the letter of the Law and circumcision are a transgressor of the Law?

Romans 3:19–20
Now we know that whatever the Law says,

it speaks to those who are *under the Law*, so that every mouth may be closed and all the world may become accountable to God; [20]because by the works of the Law no flesh will be *justified* in His sight; for through the Law comes the knowledge of sin.

Romans 5:12–13

Therefore, just as through one man sin entered into the world, and death through sin, and so death spread to all men, because all *sinned*— [13]for until *the Law* sin was in the world, but sin is not imputed when there is no law.

Romans 14:10

But you, why do you judge your brother? Or you again, why do you regard your brother with contempt? For we will all stand before the *judgment* seat of God.

OTHER PAULINE PARALLELS

1 Corinthians 4:5

Therefore do not go on passing *judgment* before the time, but wait until the Lord comes who will both bring to light the things hidden in the darkness and disclose the motives of men's *hearts*; and then each man's praise will come to him from God.

1 Corinthians 8:7

However not all men have this knowledge; but some, being accustomed to the idol until now, eat food as if it were sacrificed to an idol; and their *conscience* being weak is defiled.

1 Corinthians 9:20–21

To the Jews I became as a Jew, so that I might win Jews; to those who are *under the Law*, as under the Law though not being myself under the Law, so that I might win those who are under the Law; [21]to those who are *without law*, as without law, though not being without the law of God but under the law of Christ, so that I might win those who are without law.

OTHER BIBLICAL PARALLELS

Deuteronomy 31:12

"Assemble the people, the men and the women and children and the alien who is in your town, so that they may *hear* and learn and fear the LORD your God, and be careful to observe all the words of this *law*."

Jeremiah 31:33

"But this is the covenant which I will make with the house of Israel after those days," declares the LORD, "I will put My *law* within them and on their *heart* I will *write* it; and I will be their God, and they shall be My people."

Luke 18:9–14

And He also told this parable to some people who trusted in themselves that they were righteous, and viewed others with contempt: [10]"Two men went up into the temple to pray, one a Pharisee and the other a tax collector. [11]The Pharisee stood and was praying this to himself: 'God, I thank You that I am not like other people: swindlers, unjust, adulterers, or even like this tax collector. [12]I fast twice a week; I pay tithes of all that I get.' [13]But the tax collector, standing some distance away, was even unwilling to lift up his eyes to heaven, but was beating his breast, saying, 'God, be merciful to me, the sinner!' [14]I tell you, this man went to his house *justified* rather than the other; for everyone who exalts himself will be humbled, but he who humbles himself will be exalted."

Acts 10:34–35, 42

Opening his mouth, Peter said: "I most certainly understand now that God is not one to show partiality, [35]but in every nation the man who fears Him and does what is right is welcome to Him.... [42]And He ordered us to preach to the people, and solemnly to testify that this is the One who has been appointed by God as *Judge* of the living and the dead."

Hebrews 9:13–14

For if the blood of goats and bulls and the ashes of a heifer sprinkling those who have been defiled sanctify for the cleansing of the flesh, [14]how much more will the blood of Christ, who through the eternal Spirit offered Himself without blemish to God, cleanse your *conscience* from dead works to serve the living God?

James 1:22–25

But prove yourselves *doers* of the word, and not merely *hearers* who delude themselves. [23]For if anyone is a hearer of the word and not a doer, he is like a man who looks at his natural face in a mirror; [24]for once he has looked at himself and gone away, he has immediately forgotten what kind of person he was. [25]But one who looks intently at the perfect *law*, the law of liberty, and abides by it, not having become a forgetful hearer but an effectual doer, this man will be blessed in what he does.

James 4:11

Do not speak against one another, brethren. He who speaks against a brother or *judges* his brother, speaks against the law and judges the law; but if you judge the law, you are not a *doer of the law* but a judge of it.

1 John 3:7

Little children, make sure no one deceives you; the one who practices righteousness is righteous, just as He is righteous.

2 Esdras (4 Ezra) 3:35–36

"When have the inhabitants of the earth not *sinned* in your sight? Or what nation has kept your commandments so well? [36]You may indeed find individuals who have kept your commandments, but nations you will not find."

Testament of Judah 20:1–2

"So understand, my children, that two spirits await an opportunity with humanity: the spirit of truth and the spirit of error. [2]In between is the *conscience* of the mind which inclines as it will."

Josephus, Against Apion 2.218

Each one, having the *witness* of his *conscience*, the prophecies of the lawgiver, and the mighty assurance of divine sanction, is convinced that to those who defend *the laws* and, if necessary, willingly die for them, God has given a new and better life at the turn of the age.

Romans 2:17–24

But if you bear the name "Jew" and rely upon the Law and boast in God, [18]and know His will and approve the things that are essential, being instructed out of the Law, [19]and are confident that you yourself are a guide to the blind, a light to those who are in darkness, [20]a corrector of the foolish, a teacher of the immature, having in the Law the embodiment of knowledge and of the truth, [21]you, therefore, who teach another, do you not teach yourself? You who preach that one shall not steal, do you steal? [22]You who say that one should not commit adultery, do you commit adultery? You who abhor idols, do you rob temples? [23]You who boast in the Law, through your breaking the Law, do you dishonor God? [24]For "THE NAME OF GOD IS BLASPHEMED AMONG THE GENTILES BECAUSE OF YOU," just as it is written.

Romans 3:27

Where then is *boasting*? It is excluded. By what kind of law? Of works? No, but by a law of faith.

Romans 9:4–5

. . . who are Israelites, to whom belongs the adoption as sons, and the glory and the covenants and the giving of *the Law* and the temple service and the promises, [5]whose are the fathers, and from whom is the Christ according to the flesh, who is over all, God blessed forever. Amen.

Romans 12:2

And do not be conformed to this world, but be transformed by the renewing of your mind, so that you may prove what the *will* of God is, that which is good and acceptable and perfect.

Romans 13:9

For this, "YOU SHALL *NOT COMMIT ADULTERY*, YOU SHALL NOT MURDER, YOU *SHALL NOT STEAL*, YOU SHALL NOT COVET," and if there is any other commandment, it is summed up in this saying, "YOU SHALL LOVE YOUR NEIGHBOR AS YOURSELF."

Galatians 6:12–13

Those who desire to make a good showing in the flesh try to compel you to be circumcised, simply so that they will not be persecuted for the cross of Christ. [13]For those who are circumcised do not even keep *the*

Law themselves, but they desire to have you circumcised so that they may *boast* in your flesh.

Philippians 1:9–10
And this I pray, that your love may abound still more and more in real knowledge and all discernment, [10]so that you may *approve* the things that are excellent, in order to be sincere and blameless until the day of Christ.

1 Timothy 1:6–7
For some men, straying from these things, have turned aside to fruitless discussion, [7]wanting to be *teachers* of *the Law*, even though they do not understand either what they are saying or the matters about which they make *confident* assertions.

OTHER BIBLICAL PARALLELS

Psalm 50:16–21
But to the wicked God says, "What right have you to tell of My statutes And to take My covenant in your mouth? [17]For you hate discipline, And you cast My words behind you. [18]When you see a thief, you are pleased with him, And you associate with *adulterers*. [19]You let your mouth loose in evil And your tongue frames deceit. [20]You sit and speak against your brother; You slander your own mother's son. [21]These things you have done and I kept silence; You thought that I was just like you; I will reprove you and state the case in order before your eyes."

Isaiah 42:6–7
"I am the LORD, I have called you in righteousness, I will also hold you by the hand and watch over you, And I will appoint you as a covenant to the people, As a *light* to the nations, [7]To open *blind* eyes, To bring out prisoners from the dungeon And those who dwell in *darkness* from the prison."

Isaiah 52:5
"Now therefore, what do I have here," declares the LORD, "seeing that My people have been taken away without cause?" Again the LORD declares, "Those who rule over them howl, and My *name* is continually *blasphemed* all day long."

Ezekiel 36:20–21
"When they came to the nations where they went, they profaned My holy *name*, because

it was said of them, 'These are the people of the LORD; yet they have come out of His land.' [21]But I had concern for My holy name, which the house of Israel had profaned among the nations where they went."

Matthew 15:14
"Let them alone; they are blind *guides* of *the blind*. And if a blind man guides a blind man, both will fall into a pit."

Matthew 23:2–3
"The scribes and the Pharisees have seated themselves in the chair of Moses; [3]therefore all that they tell you, do and observe, but do not do according to their deeds; for they say things and do not do them."

John 3:10
Jesus answered and said to him, "Are you the *teacher* of Israel and do not understand these things?"

NONCANONICAL PARALLELS

Testament of Levi *14:4–5*
"For what will all the nations do if you become darkened with impiety? You will bring down a curse on our nation, because you want to destroy the *light* of *the Law* which was granted to you for the enlightenment of every man, *teaching* commandments which are opposed to God's ordinances. [5]You plunder the Lord's offerings; from his share you *steal* choice parts, contemptuously eating them with whores."

Seneca, On Anger *2.28.7–8*
But where will you find a judge this fair? He who lusts after everyone else's wife . . . will not have his own wife looked at; . . . he who prosecutes lying is himself a perjurer; . . . [8]The vices of others we keep before our eyes, our own behind our back. . . . The tyrant rages at a murderer and the *temple robber* punishes theft.

Romans 2:25–29

For indeed circumcision is of value if you practice the Law; but if you are a transgressor of the Law, your circumcision has become uncircumcision. [26]So if the uncircumcised man keeps the requirements of the Law, will not his uncircumcision be regarded as circumcision? ²⁷And he who is physically uncircumcised, if he keeps the Law, will he not judge you who though having the letter of the Law and circumcision are a transgressor of the Law? ²⁸For he is not a Jew who is one outwardly, nor is circumcision that which is outward in the flesh. ²⁹But he is a Jew who is one inwardly; and circumcision is that which is of the heart, by the Spirit, not by the letter; and his praise is not from men, but from God.

ROMANS PARALLELS

Romans 2:12–13
For all who have sinned without *the Law* will also perish without the Law, and all who have sinned under the Law will be *judged* by the Law; ¹³for it is not the hearers of the Law who are just before God, but the doers of the Law will be justified.

Romans 3:29–30
Or is God the God of *Jews* only? Is He not the God of Gentiles also? Yes, of Gentiles also, ³⁰since indeed God who will justify the *circumcised* by faith and the *uncircumcised* through faith is one.

Romans 7:6
But now we have been released from *the Law*, having died to that by which we were bound, so that we serve in newness of *the Spirit* and not in oldness of *the letter*.

Romans 8:3–4
For what the Law could not do, weak as it was through the flesh, God did: sending His own Son in the likeness of sinful flesh and as an offering for sin, He condemned sin in the flesh, ⁴so that *the requirement of the Law* might be fulfilled in us, who do not walk according to *the flesh* but according to *the Spirit*.

Romans 9:6–7
But it is not as though the word of God has failed. For they are not all Israel who are descended from Israel; ⁷nor are they all children because they are Abraham's descendants, but: "THROUGH ISAAC YOUR DESCENDANTS WILL BE NAMED."

1 Corinthians 7:19
Circumcision is nothing, and *uncircumcision* is nothing, but what matters is the keeping of the commandments of God.

2 Corinthians 3:5–6
Not that we are adequate in ourselves to consider anything as coming from ourselves, but our adequacy is from God, ⁶who also made us adequate as servants of a new covenant, not of *the letter* but of *the Spirit*; for the letter kills, but the Spirit gives life.

Galatians 5:2–3
Behold I, Paul, say to you that if you receive circumcision, Christ will be of no benefit to you. ³And I testify again to every man who receives *circumcision*, that he is under obligation to *keep the* whole *Law*.

Galatians 6:13–15
For those who are circumcised do not even *keep the Law* themselves, but they desire to have you circumcised so that they may boast in your *flesh*. ¹⁴But may it never be that I would boast, except in the cross of our Lord Jesus Christ, through which the world has been crucified to me, and I to the world. ¹⁵For neither is *circumcision* anything, nor *uncircumcision*, but a new creation.

Ephesians 2:11
Therefore remember that formerly you, the Gentiles in the flesh, who are called "*Uncircumcision*" by the so-called "*Circumcision*," which is performed *in the flesh* by human hands . . .

Philippians 3:2–3
Beware of the dogs, beware of the evil workers, beware of the false *circumcision*; ³for we are the true circumcision, who worship in *the Spirit* of God and glory in Christ Jesus and put no confidence *in the flesh*.

Colossians 2:11–12
And in Him you were also circumcised with a *circumcision* made without hands, in the removal of the body of *the flesh* by the circumcision of Christ; ¹²having been buried with Him in baptism, in which you were also raised up with Him through faith in the working of God, who raised Him from the dead.

Genesis 17:11, 14
"And you shall be *circumcised* in *the flesh* of your foreskin, and it shall be the sign of the covenant between Me and you. . . . [14]But an *uncircumcised* male who is not circumcised in the flesh of his foreskin, that person shall be cut off from his people; he has broken My covenant."

Deuteronomy 30:6
"Moreover the LORD your God will *circumcise* your *heart* and the heart of your descendants, to love the LORD your God with all your heart and with all your soul, so that you may live."

1 Samuel 16:7
"Do not look at his appearance or at the height of his stature, because I have rejected him; for God sees not as man sees, for man looks at the *outward* appearance, but the LORD looks at the *heart*."

Jeremiah 4:4
"*Circumcise* yourselves to the LORD And remove the foreskins of your *heart*, Men of Judah and inhabitants of Jerusalem, Or else My wrath will go forth like fire And burn with none to quench it, Because of the evil of your deeds."

Jeremiah 9:25
"Behold, the days are coming," declares the LORD, "that I will punish all who are *circumcised* and yet *uncircumcised*."

Matthew 23:28
"So you, too, *outwardly* appear righteous to men, but *inwardly* you are full of hypocrisy and lawlessness."

Acts 7:51–52
"You men who are stiff-necked and *uncircumcised* in *heart* and ears are always resisting *the* Holy *Spirit*; you are doing just as your fathers did. [52]Which one of the prophets did your fathers not persecute?"

Philo, Questions and Answers on Exodus 2.2
Why does [Scripture] in admonishing, "Thou shalt not oppress a sojourner," add "For ye were sojourners in the land of the Egyptians"? [Scripture] first makes it clearly apparent and demonstrable that in reality the sojourner is one who *circumcises* not his *uncircumcision* but his desires and sensual pleasures and the other passions of the soul.

Josephus, Jewish Antiquities 20.41
He [Ananias] said that the King [Izates] would be able to worship God without *circumcision* if in fact he was fully committed to embracing the customs of the Jews, for this is more important than circumcision.

Romans 3:1–8

Then what advantage has the Jew? Or what is the benefit of circumcision? [2]Great in every respect. First of all, that they were entrusted with the oracles of God. [3]What then? If some did not believe, their unbelief will not nullify the faithfulness of God, will it? [4]May it never be! Rather, let God be found true, though every man be found a liar, as it is written, "THAT YOU MAY BE JUSTIFIED IN YOUR WORDS, AND PREVAIL WHEN YOU ARE JUDGED." [5]But if our unrighteousness demonstrates the righteousness of God, what shall we say? The God who inflicts wrath is not unrighteous, is He? (I am speaking in human terms.) [6]May it never be! For otherwise, how will God judge the world? [7]But if through my lie the truth of God abounded to His glory, why am I also still being judged as a sinner? [8]And why not say (as we are slanderously reported and as some claim that we say), "Let us do evil that good may come"? Their condemnation is just.

Romans 1:18
For the *wrath* of God is revealed from heaven against all ungodliness and *unrighteousness* of men who suppress *the truth* in unrighteousness.

Romans 2:16–18
. . . on the day when, according to my gospel, God will *judge* the secrets of men through Christ Jesus. [17]But if you bear the name *"Jew"* and rely upon the Law and boast in God, [18]and know His will and approve the things that are essential, being instructed out of the Law . . .

Romans 6:1–2

What shall we say then? Are we to continue in sin so that grace may increase? [2]*May it never be*! How shall we who died to sin still live in it?

Romans 9:4–5

. . . who are Israelites, to whom belongs the adoption as sons, and the glory and the covenants and the giving of the Law and the temple service and the promises, [5]whose are the fathers, and from whom is the Christ according to the flesh, who is over all, God blessed forever. Amen.

Romans 9:14–15

What shall we say then? There is no injustice with God, is there? *May it never be!* [15]For He says to Moses, "I WILL HAVE MERCY ON WHOM I HAVE MERCY, AND I WILL HAVE COMPASSION ON WHOM I HAVE COMPASSION."

Romans 9:19–20

You will say to me then, "Why does He still find fault? For who resists His will?" [20]On the contrary, who are you, O man, who answers back to God? The thing molded will not say to the molder, "Why did you make me like this," will it?

Romans 11:20, 23

Quite right, they were broken off for their *unbelief*, but you stand by your faith. Do not be conceited, but fear; . . . [23]And they also, if they do not continue in their unbelief, will be grafted in, for God is able to graft them in again.

OTHER PAULINE PARALLELS

1 Corinthians 10:29–30

I mean not your own conscience, but the other man's; for why is my freedom *judged* by another's conscience? [30]If I partake with thankfulness, why am I *slandered* concerning that for which I give thanks?

Galatians 2:20–21

"I have been crucified with Christ; and it is no longer I who live, but Christ lives in me; and the life which I now live in the flesh I live by faith in the Son of God, who loved me and gave Himself up for me. [21]I do not *nullify* the grace of God, for if *righteousness*

comes through the Law, then Christ died needlessly."

Galatians 5:2

Behold I, Paul, say to you that if you receive *circumcision*, Christ will be of no *benefit* to you.

1 Timothy 1:12–13

I thank Christ Jesus our Lord, who has strengthened me, because He considered me faithful, putting me into service, [13]even though I was formerly a blasphemer and a persecutor and a violent aggressor. Yet I was shown mercy because I acted ignorantly in *unbelief*.

2 Timothy 2:13

If we are faithless, He remains *faithful*, for He cannot deny Himself.

OTHER BIBLICAL PARALLELS

Deuteronomy 7:9

"Know therefore that the LORD your God, He is God, the *faithful God*, who keeps His covenant and His lovingkindness to a thousandth generation with those who love Him and keep His commandments."

Psalm 51:4

Against You, You only, I have sinned And done what is evil in Your sight, So that You are *justified* when You speak And blameless when You *judge*.

Psalm 116:11

I said in my alarm, "All men are *liars*."

Psalm 147:19–20

He declares His words to Jacob, His statutes and His ordinances to Israel. [20]He has not dealt thus with any nation; And as for His ordinances, they have not known them. Praise the LORD!

Acts 7:38

"This is the one who was in the congregation in the wilderness together with the angel who was speaking to him on Mount Sinai, and who was with our fathers; and he received living *oracles* to pass on to you."

Hebrews 4:2

For indeed we have had good news preached to us, just as they also; but the word they heard did not profit them, because it was not united by faith in those who heard.

NONCANONICAL PARALLELS

Psalms of Solomon 8:26, 28–29

We have proven your name right, which is honored forever, for you are the God of *righteousness, judging* Israel in discipline. . . . [28]Bring together the dispersed of Israel with mercy and goodness, for your *faithfulness* is with us. [29]For we stiffened our necks, but you are the one who disciplines us.

Romans 3:9–20

What then? Are we better than they? Not at all; for we have already charged that both Jews and Greeks are all under sin; [10]as it is written, "THERE IS NONE RIGHTEOUS, NOT EVEN ONE; [11]THERE IS NONE WHO UNDERSTANDS, THERE IS NONE WHO SEEKS FOR GOD; [12]ALL HAVE TURNED ASIDE, TOGETHER THEY HAVE BECOME USELESS; THERE IS NONE WHO DOES GOOD, THERE IS NOT EVEN ONE." [13]"THEIR THROAT IS AN OPEN GRAVE, WITH THEIR TONGUES THEY KEEP DECEIVING," "THE POISON OF ASPS IS UNDER THEIR LIPS"; [14]"WHOSE MOUTH IS FULL OF CURSING AND BITTERNESS"; [15]"THEIR FEET ARE SWIFT TO SHED BLOOD, [16]DESTRUCTION AND MISERY ARE IN THEIR PATHS, [17]AND THE PATH OF PEACE THEY HAVE NOT KNOWN." [18]"THERE IS NO FEAR OF GOD BEFORE THEIR EYES." [19]Now we know that whatever the Law says, it speaks to those who are under the Law, so that every mouth may be closed and all the world may become accountable to God; [20]because by the works of the Law no flesh will be justified in His sight; for through the Law comes the knowledge of sin.

ROMANS PARALLELS

Romans 2:9, 12–13

There will be tribulation and distress for every soul of man who does evil, of the *Jew* first and also of the *Greek*. . . . [12]For all who have sinned without the Law will also perish without the Law, and all who have sinned *under the Law* will be judged by the Law; [13]for it is not the hearers of the Law

who are just before God, but the doers of the Law will be *justified*.

Romans 3:28

For we maintain that a man is *justified* by faith apart from *works of the Law*.

Romans 5:13, 20

For until *the Law* sin was in the world, but *sin* is not imputed when there is no law. . . . [20]The Law came in so that the transgression would increase; but where sin increased, grace abounded all the more.

Romans 7:7

What shall we say then? Is *the Law* sin? May it never be! On the contrary, I would not have come to *know sin* except through the Law.

Romans 11:30–32

For just as you once were disobedient to God, but now have been shown mercy because of their disobedience, [31]so these also now have been disobedient, that because of the mercy shown to you they also may now be shown mercy. [32]For God has shut up all in disobedience so that He may show mercy to all.

OTHER PAULINE PARALLELS

Galatians 2:15–16

"We are Jews by nature and not sinners from among the Gentiles; [16]nevertheless knowing that a man is not *justified* by *the works of the Law* but through faith in Christ Jesus . . ."

Galatians 3:10–12, 22

For as many as are of *the works of the Law* are under a curse; for it is written, "CURSED IS EVERYONE WHO DOES NOT ABIDE BY ALL THINGS WRITTEN IN THE BOOK OF THE LAW, TO PERFORM THEM." [11]Now that no one is *justified* by the Law before God is evident; for, "THE *RIGHTEOUS* MAN SHALL LIVE BY FAITH." [12]However, the Law is not of faith; on the contrary, "HE WHO PRACTICES THEM SHALL LIVE BY THEM." . . . [22]But the Scripture has shut up everyone *under sin*, so that the promise by faith in Jesus Christ might be given to those who believe.

Psalm 5:9

There is nothing reliable in what they say; Their inward part is destruction itself. *Their throat is an open grave*; They flatter *with their tongue.*

Psalm 10:7

His *mouth is full of curses* and deceit and oppression; Under his *tongue* is mischief and wickedness.

Psalm 14:1–3

The fool has said in his heart, "There is no God." They are corrupt, they have committed abominable deeds; There is no one who does good. [2]The LORD has looked down from heaven upon the sons of men To see if there are any *who understand, Who seek after God.* [3]They *have all turned aside, together they have become* corrupt; *There is no one who does good, not even one.*

Psalm 36:1

Transgression speaks to the ungodly within his heart; *There is no fear of God before* his *eyes.*

Psalm 59:7–8

Behold, they belch forth with their *mouth*; Swords are in their *lips*, For, they say, "Who hears?" [8]But You, O LORD, laugh at them; You scoff at all the nations.

Psalm 140:3

They sharpen their *tongues* as a serpent; *Poison of* a viper *is under their lips.*

Psalm 143:2

And do not enter into judgment with Your servant, For *in* Your *sight* no man living is righteous.

Proverbs 1:16

For *their feet* run to evil And they hasten to *shed blood.*

Ecclesiastes 7:20

Indeed, *there is not* a *righteous* man on earth who continually *does good* and who never sins.

Isaiah 59:7–8

Their feet run to evil, And they hasten to *shed* innocent *blood*; Their thoughts are thoughts of iniquity, Devastation and *destruction* are in their highways. [8]They do *not know* the way of *peace*, And there is no justice in their tracks; They have made their *paths* crooked, Whoever treads on them does not know peace.

James 3:8

But no one can tame the *tongue*; it is a restless evil and full of deadly *poison.*

1 Enoch *81:5*

Then the seven holy ones brought me and placed me on the ground in front of the gate of my house, and said to me, "Make everything known to your son, Methuselah, and show to all your children that *no* one of the *flesh* can be just before the Lord; for they are merely his own creation."

2 Baruch *15:5–6*

It is true that man would not have understood my judgment if he had not received *the Law* and if he were not instructed with understanding. [6]But now, because he trespassed, having understanding, he will be punished.

Jubilees *21:21*

I see, my son, every deed of mankind, that (they are) *sin* and evils; and all of their deeds are defilement and corruption and contamination; and there is no *righteousness* with them.

Halakhic Letter *(4QMMT) 106–8, 112–13*

And we are aware that part of the blessings and curses have occurred [107]that are written in the b[ook of Mo]ses. And this is the end of days, when they will return in Israel [108]to the L[aw]. . . . [112] . . . And also we have written to you [113]some of *the works* of the Torah which we think are good for you and your people.

Romans 3:21–26

But now apart from the Law the righteousness of God has been manifested, being witnessed by the Law and the Prophets, [22]even the righteousness of God through faith in Jesus Christ for all those who believe; for there is no distinction; [23]for all have sinned and fall short of the glory of God, [24]being justified as a gift by His grace through the redemption which is in Christ Jesus; [25]whom God displayed publicly as a propitiation in His blood through faith. This was to demonstrate His righteousness, because in the forbearance of God He passed over the sins previously committed; [26]for the demonstration, I say, of His righteousness at the present time, so that He would be just and the justifier of the one who has faith in Jesus.

ROMANS PARALLELS

Romans 1:16–17

For I am not ashamed of the gospel, for it is the power of God for salvation to everyone who *believes*, to the Jew first and also to the Greek. [17]For in it *the righteousness of God* is revealed from *faith* to faith; as it is written, "BUT THE RIGHTEOUS man SHALL LIVE BY FAITH."

Romans 4:5

But to the one who does not work, but *believes* in Him who *justifies* the ungodly, his *faith* is credited as *righteousness*.

Romans 5:1–2, 9

Therefore, having been *justified* by *faith*, we have peace with God through our Lord Jesus Christ, [2]through whom also we have obtained our introduction by faith into this *grace* in which we stand; and we exult in hope of *the glory of God*. . . . [9]Much more then, having now been justified by His *blood*, we shall be saved from the wrath of God through Him.

Romans 8:3–4

For what *the Law* could not do, weak as it was through the flesh, God did: sending His own Son in the likeness of sinful flesh and as an offering for *sin*, He condemned sin in the flesh, [4]so that the requirement of the Law might be fulfilled in us, who do not walk according to the flesh but according to the Spirit.

Romans 10:4, 12

For Christ is the end of *the law* for *righteousness* to everyone who *believes*. . . . [12]For *there is no distinction* between Jew and Greek; for the same Lord is Lord of all, abounding in riches for all who call on Him.

1 Corinthians 5:7

Clean out the old leaven so that you may be a new lump, just as you are in fact unleavened. For Christ our Passover also has been sacrificed.

2 Corinthians 5:21

He made Him who knew no sin to be *sin* on our behalf, so that we might become *the righteousness of God* in Him.

Galatians 2:16

". . . Nevertheless knowing that a man is not justified by the works of *the Law* but through *faith* in Christ Jesus, even we have *believed* in Christ Jesus, so that we may be *justified* by faith in Christ and not by the works of the Law; since by the works of the Law no flesh will be justified."

Galatians 3:13–14

Christ *redeemed* us from the curse of *the Law,* having become a curse for us—for it is written, "CURSED IS EVERYONE WHO HANGS ON A TREE"— [14]in order that in Christ Jesus the blessing of Abraham might come to the Gentiles, so that we would receive the promise of the Spirit through *faith.*

Galatians 3:22–24

But the Scripture has shut up everyone under sin, so that the promise by *faith* in Jesus Christ might be given to those who *believe.* [23]But before faith came, we were kept in custody under the law, being shut up to the faith which was later to be revealed. [24]Therefore *the Law* has become our tutor to lead us to Christ, so that we may be *justified* by faith.

Ephesians 1:7–8

In Him we have *redemption* through *His blood,* the forgiveness of our trespasses, according to the riches of *His grace* [8]which He lavished on us.

Ephesians 2:8

For by *grace* you have been saved through *faith*; and that not of yourselves, it is the *gift* of God; not as a result of works, so that no one may boast.

Ephesians 5:2

. . . And walk in love, just as Christ also loved you and gave Himself up for us, an offering and a sacrifice to God as a fragrant aroma.

Colossians 1:13–14

For He rescued us from the domain of darkness, and transferred us to the kingdom of His beloved Son, [14]in whom we have *redemption*, the forgiveness of *sins*.

OTHER BIBLICAL PARALLELS

Leviticus 16:11, 15–16

"Then Aaron shall offer the bull of the sin offering which is for himself and make atonement for himself and for his household. . . . [15]Then he shall slaughter the goat of the sin offering which is for the people, and bring its *blood* inside the veil and do with its blood as he did with the blood of the bull, and sprinkle it on the mercy seat and in front of the mercy seat. [16]He shall make atonement for the holy place, because of the impurities of the sons of Israel and because of their transgressions in regard to all their *sins*."

Acts 10:43

"Of Him all *the prophets* bear *witness* that through His name everyone who *believes* in Him receives forgiveness of *sins*."

Hebrews 2:17

Therefore, He had to be made like His brethren in all things, so that He might become a merciful and faithful high priest in things pertaining to God, to make *propitiation* for the *sins* of the people.

Hebrews 9:13–15

For if the blood of goats and bulls and the ashes of a heifer sprinkling those who have been defiled sanctify for the cleansing of the flesh, [14]how much more will the *blood* of Christ, who through the eternal Spirit offered Himself without blemish to God, cleanse your conscience from dead works to serve the living God? [15]For this reason He is the mediator of a new covenant, so that, since a death has taken place for the *redemption* of the transgressions that were committed under the first covenant, those who have been called may receive the promise of the eternal inheritance.

1 John 2:1–2

And if anyone sins, we have an Advocate with the Father, Jesus Christ the righteous; [2]and He Himself is the *propitiation* for our *sins*; and not for ours only, but also for those of the whole world.

NONCANONICAL PARALLELS

4 Maccabees 17:20–22

These, then, who have been consecrated for the sake of God, are honored, not only with this honor, but also by the fact that because of them our enemies did not rule over our nation, [21]the tyrant was punished, and the homeland purified—they having become, as it were, a ransom for the *sin* of our nation. [22]And through the *blood* of those devout ones and their death as an atoning sacrifice, divine Providence preserved Israel that previously had been mistreated.

Romans 3:27–31

Where then is boasting? It is excluded. By what kind of law? Of works? No, but by a law of faith. [28]For we maintain that a man is justified by faith apart from works of the Law. [29]Or is God the God of Jews only? Is He not the God of Gentiles also? Yes, of Gentiles also, [30]since indeed God who will justify the circumcised by faith and the uncircumcised through faith is one. [31]Do we then nullify the Law through faith? May it never be! On the contrary, we establish the Law.

ROMANS PARALLELS

Romans 2:17, 23

But if you bear the name *"Jew"* and rely upon the Law and *boast* in God . . . [23]You who boast in *the Law*, through your breaking the Law, do you dishonor God?

Romans 2:25–26

For indeed *circumcision* is of value if you practice *the Law*; but if you are a transgressor of the Law, your circumcision has become uncircumcision. [26]So if the *uncircumcised* man keeps the requirements of the Law, will not his uncircumcision be regarded as circumcision?

Romans 3:20

. . . because by the *works of the Law* no flesh will be *justified* in His sight; for through the Law comes the knowledge of sin.

Romans 5:1–2

Therefore, having been *justified by faith*, we have peace with God through our Lord Jesus Christ, [2]through whom also we have obtained our introduction by faith into this grace in which we stand; and we exult in hope of the glory of God.

Romans 6:15

What then? Shall we sin because we are not under law but under grace? *May it never be!*

Romans 8:3–4

For what the Law could not do, weak as it was through the flesh, God did: sending His own Son in the likeness of sinful flesh and as an offering for sin, He condemned sin in the flesh, [4]so that the requirement of *the Law* might be fulfilled in us, who do not walk according to the flesh but according to the Spirit.

Romans 9:23–24

And He did so to make known the riches of His glory upon vessels of mercy, which He prepared beforehand for glory, [24]even us, whom He also called, not from among *Jews* only, but also from among *Gentiles*.

Romans 9:30–31

What shall we say then? That *Gentiles*, who did not pursue righteousness, attained righteousness, even the righteousness which is by *faith*; [31]but Israel, pursuing a *law* of righteousness, did not arrive at that law.

Romans 10:12

For there is no distinction between *Jew* and Greek; for the same Lord is Lord of all, abounding in riches for all who call on Him.

OTHER PAULINE PARALLELS

1 Corinthians 1:30–31

But by His doing you are in Christ Jesus, who became to us wisdom from God, and righteousness and sanctification, and redemption, [31]so that, just as it is written, "LET HIM WHO *BOASTS*, BOAST IN THE LORD."

Galatians 2:15–16

"We are *Jews* by nature and not sinners from among the *Gentiles*; [16]nevertheless knowing that a man is not justified by the *works of the Law* but through faith in Christ Jesus, even we have believed in Christ Jesus, so that we may be *justified by faith* in Christ and not by the works of the Law; since by the works of the Law no flesh will be justified."

Galatians 2:19–21

"For through *the Law* I died to the Law, so that I might live to God. [20]I have been crucified with Christ; and it is no longer I who live, but Christ lives in me; and the life which I now live in the flesh I live by *faith* in the Son of God, who loved me and gave Himself up for me. [21]I do not *nullify* the grace of God, for if righteousness comes through the Law, then Christ died needlessly."

Galatians 3:8–10

The Scripture, foreseeing that God would *justify* the *Gentiles* by *faith*, preached the gospel beforehand to Abraham, saying, "ALL THE NATIONS WILL BE BLESSED IN YOU." [9]So then those who are of faith are blessed with Abraham, the believer. [10]For as many as are of the *works of the Law* are under a curse.

Galatians 3:24

Therefore *the Law* has become our tutor to lead us to Christ, so that we may be *justified by faith*.

Ephesians 2:8–9

For by grace you have been saved through *faith*; and that not of yourselves, it is the gift of God; [9]not as a result of *works*, so that no one may *boast*.

OTHER BIBLICAL PARALLELS

Deuteronomy 6:4

"Hear, O Israel! The LORD is our *God*, the LORD is *one!*"

Acts 10:34–35

Opening his mouth, Peter said: "I most certainly understand now that God is not one to show partiality, [35]but in every nation the man who fears Him and does what is right is welcome to Him."

Acts 13:38–39

"Therefore let it be known to you, brethren, that through Him forgiveness of sins is proclaimed to you, [39]and through Him everyone who believes is freed from all things, from which you could not be freed through *the Law* of Moses."

James 2:14, 18, 24, 26

What use is it, my brethren, if someone says he has faith but he has no works? Can that faith save him? . . . [18]But someone may well say, "You have faith and I have works; show me your faith without the works, and I will show you my faith by my works." . . . [24]You see that a man is *justified* by *works* and not by *faith* alone. . . . [26]For just as the body without the spirit is dead, so also faith without works is dead.

Romans 4:1–8

What then shall we say that Abraham, our forefather according to the flesh, has found? [2]For if Abraham was justified by works, he has something to boast about, but not before God. [3]For what does the Scripture say? "ABRAHAM BELIEVED GOD, AND IT WAS CREDITED TO HIM AS RIGHTEOUSNESS." [4]Now to the one who works, his wage is not credited as a favor, but as what is due. [5]But to the one who does not work, but believes in Him who justifies the ungodly, his faith is credited as righteousness, [6]just as David also speaks of the blessing on the man to whom God credits righteousness apart from works: [7]"BLESSED ARE THOSE WHOSE LAWLESS DEEDS HAVE BEEN FORGIVEN, AND WHOSE SINS HAVE BEEN COVERED. [8]BLESSED IS THE MAN WHOSE SIN THE LORD WILL NOT TAKE INTO ACCOUNT."

ROMANS PARALLELS

Romans 1:3

. . . concerning His Son, who was born of a descendant of *David* according to the flesh.

Romans 2:23

You who *boast* in the Law, through your breaking the Law, do you dishonor God?

Romans 3:19–24

Now we know that whatever the Law says, it speaks to those who are under the Law, so that every mouth may be closed and all the world may become accountable to God; [20]because by the *works* of the Law no flesh will be *justified* in His sight; for through the Law comes the knowledge of *sin*. [21]But now apart from the Law the *righteousness* of God has been manifested, being witnessed by the Law and the Prophets, [22]even the righteousness of God through *faith* in Jesus Christ for all those who *believe*; for there is no distinction; [23]for all have sinned and fall short of the glory of God, [24]being justified as a gift by His grace through the redemption which is in Christ Jesus.

Romans 4:20–24

. . . Yet, with respect to the promise of God, he did not waver in unbelief but grew strong in *faith,* giving glory to God, [21]and being fully assured that what God had promised, He was able also to perform. [22]Therefore *IT WAS ALSO CREDITED TO HIM AS RIGHTEOUSNESS.* [23]Now not for his sake only was it written that it was credited to him, [24]but for our sake also, to whom it will be credited, as those who *believe* in Him who raised Jesus our Lord from the dead.

Romans 5:6–7

For while we were still helpless, at the right time Christ died for *the ungodly.* [7]For one will hardly die for a righteous man; though perhaps for the good man someone would dare even to die.

Romans 11:6

But if it is by grace, it is no longer on the basis of *works,* otherwise grace is no longer grace.

OTHER PAULINE PARALLELS

2 Corinthians 5:18–19

Now all these things are from God, who reconciled us to Himself through Christ and gave us the ministry of reconciliation, [19]namely, that God was in Christ reconciling the world to Himself, not counting their trespasses against them, and He has committed to us the word of reconciliation.

Galatians 2:16

"Nevertheless knowing that a man is not *justified* by the *works* of the Law but through *faith* in Christ Jesus, even we have *believed* in Christ Jesus, so that we may be justified by faith in Christ and not by the works of the Law; since by the works of the Law no flesh will be justified."

Galatians 3:5–9

So then, does He who provides you with the Spirit and works miracles among you, do it by the *works* of the Law, or by hearing with *faith*? [6]Even so *Abraham BELIEVED GOD, AND IT WAS* RECKONED *TO HIM AS RIGHTEOUSNESS.* [7]Therefore, be sure that it is those who are of faith who are sons of Abraham. [8]The Scripture, foreseeing that God would *justify* the Gentiles by faith, preached the gospel beforehand to Abraham, saying, "ALL THE NATIONS WILL BE BLESSED IN YOU." [9]So then those who are of faith are blessed with Abraham, the believer.

Galatians 3:13–14

Christ redeemed us from the curse of the Law, having become a curse for us—for it is written, "CURSED IS EVERYONE WHO HANGS ON A TREE"— [14]in order that in Christ Jesus the *blessing* of *Abraham* might come to the Gentiles, so that we would receive the promise of the Spirit through *faith.*

Colossians 2:13

When you were dead in your transgressions and the uncircumcision of your flesh, He made you alive together with Him, having *forgiven* us all our transgressions.

OTHER BIBLICAL PARALLELS

Genesis 15:5–6

And He took him [Abram] outside and said, "Now look toward the heavens, and count the stars, if you are able to count them." And He said to him, "So shall your descendants be." [6]Then he *believed* in the LORD; and He reckoned it *to him as righteousness.*

Psalm 32:1–2

How *blessed* is he whose transgression is *forgiven, Whose sin* is *covered!* [2]How *blessed is the man* to whom the LORD does not impute iniquity, And in whose spirit there is no deceit!

Hebrews 11:8

By *faith Abraham*, when he was called, obeyed by going out to a place which he was to receive for an inheritance; and he went out, not knowing where he was going.

James 2:21–24

Was not *Abraham* our father *justified* by *works* when he offered up Isaac his son on the altar? [22]You see that *faith* was working with his works, and as a result of the works, faith was perfected; [23]and the Scripture was fulfilled which says, "AND *ABRAHAM BELIEVED GOD, AND IT WAS* RECKONED *TO HIM AS RIGHTEOUSNESS,*" and he was called the friend of God. [24]You see that a man is justified by works and not by faith alone.

NONCANONICAL PARALLELS

1 Maccabees 2:51–52

Remember the deeds of the ancestors, which they did in their generations; and you will receive great honor and an everlasting name. [52]Was not *Abraham* found faithful when tested, and *it was* reckoned *to him as righteousness?*

Romans 4:9–15

Is this blessing then on the circumcised, or on the uncircumcised also? For we say, "FAITH WAS CREDITED TO ABRAHAM AS RIGHTEOUSNESS." [10]How then was it credited? While he was circumcised, or uncircumcised? Not while circumcised, but while uncircumcised; [11]and he received the sign of circumcision, a seal of the righteousness of the faith which he had while uncircumcised, so that he might be the father of all who believe without being circumcised, that righteousness might be credited to them, [12]and the father of circumcision to those who not only are of the circumcision, but who also follow in the steps of the faith of our father Abraham which he had while uncircumcised. [13]For the promise to Abraham or to his descendants that he would be heir of the world was not through the Law, but through the righteousness of faith. [14]For if those who are of the Law are heirs, faith is made void and the promise is nullified; [15]for the Law brings about wrath, but where there is no law, there also is no violation.

Romans 2:26, 28–29

So if the *uncircumcised* man keeps the requirements of *the Law,* will not his uncircumcision be regarded as circumcision? . . . [28]For he is not a Jew who is one outwardly, nor is *circumcision* that which is outward in the flesh. [29]But he is a Jew who is one inwardly; and circumcision is that which is of the heart, by the Spirit, not by the letter; and his praise is not from men, but from God.

Romans 3:1–2

Then what advantage has the Jew? Or what is the benefit of *circumcision*? [2]Great in every respect. First of all, that they were entrusted with the oracles of God.

Romans 3:20–22

. . . because by the works of the Law no flesh will be justified in His sight; for through *the Law* comes the knowledge of sin. [21]But now apart from the Law the *righteousness* of God has been manifested, being witnessed by the Law and the Prophets, [22]even the righteousness of God through *faith* in Jesus Christ for all those who *believe*; for there is no distinction.

Romans 5:13, 20

. . . For until *the Law* sin was in the world, but sin is not imputed when *there is no law.* . . . [20]The Law came in so that the transgression would increase; but where sin increased, grace abounded all the more.

Romans 7:7–8

What shall we say then? Is *the Law* sin? May it never be! On the contrary, I would not have come to know sin except through the Law; for I would not have known about coveting if the Law had not said, "YOU SHALL NOT COVET." [8]But sin, taking opportunity through the commandment, produced in me coveting of every kind; for apart from the Law sin is dead.

Romans 9:7–8

. . . Nor are they all children because they are *Abraham's descendants*, but: "THROUGH ISAAC YOUR DESCENDANTS WILL BE NAMED." [8]That is, it is not the children of the flesh who are children of God, but the children of the *promise* are regarded as descendants.

1 Corinthians 15:56

The sting of death is sin, and the power of sin is the *law.*

Galatians 3:7–10

Therefore, be sure that it is those who are of *faith* who are sons of *Abraham.* [8]The Scripture, foreseeing that God would justify the Gentiles by faith, preached the gospel beforehand to Abraham, saying, "ALL THE NATIONS WILL BE BLESSED IN YOU." [9]So then those who are of faith are blessed with Abraham, the believer. [10]For as many as are of the works of *the Law* are under a curse.

Galatians 3:16–18

Now the promises were spoken to *Abraham* and to his seed. He does not say, "And to seeds," as referring to many, but rather to one, "And to your seed," that is, Christ. [17]What I am saying is this: *the Law,* which came four hundred and thirty years later, does not invalidate a covenant previously ratified by God, so as to *nullify* the *promise.* [18]For if the inheritance is based on law, it is no longer based on a promise; but God has granted it to Abraham by means of a promise.

Galatians 3:26, 29

For you are all sons of God through *faith* in Christ Jesus. . . . [29]And if you belong to Christ, then you are *Abraham's descendants*, *heirs* according to *promise.*

Genesis 15:5–6

And He took him [Abram] outside and said, "Now look toward the heavens, and count the stars, if you are able to count them." And He said to him, "So shall your *descendants* be." [6]Then he *believed* in the LORD; and He reckoned it to him *as righteousness.*

Genesis 17:4, 10–11

"As for Me, behold, My covenant is with you, And you will be the *father* of a multitude of nations. . . . [10]This is My covenant, which you shall keep, between Me and you and your *descendants* after you: every male among you shall be *circumcised.* [11]And you shall be circumcised in the flesh of your foreskin, and it shall be the sign of the covenant between Me and you."

Genesis 18:17–18

The LORD said, "Shall I hide from *Abraham* what I am about to do, [18]since Abraham will surely become a great and mighty nation, and in him all the nations of the earth will be blessed?"

Matthew 3:9

"And do not suppose that you can say to yourselves, 'We have *Abraham* for our *father*'; for I say to you that from these stones God is able to raise up children to Abraham."

Hebrews 6:13–14, 17–18

For when God made the promise to *Abraham,* since He could swear by no one greater, He swore by Himself, [14]saying, "I WILL SURELY BLESS YOU AND I WILL SURELY MULTIPLY YOU." . . . [17]In the same way God, desiring even more to show to the *heirs* of the *promise* the unchangeableness of His purpose, interposed with an oath, [18]so that by two unchangeable things in which it is impossible for God to lie, we who have taken refuge would have strong encouragement to take hold of the hope set before us.

Romans 4:16–25

For this reason it is by faith, in order that it may be in accordance with grace, so that the promise will be guaranteed to all the descendants, not only to those who are of the Law, but also to those who are of the faith of Abraham, who is the father of us all, [17](as it is written, "A FATHER OF MANY NATIONS HAVE I MADE YOU") in the presence of Him whom he believed, even God, who gives life to the dead and calls into being that which does not exist. [18]In hope against hope he believed, so that he might become a father of many nations according to that which had been spoken, "SO SHALL YOUR DESCENDANTS BE." [19]Without becoming weak in faith he contemplated his own body, now as good as dead since he was about a hundred years old, and the deadness of Sarah's womb; [20]yet, with respect to the promise of God, he did not waver in unbelief but grew strong in faith, giving glory to God, [21]and being fully assured that what God had promised, He was able also to perform. [22]Therefore IT WAS ALSO CREDITED TO HIM AS RIGHTEOUSNESS. [23]Now not for his sake only was it written that it was credited to him, [24]but for our sake also, to whom it will be credited, as those who believe in Him who raised Jesus our Lord from the dead, [25]He who was delivered over because of our transgressions, and was raised because of our justification.

NONCANONICAL PARALLELS

Sirach 44:19–21

Abraham was the great *father* of a multitude of nations, and no one has been found like him in glory. [20]He kept *the law* of the Most High, and entered into a covenant with him; he certified the covenant in his flesh, and when he was tested he proved *faithful.* [21]Therefore the Lord assured him with an oath that the nations would be blessed through his offspring; that he would make him as numerous as the dust of the earth, and exalt his offspring like the stars, and give them an inheritance from sea to sea and from the Euphrates to the ends of the earth.

ROMANS PARALLELS

Romans 3:21–24

But now apart from the *Law* the *righteousness* of God has been manifested, being witnessed by the Law and the Prophets, [22]even the righteousness of God through *faith* in Jesus Christ for all those who *believe;* for there is no distinction; [23]for all have sinned and fall short of the glory of God, [24]being justified as a gift by His *grace* through the redemption which is in Christ Jesus.

Romans 4:3–5

For what does the Scripture say? "ABRAHAM BELIEVED GOD, AND *IT WAS CREDITED TO HIM AS RIGHTEOUSNESS.*" [4]Now to the one who works, his wage is not credited as a favor, but as what is due. [5]But to the one who does not work, but *believes* in Him who justifies the ungodly, his *faith* is credited as righteousness.

Romans 8:24–25, 32

For in *hope* we have been saved, but hope that is seen is not hope; for who hopes for what he already sees? [25]But if we hope for what we do not see, with perseverance we wait eagerly for it. . . . [32]He who did not spare His own Son, but *delivered* Him *over* for us all, how will He not also with Him freely give us all things?

Romans 9:7–8

Nor are they all children because they are *Abraham's* descendants, but: "THROUGH ISAAC YOUR *DESCENDANTS* WILL BE NAMED." [8]That is, it is not the children of the flesh who are children of God, but the children of the *promise* are regarded as descendants.

Romans 10:9

If you confess with your mouth Jesus as Lord, and *believe* in your heart that God *raised* Him *from the dead*, you will be saved.

Romans 15:8–9

For I say that Christ has become a servant to the circumcision on behalf of the truth of God to confirm the *promises* given to the fathers, [9]and for the Gentiles to glorify God for His mercy.

OTHER PAULINE PARALLELS

1 Corinthians 15:20

But now Christ has been *raised from the dead*, the first fruits of those who are asleep.

2 Corinthians 5:21

He made Him who knew no sin to be sin on our behalf, so that we might become the *righteousness* of God in Him.

Galatians 3:6–7, 29

Even so Abraham *BELIEVED* GOD, AND *IT WAS* RECKONED *TO HIM AS RIGHT-EOUSNESS.* [7]Therefore, be sure that it is those who are of *faith* who are sons of *Abraham.* . . . [29]And if you belong to Christ, then you are Abraham's *descendants*, heirs according to *promise.*

Ephesians 1:18–20

I pray that the eyes of your heart may be enlightened, so that you will know what is the hope of His calling, what are the riches of the glory of His inheritance in the saints, [19]and what is the surpassing greatness of His power toward us who *believe*. These are in accordance with the working of the strength of His might [20]which He brought about in Christ, when He *raised* Him *from the dead* and seated Him at His right hand in the heavenly places.

OTHER BIBLICAL PARALLELS

Genesis 15:5–6

And He took him [Abram] outside and said, "Now look toward the heavens, and count the stars, if you are able to count them." And He said to him, "*So shall your descendants be.*" [6]Then he *believed* in the LORD; and He reckoned it *to him as righteousness.*

Genesis 17:5

"No longer shall your name be called Abram, But your name shall be *Abraham*; For *I* will *make you* the *father* of a multitude of *nations.*"

Genesis 17:17

Then *Abraham* fell on his face and laughed, and said in his heart, "Will a child be born to a man *one hundred years old*? And will *Sarah*, who is ninety years old, bear a child?"

Genesis 18:11

Now *Abraham* and Sarah were old, advanced in age; *Sarah* was past childbearing.

Isaiah 53:5

But He was pierced through for our *trans-gressions*, He was crushed for our iniquities; The chastening for our well-being fell upon Him, And by His scourging we are healed.

Hebrews 11:11–12

By *faith* even *Sarah* herself received ability to conceive, even beyond the proper time of life, since she considered Him faithful who had *promised.* [12]Therefore there was born even of one man, and him *as good as dead* at that, as many *descendants* AS THE STARS OF HEAVEN IN NUMBER, AND INNU-MERABLE AS THE SAND WHICH IS BY THE SEASHORE.

Hebrews 11:17–19

By *faith Abraham*, when he was tested, offered up Isaac, and he who had received the *promises* was offering up his only begotten son; [18]it was he to whom it was said, "IN ISAAC *YOUR DESCENDANTS* SHALL BE CALLED." [19]He considered that God is able to *raise* people even *from the dead*, from which he also received him back as a type.

NONCANONICAL PARALLELS

Philo, On the Special Laws *4.187*

God . . . wills only the good. And this was demonstrated in both the creation and ordering of the world. For God *called that which does not exist* into existence and from disorder produced order.

Romans 5:1–5

Therefore, having been justified by faith, we have peace with God through our Lord Jesus Christ, [2]through whom also we have obtained our introduction by faith into this grace in which we stand; and we exult in hope of the glory of God. [3]And not only this, but we also exult in our tribulations, knowing that tribulation brings about perseverance; [4]and perseverance, proven character; and proven character, hope; [5]and hope does not disappoint, because the love of God has been poured out within our hearts through the Holy Spirit who was given to us.

ROMANS PARALLELS

Romans 3:23–24, 28

For all have sinned and fall short of *the glory of God*, [24]being justified as a gift by His *grace* through the redemption which is in Christ Jesus; . . . [28]For we maintain that a man is *justified by faith* apart from works of the Law.

Romans 8:11, 18

But if *the Spirit* of Him who raised Jesus from the dead dwells in you, He who raised Christ Jesus from the dead will also give life to your mortal bodies through His Spirit who dwells in you. . . . [18]For I consider that the sufferings of this present time are not worthy to be compared with the *glory* that is to be revealed to us.

Romans 8:23–25

And not only this, but also we ourselves, having the first fruits of *the Spirit*, even we ourselves groan within ourselves, waiting eagerly for our adoption as sons, the redemption of our body. [24]For in *hope* we have been saved, but hope that is seen is not hope; for who hopes for what he already sees? [25]But if we hope for what we do not see, with *perseverance* we wait eagerly for it.

Romans 8:29–30

For those whom He foreknew, He also predestined to become conformed to the image of His Son, so that He would be the firstborn among many brethren; [30]and these whom He predestined, He also called; and these whom He called, He also *justified*; and these whom He justified, He also *glorified*.

Romans 8:35, 38–39

Who will separate us from the love of Christ? Will *tribulation*, or distress, or persecution, or famine, or nakedness, or peril, or sword? . . . [38]For I am convinced that neither death, nor life, nor angels, nor principalities, nor things present, nor things to come, nor powers, [39]nor height, nor depth, nor any other created thing, will be able to separate us from *the love of God*, which is in Christ Jesus our Lord.

Romans 12:10, 12

Be devoted to one another in brotherly love; give preference to one another in honor; . . . [12]rejoicing in *hope, persevering* in *tribulation*, devoted to prayer.

OTHER PAULINE PARALLELS

2 Corinthians 4:17–18

For momentary, light affliction is producing for us an eternal weight of *glory* far beyond all comparison, [18]while we look not at the things which are seen, but at the things which are not seen; for the things which are seen are temporal, but the things which are not seen are eternal.

Galatians 4:6

Because you are sons, God has sent forth *the Spirit* of His Son into our *hearts*, crying, "Abba! Father!"

Ephesians 2:13–14

But now in Christ Jesus you who formerly were far off have been brought near by the blood of Christ. [14]For He Himself is our *peace*, who made both groups into one and broke down the barrier of the dividing wall.

Colossians 1:26–27

. . . that is, the mystery which has been hidden from the past ages and generations, but has now been manifested to His saints, [27]to whom God willed to make known what is the riches of the glory of this mystery among the Gentiles, which is Christ in you, the *hope of glory*.

Titus 3:5–6

He saved us, not on the basis of deeds which we have done in righteousness, but according to His mercy, by the washing of regeneration and renewing by *the Holy Spirit*, [6]whom He *poured out* upon us richly through Jesus Christ our Savior.

OTHER BIBLICAL PARALLELS

Psalm 22:5

To You they cried out and were delivered; In You they trusted and were *not disappointed*.

Isaiah 32:17

And the work of righteousness will be *peace*, And the service of righteousness, quietness and confidence forever.

Joel 2:28

"It will come about after this That I will *pour out* My *Spirit* on all mankind; And your sons and daughters will prophesy, Your old men will dream dreams, Your young men will see visions."

John 16:33

"These things I have spoken to you, so that in Me you may have *peace*. In the world you have *tribulation*, but take courage; I have overcome the world."

Hebrews 6:13–14, 17–19

For when God made the promise to Abraham, since He could swear by no one greater, He swore by Himself, [14]saying, "I WILL SURELY BLESS YOU AND I WILL SURELY MULTIPLY YOU." . . . [17]In the same way God, desiring even more to show to the heirs of the promise the unchange-

ableness of His purpose, interposed with an oath, [18]so that by two unchangeable things in which it is impossible for God to lie, we who have taken refuge would have strong encouragement to take hold of the *hope* set before us. [19]This hope we have as an anchor of the soul, a hope both sure and steadfast and one which enters within the veil.

James 1:2–4, 12

Consider it all joy, my brethren, when you encounter various trials, [3]knowing that the testing of your *faith* produces endurance. [4]And let endurance have its perfect result, so that you may be perfect and complete, lacking in nothing. . . . [12]Blessed is a man who *perseveres* under trial; for once he has been approved, he will receive the crown of life which the Lord has promised to those who love Him.

1 Peter 5:12

Through Silvanus, our faithful brother (for so I regard him), I have written to you briefly, exhorting and testifying that this is the true *grace* of God. *Stand* firm in it!

Romans 5:6–11

For while we were still helpless, at the right time Christ died for the ungodly. [7]For one will hardly die for a righteous man; though perhaps for the good man someone would dare even to die. [8]But God demonstrates His own love toward us, in that while we were yet sinners, Christ died for us. [9]Much more then, having now been justified by His blood, we shall be saved from the wrath of God through Him. [10]For if while we were enemies we were reconciled to God through the death of His Son, much more, having been reconciled, we shall be saved by His life. [11]And not only this, but we also exult in God through our Lord Jesus Christ, through whom we have now received the reconciliation.

ROMANS PARALLELS

Romans 1:18

For *the wrath of God* is revealed from heaven against all ungodliness and unrighteousness of men who suppress the truth in unrighteousness.

Romans 3:23–25

For all have *sinned* and fall short of the glory of God, [24]being *justified* as a gift by His grace through the redemption which is in Christ Jesus; [25]whom God displayed publicly as a propitiation in *His blood* through faith. This was to demonstrate His righteousness, because in the forbearance of God He passed over the sins previously committed.

Romans 4:5

But to the one who does not work, but believes in Him who *justifies the ungodly*, his faith is credited as righteousness.

Romans 4:25

He who was delivered over because of our transgressions, and was raised because of our *justification*.

Romans 8:38–39

For I am convinced that neither death, nor life, nor angels, nor principalities, nor things present, nor things to come, nor powers, [39]nor height, nor depth, nor any other created thing, will be able to separate us from the *love* of God, which is in Christ Jesus our Lord.

Romans 10:8–9

But what does it say? "THE WORD IS NEAR YOU, in your mouth and in your heart"—that is, the word of faith which we are preaching, [9]that if you confess with your mouth Jesus as Lord, and believe in your heart that God raised Him from the dead, you will be *saved*.

Romans 11:13–15

Inasmuch then as I am an apostle of Gentiles, I magnify my ministry, [14]if somehow I might move to jealousy my fellow countrymen and *save* some of them. [15]For if their rejection is the *reconciliation* of the world, what will their acceptance be but life from the dead?

OTHER PAULINE PARALLELS

2 Corinthians 5:18–19

Now all these things are from God, who *reconciled* us to Himself through Christ and gave us the ministry of *reconciliation*, [19]namely, that God was in Christ reconciling the world to Himself, not counting their trespasses against them, and He has committed to us the word of reconciliation.

Galatians 2:20

"I have been crucified with Christ; and it is no longer I who live, but Christ lives in me; and the life which I now live in the flesh I live by faith in the Son of God, who *loved* me and gave Himself up for me."

Galatians 4:4–5

But when the fullness of the *time* came, God sent forth His Son, born of a woman, born under the Law, [5]so that He might redeem those who were under the Law, that we might receive the adoption as sons.

Ephesians 2:3–5

Among them we too all formerly lived in the lusts of our flesh, indulging the desires of the flesh and of the mind, and were by nature children of *wrath*, even as the rest. [4]But God, being rich in mercy, because of His great *love* with which He loved us, [5]even when we were dead in our transgressions, made us alive together with Christ (by grace you have been *saved*).

Ephesians 5:2

And walk in love, just as Christ also *loved* you and gave Himself up for us, an offering and a sacrifice to God as a fragrant aroma.

Colossians 1:21–22

And although you were formerly alienated and hostile in mind, engaged in evil deeds, [22]yet He has now *reconciled* you in His fleshly body *through death*, in order to present you before Him holy and blameless and beyond reproach.

1 Thessalonians 5:9–10

For God has not destined us for *wrath*, but for obtaining salvation through our Lord Jesus Christ, [10]who *died for us*, so that whether we are awake or asleep, we will live together with Him.

OTHER BIBLICAL PARALLELS

John 3:16

"For God so *loved* the world, that He gave His only begotten Son, that whoever believes in Him shall not perish, but have eternal life."

John 15:13

"Greater *love* has no one than this, that one lay down *his life* for his friends."

Hebrews 7:24–25

But Jesus, on the other hand, because He continues forever, holds His priesthood permanently. [25]Therefore He is able also to *save* forever those who draw near to God through Him, since He always lives to make intercession for them.

1 Peter 3:18

For Christ also *died* for sins once for all, the just for the unjust, so that He might bring us to God, having been put to death in the flesh, but made alive in the spirit.

1 John 4:10

In this is love, not that we loved God, but that He *loved* us and sent His Son to be the propitiation for our sins.

NONCANONICAL PARALLELS

Seneca, Moral Epistles *9.10*

Why, then, do I acquire a friend? In order to have someone for whom I may *die,* in order to have someone I may follow into exile, someone against whose death I may pledge and stake my life.

Romans 5:12–21

Therefore, just as through one man sin entered into the world, and death through sin, and so death spread to all men, because all sinned— [13]for until the Law sin was in the world, but sin is not imputed when there is no law. [14]Nevertheless death reigned from Adam until Moses, even over those who had not sinned in the likeness of the offense of Adam, who is a type of Him who was to come. [15]But the free gift is not like the transgression. For if by the transgression of the one the many died, much more did the grace of God and the gift by the grace of the one Man, Jesus Christ, abound to the many. [16]The gift is not like that which came through the one who sinned; for on the one hand the judgment arose from one transgression resulting in condemnation, but on the other hand the free gift arose from many transgressions resulting in justification. [17]For if by the trans-

gression of the one, death reigned through the one, much more those who receive the abundance of grace and of the gift of righteousness will reign in life through the One, Jesus Christ. [18]So then as through one transgression there resulted condemnation to all men, even so through one act of righteousness there resulted justification of life to all men. [19]For as through the one man's disobedience the many were made sinners, even so through the obedience of the One the many will be made righteous. [20]The Law came in so that the transgression would increase; but where sin increased, grace abounded all the more, [21]so that, as sin reigned in death, even so grace would reign through righteousness to eternal life through Jesus Christ our Lord.

ROMANS PARALLELS

Romans 3:20–25

Because by the works of the Law no flesh will be justified in His sight; for through *the Law* comes the knowledge of *sin.* [21]But now apart from the Law the *righteousness* of God has been manifested, being witnessed by the Law and the Prophets, [22]even the righteousness of God through faith in Jesus Christ for all those who believe; for there is no distinction; [23]for *all* have *sinned* and fall short of the glory of God, [24]being *justified* as a *gift* by His *grace* through the redemption which is in Christ Jesus; [25]whom God displayed publicly as a propitiation in His blood through faith. This was to demonstrate His righteousness, because in the forbearance of God He passed over the sins previously committed.

Romans 4:14–15

For if those who are of *the Law* are heirs, faith is made void and the promise is nullified; [15]for the Law brings about wrath, but where *there is no law,* there also is no violation.

Romans 4:25

He who was delivered over because of our *transgressions,* and was raised because of our *justification.*

Romans 6:23

For the wages of *sin* is *death,* but the *free gift* of God is eternal *life* in Christ Jesus our Lord.

Romans 7:7–10

What shall we say then? Is the Law sin? May it never be! On the contrary, I would not have come to know *sin* except through *the Law*; for I would not have known about coveting if the Law had not said, "YOU SHALL NOT COVET." [8]But sin, taking opportunity through the commandment, produced in me coveting of every kind; for apart from the Law sin is dead. [9]I was once alive apart from the Law; but when the commandment came, sin became alive and I died; [10]and this commandment, which was to result in *life,* proved to result in *death* for me.

OTHER PAULINE PARALLELS

1 Corinthians 15:21–22

For since by a man came *death,* by a man also came the resurrection of the dead. [22]For as in *Adam* all *die,* so also in Christ all will be made alive.

1 Corinthians 15:45–49, 54–56

So also it is written, "The first MAN, *Adam,* BECAME A LIVING SOUL." The last Adam became a life-giving spirit. [46]However, the spiritual is not first, but the natural; then the spiritual. [47]The first man is from the earth, earthy; the second man is from heaven. [48]As is the earthy, so also are those who are earthy; and as is the heavenly, so also are those who are heavenly. [49]Just as we have borne the image of the earthy, we will also bear the image of the heavenly. . . . [54]But when this perishable will have put on the imperishable, and this mortal will have put on immortality, then will come about the saying that is written, "DEATH IS SWALLOWED UP in victory. [55]O DEATH, WHERE IS YOUR VICTORY? O DEATH, WHERE IS YOUR STING?" [56]The sting of *death* is *sin,* and the power of sin is *the law.*

Galatians 3:19

Why *the Law* then? It was added because of *transgressions,* having been ordained through angels by the agency of a mediator, until the seed would come to whom the promise had been made.

Philippians 2:8

Being found in appearance as a man, He humbled Himself by becoming *obedient* to the point of death, even death on a cross.

2 Timothy 2:11–12

It is a trustworthy statement: For if we died with Him, we will also live with Him; [12]If we endure, we will also *reign* with Him; If we deny Him, He also will deny us.

OTHER BIBLICAL PARALLELS

Genesis 2:16–17

The LORD God commanded the man, saying, "From any tree of the garden you may eat freely; [17]but from the tree of the knowledge of good and evil you shall not eat, for in the day that you eat from it you will surely *die.*"

Genesis 3:17, 19

Then to *Adam* He said, "Because you have listened to the voice of your wife, and have eaten from the tree about which I commanded you, saying, 'You shall not eat from it'; Cursed is the ground because of you; In toil you will eat of it All the days of your life. . . . [19]By the sweat of your face You will eat bread, Till you return to the ground, Because from it you were taken; For you are dust, And to dust you shall return."

Isaiah 53:11–12

As a result of the anguish of His soul, He will see it and be satisfied; By His knowledge the *Righteous* One, My Servant, will *justify* the many, As He will bear their iniquities. [12]Therefore, I will allot Him a portion with the great, And He will divide the booty with the strong; Because He poured out Himself to death, And was numbered with the *transgressors*; Yet He Himself bore the *sin* of many, And interceded for the transgressors.

Hosea 6:7

But like *Adam* they have *transgressed* the covenant; There they have dealt treacherously against Me.

Revelation 22:5

And there will no longer be any night; and they will not have need of the light of a lamp nor the light of the sun, because the Lord God will illumine them; and they will *reign* forever and ever.

2 Esdras (4 Ezra) 7:118–19

O *Adam*, what have you done? For though it was you who *sinned*, the fall was not yours alone, but ours also who are your descendants. [119]For what good is it to us, if an immortal time has been promised to us, but we have done deeds that bring *death*?

2 Baruch 54:15, 19

For, although *Adam sinned* first and has brought *death* upon all who were not in his own time, yet each of them who has been born from him has prepared for himself the coming torment. . . . [19]Adam is, therefore, not the cause, except only for himself, but each of us has become our own Adam.

Romans 6:1–11

What shall we say then? Are we to continue in sin so that grace may increase? [2]May it never be! How shall we who died to sin still live in it? [3]Or do you not know that all of us who have been baptized into Christ Jesus have been baptized into His death? [4]Therefore we have been buried with Him through baptism into death, so that as Christ was raised from the dead through the glory of the Father, so we too might walk in newness of life. [5]For if we have become united with Him in the likeness of His death, certainly we shall also be in the likeness of His resurrection, [6]knowing this, that our old self was crucified with Him, in order that our body of sin might be done away with, so that we would no longer be slaves to sin; [7]for he who has died is freed from sin. [8]Now if we have died with Christ, we believe that we shall also live with Him, [9]knowing that Christ, having been raised from the dead, is never to die again; death no longer is master over Him. [10]For the death that He died, He died to sin once for all; but the life that He lives, He lives to God. [11]Even so consider yourselves to be dead to sin, but alive to God in Christ Jesus.

Romans 3:8

And why not say (as we are slanderously reported and as some claim that we say), "Let us do evil that good may come"? Their condemnation is just.

Romans 7:4–6

Therefore, my brethren, you also were made to die to the Law through the body of Christ, so that you might be joined to another, to Him who was *raised from the dead*, in order that we might bear fruit for God. [5]For while we were in the flesh, the sinful passions, which were aroused by the Law, were at work in the members of our *body* to bear fruit for death. [6]But now we have been released from the Law, having *died* to that by which we were bound, so that we serve in *newness* of the Spirit and not in oldness of the letter.

Romans 7:22–24

For I joyfully concur with the law of God in the inner man, [23]but I see a different law in the members of my *body*, waging war against the law of my mind and making me a prisoner of the law of *sin* which is in my members. [24]Wretched man that I am! Who will set me *free* from the body of this death?

Romans 8:3–4, 12–13

For what the Law could not do, weak as it was through the flesh, God did: sending His own Son in the likeness of sinful flesh and as an offering for sin, He condemned *sin* in the flesh, [4]so that the requirement of the Law might be fulfilled in us, who do not *walk* according to the flesh but according to the Spirit. . . . [12]So then, brethren, we are under obligation, not to the flesh, to live according to the flesh— [13]for if you are living according to the flesh, you must die; but if by the Spirit you are putting to *death* the deeds of the *body*, you will live.

1 Corinthians 15:20, 23–26

But now Christ has been *raised from the dead*, the first fruits of those who are asleep. . . . [23]But each in his own order: Christ the first fruits, after that those who are Christ's at His coming, [24]then comes the end, when He hands over the kingdom to the God and Father, when He has abolished all rule and all authority and power. [25]For He must reign until He has put all His enemies under His feet. [26]The last enemy that will be abolished is *death*.

1 Corinthians 15:42–43

So also is the *resurrection* of the dead. It is sown a perishable *body,* it is raised an imperishable body; [43]it is sown in dishonor, it is *raised* in *glory;* it is sown in weakness, it is raised in power.

2 Corinthians 4:10

. . . always carrying about in the *body* the *dying* of Jesus, so that the *life* of Jesus also may be manifested in our body.

2 Corinthians 5:14–15

For the love of Christ controls us, having concluded this, that one *died* for all, therefore all died; [15]and He died for all, so that they who *live* might no longer live for themselves, but for Him who died and rose again on their behalf.

Galatians 2:19–21

"For through the Law I *died* to the Law, so that I might *live* to God. [20]I have been *crucified* with Christ; and it is no longer I who live, but Christ lives in me; and the life which I now live in the flesh I live by faith in the Son of God, who loved me and gave Himself up for me. [21]I do not nullify the *grace* of God, for if righteousness comes through the Law, then Christ died needlessly."

Galatians 3:27

For all of you who were *baptized* into Christ have clothed yourselves with Christ.

Galatians 5:24

Now those who belong to Christ Jesus have *crucified* the flesh with its passions and desires.

Philippians 3:10–11

. . . that I may know Him and the power of His *resurrection* and the fellowship of His sufferings, being conformed to His *death;* [11]in order that I may attain to the resurrection from the dead.

Colossians 2:11–13

And in Him you were also circumcised with a circumcision made without hands, in the removal of the *body* of the flesh by the circumcision of Christ; [12]having been *buried with Him* in *baptism,* in which you were also raised up with Him through faith in the

working of God, who *raised* Him *from the dead.* [13]When you were dead in your transgressions and the uncircumcision of your flesh, He made you *alive* together with Him, having forgiven us all our transgressions.

Colossians 3:1, 3, 9–10

Therefore if you have been raised up with Christ, keep seeking the things above, where Christ is, seated at the right hand of God. . . . [3]For you have *died* and your *life* is hidden with Christ in God. . . . [9]Do not lie to one another, since you laid aside the *old self* with its evil practices, [10]and have put on the new self who is being renewed to a true knowledge according to the image of the One who created him.

2 Timothy 2:11–12

It is a trustworthy statement: For if we *died* with Him, we will also *live* with Him; [12]If we endure, we will also reign with Him; If we deny Him, He also will deny us.

OTHER BIBLICAL PARALLELS

Acts 2:24

But God *raised* Him up again, putting an end to the agony of *death,* since it was impossible for Him to be held in its power.

1 Peter 2:24

And He Himself bore our sins in His body on the cross, so that we might *die to sin* and *live* to righteousness; for by His wounds you were healed.

1 Peter 3:18

For Christ also *died* for *sins once for all,* the just for the unjust, so that He might bring us to God, having been put to *death* in the flesh, but made *alive* in the spirit.

NONCANONICAL PARALLELS

Apuleius, Metamorphoses *11.21*

For the gates of death and the assurance of life were in the power of the goddess [Isis], and the rite of initiation was performed in the manner of a voluntary *death* and of a life obtained by *grace.* . . . By her power she caused them in some manner to be reborn and set on a *new* course of *life.*

Romans 6:12–23

Therefore do not let sin reign in your mortal body so that you obey its lusts, [13]and do not go on presenting the members of your body to sin as instruments of unrighteousness; but present yourselves to God as those alive from the dead, and your members as instruments of righteousness to God. [14]For sin shall not be master over you, for you are not under law but under grace. [15]What then? Shall we sin because we are not under law but under grace? May it never be! [16]Do you not know that when you present yourselves to someone as slaves for obedience, you are slaves of the one whom you obey, either of sin resulting in death, or of obedience resulting in righteousness? [17]But thanks be to God that though you were slaves of sin, you became obedient from the heart to that form of teaching to which you were committed, [18]and having been freed from sin, you became slaves of righteousness. [19]I am speaking in human terms because of the weakness of your flesh. For just as you presented your members as slaves to impurity and to lawlessness, resulting in further lawlessness, so now present your members as slaves to righteousness, resulting in sanctification. [20]For when you were slaves of sin, you were free in regard to righteousness. [21]Therefore what benefit were you then deriving from the things of which you are now ashamed? For the outcome of those things is death. [22]But now having been freed from sin and enslaved to God, you derive your benefit, resulting in sanctification, and the outcome, eternal life. [23]For the wages of sin is death, but the free gift of God is eternal life in Christ Jesus our Lord.

ROMANS PARALLELS

Romans 1:24, 32

Therefore God gave them over in the *lusts* of their hearts to *impurity*, so that their bodies would be dishonored among them. . . . [32]And although they know the ordinance of God, that those who practice such things are worthy of *death*, they not only do the same, but also give hearty approval to those who practice them.

Romans 5:12, 15, 17

Therefore, just as through one man *sin* entered into the world, and *death* through sin, and so death spread to all men, because

all sinned. . . . [15]But the *free gift* is not like the transgression. For if by the transgression of the one the many died, much more did the *grace* of God and the gift by the grace of the one Man, Jesus Christ, abound to the many. . . . [17]For if by the transgression of the one, death *reigned* through the one, much more those who receive the abundance of grace and of the gift of *righteousness* will reign in *life* through the One, Jesus Christ.

Romans 5:19–21

For as through the one man's disobedience the many were made sinners, even so through the *obedience* of the One the many will be made righteous. [20]The *Law* came in so that the transgression would increase; but where sin increased, *grace* abounded all the more, [21]so that, as *sin reigned* in *death*, even so grace would reign through *righteousness* to *eternal life* through Jesus Christ our Lord.

Romans 7:22–24

For I joyfully concur with the law of God in the inner man, [23]but I see a different *law* in the *members* of my *body*, waging war against the law of my mind and making me a prisoner of the law of *sin* which is in my members. [24]Wretched man that I am! Who will set me *free* from the body of this *death*?

Romans 8:2, 10

For the law of the Spirit of life in Christ Jesus has set you *free* from the *law* of *sin* and of *death*. . . . [10]If Christ is in you, though the *body* is *dead* because of sin, yet the spirit is *alive* because of *righteousness*.

Romans 8:15

For you have not received a spirit of *slavery* leading to fear again, but you have received a spirit of adoption as sons by which we cry out, "Abba! Father!"

Romans 12:1

Therefore I urge you, brethren, by the mercies of God, to *present* your *bodies* a living and holy sacrifice, acceptable to God, which is your spiritual service of worship.

OTHER PAULINE PARALLELS

1 Corinthians 1:30

But by His doing you are in Christ Jesus, who

became to us wisdom from God, and *right-eousness* and *sanctification*, and redemption.

1 Corinthians 7:22–23

For he who was called in the Lord while a slave, is the Lord's freedman; likewise he who was called while *free*, is Christ's *slave*. [23]You were bought with a price; do not become slaves of men.

Galatians 2:21

"I do not nullify the *grace* of God, for if *righteousness* comes through the *Law*, then Christ died needlessly."

Galatians 5:18

But if you are led by the Spirit, you are *not under* the *Law*.

Ephesians 4:22–23

. . . that, in reference to your former manner of life, you lay aside the old self, which is being corrupted in accordance with the *lusts* of deceit, [23]and that you be renewed in the spirit of your mind.

Colossians 3:3, 5

For you have died and your life is hidden with Christ in God. . . . [5]Therefore consider the *members* of your earthly *body* as dead to immorality, impurity, passion, evil desire, and greed, which amounts to idolatry.

1 Thessalonians 4:7

For God has not called us for the purpose of *impurity*, but in *sanctification*.

Titus 3:3

For we also once were foolish ourselves, disobedient, deceived, *enslaved* to various *lusts* and pleasures.

Jeremiah 12:13

They have sown wheat and have reaped thorns, They have strained themselves to no profit. But be *ashamed* of your harvest Because of the fierce anger of the LORD.

Matthew 6:24

"No one can serve two *masters*; for either he will hate the one and love the other, or he will be devoted to one and despise the other. You cannot serve God and wealth."

John 8:32, 34, 36

"And you will know the truth, and the truth will make you *free*. . . . [34] . . . Truly, truly, I say to you, everyone who commits sin is the *slave of sin*. . . . [36]So if the Son makes you free, you will be free indeed."

1 Peter 2:16

Act as *free* men, and do not use your freedom as a covering for evil, but use it as *bondslaves* of God.

Plutarch, On Superstition *166D*

There is even a law for *slaves* who have lost hope of freedom, permitting them to ask for their current *master* to be exchanged for a more reasonable one.

Romans 7:1–6

Or do you not know, brethren (for I am speaking to those who know the law), that the law has jurisdiction over a person as long as he lives? [2]For the married woman is bound by law to her husband while he is living; but if her husband dies, she is released from the law concerning the husband. [3]So then, if while her husband is living she is joined to another man, she shall be called an adulteress; but if her husband dies, she is free from the law, so that she is not an adulteress though she is joined to another man. [4]Therefore, my brethren, you also were made to die to the Law through the body of Christ, so that you might be joined to another, to Him who was raised from the dead, in order that we might bear fruit for God. [5]For while we were in the flesh, the sinful passions, which were aroused by the Law, were at work in the members of our body to bear fruit for death. [6]But now we have been released from the Law, having died to that by which we were bound, so that we serve in newness of the Spirit and not in oldness of the letter.

Romans 2:12

For all who have sinned without the Law will also perish without the Law, and all who have sinned under the Law will be judged by *the Law*.

Romans 2:29

But he is a Jew who is one inwardly; and circumcision is that which is of the heart, by *the Spirit, not* by *the letter*; and his praise is not from men, but from God.

Romans 3:19

Now we know that whatever *the Law* says, it speaks to those who are under the Law, so that every mouth may be closed and all the world may become accountable to God.

Romans 4:15

For *the Law* brings about wrath, but where there is no law, there also is no violation.

Romans 5:13

For until *the Law* sin was in the world, but sin is not imputed when there is no law.

Romans 6:2–5, 7, 11

May it never be! How shall we who *died* to sin still live in it? [3]Or do you not know that all of us who have been baptized into Christ Jesus have been baptized into His death? [4]Therefore we have been buried with Him through baptism into death, so that as Christ was *raised from the dead* through the glory of the Father, so we too might walk in *newness* of life. [5]For if we have become united with Him in the likeness of His death, certainly we shall also be in the likeness of His resurrection. . . . [7]For he who has died is *freed* from sin. . . . [11]Even so consider yourselves to be dead to sin, but alive to God in Christ Jesus.

Romans 7:22–23, 25

For I joyfully concur with the law of God in the inner man, [23]but I see a different law in the *members of* my *body*, waging war against the law of my mind and making me a prisoner of *the law* of sin which is in my members. . . . [25]Thanks be to God through Jesus Christ our Lord! So then, on the one hand I myself with my mind am serving the law of God, but on the other, with my *flesh* the law of sin.

Romans 8:2, 4, 6–8

For the law of *the Spirit* of life in Christ Jesus has set you *free* from *the law* of sin and of *death*. . . . [4]so that the requirement of *the Law* might be fulfilled in us, who do not walk according to *the flesh* but according to *the Spirit*. . . . [6]For the mind set on the flesh is death, but the mind set on the Spirit is life and peace, [7]because the mind set on the flesh is hostile toward God; for it does not subject itself to the law of God, for it is not even able to do so, [8]and those who are in the flesh cannot please God.

Romans 8:10–11

If Christ is in you, though the body is dead because of sin, yet the spirit is alive because of righteousness. [11]But if *the Spirit* of Him who *raised* Jesus *from the dead* dwells in you, He who raised Christ Jesus from the dead will also give life to your mortal bodies through His Spirit who dwells in you.

OTHER PAULINE PARALLELS

1 Corinthians 6:16–17

Or do you not know that the one who *joins* himself to a prostitute is one *body* with her? For He says, "THE TWO SHALL BECOME ONE FLESH." [17]But the one who joins himself to the Lord is one spirit with Him.

1 Corinthians 7:39

A wife is *bound* as long as *her husband* lives; but if her husband is dead, she is *free* to be married to whom she wishes, only in the Lord.

2 Corinthians 3:6

. . . who also made us adequate as servants of a new covenant, *not* of *the letter* but of *the Spirit*; for the letter kills, but the Spirit gives life.

2 Corinthians 5:14–15

For the love of Christ controls us, having concluded this, that one died for all, therefore all *died*; [15]and He died for all, so that they who live might no longer live for themselves, but for Him who died and rose again on their behalf.

2 Corinthians 11:2

For I am jealous for you with a godly jealousy; for I betrothed you to one *husband*, so that to Christ I might present you as a pure virgin.

Galatians 2:19–20

"For through the Law I *died to the Law*, so that I might live to God. [20]I have been crucified with Christ; and it is no longer I who live, but Christ lives in me; and the life which I now live in *the flesh* I live by faith in the Son of God, who loved me and gave Himself up for me."

Galatians 3:23
But before faith came, we were kept in custody under *the law*, being shut up to the faith which was later to be revealed.

Colossians 1:10
. . . so that you will walk in a manner worthy of the Lord, to please Him in all respects, *bearing fruit* in every good work and increasing in the knowledge of God.

Colossians 1:21–22
And although you were formerly alienated and hostile in mind, engaged in evil deeds, [22]yet He has now reconciled you in His fleshly *body* through death, in order to present you before Him holy and blameless and beyond reproach.

OTHER BIBLICAL PARALLELS

Isaiah 45:8
"Drip down, O heavens, from above, And let the clouds pour down righteousness; Let the earth open up and salvation *bear fruit*, And righteousness spring up with it. I, the LORD, have created it."

Matthew 5:32
"But I say to you that everyone who divorces his wife, except for the reason of unchastity, makes her commit *adultery*; and whoever marries a divorced woman commits adultery."

Romans 7:7–13

What shall we say then? Is the Law sin? May it never be! On the contrary, I would not have come to know sin except through the Law; for I would not have known about coveting if the Law had not said, "YOU SHALL NOT COVET." [8]But sin, taking opportunity through the commandment, produced in me coveting of every kind; for apart from the Law sin is dead. [9]I was once alive apart from the Law; but when the commandment came, sin became alive and I died; [10]and this commandment, which was to result in life, proved to result in death for me;

[11]for sin, taking an opportunity through the commandment, deceived me and through it killed me. [12]So then, the Law is holy, and the commandment is holy and righteous and good. [13]Therefore did that which is good become a cause of death for me? May it never be! Rather it was sin, in order that it might be shown to be sin by effecting my death through that which is good, so that through the commandment sin would become utterly sinful.

ROMANS PARALLELS

Romans 3:19–20
Now we know that whatever the Law says, it speaks to those who are under the Law, so that every mouth may be closed and all the world may become accountable to God; [20]because by the works of the Law no flesh will be justified in His sight; for through *the Law* comes the knowledge of *sin*.

Romans 4:14–15
For if those who are of the Law are heirs, faith is made void and the promise is nullified; [15]for *the Law* brings about wrath, but where there is no law, there also is no violation.

Romans 5:12–14
Therefore, just as through one man sin entered into the world, and *death* through sin, and so death spread to all men, because all sinned— [13]for until *the Law* sin was in the world, but *sin* is not imputed when there is no law. [14]Nevertheless death reigned from Adam until Moses, even over those who had not sinned in the likeness of the offense of Adam, who is a type of Him who was to come.

Romans 5:20
The Law came in so that the transgression would increase; but where *sin* increased, grace abounded all the more.

Romans 10:5
For Moses writes that the man who practices the righteousness which is based on *law* shall live by that righteousness.

OTHER PAULINE PARALLELS

1 Corinthians 15:56
The sting of *death* is sin, and the power of *sin* is *the law*.

2 Corinthians 11:3

But I am afraid that, as the serpent *deceived* Eve by his craftiness, your minds will be led astray from the simplicity and purity of devotion to Christ.

Galatians 3:12

However, *the Law* is not of faith; on the contrary, "HE WHO PRACTICES THEM SHALL LIVE BY THEM."

1 Timothy 1:8–9

But we know that *the Law* is *good*, if one uses it lawfully, [9]realizing the fact that law is not made for a *righteous* person, but for those who are lawless and rebellious, for the ungodly and sinners, for the unholy and profane, for those who kill their fathers or mothers, for murderers.

OTHER BIBLICAL PARALLELS

Genesis 2:16–17

The LORD God commanded the man, saying, "From any tree of the garden you may eat freely; [17]but from the tree of the knowledge of good and evil you shall not eat, for in the day that you eat from it you will surely die."

Genesis 3:13, 17, 19

Then the LORD God said to the woman, "What is this you have done?" And the woman said, "The serpent *deceived* me, and I ate." . . . [17]Then to Adam He said, "Because you have listened to the voice of your wife, and have eaten from the tree about which I commanded you, saying, 'You shall not eat from it'; Cursed is the ground because of you; In toil you will eat of it All the days of your life. . . . [19]By the sweat of your face You will eat bread, Till you return to the ground, Because from it you were taken; For you are dust, And to dust you shall return."

Exodus 20:17

You shall not covet your neighbor's house; you shall not covet your neighbor's wife or his male servant or his female servant or his ox or his donkey or anything that belongs to your neighbor.

Leviticus 18:5

So you shall keep My statutes and My judgments, by which a man may live if he does them; I am the LORD.

James 1:13–15

Let no one say when he is tempted, "I am being tempted by God"; for God cannot be tempted by evil, and He Himself does not tempt anyone. [14]But each one is tempted when he is carried away and enticed by his own lust. [15]Then when lust has conceived, it gives birth to *sin*; and when sin is accomplished, it brings forth *death*.

NONCANONICAL PARALLELS

2 Esdras (4 Ezra) *3:6–8*

And you led him into the garden that your right hand had planted before the earth appeared. [7]And you laid upon him one *commandment* of yours; but he transgressed it, and immediately you appointed *death* for him and for his descendants. From him there sprang nations and tribes, peoples and clans without number. [8]And every nation walked after its own will; they did ungodly things in your sight and rejected your commands, and you did not hinder them.

2 Esdras (4 Ezra) *9:36–37*

"For we who have received *the law* and sinned will perish, as well as our hearts that received it; [37]the law, however, does not perish but survives in its glory."

4 Maccabees 2:5–6

Thus *the law* says, "*You shall not covet* your neighbor's wife or anything that is your neighbor's." [6]In fact, since the law has told us not to covet, I could prove to you all the more that reason is able to control desires. Just so it is with the emotions that hinder one from justice.

2 Baruch 15:5–6

It is true that man would not have understood my judgment if he had not received *the Law* and if he were not instructed with understanding. [6]But now, because he trespassed, having understanding, he will be punished.

Romans 7:14–20

For we know that the Law is spiritual, but I am of flesh, sold into bondage to sin. [15]For what I am doing, I do not understand; for I am not practicing what I would like to do, but I am doing the very thing I hate. [16]But if I do the very thing I do not want to do, I agree with the Law, confessing that the Law is good. [17]So now, no longer am I the one doing it, but sin which dwells in me. [18]For I know that nothing good dwells in me, that is, in my flesh; for the willing is present in me, but the doing of the good is not. [19]For the good that I want, I do not do, but I practice the very evil that I do not want. [20]But if I am doing the very thing I do not want, I am no longer the one doing it, but sin which dwells in me.

ROMANS PARALLELS

Romans 3:9

What then? Are we better than they? Not at all; for we have already charged that both Jews and Greeks are all under *sin*.

Romans 3:19–20

Now we know that whatever the Law says, it speaks to those who are under the Law, so that every mouth may be closed and all the world may become accountable to God; [20]because by the works of the Law no *flesh* will be justified in His sight; for through *the Law* comes the knowledge of *sin*.

Romans 6:5–7

For if we have become united with Him in the likeness of His death, certainly we shall also be in the likeness of His resurrection, [6]knowing this, that our old self was crucified with Him, in order that our body of sin might be done away with, so that we would no longer be slaves to *sin*; [7]for he who has died is freed from sin.

Romans 6:12–14

Therefore do not let *sin* reign in your mortal body so that you obey its lusts, [13]and do not go on presenting the members of your body to sin as instruments of unrighteousness; but present yourselves to God as those alive from the dead, and your members as instruments of righteousness to God. [14]For sin shall not be master over you, for you are not under *law* but under grace.

Romans 7:5

For while we were in the *flesh*, the sinful passions, which were aroused by *the Law*, were at work in the members of our body to bear fruit for death.

Romans 8:3–4

For what *the Law* could not do, weak as it was through the *flesh*, God did: sending His own Son in the likeness of sinful flesh and as an offering for sin, He condemned *sin* in the flesh, [4]so that the requirement of the Law might be fulfilled in us, who do not walk according to the flesh but according to the Spirit.

Romans 8:6–7, 9

For the mind set on the *flesh* is death, but the mind set on the Spirit is life and peace, [7]because the mind set on the flesh is hostile toward God; for it does not subject itself to *the law* of God, for it is not even able to do so. . . . [9]However, you are not in the flesh but in the Spirit, if indeed the Spirit of God *dwells* in you. But if anyone does not have the Spirit of Christ, he does not belong to Him.

Romans 8:12–13

So then, brethren, we are under obligation, not to the *flesh*, to live according to the flesh— [13]for if you are living according to the flesh, you must die; but if by the Spirit you are putting to death the deeds of the body, you will live.

OTHER PAULINE PARALLELS

1 Corinthians 3:1–3

And I, brethren, could not speak to you as to *spiritual* men, but as to men of *flesh*, as to infants in Christ. [2]I gave you milk to drink, not solid food; for you were not yet able to receive it. Indeed, even now you are not yet able, [3]for you are still fleshly. For since there is jealousy and strife among you, are you not fleshly, and are you not walking like mere men?

2 Corinthians 10:3–4

For though we walk in the *flesh*, we do not war according to the flesh, [4]for the weapons of our warfare are not of the flesh, but divinely powerful for the destruction of fortresses.

Galatians 5:17

For the *flesh* sets its desire against the Spirit, and the Spirit against the flesh; for these are in opposition to one another, so that you may *not do* the things that you please.

1 Timothy 1:8–9

But we know that *the Law is good*, if one uses it lawfully, [9]realizing the fact that law is not made for a righteous person, but for those who are lawless and rebellious, for the ungodly and sinners.

OTHER BIBLICAL PARALLELS

1 Kings 21:25

Surely there was no one like Ahab who *sold* himself to do *evil* in the sight of the Lord, because Jezebel his wife incited him.

Matthew 26:41

"Keep watching and praying that you may not enter into temptation; the spirit is *willing*, but the *flesh* is weak."

John 3:6

"That which is born of the flesh is *flesh*, and that which is born of the Spirit is spirit."

John 15:15

"No longer do I call you slaves, for the slave does not know what his master is doing; but I have called you friends, for all things that I have heard from My Father I have made known to you."

NONCANONICAL PARALLELS

The Rule of the Community (1QS) 3.17–18

He created man to rule [18]the world and placed within him two spirits so that he would walk with them until the moment of his visitation: they are the spirits of truth and deceit.

Epictetus, Discourses 2.26.1, 4

For since the one who does wrong *does not want to do* wrong but to be right, it is clear that he is not doing what he wants to do. . . . [4]And the one who can show to each person the conflict which leads him to do wrong and clearly demonstrate how he is not doing what he wants to do, and is doing what he does not want to do, is powerful in argument, both persuasion and reproof.

Romans 7:21–25

I find then the principle that evil is present in me, the one who wants to do good. [22]For I joy-

fully concur with the law of God in the inner man, [23]but I see a different law in the members of my body, waging war against the law of my mind and making me a prisoner of the law of sin which is in my members. [24]Wretched man that I am! Who will set me free from the body of this death? [25]Thanks be to God through Jesus Christ our Lord! So then, on the one hand I myself with my mind am serving the law of God, but on the other, with my flesh the law of sin.

ROMANS PARALLELS

Romans 2:14–15

For when Gentiles who do not have the Law do instinctively the things of the Law, these, not having the Law, are a *law* to themselves, [15]in that they show the work of the Law written in their hearts, their conscience bearing witness and their thoughts alternately accusing or else defending them.

Romans 3:19–20

Now we know that whatever the Law says, it speaks to those who are under the Law, so that every mouth may be closed and all the world may become accountable to God; [20]because by the works of the Law no *flesh* will be justified in His sight; for through *the Law* comes the knowledge of *sin*.

Romans 5:12–13

Therefore, just as through one man sin entered into the world, and *death* through sin, and so death spread to all men, because all sinned— [13]for until the Law sin was in the world, but *sin* is not imputed when there is no *law*.

Romans 6:5–6

For if we have become united with Him in the likeness of His death, certainly we shall also be in the likeness of His resurrection, [6]knowing this, that our old self was crucified with Him, in order that our *body* of sin might be done away with, so that we would no longer be slaves to *sin*.

Romans 6:12–14

Therefore do not let sin reign in your mortal *body* so that you obey its lusts, [13]and do not go on presenting the *members* of your body to sin as instruments of unrighteousness; but present yourselves to God as those alive from the dead, and your members as instruments of righteousness to God. [14]For *sin* shall not be master over you, for you are not under *law* but under grace.

Romans 6:16–19

Do you not know that when you present yourselves to someone as slaves for obedience, you are slaves of the one whom you obey, either of sin resulting in *death*, or of obedience resulting in righteousness? [17]But *thanks be to God* that though you were slaves of *sin*, you became obedient from the heart to that form of teaching to which you were committed, [18]and having been *freed* from sin, you became slaves of righteousness. [19]I am speaking in human terms because of the weakness of your flesh. For just as you presented your *members* as slaves to impurity and to lawlessness, resulting in further lawlessness, so now present your members as slaves to righteousness, resulting in sanctification.

Romans 7:6

But now we have been released from *the Law,* having died to that by which we were bound, so that we *serve* in newness of the Spirit and not in oldness of the letter.

Romans 8:10

If Christ is in you, though the *body* is dead because of *sin*, yet the spirit is alive because of righteousness.

Romans 12:2

And do not be conformed to this world, but be transformed by the renewing of your *mind*, so that you may prove what the will of God is, that which is *good* and acceptable and perfect.

OTHER PAULINE PARALLELS

2 Corinthians 4:16

Therefore we do not lose heart, but though our outer man is decaying, yet our *inner man* is being renewed day by day.

Galatians 5:16–17

But I say, walk by the Spirit, and you will not carry out the desire of the *flesh*. [17]For the flesh sets its desire against the Spirit, and the Spirit against the flesh; for these are in opposition to one another, so that you may not do the things that you please.

Ephesians 3:16–17

. . . that He would grant you, according to the riches of His glory, to be strengthened with power through His Spirit in *the inner man*, [17]so that Christ may dwell in your hearts through faith.

Colossians 2:11

And in Him you were also circumcised with a circumcision made without hands, in the removal of the *body* of the *flesh* by the circumcision of Christ.

OTHER BIBLICAL PARALLELS

Psalm 51:6

Behold, You desire truth in the innermost being, And in the hidden part You will make me know wisdom.

Acts 13:38–39

"Therefore let it be known to you, brethren, that through Him forgiveness of sins is proclaimed to you, [39]and through Him everyone who believes is *freed* from all things, from which you could not be freed through *the Law* of Moses."

James 4:1

What is the source of quarrels and conflicts among you? Is not the source your pleasures that *wage war* in your *members*?

1 Peter 2:11

Beloved, I urge you as aliens and strangers to abstain from fleshly lusts which *wage war* against the soul.

NONCANONICAL PARALLELS

2 Esdras (4 Ezra) 3:21–22, 26

For the first Adam, burdened with an evil heart, transgressed and was overcome, as were also all who were descended from him. [22]Thus the disease became permanent; *the law* was in the hearts of the people along with the evil root; but what was *good* departed, and the *evil* remained. . . . [26]in everything doing just as Adam and all his descendants had done, for they also had the evil heart.

The Rule of the Community (1QS) 4.23–25

Until now the spirits of truth and of injustice feud in the heart of man [24]and they walk in wisdom or in folly. In agreement with man's birthright in justice and in truth, so he abhors injustice; and according to his share in the lot of injustice he acts irreverently in it and so [25]abhors the truth.

Romans 8:1–8

Therefore there is now no condemnation for those who are in Christ Jesus. [2]For the law of the Spirit of life in Christ Jesus has set you free from the law of sin and of death. [3]For what the Law could not do, weak as it was through the flesh, God did: sending His own Son in the likeness of sinful flesh and as an offering for sin, He condemned sin in the flesh, [4]so that the requirement of the Law might be fulfilled in us, who do not walk according to the flesh but according to the Spirit. [5]For those who are according to the flesh set their minds on the things of the flesh, but those who are according to the Spirit, the things of the Spirit. [6]For the mind set on the flesh is death, but the mind set on the Spirit is life and peace, [7]because the mind set on the flesh is hostile toward God; for it does not subject itself to the law of God, for it is not even able to do so, [8]and those who are in the flesh cannot please God.

ROMANS PARALLELS

Romans 2:26

So if the uncircumcised man keeps *the requirements of the Law*, will not his uncircumcision be regarded as circumcision?

Romans 3:23–25

For all have sinned and fall short of the glory of God, [24]being justified as a gift by His grace through the redemption which is in Christ Jesus; [25]whom God displayed publicly as a propitiation in His blood through faith. This was to demonstrate His righteousness, because in the forbearance of God He passed over the sins previously committed.

Romans 5:16

The gift is not like that which came through the one who sinned; for on the one hand the judgment arose from one transgression resulting in *condemnation*, but on the other hand the free gift arose from many transgressions resulting in justification.

Romans 6:4, 14, 18

Therefore we have been buried with Him through baptism into death, so that as Christ was raised from the dead through the glory of the Father, so we too might *walk* in newness of *life*. . . . [14]For *sin* shall not be master over you, for you are not under *law* but under grace. . . . [18]and having been *freed* from sin, you became slaves of righteousness.

Romans 7:5–6

For while we were in *the flesh*, the sinful passions, which were aroused by *the Law*, were at work in the members of our body to bear fruit for *death*. [6]But now we have been released from the Law, having died to that by which we were bound, so that we serve in newness of *the Spirit* and not in oldness of the letter.

Romans 12:1–2

Therefore I urge you, brethren, by the mercies of God, to present your bodies a living and holy sacrifice, acceptable to God, which is your spiritual service of worship. [2]And do not be conformed to this world, but be transformed by the renewing of your *mind*, so that you may prove what the will of God is, that which is good and acceptable and perfect.

OTHER PAULINE PARALLELS

2 Corinthians 5:21

He made Him who knew no *sin* to be sin on our behalf, so that we might become the righteousness of God in Him.

Galatians 3:21

Is *the Law* then contrary to the promises of God? May it never be! For if a law had been given which was able to impart *life*, then righteousness would indeed have been based on law.

Galatians 4:4–5

But when the fullness of the time came, God sent forth His Son, born of a woman, born under the Law, [5]so that He might redeem those who were under *the Law*, that we might receive the adoption as sons.

Galatians 5:16–18

But I say, *walk* by *the Spirit*, and you will not carry out the desire of *the flesh*. [17]For the flesh sets its desire against the Spirit, and the Spirit against the flesh; for these are in opposition to one another, so that you may not do the things that you please. [18]But if you are led by the Spirit, you are not under *the Law*.

Philippians 2:7–8

. . . but emptied Himself, taking the form of a bond-servant, and being made in the *likeness* of men. [8]Being found in appearance as a man, He humbled Himself by becoming obedient to the point of death, even death on a cross.

Colossians 1:9–10

For this reason also, since the day we heard of it, we have not ceased to pray for you and to ask that you may be filled with the knowledge of His will in all spiritual wisdom and understanding, [10]so that you will *walk* in a manner worthy of the Lord, to *please* Him in all respects, bearing fruit in every good work and increasing in the knowledge of God.

Colossians 3:2–3

Set your *mind* on the things above, not on the things that are on earth. [3]For you have died and your *life* is hidden with Christ in God.

OTHER BIBLICAL PARALLELS

Leviticus 4:13–14

"Now if the whole congregation of Israel commits error and the matter escapes the notice of the assembly, and they commit any of the things which the LORD has commanded not to be done, and they become guilty; [14]when the sin which they have committed becomes known, then the assembly shall offer a bull of the herd for a *sin offering* and bring it before the tent of meeting."

Malachi 2:5

"My covenant with him was one of *life and peace*, and I gave them to him as an object of reverence; so he revered Me and stood in awe of My name."

Matthew 5:17

"Do not think that I came to abolish *the Law* or the Prophets; I did not come to abolish but to *fulfill*."

Acts 13:38–39

"Therefore let it be known to you, brethren, that through Him forgiveness of *sins* is proclaimed to you, [39]and through Him everyone who believes is *freed* from all things, from which you could not be freed through *the Law* of Moses."

Hebrews 7:18–19

For, on the one hand, there is a setting aside of a former commandment because of its *weakness* and uselessness [19](for *the Law* made nothing perfect), and on the other hand there is a bringing in of a better hope, through which we draw near to God.

Hebrews 13:11–12

For the bodies of those animals whose blood is brought into the holy place by the high priest as *an offering for sin*, are burned outside the camp. [12]Therefore Jesus also, that He might sanctify the people through His own blood, suffered outside the gate.

James 1:25

But one who looks intently at the perfect law, *the law* of liberty, and abides by it, not having become a forgetful hearer but an effectual doer, this man will be blessed in what he does.

Romans 8:9–11

However, you are not in the flesh but in the Spirit, if indeed the Spirit of God dwells in you. But if anyone does not have the Spirit of Christ, he does not belong to Him. [10]If Christ is in you, though the body is dead because of sin, yet the spirit is alive because of righteousness. [11]But if the Spirit of Him who raised Jesus from the dead dwells in you, He who raised Christ Jesus from the dead will also give life to your mortal bodies through His Spirit who dwells in you.

ROMANS PARALLELS

Romans 4:23–25

Now not for his sake only was it written that it was credited to him, [24]but for our sake also, to whom it will be credited, as those who believe in Him who *raised Jesus* our Lord *from the dead*, [25]He who was delivered over because of our transgressions, and was raised because of our justification.

Romans 5:12, 18

Therefore, just as through one man sin entered into the world, and death through *sin*, and so death spread to all men, because all sinned. . . . [18]So then as through one transgression there resulted condemnation to all men, even so through one act of *righteousness* there resulted justification of *life* to all men.

Romans 6:4, 6

Therefore we have been buried with Him through baptism into death, so that as Christ was *raised from the dead* through the glory of the Father, so we too might walk in newness of *life*. . . . [6]knowing this, that our old self was crucified with Him, in order that our *body* of *sin* might be done away with, so that we would no longer be slaves to sin.

Romans 6:8–9

Now if we have died with Christ, we believe that we shall also live with Him, [9]knowing that Christ, having been *raised from the dead*, is never to die again; death no longer is master over Him.

Romans 7:5–6

For while we were *in the flesh*, the sinful passions, which were aroused by the Law, were at work in the members of our *body* to bear fruit for death. [6]But now we have been released from the Law, having died to that by which we were bound, so that we serve in newness of *the Spirit* and not in oldness of the letter.

Romans 7:18, 24

For I know that nothing good *dwells* in me, that is, in my *flesh*; for the willing is present in me, but the doing of the good is not. . . . [24]Wretched man that I am! Who will set me free from *the body* of this death?

OTHER PAULINE PARALLELS

1 Corinthians 3:16

Do you not know that you are a temple of God and that *the Spirit of God dwells in you*?

1 Corinthians 6:14

Now God has not only *raised* the Lord, but will also raise us up through His power.

1 Corinthians 15:20–23

But now Christ has been *raised from the dead*, the first fruits of those who are asleep. [21]For since by a man came death, by a man also came the resurrection of the dead. [22]For as in Adam all die, so also in Christ all will be made *alive*. [23]But each in his own order: Christ the first fruits, after that those who are Christ's at His coming.

1 Corinthians 15:45

So also it is written, "The first MAN, Adam, BECAME A LIVING SOUL." The last Adam became a life-giving *spirit*.

2 Corinthians 13:5

Test yourselves to see if you are in the faith; examine yourselves! Or do you not recognize this about yourselves, that Jesus *Christ is in you*—unless indeed you fail the test?

Galatians 2:20

"I have been crucified with Christ; and it is no longer I who live, but Christ lives in me; and the *life* which I now live in *the flesh* I live by faith in the Son of God, who loved me and gave Himself up for me."

Galatians 4:6

Because you are sons, God has sent forth *the Spirit* of His Son into our hearts, crying, "Abba! Father!"

Galatians 5:24

Now those who *belong* to Christ Jesus have crucified *the flesh* with its passions and desires.

Ephesians 3:16–17

. . . that He would grant you, according to the riches of His glory, to be strengthened with power through His *Spirit* in the inner man, [17]so that Christ may *dwell* in your hearts through faith.

Philippians 3:3

For we are the true circumcision, who worship in *the Spirit of God* and glory in Christ Jesus and put no confidence in *the flesh*.

Colossians 1:26–27

. . . His saints, [27]to whom God willed to make known what is the riches of the glory of this mystery among the Gentiles, which is *Christ in you*, the hope of glory.

2 Timothy 1:14

Guard, through *the* Holy *Spirit* who *dwells* in us, the treasure which has been entrusted to you.

OTHER BIBLICAL PARALLELS

John 5:21

"For just as the Father *raises the dead* and gives them life, even so the Son also *gives life* to whom He wishes."

John 14:16–17

"I will ask the Father, and He will give you another Helper, that He may be with you forever; [17]that is *the Spirit* of truth, whom the world cannot receive, because it does not see Him or know Him, but you know Him because He abides with you and will be in you."

Acts 2:24

"But God *raised* Him up again, putting an end to the agony of death, since it was impossible for Him to be held in its power."

1 John 3:24

The one who keeps His commandments abides in Him, and He in him. We know by this that He abides in us, by *the Spirit* whom He has given us.

Romans 8:12–17

So then, brethren, we are under obligation, not to the flesh, to live according to the flesh— [13]for if you are living according to the flesh, you must die; but if by the Spirit you are putting to death the deeds of the body, you will live. [14]For all who are being led by the Spirit of God, these are sons of God. [15]For you have not received a spirit of slavery leading to fear again, but you have received a spirit of adoption as sons by which we cry out, "Abba! Father!" [16]The Spirit Himself testifies with our spirit that we are children of God, [17]and if children, heirs also, heirs of God and fellow heirs with Christ, if indeed we suffer with Him so that we may also be glorified with Him.

ROMANS PARALLELS

Romans 6:6, 12–13

Our old self was crucified with Him, in order that our *body* of sin might be done away with, so that we would no longer be *slaves* to sin; . . . [12]Therefore do not let sin reign in your mortal body so that you obey its lusts, [13]and do not go on presenting the members of your body to sin as instruments of unrighteousness.

Romans 7:5

For while we were in *the flesh*, the sinful passions, which were aroused by the Law, were at work in the members of our *body* to bear fruit for death.

Romans 8:29–30

For those whom He foreknew, He also predestined to become conformed to the image of His Son, so that He would be the firstborn among many brethren; [30]and these whom He predestined, He also called; and these whom He called, He also justified; and these whom He justified, He also *glorified*.

Romans 9:4

. . . who are Israelites, to whom belongs the *adoption as sons*, and the glory and the covenants and the giving of the Law and the temple service and the promises.

Romans 9:8

That is, it is not the children of *the flesh* who are *children of God*, but the children of the promise are regarded as descendants.

OTHER PAULINE PARALLELS

Galatians 3:26, 29

For you are all *sons of God* through faith in Christ Jesus. . . . [29]And if you belong to Christ, then you are Abraham's descendants, *heirs* according to promise.

Galatians 4:4–7

But when the fullness of the time came, God sent forth His Son, born of a woman, born under the Law, [5]so that He might redeem those who were under the Law, that we might receive the *adoption as sons*. [6]Because you are sons, God has sent forth *the Spirit* of His Son into our hearts, *crying, "Abba! Father!"* [7]Therefore you are no longer a slave, but a son; and if a son, then an *heir* through God.

Galatians 5:17–18

For *the flesh* sets its desire against the Spirit,

and the Spirit against the flesh; for these are in opposition to one another, so that you may not do the things that you please. [18]But if you are *led by the Spirit*, you are not under the Law.

Galatians 6:8
For the one who sows to his own flesh will from *the flesh* reap corruption, but the one who sows to *the Spirit* will from the Spirit reap eternal life.

Ephesians 1:5–6
He predestined us to *adoption as sons* through Jesus Christ to Himself, according to the kind intention of His will, [6]to the praise of the glory of His grace, which He freely bestowed on us in the Beloved.

Ephesians 3:5–6
. . . which in other generations was not made known to the sons of men, as it has now been revealed to His holy apostles and prophets in *the Spirit*; [6]to be specific, that the Gentiles are fellow *heirs* and fellow members of the body, and fellow partakers of the promise in Christ Jesus through the gospel.

Colossians 3:5
Therefore consider the members of your earthly *body* as dead to immorality, impurity, passion, evil desire, and greed, which amounts to idolatry.

Titus 3:5–7
He saved us, not on the basis of deeds which we have done in righteousness, but according to His mercy, by the washing of regeneration and renewing by *the* Holy *Spirit*, [6]whom He poured out upon us richly through Jesus Christ our Savior, [7]so that being justified by His grace we would be made *heirs* according to the hope of eternal life.

OTHER BIBLICAL PARALLELS

Matthew 6:9
"Pray, then, in this way: 'Our *Father* who is in heaven, Hallowed be Your name.'"

Mark 14:36
And He was saying, "*Abba*! *Father*! All things are possible for You; remove this cup from Me; yet not what I will, but what You will."

John 1:12
But as many as received Him, to them He gave the right to become *children of God*, even to those who believe in His name.

Acts 20:32
"And now I commend you to God and to the word of His grace, which is able to build you up and to give you the inheritance among all those who are sanctified."

Hebrews 1:2
In these last days [God] has spoken to us in His Son, whom He appointed *heir* of all things, through whom also He made the world.

Hebrews 2:14–15
Therefore, since the *children* share in flesh and blood, He Himself likewise also partook of the same, that through death He might render powerless him who had the power of death, that is, the devil, [15]and might free those who through fear of death were subject to *slavery* all their lives.

1 Peter 4:13
But to the degree that you share the *sufferings* of Christ, keep on rejoicing, so that also at the revelation of His glory you may rejoice with exultation.

NONCANONICAL PARALLELS

Philo, Who Is the Heir of Divine Things? *57, 63*
Thus there are two kinds of people, one which lives according to the divine *spirit*, reason, the other which lives according to blood and the pleasure of *the flesh*. The latter kind is a mold of earth, the former an accurate impression of the divine image. . . . [63] . . . Can someone who desires the life of blood . . . become the *heir* of incorporeal and divine things? No.

Romans 8:18–25

For I consider that the sufferings of this present time are not worthy to be compared with the glory that is to be revealed to us. [19]For the anxious longing of the creation waits eagerly for the revealing of the sons of God. [20]For the creation was subjected to futility, not willingly, but because of Him who subjected it, in hope

²¹that the creation itself also will be set free from its slavery to corruption into the freedom of the glory of the children of God. ²²For we know that the whole creation groans and suffers the pains of childbirth together until now. ²³And not only this, but also we ourselves, having the first fruits of the Spirit, even we ourselves groan within ourselves, waiting eagerly for our adoption as sons, the redemption of our body. ²⁴For in hope we have been saved, but hope that is seen is not hope; for who hopes for what he already sees? ²⁵But if we hope for what we do not see, with perseverance we wait eagerly for it.

ROMANS PARALLELS

Romans 3:23–24

For all have sinned and fall short of the glory of God, ²⁴being justified as a gift by His grace through the *redemption* which is in Christ Jesus.

Romans 5:2–5, 9

. . . through whom also we have obtained our introduction by faith into this grace in which we stand; and we exult in hope of the *glory* of God. ³And not only this, but we also exult in our tribulations, knowing that tribulation brings about *perseverance*; ⁴and perseverance, proven character; and proven character, *hope*; ⁵and hope does not disappoint, because the love of God has been poured out within our hearts through *the* Holy *Spirit* who was given to us. . . . ⁹Much more then, having now been justified by His blood, we shall be *saved* from the wrath of God through Him.

Romans 7:24

Wretched man that I am! Who will *set* me *free* from the body of this death?

OTHER PAULINE PARALLELS

1 Corinthians 1:7–8

You are not lacking in any gift, *awaiting eagerly* the *revelation* of our Lord Jesus Christ, ⁸who will also confirm you to the end, blameless in the day of our Lord Jesus Christ.

2 Corinthians 4:17–18

For momentary, light affliction is producing for us an eternal weight of *glory* far beyond all *comparison*, ¹⁸while we look not at the things which are seen, but at the things which are *not seen*; for the things which are seen are temporal, but the things which are not seen are eternal.

2 Corinthians 5:2–4

For indeed in this house we *groan, longing* to be clothed with our dwelling from heaven, ³inasmuch as we, having put it on, will not be found naked. ⁴For indeed while we are in this tent, we groan, being burdened, because we do not want to be unclothed but to be clothed, so that what is mortal will be swallowed up by life.

Galatians 4:4–5

But when the fullness of the time came, God sent forth His Son, born of a woman, born under the Law, ⁵so that He might redeem those who were under the Law, that we might receive the *adoption as sons*.

Ephesians 1:13–14

In Him, you also, after listening to the message of truth, the gospel of your salvation— having also believed, you were sealed in Him with *the* Holy *Spirit* of promise, ¹⁴who is given as a pledge of our inheritance, with a view to the *redemption* of God's own possession, to the praise of His *glory*.

Philippians 1:29

For to you it has been granted for Christ's sake, not only to believe in Him, but also to *suffer* for His sake.

Colossians 3:4

When Christ, who is our life, is revealed, then you also will be *revealed* with Him in *glory*.

1 Thessalonians 5:3

While they are saying, "Peace and safety!" then destruction will come upon them suddenly like labor *pains* upon a woman with child, and they will not escape.

OTHER BIBLICAL PARALLELS

Genesis 3:17

Then to Adam He said, "Because you have listened to the voice of your wife, and have eaten from the tree about which I commanded you, saying, 'You shall not eat from it'; Cursed is the ground because of you; In toil you will eat of it All the days of your life."

Isaiah 65:17

"For behold, I create new heavens and a new earth; And the former things will not be remembered or come to mind."

Jeremiah 12:4

How long is the land to mourn And the vegetation of the countryside to wither? For the wickedness of those who dwell in it, Animals and birds have been snatched away, Because men have said, "He will not see our latter ending."

Mark 13:8

"For nation will rise up against nation, and kingdom against kingdom; there will be earthquakes in various places; there will also be famines. These things are merely the beginning of *birth* pangs."

Acts 3:19–21

"Therefore repent and return, so that your sins may be wiped away, in order that times of refreshing may come from the presence of the Lord; [20]and that He may send Jesus, the Christ appointed for you, [21]whom heaven must receive until the period of restoration of all things about which God spoke by the mouth of His holy prophets from ancient time."

1 Peter 4:13

But to the degree that you share the *sufferings* of Christ, keep on rejoicing, so that also at the *revelation* of His *glory* you may rejoice with exultation.

1 John 3:2

Beloved, now we are *children of God*, and it has not appeared as yet what we will be. We know that when He appears, we will be like Him, because we will see Him just as He is.

NONCANONICAL PARALLELS

2 Esdras (4 Ezra) 7:11–14

"For I made the world for their sake, and when Adam transgressed my statutes, what had been made was judged. [12]And so the entrances of this world were made narrow and sorrowful and toilsome; they are few and evil, full of dangers and involved in great hardships. [13]But the entrances of the

greater world are broad and safe, and yield the fruit of immortality. [14]Therefore unless the living pass through the difficult and *futile* experiences, they can never receive those things that have been reserved for them."

2 Esdras (4 Ezra) 13:25–26

"This is the interpretation of the vision: As for your seeing a man come up from the heart of the sea, [26]this is he whom the Most High has been keeping for many ages, who will himself deliver his *creation*; and he will direct those who are left."

2 Baruch *15:7–8*

And with regard to the righteous ones . . . [8]For this world is to them a struggle and an effort with much trouble. And that accordingly which will come, a crown with great *glory*.

Romans 8:26–30

In the same way the Spirit also helps our weakness; for we do not know how to pray as we should, but the Spirit Himself intercedes for us with groanings too deep for words; [27]and He who searches the hearts knows what the mind of the Spirit is, because He intercedes for the saints according to the will of God. [28]And we know that God causes all things to work together for good to those who love God, to those who are called according to His purpose. [29]For those whom He foreknew, He also predestined to become conformed to the image of His Son, so that He would be the firstborn among many brethren; [30]and these whom He predestined, He also called; and these whom He called, He also justified; and these whom He justified, He also glorified.

ROMANS PARALLELS

Romans 3:23–24

For all have sinned and fall short of the glory of God, [24]being *justified* as a gift by His grace through the redemption which is in Christ Jesus.

Romans 8:15–17

For you have not received a spirit of slavery leading to fear again, but you have received a spirit of adoption as sons by which we cry out, "Abba! Father!" [16]*The Spirit* Himself testifies with our spirit that we are children of God, [17]and if children, heirs also, heirs of God and fellow heirs with Christ, if indeed we suffer with Him so that we may also be *glorified* with Him.

Romans 9:23–24

And He did so to make known the riches of His *glory* upon vessels of mercy, which He prepared beforehand for glory, [24]even us, whom He also *called*, not from among Jews only, but also from among Gentiles.

Romans 11:2

God has not rejected His people whom He *foreknew*. Or do you not know what the Scripture says in the passage about Elijah, how he pleads with God against Israel?

OTHER PAULINE PARALLELS

1 Corinthians 2:7

But we speak God's wisdom in a mystery, the hidden wisdom which God *predestined* before the ages to our *glory.*

1 Corinthians 2:10

For to us God revealed them through *the Spirit*; for the Spirit *searches* all things, even the depths of God.

1 Corinthians 8:2–3

If anyone supposes that he knows anything, he has not yet known as he ought to know; [3]but if anyone *loves God*, he is known by Him.

1 Corinthians 14:15

What is the outcome then? I will *pray* with the spirit and I will pray with the mind also; I will sing with the spirit and I will sing with the mind also.

1 Corinthians 15:49

Just as we have borne the image of the earthy, we will also bear *the image* of the heavenly.

2 Corinthians 3:18

But we all, with unveiled face, beholding as in a mirror the glory of the Lord, are being transformed into the same *image* from glory to *glory*, just as from the Lord, *the Spirit.*

Ephesians 1:11–12

Also we have obtained an inheritance, having been *predestined* according to His *purpose* who works all things after the counsel of His will, [12]to the end that we who were the first to hope in Christ would be to the praise of His *glory.*

Ephesians 6:18

With all prayer and petition *pray* at all times in *the Spirit*, and with this in view, be on the alert with all perseverance and petition for all *the saints.*

Philippians 3:10

. . . that I may know Him and the power of His resurrection and the fellowship of His sufferings, being *conformed* to His death.

Philippians 3:21

[Christ] will transform the body of our humble state into *conformity* with the body of His *glory*, by the exertion of the power that He has even to subject all things to Himself.

Colossians 1:15, 18

He is *the image* of the invisible God, the firstborn of all creation. . . . [18]He is also head of the body, the church; and He is the beginning, *the firstborn* from the dead, so that He Himself will come to have first place in everything.

Colossians 3:9–10

Do not lie to one another, since you laid aside the old self with its evil practices, [10]and have put on the new self who is being renewed to a true knowledge according to *the image* of the One who created him.

2 Thessalonians 2:13–14

But we should always give thanks to God for you, brethren beloved by the Lord, because God has chosen you from the beginning for salvation through sanctification by *the Spirit* and faith in the truth. [14]It was for this He *called* you through our gospel, that you may gain the *glory* of our Lord Jesus Christ.

OTHER BIBLICAL PARALLELS

Genesis 1:27

God created man in His own image, in *the image* of God He created him; male and female He created them.

Isaiah 53:12

Therefore, I will allot Him a portion with the great, And He will divide the booty with the strong; Because He poured out Himself to death, And was numbered with the transgressors; Yet He Himself bore the sin of many, And *interceded* for the transgressors.

John 16:13

"But when He, *the Spirit* of truth, comes, He will guide you into all the truth; for He will not speak on His own initiative, but whatever He hears, He will speak; and He will disclose to you what is to come."

Hebrews 1:6

And when He again brings *the firstborn* into the world, He says, "AND LET ALL THE ANGELS OF GOD WORSHIP HIM."

Hebrews 7:25

Therefore He is able also to save forever those who draw near to God through Him, since He always lives to make *intercession* for them.

Romans 8:31–39

What then shall we say to these things? If God is for us, who is against us? [32]He who did not spare His own Son, but delivered Him over for us all, how will He not also with Him freely give us all things? [33]Who will bring a charge against God's elect? God is the one who justifies; [34]who is the one who condemns? Christ Jesus is He who died, yes, rather who was raised, who is at the right hand of God, who also intercedes for us. [35]Who will separate us from the love of Christ? Will tribulation, or distress, or persecution, or famine, or nakedness, or peril, or sword? [36]Just as it is written, "FOR YOUR SAKE WE ARE BEING PUT TO DEATH ALL DAY LONG; WE WERE CONSIDERED AS SHEEP TO BE SLAUGHTERED." [37]But in all these things we overwhelmingly conquer through Him who loved us. [38]For I am convinced that neither death, nor life, nor angels, nor principalities, nor things present, nor things to come, nor powers, [39]nor height, nor depth, nor any other created thing, will be able to separate us from the love of God, which is in Christ Jesus our Lord.

ROMANS PARALLELS

Romans 3:23–24

For all have sinned and fall short of the glory of God, [24]being *justified* as a gift by His grace through the redemption which is in Christ.

Romans 4:25

He . . . was *delivered over* because of our transgressions, and was *raised* because of our justification.

Romans 5:3–5

And not only this, but we also exult in our *tribulations*, knowing that tribulation brings about perseverance; [4]and perseverance, proven character; and proven character, hope; [5]and hope does not disappoint, because *the love of God* has been poured out within our hearts through the Holy Spirit who was given to us.

Romans 5:8

But God demonstrates His own *love* toward us, in that while we were yet sinners, Christ *died* for us.

Romans 8:1, 3

Therefore there is now no *condemnation* for those who are in Christ Jesus. . . . [3]For what the Law could not do, weak as it was through the flesh, God did: sending His own Son in the likeness of sinful flesh and as an offering for sin, He condemned sin in the flesh.

OTHER PAULINE PARALLELS

1 Corinthians 3:22

. . . whether Paul or Apollos or Cephas or the world or *life* or *death* or *things present* or *things to come*; all things belong to you.

1 Corinthians 15:56–57

The sting of *death* is sin, and the power of sin is the law; [57]but thanks be to God, who gives us the victory through our Lord Jesus Christ.

2 Corinthians 5:14–15

For *the love of Christ* controls us, having concluded this, that one *died* for all, therefore all died; [15]and He died for all, so that they who live might no longer live for themselves, but for Him who died and rose again on their behalf.

51

2 Corinthians 12:10

Therefore I am well content with weaknesses, with insults, with *distresses*, with *persecutions*, with difficulties, for Christ's sake; for when I am weak, then I am strong.

Galatians 2:20

"I have been crucified with Christ; and it is no longer I who live, but Christ lives in me; and the life which I now live in the flesh I live by faith in the Son of God, who *loved* me and gave Himself up for me."

Ephesians 1:19–21

These are in accordance with the working of the strength of His might [20]which He brought about in Christ, when He *raised* Him from the dead and seated Him at His *right hand* in the heavenly places, [21]far above all rule and authority and *power* and dominion, and every name that is named, not only in this age but also in the one to come.

Ephesians 3:17–19

. . . and that you, being rooted and grounded in love, [18]may be able to comprehend with all the saints what is the breadth and length and *height* and *depth*, [19]and to know *the love of Christ* which surpasses knowledge, that you may be filled up to all the fullness of God.

Ephesians 5:1–2

Therefore be imitators of God, as beloved children; [2]and walk in love, just as Christ also *loved* you and gave Himself up for us, an offering and a sacrifice to God as a fragrant aroma.

OTHER BIBLICAL PARALLELS

Psalm 44:22–23

But *for Your sake we are* killed *all day long*; *We* are *considered as sheep to be slaughtered.* [23]Arouse Yourself, why do You sleep, O Lord? Awake, do not reject us forever.

Psalm 110:1

The LORD says to my Lord: "Sit at My *right hand* Until I make Your enemies a footstool for Your feet."

Psalm 118:6

The LORD is for me; I will not fear; What can man do to me?

Isaiah 50:8–9

He who vindicates Me is near; Who will contend with Me? Let us stand up to each other; Who has a case against Me? Let him draw near to Me. [9]Behold, the Lord GOD helps Me; *Who is* he *who condemns* Me? Behold, they will all wear out like a garment; The moth will eat them.

Luke 18:7

"Now, will not God bring about justice for His *elect* who cry to Him day and night, and will He delay long over them?"

Acts 2:24–25

"But God *raised* Him up again, putting an end to the agony of *death*, since it was impossible for Him to be held in its power. [25]For David says of Him, 'I SAW THE LORD ALWAYS IN MY PRESENCE; FOR HE IS AT MY *RIGHT HAND*, SO THAT I WILL NOT BE SHAKEN.'"

Hebrews 7:25

Therefore He is able also to save forever those who draw near to God through Him, since He always lives to make *intercession* for them.

1 Peter 3:21–22

Jesus Christ [22]. . . is at *the right hand of God*, having gone into heaven, after *angels* and authorities and *powers* had been subjected to Him.

Romans 9:1–5

I am telling the truth in Christ, I am not lying, my conscience testifies with me in the Holy Spirit, [2]that I have great sorrow and unceasing grief in my heart. [3]For I could wish that I myself were accursed, separated from Christ for the sake of my brethren, my kinsmen according to the flesh, [4]who are Israelites, to whom belongs the adoption as sons, and the glory and the covenants and the giving of the Law and the temple service and the promises, [5]whose are the fathers, and from whom is the Christ according to the flesh, who is over all, God blessed forever. Amen.

Romans 1:1, 3

Paul, a bond-servant of Christ Jesus, called as an apostle, set apart for the gospel of God . . . [3]concerning His Son, who was born of a descendant of David *according to the flesh* . . .

Romans 2:17, 20

But if you bear the name "Jew" and rely upon the Law and boast in God, . . . [20] . . . having in *the Law* the embodiment of knowledge and of the truth . . .

Romans 3:1–2

Then what advantage has the Jew? Or what is the benefit of circumcision? [2]Great in every respect. First of all, that they were entrusted with the oracles of God.

Romans 4:1

What then shall we say that Abraham, our forefather *according to the flesh,* has found?

Romans 8:15

For you have not received a spirit of slavery leading to fear again, but you have received a spirit of *adoption as sons* by which we cry out, "Abba! Father!"

Romans 10:1–2

Brethren, my heart's desire and my prayer to God for them is for their salvation. [2]For I *testify* about them that they have a zeal for God, but not in accordance with knowledge.

Romans 11:13–14, 28

But I am speaking to you who are Gentiles. Inasmuch then as I am an apostle of Gentiles, I magnify my ministry, [14]if somehow I might move to jealousy my fellow countrymen and save some of them. . . . [28]From the standpoint of the gospel they are enemies for your sake, but from the standpoint of God's choice they are beloved for the sake of *the fathers.*

Romans 15:8

For I say that Christ has become a servant to the circumcision on behalf of the truth of God to confirm *the promises* given to *the fathers.*

2 Corinthians 11:22

Are they Hebrews? So am I. Are they *Israelites*? So am I. Are they descendants of Abraham? So am I.

2 Corinthians 11:31

The God and Father of the Lord Jesus, He who is *blessed forever*, knows that *I am not lying.*

Galatians 1:8

But even if we, or an angel from heaven, should preach to you a gospel contrary to what we have preached to you, he is to be *accursed*!

Ephesians 2:12

Remember that you were at that time *separate from Christ*, excluded from the commonwealth of Israel, and strangers to *the covenants* of promise, having no hope and without God in the world.

Philippians 3:4–6

If anyone else has a mind to put confidence in *the flesh*, I far more: [5]circumcised the eighth day, of the nation of Israel, of the tribe of Benjamin, a Hebrew of Hebrews; as to *the Law*, a Pharisee; [6]as to zeal, a persecutor of the church; as to the righteousness which is in the Law, found blameless.

1 Timothy 2:7

For this I was appointed a preacher and an apostle (*I am telling the truth, I am not lying*) as a teacher of the Gentiles in faith and truth.

Genesis 17:2

"I will establish My *covenant* between Me and you, And I will multiply you exceedingly."

Exodus 4:22

"Then you shall say to Pharaoh, 'Thus says the LORD, "Israel is My *son*, My firstborn."'"

Exodus 32:30–32

On the next day Moses said to the people, "You yourselves have committed a great sin; and now I am going up to the LORD, perhaps I can make atonement for your sin."

³¹Then Moses returned to the LORD, and said, "Alas, this people has committed a great sin, and they have made a god of gold for themselves. ³²But now, if You will, forgive their sin—and if not, please blot me out from Your book which You have written!"

Exodus 40:34

Then the cloud covered the tent of meeting, and the *glory* of the LORD filled the tabernacle.

Deuteronomy 4:7–8

"For what great nation is there that has a god so near to it as is the LORD our God whenever we call on Him? ⁸Or what great nation is there that has statutes and judgments as righteous as this whole *law* which I am setting before you today?"

Deuteronomy 29:1

These are the words of the *covenant* which the LORD commanded Moses to make with the sons of Israel in the land of Moab, besides the *covenant* which He had made with them at Horeb.

1 Kings 9:3

"I have heard your prayer and your supplication, which you have made before Me; I have consecrated this house which you have built by putting My name there forever, and My eyes and My heart will be there perpetually."

Psalm 13:2

How long shall I take counsel in my soul, Having *sorrow in my heart* all the day?

Psalm 41:13

Blessed be the LORD, the God of Israel, From everlasting to everlasting. *Amen* and Amen.

NONCANONICAL PARALLELS

Sirach 44:1–2, 12

Let us now sing the praises of famous men, our ancestors in their generations. ²The Lord apportioned to them great *glory*, his majesty from the beginning. . . . ¹²Their descendants stand by the *covenants*; their children also, for their sake.

Romans 9:6–13

But it is not as though the word of God has failed. For they are not all Israel who are descended from Israel; ⁷nor are they all children because they are Abraham's descendants, but: "THROUGH ISAAC YOUR DESCENDANTS WILL BE NAMED." ⁸That is, it is not the children of the flesh who are children of God, but the children of the promise are regarded as descendants. ⁹For this is the word of promise: "AT THIS TIME I WILL COME, AND SARAH SHALL HAVE A SON." ¹⁰And not only this, but there was Rebekah also, when she had conceived twins by one man, our father Isaac; ¹¹for though the twins were not yet born and had not done anything good or bad, so that God's purpose according to His choice would stand, not because of works but because of Him who calls, ¹²it was said to her, "THE OLDER WILL SERVE THE YOUNGER." ¹³Just as it is written, "JACOB I LOVED, BUT ESAU I HATED."

ROMANS PARALLELS

Romans 2:28–29

For he is not a Jew who is one outwardly, nor is circumcision that which is outward in *the flesh*. ²⁹But he is a Jew who is one inwardly; and circumcision is that which is of the heart, by the Spirit, not by the letter; and his praise is not from men, but from God.

Romans 4:13, 16

For *the promise* to *Abraham* or to his *descendants* that he would be heir of the world was not through the Law, but through the righteousness of faith. . . . ¹⁶For this reason it is by faith, in order that it may be in accordance with grace, so that the promise will be guaranteed to all the descendants, not only to those who are of the Law, but also to those who are of the faith of Abraham, who is the father of us all.

Romans 8:16–17

The Spirit Himself testifies with our spirit that we are *children of God*, ¹⁷and if children, heirs also, heirs of God and fellow heirs with Christ, if indeed we suffer with Him so that we may also be glorified with Him.

Romans 8:28

And we know that God causes all things to work together for good to those who love God, to those who are *called* according to His *purpose.*

Romans 9:23–24

And He did so to make known the riches of His glory upon vessels of mercy, which He prepared beforehand for glory, [24]even us, whom He also *called,* not from among Jews only, but also from among Gentiles.

Romans 11:1, 5–6

I say then, God has not rejected His people, has He? May it never be! For I too am an Israelite, a *descendant of Abraham,* of the tribe of Benjamin. . . . [5]In the same way then, there has also come to be at the present time a remnant according to God's gracious *choice.* [6]But if it is by grace, it is no longer on the basis of *works,* otherwise grace is no longer grace.

Romans 11:28

From the standpoint of the gospel they are enemies for your sake, but from the standpoint of God's *choice* they are beloved for the sake of the fathers.

OTHER PAULINE PARALLELS

Galatians 3:13–14

Christ redeemed us from the curse of the Law, having become a curse for us—for it is written, "CURSED IS EVERYONE WHO HANGS ON A TREE"— [14]in order that in Christ Jesus the blessing of *Abraham* might come to the Gentiles, so that we would receive *the promise* of the Spirit through faith.

Galatians 3:29

And if you belong to Christ, then you are *Abraham's descendants,* heirs according to *promise.*

Galatians 4:22–23, 28

For it is written that *Abraham* had two sons, one by the bondwoman and one by the free woman. [23]But the son by the bondwoman was born according to *the flesh,* and the *son* by the free woman through the promise. . . . [28]And you brethren, like *Isaac,* are *children of promise.*

OTHER BIBLICAL PARALLELS

Genesis 18:14

"Is anything too difficult for the LORD? *At* the appointed *time I will* return to you, at this time next year, *and Sarah will have a son."*

Genesis 21:12

"Do not be distressed because of the lad and your maid; whatever Sarah tells you, listen to her, for *through Isaac your descendants* shall *be named."*

Genesis 25:21–23

Isaac prayed to the LORD on behalf of his wife, because she was barren; and the LORD answered him and *Rebekah* his wife *conceived.* [22]But the children struggled together within her; and she said, "If it is so, why then am I this way?" So she went to inquire of the LORD. [23]The LORD said to her, "Two nations are in your womb; And two peoples will be separated from your body; And one people shall be stronger than the other; And *the older* shall *serve the younger."*

Malachi 1:2–3

"I have loved you," says the LORD. But you say, "How have You loved us?" "Was not Esau Jacob's brother?" declares the LORD. "Yet *I* have *loved Jacob*; [3]*but I* have *hated Esau,* and I have made his mountains a desolation and appointed his inheritance for the jackals of the wilderness."

Matthew 3:9

"And do not suppose that you can say to yourselves, 'We have Abraham for our father'; for I say to you that from these stones God is able to raise up *children* to Abraham."

John 8:39

They answered and said to Him, "Abraham is our father." Jesus said to them, "If you are *Abraham's children,* do the deeds of Abraham."

Hebrews 11:17–18

By faith *Abraham,* when he was tested, offered up Isaac, and he who had received the promises was offering up his only begotten son; [18]it was he to whom it was said, "IN *ISAAC YOUR DESCENDANTS* SHALL BE CALLED."

Pseudo–Philo, Biblical Antiquities *32:5*

And God *loved Jacob*, but he *hated Esau* because of his deeds.

Romans 9:14–18

What shall we say then? There is no injustice with God, is there? May it never be! ¹⁵For He says to Moses, "I WILL HAVE MERCY ON WHOM I HAVE MERCY, AND I WILL HAVE COMPASSION ON WHOM I HAVE COMPASSION." ¹⁶So then it does not depend on the man who wills or the man who runs, but on God who has mercy. ¹⁷For the Scripture says to Pharaoh, "FOR THIS VERY PURPOSE I RAISED YOU UP, TO DEMONSTRATE MY POWER IN YOU, AND THAT MY NAME MIGHT BE PROCLAIMED THROUGHOUT THE WHOLE EARTH." ¹⁸So then He has mercy on whom He desires, and He hardens whom He desires.

ROMANS PARALLELS

Romans 3:5–6

But if our unrighteousness demonstrates the righteousness of God, what shall we say? The God who inflicts wrath is not unrighteous, is He? (I am speaking in human terms.) ⁶*May it never be!* For otherwise, how will God judge the world?

Romans 11:7

What then? What Israel is seeking, it has not obtained, but those who were chosen obtained it, and the rest were *hardened*.

Romans 11:25

For I do not want you, brethren, to be uninformed of this mystery—so that you will not be wise in your own estimation—that a partial *hardening* has happened to Israel until the fullness of the Gentiles has come in.

Romans 11:30–32

For just as you once were disobedient to God, but now have been shown *mercy* because of their disobedience, ³¹so these also now have been disobedient, that because of the mercy shown to you they also may now be shown mercy. ³²For God has shut up all in disobedience so that He may show mercy to all.

2 Corinthians 3:12–14

Therefore having such a hope, we use great boldness in our speech, ¹³and are not like Moses, who used to put a veil over his face so that the sons of Israel would not look intently at the end of what was fading away. ¹⁴But their minds were *hardened*; for until this very day at the reading of the old covenant the same veil remains unlifted, because it is removed in Christ.

Titus 3:5

He saved us, not on the basis of deeds which we have done in righteousness, but according to His *mercy*, by the washing of regeneration and renewing by the Holy Spirit.

OTHER BIBLICAL PARALLELS

Exodus 7:3

"But I will *harden* Pharaoh's heart that I may multiply My signs and My wonders in the land of Egypt."

Exodus 9:13, 16

"Rise up early in the morning and stand before *Pharaoh* and say to him, 'Thus says the LORD, the God of the Hebrews, "Let My people go, that they may serve Me. . . . ¹⁶But, indeed, *for this* reason I have allowed you to remain, in order to show you *My power* and in order to *proclaim My name through* all *the earth.*"'"

Exodus 33:18–19

Then Moses said, "I pray You, show me Your glory!" ¹⁹And He said, "I Myself will make all My goodness pass before you, and will proclaim the name of the LORD before you; and I will be gracious to whom I will be gracious, and *will* show *compassion on whom I* will show *compassion.*"

Deuteronomy 32:4

"The Rock! His work is perfect, For all His ways are just; A God of faithfulness and without *injustice*, Righteous and upright is He."

Job 13:7

"Will you speak what is unjust for God, And speak what is deceitful for Him?"

Zephaniah 3:5

The LORD is righteous within her; He will do *no injustice.* Every morning He brings His justice to light; He does not fail. But the unjust knows no shame.

Romans 9:19–26

You will say to me then, "Why does He still find fault? For who resists His will?" ²⁰On the contrary, who are you, O man, who answers back to God? The thing molded will not say to the molder, "Why did you make me like this," will it? ²¹Or does not the potter have a right over the clay, to make from the same lump one vessel for honorable use and another for common use? ²²What if God, although willing to demonstrate His wrath and to make His power known, endured with much patience vessels of wrath prepared for destruction? ²³And He did so to make known the riches of His glory upon vessels of mercy, which He prepared beforehand for glory, ²⁴even us, whom He also called, not from among Jews only, but also from among Gentiles. ²⁵As He says also in Hosea, "I WILL CALL THOSE WHO WERE NOT MY PEOPLE, 'MY PEOPLE,' AND HER WHO WAS NOT BELOVED, 'BELOVED.'" ²⁶"AND IT SHALL BE THAT IN THE PLACE WHERE IT WAS SAID TO THEM, 'YOU ARE NOT MY PEOPLE,' THERE THEY SHALL BE CALLED SONS OF THE LIVING GOD."

ROMANS PARALLELS

Romans 2:4–5

Or do you think lightly of *the riches* of His kindness and tolerance and *patience,* not knowing that the kindness of God leads you to repentance? ⁵But because of your stubbornness and unrepentant heart you are storing up *wrath* for yourself in the day of wrath and revelation of the righteous judgment of God.

Romans 3:5, 7

But if our unrighteousness demonstrates the righteousness of God, what shall we say? The God who inflicts *wrath* is not unrighteous, is He? . . . ⁷But if through my lie the truth of God abounded to *His glory,* why am I also still being judged as a sinner?

Romans 8:28–30

And we know that God causes all things to work together for good to those who love God, to those who are *called* according to His purpose. ²⁹For those whom He foreknew, He also predestined to become conformed to the image of His Son, so that He would be the firstborn among many brethren; ³⁰and these whom He predestined, He also called; and these whom He called, He also justified; and these whom He justified, He also *glorified.*

Romans 10:12

For there is no distinction between *Jew* and Greek; for the same Lord is Lord of all, abounding in *riches* for all who call on Him.

OTHER PAULINE PARALLELS

2 Corinthians 5:4–5

For indeed while we are in this tent, we groan, being burdened, because we do not want to be unclothed but to be clothed, so that what is mortal will be swallowed up by life. ⁵Now He who *prepared* us for this very purpose is God, who gave to us the Spirit as a pledge.

Ephesians 1:4–5

He chose us in Him before the foundation of the world, that we would be holy and blameless before Him. In love ⁵He predestined us to adoption as sons through Jesus Christ to Himself, according to the kind intention of *His will.*

Ephesians 1:18

I pray that the eyes of your heart may be enlightened, so that you will know what is the hope of His *calling,* what are *the riches* of the *glory* of His inheritance in the saints.

Ephesians 2:10

For we are His workmanship, created in Christ Jesus for good works, which God *prepared beforehand* so that we would walk in them.

2 Timothy 2:20–21

Now in a large house there are not only gold and silver *vessels,* but also vessels of wood and of earthenware, and some to *honor* and some to dishonor. ²¹Therefore, if anyone cleanses himself from these things, he will be a vessel for honor, sanctified, useful to the Master, *prepared* for every good work.

Job 9:2–4

"In truth I know that this is so; But how can a man be in the right before God? ³If one wished to dispute with Him, He could not *answer* Him once in a thousand times. ⁴Wise in heart and mighty in strength, Who has defied Him without harm?"

Proverbs 16:4

The LORD has made everything for its own purpose, Even the wicked for the day of evil.

Isaiah 29:16

You turn things around! Shall *the potter* be considered as equal with *the clay*, That what is made would say to its maker, "He did not *make me*"; Or what is formed say to him who formed it, "He has no understanding"?

Isaiah 45:9

"Woe to the one who quarrels with his Maker—An earthenware *vessel* among the vessels of earth! Will *the clay* say to *the potter*, 'What are you doing?' Or the thing you are making say, 'He has no hands'?"

Jeremiah 18:6

"Can I not, O house of Israel, deal with you as this *potter* does?" declares the LORD. "Behold, like *the clay* in the potter's hand, so are you in My hand, O house of Israel."

Daniel 4:35

"All the inhabitants of the earth are accounted as nothing, But He does according to *His will* in the host of heaven And among the inhabitants of earth; And no one can ward off His hand Or say to Him, 'What have You done?'"

Hosea 1:10

Yet the number of the sons of Israel Will be like the sand of the sea, Which cannot be measured or numbered; And *in the place Where it is said to them*, "You are not My people," It will be said to them, "You are the *sons of the living God*."

Hosea 2:23

"I will sow her for Myself in the land. I will also have compassion on her who had not obtained compassion, And *I will* say to *those who were not My people*, 'You are *My people*!' And they will say, 'You are my God!'"

1 Peter 2:9–10

But you are A CHOSEN RACE, A royal PRIESTHOOD, A HOLY NATION, A PEOPLE FOR God's OWN POSSESSION, so that you may proclaim the excellencies of Him who has *called* you out of darkness into His marvelous light; ¹⁰for you once were *NOT A PEOPLE*, but now you are THE *PEOPLE* OF GOD; you had NOT RECEIVED MERCY, but now you have RECEIVED MERCY.

Sirach 33:12–13

Some he blessed and exalted, and some he made holy and brought near to himself; but some he cursed and brought low, and turned them out of their place. ¹³Like *clay* in the hand of *the potter*, to be molded as he pleases, so all are in the hand of their Maker, to be given whatever he decides.

Romans 9:27–33

Isaiah cries out concerning Israel, "THOUGH THE NUMBER OF THE SONS OF ISRAEL BE LIKE THE SAND OF THE SEA, IT IS THE REMNANT THAT WILL BE SAVED; ²⁸FOR THE LORD WILL EXECUTE HIS WORD ON THE EARTH, THOROUGHLY AND QUICKLY." ²⁹And just as Isaiah foretold, "UNLESS THE LORD OF SABAOTH HAD LEFT TO US A POSTERITY, WE WOULD HAVE BECOME LIKE SODOM, AND WOULD HAVE RESEMBLED GOMORRAH." ³⁰What shall we say then? That Gentiles, who did not pursue righteousness, attained righteousness, even the righteousness which is by faith; ³¹but Israel, pursuing a law of righteousness, did not arrive at that law. ³²Why? Because they did not pursue it by faith, but as though it were by works. They stumbled over the stumbling stone, ³³just as it is written, "BEHOLD, I LAY IN ZION A STONE OF STUMBLING AND A ROCK OF OFFENSE, AND HE WHO BELIEVES IN HIM WILL NOT BE DISAPPOINTED."

Romans 1:16–17

For I am not ashamed of the gospel, for it is the power of God for salvation to everyone who believes, to the Jew first and also to the Greek. ¹⁷For in it the *righteousness* of God is revealed from *faith* to faith; as it is written, "BUT THE RIGHTEOUS man SHALL LIVE BY FAITH."

Romans 3:27–28

Where then is boasting? It is excluded. By what kind of *law*? Of works? No, but by a law of faith. [28]For we maintain that a man is justified by *faith* apart from *works* of the Law.

Romans 4:11, 13

And he received the sign of circumcision, a seal of the *righteousness* of the *faith* which he had while uncircumcised, so that he might be the father of all who believe without being circumcised, that righteousness might be credited to them. . . . [13]For the promise to Abraham or to his descendants that he would be heir of the world was not through the Law, but through the righteousness of faith.

Romans 10:11–12

For the Scripture says, "WHOEVER *BELIEVES IN HIM WILL NOT BE DISAPPOINTED.*" [12]For there is no distinction between Jew and Greek; for the same Lord is Lord of all, abounding in riches for all who call on Him.

Romans 10:20

And *Isaiah* is very bold and says, "I WAS FOUND BY THOSE WHO DID NOT SEEK ME, I BECAME MANIFEST TO THOSE WHO DID NOT ASK FOR ME."

Romans 11:5, 7, 9

In the same way then, there has also come to be at the present time a *remnant* according to God's gracious choice. . . . [7]What then? What *Israel* is seeking, it has not obtained, but those who were chosen obtained it, and the rest were hardened; . . . [9]And David says, "LET THEIR TABLE BECOME A SNARE AND A TRAP, AND A *STUMBLING* BLOCK AND A RETRIBUTION TO THEM."

OTHER PAULINE PARALLELS

Galatians 2:15–16

"We are Jews by nature and not sinners from among the *Gentiles*; [16]nevertheless knowing that a man is not justified by the *works* of the Law but through *faith* in Christ Jesus, even we have believed in Christ

Jesus, so that we may be justified by faith in Christ and not by the works of the Law; since by the works of the Law no flesh will be justified."

Galatians 5:4

You have been severed from Christ, you who are seeking to be justified by *law*; you have fallen from grace.

OTHER BIBLICAL PARALLELS

Deuteronomy 16:20

"Justice, and only justice, you shall *pursue,* that you may live and possess the land which the LORD your God is giving you."

Isaiah 1:8–9

The daughter of Zion is left like a shelter in a vineyard, Like a watchman's hut in a cucumber field, like a besieged city. [9]*Unless the* LORD *of hosts Had left us* a few survivors, *We would* be *like Sodom*, We *would* be like *Gomorrah.*

Isaiah 8:14

"Then He shall become a sanctuary; But to both the houses of *Israel, a stone* to strike and *a rock* to *stumble* over, And a snare and a trap for the inhabitants of Jerusalem."

Isaiah 10:22–23

For *though* your people, O *Israel*, may *be like the sand of the sea*, Only a *remnant* within them will return; A destruction is determined, overflowing with *righteousness.* [23]For a complete destruction, one that is decreed, *the Lord* GOD of hosts *will execute* in the midst of the whole land.

Isaiah 28:16

"*Behold, I* am *laying in Zion a stone*, a tested stone, A costly cornerstone for the foundation, firmly placed. *He who believes in* it *will not be* disturbed."

Isaiah 37:32

"For out of Jerusalem will go forth a *remnant* and out of Mount Zion survivors. The zeal of the LORD of hosts will perform this."

Isaiah 51:1

"Listen to me, you who *pursue righteousness*, Who seek the LORD: Look to the rock from which you were hewn And to the quarry from which you were dug."

Matthew 21:42–44

"Did you never read in the Scriptures, 'THE STONE WHICH THE BUILDERS REJECTED, THIS BECAME THE CHIEF CORNER stone; THIS CAME ABOUT FROM THE LORD, AND IT IS MARVELOUS IN OUR EYES'? [43]Therefore I say to you, the kingdom of God will be taken away from you and given to a people, producing the fruit of it. [44]And he who falls on this *stone* will be broken to pieces; but on whomever it falls, it will scatter him like dust."

1 Peter 2:6–8

For this is contained in Scripture: *"BEHOLD, I LAY IN ZION A CHOICE STONE, A PRECIOUS CORNER stone, AND HE WHO BELIEVES IN HIM WILL NOT BE DISAPPOINTED."* [7]This precious value, then, is for you who believe; but for those who disbelieve, "THE STONE WHICH THE BUILDERS REJECTED, THIS BECAME THE VERY CORNER stone," [8]and,*"A STONE OF STUMBLING AND A ROCK OF OFFENSE"*; for they *stumble* because they are disobedient to the word, and to this doom they were also appointed.

NONCANONICAL PARALLELS

The War Scroll *(1QM) 14.9*

In all our generations you have caused your favours to fall on the *rem*[*nant* of our people] during the empire of Belial. In all the mysteries of his enmity, they have not separated us from your covenant.

Romans 10:1–4

Brethren, my heart's desire and my prayer to God for them is for their salvation. [2]For I testify about them that they have a zeal for God, but not in accordance with knowledge. [3]For not knowing about God's righteousness and seeking to establish their own, they did not subject themselves to the righteousness of God. [4]For Christ is the end of the law for righteousness to everyone who believes.

ROMANS PARALLELS

Romans 1:16–17

For I am not ashamed of the gospel, for it is the power of God for *salvation* to *everyone who believes*, to the Jew first and also to the Greek. [17]For in it *the righteousness of God* is revealed from faith to faith; as it is written, "BUT THE RIGHTEOUS man SHALL LIVE BY FAITH."

Romans 2:17, 19–20

But if you bear the name "Jew" and rely upon *the Law* and boast in God . . . [19]and are confident that you yourself are a guide to the blind, a light to those who are in darkness, [20]a corrector of the foolish, a teacher of the immature, having in the Law the embodiment of *knowledge* and of the truth . . .

Romans 3:21–22

But now apart from the Law *the righteousness of God* has been manifested, being witnessed by *the Law* and the Prophets, [22]even the righteousness of God through faith in Jesus Christ for all those who *believe*; for there is no distinction.

Romans 7:4

Therefore, my brethren, you also were made to die to *the Law* through the body of Christ, so that you might be joined to another, to Him who was raised from the dead, in order that we might bear fruit for God.

Romans 8:3–4

For what the Law could not do, weak as it was through the flesh, God did: sending His own Son in the likeness of sinful flesh and as an offering for sin, He condemned sin in the flesh, [4]so that the requirement of *the Law* might be fulfilled in us, who do not walk according to the flesh but according to the Spirit.

Romans 9:1–3

I am telling the truth in Christ, I am not lying, my conscience *testifies* with me in the Holy Spirit, [2]that I have great sorrow and unceasing grief in my *heart*. [3]For I could wish that I myself were accursed, separated from Christ for the sake of my brethren, my kinsmen according to the flesh.

Romans 10:20

And Isaiah is very bold and says, "I WAS FOUND BY THOSE WHO DID NOT SEEK ME, I BECAME MANIFEST TO THOSE WHO DID NOT ASK FOR ME."

Romans 11:7

What then? What Israel is *seeking*, it has not obtained, but those who were chosen obtained it, and the rest were hardened.

OTHER PAULINE PARALLELS

2 Corinthians 3:12–14

Therefore having such a hope, we use great boldness in our speech, [13]and are not like Moses, who used to put a veil over his face so that the sons of Israel would not look intently at *the end* of what was fading away. [14]But their minds were hardened; for until this very day at the reading of the old covenant the same veil remains unlifted, because it is removed in Christ.

Galatians 3:23–24

But before faith came, we were kept in custody under *the law*, being shut up to the faith which was later to be revealed. [24]Therefore the Law has become our tutor to lead us to Christ, so that we may be justified by faith.

Galatians 4:4–5

But when the fullness of the time came, God sent forth His Son, born of a woman, born under the Law, [5]so that He might redeem those who were under *the Law*, that we might receive the adoption as sons.

Philippians 3:8–9

More than that, I count all things to be loss in view of the surpassing value of *knowing* Christ Jesus my Lord, for whom I have suffered the loss of all things, and count them but rubbish so that I may gain Christ, [9]and may be found in Him, not having a *righteousness* of my own derived from *the Law*, but that which is through faith in Christ, the righteousness which comes from God on the basis of faith.

Colossians 2:1–3

For I want you to know how great a struggle I have on your behalf and for those who are at Laodicea, and for all those who have not personally seen my face, [2]that their hearts may be encouraged, having been knit together in love, and attaining to all the wealth that comes from the full assurance of understanding, resulting in a true *knowledge* of God's mystery, that is, Christ Himself, [3]in whom are hidden all the treasures of wisdom and knowledge.

OTHER BIBLICAL PARALLELS

Deuteronomy 9:4

"Do not say in your heart when the LORD your God has driven them out before you, 'Because of my *righteousness* the LORD has brought me in to possess this land,' but it is because of the wickedness of these nations that the LORD is dispossessing them before you."

Psalm 20:3–4

May He remember all your meal offerings And find your burnt offering acceptable! Selah! [4]May He grant you your *heart's desire* And fulfill all your counsel!

Acts 21:20

And when they heard it they began glorifying God; and they said to him, "You see, brother, how many thousands there are among the Jews of those who have believed, and they are all *zealous* for *the Law*."

Acts 22:3

"I am a Jew, born in Tarsus of Cilicia, but brought up in this city, educated under Gamaliel, strictly according to *the law* of our fathers, being *zealous for God* just as you all are today."

NONCANONICAL PARALLELS

Plutarch, To an Uneducated Ruler *780E*

Justice, then, is *the end of the law*, but law is the work of a ruler.

Romans 10:5–13

For Moses writes that the man who practices the righteousness which is based on law shall live by that righteousness. [6]But the righteousness based on faith speaks as follows: "DO NOT SAY IN YOUR HEART, 'WHO WILL ASCEND INTO HEAVEN?' (that is, to bring Christ down), [7]or 'WHO WILL DESCEND INTO THE ABYSS?' (that is, to bring Christ up from the dead)."

⁸But what does it say? "THE WORD IS NEAR YOU, in your mouth and in your heart"—that is, the word of faith which we are preaching, ⁹that if you confess with your mouth Jesus as Lord, and believe in your heart that God raised Him from the dead, you will be saved; ¹⁰for with the heart a person believes, resulting in righteousness, and with the mouth he confesses, resulting in salvation. ¹¹For the Scripture says, "WHOEVER BELIEVES IN HIM WILL NOT BE DISAPPOINTED." ¹²For there is no distinction between Jew and Greek; for the same Lord is Lord of all, abounding in riches for all who call on Him; ¹³for "WHOEVER WILL CALL ON THE NAME OF THE LORD WILL BE SAVED."

ROMANS PARALLELS

Romans 2:13

For it is not the hearers of the Law who are just before God, but the doers of the *Law* will be justified.

Romans 3:21–22

But now apart from the *Law* the *righteousness* of God has been manifested, being witnessed by the Law and the Prophets, ²²even the righteousness of God through *faith* in Jesus Christ for all those who *believe*; for there is *no distinction*.

Romans 4:23–24

Now not for his sake only was it written that it was credited to him, ²⁴but for our sake also, to whom it will be credited, as those who *believe* in Him who *raised* Jesus our Lord *from the dead*.

Romans 9:30, 33

What shall we say then? That Gentiles, who did not pursue righteousness, attained *righteousness*, even the righteousness which is by *faith*; . . . ³³just as it is written, "BEHOLD, I LAY IN ZION A STONE OF STUMBLING AND A ROCK OF OFFENSE, AND HE *WHO BELIEVES IN HIM WILL NOT BE DISAPPOINTED*."

Romans 14:9

For to this end Christ died and lived again, that He might be Lord both of *the dead* and of the living.

OTHER PAULINE PARALLELS

Galatians 3:10–12

For as many as are of the works of the Law are under a curse; for it is written, "CURSED IS EVERYONE WHO DOES NOT ABIDE BY ALL THINGS WRITTEN IN THE BOOK OF THE LAW, TO PERFORM THEM." ¹¹Now that no one is justified by the Law before God is evident; for, "THE RIGHTEOUS MAN SHALL LIVE BY FAITH." ¹²However, the *Law* is not of *faith*; on the contrary, "HE WHO *PRACTICES* THEM *SHALL LIVE* BY THEM."

Ephesians 4:8–10

Therefore it says, "WHEN HE ASCENDED ON HIGH, HE LED CAPTIVE A HOST OF CAPTIVES, AND HE GAVE GIFTS TO MEN." ⁹(Now this expression, "He *ascended*," what does it mean except that He also had *descended* into the lower parts of the earth? ¹⁰He who descended is Himself also He who ascended far above all the heavens, so that He might fill all things.)

Philippians 2:10–11

At the name of Jesus EVERY KNEE WILL BOW, of those who are in heaven and on earth and under the earth, ¹¹and that every tongue will *confess* that Jesus Christ is Lord, to the glory of God the Father.

Colossians 3:11

. . . a renewal in which there is *no distinction between Greek and Jew*, circumcised and uncircumcised, barbarian, Scythian, slave and freeman, but Christ is all, and in all.

OTHER BIBLICAL PARALLELS

Leviticus 18:5

"So you shall keep My statutes and My judgments, by which a man may *live* if he does them; I am the LORD."

Deuteronomy 30:11–12, 14

"For this commandment which I command you today is not too difficult for you, nor is it out of reach. ¹²It is not in heaven, that you should say, '*Who will* go up *to heaven* for us to get it for us and make us hear it, that we may observe it?' . . . ¹⁴But *the word is* very *near you, in your mouth and in your heart*, that you may observe it."

Isaiah 28:16

Therefore thus says the Lord GOD, "Behold, I am laying in Zion a stone, a tested stone, A costly cornerstone for the foundation, firmly placed. He *who believes in* it *will not be* disturbed."

Joel 2:32

"And it will come about that *whoever calls on the name of the* LORD *Will be* delivered; For on Mount Zion and in Jerusalem There will be those who escape, As the LORD has said, Even among the survivors whom the LORD calls."

Matthew 10:32

"Therefore everyone who *confesses* Me before men, I will also confess him before My Father who is in heaven."

Acts 10:34–36

Opening his mouth, Peter said: "I most certainly understand now that God is not one to show partiality, [35]but in every nation the man who fears Him and does what is right is welcome to Him. [36]*The word* which He sent to the sons of Israel, *preaching* peace through Jesus Christ (He is *Lord of all*) . . ."

Acts 15:7, 9, 11

After there had been much debate, Peter stood up and said to them, "Brethren, you know that in the early days God made a choice among you, that by my mouth the Gentiles would hear *the word* of the gospel and *believe*. . . . [9]And He made *no distinction* between us and them, cleansing their hearts by *faith*. . . . [11]But we believe that we are *saved* through the grace of the Lord Jesus, in the same way as they also are."

1 Peter 3:18–19

For Christ also died for sins once for all, the just for the unjust, so that He might bring us to God, having been put to death in the flesh, but made alive in the spirit; [19]in which also He went and made proclamation to the spirits now in prison.

NONCANONICAL PARALLELS

Baruch 3:9, 29–30

Hear the commandments of life, O Israel; give ear, and learn wisdom! . . . [29]Who has gone up *into heaven*, and taken her, and brought her down from the clouds? [30]Who

has gone over the sea, and found her, and will buy her for pure gold?

Targum Neofiti on Deuteronomy 30:12–13

The *law* is not in the heavens, that one should say: Would that we had one like Moses the prophet who would go up *to heaven* and fetch it for us. . . . [13]Nor is the law beyond the Great Sea, that one should say: Would that we had one like Jonah the prophet who would *descend* into the depths of the Great Sea and bring it up for us.

Romans 10:14–21

How then will they call on Him in whom they have not believed? How will they believe in Him whom they have not heard? And how will they hear without a preacher? [15]How will they preach unless they are sent? Just as it is written, "HOW BEAUTIFUL ARE THE FEET OF THOSE WHO BRING GOOD NEWS OF GOOD THINGS!" [16]However, they did not all heed the good news; for Isaiah says, "LORD, WHO HAS BELIEVED OUR REPORT?" [17]So faith comes from hearing, and hearing by the word of Christ. [18]But I say, surely they have never heard, have they? Indeed they have; "THEIR VOICE HAS GONE OUT INTO ALL THE EARTH, AND THEIR WORDS TO THE ENDS OF THE WORLD." [19]But I say, surely Israel did not know, did they? First Moses says, "I WILL MAKE YOU JEALOUS BY THAT WHICH IS NOT A NATION, BY A NATION WITHOUT UNDERSTANDING WILL I ANGER YOU." [20]And Isaiah is very bold and says, "I WAS FOUND BY THOSE WHO DID NOT SEEK ME, I BECAME MANIFEST TO THOSE WHO DID NOT ASK FOR ME." [21]But as for Israel He says, "ALL THE DAY LONG I HAVE STRETCHED OUT MY HANDS TO A DISOBEDIENT AND OBSTINATE PEOPLE."

ROMANS PARALLELS

Romans 1:15–17

So, for my part, I am eager to *preach* the gospel to you also who are in Rome. [16]For I am not ashamed of the gospel, for it is the power of God for salvation to everyone who *believes*, to the Jew first and also to the Greek. [17]For in it the righteousness of God is revealed from *faith* to faith; as it is written, "BUT THE RIGHTEOUS man SHALL LIVE BY FAITH."

Romans 3:3
What then? If some did not *believe*, their unbelief will not nullify the faithfulness of God, will it?

Romans 9:30
What shall we say then? That Gentiles, who did not pursue righteousness, attained righteousness, even the righteousness which is by *faith*.

Romans 11:11
I say then, they did not stumble so as to fall, did they? May it never be! But by their transgression salvation has come to the Gentiles, to make them *jealous*.

Romans 11:25, 30–31
For I do not want you, brethren, to be uninformed of this mystery—so that you will not be wise in your own estimation—that a partial hardening has happened to *Israel* until the fullness of the Gentiles has come in; . . . ³⁰For just as you once were disobedient to God, but now have been shown mercy because of their disobedience, ³¹so these also now have been *disobedient*, that because of the mercy shown to you they also may now be shown mercy.

OTHER PAULINE PARALLELS

Galatians 3:2
This is the only thing I want to find out from you: did you receive the Spirit by the works of the Law, or by *hearing* with *faith*?

Colossians 1:5–6
. . . because of the hope laid up for you in heaven, of which you previously *heard* in *the word* of truth, the gospel ⁶which has come to you, just as in all *the world* also it is constantly bearing fruit and increasing, even as it has been doing in you also since the day you heard of it and understood the grace of God in truth.

Colossians 1:23
. . . if indeed you continue in the *faith* firmly established and steadfast, and not moved away from the hope of the gospel that you have *heard*, which was proclaimed in all creation under heaven, and of which I, Paul, was made a minister.

1 Thessalonians 2:13
For this reason we also constantly thank God that when you received *the word* of God which you *heard* from us, you accepted it not as the word of men, but for what it really is, the word of God, which also performs its work in you who *believe*.

OTHER BIBLICAL PARALLELS

Exodus 32:9
The LORD said to Moses, "I have seen this people, and behold, they are an *obstinate people*."

Deuteronomy 32:21
"They have made Me jealous with what is not God; They have provoked Me to anger with their idols. So *I will make* them *jealous* with those who are not a people; I will provoke them to *anger* with a foolish *nation*."

Psalm 19:1–4
The heavens are telling of the glory of God; And their expanse is declaring the work of His hands. ²Day to day pours forth speech, And night to night reveals knowledge. ³There is no speech, nor are there words; *Their voice* is not heard. ⁴Their line *has gone out* through *all the earth*, And their utterances *to the end of the world*.

Isaiah 52:7
How lovely on the mountains *Are the feet* of him *who brings good news*, Who announces peace And brings good news of happiness, Who announces salvation, And says to Zion, "Your God reigns!"

Isaiah 53:1
Who has believed our message? And to whom has the arm of the LORD been revealed?

Isaiah 65:1–2
"I permitted Myself to be sought by those who did not ask for Me; I permitted Myself to be *found by those who did not seek Me*. I said, 'Here am I, here am I,' To a nation which did not call on My name. ²*I have* spread *out My hands all day long to a* rebellious *people*, Who walk in the way which is not good, following their own thoughts."

Nahum 1:15
Behold, on the mountains *the feet of* him *who brings good news*, Who announces peace!

Celebrate your feasts, O Judah; Pay your vows. For never again will the wicked one pass through you; He is cut off completely.

Matthew 24:14

"This gospel of the kingdom shall be *preached* in *the* whole *world* as a testimony to all the nations, and then the end will come."

John 12:37–38

But though He had performed so many signs before them, yet they were not believing in Him. [38]This was to fulfill the word of *Isaiah* the prophet which he spoke: "LORD, WHO HAS BELIEVED OUR REPORT? AND TO WHOM HAS THE ARM OF THE LORD BEEN REVEALED?"

Acts 1:8

"But you will receive power when the Holy Spirit has come upon you; and you shall be My witnesses both in Jerusalem, and in all Judea and Samaria, and even to the remotest part of *the earth*."

Romans 11:1–6

I say then, God has not rejected His people, has He? May it never be! For I too am an Israelite, a descendant of Abraham, of the tribe of Benjamin. [2]God has not rejected His people whom He foreknew. Or do you not know what the Scripture says in the passage about Elijah, how he pleads with God against Israel? [3]"Lord, THEY HAVE KILLED YOUR PROPHETS, THEY HAVE TORN DOWN YOUR ALTARS, AND I ALONE AM LEFT, AND THEY ARE SEEKING MY LIFE." [4]But what is the divine response to him? "I HAVE KEPT for Myself SEVEN THOUSAND MEN WHO HAVE NOT BOWED THE KNEE TO BAAL." [5]In the same way then, there has also come to be at the present time a remnant according to God's gracious choice. [6]But if it is by grace, it is no longer on the basis of works, otherwise grace is no longer grace.

ROMANS PARALLELS

Romans 3:3

What then? If some did not believe, their unbelief will not nullify the faithfulness of God, will it?

Romans 3:28–30

For we maintain that a man is justified by faith apart from *works* of the Law. [29]Or is God the God of Jews only? Is He not the God of Gentiles also? Yes, of Gentiles also, [30]since indeed God who will justify the circumcised by faith and the uncircumcised through faith is one.

Romans 4:16

For this reason it is by faith, in order that it may be in accordance with *grace,* so that the promise will be guaranteed to all the *descendants,* not only to those who are of the Law, but also to those who are of the faith of *Abraham,* who is the father of us all.

Romans 8:29

For those whom He *foreknew,* He also predestined to become conformed to the image of His Son, so that He would be the first-born among many brethren.

Romans 9:3–4

For I could wish that I myself were accursed, separated from Christ for the sake of my brethren, my kinsmen according to the flesh, [4]who are *Israelites,* to whom belongs the adoption as sons, and the glory and the covenants and the giving of the Law and the temple service and the promises.

Romans 9:10–11

And not only this, but there was Rebekah also, when she had conceived twins by one man, our father Isaac; [11]for though the twins were not yet born and had not done anything good or bad, so that God's purpose according to His *choice* would stand, not because of *works* but because of Him who calls.

Romans 9:27

Isaiah cries out concerning Israel, "THOUGH THE NUMBER OF THE SONS OF *ISRAEL* BE LIKE THE SAND OF THE SEA, IT IS THE *REMNANT* THAT WILL BE SAVED.

Romans 11:28

From the standpoint of the gospel they are enemies for your sake, but from the standpoint of God's *choice* they are beloved for the sake of the fathers.

2 Corinthians 11:22

Are they Hebrews? So am I. Are they Israelites? So am I. Are they *descendants of Abraham*? So am I.

Philippians 3:4–6

If anyone else has a mind to put confidence in the flesh, I far more: ⁵circumcised the eighth day, of the nation of Israel, *of the tribe of Benjamin*, a Hebrew of Hebrews; as to the Law, a Pharisee; ⁶as to zeal, a persecutor of the church; as to the righteousness which is in the Law, found blameless.

2 Timothy 1:8–9

Therefore do not be ashamed of the testimony of our Lord or of me His prisoner, but join with me in suffering for the gospel according to the power of God, ⁹who has saved us and called us with a holy calling, not according to our *works*, but according to His own purpose and *grace* which was granted us in Christ Jesus from all eternity.

Leviticus 26:44

"Yet in spite of this, when they are in the land of their enemies, I will *not reject* them, nor will I so abhor them as to destroy them, breaking My covenant with them; for I am the LORD their God."

1 Kings 19:9–10, 15, 18

Then he came there to a cave and lodged there; and behold, the word of the LORD came to him, and He said to him, "What are you doing here, *Elijah*?" ¹⁰He said, "I have been very zealous for the LORD, the God of hosts; for the sons of *Israel* have forsaken Your covenant, *torn down Your altars and killed Your prophets* with the sword. *And I alone am left; and they seek my life*, to take it away." . . . ¹⁵The LORD said to him, "Go, return on your way to the wilderness of Damascus. . . . ¹⁸Yet I will leave *7,000* in Israel, all *the knees* that have *not bowed to Baal* and every mouth that has not kissed him."

2 Kings 19:4

"Perhaps the LORD your God will hear all the words of Rabshakeh, whom his master the king of Assyria has sent to reproach the living God, and will rebuke the words which the LORD your God has heard. Therefore, offer a prayer for the *remnant* that is left."

Psalm 94:14

For the LORD will not abandon *His people*, Nor will He forsake His inheritance.

Jeremiah 33:25–26

"'If My covenant for day and night stand not, and the fixed patterns of heaven and earth I have not established, ²⁶then I would *reject* the descendants of Jacob and David My servant, not taking from his descendants rulers over the *descendants of Abraham*, Isaac and Jacob. But I will restore their fortunes and will have mercy on them.'"

Zechariah 10:6

"I will strengthen the house of Judah, And I will save the house of Joseph, And I will bring them back, Because I have had compassion on them; And they will be as though I had *not rejected* them, For I am the LORD their God and I will answer them."

Sirach 47:22

But the Lord will never give up his mercy, or cause any of his works to perish; he will never blot out the *descendants* of his chosen one, or destroy the family line of him who loved him. So he gave *a remnant* to Jacob, and to David a root from his own family.

2 Esdras (4 Ezra) 12:34

"But in mercy he will set free the *remnant* of my people, those who have been saved throughout my borders, and he will make them joyful until the end comes, the day of judgment, of which I spoke to you at the beginning."

Romans 11:7–16

What then? What Israel is seeking, it has not obtained, but those who were chosen obtained it, and the rest were hardened; ⁸just as it is written, "GOD GAVE THEM A SPIRIT OF STUPOR, EYES TO SEE NOT AND EARS TO HEAR NOT, DOWN TO THIS VERY DAY." ⁹And David says, "LET THEIR TABLE BECOME A SNARE AND A TRAP, AND A STUMBLING BLOCK AND A RETRIBUTION TO THEM. ¹⁰LET THEIR EYES BE

DARKENED TO SEE NOT, AND BEND THEIR BACKS FOREVER." [11]I say then, they did not stumble so as to fall, did they? May it never be! But by their transgression salvation has come to the Gentiles, to make them jealous. [12]Now if their transgression is riches for the world and their failure is riches for the Gentiles, how much more will their fulfillment be! [13]But I am speaking to you who are Gentiles. Inasmuch then as I am an apostle of Gentiles, I magnify my ministry, [14]if somehow I might move to jealousy my fellow countrymen and save some of them. [15]For if their rejection is the reconciliation of the world, what will their acceptance be but life from the dead? [16]If the first piece of dough is holy, the lump is also; and if the root is holy, the branches are too.

ROMANS PARALLELS

Romans 1:4–5

. . . Jesus Christ our Lord, [5]through whom we have received grace and *apostleship* to bring about the obedience of faith among all *the Gentiles* for His name's sake.

Romans 1:16

For I am not ashamed of the gospel, for it is the power of God for *salvation* to everyone who believes, to the Jew first and also to the Greek.

Romans 5:10–11

For if while we were enemies we were reconciled to God through the death of His Son, much more, having been reconciled, we shall be *saved* by His life. [11]And not only this, but we also exult in God through our Lord Jesus Christ, through whom we have now received the *reconciliation*.

Romans 8:11

But if the Spirit of Him who raised Jesus from the dead dwells in you, He who raised Christ Jesus *from the dead* will also give *life* to your mortal bodies through His Spirit who dwells in you.

Romans 9:31–32

But *Israel*, pursuing a law of righteousness, did not arrive at that law. [32]Why? Because they did not pursue it by faith, but as though it were by works. They *stumbled* over the stumbling stone.

Romans 10:19

But I say, surely *Israel* did not know, did they? First Moses says, "I WILL MAKE YOU *JEALOUS* BY THAT WHICH IS NOT A NATION, BY A NATION WITHOUT UNDERSTANDING WILL I ANGER YOU."

Romans 11:25–26

For I do not want you, brethren, to be uninformed of this mystery—so that you will not be wise in your own estimation—that a partial *hardening* has happened to *Israel* until the fullness of *the Gentiles* has come in; [26]and so all Israel will be *saved*; just as it is written, "THE DELIVERER WILL COME FROM ZION, HE WILL REMOVE UNGODLINESS FROM JACOB."

OTHER PAULINE PARALLELS

1 Corinthians 1:23

But we preach Christ crucified, to Jews *a stumbling block* and to *Gentiles* foolishness.

1 Corinthians 9:20, 22

To the Jews I became as a Jew, so that I might win Jews; to those who are under the Law, as under the Law though not being myself under the Law, so that I might win those who are under the Law; . . . [22]To the weak I became weak, that I might win the weak; I have become all things to all men, so that I may by all means *save some*.

2 Corinthians 3:14–15

But their minds were *hardened*; for until this very day at the reading of the old covenant the same veil remains unlifted, because it is removed in Christ. [15]But to this day whenever Moses is read, a veil lies over their heart.

2 Corinthians 5:18–19

Now all these things are from God, who reconciled us to Himself through Christ and gave us the ministry of *reconciliation*, [19]namely, that God was in Christ reconciling *the world* to Himself, not counting their trespasses against them, and He has committed to us the word of reconciliation.

Galatians 2:9

And recognizing the grace that had been given to me, James and Cephas and John, who were reputed to be pillars, gave to me and Barnabas the right hand of fellowship, so that we might go to *the Gentiles* and they to the circumcised.

1 Timothy 2:7

For this I was appointed a preacher and *an apostle* (I am telling the truth, I am not lying) as a teacher of *the Gentiles* in faith and truth.

Numbers 15:21

"'From the *first* of your *dough* you shall give to the LORD an offering throughout your generations.'"

Deuteronomy 29:4

"Yet *to this day* the LORD has not given you a heart to know, nor *eyes to see*, nor *ears to hear*."

Psalm 69:22–23

May *their table* before them *become a snare*; And when they are in peace, may it become *a trap*. [23]May *their eyes* grow dim so that they *cannot see*, And make their loins shake continually.

Isaiah 29:10

For the LORD has poured over you *a spirit* of deep sleep, He has shut your *eyes*, the prophets; And He has covered your heads, the seers.

Acts 13:45–46

But when the Jews saw the crowds, they were filled with *jealousy* and began contradicting the things spoken by Paul, and were blaspheming. [46]Paul and Barnabas spoke out boldly and said, "It was necessary that the word of God be spoken to you first; since you repudiate it and judge yourselves unworthy of eternal *life*, behold, we are turning to *the Gentiles*."

Acts 28:25–28

And when they did not agree with one another, they began leaving after Paul had spoken one parting word, "The Holy Spirit rightly spoke through Isaiah the prophet to your fathers, [26]saying,'GO TO THIS PEOPLE AND SAY, "YOU WILL KEEP ON HEARING, BUT WILL NOT UNDER-STAND; AND YOU WILL KEEP ON SEEING, BUT WILL NOT PERCEIVE; [27]FOR THE HEART OF THIS PEOPLE HAS BECOME DULL, AND WITH THEIR *EARS* THEY SCARCELY *HEAR*, AND THEY HAVE CLOSED THEIR *EYES*; OTHERWISE THEY MIGHT SEE WITH THEIR EYES, AND HEAR WITH THEIR EARS, AND UNDERSTAND WITH THEIR HEART AND RETURN, AND I WOULD HEAL THEM."' [28]Therefore let it be known to you that this *salvation* of God has been sent to *the Gentiles*; they will also listen."

Romans 11:17–24

But if some of the branches were broken off, and you, being a wild olive, were grafted in among them and became partaker with them of the rich root of the olive tree, [18]do not be arrogant toward the branches; but if you are arrogant, remember that it is not you who supports the root, but the root supports you. [19]You will say then, "Branches were broken off so that I might be grafted in." [20]Quite right, they were broken off for their unbelief, but you stand by your faith. Do not be conceited, but fear; [21]for if God did not spare the natural branches, He will not spare you, either. [22]Behold then the kindness and severity of God; to those who fell, severity, but to you, God's kindness, if you continue in His kindness; otherwise you also will be cut off. [23]And they also, if they do not continue in their unbelief, will be grafted in, for God is able to graft them in again. [24]For if you were cut off from what is by nature a wild olive tree, and were grafted contrary to nature into a cultivated olive tree, how much more will these who are the natural branches be grafted into their own olive tree?

Romans 2:4–5, 9

Or do you think lightly of the riches of His *kindness* and tolerance and patience, not knowing that the kindness of God leads you to repentance? [5]But because of your stubbornness and unrepentant heart you are storing up wrath for yourself in the day of wrath and revelation of the righteous judgment of God. . . . [9]There will be tribulation and distress for every soul of man who does evil, of the Jew first and also of the Greek.

Romans 3:1–3

Then what advantage has the Jew? Or what is the benefit of circumcision? [2]Great in every respect. First of all, that they were entrusted with the oracles of God. [3]What then? If some did not believe, their *unbelief* will not nullify the faithfulness of God, will it?

Romans 5:1–2

Therefore, having been justified by faith, we have peace with God through our Lord Jesus Christ, [2]through whom also we have obtained our introduction by *faith* into this grace in which we *stand*; and we exult in hope of the glory of God.

OTHER PAULINE PARALLELS

1 Corinthians 10:12

Therefore let him who thinks he *stands* take heed that he does not fall.

1 Corinthians 13:4

Love is patient, love is kind and is not jealous; love does not brag and is not *arrogant*.

2 Corinthians 3:14–16

But their minds were hardened; for until this very day at the reading of the old covenant the same veil remains unlifted, because it is removed in Christ. [15]But to this day whenever Moses is read, a veil lies over their heart; [16]but whenever a person turns to the Lord, the veil is taken away.

Ephesians 2:11–14

Therefore remember that formerly you, the Gentiles in the flesh, who are called "Uncircumcision" by the so-called "Circumcision," which is performed in the flesh by human hands— [12]remember that you were at that time separate from Christ, excluded from the commonwealth of Israel, and strangers to the covenants of promise, having no hope and without God in the world. [13]But now in Christ Jesus you who formerly were far off have been brought near by the blood of Christ. [14]For He Himself is our peace, who made both groups into one and broke down the barrier of the dividing wall.

Ephesians 3:4–6

By referring to this, when you read you can understand my insight into the mystery of Christ, [5]which in other generations was not made known to the sons of men, as it has now been revealed to His holy apostles and prophets in the Spirit; [6]to be specific, that the Gentiles are fellow heirs and fellow members of the body, and fellow *partakers* of the promise in Christ Jesus through the gospel.

OTHER BIBLICAL PARALLELS

Judges 9:8–9

"Once the trees went forth to anoint a king over them, and they said to *the olive tree*, 'Reign over us!' [9]But the olive tree said to them, 'Shall I leave my fatness with which God and men are honored, and go to wave over the trees?'"

Psalm 52:8

But as for me, I am like a green *olive tree* in the house of God; I trust in the lovingkindness of God forever and ever.

Jeremiah 11:16–17

The LORD called your name, "A green *olive tree*, beautiful in fruit and form"; With the noise of a great tumult He has kindled fire on it, And its *branches* are worthless. [17]The LORD of hosts, who planted you, has pronounced evil against you because of the evil of the house of Israel and of the house of Judah, which they have done to provoke Me by offering up sacrifices to Baal.

Hosea 14:6

His shoots will sprout, And his beauty will be like *the olive tree*, And his fragrance like the cedars of Lebanon.

Zechariah 4:1–3, 12–14

Then the angel who was speaking with me returned and roused me, as a man who is awakened from his sleep. [2]He said to me, "What do you see?" And I said, "I see, and behold, a lampstand all of gold with its bowl on the top of it, and its seven lamps on it with seven spouts belonging to each of the lamps which are on the top of it; [3]also two *olive trees* by it, one on the right side of the bowl and the other on its left side." . . . [12]And I answered the second time and said to him, "What are the two *olive branches* which are beside the two golden pipes, which empty the golden oil from themselves?" [13]So he answered me, saying, "Do you not know what these are?" And I said, "No, my lord." [14]Then he said, "These are the two anointed ones who are standing by the Lord of the whole earth."

John 15:1–2, 5
"I am the true vine, and My Father is the vinedresser. [2]Every branch in Me that does not bear fruit, He takes away; and every branch that bears fruit, He prunes it so that it may bear more fruit. . . . [5]I am the vine, you are the *branches*; he who abides in Me and I in him, he bears much fruit, for apart from Me you can do nothing."

Sirach 24:1, 14
Wisdom praises herself, and tells of her glory in the midst of her people. . . . [14]I grew tall like a palm tree in En–gedi, and like rosebushes in Jericho; like a fair *olive tree* in the field, and like a plane tree beside water I grew tall.

The Genesis Apocryphon (1Q20) 13.13–17
I turned around to look at *the olive tree*; for behold the olive tree (was) growing in height and (for) many hours with the glory of many leaves [14][and] fru[its] in abundance. . . . [15] . . . I was quite amazed. . . . [16][The four] winds of the heavens (were) blowing with vehemence, and they damaged this olive tree, debranching it and breaking it to pieces. First [came] [17][the wind from] the west, and it struck and stripped it of its leaves and its fruit, and scattered it to the winds.

Mishnah Kil'ayim 1:7
They do not *graft* [either] a tree onto a tree [of a different kind], [or] a vegetable onto a vegetable [of a different kind], and neither [do they graft] a tree onto a vegetable, nor a vegetable onto a tree. R. Judah permits [the grafting of] a vegetable onto a tree.

Romans 11:25–32

For I do not want you, brethren, to be uninformed of this mystery — so that you will not be wise in your own estimation — that a partial

hardening has happened to Israel until the fullness of the Gentiles has come in; [26]and so all Israel will be saved; just as it is written, "THE DELIVERER WILL COME FROM ZION, HE WILL REMOVE UNGODLINESS FROM JACOB." [27]"THIS IS MY COVENANT WITH THEM, WHEN I TAKE AWAY THEIR SINS." [28]From the standpoint of the gospel they are enemies for your sake, but from the standpoint of God's choice they are beloved for the sake of the fathers; [29]for the gifts and the calling of God are irrevocable. [30]For just as you once were disobedient to God, but now have been shown mercy because of their disobedience, [31]so these also now have been disobedient, that because of the mercy shown to you they also may now be shown mercy. [32]For God has shut up all in disobedience so that He may show mercy to all.

Romans 5:10
For if while we were *enemies* we were reconciled to God through the death of His Son, much more, having been reconciled, we shall be *saved* by His life.

Romans 9:4–5
. . . who are Israelites, to whom belongs the adoption as sons, and the glory and the *covenants* and the giving of the Law and the temple service and the promises, [5]whose are *the fathers*, and from whom is the Christ according to the flesh, who is over all, God blessed forever. Amen.

Romans 9:18
So then He has *mercy* on whom He desires, and He *hardens* whom He desires.

Romans 9:22–24
What if God, although willing to demonstrate His wrath and to make His power known, endured with much patience vessels of wrath prepared for destruction? [23]And He did so to make known the riches of His glory upon vessels of *mercy*, which He prepared beforehand for glory, [24]even us, whom He also *called*, not from among Jews only, but also from among *Gentiles*.

Romans 10:21
But as for *Israel* He says, "ALL THE DAY LONG I HAVE STRETCHED OUT MY HANDS TO A *DISOBEDIENT* AND OBSTINATE PEOPLE."

Romans 11:7, 11–12

What then? What *Israel* is seeking, it has not obtained, but those who were chosen obtained it, and the rest were *hardened*; . . . [11]I say then, they did not stumble so as to fall, did they? May it never be! But by their transgression salvation has come to *the Gentiles*, to make them jealous. [12]Now if their transgression is riches for the world and their failure is riches for the Gentiles, how much more will their fulfillment be!

Romans 12:16

Be of the same mind toward one another; do not be haughty in mind, but associate with the lowly. Do *not be wise in your own estimation.*

Romans 15:8–9

For I say that Christ has become a servant to the circumcision on behalf of the truth of God to confirm the promises given to *the fathers,* [9]and for *the Gentiles* to glorify God for His *mercy.*

Galatians 3:22

But the Scripture has *shut up* everyone under sin, so that the promise by faith in Jesus Christ might be given to those who believe.

Ephesians 3:4–6

By referring to this, when you read you can understand my insight into the *mystery* of Christ, [5]which in other generations was not made known to the sons of men, as it has now been revealed to His holy apostles and prophets in the Spirit; [6]to be specific, that *the Gentiles* are fellow heirs and fellow members of the body, and fellow partakers of the promise in Christ Jesus through the gospel.

Colossians 1:25–27

. . . the word of God, [26]that is, the *mystery* which has been hidden from the past ages and generations, but has now been manifested to His saints, [27]to whom God willed to make known what is the riches of the glory of this mystery among *the Gentiles,* which is Christ in you, the hope of glory.

Titus 3:3

For we also *once were* foolish ourselves, *disobedient*, deceived, enslaved to various lusts and pleasures, spending our life in malice and envy, hateful, hating one another.

Deuteronomy 10:15

"Yet on your *fathers* did the LORD set His affection to love them, and He chose their descendants after them, even you above all peoples, as it is this day."

Psalm 14:7

Oh, that the salvation of *Israel* would *come* out of *Zion*! When the LORD restores His captive people, *Jacob* will rejoice, Israel will be glad.

Isaiah 27:9

Therefore through this *Jacob's* iniquity will be forgiven; And this will be the full price of the pardoning of his *sin*: When he makes all the altar stones like pulverized chalk stones; When Asherim and incense altars will not stand.

Isaiah 59:20–21

"A Redeemer *will come to Zion*, And to those who turn from transgression in *Jacob*," declares the LORD. [21]"As for Me, *this is My covenant with them*," says the LORD: "My Spirit which is upon you, and My words which I have put in your mouth shall not depart from your mouth, nor from the mouth of your offspring, nor from the mouth of your offspring's offspring," says the LORD, "from now and forever."

Jeremiah 31:33

"But this is the *covenant* which I will make with the house of Israel after those days," declares the LORD, "I will put My law within them and on their heart I will write it; and I will be their God, and they shall be My people."

2 Esdras (4 Ezra) 4:35–37

"Did not the souls of the righteous in their chambers ask about these matters, saying, 'How long are we to remain here? And when will the harvest of our reward come?' [36]And the archangel Jeremiel answered and said, 'When the number of those like yourselves is completed; for he has weighed the age in the balance, [37]and measured the times by measure, and numbered the times by number; and he will not move or arouse them until that measure is fulfilled.'"

Testament of Zebulon 9:5, 7–8
"In the last days you shall defect from the Lord, and you shall be divided in *Israel*. . . . [7]And thereafter you will remember the Lord and repent, and he will turn you around because he is *merciful* and compassionate. . . . [8]And thereafter the Lord himself will arise upon you, the light of righteousness with healing and compassion in his wings. He will liberate every captive of the sons of men from Beliar. He will turn all nations to being zealous for him."

Romans 11:33–36

Oh, the depth of the riches both of the wisdom and knowledge of God! How unsearchable are His judgments and unfathomable His ways! [34]For WHO HAS KNOWN THE MIND OF THE LORD, OR WHO BECAME HIS COUNSELOR? [35]Or WHO HAS FIRST GIVEN TO HIM THAT IT MIGHT BE PAID BACK TO HIM AGAIN? [36]For from Him and through Him and to Him are all things. To Him be the glory forever. Amen.

ROMANS PARALLELS

Romans 9:5
. . . whose are the fathers, and from whom is the Christ according to the flesh, who is over all, God blessed *forever. Amen.*

Romans 9:23
And He did so to make known *the riches* of His glory upon vessels of mercy, which He prepared beforehand for glory.

Romans 16:25–27
Now to Him who is able to establish you according to my gospel and the preaching of Jesus Christ, according to the revelation of the mystery which has been kept secret for long ages past, [26]but now is manifested, and by the Scriptures of the prophets, according to the commandment of the eternal God, has been made known to all the nations, leading to obedience of faith; [27]to the only wise God, through Jesus Christ, *be the glory forever. Amen.*

OTHER PAULINE PARALLELS

1 Corinthians 2:6–7
Yet we do speak wisdom among those who are mature; a wisdom, however, not of this age nor of the rulers of this age, who are passing away; [7]but we speak *God's wisdom* in a mystery, the hidden wisdom which God predestined before the ages to our glory.

1 Corinthians 2:15–16
But he who is spiritual appraises all things, yet he himself is appraised by no one. [16]*For WHO HAS KNOWN THE MIND OF THE LORD, THAT HE WILL INSTRUCT HIM?* But we have the mind of Christ.

1 Corinthians 8:6
Yet for us there is but one God, the Father, from whom are *all things* and we exist for Him; and one Lord, Jesus Christ, by whom are all things, and we exist through Him.

Ephesians 3:8–10
To me, the very least of all saints, this grace was given, to preach to the Gentiles *the unfathomable riches* of Christ, [9]and to bring to light what is the administration of the mystery which for ages has been hidden in God who created *all things*; [10]so that the manifold *wisdom of God* might now be made known through the church to the rulers and the authorities in the heavenly places.

Ephesians 3:20–21
Now to Him who is able to do far more abundantly beyond all that we ask or think, according to the power that works within us, [21]*to Him be the glory* in the church and in Christ Jesus to all generations *forever* and ever. *Amen.*

Philippians 4:20
Now to our God and Father *be the glory forever* and ever. *Amen.*

Colossians 1:16
For by Him *all things* were created, both in the heavens and on earth, visible and invisible, whether thrones or dominions or rulers or authorities—all things have been created *through Him* and for Him.

Colossians 2:2–3
. . . that their hearts may be encouraged, having been knit together in love, and attaining

to all the wealth that comes from the full assurance of understanding, resulting in a true knowledge of God's mystery, that is, Christ Himself, [3]in whom are hidden all the treasures of *wisdom and knowledge.*

1 Timothy 1:16–17

Yet for this reason I found mercy, so that in me as the foremost, Jesus Christ might demonstrate His perfect patience as an example for those who would believe in Him for eternal life. [17]Now to the King eternal, immortal, invisible, the only God, *be* honor and *glory forever* and ever. *Amen.*

Job 5:8–9

"But as for me, I would seek God, And I would place my cause before God; [9]Who does great and *unsearchable* things, Wonders without number."

Job 9:10

"[It is God] who does great things, *unfathomable*, And wondrous works without number."

Job 11:7

"Can you discover *the depths* of God? Can you discover the limits of the Almighty?"

Job 15:8

"Do you hear the secret counsel of God, And limit wisdom to yourself?"

Job 35:7

"If you are righteous, what do you *give to Him*, Or what does He receive from your hand?"

Job 41:11

"*Who has given to* Me *that* I should repay *him*? Whatever is under the whole heaven is Mine."

Psalm 145:3

Great is the Lᴏʀᴅ, and highly to be praised, And His greatness is *unsearchable.*

Isaiah 40:13–14

Who has directed the Spirit *of the* Lᴏʀᴅ, Or as *His counselor* has informed Him? [14]With whom did He consult and who gave Him understanding? And who taught Him in the path of justice and taught Him *knowledge* And informed Him of the way of understanding?

Hebrews 2:10

For it was fitting for Him, for whom are all things, and through whom are *all things*, in bringing many sons to glory, to perfect the author of their salvation through sufferings.

2 Baruch 14:8–9

O Lord, my Lord, who can understand your *judgment*? Or who can explore *the depth* of your *way*? [9]Or who can discern the majesty of your path? Or who can discern your incomprehensible counsel? Or who of those who are born has ever discovered the beginning and the end of your *wisdom*?

Marcus Aurelius, Meditations 4.23

All that is harmonious with you, O Cosmos, is harmonious with me. . . . From you are *all things*, in you all things, to you all things.

Romans 12:1–2

Therefore I urge you, brethren, by the mercies of God, to present your bodies a living and holy sacrifice, acceptable to God, which is your spiritual service of worship. [2]And do not be conformed to this world, but be transformed by the renewing of your mind, so that you may prove what the will of God is, that which is good and acceptable and perfect.

Romans 1:24, 28

Therefore God gave them over in the lusts of their hearts to impurity, so that their *bodies* would be dishonored among them. . . . [28]And just as they did not see fit to acknowledge God any longer, God gave them over to a depraved *mind*, to do those things which are not proper.

Romans 2:17–18

But if you bear the name "Jew" and rely upon the Law and boast in God, [18]and know His *will* and *approve* the things that are essential, being instructed out of the Law . . .

Romans 6:13

And do not go on *presenting* the members of your *body* to sin as instruments of unrighteousness; but *present* yourselves to God as those alive from the dead, and your members as instruments of righteousness to God.

Romans 6:19

I am speaking in human terms because of the weakness of your flesh. For just as you presented your members as slaves to impurity and to lawlessness, resulting in further lawlessness, so now *present* your members as slaves to righteousness, resulting in sanctification.

Romans 8:5

For those who are according to the flesh set their *minds* on the things of the flesh, but those who are according to the Spirit, the things of the Spirit.

Romans 8:29

For those whom He foreknew, He also predestined to become *conformed* to the image of His Son, so that He would be the firstborn among many brethren.

Romans 11:32

For God has shut up all in disobedience so that He may show *mercy* to all.

OTHER PAULINE PARALLELS

2 Corinthians 1:3

Blessed be the God and Father of our Lord Jesus Christ, the Father of *mercies* and God of all comfort.

2 Corinthians 3:18

But we all, with unveiled face, beholding as in a mirror the glory of the Lord, are being *transformed* into the same image from glory to glory, just as from the Lord, the Spirit.

2 Corinthians 4:16

Therefore we do not lose heart, but though our outer man is decaying, yet our inner man is being *renewed* day by day.

Ephesians 4:22–24

. . . that, in reference to your former manner of life, you lay aside the old self, which is being corrupted in accordance with the lusts of deceit, [23]and that you be *renewed* in the spirit of your *mind*, [24]and put on the new

self, which in the likeness of God has been created in righteousness and holiness of the truth.

Philippians 1:9–10

And this I pray, that your love may abound still more and more in real knowledge and all discernment, [10]so that you may *approve* the things that are excellent, in order to be sincere and blameless until the day of Christ.

Philippians 3:3

For we are the true circumcision, who *worship* in the Spirit of God and glory in Christ Jesus and put no confidence in the flesh.

Philippians 3:20–21

For our citizenship is in heaven, from which also we eagerly wait for a Savior, the Lord Jesus Christ; [21]who will *transform* the body of our humble state into *conformity* with the body of His glory, by the exertion of the power that He has even to subject all things to Himself.

Colossians 1:9

For this reason also, since the day we heard of it, we have not ceased to pray for you and to ask that you may be filled with the knowledge of His *will* in all spiritual wisdom and understanding.

Colossians 3:10

. . . and have put on the new self who is being *renewed* to a true knowledge according to the image of the One who created him.

Titus 3:5

He saved us, not on the basis of deeds which we have done in righteousness, but according to His *mercy*, by the washing of regeneration and *renewing* by the Holy Spirit.

OTHER BIBLICAL PARALLELS

James 4:4

You adulteresses, do you not know that friendship with the *world* is hostility toward God? Therefore whoever wishes to be a friend of the world makes himself an enemy of God.

1 Peter 1:14–15

As obedient children, *do not be conformed* to the former lusts which were yours in your ignorance, [15]but like the Holy One who called you, be *holy* yourselves also in all your behavior.

1 Peter 2:4–5

And coming to Him as to a living stone which has been rejected by men, but is choice and precious in the sight of God, [5]you also, as living stones, are being built up as a spiritual house for a holy priesthood, to offer up *spiritual sacrifices acceptable to God* through Jesus Christ.

1 John 2:15

Do not love the *world* nor the things in the world. If anyone loves the world, the love of the Father is not in him.

Seneca, Moral Epistles *94.48*

It is said that philosophy is divided into learning and state of mind. For one who has learned and knows what to do and what to shun does not become a sage until his *mind* is transfigured into the shape of that which he has learned.

Romans 12:3–8

For through the grace given to me I say to everyone among you not to think more highly of himself than he ought to think; but to think so as to have sound judgment, as God has allotted to each a measure of faith. [4]For just as we have many members in one body and all the members do not have the same function, [5]so we, who are many, are one body in Christ, and individually members one of another. [6]Since we have gifts that differ according to the grace given to us, each of us is to exercise them accordingly: if prophecy, according to the proportion of his faith; [7]if service, in his serving; or he who teaches, in his teaching; [8]or he who exhorts, in his exhortation; he who gives, with liberality; he who leads, with diligence; he who shows mercy, with cheerfulness.

Romans 1:4–5

. . . Jesus Christ our Lord, [5]through whom we have received *grace* and apostleship to bring about the obedience of *faith* among all the Gentiles for His name's sake.

Romans 5:1–2

Therefore, having been justified by *faith*, we have peace with God through our Lord Jesus Christ, [2]through whom also we have obtained our introduction by faith into this *grace* in which we stand; and we exult in hope of the glory of God.

Romans 12:16

Be of the same mind toward one another; do not be haughty in mind, but associate with the lowly. Do not be wise in your own estimation.

Romans 15:15

But I have written very boldly to you on some points so as to remind you again, because of *the grace* that was *given me* from God.

1 Corinthians 7:7, 17

Yet I wish that all men were even as I myself am. However, each man has his own *gift* from God, one in this manner, and another in that. . . . [17]Only, as the Lord has assigned to each one, as God has called each, in this manner let him walk. And so I direct in all the churches.

1 Corinthians 12:4, 8–10

Now there are varieties of *gifts*, but the same Spirit. . . . [8]For to one is given the word of wisdom through the Spirit, and to another the word of knowledge according to the same Spirit; [9]to another *faith* by the same Spirit, and to another gifts of healing by the one Spirit, [10]and to another the effecting of miracles, and to another *prophecy*, and to another the distinguishing of spirits, to another various kinds of tongues, and to another the interpretation of tongues.

1 Corinthians 12:12, 18, 20

For even as the body is one and yet has *many members*, and all the members of the body, though they are many, are *one body*, so also is Christ. . . . [18]But now God has placed the members, each one of them, in the body, just as He desired. . . . 20But now there are many members, but one body.

1 Corinthians 12:27–28

Now you are Christ's *body*, and *individually members* of it. 28And God has appointed in the church, first apostles, second *prophets*, third *teachers*, then miracles, then *gifts* of healings, helps, administrations, various kinds of tongues.

2 Corinthians 8:1–2

Now, brethren, we wish to make known to you *the grace* of God which has been *given* in the churches of Macedonia, 2that in a great ordeal of affliction their abundance of joy and their deep poverty overflowed in the wealth of their *liberality*.

Ephesians 4:4, 7, 11–12

There is *one body* and one Spirit, just as also you were called in one hope of your calling; . . . 7But to each one of us *grace* was *given* according to the *measure* of Christ's *gift*. . . . 11And He gave some as apostles, and some as *prophets*, and some as evangelists, and some as pastors and *teachers*, 12for the equipping of the saints for the work of *service*, to the building up of the body of Christ.

Colossians 3:15

Let the peace of Christ rule in your hearts, to which indeed you were called in one *body*; and be thankful.

1 Thessalonians 5:12

But we request of you, brethren, that you appreciate those who *diligently* labor among you, and have charge over you in the Lord and give you instruction.

1 Timothy 4:13–14

Until I come, give attention to the public reading of Scripture, to *exhortation* and *teaching*. 14Do not neglect the spiritual *gift* within you, which was bestowed on you through prophetic utterance with the laying on of hands by the presbytery.

1 Timothy 5:17

The elders who rule well are to be considered worthy of double honor, especially those who work hard at *preaching* and *teaching*.

Acts 13:1

Now there were at Antioch, in the church that was there, *prophets* and *teachers*: Barnabas, and Simeon who was called Niger, and Lucius of Cyrene, and Manaen who had been brought up with Herod the tetrarch, and Saul.

1 Peter 4:10–11

As each one has received a special *gift*, employ it in serving one another as good stewards of the manifold *grace* of God. 11Whoever speaks, is to do so as one who is speaking the utterances of God; whoever *serves* is to do so as one who is serving by the strength which God supplies; so that in all things God may be glorified through Jesus Christ, to whom belongs the glory and dominion forever and ever. Amen.

Epictetus, Discourses *2.10.4*

So what is the profession of a citizen? To have nothing as a private interest and to deliberate about nothing as though separate, but as the hand or the foot, if they had reason and understood the natural constitution of things, would never express desire or yearning except with reference to the whole.

Romans 12:9–13

Let love be without hypocrisy. Abhor what is evil; cling to what is good. 10Be devoted to one another in brotherly love; give preference to one another in honor; 11not lagging behind in diligence, fervent in spirit, serving the Lord; 12rejoicing in hope, persevering in tribulation, devoted to prayer, 13contributing to the needs of the saints, practicing hospitality.

Romans 5:2–5

. . . through whom also we have obtained our introduction by faith into this grace in which we stand; and we exult in hope of the glory of God. 3And not only this, but we also exult in our *tribulations*, knowing that tribulation brings about *perseverance*; 4and perseverance, proven character; and proven character, *hope*; [5]and hope does not disappoint, because the *love* of God has been poured out within our hearts through the Holy Spirit who was given to us.

Romans 8:26
In the same way the Spirit also helps our weakness; for we do not know how to *pray* as we should, but the Spirit Himself intercedes for us with groanings too deep for words.

Romans 13:7
Render to all what is due them: tax to whom tax is due; custom to whom custom; fear to whom fear; *honor* to whom honor.

Romans 15:25–26
But now, I am going to Jerusalem serving *the saints*. [26]For Macedonia and Achaia have been pleased to make a *contribution* for the poor among the saints in Jerusalem.

OTHER PAULINE PARALLELS

1 Corinthians 13:4–7
Love is patient, love is kind and is not jealous; love does not brag and is not arrogant, [5]does not act unbecomingly; it does not seek its own, is not provoked, does not take into account a wrong suffered, [6]does not rejoice in unrighteousness, but rejoices with the truth; [7]bears all things, believes all things, *hopes* all things, endures all things.

2 Corinthians 6:4, 6
But in everything commending ourselves as servants of God, in much endurance, in afflictions, in hardships, in distresses, . . . [6]in purity, in knowledge, in patience, in kindness, in the Holy Spirit, in genuine *love*.

Ephesians 4:1–3
Therefore I, the prisoner of the Lord, implore you to walk in a manner worthy of the calling with which you have been called, [2]with all humility and gentleness, with patience, showing tolerance for one another in *love*, [3]being *diligent* to preserve the unity of the Spirit in the bond of peace.

Ephesians 6:18
With all *prayer* and petition pray at all times in the Spirit, and with this in view, be on the alert with all *perseverance* and petition for all *the saints*.

Colossians 4:2
Devote yourselves to *prayer*, keeping alert in it with an attitude of thanksgiving.

1 Thessalonians 4:9
Now as to the *love* of the brethren, you have no need for anyone to write to you, for you yourselves are taught by God to love one another.

1 Thessalonians 5:16–22
Rejoice always; [17]*pray* without ceasing; [18]in everything give thanks; for this is God's will for you in Christ Jesus. [19]Do not quench the Spirit; [20]do not despise prophetic utterances. [21]But examine everything carefully; hold fast to that which is *good*; [22]abstain from every form of *evil*.

1 Timothy 1:5
But the goal of our instruction is *love* from a pure heart and a good conscience and a sincere faith.

1 Timothy 5:9–10
A widow is to be put on the list only if she is not less than sixty years old, having been the wife of one man, [10]having a reputation for good works; and if she has brought up children, if she has shown *hospitality* to strangers, if she has washed *the saints'* feet, if she has assisted those in distress, and if she has devoted herself to every good work.

OTHER BIBLICAL PARALLELS

Psalm 34:14
Depart from *evil* and do *good*; Seek peace and pursue it.

Amos 5:15
Hate *evil*, love *good*, And establish justice in the gate! Perhaps the LORD God of hosts May be gracious to the remnant of Joseph.

John 13:34
A new commandment I give to you, that you *love* one another, even as I have loved you, that you also love one another.

Hebrews 13:1–2
Let *love of the brethren* continue. [2]Do not neglect to show *hospitality* to strangers, for by this some have entertained angels without knowing it.

1 Peter 2:17

Honor all people, *love* the brotherhood, fear God, honor the king.

1 Peter 3:8–11

To sum up, all of you be harmonious, sympathetic, *brotherly*, kindhearted, and humble in spirit; [9]not returning evil for evil or insult for insult, but giving a blessing instead; for you were called for the very purpose that you might inherit a blessing. [10]For,"THE ONE WHO DESIRES LIFE, TO *LOVE* AND SEE GOOD DAYS, MUST KEEP HIS TONGUE FROM EVIL AND HIS LIPS FROM SPEAKING DECEIT. [11]HE MUST TURN AWAY FROM *EVIL* AND DO *GOOD*; HE MUST SEEK PEACE AND PURSUE IT."

1 Peter 4:8–9

Above all, keep fervent in your *love* for one another, because love covers a multitude of sins. [9]Be *hospitable* to one another without complaint.

2 Peter 1:5–7

Now for this very reason also, applying all *diligence*, in your faith supply moral excellence, and in your moral excellence, knowledge, [6]and in your knowledge, self-control, and in your self-control, *perseverance*, and in your perseverance, godliness, [7]and in your godliness, *brotherly* kindness, and in your brotherly kindness, *love*.

Mishnah 'Abot 4:12

The *honor* owing to your disciple should be as precious to you as yours. And the honor owing to your fellow should be like the reverence owing to your master.

Menander, Sentences 554

Welcome strangers, lest you become a stranger.

Romans 12:14–21

Bless those who persecute you; bless and do not curse. [15]Rejoice with those who rejoice, and weep with those who weep. [16]Be of the same mind toward one another; do not be haughty in mind, but associate with the lowly.

Do not be wise in your own estimation. [17]Never pay back evil for evil to anyone. Respect what is right in the sight of all men. [18]If possible, so far as it depends on you, be at peace with all men. [19]Never take your own revenge, beloved, but leave room for the wrath of God, for it is written, "VENGEANCE IS MINE, I WILL REPAY," says the Lord. [20]"BUT IF YOUR ENEMY IS HUNGRY, FEED HIM, AND IF HE IS THIRSTY, GIVE HIM A DRINK; FOR IN SO DOING YOU WILL HEAP BURNING COALS ON HIS HEAD." [21]Do not be overcome by evil, but overcome evil with good.

Romans 1:18

For *the wrath of God* is revealed from heaven against all ungodliness and unrighteousness of men who suppress the truth in unrighteousness.

Romans 11:20, 25

Quite right, they were broken off for their unbelief, but you stand by your faith. Do not be conceited, but fear; . . . [25]For I do not want you, brethren, to be uninformed of this mystery—so that you will *not be wise in your own estimation*—that a partial hardening has happened to Israel until the fullness of the Gentiles has come in.

Romans 14:19

So then we pursue the things which make for *peace* and the building up of one another.

Romans 15:5–6

Now may the God who gives perseverance and encouragement grant you to *be of the same mind* with *one another* according to Christ Jesus, [6]so that with one accord you may with one voice glorify the God and Father of our Lord Jesus Christ.

1 Corinthians 3:18

Let no man deceive himself. If any man among you thinks that he is *wise* in this age, he must become foolish, so that he may become wise.

1 Corinthians 4:12–13

And we toil, working with our own hands; when we are reviled, we *bless*; when we are *persecuted*, we endure; [13]when we are slandered, we try to conciliate; we have become as the scum of the world, the dregs of all things, even until now.

2 Corinthians 8:21

We have regard for what is honorable, not only in the sight of the Lord, but also *in the sight of men.*

2 Corinthians 13:11

Finally, brethren, *rejoice,* be made complete, be comforted, be like-minded, live in *peace*; and the God of love and peace will be with you.

Philippians 2:1–3

Therefore if there is any encouragement in Christ, if there is any consolation of love, if there is any fellowship of the Spirit, if any affection and compassion, [2]make my joy complete by *being of the same mind*, maintaining the same love, united in spirit, intent on one purpose. [3]Do nothing from selfishness or empty conceit, but with humility of mind regard one another as more important than yourselves.

1 Thessalonians 5:13–15

Live in *peace* with one another. [14]We urge you, brethren, admonish the unruly, encourage the fainthearted, help the weak, be patient with everyone. [15]See that no one *repays* another with *evil for evil*, but always seek after that which is *good* for one another and for all people.

Proverbs 3:4

So you will find favor and good repute *In the sight of* God and *man.*

Proverbs 3:7

Do not be wise in your own eyes; Fear the LORD and turn away from *evil.*

Proverbs 20:22

Do not say, "I will *repay evil*"; Wait for the LORD, and He will save you.

Proverbs 25:21–22

If your enemy is hungry, give him food to eat; *And if he is thirsty, give him* water *to drink;* [22]*For you will heap burning coals on his head,* And the LORD will reward you.

Matthew 5:44

"But I say to you, love your enemies and pray for those who *persecute* you."

Luke 6:27–28

"But I say to you who hear, love your enemies, do good to those who hate you, [28]*bless* those who *curse* you, pray for those who mistreat you."

1 Peter 3:8–9

To sum up, all of you be harmonious, sympathetic, brotherly, kindhearted, and humble in spirit; [9]not returning *evil for evil* or insult for insult, but giving a *blessing* instead; for you were called for the very purpose that you might inherit a blessing.

OTHER BIBLICAL PARALLELS

Leviticus 19:18

"You shall not take *vengeance,* nor bear any grudge against the sons of your people, but you shall love your neighbor as yourself; I am the LORD."

Deuteronomy 32:35

"*Vengeance is Mine,* and retribution, In due time their foot will slip; For the day of their calamity is near, And the impending things are hastening upon them."

Job 30:25

"Have I not *wept* for the one whose life is hard? Was not my soul grieved for the needy?"

NONCANONICAL PARALLELS

Sirach 7:34

Do not avoid those who *weep,* but mourn with those who mourn.

Testament of Benjamin 4:2–3

"For a good man does not have a blind eye, but he is merciful to all, even though they may be sinners. [3]And even if persons plot against him for evil ends, by doing *good* this man conquers *evil,* being watched over by God."

Joseph and Aseneth 28:5

"And we know that our brothers are men who worship God and do not *repay* anyone *evil for evil.*"

Every person is to be in subjection to the governing authorities. For there is no authority except from God, and those which exist are established by God. [2]Therefore whoever resists authority has opposed the ordinance of God; and they who have opposed will receive condemnation upon themselves. [3]For rulers are not a cause of fear for good behavior, but for evil. Do you want to have no fear of authority? Do what is good and you will have praise from the same; [4]for it is a minister of God to you for good. But if you do what is evil, be afraid; for it does not bear the sword for nothing; for it is a minister of God, an avenger who brings wrath on the one who practices evil. [5]Therefore it is necessary to be in subjection, not only because of wrath, but also for conscience' sake. [6]For because of this you also pay taxes, for rulers are servants of God, devoting themselves to this very thing. [7]Render to all what is due them: tax to whom tax is due; custom to whom custom; fear to whom fear; honor to whom honor.

ROMANS PARALLELS

Romans 1:18

For the *wrath* of God is revealed from heaven against all ungodliness and unrighteousness of men who suppress the truth in unrighteousness.

Romans 2:14–15

For when Gentiles who do not have the Law do instinctively the things of the Law, these, not having the Law, are a law to themselves, [15]in that they show the work of the Law written in their hearts, their *conscience* bearing witness and their thoughts alternately accusing or else defending them.

Romans 2:29

But he is a Jew who is one inwardly; and circumcision is that which is of the heart, by the Spirit, not by the letter; and his *praise* is not from men, but from God.

Romans 12:10

Be devoted to one another in brotherly love; give preference to one another in *honor*.

OTHER PAULINE PARALLELS

1 Thessalonians 4:6

. . . and that no man transgress and defraud his brother in the matter because the Lord is the *avenger* in all these things, just as we also told you before and solemnly warned you.

1 Timothy 2:1–2

First of all, then, I urge that entreaties and prayers, petitions and thanksgivings, be made on behalf of all men, [2]for kings and all who are in *authority*, so that we may lead a tranquil and quiet life in all godliness and dignity.

Titus 3:1–2

Remind them to be subject to *rulers*, to *authorities*, to be obedient, to be ready for every *good* deed, [2]to malign no one, to be peaceable, gentle, showing every consideration for all men.

OTHER BIBLICAL PARALLELS

Proverbs 3:27

Do not withhold good from those to whom it is *due*, When it is in your power to do it.

Daniel 2:21

"It is He who changes the times and the epochs; He removes kings and *establishes* kings; He gives wisdom to wise men And knowledge to men of understanding."

Matthew 17:24–25

When they came to Capernaum, those who collected the two-drachma tax came to Peter and said, "Does your teacher not *pay* the two-drachma *tax*?" [25]He said, "Yes." And when he came into the house, Jesus spoke to him first, saying, "What do you think, Simon? From whom do the kings of the earth collect customs or poll-tax, from their sons or from strangers?"

Matthew 22:19–21

"Show Me the coin used for the *poll-tax*." And they brought Him a denarius. [20]And He said to them, "Whose likeness and inscription is this?" [21]They said to Him, "Caesar's." Then He said to them, "Then *render* to Caesar the things that are Caesar's; and to God the things that are God's."

John 19:10–11

So Pilate said to Him, "You do not speak to me? Do You not know that I have *authority* to release You, and I have authority to crucify You?" [11]Jesus answered, "You would have no authority over Me, unless it had been given you from above; for this reason he who delivered Me to you has the greater sin."

1 Peter 2:13–14, 17

Submit yourselves for the Lord's sake to every human institution, whether to a king as the one in *authority*, [14]or to governors as sent by him for the punishment of *evildoers* and the *praise* of those who do right. . . . [17]Honor all people, love the brotherhood, *fear* God, *honor* the king.

NONCANONICAL PARALLELS

Wisdom of Solomon 6:2–3

Give ear, you that *rule* over multitudes, and boast of many nations. [3]For your dominion was given you from the Lord, and your sovereignty from the Most High; he will search out your works and inquire into your plans.

Sirach 10:4

The government of the earth is in the hand of the Lord, and over it he will raise up the right leader for the time.

1 Enoch 46:5

He shall depose the kings from their thrones and kingdoms. For they do not extol and glorify him, and neither do they obey him, the source of their kingship.

Romans 13:8–14

Owe nothing to anyone except to love one another; for he who loves his neighbor has fulfilled the law. [9]For this, "YOU SHALL NOT COMMIT ADULTERY, YOU SHALL NOT MURDER, YOU SHALL NOT STEAL, YOU SHALL NOT COVET," and if there is any other commandment, it is summed up in this saying, "YOU SHALL LOVE YOUR NEIGHBOR AS YOURSELF." [10]Love does no wrong to a neighbor; therefore love is the fulfillment of the law. [11]Do this, knowing the time, that it is already the hour for you to awaken from sleep; for now salvation is nearer to us than when we believed. [12]The night is

almost gone, and the day is near. Therefore let us lay aside the deeds of darkness and put on the armor of light. [13]Let us behave properly as in the day, not in carousing and drunkenness, not in sexual promiscuity and sensuality, not in strife and jealousy. [14]But put on the Lord Jesus Christ, and make no provision for the flesh in regard to its lusts.

ROMANS PARALLELS

Romans 1:26, 28–29

For this reason God gave them over to degrading passions; . . . [28]And just as they did not see fit to acknowledge God any longer, God gave them over to a depraved mind, to do those things which are not proper, [29]being filled with all unrighteousness, wickedness, greed, evil; full of envy, *murder, strife*, deceit, malice.

Romans 2:5, 21–22

But because of your stubbornness and unrepentant heart you are storing up wrath for yourself in *the day* of wrath and revelation of the righteous judgment of God. . . . [21]you, therefore, who teach another, do you not teach yourself? You who preach that one *shall not steal*, do you steal? [22]You who say that one should *not commit adultery*, do you commit adultery? You who abhor idols, do you rob temples?

Romans 8:3–4

Sending His own Son in the likeness of sinful flesh and as an offering for sin, He condemned sin in the flesh, [4]so that the requirement of *the Law* might be *fulfilled* in us, who do not walk according to *the flesh* but according to the Spirit.

Romans 12:9

Let *love* be without hypocrisy. Abhor what is evil; cling to what is good.

OTHER PAULINE PARALLELS

1 Corinthians 13:4–6

Love is patient, love is kind and is not *jealous*; love does not brag and is not arrogant, [5]does not act unbecomingly; it does not seek its own, is not provoked, does not take into account a wrong suffered, [6]does not rejoice in unrighteousness, but rejoices with the truth.

Galatians 5:14, 19–21

For *the* whole *Law* is *fulfilled* in one word, in the statement, "*YOU SHALL LOVE YOUR NEIGHBOR AS YOURSELF*." . . . [19]Now the deeds of *the flesh* are evident, which are: immorality, impurity, *sensuality,* [20]idolatry, sorcery, enmities, *strife, jealous*y, outbursts of anger, disputes, dissensions, factions, [21]envying, *drunkenness, carousing,* and things like these.

Ephesians 4:22–24

. . . that, in reference to your former manner of life, you lay aside the old self, which is being corrupted in accordance with the *lusts* of deceit, [23]and that you be renewed in the spirit of your mind, [24]and *put on* the new self, which in the likeness of God has been created in righteousness and holiness of the truth.

Ephesians 5:8, 11, 14, 18

For you were formerly darkness, but now you are *Light* in the Lord; walk as children of Light. . . . [11]Do not participate in the unfruitful *deeds of darkness*, but instead even expose them; . . . [14]For this reason it says, "*Awake, sleeper,* And arise from the dead, And Christ will shine on you." . . . [18]And do not get *drunk* with wine, for that is dissipation, but be filled with the Spirit.

Ephesians 6:11–12

Put on the full *armor* of God, so that you will be able to stand firm against the schemes of the devil. [12]For our struggle is not against flesh and blood, but against the rulers, against the powers, against the world forces of this *darkness*, against the spiritual forces of wickedness in the heavenly places.

1 Thessalonians 5:4–8

But you, brethren, are not in *darkness*, that *the day* would overtake you like a thief; [5]for you are all sons of *light* and sons of day. We are not of *night* nor of darkness; [6]so then let us not *sleep* as others do, but let us be alert and sober. [7]For those who sleep do their sleeping at night, and those who get *drunk* get drunk at night. [8]But since we are of the day, let us be sober, having *put on* the breastplate of faith and *love*, and as a helmet, the hope of salvation.

Exodus 20:13–17

"*You shall not murder.* [14]*You shall not commit adultery.* [15]*You shall not steal.* [16]You shall not bear false witness against your neighbor. [17]*You shall not covet* your neighbor's house; you shall not covet your neighbor's wife or his male servant or his female servant or his ox or his donkey or anything that belongs to your neighbor."

Leviticus 19:18

"You shall not take vengeance, nor bear any grudge against the sons of your people, but *you shall love your neighbor as yourself*; I am the LORD."

Proverbs 4:18–19

But the path of the righteous is like the *light* of dawn, That shines brighter and brighter until the full *day*. [19]The way of the wicked is like *darkness*; They do not know over what they stumble.

Matthew 19:17–19

And He said to him, "Why are you asking Me about what is good? There is only One who is good; but if you wish to enter into life, keep the *commandments*." [18]Then he said to Him, "Which ones?" And Jesus said, "*YOU SHALL NOT* COMMIT *MURDER*; *YOU SHALL NOT COMMIT ADULTERY*; *YOU SHALL NOT STEAL*; YOU SHALL NOT BEAR FALSE WITNESS; [19]HONOR YOUR FATHER AND MOTHER; and *YOU SHALL LOVE YOUR NEIGHBOR AS YOURSELF*."

Matthew 22:36–39

"Teacher, which is the great *commandment* in the Law?" [37]And He said to him, "'YOU SHALL LOVE THE LORD YOUR GOD WITH ALL YOUR HEART, AND WITH ALL YOUR SOUL, AND WITH ALL YOUR MIND.' [38]This is the great and foremost commandment. [39]The second is like it, 'YOU SHALL LOVE YOUR NEIGHBOR AS YOURSELF.'"

Luke 21:34

"Be on guard, so that your hearts will not be weighted down with dissipation and *drunkenness* and the worries of life, and that *day* will not come on you suddenly like a trap."

James 2:8

If, however, you are *fulfilling the* royal *law* according to the Scripture, *"YOU SHALL LOVE YOUR NEIGHBOR AS YOURSELF,"* you are doing well.

1 Peter 4:3

For the time already past is sufficient for you to have carried out the desire of the Gentiles, having pursued a course of *sensuality, lusts, drunkenness, carousing,* drinking parties and abominable idolatries.

Romans 14:1–4

Now accept the one who is weak in faith, but not for the purpose of passing judgment on his opinions. ²One person has faith that he may eat all things, but he who is weak eats vegetables only. ³The one who eats is not to regard with contempt the one who does not eat, and the one who does not eat is not to judge the one who eats, for God has accepted him. ⁴Who are you to judge the servant of another? To his own master he stands or falls; and he will stand, for the Lord is able to make him stand.

ROMANS PARALLELS

Romans 2:1–2

Therefore you have no excuse, everyone of you who *passes judgment,* for in that which you judge another, you condemn yourself; for you who judge practice the same things. ²And we know that the judgment of God rightly falls upon those who practice such things.

Romans 4:19

Without becoming *weak in faith* he contemplated his own body, now as good as dead since he was about a hundred years old, and the deadness of Sarah's womb.

Romans 11:20

Quite right, they were broken off for their unbelief, but you *stand* by your faith. Do not be conceited, but fear.

Romans 14:13

Therefore let us not *judge* one another anymore, but rather determine this—not to put an obstacle or a stumbling block in a brother's way.

Romans 14:16–18

Therefore do not let what is for you a good thing be spoken of as evil; ¹⁷for the kingdom of God is not *eating* and drinking, but righteousness and peace and joy in the Holy Spirit. ¹⁸For he who in this way serves Christ is *acceptable* to God and approved by men.

Romans 14:21–23

It is good not to *eat* meat or to drink wine, or to do anything by which your brother stumbles. ²²The *faith* which you have, have as your own conviction before God. Happy is he who does not condemn himself in what he approves. ²³But he who doubts is condemned if he eats, because his eating is not from faith; and whatever is not from faith is sin.

Romans 15:1, 7

Now we who are strong ought to bear the *weaknesses* of those without strength and not just please ourselves. . . . ⁷Therefore, *accept* one another, just as Christ also *accepted* us to the glory of God.

OTHER PAULINE PARALLELS

1 Corinthians 8:8–13

But food will not commend us to God; we are neither the worse if we do not *eat,* nor the better if we do eat. ⁹But take care that this liberty of yours does not somehow become a stumbling block to the weak. ¹⁰For if someone sees you, who have knowledge, dining in an idol's temple, will not his conscience, if he is weak, be strengthened to eat things sacrificed to idols? ¹¹For through your knowledge *he who is weak* is ruined, the brother for whose sake Christ died. ¹²And so, by sinning against the brethren and wounding their conscience when it is weak, you sin against Christ. ¹³Therefore, if food causes my brother to stumble, I will never eat meat again, so that I will not cause my brother to stumble.

1 Corinthians 9:22

To the *weak* I became weak, that I might win the weak; I have become all things to all men, so that I may by all means save some.

1 Corinthians 10:12

Therefore let him who thinks he *stands* take heed that he does not *fall.*

1 Corinthians 10:31–33

Whether, then, you *eat* or drink or whatever you do, do all to the glory of God. [32]Give no offense either to Jews or to Greeks or to the church of God; [33]just as I also please all men in all things, not seeking my own profit but the profit of the many, so that they may be saved.

Colossians 2:16–17

Therefore no one is to act as your *judge* in regard to food or drink or in respect to a festival or a new moon or a Sabbath day— [17]things which are a mere shadow of what is to come; but the substance belongs to Christ.

Colossians 4:1

Masters, grant to your slaves justice and fairness, knowing that you too have a *Master* in heaven.

OTHER BIBLICAL PARALLELS

Daniel 1:8, 12, 16

But Daniel made up his mind that he would not defile himself with the king's choice food or with the wine which he drank; so he sought permission from the commander of the officials that he might not defile himself. . . . [12]"Please test your servants for ten days, and let us be given some *vegetables* to *eat* and water to drink." . . . [16]So the overseer continued to withhold their choice food and the wine they were to drink, and kept giving them vegetables.

James 4:12

There is only one Lawgiver and Judge, the One who is able to save and to destroy; but who are you who *judge* your neighbor?

NONCANONICAL PARALLELS

Josephus, Life 13–14

When Felix was procurator of Judea, certain priests of my acquaintance . . . were on a minor and trifling charge sent by him in bonds to Rome to plead their case before Caesar. [14]I wanted to obtain some manner of release for them, especially after learning that, even in their afflictions, they had not forgotten piety towards God and supported themselves on figs and nuts.

Romans 14:5–12

One person regards one day above another, another regards every day alike. Each person must be fully convinced in his own mind. [6]He who observes the day, observes it for the Lord, and he who eats, does so for the Lord, for he gives thanks to God; and he who eats not, for the Lord he does not eat, and gives thanks to God. [7]For not one of us lives for himself, and not one dies for himself; [8]for if we live, we live for the Lord, or if we die, we die for the Lord; therefore whether we live or die, we are the Lord's. [9]For to this end Christ died and lived again, that He might be Lord both of the dead and of the living. [10]But you, why do you judge your brother? Or you again, why do you regard your brother with contempt? For we will all stand before the judgment seat of God. [11]For it is written, "AS I LIVE, SAYS THE LORD, EVERY KNEE SHALL BOW TO ME, AND EVERY TONGUE SHALL GIVE PRAISE TO GOD." [12]So then each one of us will give an account of himself to God.

ROMANS PARALLELS

Romans 2:16

. . . on the day when, according to my gospel, God will *judge* the secrets of men through Christ Jesus.

Romans 3:19

Now we know that whatever the Law says, it speaks to those who are under the Law, so that every mouth may be closed and all the world may become *accountable* to God.

Romans 6:8–11

Now if we have *died* with Christ, we believe that we shall also *live* with Him, [9]knowing that Christ, having been raised from the dead, is never to die again; death no longer is master over Him. [10]For the death that He died, He died to sin once for all; but the life that He lives, He lives to God. [11]Even so consider yourselves to be dead to sin, but alive to God in Christ Jesus.

Romans 8:34

Christ Jesus is He who *died*, yes, rather who was raised, who is at the right hand of God, who also intercedes for us.

1 Corinthians 10:30–31

If I partake with thankfulness, why am I slandered concerning that for which I *give thanks*? [31]Whether, then, you *eat* or drink or whatever you do, do all to the glory of God.

2 Corinthians 5:10

For we must all appear before *the judgment seat* of Christ, so that each one may be recompensed for his deeds in the body, according to what he has done, whether good or bad.

2 Corinthians 5:14–15

For the love of Christ controls us, having concluded this, that one *died* for all, therefore all died; [15]and He died for all, so that they who *live* might no longer live for themselves, but for Him who died and rose again on their behalf.

2 Corinthians 13:4

For indeed He was crucified because of weakness, yet He *lives* because of the power of God. For we also are weak in Him, yet we will live with Him because of the power of God directed toward you.

Galatians 2:19–20

"For through the Law I *died* to the Law, so that I might *live* to God. [20]I have been crucified with Christ; and it is no longer I who live, but Christ lives in me; and the life which I now live in the flesh I live by faith in the Son of God, who loved me and gave Himself up for me."

Galatians 4:9–10

But now that you have come to know God, or rather to be known by God, how is it that you turn back again to the weak and worthless elemental things, to which you desire to be enslaved all over again? [10]You observe *days* and months and seasons and years.

Philippians 2:10–11

. . . so that at the name of Jesus EVERY KNEE WILL BOW, of those who are in heaven and on earth and under the earth, [11]and that every tongue will confess that Jesus Christ is Lord, to the glory of God the Father.

Colossians 2:16–17

Therefore no one is to act as your *judge* in regard to food or drink or in respect to a festival or a new moon or a Sabbath *day*— [17]things which are a mere shadow of what is to come; but the substance belongs to Christ.

1 Timothy 4:1, 3–4

But the Spirit explicitly says that in later times some will fall away from the faith, paying attention to deceitful spirits and doctrines of demons, . . . [3]men who forbid marriage and advocate abstaining from foods which God has created to be gratefully shared in by those who believe and know the truth. [4]For everything created by God is good, and nothing is to be rejected if it is received with gratitude.

OTHER BIBLICAL PARALLELS

Isaiah 45:23

"I have sworn by Myself, The word has gone forth from My mouth in righteousness And will not turn back, That *to Me every knee* will *bow, every tongue* will swear allegiance."

Matthew 7:1–2

"Do not *judge* so that you will not be judged. [2]For in the way you judge, you will be judged; and by your standard of measure, it will be measured to you."

Luke 20:38

"Now He is not the God of *the dead* but of *the living*; for all live to Him."

Acts 17:30–31

"Therefore having overlooked the times of ignorance, God is now declaring to men that all people everywhere should repent, [31]because He has fixed a day in which He will *judge* the world in righteousness through a Man whom He has appointed, having furnished proof to all men by raising Him from *the dead*."

NONCANONICAL PARALLELS

4 Maccabees 16:25

They knew also that those who *die* for the sake of God *live* to God, as do Abraham and Isaac and Jacob and all the patriarchs.

For it is shameful both to *live* and to *die* only
for oneself.

Romans 14:13–23

Therefore let us not judge one another anymore, but rather determine this—not to put an
obstacle or a stumbling block in a brother's
way. [14]I know and am convinced in the Lord
Jesus that nothing is unclean in itself; but to
him who thinks anything to be unclean, to him
it is unclean. [15]For if because of food your
brother is hurt, you are no longer walking
according to love. Do not destroy with your
food him for whom Christ died. [16]Therefore do
not let what is for you a good thing be spoken
of as evil; [17]for the kingdom of God is not eating and drinking, but righteousness and peace
and joy in the Holy Spirit. [18]For he who in this
way serves Christ is acceptable to God and
approved by men. [19]So then we pursue the
things which make for peace and the building
up of one another. [20]Do not tear down the work
of God for the sake of food. All things indeed
are clean, but they are evil for the man who
eats and gives offense. [21]It is good not to eat
meat or to drink wine, or to do anything by
which your brother stumbles. [22]The faith which
you have, have as your own conviction before
God. Happy is he who does not condemn himself in what he approves. [23]But he who doubts
is condemned if he eats, because his eating
is not from faith; and whatever is not from faith
is sin.

ROMANS PARALLELS

Romans 4:5

But to the one who does not work, but
believes in Him who justifies the ungodly,
his *faith* is credited as *righteousness.*

Romans 9:31–32

But Israel, pursuing a law of *righteousness,*
did not arrive at that law. [32]Why? Because
they did not pursue it by *faith,* but as though
it were by works. They stumbled over the
stumbling stone.

Romans 12:18

If possible, so far as it depends on you, be at
peace with all men.

Romans 13:10

Love does no wrong to a neighbor; therefore
love is the fulfillment of the law.

Romans 14:1–3

Now accept the one who is weak in faith,
but not for the purpose of passing judgment
on his opinions. [2]One person has *faith* that
he may *eat* all things, but he who is weak
eats vegetables only. [3]The one who eats is
not to regard with contempt the one who
does not eat, and the one who does not eat
is not to *judge* the one who eats, for God has
accepted him.

Romans 15:13

Now may the God of hope fill you with all
joy and *peace* in believing, so that you will
abound in hope by the power of *the Holy
Spirit.*

OTHER PAULINE PARALLELS

1 Corinthians 8:1, 7–9

Now concerning things sacrificed to idols,
we know that we all have knowledge.
Knowledge makes arrogant, but *love* edifies.
. . . [7]However not all men have this knowledge; but some, being accustomed to the
idol until now, eat *food* as if it were sacrificed to an idol; and their conscience being
weak is defiled. [8]But food will not commend
us to God; we are neither the worse if we do
not *eat,* nor the better if we do eat. [9]But take
care that this liberty of yours does not somehow become *a stumbling block* to the weak.

1 Corinthians 8:11, 13

For through your knowledge he who is
weak is ruined, the *brother* for whose sake
Christ died. . . . [13]Therefore, if *food* causes
my brother to *stumble,* I will never *eat meat*
again, so that I will not cause my brother to
stumble.

1 Corinthians 10:23, 31–32

All things are lawful, but not all things are
profitable. All things are lawful, but not all
things edify. . . . [31]Whether, then, you *eat* or
drink or whatever you do, do all to the glory
of God. [32]Give no offense either to Jews or
to Greeks or to the church of God.

Galatians 5:20–22

. . . idolatry, sorcery, enmities, strife, jealousy, outbursts of anger, disputes, dissen-

sions, factions, [21]envying, drunkenness, carousing, and things like these, of which I forewarn you, just as I have forewarned you, that those who practice such things will not inherit *the kingdom of God.* [22]But the fruit of the Spirit is *love, joy, peace,* patience, kindness, goodness, faithfulness.

Ephesians 5:1–2
Therefore be imitators of God, as beloved children; [2]and *walk* in *love,* just as Christ also loved you and gave Himself up for us, an offering and a sacrifice to God as a fragrant aroma.

1 Thessalonians 5:11
Therefore encourage one another and *build up one another*, just as you also are doing.

Leviticus 11:4, 8
"Nevertheless, you are not to *eat* of these, among those which chew the cud, or among those which divide the hoof. . . . [8]You shall not eat of their flesh nor touch their carcasses; they are *unclean* to you."

Psalm 34:14
Depart from evil and do good; Seek *peace* and *pursue* it.

Daniel 1:8, 12, 16
But Daniel made up his mind that he would not defile himself with the king's choice *food* or with the wine which he drank; so he sought permission from the commander of the officials that he might not defile himself. . . . [12]"Please test your servants for ten days, and let us be given some vegetables to *eat* and water to drink." . . . [16]So the overseer continued to withhold their choice food and the *wine* they were to *drink*, and kept giving them vegetables.

Mark 7:18–19
And He said to them, "Are you so lacking in understanding also? Do you not understand that whatever goes into the man from outside cannot defile him, [19]because it does not go into his heart, but into his stomach, and is eliminated?" (Thus He declared all *foods clean*.)

Acts 10:14–15
But Peter said, "By no means, Lord, for I have never *eaten* anything unholy and *unclean*." [15]Again a voice came to him a second time, "What God has cleansed, no longer consider unholy."

1 John 2:10
The one who *loves* his *brother* abides in the Light and there is no cause for *stumbling* in him.

1 Maccabees 1:62–63
But many in Israel stood firm and were resolved in their hearts not to *eat unclean food.* [63]They chose to die rather than to be defiled by food or to profane the holy covenant; and they did die.

Romans 15:1–6

Now we who are strong ought to bear the weaknesses of those without strength and not just please ourselves. [2]Each of us is to please his neighbor for his good, to his edification. [3]For even Christ did not please Himself; but as it is written, "THE REPROACHES OF THOSE WHO REPROACHED YOU FELL ON ME." [4]For whatever was written in earlier times was written for our instruction, so that through perseverance and the encouragement of the Scriptures we might have hope. [5]Now may the God who gives perseverance and encouragement grant you to be of the same mind with one another according to Christ Jesus, [6]so that with one accord you may with one voice glorify the God and Father of our Lord Jesus Christ.

Romans 4:23–24
Now not for his sake only *was* it *written* that it was credited to him, [24]but for our sake also, to whom it will be credited, as those who believe in Him who raised Jesus our Lord from the dead.

Romans 5:3–5
And not only this, but we also exult in our tribulations, knowing that tribulation brings about *perseverance*; [4]and perseverance, proven character; and proven character,

hope; [5]and hope does not disappoint, because the love of God has been poured out within our hearts through the Holy Spirit who was given to us.

Romans 12:16

Be of the same mind toward one another; do not be haughty in mind, but associate with the lowly. Do not be wise in your own estimation.

Romans 14:1

Now accept the one who is *weak* in faith, but not for the purpose of passing judgment on his opinions.

OTHER PAULINE PARALLELS

1 Corinthians 1:10

Now I exhort you, brethren, by the name of our Lord Jesus Christ, that you all agree and that there be no divisions among you, but that you be made complete in *the same mind* and in the same judgment.

1 Corinthians 6:20

For you have been bought with a price: therefore *glorify God* in your body.

1 Corinthians 9:22

To the *weak* I became weak, that I might win the weak; I have become all things to all men, so that I may by all means save some.

1 Corinthians 10:11–12

Now these things happened to them as an example, and they were *written for our instruction*, upon whom the ends of the ages have come. [12]Therefore let him who thinks he stands take heed that he does not fall.

1 Corinthians 10:23–24

All things are lawful, but not all things are profitable. All things are lawful, but not all things *edify*. [24]Let no one seek his own good, but that of his *neighbor*.

1 Corinthians 10:31–33

Whether, then, you eat or drink or whatever you do, do all to the glory of God. [32]Give no offense either to Jews or to Greeks or to the church of God; [33]just as I also *please* all men in all things, not seeking my own profit but the profit of the many, so that they may be saved.

2 Corinthians 8:9

For you know the grace of our Lord Jesus Christ, that though He was rich, yet for your sake He became poor, so that you through His poverty might become rich.

Galatians 6:2

Bear one another's burdens, and thereby fulfill the law of Christ.

Ephesians 4:29

Let no unwholesome word proceed from your mouth, but only such a word as is good for *edification* according to the need of the moment, so that it will give grace to those who hear.

Philippians 2:1–2

Therefore if there is any *encouragement* in Christ, if there is any consolation of love, if there is any fellowship of the Spirit, if any affection and compassion, [2]make my joy complete by *being of the same mind*, maintaining the same love, united in spirit, intent on one purpose.

OTHER BIBLICAL PARALLELS

2 Chronicles 5:12–13

. . . and with them one hundred and twenty priests blowing trumpets [13]in unison when the trumpeters and the singers were to make themselves heard with *one voice* to praise and to *glorify* the LORD.

Psalm 69:9

For zeal for Your house has consumed me, And *the reproaches of those who reproach You* have *fallen on me.*

Acts 4:24

And when they heard this, they lifted their *voices* to God with *one accord* and said, "O Lord, it is You who MADE THE HEAVEN AND THE EARTH AND THE SEA, AND ALL THAT IS IN THEM."

NONCANONICAL PARALLELS

Philo, On Abraham 4

They [The patriarchs] are such persons who have lived irreproachable and noble lives, whose virtues are permanently inscribed in the most holy *scriptures*, not only to praise them, but also in order to *encourage* the readers and to lead them to aspire to the same.

Romans 15:7–13

Therefore, accept one another, just as Christ also accepted us to the glory of God. [8]For I say that Christ has become a servant to the circumcision on behalf of the truth of God to confirm the promises given to the fathers, [9]and for the Gentiles to glorify God for His mercy; as it is written, "THEREFORE I WILL GIVE PRAISE TO YOU AMONG THE GENTILES, AND I WILL SING TO YOUR NAME." [10]Again he says, "REJOICE, O GENTILES, WITH HIS PEOPLE." [11]And again, "PRAISE THE LORD ALL YOU GENTILES, AND LET ALL THE PEOPLES PRAISE HIM." [12]Again Isaiah says, "THERE SHALL COME THE ROOT OF JESSE, AND HE WHO ARISES TO RULE OVER THE GENTILES, IN HIM SHALL THE GENTILES HOPE." [13]Now may the God of hope fill you with all joy and peace in believing, so that you will abound in hope by the power of the Holy Spirit.

ROMANS PARALLELS

Romans 1:16
For I am not ashamed of the gospel, for it is the power of God for salvation to everyone who believes, to the Jew first and also to the Greek.

Romans 3:29–30
Or is God the God of Jews only? Is He not the God of *Gentiles* also? Yes, of Gentiles also, [30]since indeed God who will justify the *circumcised* by faith and the uncircumcised through faith is one.

Romans 4:16
For this reason it is by faith, in order that it may be in accordance with grace, so that *the promise* will be guaranteed to all the descendants, not only to those who are of the Law, but also to those who are of the faith of Abraham, who is the *father* of us all.

Romans 5:5
And *hope* does not disappoint, because the love of God has been poured out within our hearts through *the Holy Spirit* who was given to us.

Romans 9:4–5
. . . who are Israelites, to whom belongs the adoption as sons, and the glory and the covenants and the giving of the Law and the temple service and *the promises*, [5]whose are *the fathers*, and from whom is the Christ according to the flesh, who is over all, God blessed forever. Amen.

Romans 11:28, 30–31
From the standpoint of the gospel they are enemies for your sake, but from the standpoint of God's choice they are beloved for the sake of *the fathers*. . . . [30]For just as you once were disobedient to God, but now have been shown *mercy* because of their disobedience, [31]so these also now have been disobedient, that because of the mercy shown to you they also may now be shown mercy.

Romans 14:1, 3
Now *accept* the one who is weak in faith, but not for the purpose of passing judgment on his opinions. . . . [3]The one who eats is not to regard with contempt the one who does not eat, and the one who does not eat is not to judge the one who eats, for God has *accepted* him.

Romans 14:17
For the kingdom of God is not eating and drinking, but righteousness and *peace* and *joy* in *the Holy Spirit*.

OTHER BIBLICAL PARALLELS

Deuteronomy 32:43
"*Rejoice, O* nations, *with His people*; For He will avenge the blood of His servants, And will render vengeance on His adversaries, And will atone for His land and His people."

Psalm 18:49
Therefore I will give thanks *to You among the* nations, O LORD, *And I will sing* praises *to Your name.*

Psalm 86:9
All nations whom You have made shall come and worship before You, O Lord, And they shall *glorify* Your name.

Psalm 117:1
Praise the LORD, *all* nations; Laud Him, *all peoples!*

Isaiah 11:10

Then in that day The nations will resort to *the root of Jesse*, Who will stand as a signal for the peoples; And His resting place will be glorious.

Matthew 12:15–21

Many followed Him, and He healed them all, [16]and warned them not to tell who He was. [17]This was to fulfill what was spoken through *Isaiah* the prophet: [18]"BEHOLD, MY *SERVANT* WHOM I HAVE CHOSEN; MY BELOVED IN WHOM MY SOUL is WELL-PLEASED; I WILL PUT MY SPIRIT UPON HIM, AND HE SHALL PROCLAIM JUSTICE TO *THE GENTILES*. [19]HE WILL NOT QUARREL, NOR CRY OUT; NOR WILL ANYONE HEAR HIS VOICE IN THE STREETS. [20]A BATTERED REED HE WILL NOT BREAK OFF, AND A SMOLDERING WICK HE WILL NOT PUT OUT, UNTIL HE LEADS JUSTICE TO VICTORY. [21]AND IN HIS NAME *THE GENTILES* WILL *HOPE*."

Matthew 15:24

"I was sent only to the lost sheep of the house of Israel."

Mark 10:45

"For even the Son of Man did not come to be served, but to *serve*, and to give His life a ransom for many."

Acts 3:12, 25–26

But when Peter saw this, he replied to the people, "Men of Israel, why are you amazed at this, or why do you gaze at us, as if by our own power or piety we had made him walk? . . . [25]It is you who are the sons of the prophets and of the covenant which God made with your *fathers*, saying to Abraham, 'AND IN YOUR SEED ALL THE FAMILIES OF THE EARTH SHALL BE BLESSED.' [26]For you first, God raised up His *Servant* and sent Him to bless you by turning every one of you from your wicked ways."

Acts 13:46, 48

Paul and Barnabas spoke out boldly and said, "It was necessary that the word of God be spoken to you first; since you repudiate it and judge yourselves unworthy of eternal life, behold, we are turning to the Gentiles."

. . . [48]When *the Gentiles* heard this, they began rejoicing and *glorifying* the word of the Lord; and as many as had been appointed to eternal life believed.

Revelation 5:5

And one of the elders said to me, "Stop weeping; behold, the Lion that is from the tribe of Judah, *the Root* of David, has overcome so as to open the book and its seven seals."

Revelation 22:16

"I, Jesus, have sent My angel to testify to you these things for the churches. I am *the root* and the descendant of David, the bright morning star."

Romans 15:14–21

And concerning you, my brethren, I myself also am convinced that you yourselves are full of goodness, filled with all knowledge and able also to admonish one another. [15]But I have written very boldly to you on some points so as to remind you again, because of the grace that was given me from God, [16]to be a minister of Christ Jesus to the Gentiles, ministering as a priest the gospel of God, so that my offering of the Gentiles may become acceptable, sanctified by the Holy Spirit. [17]Therefore in Christ Jesus I have found reason for boasting in things pertaining to God. [18]For I will not presume to speak of anything except what Christ has accomplished through me, resulting in the obedience of the Gentiles by word and deed, [19]in the power of signs and wonders, in the power of the Spirit; so that from Jerusalem and round about as far as Illyricum I have fully preached the gospel of Christ. [20]And thus I aspired to preach the gospel, not where Christ was already named, so that I would not build on another man's foundation; [21]but as it is written, "THEY WHO HAD NO NEWS OF HIM SHALL SEE, AND THEY WHO HAVE NOT HEARD SHALL UNDERSTAND."

ROMANS PARALLELS

Romans 1:1, 3, 5

Paul, a bond-servant of Christ Jesus, called as an apostle, set apart for *the gospel of God*, . . . [3]concerning His Son, . . . [5]through whom we have received *grace* and apostleship to bring about *the obedience* of faith among all *the Gentiles* for His name's sake.

Romans 1:15

So, for my part, I am eager *to preach the gospel* to you also who are in Rome.

Romans 11:13

But I am speaking to you who are Gentiles. Inasmuch then as I am an apostle of *Gentiles*, I magnify my ministry.

Romans 12:1

Therefore I urge you, brethren, by the mercies of God, to present your bodies a living and holy sacrifice, *acceptable* to God, which is your spiritual service of worship.

OTHER PAULINE PARALLELS

1 Corinthians 2:2, 4

For I determined to know nothing among you except Jesus Christ, and Him crucified. . . . [4]And my message and my *preaching* were not in persuasive words of wisdom, but in demonstration of *the Spirit* and of *power*.

1 Corinthians 3:10

According to *the grace* of God which *was given* to *me*, like a wise master builder I laid a *foundation*, and another is building on it. But each man must be careful how he *builds on* it.

2 Corinthians 10:14–16

For we are not overextending ourselves, as if we did not reach to you, for we were the first to come even as far as you in the gospel of Christ; [15]not *boasting* beyond our measure, that is, in other men's labors, but with the hope that as your faith grows, we will be, within our sphere, enlarged even more by you, [16]so as *to preach the gospel* even to the regions beyond you, and not to boast in what has been accomplished in the sphere of another.

2 Corinthians 12:12

The signs of a true apostle were performed among you with all perseverance, by *signs and wonders* and miracles.

Galatians 2:1–2

Then after an interval of fourteen years I went up again to *Jerusalem* with Barnabas, taking Titus along also. [2]It was because of a revelation that I went up; and I submitted to them *the gospel* which *I preach* among *the Gentiles*, but I did so in private to those who were of reputation, for fear that I might be running, or had run, in vain.

Ephesians 3:7–8

. . . of which I was made a *minister*, according to the gift of God's *grace* which *was given* to *me* according to the working of His *power*. [8]To me, the very least of all saints, this grace was given, *to preach* to *the Gentiles* the unfathomable riches of Christ.

Ephesians 6:19–20

Pray on my behalf, that utterance may be given to me in the opening of my mouth, to make known with boldness the mystery of *the gospel*, [20]for which I am an ambassador in chains; that in proclaiming it I may speak *boldly*, as I ought to speak.

Colossians 3:16

Let the word of Christ richly dwell within you, with all wisdom teaching and *admonishing one another* with psalms and hymns and spiritual songs, singing with thankfulness in your hearts to God.

OTHER BIBLICAL PARALLELS

Exodus 28:1

"Then bring near to yourself Aaron your brother, and his sons with him, from among the sons of Israel, to *minister as priest* to Me."

Psalm 20:3

May He remember all your meal offerings And find your burnt *offering acceptable*!

Isaiah 52:15

Thus He will sprinkle many nations, Kings will shut their mouths on account of Him; For what had not been told them *they* will *see*, And what they had *not heard* they will *understand*.

Isaiah 66:20

"Then they shall bring all your brethren from all the nations as a grain *offering* to the LORD, on horses, in chariots, in litters, on mules and on camels, to My holy mountain Jerusalem," says the LORD, "just as the sons of Israel bring their grain offering in a clean vessel to the house of the LORD."

Acts 9:15

But the Lord said to him [Ananias], "Go, for he is a chosen instrument of Mine, to bear My name before *the Gentiles* and kings and the sons of Israel."

Acts 14:3

Therefore they [Paul and Barnabas] spent a long time there speaking *boldly* with reliance upon the Lord, who was testifying to the word of His grace, granting that *signs and wonders* be done by their hands.

Acts 19:21

Now after these things were finished, Paul purposed in the spirit to go to *Jerusalem* after he had passed through Macedonia and Achaia, saying, "After I have been there, I must also see Rome."

Acts 24:17–18

"Now after several years I came to bring alms to my nation and to present *offerings*; [18]in which they found me occupied in the temple, having been purified, without any crowd or uproar."

Hebrews 5:1

For every high *priest* taken from among men is appointed on behalf of men *in things pertaining to God*, in order to *offer* both gifts and sacrifices for sins.

Romans 15:22–29

For this reason I have often been prevented from coming to you; [23]but now, with no further place for me in these regions, and since I have had for many years a longing to come to you [24]whenever I go to Spain—for I hope to see you in passing, and to be helped on my way there by you, when I have first enjoyed your company for a while— [25]but now, I am going to Jerusalem serving the saints. [26]For Macedonia and Achaia have been pleased to make a contribution for the poor among the saints in Jerusalem. [27]Yes, they were pleased to do so, and they are indebted to them. For if the Gentiles have shared in their spiritual things, they are indebted to minister to them also in material things. [28]Therefore, when I have finished this, and have put my seal on this fruit of theirs, I will go on by way of you to Spain.

[29]I know that when I come to you, I will come in the fullness of the blessing of Christ.

Romans 1:10–13

. . . always in my prayers making request, if perhaps now at last by the will of God I may succeed in *coming to you*. [11]For I *long* to see you so that I may impart some spiritual gift to you, that you may be established; [12]that is, that I may be encouraged together with you while among you, each of us by the other's faith, both yours and mine. [13]I do not want you to be unaware, brethren, that often I have planned to come to you (and *have been prevented* so far) so that I may obtain some fruit among you also, even as among the rest of *the Gentiles*.

Romans 12:10, 13

Be devoted to one another in brotherly love; give preference to one another in honor; . . . [13]*contributing* to the needs of *the saints*, practicing hospitality.

1 Corinthians 9:11

If we sowed *spiritual things* in you, is it too much if we reap *material things* from you?

1 Corinthians 16:1–4

Now concerning the collection for *the saints*, as I directed the churches of Galatia, so do you also. [2]On the first day of every week each one of you is to put aside and save, as he may prosper, so that no collections be made when I come. [3]When I arrive, whomever you may approve, I will send them with letters to carry your gift to *Jerusalem*; [4]and if it is fitting for me to go also, they will go with me.

1 Corinthians 16:6

And perhaps I will stay with you, or even spend the winter, so that you may send me *on my way* wherever I may go.

2 Corinthians 1:15

In this confidence I intended at first *to come to you*, so that you might twice receive a *blessing*.

2 Corinthians 8:1, 3–4

Now, brethren, we wish to make known to you the grace of God which has been given in the churches of *Macedonia.* . . . ³For I testify that according to their ability, and beyond their ability, they gave of their own accord, ⁴begging us with much urging for the favor of participation in the support of *the saints.*

2 Corinthians 9:1–2

For it is superfluous for me to write to you about this ministry to *the saints*; ²for I know your readiness, of which I boast about you to the *Macedonians*, namely, that *Achaia* has been prepared since last year, and your zeal has stirred up most of them.

2 Corinthians 9:12–14

For the ministry of this *service* is not only fully supplying the needs of *the saints*, but is also overflowing through many thanksgivings to God. ¹³Because of the proof given by this ministry, they will glorify God for your obedience to your confession of the gospel of Christ and for the liberality of your *contribution* to them and to all, ¹⁴while they also, by prayer on your behalf, yearn for you because of the surpassing grace of God in you.

Galatians 2:9–10

And recognizing the grace that had been given to me, James and Cephas and John, who were reputed to be pillars, gave to me and Barnabas the right hand of fellowship, so that we might go to *the Gentiles* and they to the circumcised. ¹⁰They only asked us to remember *the poor*—the very thing I also was eager to do.

OTHER BIBLICAL PARALLELS

Isaiah 60:5–7

"Then you will see and be radiant, And your heart will thrill and rejoice; Because the abundance of the sea will be turned to you, The wealth of the nations will come to you. ⁶A multitude of camels will cover you. . . . They will bring gold and frankincense, And will bear good news of the praises of the LORD. ⁷All the flocks of Kedar will be gathered together to you. . . . They will go up with acceptance on My altar, And I shall glorify My glorious house."

Acts 11:29

And in the proportion that any of the disciples had means, each of them determined to send *a contribution* for the relief of the brethren living in Judea.

Acts 19:21

Now after these things were finished, Paul purposed in the spirit to go to *Jerusalem* after he had passed through *Macedonia and Achaia*, saying, "After I have been there, I must also see Rome."

Acts 20:22

"And now, behold, bound in spirit, I am on my way to *Jerusalem*, not knowing what will happen to me there."

Acts 24:17–18

"Now after several years I came to bring alms to my nation and to present offerings; ¹⁸in which they found me occupied in the temple, having been purified, without any crowd or uproar."

NONCANONICAL PARALLELS

Testament of Job 11:2–3

And there were still others, at the time without resources and unable to invest in a thing, who came and entreated me, saying, "We beg you, may we also engage in this service. ³We own nothing, however. Show mercy on us and lend us money so we may leave for distant cities on business and be able to do *the poor* a service."

1 Clement 5:7

He [Paul] taught righteousness to the whole world, and went to the limits of the West, and gave testimony before the rulers.

Romans 15:30–33

Now I urge you, brethren, by our Lord Jesus Christ and by the love of the Spirit, to strive together with me in your prayers to God for me, ³¹that I may be rescued from those who are disobedient in Judea, and that my service for Jerusalem may prove acceptable to the saints; ³²so that I may come to you in joy by the will of God and find refreshing rest in your company. ³³Now the God of peace be with you all. Amen.

Romans 1:10–11

. . . always in my *prayers* making request, if perhaps now at last by *the will of God* I may succeed in *coming to you.* [11]For I long to see you so that I may impart some spiritual gift to you, that you may be established.

Romans 5:5

And hope does not disappoint, because the *love* of God has been poured out within our hearts through *the* Holy *Spirit* who was given to us.

Romans 11:30–31

For just as you once were disobedient to God, but now have been shown mercy because of their disobedience, [31]so these also now have been *disobedient*, that because of the mercy shown to you they also may now be shown mercy.

Romans 16:20

The God of peace will soon crush Satan under your feet. The grace of our Lord Jesus be with you.

1 Corinthians 16:1–3

Now concerning the collection for *the saints*, as I directed the churches of Galatia, so do you also. [2]On the first day of every week each one of you is to put aside and save, as he may prosper, so that no collections be made when I come. [3]When I arrive, whomever you may approve, I will send them with letters to carry your gift to *Jerusalem.*

2 Corinthians 1:9–11

Indeed, we had the sentence of death within ourselves so that we would not trust in ourselves, but in God who raises the dead; [10]who delivered us from so great a peril of death, and will deliver us, He on whom we have set our hope. And He will yet deliver us, [11]you also joining in helping us through *your prayers*, so that thanks may be given by many persons on our behalf for the favor bestowed on us through the prayers of many.

2 Corinthians 8:12

For if the readiness is present, it is *acceptable* according to what a person has, not according to what he does not have.

2 Corinthians 9:12

For the ministry of this *service* is not only fully supplying the needs of *the saints*, but is also overflowing through many thanksgivings to God.

2 Corinthians 13:11

Finally, brethren, rejoice, be made complete, be comforted, be like-minded, live in peace; and *the God of* love and *peace* will *be with you.*

Galatians 2:1, 3–4

Then after an interval of fourteen years I went up again to *Jerusalem* with Barnabas, taking Titus along also. . . . [3]But not even Titus, who was with me, though he was a Greek, was compelled to be circumcised. [4]But it was because of the false brethren secretly brought in, who had sneaked in to spy out our liberty which we have in Christ Jesus, in order to bring us into bondage.

Philippians 4:9

The things you have learned and received and heard and seen in me, practice these things, and *the God of peace* will *be with you.*

Colossians 4:3

. . . *praying* at the same time for us as well, that God will open up to us a door for the word, so that we may speak forth the mystery of Christ, for which I have also been imprisoned.

1 Thessalonians 2:14–16

For you, brethren, became imitators of the churches of God in Christ Jesus that are in *Judea*, for you also endured the same sufferings at the hands of your own countrymen, even as they did from the Jews, [15]who both killed the Lord Jesus and the prophets, and drove us out. They are not pleasing to God, but hostile to all men, [16]hindering us from speaking to the Gentiles so that they may be saved; with the result that they always fill up the measure of their sins. But wrath has come upon them to the utmost.

2 Thessalonians 3:1–2

Finally, brethren, *pray* for us that the word of the Lord will spread rapidly and be glorified, just as it did also with you; ²and that we will be *rescued* from perverse and evil men; for not all have faith.

2 Thessalonians 3:16

Now may the Lord of *peace* Himself continually grant you peace in every circumstance. The Lord be with you all!

2 Timothy 1:3–4

I thank God, whom I serve with a clear conscience the way my forefathers did, as I constantly remember you in my *prayers* night and day, ⁴longing to see you, even as I recall your tears, so that I may be filled with *joy*.

2 Timothy 1:16

The Lord grant mercy to the house of Onesiphorus, for he often *refreshed* me and was not ashamed of my chains.

2 Timothy 4:18

The Lord will *rescue* me from every evil deed, and will bring me safely to His heavenly kingdom; to Him be the glory forever and ever. *Amen.*

OTHER BIBLICAL PARALLELS

Acts 20:22

"And now, behold, bound in spirit, I am on my way to *Jerusalem*, not knowing what will happen to me there."

Acts 21:13

"What are you doing, weeping and breaking my heart? For I am ready not only to be bound, but even to die at *Jerusalem* for the name of the Lord Jesus."

Hebrews 13:18, 20–21

Pray for us, for we are sure that we have a good conscience, desiring to conduct ourselves honorably in all things. . . . ²⁰Now *the God of peace*, who brought up from the dead the great Shepherd of the sheep through the blood of the eternal covenant, even Jesus our Lord, ²¹equip you in every good thing to do His will, working in us that which is pleasing in His sight, through Jesus Christ, to whom be the glory forever and ever. *Amen.*

I commend to you our sister Phoebe, who is a servant of the church which is at Cenchrea; ²that you receive her in the Lord in a manner worthy of the saints, and that you help her in whatever matter she may have need of you; for she herself has also been a helper of many, and of myself as well. ³Greet Prisca and Aquila, my fellow workers in Christ Jesus, ⁴who for my life risked their own necks, to whom not only do I give thanks, but also all the churches of the Gentiles; ⁵also greet the church that is in their house. Greet Epaenetus, my beloved, who is the first convert to Christ from Asia. ⁶Greet Mary, who has worked hard for you. ⁷Greet Andronicus and Junias, my kinsmen and my fellow prisoners, who are outstanding among the apostles, who also were in Christ before me. ⁸Greet Ampliatus, my beloved in the Lord. ⁹Greet Urbanus, our fellow worker in Christ, and Stachys my beloved. ¹⁰Greet Apelles, the approved in Christ. Greet those who are of the household of Aristobulus. ¹¹Greet Herodion, my kinsman. Greet those of the household of Narcissus, who are in the Lord. ¹²Greet Tryphaena and Tryphosa, workers in the Lord. Greet Persis the beloved, who has worked hard in the Lord. ¹³Greet Rufus, a choice man in the Lord, also his mother and mine. ¹⁴Greet Asyncritus, Phlegon, Hermes, Patrobas, Hermas and the brethren with them. ¹⁵Greet Philologus and Julia, Nereus and his sister, and Olympas, and all the saints who are with them. ¹⁶Greet one another with a holy kiss. All the churches of Christ greet you.

ROMANS PARALLELS

Romans 1:7

To all who are *beloved* of God in Rome, called as saints: Grace to you and peace from God our Father and the Lord Jesus Christ.

Romans 9:3

For I could wish that I myself were accursed, separated from Christ for the sake of my brethren, *my kinsmen* according to the flesh.

OTHER PAULINE PARALLELS

1 Corinthians 15:6–7

After that He appeared to more than five hundred brethren at one time, most of whom remain until now, but some have fallen asleep; [7]then He appeared to James, then to all *the apostles.*

1 Corinthians 16:19–20
The churches of *Asia* greet you. *Aquila* and *Prisca* greet you heartily in the Lord, with *the church that is in their house.* [20]*All the* brethren *greet you. Greet one another with a holy kiss.*

2 Corinthians 3:1
Are we beginning to *commend* ourselves again? Or do we need, as some, letters of commendation to you or from you?

2 Corinthians 13:12–13
Greet one another with a holy kiss. [13]*All* the saints *greet you.*

Philippians 2:25, 29
But I thought it necessary to send to you Epaphroditus, my brother and *fellow worker* and fellow soldier, who is also your messenger and minister to my need; . . . [29]*Receive* him then in the Lord with all joy, and hold men like him in high regard.

Colossians 4:10
Aristarchus, *my fellow prisoner,* sends you his greetings; and also Barnabas's cousin Mark (about whom you received instructions; if he comes to you, welcome him).

2 Timothy 4:19
Greet Prisca and Aquila, and the household of Onesiphorus.

Mark 15:21
They pressed into service a passer-by coming from the country, Simon of Cyrene (the father of Alexander and *Rufus*), to bear His cross.

Acts 18:1–3
After these things he [Paul] left Athens and went to Corinth. [2]And he found a Jew named *Aquila,* a native of Pontus, having recently come from Italy with his wife *Priscilla,* because Claudius had commanded all the Jews to leave Rome. He came to them, [3]and because he was of the same trade, he stayed with them and they were working, for by trade they were tent-makers.

Acts 18:18
Paul, having remained many days longer, took leave of the brethren and put out to sea for Syria, and with him were *Priscilla and Aquila.* In *Cenchrea* he had his hair cut, for he was keeping a vow.

Josephus, Jewish War *2.219, 221–22*
He [Agrippa] died in Caesarea having reigned three years. . . . [221]Later [his brother] Herod, king of Chalcis, died. . . . Another brother, *Aristobulus,* died a private person. . . . [222]These three, as I said before, were the children of Aristobulus, son of Herod (the Great).

Cicero, Letters to his Friends *13.77.2*
I strongly *commend to you* M. Bolanus, a good and noble man possessed of every good quality and an old friend of mine. You would do me a favor if you endeavor to make him see that this recommendation has proven to be of assistance to him.

Romans 16:17–20

Now I urge you, brethren, keep your eye on those who cause dissensions and hindrances contrary to the teaching which you learned, and turn away from them. [18]For such men are slaves, not of our Lord Christ but of their own appetites; and by their smooth and flattering speech they deceive the hearts of the unsuspecting. [19]For the report of your obedience has reached to all; therefore I am rejoicing over you, but I want you to be wise in what is good and innocent in what is evil. [20]The God of peace will soon crush Satan under your feet. The grace of our Lord Jesus be with you.

Romans 1:8
First, I thank my God through Jesus Christ for you all, because your faith is being proclaimed throughout the whole world.

Romans 6:17
But thanks be to God that though you were slaves of sin, you became *obedient* from the heart to that form of *teaching* to which you were committed.

Romans 6:19

I am speaking in human terms because of the weakness of your flesh. For just as you presented your members as *slaves* to impurity and to lawlessness, resulting in further lawlessness, so now present your members as slaves to righteousness, resulting in sanctification.

Romans 15:33

Now *the God of peace* be with you all. Amen.

OTHER PAULINE PARALLELS

1 Corinthians 5:11

But actually, I wrote to you not to associate with any so-called brother if he is an immoral person, or covetous, or an idolater, or a reviler, or a drunkard, or a swindler—not even to eat with such a one.

1 Corinthians 16:23

The grace of the Lord Jesus *be with you.*

2 Corinthians 11:13–14

For such men are false apostles, deceitful workers, disguising themselves as apostles of Christ. [14]No wonder, for even Satan disguises himself as an angel of light.

Galatians 1:9

As we have said before, so I say again now, if any man is preaching to you a gospel contrary to what you received, he is to be accursed!

Galatians 5:19–20

Now the deeds of the flesh are evident, which are: immorality, impurity, sensuality, [20]idolatry, sorcery, enmities, strife, jealousy, outbursts of anger, disputes, *dissensions*, factions.

Galatians 6:18

The grace of our Lord Jesus Christ *be with* your spirit, *brethren.* Amen.

Ephesians 5:6

Let no one *deceive* you with empty words, for because of these things the wrath of God comes upon the sons of disobedience.

Philippians 2:15

. . . so that you will prove yourselves to be blameless and *innocent,* children of God above reproach in the midst of a crooked and perverse generation, among whom you appear as lights in the world.

Philippians 3:18–19

For many walk, of whom I often told you, and now tell you even weeping, that they are enemies of the cross of Christ, [19]whose end is destruction, whose god is their *appetite*, and whose glory is in their shame, who set their minds on earthly things.

Colossians 2:4, 8

I say this so that no one will delude you with persuasive argument. . . . [8]See to it that no one takes you captive through philosophy and empty deception, according to the tradition of men, according to the elementary principles of the world, rather than according to Christ.

1 Thessalonians 2:5–6

For we never came with *flattering speech*, as you know, nor with a pretext for greed—God is witness— [6]nor did we seek glory from men, either from you or from others, even though as apostles of Christ we might have asserted our authority.

2 Thessalonians 3:6

Now we command you, brethren, in the name of our Lord Jesus Christ, that you keep away from every brother who leads an unruly life and not according to the tradition which you received from us.

2 Timothy 3:13–14

But evil men and impostors will proceed from bad to worse, *deceiving* and being deceived. [14]You, however, continue in the things you have *learned* and become convinced of, knowing from whom you have learned them.

OTHER BIBLICAL PARALLELS

Genesis 3:14–15

The LORD God said to the serpent, "Because you have done this, Cursed are you more than all cattle, And more than every beast of the field; On your belly you will go, And dust you will eat All the days of your life; [15]And I will put enmity Between you and the woman, And between your seed and her seed; He shall bruise you on the head, And you shall bruise him on the heel."

Matthew 10:16

"Behold, I send you out as sheep in the midst of wolves; so be shrewd as serpents and *innocent* as doves."

2 Peter 2:2–3

Many will follow their sensuality, and because of them the way of the truth will be maligned; ³and in their greed they will exploit you with false words; their judgment from long ago is not idle, and their destruction is not asleep.

2 John 10

If anyone comes to you and does not bring this *teaching,* do not receive him into your house, and do not give him a greeting.

NONCANONICAL PARALLELS

Testament of Moses 7:1, 3–4

"When this has taken place, the times will quickly come to an end . . . ³Then will rule destructive and godless men, who represent themselves as being righteous, ⁴but who will (in fact) arouse their inner wrath, for they will be deceitful men, pleasing themselves, false in every way imaginable, . . . devouring, gluttonous."

Romans 16:21–27

Timothy my fellow worker greets you, and so do Lucius and Jason and Sosipater, my kinsmen. ²²I, Tertius, who write this letter, greet you in the Lord. ²³Gaius, host to me and to the whole church, greets you. Erastus, the city treasurer greets you, and Quartus, the brother. ²⁴[The grace of our Lord Jesus Christ be with you all. Amen.] ²⁵Now to Him who is able to establish you according to my gospel and the preaching of Jesus Christ, according to the revelation of the mystery which has been kept secret for long ages past, ²⁶but now is manifested, and by the Scriptures of the prophets, according to the commandment of the eternal God, has been made known to all the nations, leading to obedience of faith; ²⁷to the only wise God, through Jesus Christ, be the glory forever. Amen.

ROMANS PARALLELS

Romans 1:1–3, 5

Paul, a bond-servant of Christ Jesus, called as an apostle, set apart for the *gospel* of God, ²which He promised beforehand through His *prophets* in *the* holy *Scriptures,* ³concerning His Son, . . . ⁵through whom we have received grace and apostleship to bring about the *obedience of faith* among all the Gentiles for His name's sake.

Romans 1:9, 11

For God, whom I serve in my spirit in the *preaching* of the *gospel* of His Son, is my witness as to how unceasingly I make mention of you. . . . ¹¹For I long to see you so that I may impart some spiritual gift to you, that you may be *established.*

Romans 3:21

But now apart from the Law the righteousness of God has been *manifested,* being witnessed by the Law and *the Prophets.*

Romans 11:25, 33, 36

For I do not want you, brethren, to be uninformed of this *mystery*—so that you will not be wise in your own estimation—that a partial hardening has happened to Israel until the fullness of the Gentiles has come in; . . . ³³Oh, the depth of the riches both of the *wisdom* and knowledge of God! How unsearchable are His judgments and unfathomable His ways! . . . ³⁶For from Him and through Him and to Him are all things. To Him be *the glory forever. Amen.*

OTHER PAULINE PARALLELS

1 Corinthians 1:14

I thank God that I baptized none of you except Crispus and *Gaius.*

1 Corinthians 2:7

But we speak God's *wisdom* in a *mystery,* the hidden wisdom which God predestined before the *ages* to our glory.

1 Corinthians 4:17

For this reason I have sent to you *Timothy,* who is my beloved and faithful child in the Lord, and he will remind you of my ways which are in Christ, just as I teach everywhere in every church.

Ephesians 3:8–9
To me, the very least of all saints, this grace was given, to *preach* to the Gentiles the unfathomable riches of Christ, [9]and to bring to light what is the administration of the *mystery* which for *ages* has been hidden in God who created all things.

Philippians 4:20
Now to our God and Father *be the glory forever* and ever. *Amen.*

Colossians 1:25–27
Of this church I was made a minister according to the stewardship from God bestowed on me for your benefit, so that I might fully carry out the *preaching* of the word of God, [26]that is, *the mystery* which has been hidden from the *past ages* and generations, *but* has *now* been *manifested* to His saints, [27]to whom God willed to make known what is the riches of the glory of this mystery among the Gentiles, which is Christ in you, the hope of glory.

2 Thessalonians 3:18
The grace of our Lord Jesus Christ be with you all.

1 Timothy 1:17
Now to the King *eternal*, immortal, invisible, the only God, *be* honor and *glory forever* and ever. *Amen.*

2 Timothy 4:20
Erastus remained at Corinth, but Trophimus I left sick at Miletus.

Titus 1:2–3
. . . in the hope of eternal life, which God, who cannot lie, promised *long ages* ago, [3]but at the proper time *manifested*, even His word, in the proclamation with which I was entrusted *according to the commandment of God* our Savior.

OTHER BIBLICAL PARALLELS

Acts 13:1
Now there were at Antioch, in the church that was there, prophets and teachers: Barnabas, and Simeon who was called Niger, and *Lucius* of Cyrene, and Manaen who had been brought up with Herod the tetrarch, and Saul.

Acts 16:1
Paul came also to Derbe and to Lystra. And a disciple was there, named *Timothy*, the son of a Jewish woman who was a believer, but his father was a Greek.

Acts 17:5
But the Jews, becoming jealous and taking along some wicked men from the market place, formed a mob and set the city in an uproar; and attacking the house of *Jason*, they were seeking to bring them out to the people.

Acts 19:22
And having sent into Macedonia two of those who ministered to him, *Timothy* and *Erastus*, he [Paul] himself stayed in Asia for a while.

Acts 19:29
The city was filled with the confusion, and they rushed with one accord into the theater, dragging along *Gaius* and Aristarchus, Paul's traveling companions from Macedonia.

Acts 20:4
And he [Paul] was accompanied by Sopater of Berea, the son of Pyrrhus, and by Aristarchus and Secundus of the Thessalonians, and *Gaius* of Derbe, and *Timothy*, and Tychicus and Trophimus of Asia.

NONCANONICAL PARALLELS

Corinth: Inscription (CI 232)
In return for his aedileship *Erastus* had (this pavement) laid with his own money.

1 Corinthians

1 Corinthians 1:1–3

Paul, called as an apostle of Jesus Christ by the will of God, and Sosthenes our brother, [2]To the church of God which is at Corinth, to those who have been sanctified in Christ Jesus, saints by calling, with all who in every place call on the name of our Lord Jesus Christ, their Lord and ours: [3]Grace to you and peace from God our Father and the Lord Jesus Christ.

1 CORINTHIANS PARALLELS

1 Corinthians 1:30

But by His doing you are in Christ Jesus, who became to us wisdom from God, and righteousness and *sanctification*, and redemption.

1 Corinthians 4:9–10

For, I think, God has exhibited us *apostles* last of all, as men condemned to death; because we have become a spectacle to the world, both to angels and to men. [10]We are fools for Christ's sake, but you are prudent in Christ; we are weak, but you are strong; you are distinguished, but we are without honor.

1 Corinthians 6:11

Such were some of you; but you were washed, but you were *sanctified*, but you were justified in *the name of* the *Lord Jesus Christ* and in the Spirit of our God.

1 Corinthians 8:5–6

For even if there are so-called gods whether in heaven or on earth, as indeed there are many gods and many lords, [6]yet for us there is but one *God*, the *Father*, from whom are all things and we exist for Him; and one *Lord*, *Jesus Christ*, by whom are all things, and we exist through Him.

1 Corinthians 9:1–2

Am I not free? Am I not *an apostle*? Have I not seen Jesus our Lord? Are you not my work in the Lord? [2]If to others I am not an apostle, at least I am to you; for you are the seal of my apostleship in the Lord.

1 Corinthians 10:32–33

Give no offense either to Jews or to Greeks or to *the church of God*; [33]just as I also please all men in all things, not seeking my own profit but the profit of the many, so that they may be saved.

1 Corinthians 11:22

What! Do you not have houses in which to eat and drink? Or do you despise *the church of God* and shame those who have nothing? What shall I say to you? Shall I praise you? In this I will not praise you.

1 Corinthians 15:9

For I am the least of the apostles, and not fit to be called *an apostle*, because I persecuted *the church of God*.

OTHER PAULINE PARALLELS

Romans 1:1, 7

Paul, a bond-servant of Christ Jesus, *called as an apostle*, set apart for the gospel of God, . . . [7]to all who are beloved of God in Rome, *called* as *saints*: *Grace to you and peace from God our Father and the Lord Jesus Christ.*

Romans 10:12–13

For there is no distinction between Jew and Greek; for the same Lord is Lord of all, abounding in riches for all who call on Him; [13]for "WHOEVER WILL *CALL ON THE NAME OF* THE *LORD* WILL BE SAVED."

2 Corinthians 1:1–2

Paul, an apostle of Christ Jesus by the will of God, and Timothy our brother, To the church of God which is at Corinth with all the saints who are throughout Achaia: ²Grace to you and peace from God our Father and the Lord Jesus Christ.

Ephesians 1:1–2

Paul, an apostle of Christ Jesus by the will of God, To the saints who are at Ephesus and who are faithful in Christ Jesus: ²Grace to you and peace from God our Father and the Lord Jesus Christ.

Colossians 1:1–2

Paul, an apostle of Jesus Christ by the will of God, and Timothy our brother, ²To the saints and faithful brethren in Christ who are at Colossae: Grace to you and peace from God our Father.

2 Timothy 1:1–2

Paul, an apostle of Christ Jesus by the will of God, according to the promise of life in Christ Jesus, ²To Timothy, my beloved son: Grace, mercy and peace from God the Father and Christ Jesus our Lord.

OTHER BIBLICAL PARALLELS

Psalm 116:13, 17

I shall lift up the cup of salvation And call upon the name of the LORD. . . . ¹⁷To You I shall offer a sacrifice of thanksgiving, And call upon the name of the LORD.

Joel 2:31–32

"The sun will be turned into darkness And the moon into blood Before the great and awesome day of the LORD comes. ³²And it will come about that whoever calls on the name of the LORD Will be delivered; For on Mount Zion and in Jerusalem There will be those who escape, As the LORD has said, Even among the survivors whom the LORD calls."

Zephaniah 3:9

"For then I will give to the peoples purified lips, That all of them may call on the name of the LORD, To serve Him shoulder to shoulder."

Acts 18:1–5

After these things he left Athens and went to Corinth. ²And he found a Jew named Aquila, a native of Pontus, having recently come from Italy with his wife Priscilla, because Claudius had commanded all the Jews to leave Rome. He came to them, ³and because he was of the same trade, he stayed with them and they were working, for by trade they were tent-makers. ⁴And he was reasoning in the synagogue every Sabbath and trying to persuade Jews and Greeks. ⁵But when Silas and Timothy came down from Macedonia, Paul began devoting himself completely to the word, solemnly testifying to the Jews that Jesus was the Christ.

Acts 18:12–17

But while Gallio was proconsul of Achaia, the Jews with one accord rose up against Paul and brought him before the judgment seat, ¹³saying, "This man persuades men to worship God contrary to the law." ¹⁴But when Paul was about to open his mouth, Gallio said to the Jews, "If it were a matter of wrong or of vicious crime, O Jews, it would be reasonable for me to put up with you; ¹⁵but if there are questions about words and names and your own law, look after it yourselves; I am unwilling to be a judge of these matters." ¹⁶And he drove them away from the judgment seat. ¹⁷And they all took hold of Sosthenes, the leader of the synagogue, and began beating him in front of the judgment seat. But Gallio was not concerned about any of these things.

1 Corinthians 1:4–9

I thank my God always concerning you for the grace of God which was given you in Christ Jesus, ⁵that in everything you were enriched in Him, in all speech and all knowledge, ⁶even as the testimony concerning Christ was confirmed in you, ⁷so that you are not lacking in any gift, awaiting eagerly the revelation of our Lord Jesus Christ, ⁸who will also confirm you to the end, blameless in the day of our Lord Jesus Christ. ⁹God is faithful, through whom you were called into fellowship with His Son, Jesus Christ our Lord.

1 Corinthians 2:1
And when I came to you, brethren, I did not come with superiority of *speech* or of wisdom, proclaiming to you *the testimony* of God.

1 Corinthians 3:12–13
Now if any man builds on the foundation with gold, silver, precious stones, wood, hay, straw, [13]each man's work will become evident; for *the day* will show it because it is to be revealed with fire, and the fire itself will test the quality of each man's work.

1 Corinthians 4:7–8
For who regards you as superior? What do you have that you did not receive? And if you did receive it, why do you boast as if you had not received it? [8]You are already filled, you have already become *rich*, you have become kings without us; and indeed, I wish that you had become kings so that we also might reign with you.

1 Corinthians 8:1–3
Now concerning things sacrificed to idols, we know that we all have *knowledge*. Knowledge makes arrogant, but love edifies. [2]If anyone supposes that he knows anything, he has not yet known as he ought to know; [3]but if anyone loves God, he is known by Him.

1 Corinthians 8:6–7
Yet for us there is but one God, the Father, from whom are all things and we exist for Him; and one Lord, Jesus Christ, by whom are all things, and we exist through Him. [7]However not all men have this *knowledge*; but some, being accustomed to the idol until now, eat food as if it were sacrificed to an idol; and their conscience being weak is defiled.

1 Corinthians 10:13
No temptation has overtaken you but such as is common to man; and *God is faithful*, who will not allow you to be tempted beyond what you are able, but with the temptation will provide the way of escape also, so that you will be able to endure it.

1 Corinthians 12:4, 8
Now there are varieties of *gifts*, but the same Spirit. . . . [8]For to one is given the word of wisdom through the Spirit, and to another the word of *knowledge* according to the same Spirit.

1 Corinthians 13:2, 8
If I have the *gift* of prophecy, and know all mysteries and all *knowledge*; and if I have all faith, so as to remove mountains, but do not have love, I am nothing. . . . [8]Love never fails; but if there are gifts of prophecy, they will be done away; if there are tongues, they will cease; if there is knowledge, it will be done away.

1 Corinthians 15:34
Become sober-minded as you ought, and stop sinning; for some have no *knowledge* of God. I speak this to your shame.

Romans 8:19
For the anxious longing of the creation *waits eagerly* for *the revealing* of the sons of God.

2 Corinthians 1:13–14
For we write nothing else to you than what you read and understand, and I hope you will understand until *the end*; [14]just as you also partially did understand us, that we are your reason to be proud as you also are ours, in *the day of our Lord Jesus*.

2 Corinthians 8:7, 9
But just as you abound in everything, in faith and utterance and *knowledge* and in all earnestness and in the love we inspired in you, see that you abound in this gracious work also. . . . [9]For you know the *grace* of our Lord Jesus Christ, that though He was rich, yet for your sake He became poor, so that you through His poverty might become *rich*.

2 Corinthians 11:6
But even if I am unskilled in *speech*, yet I am not so in *knowledge*; in fact, in every way we have made this evident to you in all things.

Philippians 1:3–6, 9–10
I thank my God in all my remembrance of you, [4]*always* offering prayer with joy in my every prayer for you all, [5]in view of your participation in the gospel from the first day until now. [6]For I am confident of this very

thing, that He who began a good work in you will perfect it until the day of Christ Jesus. . . . ⁹And this I pray, that your love may abound still more and more in real *knowledge* and all discernment, ¹⁰so that you may approve the things that are excellent, in order to be sincere and *blameless* until *the day of Christ.*

1 Thessalonians 5:23–24

Now may the God of peace Himself sanctify you entirely; and may your spirit and soul and body be preserved complete, without *blame* at the coming of our Lord Jesus Christ. ²⁴*Faithful* is He who *calls* you, and He also will bring it to pass.

OTHER BIBLICAL PARALLELS

Deuteronomy 7:9

"Know therefore that the LORD your God, He is God, the *faithful God*, who keeps His covenant and His lovingkindness to a thousandth generation with those who love Him and keep His commandments."

Isaiah 13:9

Behold, *the day of* the LORD is coming, Cruel, with fury and burning anger, To make the land a desolation; And He will exterminate its sinners from it.

Joel 2:31–32

"The sun will be turned into darkness And the moon into blood Before *the* great and awesome *day of* the LORD comes. ³²And it will come about that whoever calls on the name of the LORD Will be delivered; For on Mount Zion and in Jerusalem There will be those who escape, As the LORD has said, Even among the survivors whom the LORD *calls.*"

1 Peter 1:13

Therefore, prepare your minds for action, keep sober in spirit, fix your hope completely on the *grace* to be brought to you at *the revelation of Jesus Christ.*

NONCANONICAL PARALLELS

Strabo, Geography *8.6.20*

Corinth is called "wealthy" on account of its commerce, lying on the Isthmus and master of two harbors, one nearer Asia, the other Italy.

1 Corinthians 1:10–17

Now I exhort you, brethren, by the name of our Lord Jesus Christ, that you all agree and that there be no divisions among you, but that you be made complete in the same mind and in the same judgment. ¹¹For I have been informed concerning you, my brethren, by Chloe's people, that there are quarrels among you. ¹²Now I mean this, that each one of you is saying, "I am of Paul," and "I of Apollos," and "I of Cephas," and "I of Christ." ¹³Has Christ been divided? Paul was not crucified for you, was he? Or were you baptized in the name of Paul? ¹⁴I thank God that I baptized none of you except Crispus and Gaius, ¹⁵so that no one would say you were baptized in my name. ¹⁶Now I did baptize also the household of Stephanas; beyond that, I do not know whether I baptized any other. ¹⁷For Christ did not send me to baptize, but to preach the gospel, not in cleverness of speech, so that the cross of Christ would not be made void.

1 CORINTHIANS PARALLELS

1 Corinthians 2:2–5

For I determined to know nothing among you except Jesus Christ, and Him *crucified.* ³I was with you in weakness and in fear and in much trembling, ⁴and my message and my *preaching* were not in persuasive words of wisdom, but in demonstration of the Spirit and of power, ⁵so that your faith would not rest on the wisdom of men, but on the power of God.

1 Corinthians 3:3–6

For since there is jealousy and strife among you, are you not fleshly, and are you not walking like mere men? ⁴For when *one says,* "I am of Paul," and another, "I am *of Apollos,*" are you not mere men? ⁵What then is Apollos? And what is Paul? Servants through whom you believed, even as the Lord gave opportunity to each one. ⁶I planted, Apollos watered, but God was causing the growth.

1 Corinthians 3:21–23

So then let no one boast in men. For all things belong to you, ²²whether *Paul* or *Apollos* or *Cephas* or the world or life or death or things present or things to come; all things belong to you, [23]and you belong to Christ; and Christ belongs to God.

1 Corinthians 4:6

Now these things, brethren, I have figuratively applied to myself and *Apollos* for your sakes, so that in us you may learn not to exceed what is written, so that no one of you will become arrogant in behalf of one against the other.

1 Corinthians 11:17–18

But in giving this instruction, I do not praise you, because you come together not for the better but for the worse. [18]For, in the first place, when you come together as a church, I hear that *divisions* exist *among you*; and in part I believe it.

1 Corinthians 12:12–13

For even as the body is one and yet has many members, and all the members of the body, though they are many, are one body, so also is Christ. [13]For by one Spirit we were all *baptized* into one body, whether Jews or Greeks, whether slaves or free, and we were all made to drink of one Spirit.

1 Corinthians 16:12, 15–17

But concerning *Apollos* our brother, I encouraged him greatly to come to you with the brethren; and it was not at all his desire to come now, but he will come when he has opportunity. . . . [15]Now I urge you, brethren (you know *the household of Stephanas*, that they were the first fruits of Achaia, and that they have devoted themselves for ministry to the saints), [16]that you also be in subjection to such men and to everyone who helps in the work and labors. [17]I rejoice over the coming of Stephanas and Fortunatus and Achaicus, because they have supplied what was lacking on your part.

OTHER PAULINE PARALLELS

Romans 6:2–3

May it never be! How shall we who died to sin still live in it? [3]Or do you not know that all of us who have been *baptized* into Christ Jesus have been baptized into His death?

Romans 16:23

Gaius, host to me and to the whole church, greets you. Erastus, the city treasurer greets you, and Quartus, the brother.

2 Corinthians 10:10

For they say, "His letters are weighty and strong, but his personal presence is unimpressive and his *speech* contemptible."

Galatians 2:11–12

But when *Cephas* came to Antioch, I opposed him to his face, because he stood condemned. [12]For prior to the coming of certain men from James, he used to eat with the Gentiles; but when they came, he began to withdraw and hold himself aloof, fearing the party of the circumcision.

Philippians 2:1–2

Therefore if there is any encouragement in Christ, if there is any consolation of love, if there is any fellowship of the Spirit, if any affection and compassion, [2]make my joy complete by being of *the same mind*, maintaining the same love, united in spirit, intent on one purpose.

2 Timothy 2:22–23

Now flee from youthful lusts and pursue righteousness, faith, love and peace, with those who call on the Lord from a pure heart. [23]But refuse foolish and ignorant speculations, knowing that they produce *quarrels*.

OTHER BIBLICAL PARALLELS

Acts 2:38

"Repent, and each of you be *baptized in the name of* Jesus Christ for the forgiveness of your sins; and you will receive the gift of the Holy Spirit."

Acts 18:8

Crispus, the leader of the synagogue, believed in the Lord with all his household, and many of the Corinthians when they heard were believing and being *baptized*.

Acts 18:24–27

Now a Jew named *Apollos*, an Alexandrian by birth, an eloquent man, came to Ephesus; and he was mighty in the Scriptures. [25]This man had been instructed in the way of the Lord; and being fervent in spirit, he was speaking and teaching accurately the things concerning Jesus, being acquainted only with the *baptism* of John; [26]and he began to speak out boldly in the synagogue. But when Priscilla and Aquila heard him, they took him aside and explained to him the way of God more accurately. ²⁷And when he wanted to go across to Achaia, the brethren encouraged him and wrote to the disciples to welcome him; and when he had arrived, he greatly helped those who had believed through grace.

Acts 19:28–29

When they heard this and were filled with rage, they began crying out, saying, "Great is Artemis of the Ephesians!" ²⁹The city was filled with the confusion, and they rushed with one accord into the theater, dragging along *Gaius* and Aristarchus, Paul's traveling companions from Macedonia.

NONCANONICAL PARALLELS

Polybius, Histories *5.104.1*

Above all the Greeks must not wage war on each other, but regard it as a great gift from the gods if they *all agree*, joined arm in arm like men fording a river.

1 Corinthians 1:18–25

For the word of the cross is foolishness to those who are perishing, but to us who are being saved it is the power of God. ¹⁹For it is written, "I WILL DESTROY THE WISDOM OF THE WISE, AND THE CLEVERNESS OF THE CLEVER I WILL SET ASIDE." ²⁰Where is the wise man? Where is the scribe? Where is the debater of this age? Has not God made foolish the wisdom of the world? ²¹For since in the wisdom of God the world through its wisdom did not come to know God, God was well-pleased through the foolishness of the message preached to save those who believe. ²²For indeed Jews ask for signs and Greeks search for wisdom; ²³but we preach Christ crucified, to Jews a stumbling block and to Gentiles foolishness, ²⁴but to those who are the called, both Jews and Greeks, Christ the power of God and the wisdom of God. ²⁵Because the foolishness of God is wiser than men, and the weakness of God is stronger than men.

1 CORINTHIANS PARALLELS

1 Corinthians 2:1–6

And when I came to you, brethren, I did not come with superiority of speech or of *wis-*

dom, proclaiming to you the testimony of God. ²For I determined to know nothing among you except Jesus Christ, and Him *crucified.* ³I was with you in *weakness* and in fear and in much trembling, ⁴and my message and my *preaching* were not in persuasive words of wisdom, but in demonstration of the Spirit and of power, ⁵so that your faith would not rest on the wisdom of men, but on *the power of God.* ⁶Yet we do speak wisdom among those who are mature; a wisdom, however, not *of this age* nor of the rulers of this age, who are passing away.

1 Corinthians 2:14

But a natural man does not accept the things of the Spirit of God, for they are *foolishness* to him; and he cannot understand them, because they are spiritually appraised.

1 Corinthians 3:18–19

Let no man deceive himself. If any man among you thinks that he is *wise* in *this age*, he must become foolish, so that he may become wise. ¹⁹For *the wisdom of* this *world* is *foolishness* before God. For it is written, "He is THE ONE WHO CATCHES *THE WISE* IN THEIR CRAFTINESS."

1 Corinthians 4:10

We are *fools* for Christ's sake, but you are prudent in Christ; we are *weak*, but you are strong; you are distinguished, but we are without honor.

1 Corinthians 12:13

For by one Spirit we were all baptized into one body, whether *Jews* or *Greeks*, whether slaves or free, and we were all made to drink of one Spirit.

OTHER PAULINE PARALLELS

Romans 1:16

For I am not ashamed of the gospel, for it is *the power of God* for salvation to everyone who *believes*, to the *Jew* first and also to the *Greek*.

Romans 1:20–23

For since the creation of the world His invisible attributes, His eternal *power* and divine nature, have been clearly seen, being understood through what has been made, so that they are without excuse. ²¹For even though they *knew God*, they did not honor

Him as God or give thanks, but they became futile in their speculations, and their foolish heart was darkened. [22]Professing to be *wise*, they became *fools*, [23]and exchanged the glory of the incorruptible God for an image in the form of corruptible man and of birds and four-footed animals and crawling creatures.

Romans 9:30–33

Gentiles, who did not pursue righteousness, attained righteousness, even the righteousness which is by faith; [31]but Israel, pursuing a law of righteousness, did not arrive at that law. [32]Why? Because they did not pursue it by faith, but as though it were by works. They stumbled over the *stumbling* stone, [33]just as it is written, "BEHOLD, I LAY IN ZION A STONE OF STUMBLING AND A ROCK OF OFFENSE, AND HE WHO *BELIEVES* IN HIM WILL NOT BE DISAPPOINTED."

Romans 11:33–34

Oh, the depth of the riches both of the *wisdom* and knowledge of God! How unsearchable are His judgments and unfathomable His ways! [34]For WHO HAS KNOWN THE MIND OF THE LORD, OR WHO BECAME HIS COUNSELOR?

2 Corinthians 2:15–16

For we are a fragrance of Christ to God among those *who are being saved* and among *those who are perishing*; [16]to the one an aroma from death to death, to the other an aroma from life to life. And who is adequate for these things?

2 Corinthians 12:9

And He has said to me, "My grace is sufficient for you, for *power* is perfected in *weakness*." Most gladly, therefore, I will rather boast about my weaknesses, so that the *power* of Christ may dwell in me.

Galatians 6:14

But may it never be that I would boast, except in *the cross* of our Lord Jesus Christ, through which the world has been crucified to me, and I to *the world*.

Job 12:13, 17

"With Him are *wisdom* and might; To Him belong counsel and understanding. . . .[17]He makes counselors walk barefoot And *makes fools* of judges."

Isaiah 19:11–12

The princes of Zoan are mere *fools*; The advice of Pharaoh's wisest advisers has become stupid. How can you men say to Pharaoh, "I am a son of *the wise*, a son of ancient kings"? [12]Well then, *where are* your *wise men*? Please let them tell you, And let them understand what the LORD of hosts Has purposed against Egypt.

Isaiah 29:14

"Therefore behold, I will once again deal marvelously with this people, wondrously marvelous; And *the wisdom of* their *wise* men will perish, And the discernment of their discerning men will be concealed."

Isaiah 33:18

Your heart will meditate on terror: "*Where is* he who counts? Where is he who weighs? Where is he who counts the towers?"

Isaiah 44:24–25

Thus says the LORD, your Redeemer, and the one who formed you from the womb, "I, the LORD, am the maker of all things, Stretching out the heavens by Myself And spreading out the earth all alone, [25]Causing the omens of boasters to fail, *Making fools* out of diviners, Causing *wise* men to draw back And turning their knowledge into *foolishness*.

Matthew 16:1

The Pharisees and Sadducees came up, and testing Jesus, they *asked* Him to show them a *sign* from heaven.

Plato, Apology 20D–E, 23A

For I have earned this reputation, men of Athens, through nothing other than a certain kind of *wisdom*. . . . [E]Of my wisdom, if indeed it is some sort of wisdom, I will present as a witness the god that is in Delphi. . . . [23A]Then it is probable, gentlemen, that the god is in fact *wise* and through this oracle is saying this, that human wisdom is of little or no value.

1 Corinthians 1:26–31

For consider your calling, brethren, that there were not many wise according to the flesh, not many mighty, not many noble; ²⁷but God has chosen the foolish things of the world to shame the wise, and God has chosen the weak things of the world to shame the things which are strong, ²⁸and the base things of the world and the despised God has chosen, the things that are not, so that He may nullify the things that are, ²⁹so that no man may boast before God. ³⁰But by His doing you are in Christ Jesus, who became to us wisdom from God, and righteousness and sanctification, and redemption, ³¹so that, just as it is written, "LET HIM WHO BOASTS, BOAST IN THE LORD."

1 CORINTHIANS PARALLELS

1 Corinthians 1:2

To the church of God which is at Corinth, to those who have been *sanctified* in Christ Jesus, saints by *calling*, with all who in every place call on the name of our Lord Jesus Christ, their Lord and ours . . .

1 Corinthians 2:6, 8

Yet we do speak *wisdom* among those who are mature; a wisdom, however, not of this age nor of the rulers of this age, who are passing away, . . .⁸the wisdom which none of the rulers of this age has understood; for if they had understood it they would not have crucified the Lord of glory.

1 Corinthians 3:18–21

Let no man deceive himself. If any man among you thinks that he is *wise* in this age, he must become *foolish*, so that he may become wise. ¹⁹For the wisdom *of* this *world* is foolishness before God. For it is written, "He is THE ONE WHO CATCHES *THE WISE* IN THEIR CRAFTINESS"; ²⁰and again, "THE LORD KNOWS THE REASONINGS of the wise, THAT THEY ARE USELESS." ²¹So then let no one *boast* in men.

1 Corinthians 4:10

We are *fools* for Christ's sake, but you are prudent in Christ; we are *weak*, but you are *strong*; you are distinguished, but we are without honor.

1 Corinthians 5:6

Your *boasting* is not good. Do you not know that a little leaven leavens the whole lump of dough?

1 Corinthians 6:11

Such were some of you; but you were washed, but you were *sanctified*, but you were justified in the name of the Lord Jesus Christ and in the Spirit of our God.

1 Corinthians 8:9–11

But take care that this liberty of yours does not somehow become a stumbling block to the weak. ¹⁰For if someone sees you, who have knowledge, dining in an idol's temple, will not his conscience, if he is *weak*, be strengthened to eat things sacrificed to idols? ¹¹For through your knowledge he who is weak is ruined, the brother for whose sake Christ died.

OTHER PAULINE PARALLELS

Romans 3:21–25, 27

But now apart from the Law the *righteousness* of God has been manifested, being witnessed by the Law and the Prophets, ²²even the righteousness of God through faith in Jesus Christ for all those who believe; for there is no distinction; ²³for all have sinned and fall short of the glory of God, ²⁴being justified as a gift by His grace through the *redemption* which is in Christ Jesus; ²⁵whom God displayed publicly as a propitiation in His blood through faith. This was to demonstrate His righteousness, because in the forbearance of God He passed over the sins previously committed. . . .²⁷Where then is *boasting*? It is excluded. By what kind of law? Of works? No, but by a law of faith.

2 Corinthians 10:14–17

For we are not overextending ourselves, as if we did not reach to you, for we were the first to come even as far as you in the gospel of Christ; ¹⁵not boasting beyond our measure, that is, in other men's labors, but with the hope that as your faith grows, we will be, within our sphere, enlarged even more by you, [16]so as to preach the gospel even to the regions beyond you, and not to boast in what has been accomplished in the sphere of another. [17]But HE WHO BOASTS IS TO BOAST IN THE LORD.

2 Corinthians 11:29–30

Who is *weak* without my being weak? Who is led into sin without my intense concern? [30]If I have to *boast*, I will boast of what pertains to my weakness.

Galatians 6:14

But may it never be that I would *boast*, except in the cross of our Lord Jesus Christ, through which *the world* has been crucified to me, and I to the world.

Ephesians 2:8–9

For by grace you have been saved through faith; and that not of yourselves, it is the gift of God; [9]not as a result of works, *so that no one may boast.*

Ephesians 4:1

Therefore I, the prisoner of the Lord, implore you to walk in a manner worthy of the *calling* with which you have been called.

2 Thessalonians 2:13

But we should always give thanks to God for you, brethren beloved by the Lord, because God has *chosen* you from the beginning for salvation through *sanctification* by the Spirit and faith in the truth.

Jeremiah 9:23–24

"Let not a *wise* man boast of his *wisdom*, and let not the *mighty* man boast of his might, let not a rich man boast of his riches; [24]but *let him who boasts boast* of this, that he understands and knows Me, that I am *the* LORD who exercises lovingkindness, justice and *righteousness* on earth; for I delight in these things."

Matthew 11:25

"I praise You, Father, Lord of heaven and earth, that You have hidden these things from *the wise* and intelligent and have revealed them to infants."

James 2:5

Listen, my beloved brethren: did not *God choose* the poor of this *world* to be rich in faith and heirs of the kingdom which He promised to those who love Him?

Wisdom of Solomon 10:1–2, 5–6, 10, 12

Wisdom protected the first-formed father of the world, when he alone had been created; she delivered him from his transgression, [2]and gave him strength to rule all things. . . . [5]Wisdom also, when the nations in wicked agreement had been put to confusion, recognized the righteous man and preserved him blameless before God, and kept him strong in the face of his compassion for his child. [6]Wisdom rescued a righteous man when the ungodly were perishing; he escaped the fire that descended on the Five Cities. . . . [10]When a righteous man fled from his brother's wrath, she guided him on straight paths; she showed him the kingdom of God, and gave him knowledge of holy things; she prospered him in his labors, and increased the fruit of his toil. . . . [12]She protected him from his enemies, and kept him safe from those who lay in wait for him; in his arduous contest she gave him the victory, so that he might learn that godliness is more powerful than anything else.

1 Corinthians 2:1–5

And when I came to you, brethren, I did not come with superiority of speech or of wisdom, proclaiming to you the testimony of God. [2]For I determined to know nothing among you except Jesus Christ, and Him crucified. [3]I was with you in weakness and in fear and in much trembling, [4]and my message and my preaching were not in persuasive words of wisdom, but in demonstration of the Spirit and of power, [5]so that your faith would not rest on the wisdom of men, but on the power of God.

1 Corinthians 1:4–6

I thank my God always concerning you for the grace of God which was given you in Christ Jesus, [5]that in everything you were enriched in Him, in all *speech* and all knowledge, [6]even as *the testimony* concerning Christ was confirmed in you.

1 Corinthians 1:17

For Christ did not send me to baptize, but to *preach* the gospel, not in cleverness of *speech*, so that the cross of Christ would not be made void.

1 Corinthians 1:21

For since in the *wisdom* of God the world through its wisdom did not come to know God, God was well-pleased through the foolishness of the *message preached* to save those who believe.

1 Corinthians 4:1, 10

Let a man regard us in this manner, as servants of Christ and stewards of the mysteries of God. . . . [10]We are fools for Christ's sake, but you are prudent in Christ; we are *weak*, but you are strong; you are distinguished, but we are without honor.

1 Corinthians 4:19–20

But I will come to you soon, if the Lord wills, and I shall find out, not the *words* of those who are arrogant but their *power*. [20]For the kingdom of God does not consist in words but in power.

OTHER PAULINE PARALLELS

Romans 15:18–19

For I will not presume to speak of anything except what Christ has accomplished through me, resulting in the obedience of the Gentiles by word and deed, [19]in the power of signs and wonders, in the *power* of *the Spirit*; so that from Jerusalem and round about as far as Illyricum I have fully *preached* the gospel of Christ.

2 Corinthians 1:12

For our proud confidence is this: the testimony of our conscience, that in holiness and godly sincerity, not in fleshly *wisdom* but in the grace of God, we have conducted ourselves in the world, and especially toward you.

2 Corinthians 4:7

But we have this treasure in earthen vessels, so that the surpassing greatness of *the power* will be of God and not from ourselves.

2 Corinthians 7:14–15

For if in anything I have boasted to him about you, I was not put to shame; but as we spoke all things to you in truth, so also our boasting before Titus proved to be the truth. [15]His affection abounds all the more toward you, as he remembers the obedience of you all, how you received him with *fear* and *trembling*.

2 Corinthians 10:10

For they say, "His letters are weighty and strong, but his personal presence is unimpressive and his *speech* contemptible."

2 Corinthians 11:6

But even if I am unskilled in *speech*, yet I am not so in knowledge; in fact, in every way we have made this evident to you in all things.

2 Corinthians 12:9–10

And He has said to me, "My grace is sufficient for you, for *power* is perfected in *weakness*." Most gladly, therefore, I will rather boast about my weaknesses, so that the power of Christ may dwell in me. [10]Therefore I am well content with weaknesses, with insults, with distresses, with persecutions, with difficulties, for Christ's sake; for when I am weak, then I am strong.

2 Corinthians 13:4

For indeed He was *crucified* because of *weakness*, yet He lives because of *the power of God*. For we also are weak in Him, yet we will live with Him because of the power of God directed toward you.

Colossians 2:2–4

. . . that their hearts may be encouraged, having been knit together in love, and attaining to all the wealth that comes from the full assurance of understanding, resulting in a true knowledge of God's mystery, that is, Christ Himself, [3]in whom are hidden all the treasures of *wisdom* and knowledge. [4]I say this so that no one will delude you with *persuasive* argument.

1 Thessalonians 1:5

For our gospel did not come to you in *word* only, but also in *power* and in *the* Holy *Spirit* and with full conviction; just as you know what kind of men we proved to be among you for your sake.

Jeremiah 8:9

The wise men are put to shame, They are dismayed and caught; Behold, they have rejected the word of the LORD, And what kind of *wisdom* do they have?

Daniel 2:20

"Let the name of God be blessed forever and ever, For *wisdom* and *power* belong to Him."

1 Corinthians 2:6–13

Yet we do speak wisdom among those who are mature; a wisdom, however, not of this age nor of the rulers of this age, who are passing away; [7]but we speak God's wisdom in a mystery, the hidden wisdom which God predestined before the ages to our glory; [8]the wisdom which none of the rulers of this age has understood; for if they had understood it they would not have crucified the Lord of glory; [9]but just as it is written, "THINGS WHICH EYE HAS NOT SEEN AND EAR HAS NOT HEARD, AND which HAVE NOT ENTERED THE HEART OF MAN, ALL THAT GOD HAS PREPARED FOR THOSE WHO LOVE HIM." [10]For to us God revealed them through the Spirit; for the Spirit searches all things, even the depths of God. [11]For who among men knows the thoughts of a man except the spirit of the man which is in him? Even so the thoughts of God no one knows except the Spirit of God. [12]Now we have received, not the spirit of the world, but the Spirit who is from God, so that we may know the things freely given to us by God, [13]which things we also speak, not in words taught by human wisdom, but in those taught by the Spirit, combining spiritual thoughts with spiritual words.

1 CORINTHIANS PARALLELS

1 Corinthians 1:20

Where is the wise man? Where is the scribe? Where is the debater of *this age*? Has not God made foolish the *wisdom* of *the world*?

1 Corinthians 12:4, 13

Now there are varieties of gifts, but the same *Spirit*. . . .[13]For by one Spirit we were all baptized into one body, whether Jews or Greeks, whether slaves or free, and we were all made to drink of one Spirit.

1 Corinthians 15:24

Then comes the end, when He hands over the kingdom to the God and Father, when He has abolished all *rule* and all authority and power.

OTHER PAULINE PARALLELS

Romans 8:15

For you have *not received* a *spirit* of slavery leading to fear again, but you *have received* a *spirit* of adoption as sons by which we cry out, "Abba! Father!"

Romans 8:26–30

In the same way *the Spirit* also helps our weakness; for we do not know how to pray as we should, but the Spirit Himself intercedes for us with groanings too deep for words; [27]and He who *searches* the hearts knows what the mind of the Spirit is, because He intercedes for the saints according to the will of God. [28]And we know that God causes all things to work together for good to *those who love* God, to those who are called according to His purpose. [29]For those whom He foreknew, He also *predestined* to become conformed to the image of His Son, so that He would be the firstborn among many brethren; [30]and these whom He predestined, He also called; and these whom He called, He also justified; and these whom He justified, He also *glorified*.

Ephesians 1:3–5

Blessed be the God and Father of our Lord Jesus Christ, who has blessed us with every *spiritual* blessing in the heavenly places in Christ, [4]just as He chose us in Him before the foundation of the world, that we would be holy and blameless before Him. In love [5]He *predestined* us to adoption as sons through Jesus Christ to Himself, according to the kind intention of His will.

Ephesians 3:4–5

By referring to this, when you read you can *understand* my insight into the *mystery* of Christ, [5]which in other generations was not made known to the sons of men, as it has now been *revealed* to His holy apostles and prophets in *the Spirit*.

Colossians 1:25–28

Of this church I was made a minister according to the stewardship from God bestowed on me for your benefit, so that I might fully carry out the preaching of the word of God, ²⁶that is, the *mystery* which has been *hidden* from the past ages and generations, but has now been manifested to His saints, ²⁷to whom God willed to make known what is the riches of the *glory* of this mystery among the Gentiles, which is Christ in you, the hope of glory. ²⁸We proclaim Him, admonishing every man and teaching every man with all *wisdom*, so that we may present every man complete in Christ.

OTHER BIBLICAL PARALLELS

Proverbs 20:27

The *spirit of man* is the lamp of the LORD, *Searching* all the innermost parts of his being.

Isaiah 52:15

Thus He will sprinkle many nations, Kings will shut their mouths on account of Him; For what had not been told them they will *see*, And what they had *not heard* they will *understand*.

Isaiah 64:4

For from days of old they have *not heard* or perceived by *ear*, Nor has the *eye seen* a God besides You, Who acts in behalf of the one who waits for Him.

Daniel 2:22–23

"It is He who *reveals* the profound and *hidden* things; He knows what is in the darkness, And the light dwells with Him. ²³To You, O God of my fathers, I give thanks and praise, For You have *given* me *wisdom* and power."

Luke 10:21

At that very time He rejoiced greatly in the Holy *Spirit*, and said, "I praise You, O Father, Lord of heaven and earth, that You have *hidden* these things from the wise and intelligent and have *revealed* them to infants. Yes, Father, for this way was well–pleasing in Your sight."

Acts 13:27–28

"For those who live in Jerusalem, and their *rulers*, recognizing neither Him nor the utterances of the prophets which are read every Sabbath, fulfilled these by condemning Him. ²⁸And though they found no ground for putting Him to death, they asked Pilate that He be executed."

NONCANONICAL PARALLELS

Wisdom of Solomon 9:17–18

"Who has learned your counsel, unless you have given *wisdom* and sent your holy *spirit* from on high? ¹⁸And thus the paths of those on earth were set right, and people were taught what pleases you, and were saved by wisdom."

Sirach 1:1, 9–10

All *wisdom* is from the Lord, and with him it remains forever. . . . ⁹It is he who created her; he saw her and took her measure; he poured her out upon all his works, ¹⁰upon all the living according to his gift; he lavished her upon *those who love him*.

1 Enoch 62:1–2, 7

Thus the Lord commanded the kings, the governors, the high officials, and the landlords and said, "Open your eyes and lift up your eyebrows—if you are able to recognize the Elect One!" ²The Lord of the Spirits has sat down on the throne of his *glory*, and the spirit of righteousness has been poured out upon him. . . . ⁷For the Son of Man was concealed from the beginning, and the Most High One preserved him in the presence of his power; then he *revealed* him to the holy and the elect ones.

1 Corinthians 2:14–16

¹⁴But a natural man does not accept the things of the Spirit of God, for they are foolishness to him; and he cannot understand them, because they are spiritually appraised. ¹⁵But he who is spiritual appraises all things, yet he himself is appraised by no one. ¹⁶For WHO HAS KNOWN THE MIND OF THE LORD, THAT HE WILL INSTRUCT HIM? But we have the mind of Christ.

1 CORINTHIANS PARALLELS

1 Corinthians 1:18, 20–21

For the word of the cross is *foolishness* to those who are perishing, but to us who are being saved it is the power of God. . . . [20]Where is the wise man? Where is the scribe? Where is the debater of this age? Has not God made foolish the wisdom of the world? [21]For since in the wisdom of God the world through its wisdom did not come to know God, God was well-pleased through the foolishness of the message preached to save those who believe.

1 Corinthians 3:16

Do you not know that you are a temple of God and that *the Spirit of God* dwells in you?

1 Corinthians 8:2–3

If anyone supposes that he knows anything, he has not yet *known* as he ought to know; [3]but if anyone loves God, he is known by Him.

1 Corinthians 14:37

If anyone thinks he is a prophet or *spiritual*, let him recognize that the things which I write to you are the Lord's commandment.

OTHER PAULINE PARALLELS

Romans 8:9

However, you are not in the flesh but in the Spirit, if indeed *the Spirit of God* dwells in you. But if anyone does not have the Spirit of Christ, he does not belong to Him.

Romans 8:26–27

In the same way *the Spirit* also helps our weakness; for we do not know how to pray as we should, but the Spirit Himself intercedes for us with groanings too deep for words; [27]and He who searches the hearts *knows* what *the mind* of the Spirit is, because He intercedes for the saints according to the will of God.

Romans 11:33–34

Oh, the depth of the riches both of the wisdom and knowledge of God! How unsearchable are His judgments and unfathomable His ways! [34]For WHO HAS KNOWN THE MIND OF THE LORD, OR WHO BECAME HIS COUNSELOR?

Romans 12:2

And do not be conformed to this world, but be transformed by the renewing of your *mind*, so that you may prove what the will of God is, that which is good and acceptable and perfect.

Galatians 6:1

Brethren, even if anyone is caught in any trespass, you who are *spiritual*, restore such a one in a spirit of gentleness; each one looking to yourself, so that you too will not be tempted.

Philippians 2:3–5

Do nothing from selfishness or empty conceit, but with humility of *mind* regard one another as more important than yourselves; [4]do not merely look out for your own personal interests, but also for the interests of others. [5]Have this attitude in yourselves which was also in Christ Jesus.

OTHER BIBLICAL PARALLELS

Job 11:7

"Can you discover the depths of God? Can you discover the limits of the Almighty?"

Isaiah 40:13

Who has directed the Spirit of the LORD, Or as His counselor has informed Him?

John 14:17, 26

". . . that is *the Spirit* of truth, whom the world cannot receive, because it does not see Him or *know* Him, but you know Him because He abides with you and will be in you. . . . [26]But the Helper, the Holy Spirit, whom the Father will send in My name, He will teach you all things, and bring to your remembrance all that I said to you."

James 3:14–15

But if you have bitter jealousy and selfish ambition in your heart, do not be arrogant and so lie against the truth. [15]This wisdom is not that which comes down from above, but is earthly, *natural*, demonic.

NONCANONICAL PARALLELS

Posidonius (cited by Galen, On the Teaching of Hippocrates and Plato 4.7)

The cause of the passions—the cause, that is, of disharmony and of the unhappy life—is that men do not follow absolutely the daemon that is in them, which is akin to, and has a like nature with, the Power governing the whole cosmos, but turn aside after the lower animal principle, and let it run away with them. Those who fail to see this . . . do not perceive that the very first point in happiness is to be led in nothing by the irrational, unhappy, godless element in the soul.

1 Corinthians 3:1–9

And I, brethren, could not speak to you as to spiritual men, but as to men of flesh, as to infants in Christ. ²I gave you milk to drink, not solid food; for you were not yet able to receive it. Indeed, even now you are not yet able, ³for you are still fleshly. For since there is jealousy and strife among you, are you not fleshly, and are you not walking like mere men? ⁴For when one says, "I am of Paul," and another, "I am of Apollos," are you not mere men? ⁵What then is Apollos? And what is Paul? Servants through whom you believed, even as the Lord gave opportunity to each one. ⁶I planted, Apollos watered, but God was causing the growth. ⁷So then neither the one who plants nor the one who waters is anything, but God who causes the growth. ⁸Now he who plants and he who waters are one; but each will receive his own reward according to his own labor. ⁹For we are God's fellow workers; you are God's field, God's building.

1 CORINTHIANS PARALLELS

1 Corinthians 1:11–12

For I have been informed concerning you, my brethren, by Chloe's people, that there are quarrels among you. ¹²Now I mean this, that each one of you is saying, "*I am of Paul*," and "*I of Apollos*," and "I of Cephas," and "I of Christ."

1 Corinthians 4:1

Let a man regard us in this manner, as *servants* of Christ and stewards of the mysteries of God.

1 Corinthians 4:6

Now these things, brethren, I have figuratively applied to myself and *Apollos* for your sakes, so that in us you may learn not to exceed what is written, so that no one of you will become arrogant in behalf of one against the other.

1 Corinthians 9:7, 11

Who at any time serves as a soldier at his own expense? Who *plants* a vineyard and does not eat the fruit of it? Or who tends a flock and does not use the milk of the flock? . . .¹¹If we sowed *spiritual* things in you, is it too much if we reap material things from you?

1 Corinthians 14:20

Brethren, do not be children in your thinking; yet in evil be *infants*, but in your thinking be mature.

1 Corinthians 16:12

But concerning *Apollos* our brother, I encouraged him greatly to come to you with the brethren; and it was not at all his desire to come now, but he will come when he has opportunity.

OTHER PAULINE PARALLELS

Romans 13:13–14

Let us behave properly as in the day, not in carousing and drunkenness, not in sexual promiscuity and sensuality, not in *strife* and *jealousy*. ¹⁴But put on the Lord Jesus Christ, and make no provision for the *flesh* in regard to its lusts.

2 Corinthians 1:12

For our proud confidence is this: the testimony of our conscience, that in holiness and godly sincerity, not in *fleshly* wisdom but in the grace of God, we have conducted ourselves in the world, and especially toward you.

2 Corinthians 1:24

Not that we lord it over your faith, but are *workers* with you for your joy; for in your faith you are standing firm.

2 Corinthians 12:21

I am afraid that when I come again my God may humiliate me before you, and I may mourn over many of those who have sinned in the past and not repented of the impurity, immorality and sensuality which they have practiced.

Ephesians 2:19–22

So then you are no longer strangers and aliens, but you are fellow citizens with the saints, and are of God's household, ²⁰having been built on the foundation of the apostles and prophets, Christ Jesus Himself being the corner stone, [21]in whom the whole *building*, being fitted together, is growing into a holy temple in the Lord, [22]in whom you also are being built together into a dwelling of God in the Spirit.

Ephesians 3:6–7
. . . the gospel, [7]of which I was made a minister, according to the gift of God's grace which was given to me according to the working of His power.

OTHER BIBLICAL PARALLELS

Isaiah 5:1–2, 7
My well-beloved had a vineyard on a fertile hill. [2]He dug it all around, removed its stones, And *planted* it with the choicest vine. And He built a tower in the middle of it And also hewed out a wine vat in it; Then He expected it to produce good grapes, But it produced only worthless ones. . . . [7]For the vineyard of the LORD of hosts is the house of Israel And the men of Judah His delightful plant.

Acts 18:1, 11, 24–28
After these things he left Athens and went to Corinth. . . . [11]And he settled there a year and six months, teaching the word of God among them. . . . [24]Now a Jew named *Apollos*, an Alexandrian by birth, an eloquent man, came to Ephesus; and he was mighty in the Scriptures. [25]This man had been instructed in the way of the Lord; and being fervent in spirit, he was speaking and teaching accurately the things concerning Jesus, being acquainted only with the baptism of John; [26]and he began to speak out boldly in the synagogue. But when Priscilla and Aquila heard him, they took him aside and explained to him the way of God more accurately. [27]And when he wanted to go across to Achaia, the brethren encouraged him and wrote to the disciples to welcome him; and when he had arrived, he greatly helped those who had *believed* through grace, [28]for he powerfully refuted the Jews in public, demonstrating by the Scriptures that Jesus was the Christ.

Hebrews 5:11–14
Concerning him we have much to say, and it is hard to explain, since you have become dull of hearing. [12]For though by this time you ought to be teachers, you have need again for someone to teach you the elementary principles of the oracles of God, and you have come to need *milk* and *not solid food*. [13]For everyone who partakes only of milk is not accustomed to the word of righteousness, for he is an *infant*. [14]But solid food is for the mature, who because of practice have their senses trained to discern good and evil.

1 Peter 2:1–3
Therefore, putting aside all malice and all deceit and hypocrisy and envy and all slander, [2]like newborn babies, long for the pure *milk* of the word, so that by it you may grow in respect to salvation, [3]if you have tasted the kindness of the Lord.

NONCANONICAL PARALLELS

Philo, On Husbandry 7–9
Husbandry of the soul . . . [8]has as its concern to sow or plant . . . everything likely to yield annual tributes to the person who rules; . . . [9]and who else could this person be except the intellect in each of us, whose role it is to reap the advantages from what has been sown and *planted*? But since *milk* is food for *infants*, but for adults bread made from wheat, so also the soul must have milk-like nourishment in its time of childhood.

1 Corinthians 3:10–17

According to the grace of God which was given to me, like a wise master builder I laid a foundation, and another is building on it. But each man must be careful how he builds on it. [11]For no man can lay a foundation other than the one which is laid, which is Jesus Christ. [12]Now if any man builds on the foundation with gold, silver, precious stones, wood, hay, straw, [13]each man's work will become evident; for the day will show it because it is to be revealed with fire, and the fire itself will test the quality of each man's work. [14]If any man's work which he has built on it remains, he will receive a reward. [15]If any man's work is burned up, he will suffer loss; but he himself will be saved, yet so as through fire. [16]Do you not know that you are a temple of God and that the Spirit of God dwells in you? [17]If any man destroys the temple of God, God will destroy him, for the temple of God is holy, and that is what you are.

1 CORINTHIANS PARALLELS

1 Corinthians 1:7–8

You are not lacking in any gift, awaiting eagerly the revelation of our Lord Jesus Christ, [8]who will also confirm you to the end, blameless in *the day* of our Lord Jesus Christ.

1 Corinthians 4:5

Therefore do not go on passing judgment before the time, but wait until the Lord comes who will both bring to light the things hidden in the darkness and disclose the motives of men's hearts; and then each man's praise will come to him from God.

1 Corinthians 6:11, 19

Such were some of you; but you were washed, but you were sanctified, but you were justified in the name of the Lord Jesus Christ and in *the Spirit of* our *God*. . . .[19]Or do you not know that your body is a *temple* of the Holy Spirit who is in you, whom you have from God, and that you are not your own?

1 Corinthians 9:17

For if I do this voluntarily, I have *a reward*; but if against my will, I have a stewardship entrusted to me.

1 Corinthians 15:10

But by *the grace of God* I am what I am, and His grace toward me did not prove vain; but I labored even more than all of them, yet not I, but the grace of God with me.

OTHER PAULINE PARALLELS

Romans 8:9

However, you are not in the flesh but in the Spirit, if indeed *the Spirit of God dwells in you*. But if anyone does not have the Spirit of Christ, he does not belong to Him.

Romans 15:20

And thus I aspired to preach the gospel, not where Christ was already named, so that I would not *build on* another man's *foundation*.

2 Corinthians 6:16

Or what agreement has *the temple of God* with idols? For we are the temple of the living God; just as God said "I WILL DWELL IN THEM AND WALK AMONG THEM; AND I WILL BE THEIR GOD, AND THEY SHALL BE MY PEOPLE."

Ephesians 2:19–22

So then you are no longer strangers and aliens, but you are fellow citizens with the saints, and are of God's household, [20]having been *built on* the *foundation* of the apostles and prophets, Christ Jesus Himself being the corner stone, [21]in whom the whole building, being fitted together, is growing into a *holy temple* in the Lord, [22]in whom you also are being built together into a *dwelling* of *God* in *the Spirit*.

2 Timothy 2:19–21

Nevertheless, the firm *foundation* of God stands, having this seal, "The Lord knows those who are His," and, "Everyone who names the name of the Lord is to abstain from wickedness." [20]Now in a large house there are not only *gold* and *silver* vessels, but also vessels of *wood* and of earthenware, and some to honor and some to dishonor. [21]Therefore, if anyone cleanses himself from these things, he will be a vessel for honor, sanctified, useful to the Master, prepared for every good work.

OTHER BIBLICAL PARALLELS

Zechariah 13:9

"And I will bring the third part through the *fire*, Refine them as *silver* is refined, And *test* them as *gold* is tested. They will call on My name, And I will answer them; I will say, 'They are My people,' And they will say, 'The LORD is my God.'"

Malachi 4:1

"For behold, *the day* is coming, *burning* like a furnace; and all the arrogant and every evildoer will be chaff; and the day that is coming will set them ablaze," says the LORD of hosts, "so that it will leave them neither root nor branch."

Hebrews 11:9–10

By faith he [Abraham] lived as an alien in the land of promise, as in a foreign land, dwelling in tents with Isaac and Jacob, fellow heirs of the same promise; [10]for he was looking for the city which has *foundations*, whose architect and *builder* is God.

1 Peter 1:6–7

In this you greatly rejoice, even though now for a little while, if necessary, you have been distressed by various trials, [7]so that the proof of your faith, being more precious than *gold* which is perishable, even though *tested* by *fire*, may be found to result in praise and glory and honor at the revelation of Jesus Christ.

1 Peter 2:4–5

And coming to Him as to a living stone which has been rejected by men, but is choice and precious in the sight of God, [5]you also, as living stones, are being *built* up as a spiritual house for a holy priesthood, to offer up spiritual sacrifices acceptable to God through Jesus Christ.

NONCANONICAL PARALLELS

Testament of Abraham (A) *13:11–13*

The archangel Purouel . . . *tests* the *work* of men through *fire*. [12]And if the fire *burns up* the work of anyone, immediately the angel of judgment takes him and carries him away to the place of sinners. . . . [13]But if the fire tests the work of anyone and does not touch it, this person is justified.

The Rule of the Community *(1QS) 8.4–6*

When these things exist in Israel [5]the Community council shall be founded on truth, like an everlasting plantation, a holy house for Israel and the *foundation* of the holy of [6]holies for Aaron.

1 Corinthians 3:18–23

Let no man deceive himself. If any man among you thinks that he is wise in this age, he must become foolish, so that he may become wise. [19]For the wisdom of this world is foolishness before God. For it is written, "He is THE ONE WHO CATCHES THE WISE IN THEIR CRAFTINESS"; [20]and again, "THE LORD KNOWS THE REASONINGS of the wise, THAT THEY ARE USELESS." [21]So then let no one boast in men. For all things belong to you, [22]whether Paul or Apollos or Cephas or the world or life or death or things present or things to come; all things belong to you, [23]and you belong to Christ; and Christ belongs to God.

1 CORINTHIANS PARALLELS

1 Corinthians 1:12

Now I mean this, that each one of you is saying, "I am of *Paul*," and "I of *Apollos*," and "I of *Cephas*," and "I of Christ."

1 Corinthians 1:19–20

For it is written, "I WILL DESTROY THE WISDOM OF *THE WISE*, AND THE CLEVERNESS OF THE CLEVER I WILL SET ASIDE." [20]Where is the wise man? Where is the scribe? Where is the debater of *this age*? Has not God made *foolish the wisdom of* the *world*?

1 Corinthians 1:26–29

For consider your calling, brethren, that there were not many *wise* according to the flesh, not many mighty, not many noble; [27]but God has chosen the *foolish* things of the world to shame the wise, and God has chosen the weak things of the world to shame the things which are strong, [28]and the base things of the world and the despised God has chosen, the things that are not, so that He may nullify the things that are, [29]so that no man may *boast* before God.

1 Corinthians 2:6

Yet we do speak *wisdom* among those who are mature; a wisdom, however, not of *this age* nor of the rulers of this age, who are passing away.

1 Corinthians 3:5

What then is *Apollos*? And what is *Paul*? Servants through whom you believed, even as the Lord gave opportunity to each one.

1 Corinthians 4:10

We are *fools* for Christ's sake, but you are prudent in Christ; we are *weak*, but you are strong; you are distinguished, but we are without honor.

1 Corinthians 7:22

For he who was called in the Lord while a slave, is the Lord's freedman; likewise he who was called while free, is Christ's slave.

1 Corinthians 8:2–3

If anyone supposes that he knows anything, he has not yet known as he ought to know; [3]but if anyone loves God, he is known by Him.

1 Corinthians 15:23, 26, 28

But each in his own order: Christ the first fruits, after that those who are Christ's at His coming. . . . [26]The last enemy that will be abolished is *death*. . . . [28]When all things are subjected to Him, then the Son Himself also will be subjected to the One who subjected all things to Him, so that God may be all in all.

OTHER PAULINE PARALLELS

Romans 8:32, 38–39

He who did not spare His own Son, but delivered Him over for us all, how will He not also with Him freely give us *all things?* . . . [38]For I am convinced that neither *death,* nor *life,* nor angels, nor principalities, nor *things present,* nor *things to come,* nor powers, [39]nor height, nor depth, nor any other created thing, will be able to separate us from the love of God, which is in Christ Jesus our Lord.

Galatians 5:24

Now those who *belong to Christ* Jesus have crucified the flesh with its passions and desires.

Galatians 6:3

For if anyone thinks he is something when he is nothing, he *deceives himself.*

OTHER BIBLICAL PARALLELS

Job 5:13

"He captures *the wise* by their own shrewdness, And the advice of the cunning is quickly thwarted."

Psalm 94:11

The LORD *knows* the thoughts of man, *That they are* a mere breath.

Proverbs 3:7

Do not be *wise* in your own eyes; Fear the LORD and turn away from evil.

1 Corinthians 4:1–7

Let a man regard us in this manner, as servants of Christ and stewards of the mysteries of God. [2]In this case, moreover, it is required of stewards that one be found trustworthy. [3]But to me it is a very small thing that I may be examined by you, or by any human court; in fact, I do not even examine myself. [4]For I am conscious of nothing against myself, yet I am not by this acquitted; but the one who examines me is the Lord. [5]Therefore do not go on passing judgment before the time, but wait until the Lord comes who will both bring to light the things hidden in the darkness and disclose the motives of men's hearts; and then each man's praise will come to him from God. [6]Now these things, brethren, I have figuratively applied to myself and Apollos for your sakes, so that in us you may learn not to exceed what is written, so that no one of you will become arrogant in behalf of one against the other. [7]For who regards you as superior? What do you have that you did not receive? And if you did receive it, why do you boast as if you had not received it?

1 CORINTHIANS PARALLELS

1 Corinthians 2:12

Now we have *received,* not the spirit of the world, but the Spirit who is from God, so that we may know the things freely given to us by God.

1 Corinthians 3:4–5

For when one says, "I am of Paul," and another, "I am of *Apollos,*" are you not mere men? [5]What then is Apollos? And what is Paul? *Servants* through whom you believed, even as the Lord gave opportunity to each one.

1 Corinthians 3:12–14

Now if any man builds on the foundation with gold, silver, precious stones, wood, hay, straw, [13]each man's work will become evident; for the day will show it because it is to be revealed with fire, and the fire itself will test the quality of each man's work. [14]If any man's work which he has built on it remains, he will receive a reward.

1 Corinthians 4:18–19

Now some have become *arrogant,* as though I were not coming to you. [19]But I will come to you soon, if the Lord wills, and I shall find out, not the words of those who are arrogant but their power.

1 Corinthians 5:6

Your *boasting* is not good. Do you not know that a little leaven leavens the whole lump of dough?

1 Corinthians 6:2–3

Or do you not know that the saints will judge the world? If the world is *judged* by you, are you not competent to constitute the smallest law *courts*? [3]Do you not know that we will judge angels? How much more matters of this life?

1 Corinthians 7:25

Now concerning virgins I have no command of the Lord, but I give an opinion as one who by the mercy of the Lord is *trustworthy*.

1 Corinthians 8:1

Now concerning things sacrificed to idols, we know that we all have knowledge. Knowledge makes *arrogant*, but love edifies.

OTHER PAULINE PARALLELS

Romans 2:1

Therefore you have no excuse, everyone of you who *passes judgment*, for in that which you judge another, you condemn yourself; for you who judge practice the same things.

Romans 2:14–16

For when Gentiles who do not have the Law do instinctively the things of the Law, these, not having the Law, are a law to themselves, [15]in that they show the work of the Law written in their *hearts*, their conscience bearing witness and their thoughts alternately accusing or else defending them, [16]on the day when, according to my gospel, God will judge the secrets of men through Christ Jesus.

2 Corinthians 5:10

For we must all appear before the *judgment* seat of Christ, so that each one may be recompensed for his deeds in the body, according to what he has done, whether good or bad.

2 Corinthians 10:18

For it is not he who commends himself that is approved, but he whom the Lord commends.

Colossians 1:25

Of this church I was made a minister according to the *stewardship* from God bestowed on me for your benefit, so that I might fully carry out the preaching of the word of God.

1 Thessalonians 2:4

Just as we have been approved by God to be entrusted with the gospel, so we speak, not as pleasing men, but God who *examines* our *hearts*.

OTHER BIBLICAL PARALLELS

Job 27:6

"I hold fast my righteousness and will not let it go. My *heart* does not reproach any of my days."

Psalm 7:8

The LORD *judges* the peoples; Vindicate me, O LORD, according to my righteousness and my integrity that is in me.

Acts 23:1

Paul, looking intently at the Council, said, "Brethren, I have lived my life with a perfectly good conscience before God up to this day."

1 Peter 4:10

As each one has received a special gift, employ it in serving one another as good *stewards* of the manifold grace of God.

NONCANONICAL PARALLELS

Sirach 42:18–19

He searches out the abyss and the human *heart*; he understands their innermost secrets. For the Most High knows all that may be known; he sees from of old the things that are to come. [19]He *discloses* what has been and what is to be, and he reveals the traces of *hidden things*.

You are already filled, you have already become rich, you have become kings without us; and indeed, I wish that you had become kings so that we also might reign with you. [9]For, I think, God has exhibited us apostles last of all, as men condemned to death; because we have become a spectacle to the world, both to angels and to men. [10]We are fools for Christ's sake, but you are prudent in Christ; we are weak, but you are strong; you are distinguished, but we are without honor. [11]To this present hour we are both hungry and thirsty, and are poorly clothed, and are roughly treated, and are homeless; [12]and we toil, working with our own hands; when we are reviled, we bless; when we are persecuted, we endure; [13]when we are slandered, we try to conciliate; we have become as the scum of the world, the dregs of all things, even until now.

1 CORINTHIANS PARALLELS

1 Corinthians 1:4–5

I thank my God always concerning you for the grace of God which was given you in Christ Jesus, [5]that in everything you were *enriched* in Him, in all speech and all knowledge.

1 Corinthians 1:25, 27–28

Because the foolishness of God is wiser than men, and the weakness of God is stronger than men. . . . [27]But God has chosen the *foolish* things of the world to shame the wise, and God has chosen the *weak* things of the world to shame the things which are *strong*, [28]and the base things of the world and the despised God has chosen, the things that are not, so that He may nullify the things that are.

1 Corinthians 2:1–3

And when I came to you, brethren, I did not come with superiority of speech or of wisdom, proclaiming to you the testimony of God. [2]For I determined to know nothing among you except Jesus Christ, and Him crucified. [3]I was with you in *weakness* and in fear and in much trembling,

1 Corinthians 15:30–32

Why are we also in danger every hour? [31]I affirm, brethren, by the boasting in you which I have in Christ Jesus our Lord, I die daily. [32]If from human motives I fought with wild beasts at Ephesus, what does it profit me?

OTHER PAULINE PARALLELS

Romans 8:35

Who will separate us from the love of Christ? Will tribulation, or distress, or *persecution*, or famine, or nakedness, or peril, or sword?

Romans 12:14

Bless those who *persecute* you; bless and do not curse.

2 Corinthians 4:7–10

But we have this treasure in earthen vessels, so that the surpassing greatness of the power will be of God and not from ourselves; [8]we are afflicted in every way, but not crushed; perplexed, but not despairing; [9]*persecuted*, but not forsaken; struck down, but not destroyed; [10]always carrying about in the body the dying of Jesus, so that the life of Jesus also may be manifested in our body.

2 Corinthians 6:1, 4–5

And working together with Him, we also urge you not to receive the grace of God in vain, . . . [4]but in everything commending ourselves as servants of God, in much *endurance*, in afflictions, in hardships, in distresses, [5]in beatings, in imprisonments, in tumults, in labors, in sleeplessness, in *hunger*.

2 Corinthians 11:18–19

Since many boast according to the flesh, I will boast also. [19]For you, being so wise, tolerate the *foolish* gladly.

2 Corinthians 11:25–29

Three times I was beaten with rods, once I was stoned, three times I was shipwrecked, a night and a day I have spent in the deep. [26]I have been on frequent journeys, in dangers from rivers, dangers from robbers, dangers from my countrymen, dangers from the Gentiles, dangers in the city, dangers in the wilderness, dangers on the sea, dangers among false brethren; [27]I have been in labor and hardship, through many sleepless nights, in *hunger* and *thirst*, often without food, in cold and exposure. [28]Apart from such external things, there is the daily pressure on me of concern for all the churches. [29]Who is weak without my being *weak*? Who is led into sin without my intense concern?

2 Corinthians 12:10
Therefore I am well content with weaknesses, with insults, with distresses, with *persecutions*, with difficulties, for Christ's sake; for when I am *weak*, then I am *strong*.

1 Thessalonians 2:9
For you recall, brethren, our labor and hardship, how *working* night and day so as not to be a burden to any of you, we proclaimed to you the gospel of God.

OTHER BIBLICAL PARALLELS

Lamentations 3:45
You have made us mere offscouring and refuse In the midst of the peoples.

Nahum 3:6
"I will throw filth on you And make you vile, And set you up as *a spectacle*."

Luke 6:27–28
"But I say to you who hear, love your enemies, do good to those who hate you, [28]*bless* those who curse you, pray for those who mistreat you."

Acts 20:34–35
"You yourselves know that these *hands* ministered to my own needs and to the men who were with me. [35]In everything I showed you that by *working* hard in this manner you must help the *weak* and remember the words of the Lord Jesus, that He Himself said, 'It is more blessed to give than to receive.'"

Hebrews 10:32–33
But remember the former days, when, after being enlightened, you *endured* a great conflict of sufferings, [33]partly by being made a public *spectacle* through reproaches and tribulations, and partly by becoming sharers with those who were so treated.

1 Peter 3:15–16
But sanctify Christ as Lord in your hearts, always being ready to make a defense to everyone who asks you to give an account for the hope that is in you, yet with gentle-

ness and reverence; [16]and keep a good conscience so that in the thing in which you are *slandered*, those who *revile* your good behavior in Christ will be put to shame.

Revelation 3:14, 17
"To the angel of the church in Laodicea write, . . . [17]'Because you say, "I am *rich*, and have become wealthy, and have need of nothing," and you do not know that you are wretched and miserable and poor and blind and naked . . . '"

NONCANONICAL PARALLELS

Dio Chrysostom, Orations *8.15–16*
One who is noble . . . fears none of his opponents . . . [16]but challenges them all one after another, struggling with *hunger* and cold, enduring *thirst*, and showing no softness even when he must bear whips, cuts, and burns. Hunger, exile, disrepute, and such things bring no terror to him.

1 Corinthians 4:14–21

I do not write these things to shame you, but to admonish you as my beloved children. [15]For if you were to have countless tutors in Christ, yet you would not have many fathers, for in Christ Jesus I became your father through the gospel. [16]Therefore I exhort you, be imitators of me. [17]For this reason I have sent to you Timothy, who is my beloved and faithful child in the Lord, and he will remind you of my ways which are in Christ, just as I teach everywhere in every church. [18]Now some have become arrogant, as though I were not coming to you. [19]But I will come to you soon, if the Lord wills, and I shall find out, not the words of those who are arrogant but their power. [20]For the kingdom of God does not consist in words but in power. [21]What do you desire? Shall I come to you with a rod, or with love and a spirit of gentleness?

1 CORINTHIANS PARALLELS

1 Corinthians 2:3–4
I was with you in weakness and in fear and in much trembling, [4]and my message and my preaching were not in persuasive *words* of wisdom, but in demonstration of the Spirit and of *power*.

1 Corinthians 4:6

Now these things, brethren, I have figuratively applied to myself and Apollos for your sakes, so that in us you may learn not to exceed what is written, so that no one of you will become *arrogant* in behalf of one against the other.

1 Corinthians 6:5–6

I say this to your *shame*. Is it so, that there is not among you one wise man who will be able to decide between his brethren, ⁶but brother goes to law with brother, and that before unbelievers?

1 Corinthians 10:32–11:1

Give no offense either to Jews or to Greeks or to the church of God; ³³just as I also please all men in all things, not seeking my own profit but the profit of the many, so that they may be saved. ¹¹:¹*Be imitators of me*, just as I also am of Christ.

1 Corinthians 11:16

But if one is inclined to be contentious, we have no other practice, nor have the *churches* of God.

1 Corinthians 13:4

Love is patient, love is kind and is not jealous; love does not brag and is not *arrogant*.

1 Corinthians 15:33–34

Do not be deceived: "Bad company corrupts good morals." ³⁴Become sober-minded as you ought, and stop sinning; for some have no knowledge of God. I speak this to your *shame*.

1 Corinthians 16:5, 7, 10–11

But *I will come to you* after I go through Macedonia, for I am going through Macedonia; . . . ⁷For I do not wish to see you now just in passing; for I hope to remain with you for some time, *if the Lord* permits. . . . ¹⁰Now if *Timothy* comes, see that he is with you without cause to be afraid, for he is doing the Lord's work, as I also am. ¹¹So let no one despise him. But send him on his way in peace, so that he may come to me; for I expect him with the brethren.

OTHER PAULINE PARALLELS

2 Corinthians 1:19

For the Son of God, Christ Jesus, who was preached among you by us—by me and Sil-

vanus and *Timothy*—was not yes and no, but is yes in Him.

2 Corinthians 6:12–13

You are not restrained by us, but you are restrained in your own affections. ¹³Now in a like exchange—I speak as to *children*—open wide to us also.

2 Corinthians 13:2–3

I have previously said when present the second time, and though now absent I say in advance to those who have sinned in the past and to all the rest as well, that if *I come* again I will not spare anyone, ³since you are seeking for proof of the Christ who speaks in me, and who is not weak toward you, but mighty in you.

Galatians 6:1

Brethren, even if anyone is caught in any trespass, you who are spiritual, restore such a one in *a spirit of gentleness*; each one looking to yourself, so that you too will not be tempted.

Ephesians 5:1–2

Therefore *be imitators* of God, as *beloved children*; ²and walk in love, just as Christ also loved you and gave Himself up for us, an offering and a sacrifice to God as a fragrant aroma.

Philippians 3:17

Brethren, join in following my example, and observe those who walk according to the pattern you have in us.

Colossians 1:28

We proclaim Him, *admonishing* every man and *teaching* every man with all wisdom, so that we may present every man complete in Christ.

1 Thessalonians 2:11–12

. . . just as you know how we were *exhorting* and encouraging and imploring each one of you as a *father* would his own *children*, ¹²so that you would walk in a manner worthy of the God who calls you into His own *kingdom* and glory.

1 Thessalonians 3:1–2

Therefore when we could endure it no longer, we thought it best to be left behind at Athens alone, ²and we *sent Timothy*, our brother and God's fellow worker in the gospel of Christ, to strengthen and encourage you as to your faith.

2 Timothy 2:14

Remind them of these things, and solemnly charge them in the presence of God not to wrangle about *words,* which is useless and leads to the ruin of the hearers.

OTHER BIBLICAL PARALLELS

2 Samuel 7:14

"I will be a *father* to him and he will be a son to Me; when he commits iniquity, I will correct him with the *rod* of men and the strokes of the sons of men."

Proverbs 22:15

Foolishness is bound up in the heart of a *child*; The *rod* of discipline will remove it far from him.

Acts 16:1–3

Paul came also to Derbe and to Lystra. And a disciple was there, named *Timothy*, the son of a Jewish woman who was a believer, but his father was a Greek, [2]and he was well spoken of by the brethren who were in Lystra and Iconium. [3]Paul wanted this man to go with him; and he took him and circumcised him because of the Jews who were in those parts, for they all knew that his father was a Greek.

Acts 18:1, 5

After these things he left Athens and went to Corinth. . . . [5]But when Silas and *Timothy* came down from Macedonia, Paul began devoting himself completely to the word, solemnly testifying to the Jews that Jesus was the Christ.

1 Corinthians 5:1–8

It is actually reported that there is immorality among you, and immorality of such a kind as does not exist even among the Gentiles, that someone has his father's wife. [2]You have become arrogant and have not mourned instead, so that the one who had done this deed would be removed from your midst. [3]For I, on my part, though absent in body but present in spirit, have already judged him who has so committed this, as though I were present. [4]In the name of our Lord Jesus, when you are assembled, and I with you in spirit, with the power of our Lord Jesus, [5]I have decided to deliver such a one to Satan for the destruction of his flesh, so that his spirit may be saved in the day of the Lord Jesus. [6]Your boasting is not good. Do you not know that a little leaven leavens the whole lump of dough? [7]Clean out the old leaven so that you may be a new lump, just as you are in fact unleavened. For Christ our Passover also has been sacrificed. [8]Therefore let us celebrate the feast, not with old leaven, nor with the leaven of malice and wickedness, but with the unleavened bread of sincerity and truth.

1 CORINTHIANS PARALLELS

1 Corinthians 3:12–13

Now if any man builds on the foundation with gold, silver, precious stones, wood, hay, straw, [13]each man's work will become evident; for *the day* will show it because it is to be revealed with fire, and the fire itself will test the quality of each man's work.

1 Corinthians 4:6–7

Now these things, brethren, I have figuratively applied to myself and Apollos for your sakes, so that in us you may learn not to exceed what is written, so that no one of you will become *arrogant* in behalf of one against the other. [7]For who regards you as superior? What do you have that you did not receive? And if you did receive it, why do you *boast* as if you had not received it?

1 Corinthians 11:32

But when we are *judged*, we are disciplined by the Lord so that we will not be condemned along with the world.

OTHER PAULINE PARALLELS

2 Corinthians 2:10–11

But one whom you forgive anything, I forgive also; for indeed what I have forgiven, if I have forgiven anything, I did it for your sakes in the presence of Christ, [11]so that no advantage would be taken of us by *Satan*, for we are not ignorant of his schemes.

Galatians 5:7–10

You were running well; who hindered you from obeying the truth? [8]This persuasion did not come from Him who calls you. [9]*A little leaven leavens the whole lump of dough.* [10]I have confidence in you in the Lord that you will adopt no other view; but the one who is disturbing you will bear his *judgment*, whoever he is.

Colossians 2:5

For even *though I am absent in body*, nevertheless I am with you *in spirit*, rejoicing to see your good discipline and the stability of your faith in Christ.

1 Thessalonians 4:3–5

For this is the will of God, your sanctification; that is, that you abstain from sexual *immorality*; [4]that each of you know how to possess his own vessel in sanctification and honor, [5]not in lustful passion, like *the Gentiles* who do not know God.

2 Thessalonians 3:6

Now we command you, brethren, *in the name of our Lord Jesus* Christ, that you keep away from every brother who leads an unruly life and not according to the tradition which you received from us.

1 Timothy 1:18–20

This command I entrust to you, Timothy, my son, in accordance with the prophecies previously made concerning you, that by them you fight the good fight, [19]keeping faith and a good conscience, which some have rejected and suffered shipwreck in regard to their faith. [20]Among these are Hymenaeus and Alexander, whom I have handed over to *Satan*, so that they will be taught not to blaspheme.

OTHER BIBLICAL PARALLELS

Exodus 12:3, 6, 8, 14, 27

"On the tenth of this month they are each one to take a lamb for themselves. . . . [6]You shall keep it until the fourteenth day of the same month, then the whole assembly of the congregation of Israel is to kill it at twilight. . . . [8]They shall eat the flesh that same night, roasted with fire, and they shall eat it with *unleavened bread* and bitter herbs. . . . [14]Now this day will be a memorial to you, and you shall *celebrate* it as a *feast* to the LORD; throughout your generations you are to celebrate it as a permanent ordinance. . . .

[27]You shall say, 'It is a *Passover sacrifice* to the LORD.'"

Leviticus 18:8, 29

"You shall not uncover the nakedness of your *father's wife*; it is your father's nakedness. . . . [29]For whoever does any of these abominations, those persons who do so shall be cut off from among their people."

Hosea 7:4

They are all adulterers, Like an oven heated by the baker Who ceases to stir up the fire From the kneading of the dough until it is *leavened*.

Matthew 18:18, 20

"Truly I say to you, whatever you bind on earth shall have been bound in heaven; and whatever you loose on earth shall have been loosed in heaven. . . . [20]For where two or three have gathered together in My *name*, I am there in their midst."

Luke 12:1

Under these circumstances, after so many thousands of people had gathered together that they were stepping on one another, He began saying to His disciples first of all, "Beware of the *leaven* of the Pharisees, which is hypocrisy."

John 1:29

The next day he [John] saw Jesus coming to him and said, "Behold, the Lamb of God who takes away the sin of the world!"

John 19:13–16

Therefore when Pilate heard these words, he brought Jesus out. . . . [14]Now it was the day of preparation for the *Passover*; it was about the sixth hour. And he said to the Jews, "Behold, your King!" [15]So they cried out, "Away with Him, away with Him, crucify Him!" . . . [16]So he then handed Him over to them to be crucified.

1 Peter 1:17–19

Conduct yourselves in fear during the time of your stay on earth; [18]knowing that you were not redeemed with perishable things like silver or gold from your futile way of life inherited from your forefathers, [19]but with precious blood, as of a lamb unblemished and spotless, the blood of Christ.

These are the [the felons] who are put to death by stoning: He who has sexual relations with his mother, with the *wife of his father*, with his daughter-in-law, with a male, or with a cow.

1 Corinthians 5:9–13

I wrote you in my letter not to associate with immoral people; ¹⁰I did not at all mean with the immoral people of this world, or with the covetous and swindlers, or with idolaters, for then you would have to go out of the world. ¹¹But actually, I wrote to you not to associate with any so-called brother if he is an immoral person, or covetous, or an idolater, or a reviler, or a drunkard, or a swindler—not even to eat with such a one. ¹²For what have I to do with judging outsiders? Do you not judge those who are within the church? ¹³But those who are outside, God judges. REMOVE THE WICKED MAN FROM AMONG YOURSELVES.

1 CORINTHIANS PARALLELS

1 Corinthians 4:5
Therefore do not go on passing *judgment* before the time, but wait until the Lord comes who will both bring to light the things hidden in the darkness and disclose the motives of men's hearts; and then each man's praise will come to him from God.

1 Corinthians 6:9–10
Do not be deceived; neither fornicators, nor *idolaters*, nor adulterers, nor effeminate, nor homosexuals, ¹⁰nor thieves, nor the *covetous*, nor *drunkards*, nor *revilers*, nor *swindlers*, will inherit the kingdom of God.

1 Corinthians 7:30–31
. . . and those who weep, as though they did not weep; and those who rejoice, as though they did not rejoice; and those who buy, as though they did not possess; ³¹and those who use the world, as though they did not make full use of it; for the form of *this world* is passing away.

1 Corinthians 10:7–8
Do not be *idolaters*, as some of them were; as it is written, "THE PEOPLE SAT DOWN TO EAT AND DRINK, AND STOOD UP TO PLAY." ⁸Nor let us act *immorally*, as some of them did, and twenty-three thousand fell in one day.

OTHER PAULINE PARALLELS

Romans 16:17
Now I urge you, brethren, keep your eye on those who cause dissensions and hindrances contrary to the teaching which you learned, and turn away from them.

2 Corinthians 6:14
Do not be bound together with unbelievers; for what partnership have righteousness and lawlessness, or what fellowship has light with darkness?

Ephesians 5:5–6
For this you know with certainty, that no *immoral* or impure *person* or *covetous* man, who is an *idolater*, has an inheritance in the kingdom of Christ and God. ⁶Let no one deceive you with empty words, for because of these things the wrath of God comes upon the sons of disobedience.

Colossians 3:5–6
Therefore consider the members of your earthly body as dead to *immorality*, impurity, passion, evil desire, and greed, which amounts to *idolatry*. ⁶For it is because of these things that the wrath of God will come upon the sons of disobedience.

Colossians 4:5
Conduct yourselves with wisdom toward *outsiders*, making the most of the opportunity.

2 Thessalonians 3:14
If anyone does not obey our instruction in this letter, take special note of that person and do *not associate* with him, so that he will be put to shame.

OTHER BIBLICAL PARALLELS

Deuteronomy 17:2–3, 5, 7
"If there is found in your midst, in any of your towns, which the LORD your God is

giving you, a man or a woman who does what is evil in the sight of the LORD your God, by transgressing His covenant, [3]and has gone and served other gods and worshiped them, or the sun or the moon or any of the heavenly host, which I have not commanded, . . .[5]then you shall bring out that man or that woman who has done this evil deed to your gates, that is, the man or the woman, and you shall stone them to death. . . . [7]The hand of the witnesses shall be first against him to put him to death, and afterward the hand of all the people. So you shall purge the evil from your midst."

Hebrews 13:4

Marriage is to be held in honor among all, and the marriage bed is to be undefiled; for fornicators and adulterers God will *judge*.

1 Peter 4:3

For the time already past is sufficient for you to have carried out the desire of the Gentiles, having pursued a course of sensuality, lusts, *drunkenness*, carousing, drinking parties and abominable *idolatries*.

1 Corinthians 6:1–8

Does any one of you, when he has a case against his neighbor, dare to go to law before the unrighteous and not before the saints? [2]Or do you not know that the saints will judge the world? If the world is judged by you, are you not competent to constitute the smallest law courts? [3]Do you not know that we will judge angels? How much more matters of this life? [4]So if you have law courts dealing with matters of this life, do you appoint them as judges who are of no account in the church? [5]I say this to your shame. Is it so, that there is not among you one wise man who will be able to decide between his brethren, [6]but brother goes to law with brother, and that before unbelievers? [7]Actually, then, it is already a defeat for you, that you have lawsuits with one another. Why not rather be wronged? Why not rather be defrauded? [8]On the contrary, you yourselves wrong and defraud. You do this even to your brethren.

1 Corinthians 1:26–28

For consider your calling, brethren, that there were not many *wise* according to the flesh, not many mighty, not many noble; [27]but God has chosen the foolish things of the world to shame the wise, and God has chosen the weak things of the world to shame the things which are strong, [28]and the base things of the world and the despised God has chosen, the things that are not, so that He may nullify the things that are.

1 Corinthians 4:5

Therefore do not go on passing *judgment* before the time, but wait until the Lord comes who will both bring to light the things hidden in the darkness and disclose the motives of men's hearts; and then each man's praise will come to him from God.

1 Corinthians 15:33–34

Do not be deceived: "Bad company corrupts good morals." [34]Become sober-minded as you ought, and stop sinning; for some have no knowledge of God. *I speak this to your shame.*

OTHER PAULINE PARALLELS

2 Corinthians 6:15

Or what harmony has Christ with Belial, or what has a believer in common with an *unbeliever*?

1 Thessalonians 4:3–6

For this is the will of God, your sanctification; that is, that you abstain from sexual immorality; [4]that each of you know how to possess his own vessel in sanctification and honor, [5]not in lustful passion, like the Gentiles who do not know God; [6]and that no man transgress and *defraud* his brother in the matter because the Lord is the avenger in all these things, just as we also told you before and solemnly warned you.

OTHER BIBLICAL PARALLELS

Isaiah 24:21

So it will happen in that day, That the LORD will punish the host of heaven on high, And the kings of the earth on earth.

Matthew 5:39–40

"But I say to you, do not resist an evil person; but whoever slaps you on your right cheek, turn the other to him also. [40]If anyone wants to sue you and take your shirt, let him have your coat also."

Matthew 18:15–17

"If your *brother* sins, go and show him his fault in private; if he listens to you, you have won your brother. [16]But if he does not listen to you, take one or two more with you, so that BY THE MOUTH OF TWO OR THREE WITNESSES EVERY FACT MAY BE CONFIRMED. [17]If he refuses to listen to them, tell it to *the church*; and if he refuses to listen even to the church, let him be to you as a Gentile and a tax collector."

Matthew 19:28

"Truly I say to you, that you who have followed Me, in the regeneration when the Son of Man will sit on His glorious throne, you also shall sit upon twelve thrones, *judging* the twelve tribes of Israel."

Mark 10:19

"You know the commandments, 'DO NOT MURDER, DO NOT COMMIT ADULTERY, DO NOT STEAL, DO NOT BEAR FALSE WITNESS, Do not *defraud*, HONOR YOUR FATHER AND MOTHER.'"

Jude 6–7

And *angels* who did not keep their own domain, but abandoned their proper abode, He has kept in eternal bonds under darkness for the *judgment* of the great day, [7]just as Sodom and Gomorrah and the cities around them, since they in the same way as these indulged in gross immorality and went after strange flesh, are exhibited as an example in undergoing the punishment of eternal fire.

NONCANONICAL PARALLELS

Sirach 4:11, 15

Wisdom teaches her children and gives help to those who seek her. . . . [15]Those who obey her will *judge* the nations, and all who listen to her will live secure.

The Rule of the Community *(1QS) 9.7*

Only the sons of Aaron will have authority in the matter of *judgment* and goods, and their word will settle the lot of all provision for the men of the Community.

1QHabakkuk Pesher *(1QpHab) 5.3–6*

God is not to destroy his people at the hand of nations, [4]but by means of his chosen ones God will *judge* all the nations; [5]all the evildoers of his people will be pronounced guilty for the reproof of those who kept his commandments [6]in their hardship.

1 Corinthians 6:9–11

Or do you not know that the unrighteous will not inherit the kingdom of God? Do not be deceived; neither fornicators, nor idolaters, nor adulterers, nor effeminate, nor homosexuals, [10]nor thieves, nor the covetous, nor drunkards, nor revilers, nor swindlers, will inherit the kingdom of God. [11]Such were some of you; but you were washed, but you were sanctified, but you were justified in the name of the Lord Jesus Christ and in the Spirit of our God.

1 CORINTHIANS PARALLELS

1 Corinthians 1:2

To the church of God which is at Corinth, to those who have been *sanctified* in Christ Jesus, saints by calling, with all who in every place call on *the name of* our *Lord Jesus Christ*, their Lord and ours . . .

1 Corinthians 1:13

Has Christ been divided? Paul was not crucified for you, was he? Or were you baptized *in the name of* Paul?

1 Corinthians 5:9–11

I wrote you in my letter not to associate with immoral people; [10]I did not at all mean with the immoral people of this world, or with the *covetous* and *swindlers*, or with *idolaters*, for then you would have to go out of the world. [11]But actually, I wrote to you not to associate with any so-called brother if he is an immoral person, or covetous, or an idolater, or a *reviler*, or a *drunkard*, or a swindler—not even to eat with such a one.

1 Corinthians 12:2

You know that when you were pagans, you were led astray to the mute *idols*, however you were led.

1 Corinthians 15:33–34

Do not be deceived: "Bad company corrupts good morals." [34]Become sober-minded as you ought, and stop sinning; for some have no knowledge of God. I speak this to your shame.

1 Corinthians 15:50

Now I say this, brethren, that flesh and blood cannot *inherit the kingdom of God*; nor does the perishable inherit the imperishable.

OTHER PAULINE PARALLELS

Romans 1:26–27, 29

For this reason God gave them over to degrading passions; for their women exchanged the natural function for that which is unnatural, [27]and in the same way also the men abandoned the natural function of the woman and burned in their desire toward one another, men with men committing indecent acts and receiving in their own persons the due penalty of their error, . . . [29]being filled with all *unrighteousness*, wickedness, greed, evil; full of envy, murder, strife, deceit, malice.

Galatians 5:19–21

Now the deeds of the flesh are evident, which are: immorality, impurity, sensuality, [20]*idolatry*, sorcery, enmities, strife, jealousy, outbursts of anger, disputes, dissensions, factions, [21]envying, *drunkenness*, carousing, and things like these, of which I forewarn you, just as I have forewarned you, that those who practice such things *will not inherit the kingdom of God.*

Ephesians 5:5

For this you know with certainty, that no immoral or impure person or *covetous* man, who is an *idolater*, has an *inheritance in the kingdom of* Christ and God.

Colossians 3:5–7

Therefore consider the members of your earthly body as dead to immorality, impurity, passion, evil desire, and greed, which amounts to *idolatry*. [6]For it is because of these things that the wrath of God will come upon the sons of disobedience, [7]and in them you also once walked, when you were living in them.

1 Thessalonians 4:3–6

For this is the will of God, your *sanctification*; that is, that you abstain from sexual immorality; [4]that each of you know how to possess his own vessel in sanctification and honor, [5]not in lustful passion, like the Gentiles who do not know God; [6]and that no man transgress and defraud his brother in the matter because the Lord is the avenger in all these things, just as we also told you before and solemnly warned you.

1 Timothy 1:9–10

Law is not made for a righteous person, but for those who are lawless and rebellious, for the ungodly and sinners, for the unholy and profane, for those who kill their fathers or mothers, for murderers [10]and immoral men and *homosexuals* and kidnappers and liars and perjurers, and whatever else is contrary to sound teaching.

Titus 3:3

For we also once were foolish ourselves, disobedient, *deceived*, enslaved to various lusts and pleasures, spending our life in malice and envy, hateful, hating one another.

OTHER BIBLICAL PARALLELS

Exodus 20:4, 14–16

"You shall not make for yourself an *idol*, or any likeness of what is in heaven above or on the earth beneath or in the water under the earth. . . . [14]You shall not commit *adultery*. [15]You shall not steal. [16]You shall not bear false witness against your neighbor."

Leviticus 18:22

"You shall not lie with a male as one lies with a female; it is an abomination."

Acts 15:19–20

"Therefore it is my judgment that we do not trouble those who are turning to God from among the Gentiles, [20]but that we write to them that they abstain from things contaminated by *idols* and from *fornication* and from what is strangled and from blood."

Acts 22:16

"Now why do you delay? Get up and be baptized, and *wash* away your sins, calling on His *name*."

Hebrews 13:4
Marriage is to be held in honor among all, and the marriage bed is to be undefiled; for *fornicators* and *adulterers* God will judge.

Wisdom of Solomon 14:24–27
They no longer keep either their lives or their marriages pure, but they either treacherously kill one another, or grieve one another by *adultery*, [25]and all is a raging riot of blood and murder, *theft* and deceit, corruption, faithlessness, tumult, perjury, [26]confusion over what is good, forgetfulness of favors, defiling of souls, sexual perversion, disorder in marriages, adultery, and debauchery. [27]For the worship of *idols* not to be named is the beginning and cause and end of every evil.

Musonius Rufus, fragment 12
Of all couplings those that entail *adultery* are most unlawful, and no more acceptable are those of males with males, because it is an affront contrary to nature.

1 Corinthians 6:12–20

All things are lawful for me, but not all things are profitable. All things are lawful for me, but I will not be mastered by anything. [13]Food is for the stomach and the stomach is for food, but God will do away with both of them. Yet the body is not for immorality, but for the Lord, and the Lord is for the body. [14]Now God has not only raised the Lord, but will also raise us up through His power. [15]Do you not know that your bodies are members of Christ? Shall I then take away the members of Christ and make them members of a prostitute? May it never be! [16]Or do you not know that the one who joins himself to a prostitute is one body with her? For He says, "THE TWO SHALL BECOME ONE FLESH." [17]But the one who joins himself to the Lord is one spirit with Him. [18]Flee immorality. Every other sin that a man commits is outside the body, but the immoral man sins against his own body. [19]Or do you not know that your body is a temple of the Holy Spirit who is in you, whom you have from God, and that you are not your own? [20]For you have been bought with a price: therefore glorify God in your body.

1 Corinthians 3:16–17
Do you not know that you are *a temple* of God and that *the Spirit* of God dwells in you? [17]If any man destroys the temple of God, God will destroy him, for the temple of God is holy, and that is what you are.

1 Corinthians 7:23
You were *bought with a price*; do not become slaves of men.

1 Corinthians 8:8
But *food* will not commend us to God; we are neither the worse if we do not eat, nor the better if we do eat.

1 Corinthians 10:23–24
All things are lawful, but not all things are profitable. All things are lawful, but not all things edify. [24]Let no one seek his own good, but that of his neighbor.

1 Corinthians 12:12–13
For even as *the body* is one and yet has many *members*, and all the members of the body, though they are many, are *one body*, so also is Christ. [13]For by *one Spirit* we were all baptized into one body, whether Jews or Greeks, whether slaves or free, and we were all made to drink of one Spirit.

1 Corinthians 15:20, 23
But now Christ has been *raised* from the dead, the first fruits of those who are asleep. . . . [23]But each in his own order: Christ the first fruits, after that those who are Christ's at His coming.

1 Corinthians 15:42–43
So also is the resurrection of the dead. It is sown a perishable *body*, it is raised an imperishable body; [43]it is sown in dishonor, it is *raised* in glory; it is sown in weakness, it is raised in *power*.

Romans 8:11
But if *the Spirit* of Him who *raised* Jesus from the dead dwells *in you*, He who raised Christ Jesus from the dead will also give life to your mortal *bodies* through His Spirit who dwells in you.

Romans 12:1, 4–5

Therefore I urge you, brethren, by the mercies of God, to present your *bodies* a living and holy sacrifice, acceptable to God, which is your spiritual service of worship. . . . [4]For just as we have many *members* in *one body* and all the members do not have the same function, [5]so we, who are many, are one body in Christ, and individually members one of another.

Romans 14:15

For if because of *food* your brother is hurt, you are no longer walking according to love. Do not destroy with your food him for whom Christ died.

2 Corinthians 4:13–14

But having the same spirit of faith, according to what is written, "I BELIEVED, THEREFORE I SPOKE," we also believe, therefore we also speak, [14]knowing that He who *raised the Lord* Jesus *will raise us also* with Jesus and will present us with you.

2 Corinthians 6:16

Or what agreement has the temple of God with idols? For we are the *temple* of the living God; just as God said, "I WILL DWELL IN THEM AND WALK AMONG THEM; AND I WILL BE THEIR GOD, AND THEY SHALL BE MY PEOPLE."

Ephesians 5:28–31

So husbands ought also to love their own wives as their own *bodies*. He who loves his own wife loves himself; [29]for no one ever hated his own flesh, but nourishes and cherishes it, just as Christ also does the church, [30]because we are *members* of His *body*. [31]FOR THIS REASON A MAN SHALL LEAVE HIS FATHER AND MOTHER AND SHALL BE JOINED TO HIS WIFE, AND *THE TWO SHALL BECOME ONE FLESH.*

1 Thessalonians 4:3–4

For this is the will of God, your sanctification; that is, that you abstain from sexual *immorality*; [4]that each of you know how to possess his own vessel in sanctification and honor.

Genesis 2:24

For this reason a man shall leave his father and his mother, and be joined to his wife; and they *shall become one flesh*.

Matthew 15:17

"Do you not understand that everything that goes into the mouth passes into *the stomach*, and is eliminated?"

Sirach 19:2–3

Wine and women lead intelligent men astray, and the man who consorts with *prostitutes* is reckless. [3]Decay and worms will take possession of him, and the reckless person will be snatched away.

Sirach 37:28

For not everything is good for everyone, and no one enjoys everything.

Strabo, Geography 8.6.20

Corinth is called "wealthy" on account of its commerce, lying on the Isthmus and master of two harbors. . . . And the temple of Aphrodite there is so wealthy that it has over a thousand temple-slaves, courtesans, whom both men and women have dedicated to the goddess.

Epictetus, Discourses 2.8.11–13

You are a piece of God. You have inside you some part of him. Why, then, are you ignorant of your own kinship? . . . [12]Will you not remember, whenever you eat, who you are that eats and whom you are feeding? Whenever you have intercourse, who you are that does this? . . . [13]You are carrying him around inside yourself and do not realize that you defile him with unclean thoughts and foul actions.

1 Corinthians 7:1–7

Now concerning the things about which you wrote, it is good for a man not to touch a woman. [2]But because of immoralities, each man is to have his own wife, and each woman is to have her own husband. [3]The husband must fulfill his duty to his wife, and likewise also the wife to her husband. [4]The wife does not have authority over her own body, but the husband does; and likewise also the husband does not have authority over his own body, but the wife does. [5]Stop depriving one another, except by agreement for a time, so that you may devote yourselves to prayer, and come together again so that Satan will not tempt you because of your lack of self-control. [6]But this I say by way of concession, not of command. [7]Yet I wish that all men were even as I myself am. However, each man has his own gift from God, one in this manner, and another in that.

1 CORINTHIANS PARALLELS

1 Corinthians 5:1, 5
It is actually reported that there is *immorality* among you, and immorality of such a kind as does not exist even among the Gentiles, that someone has his father's *wife.* . . . [5]I have decided to deliver such a one to *Satan* for the destruction of his flesh, so that his spirit may be saved in the day of the Lord Jesus.

1 Corinthians 5:9–10
I wrote you in my letter not to associate with *immoral* people; [10]I did not at all mean with the immoral people of this world, or with the covetous and swindlers, or with idolaters, for then you would have to go out of the world.

1 Corinthians 7:25
Now concerning virgins I have *no command* of the Lord, but I give an opinion as one who by the mercy of the Lord is trustworthy.

1 Corinthians 7:39–40
A *wife* is bound as long as her *husband* lives; but if her husband is dead, she is free to be married to whom she wishes, only in the Lord. [40]But in my opinion she is happier if she remains as she is; and I think that I also have the Spirit of God.

1 Corinthians 9:5, 15
Do we not have a right to take along a believing *wife*, even as the rest of the apostles and the brothers of the Lord and Cephas? . . . [15]But I have used none of these things. And I am not writing these things so that it will be done so in my case; for it would be better for me to die than have any man make my boast an empty one.

1 Corinthians 12:4, 7
Now there are varieties of *gifts*, but the same Spirit. . . . [7]But to each one is given the manifestation of the Spirit for the common good.

OTHER PAULINE PARALLELS

Romans 12:6
Since we have *gifts* that differ according to the grace given to us, each of us is to exercise them accordingly.

Colossians 2:20–22
If you have died with Christ to the elementary principles of the world, why, as if you were living in the world, do you submit yourself to decrees, such as, [21]"Do not handle, do not taste, do *not touch!*" [22](which all refer to things destined to perish with use)—in accordance with the commandments and teachings of men?

Colossians 4:2
Devote yourselves to prayer, keeping alert in it with an attitude of thanksgiving.

1 Thessalonians 4:3–5
For this is the will of God, your sanctification; that is, that you abstain from sexual *immorality*; [4]that each of you know how to possess his own vessel in sanctification and honor, [5]not in lustful passion, like the Gentiles who do not know God.

1 Timothy 5:14–15
Therefore, I want younger widows to get married, bear children, keep house, and give the enemy no occasion for reproach; [15]for some have already turned aside to follow *Satan*.

OTHER BIBLICAL PARALLELS

Proverbs 6:29
So is the one who goes in to his neighbor's *wife*; Whoever *touches* her will not go unpunished.

Matthew 19:10–12
The disciples said to Him, "If the relationship of the man with his *wife* is like this, it is better not to marry." [11]But He said to them, "Not all men can accept this statement, but only those to whom it has been given. [12]For there are eunuchs who were born that way from their mother's womb; and there are

eunuchs who were made eunuchs by men; and there are also eunuchs who made themselves eunuchs for the sake of the kingdom of heaven. He who is able to accept this, let him accept it."

Mark 1:13

And He was in the wilderness forty days being *tempted* by *Satan*; and He was with the wild beasts, and the angels were ministering to Him.

James 1:13–14

Let no one say when he is *tempted*, "I am being tempted by God"; for God cannot be tempted by evil, and He Himself does not tempt anyone. [14]But each one is tempted when he is carried away and enticed by his own lust.

NONCANONICAL PARALLELS

Testament of Naphtali 8:7–8

"The commandments of the Lord are double, and they are to be fulfilled with regularity. [8]There is a time for having intercourse with one's *wife* and a time to abstain for the purpose of *prayer*."

Mishnah Ketubbot 5:6

He who takes a vow not to have sexual relations with his *wife*—the House of Shammai say, "[He may allow this situation to continue] for two weeks." And the House of Hillel say, "For one week."

Pseudo-Diogenes, Epistle 47

Let no one marry or raise children, since our race is weak, and marriage and offspring overload human weakness with sorrows.

1 Corinthians 7:8–16

But I say to the unmarried and to widows that it is good for them if they remain even as I. [9]But if they do not have self-control, let them marry; for it is better to marry than to burn with passion. [10]But to the married I give instructions, not I, but the Lord, that the wife should not leave her husband [11](but if she does leave, she must remain unmarried, or else be reconciled to her husband), and that the husband should not divorce his wife. [12]But to the rest I say, not the Lord, that if any brother has a wife who is an unbeliever, and she consents to live with him, he must not divorce her. [13]And a woman who has an unbelieving husband, and he consents to live with her, she must not send her husband away. [14]For the unbelieving husband is sanctified through his wife, and the unbelieving wife is sanctified through her believing husband; for otherwise your children are unclean, but now they are holy. [15]Yet if the unbelieving one leaves, let him leave; the brother or the sister is not under bondage in such cases, but God has called us to peace. [16]For how do you know, O wife, whether you will save your husband? Or how do you know, O husband, whether you will save your wife?

1 CORINTHIANS PARALLELS

1 Corinthians 7:27

Are you bound to a *wife*? Do not seek to be released. Are you released from a wife? Do not seek a wife.

1 Corinthians 7:32–34

But I want you to be free from concern. One who is *unmarried* is concerned about the things of the Lord, how he may please the Lord; [33]but one who is *married* is concerned about the things of the world, how he may please his *wife*, [34]and his interests are divided. The woman who is unmarried, and the virgin, is concerned about the things of the Lord, that she may be *holy* both in body and spirit; but one who is married is concerned about the things of the world, how she may please her *husband*.

1 Corinthians 7:39–40

A *wife* is bound as long as her *husband* lives; but if her husband is dead, she is free to be *married* to whom she wishes, only in the Lord. [40]But in my opinion she is happier if she *remains* as she is; and I think that I also have the Spirit of God.

1 Corinthians 9:5

Do we not have a right to take along a *believing wife*, even as the rest of the apostles and the brothers of the Lord and Cephas?

1 Corinthians 9:22

To the weak I became weak, that I might win the weak; I have become all things to all men, so that I may by all means *save* some.

1 Corinthians 14:31–33

For you can all prophesy one by one, so that all may learn and all may be exhorted; [32]and the spirits of prophets are subject to prophets; [33]for God is not a God of confusion but of *peace*, as in all the churches of the saints.

OTHER PAULINE PARALLELS

Romans 7:2

For the *married woman* is bound by law to her *husband* while he is living; but if her husband dies, she is released from the law concerning the husband.

Romans 14:19

So then we pursue the things which make for *peace* and the building up of one another.

2 Corinthians 6:14–15

Do not be bound together with *unbelievers*; for what partnership have righteousness and lawlessness, or what fellowship has light with darkness? [15]Or what harmony has Christ with Belial, or what has a believer in common with an unbeliever?

1 Timothy 5:14

Therefore, I want younger *widows* to get *married*, bear *children*, keep house, and give the enemy no occasion for reproach.

OTHER BIBLICAL PARALLELS

Malachi 2:15–16

"Take heed then to your spirit, and let no one deal treacherously against the *wife* of your youth. [16]For I hate *divorce*," says the LORD.

Matthew 5:31–32

"It was said, 'WHOEVER SENDS HIS WIFE AWAY, LET HIM GIVE HER A CERTIFICATE OF DIVORCE'; [32]but I say to you that everyone who *divorces his wife*, except for the reason of unchastity, makes her commit adultery; and whoever marries a divorced woman commits adultery."

Matthew 19:8–9

"Because of your hardness of heart Moses permitted you to divorce your wives; but from the beginning it has not been this way. [9]And I say to you, whoever *divorces his wife*, except for immorality, and marries another woman commits adultery."

Mark 10:11–12

"Whoever *divorces his wife* and marries another woman commits adultery against her; [12]and if she herself divorces her *husband* and marries another man, she is committing adultery."

Luke 16:18

"Everyone who *divorces his wife* and marries another commits adultery, and he who marries one who is divorced from a husband commits adultery."

1 Peter 3:1–2

In the same way, you *wives*, be submissive to your own *husbands* so that even if any of them are disobedient to the word, they may be won without a word by the behavior of their wives, [2]as they observe your chaste and respectful behavior.

NONCANONICAL PARALLELS

4 Maccabees 1:31–32

Self-control, then, is dominance over the desires. [32]Some desires are mental, others are physical, and reason obviously rules over both.

Mishnah Gittin *9:10*

The House of Shammai say, "A man should *divorce his wife* only because he has found grounds for it in unchastity." . . . And the House of Hillel say, "Even if she spoiled his dish."

Plutarch, Advice to Bride and Groom *140D*

A *wife* should not make friends of her own but have them in common with her *husband*; and the gods are the first and greatest friends. Therefore it is proper for a wife to worship the same gods her husband believes in and to shut the door to elaborate rituals and strange superstitions.

1 Corinthians 7:17–24

Only, as the Lord has assigned to each one, as God has called each, in this manner let him walk. And so I direct in all the churches. [18]Was any man called when he was already circumcised? He is not to become uncircumcised. Has anyone been called in uncircumcision? He is not to be circumcised. [19]Circumcision is nothing, and uncircumcision is nothing, but what matters is the keeping of the commandments of God. ²⁰Each man must remain in that condition in which he was called. ²¹Were you called while a slave? Do not worry about it; but if you are able also to become free, rather do that. ²²For he who was called in the Lord while a slave, is the Lord's freedman; likewise he who was called while free, is Christ's slave. ²³You were bought with a price; do not become slaves of men. ²⁴Brethren, each one is to remain with God in that condition in which he was called.

1 CORINTHIANS PARALLELS

1 Corinthians 1:23–24
But we preach Christ crucified, to Jews a stumbling block and to Gentiles foolishness, ²⁴but to those who are the *called*, both Jews and Greeks, Christ the power of God and the wisdom of God.

1 Corinthians 4:1
Let a man regard us in this manner, as servants of Christ and stewards of the mysteries of God.

1 Corinthians 4:17
For this reason I have sent to you Timothy, who is my beloved and faithful child in the Lord, and he will remind you of my ways which are in Christ, just as I teach everywhere *in every church*.

1 Corinthians 6:19–20
Or do you not know that your body is a temple of the Holy Spirit who is in you, whom you have from God, and that you are not your own? ²⁰For *you* have been *bought with a price*: therefore glorify God in your body.

1 Corinthians 12:13
For by one Spirit we were all baptized into one body, whether Jews or Greeks, whether *slaves* or *free*, and we were all made to drink of one Spirit.

OTHER PAULINE PARALLELS

Romans 6:16–18, 22
Do you not know that when you present yourselves to someone as *slaves* for obedience, you are slaves of the one whom you obey, either of sin resulting in death, or of obedience resulting in righteousness? ¹⁷But thanks be to God that though you were

slaves of sin, you became obedient from the heart to that form of teaching to which you were committed, ¹⁸and having been *freed* from sin, you became slaves of righteousness. . . . ²²But now having been freed from sin and enslaved to God, you derive your benefit, resulting in sanctification, and the outcome, eternal life.

Galatians 1:10
For am I now seeking the favor of men, or of God? Or am I striving to please men? If I were still trying to please men, I would not be a bond-servant of Christ.

Galatians 4:6–7
Because you are sons, God has sent forth the Spirit of His Son into our hearts, crying, "Abba! Father!" ⁷Therefore you are no longer *a slave*, but a son; and if a son, then an heir through God.

Galatians 5:1–2, 6
It was for freedom that Christ set us *free*; therefore keep standing firm and do not be subject again to a yoke of *slavery*. ²Behold I, Paul, say to you that if you receive circumcision, Christ will be of no benefit to you. . . . ⁶For in Christ Jesus neither *circumcision* nor *uncircumcision* means anything, but faith working through love.

Galatians 6:15
For neither is *circumcision* anything, nor *uncircumcision*, but a new creation.

Ephesians 4:1, 3
Therefore I, the prisoner of the Lord, implore you to *walk* in a manner worthy of the calling with which you have been *called,* . . .³being diligent to preserve the unity of the Spirit in the bond of peace.

Ephesians 6:5–6
Slaves, be obedient to those who are your masters according to the flesh, with fear and trembling, in the sincerity of your heart, as to Christ; ⁶not by way of eyeservice, as men-pleasers, but as *slaves of Christ*, doing the will of God from the heart.

Philemon 15–16
For perhaps he was for this reason separated from you for a while, that you would have him back forever, ¹⁶no longer as a *slave*, but more than a slave, a beloved

brother, especially to me, but how much more to you, both in the flesh and in the Lord.

Deuteronomy 6:17

"You should diligently *keep the commandments of* the LORD your *God,* and His testimonies and His statutes which He has commanded you."

Mark 13:34

"It is like a man away on a journey, who upon leaving his house and putting his *slaves* in charge, *assigning to each one* his task, also commanded the doorkeeper to stay on the alert."

1 Peter 2:16

Act as *free* men, and do not use your freedom as a covering for evil, but use it as *bondslaves* of God.

1 Maccabees 1:11, 14–15

In those days certain renegades came out from Israel and misled many, saying, "Let us go and make a covenant with the Gentiles around us, for since we separated from them many disasters have come upon us." . . . ¹⁴So they built a gymnasium in Jerusalem, according to Gentile custom, ¹⁵and removed the marks of *circumcision,* and abandoned the holy covenant. They joined with the Gentiles and sold themselves to do evil.

Teles, On Self-Sufficiency *10H*

Therefore we must try not to change circumstances but to prepare for them however they are. . . . You have grown old: do not seek the things of a young man. Again, you are weak: do not seek to bear and submit your neck to the burdens of someone who is strong.

1 Corinthians 7:25–31

Now concerning virgins I have no command of the Lord, but I give an opinion as one who by

the mercy of the Lord is trustworthy. ²⁶I think then that this is good in view of the present distress, that it is good for a man to remain as he is. ²⁷Are you bound to a wife? Do not seek to be released. Are you released from a wife? Do not seek a wife. ²⁸But if you marry, you have not sinned; and if a virgin marries, she has not sinned. Yet such will have trouble in this life, and I am trying to spare you. ²⁹But this I say, brethren, the time has been shortened, so that from now on those who have wives should be as though they had none; ³⁰and those who weep, as though they did not weep; and those who rejoice, as though they did not rejoice; and those who buy, as though they did not possess; ³¹and those who use the world, as though they did not make full use of it; for the form of this world is passing away.

1 Corinthians 1:7–8

You are not lacking in any gift, awaiting eagerly the revelation of our Lord Jesus Christ, ⁸who will also confirm you to the end, blameless in the day of our Lord Jesus Christ.

1 Corinthians 4:1–2

Let a man regard us in this manner, as servants of Christ and stewards of the mysteries of God. ²In this case, moreover, it is required of stewards that one be found *trustworthy.*

1 Corinthians 4:5

Therefore do not go on passing judgment before *the time,* but wait until the Lord comes who will both bring to light the things hidden in the darkness and disclose the motives of men's hearts; and then each man's praise will come to him from God.

1 Corinthians 7:8–11

But I say to the unmarried and to widows that *it is good* for them if they *remain* even as I. ⁹But if they do not have self-control, let them *marry;* for it is better to marry than to burn with passion. ¹⁰But to the married I give instructions, not I, but the Lord, that the *wife* should not leave her husband ¹¹(but if she does leave, she must remain unmarried, or else be reconciled to her husband), and that the husband should not divorce his wife.

Romans 12:15

Rejoice with those who rejoice, and *weep* with those who weep.

Romans 13:11

Do this, knowing *the time*, that it is already the hour for you to awaken from sleep; for now salvation is nearer to us than when we believed.

1 Timothy 1:12–13

I thank Christ Jesus our Lord, who has strengthened me, because He considered me faithful, putting me into service, [13]even though I was formerly a blasphemer and a persecutor and a violent aggressor. Yet I was shown *mercy* because I acted ignorantly in unbelief.

OTHER BIBLICAL PARALLELS

Ezekiel 7:12

The time has come, the day has arrived. Let not the *buyer rejoice* nor the seller mourn; for wrath is against all their multitude.

Mark 13:19–20

"For those days will be a time of tribulation such as has not occurred since the beginning of the creation which God created until now, and never will. [20]Unless the Lord had *shortened* those days, no life would have been saved; but for the sake of the elect, whom He chose, He shortened the days."

Luke 14:26

"If anyone comes to Me, and does not hate his own father and mother and *wife* and children and brothers and sisters, yes, and even his own life, he cannot be My disciple."

Luke 21:23

"Woe to those who are pregnant and to those who are nursing babies in those days; for there will be great *distress* upon the land and wrath to this people."

2 Peter 3:10

But the day of the Lord will come like a thief, in which the heavens will *pass away* with a roar and the elements will be destroyed with intense heat, and the earth and its works will be burned up.

1 John 2:17

The *world is passing away*, and also its lusts; but the one who does the will of God lives forever.

Revelation 21:1

Then I saw a new heaven and a new earth; for the first heaven and the first earth *passed away*, and there is no longer any sea.

NONCANONICAL PARALLELS

2 Esdras (4 Ezra) 6:20

When the seal is placed upon the age that is about to *pass away*, then I will show these signs: the books shall be opened before the face of the firmament, and all shall see my judgment together.

2 Esdras (6 Ezra) 16:40–44

Hear my words, O my people; prepare for battle, and in the midst of the calamities be like strangers on the earth. [41]Let the one who sells be like one who will flee; let the one *who buys* be like one who will lose; [42]let the one who does business be like one who will not make a profit; and let the one who builds a house be like one who will not live in it; [43]let the one who sows be like one who will not reap; so also the one who prunes the vines, like one who will not gather the grapes; [44]those who *marry*, like those who will have no children; and those who do not marry, like those who are widowed.

1 Corinthians 7:32–40

But I want you to be free from concern. One who is unmarried is concerned about the things of the Lord, how he may please the Lord; [33]but one who is married is concerned about the things of the world, how he may please his wife, [34]and his interests are divided. The woman who is unmarried, and the virgin, is concerned about the things of the Lord, that she may be holy both in body and spirit; but one who is married is concerned about the things of the world, how she may please her husband. [35]This I say for your own benefit; not to put a restraint upon you, but to promote what is appropriate and to secure undistracted devotion to the Lord. [36]But if any man thinks that he is acting unbecomingly toward his virgin daughter, if she is past her youth, and if it must be so, let him do what he wishes, he does not sin; let her marry. [37]But he who stands firm in his heart, being under no constraint, but has authority over his own will, and has decided this in his own heart, to keep his own virgin daughter, he will do well. [38]So then both he who gives his own virgin daughter in marriage does well, and he who does not give her in marriage will do better. [39]A wife is bound as long as her husband lives; but if her husband is dead, she is free to be married to whom she wishes, only in the Lord. [40]But in my opinion she is happier if she remains as she is; and I think that I also have the Spirit of God.

1 CORINTHIANS PARALLELS

1 Corinthians 2:11–12
For who among men knows the thoughts of a man except the spirit of the man which is in him? Even so the thoughts of God no one knows except *the Spirit of God.* [12]Now we have received, not the spirit of *the world,* but the Spirit who is from God, so that we may know the things freely given to us by God.

1 Corinthians 3:17
If any man destroys the temple of God, God will destroy him, for the temple of God is *holy,* and that is what you are.

1 Corinthians 6:12, 19
All things are lawful for me, but not all things are profitable. All things are lawful for me, but I will not be mastered by anything. . . . [19]Or do you not know that your *body* is a temple of the Holy Spirit who is in you, whom you have from God, and that you are not your own?

1 Corinthians 7:1–2, 7–11
Now concerning the things about which you wrote, it is good for a man not to touch a woman. [2]But because of immoralities, each man is to have his own *wife,* and each woman is to have her own *husband.* . . . [7]Yet I wish that all men were even as I myself am. However, each man has his own gift from God, one in this manner, and another in that. [8]But I say to the *unmarried* and to widows that it is good for them if they *remain* even as I. [9]But if they do not have self-control, let them *marry;* for it is better to marry than to burn with passion. [10]But to the *married* I give instructions, not I, but the

Lord, that the wife should not leave her husband [11](but if she does leave, she must remain unmarried, or else be reconciled to her husband), and that the husband should not divorce his wife.

OTHER PAULINE PARALLELS

Romans 7:2
For the married woman is *bound* by law to *her husband* while he is *living; but if her husband dies,* she is released from the law concerning the husband.

2 Corinthians 11:2–3
For I am jealous for you with a godly jealousy; for I betrothed you to one *husband,* so that to Christ I might present you as a pure *virgin.* [3]But I am afraid that, as the serpent deceived Eve by his craftiness, your minds will be led astray from the simplicity and purity of *devotion* to Christ.

2 Corinthians 11:28
Apart from such external things, there is the daily pressure on me of *concern* for all the churches.

Ephesians 5:28–29
So *husbands* ought also to love their own wives as their own bodies. He who loves his own *wife* loves himself; [29]for no one ever hated his own flesh, but nourishes and cherishes it, just as Christ also does the church.

1 Thessalonians 4:3–5
For this is the will of God, your sanctification; that is, that you abstain from sexual immorality; [4]that each of you know how to possess his own vessel in sanctification and honor, [5]not in lustful passion, like the Gentiles who do not know God.

1 Timothy 5:5
Now she who is a widow indeed and who has been left alone, has fixed her hope on God and continues in entreaties and prayers night and day.

OTHER BIBLICAL PARALLELS

Matthew 22:30
"For in the resurrection they neither *marry* nor are *given in marriage,* but are like angels in heaven."

Epictetus, Discourses *3.22.69–70*

But given the current circumstances—rather like a battle formation—it is worth considering whether the Cynic needs to be unhindered, committed completely to the service of God, . . . not bound by private responsibilities or entangled in relationships. . . . [70]For see, he must show certain services to his father-in-law and to the rest of his wife's relatives and to *his wife* herself.

1 Corinthians 8:1–6

Now concerning things sacrificed to idols, we know that we all have knowledge. Knowledge makes arrogant, but love edifies. [2]If anyone supposes that he knows anything, he has not yet known as he ought to know; [3]but if anyone loves God, he is known by Him. [4]Therefore concerning the eating of things sacrificed to idols, we know that there is no such thing as an idol in the world, and that there is no God but one. [5]For even if there are so-called gods whether in heaven or on earth, as indeed there are many gods and many lords, [6]yet for us there is but one God, the Father, from whom are all things and we exist for Him; and one Lord, Jesus Christ, by whom are all things, and we exist through Him.

1 CORINTHIANS PARALLELS

1 Corinthians 2:9

But just as it is written, "THINGS WHICH EYE HAS NOT SEEN AND EAR HAS NOT HEARD, AND which HAVE NOT ENTERED THE HEART OF MAN, ALL THAT GOD HAS PREPARED FOR THOSE WHO *LOVE* HIM."

1 Corinthians 3:18

Let no man deceive himself. If any man among you thinks that he is wise in this age, he must become foolish, so that he may become wise.

1 Corinthians 4:6

Now these things, brethren, I have figuratively applied to myself and Apollos for your sakes, so that in us you may learn not to exceed what is written, so that no one of you will become *arrogant* in behalf of one against the other.

1 Corinthians 10:14, 19–20, 23

Therefore, my beloved, flee from idolatry. . . . [19]What do I mean then? That a *thing sacrificed to idols* is anything, or that *an idol* is anything? [20]No, but I say that the things which the Gentiles sacrifice, they sacrifice to demons and not to God; and I do not want you to become sharers in demons. . . . [23]All things are lawful, but not all things are profitable. All things are lawful, but not all things *edify.*

1 Corinthians 13:2, 4, 12

If I have the gift of prophecy, and know all mysteries and all *knowledge*; and if I have all faith, so as to remove mountains, but do not have *love*, I am nothing. . . . [4]Love is patient, love is kind and is not jealous; love does not brag and is not *arrogant.* . . . [12]For now we see in a mirror dimly, but then face to face; now I *know* in part, but then I will know fully just as I also have been fully *known.*

OTHER PAULINE PARALLELS

Romans 11:34, 36

For WHO HAS *KNOWN* THE MIND OF THE LORD, OR WHO BECAME HIS COUNSELOR? . . . [36]For *from* Him and *through Him* and to Him are *all things.*

Romans 14:15, 19–20

For if because of food your brother is hurt, you are no longer walking according to *love.* Do not destroy with your food him for whom Christ died. . . . [19]So then we pursue the things which make for peace and the building up of one another. [20]Do not tear down the work of God for the sake of food. All things indeed are clean, but they are evil for the man who *eats* and gives offense.

Galatians 4:8–9

However at that time, when you did not know God, you were slaves to those which by nature are no *gods.* [9]But now that you have come to know God, or rather to be *known* by God, how is it that you turn back again to the weak and worthless elemental things, to which you desire to be enslaved all over again?

Galatians 5:13

For you were called to freedom, brethren; only do not turn your freedom into an opportunity for the flesh, but through *love* serve one another.

Ephesians 4:4–6
There is one body and one Spirit, just as also you were called in one hope of your calling; [5]*one Lord*, one faith, one baptism, [6]*one God* and *Father* of all who is over all and through all and in all.

Colossians 1:16
For by Him *all things* were created, both *in* the *heavens* and *on earth*, visible and invisible, whether thrones or dominions or rulers or authorities—all things have been created *through Him* and *for Him*.

OTHER BIBLICAL PARALLELS

Exodus 20:4–5
"You shall not make for yourself *an idol*, or any likeness of what is *in heaven* above or *on* the *earth* beneath or in the water under the earth. [5]You shall not worship them or serve them; for I, the LORD your God, am a jealous God, visiting the iniquity of the fathers on the children, on the third and the fourth generations of those who hate Me."

Exodus 33:17
The LORD said to Moses, "I will also do this thing of which you have spoken; for you have found favor in My sight and I have *known* you by name."

Deuteronomy 6:4–5
"Hear, O Israel! The LORD is our *God*, the LORD is *one*! [5]You shall *love* the LORD your *God* with all your heart and with all your soul and with all your might."

Jeremiah 10:3–6
"For the customs of the peoples are delusion; Because it is wood cut from the forest, The work of the hands of a craftsman with a cutting tool. [4]They decorate it with silver and with gold; They fasten it with nails and with hammers So that it will not totter. [5]Like a scarecrow in a cucumber field are they, And they cannot speak; They must be carried, Because they cannot walk! Do not fear them, For they can do no harm, Nor can they do any good." [6]There is none like You, O LORD; You are great, and great is Your name in might.

Malachi 2:10
"Do we not all have one *father*? Has not *one God* created us? Why do we deal treacherously each against his brother so as to profane the covenant of our fathers?"

Acts 15:19–20
"Therefore it is my judgment that we do not trouble those who are turning to God from among the Gentiles, [20]but that we write to them that they abstain from things contaminated by *idols* and from fornication and from what is strangled and from blood."

Acts 17:28
"In Him *we* live and move and *exist*, as even some of your own poets have said, 'For we also are His children.'"

Hebrews 2:10
For it was fitting for Him, *for* whom are *all things*, and *through* whom are all things, in bringing many sons to glory, to perfect the author of their salvation through sufferings.

NONCANONICAL PARALLELS

Wisdom of Solomon 13:10
But miserable, with their hopes set on dead things, are those who give the name *"gods"* to the works of human hands, gold and silver fashioned with skill, and likenesses of animals, or a useless stone, the work of an ancient hand.

1 Corinthians 8:7–13

However not all men have this knowledge; but some, being accustomed to the idol until now, eat food as if it were sacrificed to an idol; and their conscience being weak is defiled. [8]But food will not commend us to God; we are neither the worse if we do not eat, nor the better if we do eat. [9]But take care that this liberty of yours does not somehow become a stumbling block to the weak. [10]For if someone sees you, who have knowledge, dining in an idol's temple, will not his conscience, if he is weak, be strengthened to eat things sacrificed to idols? [11]For through your knowledge he who is weak is ruined, the brother for whose sake Christ died. [12]And so, by sinning against the brethren and wounding their conscience when it is weak, you sin against Christ. [13]Therefore, if food causes my brother to stumble, I will never eat meat again, so that I will not cause my brother to stumble.

1 CORINTHIANS PARALLELS

1 Corinthians 1:4–5
I thank my God always concerning you for the grace of God which was given you in Christ Jesus, ⁵that in everything you were enriched in Him, in all speech and all *knowledge.*

1 Corinthians 1:26–27
For consider your calling, brethren, that there were not many wise according to the flesh, not many mighty, not many noble; ²⁷but God has chosen the foolish things of the world to shame the wise, and God has chosen *the weak* things of the world to shame the things which are strong.

1 Corinthians 4:10
We are fools for Christ's sake, but you are prudent in Christ; we are *weak*, but you are strong; you are distinguished, but we are without honor.

1 Corinthians 9:22
To *the weak* I became weak, that I might win the weak; I have become all things to all men, so that I may by all means save some.

1 Corinthians 10:25–29
Eat anything that is sold in the *meat* market without asking questions for *conscience'* sake; ²⁶FOR THE EARTH IS THE LORD'S, AND ALL IT CONTAINS. ²⁷If one of the unbelievers invites you and you want to go, eat anything that is set before you without asking questions for conscience' sake. ²⁸But if anyone says to you, "This is meat *sacrificed to idols,*" do not eat it, for the sake of the one who informed you, and for conscience' sake; ²⁹I mean not your own conscience, but the other man's; for why is my freedom judged by another's conscience?

1 Corinthians 12:2
You know that when you were pagans, you were led astray to the mute *idols,* however you were led.

Romans 2:14–15
For when Gentiles who do not have the Law do instinctively the things of the Law, these, not having the Law, are a law to themselves, ¹⁵in that they show the work of the Law written in their hearts, their *conscience* bearing witness and their thoughts alternately accusing or else defending them.

Romans 5:6
For while we were still helpless, at the right time *Christ died* for the ungodly.

Romans 14:1–3, 13, 15, 17, 20–21
Now accept the one who is *weak* in faith, but not for the purpose of passing judgment on his opinions. ²One person has faith that he may *eat* all things, but he who is weak eats vegetables only. ³The one who eats is not to regard with contempt the one who does not eat, and the one who does not eat is not to judge the one who eats, for God has accepted him. . . . ¹³Therefore let us not judge one another anymore, but rather determine this—not to put an obstacle or *a stumbling block* in a *brother's* way. . . . ¹⁵For if because of *food* your brother is hurt, you are no longer walking according to love. Do not destroy with your food him for whom *Christ died.* . . . ¹⁷For the kingdom of God is not eating and drinking, but righteousness and peace and joy in the Holy Spirit. . . . ²⁰Do not tear down the work of God for the sake of food. All things indeed are clean, but they are evil for the man who eats and gives offense. ²¹It is good not to eat *meat* or to drink wine, or to do anything by which your brother *stumbles.*

Romans 15:1
Now we who are strong ought to bear the *weaknesses* of those without strength and not just please ourselves.

2 Corinthians 11:29
Who is *weak* without my being weak? Who is led into *sin* without my intense concern?

Titus 1:15
To the pure, all things are pure; but to those who are *defiled* and unbelieving, nothing is pure, but both their mind and their *conscience* are defiled.

Matthew 18:6

"Whoever causes one of these little ones who believe in Me to *stumble*, it would be better for him to have a heavy millstone hung around his neck, and to be drowned in the depth of the sea."

Matthew 25:40

"The King will answer and say to them, 'Truly I say to you, to the extent that you did it to one of these *brothers* of Mine, even the least of them, you did it to Me.'"

Hebrews 10:22

Let us draw near with a sincere heart in full assurance of faith, having our hearts sprinkled clean from an evil *conscience* and our bodies washed with pure water.

Hebrews 13:9

Do not be carried away by varied and strange teachings; for it is good for the heart to be *strengthened* by grace, not by *foods*, through which those who were so occupied were not benefited.

NONCANONICAL PARALLELS

2 Esdras (6 Ezra) 16:68–69

The burning wrath of a great multitude is kindled over you; they shall drag some of you away and force you to *eat* what was *sacrificed to idols.* [69]And those who consent to eat shall be held in derision and contempt, and shall be trampled under foot.

4 Maccabees 5:1–2

The tyrant Antiochus . . . [2]ordered the guards to seize each and every Hebrew and compel them to *eat* pork and food *sacrificed to idols.*

Dinner Invitation (P.Oxy. 1.110)

Chaeremon asks you to dine at the table of Lord Serapis in the Serapaeum tomorrow, which is the fifteenth, at nine o'clock.

1 Corinthians 9:1–7

Am I not free? Am I not an apostle? Have I not seen Jesus our Lord? Are you not my work in the Lord? [2]If to others I am not an apostle, at least I am to you; for you are the seal of my apostleship in the Lord. [3]My defense to those who examine me is this: [4]Do we not have a right to eat and drink? [5]Do we not have a right to take along a believing wife, even as the rest of the apostles and the brothers of the Lord and Cephas? [6]Or do only Barnabas and I not have a right to refrain from working? [7]Who at any time serves as a soldier at his own expense? Who plants a vineyard and does not eat the fruit of it? Or who tends a flock and does not use the milk of the flock?

1 CORINTHIANS PARALLELS

1 Corinthians 1:12

Now I mean this, that each one of you is saying, "I am of Paul," and "I of Apollos," and "I of *Cephas*," and "I of Christ."

1 Corinthians 3:6, 8

I planted, Apollos watered, but God was causing the growth. . . . [8]Now he who *plants* and he who waters are one; but each will receive his own reward according to his own labor.

1 Corinthians 4:3–4

But to me it is a very small thing that I may be *examined* by you, or by any human court; in fact, I do not even examine myself. [4]For I am conscious of nothing against myself, yet I am not by this acquitted; but the one who examines me is the Lord.

1 Corinthians 7:8

But I say to the unmarried and to widows that it is good for them if they remain even as I.

1 Corinthians 9:19

For though *I am free* from all men, I have made myself a slave to all, so that I may win more.

1 Corinthians 15:3–5, 7–8

For I delivered to you as of first importance what I also received, that Christ died for our sins according to the Scriptures, [4]and that He was buried, and that He was raised on the third day according to the Scriptures, [5]and that He appeared to *Cephas*, then to the twelve. . . . [7]Then He appeared to James, then to all the *apostles*; [8]and last of all, as to one untimely born, He appeared to me also.

OTHER PAULINE PARALLELS

2 Corinthians 12:12, 19

The signs of a true *apostle* were performed among you with all perseverance, by signs and wonders and miracles. . . . [19]All this time you have been thinking that we are *defending* ourselves to you. Actually, it is in the sight of God that we have been speaking in Christ; and all for your upbuilding, beloved.

Galatians 2:1, 9

Then after an interval of fourteen years I went up again to Jerusalem with *Barnabas*, taking Titus along also. . . . [9]And recognizing the grace that had been given to me, James and *Cephas* and John, who were reputed to be pillars, gave to me and Barnabas the right hand of fellowship, so that we might go to the Gentiles and they to the circumcised.

1 Thessalonians 2:9

For you recall, brethren, our labor and hardship, how *working* night and day so as not to be a burden to any of you, we proclaimed to you the gospel of God.

2 Thessalonians 3:7–9

For you yourselves know how you ought to follow our example, because we did not act in an undisciplined manner among you, [8]nor did we *eat* anyone's bread without paying for it, but with labor and hardship we kept *working* night and day so that we would not be a burden to any of you; [9]not because we do not have the *right* to this, but in order to offer ourselves as a model for you, so that you would follow our example.

2 Timothy 2:4

No *soldier* in active service entangles himself in the affairs of everyday life, so that he may please the one who enlisted him as a soldier.

OTHER BIBLICAL PARALLELS

Deuteronomy 20:6

"Who is the man that has *planted a vineyard* and has not begun to use its *fruit*? Let him depart and return to his house, otherwise he might die in the battle and another man would begin to use its fruit."

Jeremiah 23:2

Therefore thus says the LORD God of Israel concerning the shepherds who are *tending* My people: "You have scattered My *flock* and driven them away, and have not attended to them; behold, I am about to attend to you for the evil of your deeds," declares the LORD.

Mark 1:30

Now Simon's mother-in-law was lying sick with a fever; and immediately they spoke to Jesus about her.

Mark 6:3

"Is not this the carpenter, the son of Mary, and *brother* of James and Joses and Judas and Simon? Are not His sisters here with us?"

Acts 9:26–27

When he [Saul] came to Jerusalem, he was trying to associate with the disciples; but they were all afraid of him, not believing that he was a disciple. [27]But *Barnabas* took hold of him and brought him to the *apostles* and described to them how he *had seen* the *Lord* on the road, and that He had talked to him, and how at Damascus he had spoken out boldly in the name of Jesus.

Acts 13:1–2

Now there were at Antioch, in the church that was there, prophets and teachers: *Barnabas*, and Simeon who was called Niger, and Lucius of Cyrene, and Manaen who had been brought up with Herod the tetrarch, and Saul. [2]While they were ministering to the Lord and fasting, the Holy Spirit said, "Set apart for Me Barnabas and Saul for the work to which I have called them."

Acts 18:1–3

After these things he left Athens and went to Corinth. [2]And he found a Jew named Aquila, a native of Pontus, having recently come from Italy with his wife Priscilla, because Claudius had commanded all the Jews to leave Rome. He came to them, [3]and because he was of the same trade, he stayed with them and they were *working*, for by trade they were tent-makers.

Acts 20:28

"Be on guard for yourselves and for all the *flock*, among which the Holy Spirit has made you overseers, to shepherd the church of God which He purchased with His own blood."

1 Corinthians 9:8–18

I am not speaking these things according to human judgment, am I? Or does not the Law also say these things? [9]For it is written in the Law of Moses, "YOU SHALL NOT MUZZLE THE OX WHILE HE IS THRESHING." God is not concerned about oxen, is He? [10]Or is He speaking altogether for our sake? Yes, for our sake it was written, because the plowman ought to plow in hope, and the thresher to thresh in hope of sharing the crops. [11]If we sowed spiritual things in you, is it too much if we reap material things from you? [12]If others share the right over you, do we not more? Nevertheless, we did not use this right, but we endure all things so that we will cause no hindrance to the gospel of Christ. [13]Do you not know that those who perform sacred services eat the food of the temple, and those who attend regularly to the altar have their share from the altar? [14]So also the Lord directed those who proclaim the gospel to get their living from the gospel. [15]But I have used none of these things. And I am not writing these things so that it will be done so in my case; for it would be better for me to die than have any man make my boast an empty one. [16]For if I preach the gospel, I have nothing to boast of, for I am under compulsion; for woe is me if I do not preach the gospel. [17]For if I do this voluntarily, I have a reward; but if against my will, I have a stewardship entrusted to me. [18]What then is my reward? That, when I preach the gospel, I may offer the gospel without charge, so as not to make full use of my right in the gospel.

1 CORINTHIANS PARALLELS

1 Corinthians 1:17
For Christ did not send me to baptize, but to *preach the gospel*, not in cleverness of speech, so that the cross of Christ would not be made void.

1 Corinthians 3:6, 8
I planted, Apollos watered, but God was causing the growth. . . . [8]Now he who plants and he who waters are one; but each will receive his own *reward* according to his own labor.

1 Corinthians 4:1–2
Let a man regard us in this manner, as servants of Christ and *stewards* of the mysteries of God. [2]In this case, moreover, it is required of stewards that one be found trustworthy.

1 Corinthians 10:18
Look at the nation Israel; are not those who *eat* the sacrifices *sharers* in *the altar*?

OTHER PAULINE PARALLELS

Romans 15:4
For whatever was written in earlier times was *written* for our instruction, so that through perseverance and the encouragement of the Scriptures we might have *hope.*

Romans 15:26–27
For Macedonia and Achaia have been pleased to make a contribution for the poor among the saints in Jerusalem. [27]Yes, they were pleased to do so, and they are indebted to them. For if the Gentiles have *shared* in their *spiritual things*, they are indebted to minister to them also in *material things.*

2 Corinthians 11:7–10
Or did I commit a sin in humbling myself so that you might be exalted, because I *preached the gospel* of God to you *without charge*? [8]I robbed other churches by taking wages from them to serve you; [9]and when I was present with you and was in need, I was not a burden to anyone; for when the brethren came from Macedonia they fully supplied my need, and in everything I kept myself from being a burden to you, and will continue to do so. [10]As the truth of Christ is in me, this *boasting* of mine will not be stopped in the regions of Achaia.

Galatians 6:6
The one who is taught the word is to *share* all good things with the one who teaches him.

Colossians 1:25
Of this church I was made a minister according to the *stewardship* from God bestowed on me for your benefit, so that I might fully carry out the preaching of the word of God.

1 Thessalonians 2:4, 9

But just as we have been approved by God to be *entrusted* with *the gospel*, so we speak, not as pleasing men, but God who examines our hearts. . . . [9]For you recall, brethren, our labor and hardship, how working night and day so as not to be a burden to any of you, we *proclaimed* to you the gospel of God.

2 Thessalonians 3:7–9

For you yourselves know how you ought to follow our example, because we did not act in an undisciplined manner among you, [8]nor did we *eat* anyone's bread without paying for it, but with labor and hardship we kept working night and day so that we would not be a burden to any of you; [9]not because we do not have *the right* to this, but in order to offer ourselves as a model for you, so that you would follow our example.

1 Timothy 5:17–18

The elders who rule well are to be considered worthy of double honor, especially those who work hard at *preaching* and teaching. [18]For the Scripture says, *"YOU SHALL NOT MUZZLE THE OX WHILE HE IS THRESHING,"* and "The laborer is worthy of his wages."

2 Timothy 2:6

The hard-working farmer ought to be the first to receive his *share* of *the crops*.

OTHER BIBLICAL PARALLELS

Deuteronomy 18:1

"The Levitical priests, the whole tribe of Levi, shall have no portion or inheritance with Israel; they shall *eat* the LORD's offerings by fire and His portion."

Deuteronomy 25:4

"You shall not muzzle the ox while he is threshing."

Matthew 10:7–10

"And as you go, *preach*, saying, 'The kingdom of heaven is at hand.' [8]Heal the sick, raise the dead, cleanse the lepers, cast out demons. Freely you received, freely give. [9]Do not acquire gold, or silver, or copper for your money belts, [10]or a bag for your journey, or even two coats, or sandals, or a staff; for the worker is worthy of his support."

Luke 10:7

"Stay in that house, *eating* and drinking what they give you; for the laborer is worthy of his wages. Do not keep moving from house to house."

NONCANONICAL PARALLELS

Philo, On the Special Laws 1.260

For you will discover that all this accurate investigation regarding the [sacrificial] animal signifies the improvement of your conduct; for *the Law* is not for unreasoning creatures but for those possessed of intellect and reason.

1 Corinthians 9:19–27

For though I am free from all men, I have made myself a slave to all, so that I may win more. [20]To the Jews I became as a Jew, so that I might win Jews; to those who are under the Law, as under the Law though not being myself under the Law, so that I might win those who are under the Law; [21]to those who are without law, as without law, though not being without the law of God but under the law of Christ, so that I might win those who are without law. [22]To the weak I became weak, that I might win the weak; I have become all things to all men, so that I may by all means save some. [23]I do all things for the sake of the gospel, so that I may become a fellow partaker of it. [24]Do you not know that those who run in a race all run, but only one receives the prize? Run in such a way that you may win. [25]Everyone who competes in the games exercises self-control in all things. They then do it to receive a perishable wreath, but we an imperishable. [26]Therefore I run in such a way, as not without aim; I box in such a way, as not beating the air; [27]but I discipline my body and make it my slave, so that, after I have preached to others, I myself will not be disqualified.

1 CORINTHIANS PARALLELS

1 Corinthians 1:26–27

For consider your calling, brethren, that there were not many wise according to the flesh, not many mighty, not many noble; [27]but God has chosen the foolish things of the world to shame the wise, and God has chosen *the weak* things of the world to shame the things which are strong.

1 Corinthians 8:9, 12–13
But take care that this liberty of yours does not somehow become a stumbling block to *the weak.* . . . ¹²And so, by sinning against the brethren and wounding their conscience when it is weak, you sin against Christ. ¹³Therefore, if food causes my brother to stumble, I will never eat meat again, so that I will not cause my brother to stumble.

1 Corinthians 9:1
Am I not *free*? Am I not an apostle? Have I not seen Jesus our Lord? Are you not my work in the Lord?

1 Corinthians 10:32–33
Give no offense either to *Jews* or to Greeks or to the church of God; ³³just as I also please *all men* in all things, not seeking my own profit but the profit of the many, so that they may be *saved.*

1 Corinthians 15:50, 53
Now I say this, brethren, that flesh and blood cannot inherit the kingdom of God; nor does the *perishable* inherit the *imperishable.* . . . ⁵³For this perishable must put on the imperishable, and this mortal must put on immortality.

OTHER PAULINE PARALLELS

Romans 15:1
Now we who are strong ought to bear the *weaknesses* of those without strength and not just please ourselves.

2 Corinthians 4:5
For we do not *preach* ourselves but Christ Jesus as Lord, and ourselves as your bond-servants for Jesus' sake.

2 Corinthians 11:29
Who is *weak* without my being weak? Who is led into sin without my intense concern?

Galatians 2:2
It was because of a revelation that I went up; and I submitted to them *the gospel* which I *preach* among the Gentiles, but I did so in private to those who were of reputation, for fear that I might be running, or had run, in vain.

Galatians 2:19
"For through *the Law* I died to the Law, so that I might live to God."

Galatians 6:2
Bear one another's burdens, and thereby fulfill *the law of Christ.*

Philippians 3:14
I press on toward the goal for *the prize* of the upward call of God in Christ Jesus.

2 Timothy 2:5
Also if anyone *competes* as an athlete, he does not *win the prize* unless he competes according to the rules.

2 Timothy 4:7
I have fought the good fight, I have finished the course, I have kept the faith.

OTHER BIBLICAL PARALLELS

Mark 10:43–44
"But it is not this way among you, but whoever wishes to become great among you shall be your servant; ⁴⁴and whoever wishes to be first among you shall be *slave* of all."

Acts 16:1, 3
Paul came also to Derbe and to Lystra. And a disciple was there, named Timothy, the son of a Jewish woman who was a believer, but his father was a Greek. . . . ³Paul wanted this man to go with him; and he took him and circumcised him because of *the Jews* who were in those parts, for they all knew that his father was a Greek.

Hebrews 12:1
Therefore, since we have so great a cloud of witnesses surrounding us, let us also lay aside every encumbrance and the sin which so easily entangles us, and let us *run* with endurance the *race* that is set before us.

NONCANONICAL PARALLELS

Wisdom of Solomon 4:1–2
Better than this is childlessness with virtue, for in the memory of virtue is immortality, because it is known both by God and by mortals. ²When it is present, people imitate it, and they long for it when it has gone; throughout all time it marches, crowned in

triumph, victor in the contest for *prizes* that are undefiled.

4 Maccabees 17:11–15

Truly the contest in which they were engaged was divine, [12]for on that day virtue gave the awards and tested them for their endurance. *The prize* was immortality in endless life. [13]Eleazar was the first contestant, the mother of the seven sons entered the *competition*, and the brothers contended. [14]The tyrant was the antagonist, and the world and the human race were the spectators. [15]Reverence for God was victor and gave the crown to its own athletes.

Strabo, Geography *8.6.20*

Corinth is called "wealthy" on account of its commerce, lying on the Isthmus and master of two harbors; . . . also the Isthmian *Games,* which are celebrated there, draw crowds of people.

Dio Chrysostom, Orations *8.15, 18*

The noble man considers his hardships to be his greatest antagonists, and with them he desires to fight both night and day, not for a sprig of parsley, as goats might do, or a bit of wild olive or of pine, but for happiness and virtue. . . . [18] . . . For in fact, just as skillful *boxers,* if they seize their antagonist first, are not struck at all. . . . Likewise, if we accept our hardships, thinking little of them, and approach them eagerly, they do not prevail against us very much.

1 Corinthians 10:1–10

For I do not want you to be unaware, brethren, that our fathers were all under the cloud and all passed through the sea; [2]and all were baptized into Moses in the cloud and in the sea; [3]and all ate the same spiritual food; [4]and all drank the same spiritual drink, for they were drinking from a spiritual rock which followed them; and the rock was Christ. [5]Nevertheless, with most of them God was not well-pleased; for they were laid low in the wilderness. [6]Now these things happened as examples for us, so that we would not crave evil things as they also craved. [7]Do not be idolaters, as some of them were; as it is written, "THE PEOPLE SAT DOWN TO EAT AND DRINK, AND STOOD UP TO PLAY." [8]Nor let us act immorally, as some of them did,

and twenty-three thousand fell in one day. [9]Nor let us try the Lord, as some of them did, and were destroyed by the serpents. [10]Nor grumble, as some of them did, and were destroyed by the destroyer.

1 CORINTHIANS PARALLELS

1 Corinthians 1:13

Has Christ been divided? Paul was not crucified for you, was he? Or were you *baptized* in the name of Paul?

1 Corinthians 5:1, 11

It is actually reported that there is *immorality* among you, and immorality of such a kind as does not exist even among the Gentiles, that someone has his father's wife. . . . [11]But actually, I wrote to you not to associate with any so-called brother if he is an immoral person, or covetous, or an *idolater,* or a reviler, or a drunkard, or a swindler— not even to eat with such a one.

1 Corinthians 11:29–30

For he who *eats* and *drinks,* eats and drinks judgment to himself if he does not judge the body rightly. [30]For this reason many among you are weak and sick, and a number sleep.

OTHER PAULINE PARALLELS

2 Corinthians 12:21

I am afraid that when I come again my God may humiliate me before you, and I may mourn over many of those who have sinned in the past and not repented of the impurity, *immorality* and sensuality which they have practiced.

Ephesians 5:5

For this you know with certainty, that no *immoral* or impure person or covetous man, who is an *idolater,* has an inheritance in the kingdom of Christ and God.

OTHER BIBLICAL PARALLELS

Exodus 12:23

"For the LORD will pass through to smite the Egyptians; and when He sees the blood on the lintel and on the two doorposts, the LORD will pass over the door and will not allow *the destroyer* to come in to your houses to smite you."

The LORD was going before them in a pillar of *cloud* by day to lead them on the way, and in a pillar of fire by night to give them light, that they might travel by day and by night.

Exodus 14:22

The sons of Israel went *through* the midst of *the sea* on the dry land, and the waters were like a wall to them on their right hand and on their left.

Exodus 16:4

"Behold, I will rain bread from heaven for you; and the people shall go out and gather a day's portion every day, that I may test them, whether or not they will walk in My instruction."

Exodus 17:6

"Behold, I will stand before you there on *the rock* at Horeb; and you shall strike the rock, and water will come out of it, that the people may *drink*."

Exodus 32:3–4, 6

Then all the people tore off the gold rings which were in their ears and brought them to Aaron. [4]He took this from their hand, and fashioned it with a graving tool and made it into a molten calf; and they said, "This is your god, O Israel, who brought you up from the land of Egypt." . . . [6]So the next day they rose early and offered burnt offerings, and brought peace offerings; and *the people sat down to eat and* to *drink, and* rose *up to play*.

Numbers 11:4–6

The rabble who were among them had greedy desires; and also the sons of Israel wept again and said, "Who will give us meat to eat? [5]We remember the fish which we used to eat free in Egypt, the cucumbers and the melons and the leeks and the onions and the garlic, [6]but now our appetite is gone. There is nothing at all to look at except this manna."

Numbers 16:41, 46, 49

But on the next day all the congregation of the sons of Israel *grumbled* against Moses and Aaron, saying, "You are the ones who have caused the death of the LORD's people." . . . [46]Moses said to Aaron, "Take your censer and put in it fire from the altar, and

lay incense on it; then bring it quickly to the congregation and make atonement for them, for wrath has gone forth from the LORD, the plague has begun!" . . . [49]But those who died by the plague were 14,700, besides those who died on account of Korah.

Numbers 21:5–6

The people spoke against God and Moses, "Why have you brought us up out of Egypt to die *in the wilderness*? For there is no food and no water, and we loathe this miserable *food*." [6]The LORD sent fiery *serpents* among the people and they bit the people, so that many people of Israel died.

Numbers 25:1–3, 9

While Israel remained at Shittim, the people began to play the harlot with the daughters of Moab. [2]For they invited the people to the sacrifices of their gods, and the people ate and bowed down to their gods. [3]So Israel joined themselves to Baal of Peor, and the LORD was angry against Israel. . . . [9]Those who died by the plague were 24,000.

Deuteronomy 6:16

"You shall not put the LORD your God to the test, as you tested Him at Massah."

John 6:49

"Your *fathers ate* the manna *in the wilderness*, and they died."

Jude 5

Now I desire to remind you, though you know all things once for all, that the Lord, after saving a people out of the land of Egypt, subsequently *destroyed* those who did not believe.

NONCANONICAL PARALLELS

Philo, Allegorical Interpretation *2.86*

The flinty *rock* is the wisdom of God, which he marked off as the highest and foremost of his powers, and from which he quenches the thirst of those souls that love him.

1 Corinthians 10:11–22

Now these things happened to them as an example, and they were written for our instruction, upon whom the ends of the ages have come. [12]Therefore let him who thinks he stands take heed that he does not fall. [13]No temptation has overtaken you but such as is common to man; and God is faithful, who will not allow you to be tempted beyond what you are able, but with the temptation will provide the way of escape also, so that you will be able to endure it.[14]Therefore, my beloved, flee from idolatry. [15]I speak as to wise men; you judge what I say. [16]Is not the cup of blessing which we bless a sharing in the blood of Christ? Is not the bread which we break a sharing in the body of Christ? [17]Since there is one bread, we who are many are one body; for we all partake of the one bread. [18]Look at the nation Israel; are not those who eat the sacrifices sharers in the altar? [19]What do I mean then? That a thing sacrificed to idols is anything, or that an idol is anything? [20]No, but I say that the things which the Gentiles sacrifice, they sacrifice to demons and not to God; and I do not want you to become sharers in demons. [21]You cannot drink the cup of the Lord and the cup of demons; you cannot partake of the table of the Lord and the table of demons. [22]Or do we provoke the Lord to jealousy? We are not stronger than He, are we?

1 CORINTHIANS PARALLELS

1 Corinthians 1:7–9
You are not lacking in any gift, awaiting eagerly the revelation of our Lord Jesus Christ, [8]who will also confirm you to *the end*, blameless in the day of our Lord Jesus Christ. [9]*God is faithful*, through whom you were called into fellowship with His Son, Jesus Christ our Lord.

1 Corinthians 8:1, 4
Now concerning *things sacrificed to idols*, we know that we all have knowledge. Knowledge makes arrogant, but love edifies. . . . [4]Therefore concerning the *eating of* things sacrificed to idols, we know that there is no such thing as an idol in the world, and that there is no God but one.

1 Corinthians 9:13
Do you not know that those who perform sacred services *eat* the food of the temple, and those who attend regularly to the altar have their *share* from *the altar*?

1 Corinthians 11:23–25
For I received from the Lord that which I also delivered to you, that the Lord Jesus in

the night in which He was betrayed took *bread*; [24]and when He had given thanks, He *broke* it and said, "This is My *body*, which is for you; do this in remembrance of Me." [25]In the same way He took *the cup* also after supper, saying, "This cup is the new covenant in My *blood*; do this, as often as you drink it, in remembrance of Me."

1 Corinthians 12:2
You know that when you were pagans, you were led astray to the mute *idols*, however you were led.

1 Corinthians 12:12
For even as the body is one and yet has many members, and all the members of the body, though they are many, are *one body*, so also is Christ.

OTHER PAULINE PARALLELS

Romans 11:20–21
Quite right, they were broken off for their unbelief, but you *stand* by your faith. Do not be conceited, but fear; [21]for if God did not spare the natural branches, He will not spare you, either.

Romans 15:4
For whatever was written in earlier times *was written for our instruction*, so that through perseverance and the encouragement of the Scriptures we might have hope.

2 Corinthians 6:15–16
Or what harmony has Christ with Belial, or what has a believer in common with an unbeliever? [16]Or what agreement has the temple of God with *idols*? For we are the temple of the living God.

2 Thessalonians 3:3
But the Lord is *faithful*, and He will strengthen and protect you from the evil one.

OTHER BIBLICAL PARALLELS

Leviticus 7:5–6
"The priest shall offer them up in smoke on *the altar* as an offering by fire to the LORD; it is a guilt offering. [6]Every male among the priests may *eat* of it. It shall be eaten in a holy place; it is most holy."

Deuteronomy 7:9

"Know therefore that the LORD your God, He is God, the *faithful God*, who keeps His covenant and His lovingkindness to a thousandth generation with those who love Him and keep His commandments."

Deuteronomy 32:16–17

"They made Him *jealous* with strange gods; With abominations they *provoked* Him to anger. [17]They *sacrificed to demons* who were not God, To gods whom they have not known, New gods who came lately, Whom your fathers did not dread."

Isaiah 65:11–12

"But you who forsake the LORD, Who forget My holy mountain, Who set a *table* for Fortune, And who fill *cups* with mixed wine for Destiny, [12]I will destine you for the sword, And all of you will bow down to the slaughter. Because I called, but you did not answer; I spoke, but you did not hear. And you did evil in My sight And chose that in which I did not delight."

Matthew 26:26–28

While they were eating, Jesus took some *bread*, and after a *blessing*, He *broke* it and gave it to the disciples, and said, "Take, eat; this is My *body*." [27]And when He had taken a *cup* and given thanks, He gave it to them, saying, "*Drink* from it, all of you; [28]for this is My *blood* of the covenant, which is poured out for many for forgiveness of sins."

2 Peter 2:7, 9

And if He rescued righteous Lot, oppressed by the sensual conduct of unprincipled men, . . . [9]then the Lord knows how to rescue the godly from *temptation*, and to keep the unrighteous under punishment for the day of judgment.

1 John 5:21

Little children, guard yourselves from *idols*.

NONCANONICAL PARALLELS

Didache *9.1, 3–4*

Concerning the Eucharist . . . [3]And concerning *the bread* [say]: "We give thanks to you, our Father. . . . [4]As this bread was scattered upon the mountains and when gathered became *one*, so may your church be gathered from the ends of the earth into your kingdom."

1 Corinthians 10:23–11:1

All things are lawful, but not all things are profitable. All things are lawful, but not all things edify. [24]Let no one seek his own good, but that of his neighbor. [25]Eat anything that is sold in the meat market without asking questions for conscience' sake; [26]FOR THE EARTH IS THE LORD'S, AND ALL IT CONTAINS. [27]If one of the unbelievers invites you and you want to go, eat anything that is set before you without asking questions for conscience' sake. [28]But if anyone says to you, "This is meat sacrificed to idols," do not eat it, for the sake of the one who informed you, and for conscience' sake; [29]I mean not your own conscience, but the other man's; for why is my freedom judged by another's conscience? [30]If I partake with thankfulness, why am I slandered concerning that for which I give thanks? [31]Whether, then, you eat or drink or whatever you do, do all to the glory of God. [32]Give no offense either to Jews or to Greeks or to the church of God; [33]just as I also please all men in all things, not seeking my own profit but the profit of the many, so that they may be saved. [11:1]Be imitators of me, just as I also am of Christ.

1 CORINTHIANS PARALLELS

1 Corinthians 4:15–16

For if you were to have countless tutors in Christ, yet you would not have many fathers, for in Christ Jesus I became your father through the gospel. [16]Therefore I exhort you, *be imitators of me*.

1 Corinthians 6:12–13

All things are lawful for me, *but not all things are profitable. All things are lawful* for me, but I will not be mastered by anything. [13]Food is for the stomach and the stomach is for food, but God will do away with both of them. Yet the body is not for immorality, but for the Lord, and the Lord is for the body.

1 Corinthians 7:12–13

But to the rest I say, not the Lord, that if any brother has a wife who is an *unbeliever*, and she consents to live with him, he must not divorce her. [13]And a woman who has an unbelieving husband, and he consents to live with her, she must not send her husband away.

1 Corinthians 8:1, 7, 13

Now concerning things *sacrificed to idols*, we know that we all have knowledge. Knowledge makes arrogant, but love *edifies*. . . . [7]However not all men have this knowledge; but some, being accustomed to the idol until now, eat food as if it were sacrificed to an idol; and their *conscience* being weak is defiled. . . .[13]Therefore, if food causes my brother to stumble, I will never *eat meat* again, so that I will not cause my brother to stumble.

1 Corinthians 9:20–22

To the *Jews* I became as a Jew, so that I might win Jews; to those who are under the Law, as under the Law though not being myself under the Law, so that I might win those who are under the Law; [21]to those who are without law, as without law, though not being without the law of God but under the law of Christ, so that I might win those who are without law. [22]To the weak I became weak, that I might win the weak; I have become all things to all men, so that I may by all means *save* some.

1 Corinthians 11:22

What! Do you not have houses in which to *eat* and *drink*? Or do you despise *the church of God* and shame those who have nothing? What shall I say to you? Shall I praise you? In this I will not praise you.

1 Corinthians 13:4–5

Love is patient, love is kind and is not jealous; love does not brag and is not arrogant, [5]does not act unbecomingly; it does *not seek* its *own*, is not provoked, does not take into account a wrong suffered.

OTHER PAULINE PARALLELS

Romans 2:14–15

For when Gentiles who do not have the Law do instinctively the things of the Law, these, not having the Law, are a law to themselves, [15]in that they show the work of the Law written in their hearts, their *conscience* bearing witness and their thoughts alternately accusing or else defending them.

Romans 14:6, 13, 17, 20–21

He who observes the day, observes it for the Lord, and he who *eats*, does so for the Lord, for he *gives thanks* to God; and he who eats not, for the Lord he does not eat, and gives thanks to God. . . . [13]Therefore let us not *judge* one another anymore, but rather determine this—not to put an obstacle or a stumbling block in a brother's way. . . . [17]For the kingdom of God is not *eating* and *drinking*, but righteousness and peace and joy in the Holy Spirit. . . . [20]Do not tear down the work of God for the sake of food. All things indeed are clean, but they are evil for the man who eats and *gives offense.* [21]It is good not to eat *meat* or to drink wine, or to do anything by which your brother stumbles.

Romans 15:1–2

Now we who are strong ought to bear the weaknesses of those without strength and not just *please* ourselves. [2]Each of us is to please *his neighbor* for his good, to his *edification.*

Galatians 5:13

For you were called to *freedom*, brethren; only do not turn your freedom into an opportunity for the flesh, but through love serve one another.

1 Timothy 4:4

For everything created by God is good, and nothing is to be rejected if it is received with gratitude.

OTHER BIBLICAL PARALLELS

Psalm 24:1

The *earth is the LORD'S, and all it contains,* The world, and those who dwell in it.

Luke 10:8

"Whatever city you enter and they receive you, *eat* what is *set before you.*"

Hebrews 13:9

Do not be carried away by varied and strange teachings; for it is good for the heart to be strengthened by grace, not by foods, through which those who were so occupied were not benefited.

1 Peter 2:16

Act as free men, and do not use your *freedom* as a covering for evil, but use it as bondslaves of God.

And keep a good *conscience* so that in the thing in which you are *slandered*, those who revile your good behavior in Christ will be put to shame.

Sirach 37:27–28

My child, test yourself while you live; see what is bad for you and do not give in to it. [28]For not everything is good for everyone, and no one enjoys everything.

Dinner Invitation (P.Oxy. 12.1484)

Apollonius asks you to dine at the table of Lord Serapis on the occasion of the coming of age of his [brothers] in [the temple of] Thoeris.

1 Corinthians 11:2–16

Now I praise you because you remember me in everything and hold firmly to the traditions, just as I delivered them to you. [3]But I want you to understand that Christ is the head of every man, and the man is the head of a woman, and God is the head of Christ. [4]Every man who has something on his head while praying or prophesying disgraces his head. [5]But every woman who has her head uncovered while praying or prophesying disgraces her head, for she is one and the same as the woman whose head is shaved. [6]For if a woman does not cover her head, let her also have her hair cut off; but if it is disgraceful for a woman to have her hair cut off or her head shaved, let her cover her head. [7]For a man ought not to have his head covered, since he is the image and glory of God; but the woman is the glory of man. [8]For man does not originate from woman, but woman from man; [9]for indeed man was not created for the woman's sake, but woman for the man's sake. [10]Therefore the woman ought to have a symbol of authority on her head, because of the angels. [11]However, in the Lord, neither is woman independent of man, nor is man independent of woman. [12]For as the woman originates from the man, so also the man has his birth through the woman; and all things originate from God. [13]Judge for yourselves: is it proper for a woman to pray to God with her head uncovered? [14]Does not even nature itself teach you that if a man has long hair, it is a dishonor to him, [15]but if a woman has long hair, it is a glory to her? For her hair is given to her for a covering. [16]But if one is inclined to be contentious, we have no other practice, nor have the churches of God.

1 Corinthians 3:21, 23

So then let no one boast in men. For all things belong to you . . . [23]and you belong to Christ; and Christ belongs to God.

1 Corinthians 4:9

For, I think, God has exhibited us apostles last of all, as men condemned to death; because we have become a spectacle to the world, both to *angels* and to men.

1 Corinthians 7:4

The wife does not have *authority* over her own body, but the husband does; and likewise also the husband does not have authority over his own body, but the wife does.

1 Corinthians 14:14–15

For if I *pray* in a tongue, my spirit prays, but my mind is unfruitful. [15]What is the outcome then? I will pray with the spirit and I will pray with the mind also; I will sing with the spirit and I will sing with the mind also.

1 Corinthians 14:31–35

For you can all *prophesy* one by one, so that all may learn and all may be exhorted; [32]and the spirits of prophets are subject to prophets; [33]for God is not a God of confusion but of peace, as in all *the churches* of the saints. [34]The women are to keep silent in the churches; for they are not permitted to speak, but are to subject themselves, just as the Law also says. [35]If they desire to learn anything, let them ask their own husbands at home; for it is improper for a *woman* to speak in church.

Ephesians 5:23

For the husband is *the head* of the wife, as Christ also is the head of the church, He Himself being the Savior of the body.

2 Thessalonians 2:15

So then, brethren, stand firm and *hold to the traditions* which you were taught, whether by word of mouth or by letter from us.

But I do not allow *a woman* to teach or exercise *authority* over a man, but to remain quiet. [13]For it was Adam who was first *created*, and then Eve.

OTHER BIBLICAL PARALLELS

Genesis 1:27

God *created man* in His own *image*, in the image of God He created him; male and female He created them.

Genesis 2:18, 22

Then the LORD God said, "It is not good for the man to be alone; I will make him a helper suitable for him." . . . [22]The LORD God fashioned into *a woman* the rib which He had taken *from* the *man*, and brought her to the man.

Genesis 3:16

To the *woman* He said, "I will greatly multiply Your pain in childbirth, In pain you will bring forth children; Yet your desire will be for your husband, And he will rule over you."

Genesis 6:1–2

Now it came about, when men began to multiply on the face of the land, and daughters were born to them, [2]that the sons of God saw that the daughters of men were beautiful; and they took wives for themselves, whomever they chose.

2 Samuel 15:30

And David went up the ascent of the Mount of Olives, and wept as he went, and his *head* was *covered* and he walked barefoot. Then all the people who were with him each covered his head and went up weeping as they went.

Acts 18:18

Paul, having remained many days longer, took leave of the brethren and put out to sea for Syria, and with him were Priscilla and Aquila. In Cenchrea he had his *hair cut*, for he was keeping a vow.

Acts 21:8–9

On the next day we left and came to Caesarea, and entering the house of Philip the evangelist, who was one of the seven, we stayed with him. [9]Now this man had four virgin daughters who were *prophetesses*.

NONCANONICAL PARALLELS

Pseudo-Phocylides, Sentences *210–12*

Do not grow locks in the hair of a male child. [211]Braid not his crown or the cross-knots on the top of his *head*. [212]For men to wear *long hair* is not seemly, only for sensual women.

Philo, On the Virtues *73–74*

Moses convened a divine assembly . . . and in its midst sang hymns with every kind of harmony and melody. [74]He did this so that both human beings and ministering *angels* would take heed, . . . the latter as witnesses seeing . . . whether there was anything dissonant about his song.

Plutarch, The Roman Questions *267A*

It is more customary for women to go out in public with their heads *covered*, and men with their heads *uncovered*.

1 Corinthians 11:17–26

But in giving this instruction, I do not praise you, because you come together not for the better but for the worse. [18]For, in the first place, when you come together as a church, I hear that divisions exist among you; and in part I believe it. [19]For there must also be factions among you, so that those who are approved may become evident among you. [20]Therefore when you meet together, it is not to eat the Lord's Supper, [21]for in your eating each one takes his own supper first; and one is hungry and another is drunk. [22]What! Do you not have houses in which to eat and drink? Or do you despise the church of God and shame those who have nothing? What shall I say to you? Shall I praise you? In this I will not praise you. [23]For I received from the Lord that which I also delivered to you, that the Lord Jesus in the night in which He was betrayed took bread; [24]and when He had given thanks, He broke it and said, "This is My body, which is for you; do this in remembrance of Me." [25]In the same way He took the cup also after supper, saying, "This cup is the new covenant in My blood; do this, as often as you drink it, in remembrance of Me." [26]For as often as you eat this bread and drink the cup, you proclaim the Lord's death until He comes.

1 CORINTHIANS PARALLELS

1 Corinthians 1:10
Now I exhort you, brethren, by the name of our Lord Jesus Christ, that you all agree and that there be no *divisions among you,* but that you be made complete in the same mind and in the same judgment.

1 Corinthians 5:11
But actually, I wrote to you not to associate with any so-called brother if he is an immoral person, or covetous, or an idolater, or a reviler, or a *drunkard,* or a swindler—not even to *eat* with such a one.

1 Corinthians 10:16–17
Is not *the cup* of blessing which we bless a sharing in the *blood* of Christ? Is not the *bread* which we *break* a sharing in the *body* of Christ? [17]Since there is one bread, we who are many are one body; for we all partake of the one bread.

1 Corinthians 10:32
Give no offense either to Jews or to Greeks or to *the church of God.*

1 Corinthians 12:24–25
But God has so composed the *body,* giving more abundant honor to that member which lacked, [25]so that there may be no *division* in the body, but that the members may have the same care for one another.

1 Corinthians 14:26
What is the outcome then, brethren? When you assemble, each one has a psalm, has a teaching, has a revelation, has a tongue, has an interpretation. Let all things be done for edification.

1 Corinthians 15:3
For *I delivered to you* as of first importance what *I* also *received,* that Christ died for our sins according to the Scriptures.

OTHER PAULINE PARALLELS

2 Corinthians 2:9
For to this end also I wrote, so that I might put you to the test, whether you are obedient in all things.

Galatians 5:19–21
Now the deeds of the flesh are evident, which are: immorality, impurity, sensuality, [20]idolatry, sorcery, enmities, strife, jealousy, outbursts of anger, disputes, dissensions, *factions,* [21]envying, *drunkenness,* carousing, and things like these, of which I forewarn you, just as I have forewarned you, that those who practice such things will not inherit the kingdom of God.

Ephesians 5:18
And do not get *drunk* with wine, for that is dissipation, but be filled with the Spirit.

Titus 3:10–11
Reject a *factious* man after a first and second warning, [11]knowing that such a man is perverted and is sinning, being self-condemned.

OTHER BIBLICAL PARALLELS

Exodus 24:8
So Moses took the blood and sprinkled it on the people, and said, "Behold the *blood* of the *covenant,* which the LORD has made with you in accordance with all these words."

Jeremiah 31:31
"Behold, days are coming," declares the LORD, "when I will make a *new covenant* with the house of Israel and with the house of Judah."

Luke 22:19–21
And when He had *taken* some *bread* and *given thanks, He broke it* and gave it to them, *saying, "This is My body which is* given *for you; do this in remembrance of Me."* [20]And *in the same way He took the cup after* they had eaten, *saying, "This cup* which is poured out for you *is the new covenant in My blood.* [21]But behold, the hand of the one *betraying* Me is with Mine on the table."

Hebrews 9:15
For this reason He is the mediator of a *new covenant,* so that, since a *death* has taken place for the redemption of the transgressions that were committed under the first covenant, those who have been called may receive the promise of the eternal inheritance.

James 1:12

Blessed is a man who perseveres under trial; for once he has been *approved*, he will receive the crown of life which the Lord has promised to those who love Him.

James 2:2–4, 6

For if a man comes into your assembly with a gold ring and dressed in fine clothes, and there also comes in a poor man in dirty clothes, [3]and you pay special attention to the one who is wearing the fine clothes, and say, "You sit here in a good place," and you say to the poor man, "You stand over there, or sit down by my footstool," [4]have you not made distinctions among yourselves, and become judges with evil motives? . . . [6]But you have dishonored the poor man. Is it not the rich who oppress you and personally drag you into court?

NONCANONICAL PARALLELS

Statutes of a Cultic Fellowship (P.Lond. 2710)

The statutes which the members of the association of Zeus most High gave themselves: . . . none of them is to be permitted . . . to form *factions* or to leave the fraternity of the president for another fraternity. No one is to ask questions at the *drinking* feast about the origins of another member, or to show contempt for him.

1 Corinthians 11:27–34

Therefore whoever eats the bread or drinks the cup of the Lord in an unworthy manner, shall be guilty of the body and the blood of the Lord. [28]But a man must examine himself, and in so doing he is to eat of the bread and drink of the cup. [29]For he who eats and drinks, eats and drinks judgment to himself if he does not judge the body rightly. [30]For this reason many among you are weak and sick, and a number sleep. [31]But if we judged ourselves rightly, we would not be judged. [32]But when we are judged, we are disciplined by the Lord so that we will not be condemned along with the world. [33]So then, my brethren, when you come together to eat, wait for one another. [34]If anyone is hungry, let him eat at home, so that you will not come together for judgment. The remaining matters I will arrange when I come.

1 CORINTHIANS PARALLELS

1 Corinthians 4:3–4

But to me it is a very small thing that I may be examined by you, or by any human court; in fact, I do not even *examine* myself. [4]For I am conscious of nothing against myself, yet I am not by this acquitted; but the one who examines me is the Lord.

1 Corinthians 4:19–21

But I will come to you soon, if the Lord wills, and I shall find out, not the words of those who are arrogant but their power. [20]For the kingdom of God does not consist in words but in power. [21]What do you desire? Shall *I come* to you with a rod, or with love and a spirit of gentleness?

1 Corinthians 5:12

For what have I to do with judging outsiders? Do you not *judge* those who are within the church? [13]But those who are outside, God judges.

1 Corinthians 8:12

And so, by sinning against the brethren and wounding their conscience when it is weak, you sin against Christ.

1 Corinthians 10:16–17

Is not *the cup* of blessing which we bless a sharing in *the blood* of Christ? Is not *the bread* which we break a sharing in *the body* of Christ? [17]Since there is one bread, we who are many are one body; for we all partake of the one bread.

1 Corinthians 12:12–13

For even as *the body* is one and yet has many members, and all the members of the body, though they are many, are one body, so also is Christ. [13]For by one Spirit we were all baptized into one body, whether Jews or Greeks, whether slaves or free, and we were all made to *drink* of one Spirit.

1 Corinthians 12:24–25

But God has so composed *the body*, giving more abundant honor to that member which lacked, [25]so that there may be no division in the body, but that the members may have the same care for one another.

1 Corinthians 15:6

After that He appeared to more than five hundred brethren at one time, most of whom remain until now, but some have fallen *asleep.*

1 Corinthians 16:5–6

But *I* will *come* to you after I go through Macedonia, for I am going through Macedonia; [6]and perhaps I will stay with you, or even spend the winter, so that you may send me on my way wherever I may go.

OTHER PAULINE PARALLELS

Romans 14:22–23

The faith which you have, have as your own conviction before God. Happy is he who does not condemn himself in what he approves. [23]But he who doubts is *condemned* if he *eats,* because his eating is not from faith; and whatever is not from faith is sin.

2 Corinthians 13:5

Test yourselves to see if you are in the faith; *examine* yourselves! Or do you not recognize this about yourselves, that Jesus Christ is in you—unless indeed you fail the test?

Galatians 6:4

But each one must *examine* his own work, and then he will have reason for boasting in regard to himself alone, and not in regard to another.

OTHER BIBLICAL PARALLELS

Deuteronomy 8:5–6

Thus you are to know in your heart that the LORD your God was *disciplining* you just as a man disciplines his son. [6]Therefore, you shall keep the commandments of the LORD your God, to walk in His ways and to fear Him.

Psalm 94:12–13

Blessed is the man whom You chasten, O LORD, And whom You teach out of Your law; [13]That You may grant him relief from the days of adversity, Until a pit is dug for the wicked.

Hebrews 6:4–6

For in the case of those who have once been enlightened and have tasted of the heavenly gift and have been made partakers of the Holy Spirit, [5]and have tasted the good word of God and the powers of the age to come, [6]and then have fallen away, it is impossible to renew them again to repentance, since they again crucify to themselves the Son of God and put Him to open shame.

Hebrews 10:28–29

Anyone who has set aside the Law of Moses dies without mercy on the testimony of two or three witnesses. [29]How much severer punishment do you think he will deserve who has trampled under foot the Son of God, and has regarded as unclean *the blood* of the covenant by which he was sanctified, and has insulted the Spirit of grace?

Hebrews 12:7–11

It is for discipline that you endure; God deals with you as with sons; for what son is there whom his father does not discipline? [8]But if you are without discipline, of which all have become partakers, then you are illegitimate children and not sons. [9]Furthermore, we had earthly fathers to discipline us, and we respected them; shall we not much rather be subject to the Father of spirits, and live? [10]For they disciplined us for a short time as seemed best to them, but He *disciplines* us for our good, so that we may share His holiness. [11]All discipline for the moment seems not to be joyful, but sorrowful; yet to those who have been trained by it, afterwards it yields the peaceful fruit of righteousness.

1 Peter 4:17

For it is time for *judgment* to begin with the household of God; and if it begins with us first, what will be the outcome for those who do not obey the gospel of God?

NONCANONICAL PARALLELS

Wisdom of Solomon 11:9–10

For when they were tried, though they were being *disciplined* in mercy, they learned how the ungodly were tormented when *judged* in wrath. [10]For you tested them as a parent does in warning, but you *examined* the ungodly as a stern king does in *condemnation.*

1 Corinthians 12:1–11

Now concerning spiritual gifts, brethren, I do not want you to be unaware. ²You know that when you were pagans, you were led astray to the mute idols, however you were led. ³Therefore I make known to you that no one speaking by the Spirit of God says, "Jesus is accursed"; and no one can say, "Jesus is Lord," except by the Holy Spirit. ⁴Now there are varieties of gifts, but the same Spirit. ⁵And there are varieties of ministries, and the same Lord. ⁶There are varieties of effects, but the same God who works all things in all persons. ⁷But to each one is given the manifestation of the Spirit for the common good. ⁸For to one is given the word of wisdom through the Spirit, and to another the word of knowledge according to the same Spirit; ⁹to another faith by the same Spirit, and to another gifts of healing by the one Spirit, ¹⁰and to another the effecting of miracles, and to another prophecy, and to another the distinguishing of spirits, to another various kinds of tongues, and to another the interpretation of tongues. ¹¹But one and the same Spirit works all these things, distributing to each one individually just as He wills.

1 CORINTHIANS PARALLELS

1 Corinthians 1:4–5, 7

I thank my God always concerning you for the grace of God which was given you in Christ Jesus, ⁵that in everything you were enriched in Him, in all speech and all *knowledge*, . . . ⁷so that you are not lacking in any *gift*, awaiting eagerly the revelation of our Lord Jesus Christ.

1 Corinthians 2:12–13

Now we have received, not the spirit of the world, but *the Spirit* who is from God, so that we may know the things freely given to us by God, ¹³which things we also *speak*, not in words taught by human wisdom, but in those taught by the Spirit, combining spiritual thoughts with spiritual words.

1 Corinthians 7:7

Yet I wish that all men were even as I myself am. However, each man has his own *gift* from God, one in this manner, and another in that.

1 Corinthians 8:4, 6

Therefore concerning the eating of things sacrificed to *idols*, we know that there is no such thing as an idol in the world, and that there is no God but one. . . . ⁶Yet for us there is but one God, the Father, from whom are all things and we exist for Him; and one Lord, Jesus Christ, by whom are all things, and we exist through Him.

1 Corinthians 12:28

And God has appointed in the church, first apostles, second *prophets*, third teachers, then *miracles*, then *gifts of healings*, helps, administrations, *various kinds of tongues*.

1 Corinthians 13:1–2

If I speak with the *tongues* of men and of angels, but do not have love, I have become a noisy gong or a clanging cymbal. ²If I have the *gift* of *prophecy*, and know all mysteries and all *knowledge*; and if I have all *faith*, so as to remove mountains, but do not have love, I am nothing.

1 Corinthians 14:5–6

Now I wish that you all spoke in *tongues*, but even more that you would prophesy; and greater is one who prophesies than one who speaks in tongues, unless he *interprets*, so that the church may receive edifying. ⁶But now, brethren, if I come to you speaking in tongues, what will I profit you unless I speak to you either by way of revelation or of *knowledge* or of *prophecy* or of teaching?

OTHER PAULINE PARALLELS

Romans 10:9

If you confess with your mouth *Jesus* as *Lord*, and believe in your heart that God raised Him from the dead, you will be saved.

Romans 12:6–8

Since we have *gifts* that differ according to the grace given to us, each of us is to exercise them accordingly: if *prophecy*, according to the proportion of his *faith*; ⁷if service, in his serving; or he who teaches, in his teaching; ⁸or he who exhorts, in his exhortation; he who gives, with liberality; he who leads, with diligence; he who shows mercy, with cheerfulness.

2 Corinthians 12:12

The signs of a true apostle were performed among you with all perseverance, by signs and wonders and *miracles*.

Galatians 1:8

But even if we, or an angel from heaven, should preach to you a gospel contrary to what we have preached to you, he is to be *accursed*!

Galatians 3:5

So then, does He who provides you with *the Spirit* and works *miracles* among you, do it by the works of the Law, or by hearing with *faith*?

Galatians 4:8

However at that time, when you did not know God, you were slaves to those which by nature are no gods.

1 Thessalonians 1:9

For they themselves report about us what kind of a reception we had with you, and how you turned to God from *idols* to serve a living and true God.

Psalm 115:4–5

Their *idols* are silver and gold, The work of man's hands. [5]They have mouths, but they cannot speak; They have eyes, but they cannot see.

Acts 2:4

And they were all filled with *the Holy Spirit* and began to speak with other *tongues*, as the Spirit was giving them utterance.

Hebrews 2:3–4

How will we escape if we neglect so great a salvation? After it was at the first spoken through the Lord, it was confirmed to us by those who heard, [4]God also testifying with them, both by signs and wonders and by various *miracles* and by *gifts* of *the Holy Spirit* according to His own will.

1 Peter 4:10–11

As *each one* has received a special *gift*, employ it in serving one another as good stewards of the manifold grace of God. [11]Whoever speaks, is to do so as one who is *speaking* the utterances of God; whoever serves is to do so as one who is serving by the strength which God supplies; so that in all things God may be glorified through Jesus Christ, to whom belongs the glory and dominion forever and ever. Amen.

1 John 4:1–3

Beloved, do not believe every spirit, but test the *spirits* to see whether they are from God, because many false prophets have gone out into the world. [2]By this you know *the Spirit of God*: every spirit that confesses that Jesus Christ has come in the flesh is from God; [3]and every spirit that does not confess Jesus is not from God; this is the spirit of the antichrist, of which you have heard that it is coming, and now it is already in the world.

1 Corinthians 12:12–21

For even as the body is one and yet has many members, and all the members of the body, though they are many, are one body, so also is Christ. [13]For by one Spirit we were all baptized into one body, whether Jews or Greeks, whether slaves or free, and we were all made to drink of one Spirit. [14]For the body is not one member, but many. [15]If the foot says, "Because I am not a hand, I am not a part of the body," it is not for this reason any the less a part of the body. [16]And if the ear says, "Because I am not an eye, I am not a part of the body," it is not for this reason any the less a part of the body. [17]If the whole body were an eye, where would the hearing be? If the whole were hearing, where would the sense of smell be? [18]But now God has placed the members, each one of them, in the body, just as He desired. [19]If they were all one member, where would the body be? [20]But now there are many members, but one body. [21]And the eye cannot say to the hand, "I have no need of you"; or again the head to the feet, "I have no need of you."

1 Corinthians 1:13

Has Christ been divided? Paul was not crucified for you, was he? Or were you *baptized* in the name of Paul?

1 Corinthians 1:23–24

But we preach Christ crucified, to Jews a stumbling block and to Gentiles foolishness, [24]but to those who are the called, both *Jews* and *Greeks*, Christ the power of God and the wisdom of God.

1 Corinthians 6:15

Do you not know that your bodies are *members* of Christ? Shall I then take away the members of Christ and make them members of a prostitute? May it never be!

1 Corinthians 7:19, 22

Circumcision is nothing, and uncircumcision is nothing, but what matters is the keeping of the commandments of God. . . . [22]For he who was called in the Lord while a *slave*, is the Lord's freedman; likewise he who was called while *free*, is Christ's slave.

1 Corinthians 10:1, 4

For I do not want you to be unaware, brethren, that our fathers were all under the cloud and all passed through the sea; . . . [4]and all drank the same spiritual *drink*, for they were drinking from a spiritual rock which followed them; and the rock was Christ.

1 Corinthians 10:16–17

Is not the cup of blessing which we bless a sharing in the blood of Christ? Is not the bread which we break a sharing in *the body* of Christ? [17]Since there is one bread, we who are *many* are *one body*; for we all partake of the one bread.

1 Corinthians 10:21

You cannot *drink* the cup of the Lord and the cup of demons; you cannot partake of the table of the Lord and the table of demons.

1 Corinthians 10:32

Give no offense either to *Jews* or to *Greeks* or to the church of God.

OTHER PAULINE PARALLELS

Romans 12:3–5

For through the grace given to me I say to everyone among you not to think more highly of himself than he ought to think; but to think so as to have sound judgment, as God has allotted to each a measure of faith. [4]For just as we have *many members* in one

body and all the members do not have the same function, [5]so we, who are many, are one body in Christ, and individually members one of another.

Galatians 3:27–28

For all of you who were *baptized* into Christ have clothed yourselves with Christ. [28]There is neither *Jew* nor *Greek*, there is neither *slave* nor *free* man, there is neither male nor female; for you are all *one* in Christ Jesus.

Ephesians 4:4–6

There is *one body* and *one Spirit*, just as also you were called in one hope of your calling; [5]one Lord, one faith, one *baptism*, [6]one God and Father of all who is over all and through all and in all.

Colossians 3:10–11, 15

. . . and have put on the new self who is being renewed to a true knowledge according to the image of the One who created him— [11]a renewal in which there is no distinction between *Greek* and *Jew*, circumcised and uncircumcised, barbarian, Scythian, *slave* and *freeman*, but Christ is all, and in all. . . . [15]Let the peace of Christ rule in your hearts, to which indeed you were called in *one body*; and be thankful.

OTHER BIBLICAL PARALLELS

Matthew 28:19

"Go therefore and make disciples of all the nations, *baptizing* them in the name of the Father and the Son and the Holy *Spirit*."

John 7:37–39

Now on the last day, the great day of the feast, Jesus stood and cried out, saying, "If anyone is thirsty, let him come to Me and *drink*. [38]He who believes in Me, as the Scripture said, 'From his innermost being will flow rivers of living water.'" [39]But this He spoke of the *Spirit*, whom those who believed in Him were to receive; for the Spirit was not yet given, because Jesus was not yet glorified.

NONCANONICAL PARALLELS

Dionysius of Halicarnassus, Roman Antiquities *6.86.1–3*

A city resembles to some extent a human body. For each of them is composite and has many *members*, no one of which has the same function or performs the same service as the others. [2]If the members of the human body, then, were to be endowed each with its own perception and voice, and a conflict were to arise among them, all of them united against the belly, then *the feet* would say that *the whole body* rests on them; the *hands* that they ply the crafts; . . . the head, that it sees and *hears*. . . . [3] . . . If indeed they did decide on this course and none of the members continued to perform its function, could the body possibly survive for any length of time?

1 Corinthians 12:22–31

On the contrary, it is much truer that the members of the body which seem to be weaker are necessary; [23]and those members of the body which we deem less honorable, on these we bestow more abundant honor, and our less presentable members become much more presentable, [24]whereas our more presentable members have no need of it. But God has so composed the body, giving more abundant honor to that member which lacked, [25]so that there may be no division in the body, but that the members may have the same care for one another. [26]And if one member suffers, all the members suffer with it; if one member is honored, all the members rejoice with it. [27]Now you are Christ's body, and individually members of it. [28]And God has appointed in the church, first apostles, second prophets, third teachers, then miracles, then gifts of healings, helps, administrations, various kinds of tongues. [29]All are not apostles, are they? All are not prophets, are they? All are not teachers, are they? All are not workers of miracles, are they? [30]All do not have gifts of healings, do they? All do not speak with tongues, do they? All do not interpret, do they? [31]But earnestly desire the greater gifts. And I show you a still more excellent way.

1 CORINTHIANS PARALLELS

1 Corinthians 1:10
Now I exhort you, brethren, by the name of our Lord Jesus Christ, that you all agree and that there be *no divisions* among you, but that you be made complete in the same mind and in the same judgment.

1 Corinthians 4:10
We are fools for Christ's sake, but you are prudent in Christ; we are *weak*, but you are strong; you are distinguished, but we are without *honor*.

1 Corinthians 6:15
Do you not know that your bodies are *members* of Christ? Shall I then take away the members of Christ and make them members of a prostitute? May it never be!

1 Corinthians 8:9–10
But take care that this liberty of yours does not somehow become a stumbling block to the *weak*. [10]For if someone sees you, who have knowledge, dining in an idol's temple, will not his conscience, if he is weak, be strengthened to eat things sacrificed to idols?

1 Corinthians 9:22
To the *weak* I became weak, that I might win the weak; I have become all things to all men, so that I may by all means save some.

1 Corinthians 10:17
Since there is one bread, we who are many are one *body*; for we all partake of the one bread.

1 Corinthians 11:18
For, in the first place, when you come together as a church, I hear that *divisions* exist among you; and in part I believe it.

1 Corinthians 12:8–10
For to one is given the word of wisdom through the Spirit, and to another the word of knowledge according to the same Spirit; [9]to another faith by the same Spirit, and to another *gifts of healing* by the one Spirit, [10]and to another the effecting of *miracles*, and to another *prophecy*, and to another the distinguishing of spirits, to another *various kinds of tongues*, and to another the *interpretation* of tongues.

1 Corinthians 14:1, 5, 12
Pursue love, yet desire earnestly spiritual *gifts*, but especially that you may *prophesy*. . . . [5]Now I wish that you all spoke in tongues, but even more that you would prophesy; and greater is one who prophesies than one who *speaks* in *tongues*, unless he *interprets*, so that the church may receive edifying. . . .

[12]So also you, since you are zealous of spiritual gifts, seek to abound for the edification of the church.

OTHER PAULINE PARALLELS

Romans 12:3–8, 10

For through the grace given to me I say to everyone among you not to think more highly of himself than he ought to think; but to think so as to have sound judgment, as God has allotted to each a measure of faith. [4]For just as we have many *members* in one *body* and all the members do not have the same function, [5]so we, who are many, are one body in Christ, and *individually members* one of another. [6]Since we have *gifts* that differ according to the grace given to us, each of us is to exercise them accordingly: if *prophecy*, according to the proportion of his faith; [7]if service, in his serving; or he who *teaches*, in his teaching; [8]or he who exhorts, in his exhortation; he who gives, with liberality; he who leads, with diligence; he who shows mercy, with cheerfulness. . . . [10]Be devoted to one another in brotherly love; give preference to one another in *honor*.

Romans 12:15–16

Rejoice with those who rejoice, and weep with those who weep. [16]Be of the same mind toward one another; do not be haughty in mind, but associate with the lowly. Do not be wise in your own estimation.

Ephesians 4:7, 11–12, 15–16

But to each one of us grace was given according to the measure of Christ's *gift*. . . . [11]And He gave some as *apostles*, and some as *prophets*, and some as evangelists, and some as pastors and *teachers*, [12]for the equipping of the saints for the work of service, to the building up of *the body* of Christ; . . .[15]but speaking the truth in love, we are to grow up in all aspects into Him who is the head, even Christ, [16]from whom the whole body, being fitted and held together by what every joint supplies, according to the proper working of each individual part, causes the growth of the body for the building up of itself in love.

Ephesians 5:28–30

He who loves his own wife loves himself; [29]for no one ever hated his own flesh, but nourishes and cherishes it, just as Christ also does the church, [30]because we are *members* of His *body*.

OTHER BIBLICAL PARALLELS

Acts 2:4

And they were all filled with the Holy Spirit and began to *speak with* other *tongues*, as the Spirit was giving them utterance.

Acts 10:45–46

All the circumcised believers who came with Peter were amazed, because the *gift* of the Holy Spirit had been poured out on the Gentiles also. [46]For they were hearing them *speaking with tongues* and exalting God.

Acts 13:1

Now there were at Antioch, in the church that was there, *prophets* and *teachers*: Barnabas, and Simeon who was called Niger, and Lucius of Cyrene, and Manaen who had been brought up with Herod the tetrarch, and Saul.

Acts 19:6

And when Paul had laid his hands upon them, the Holy Spirit came on them, and they began *speaking with tongues* and *prophesying*.

NONCANONICAL PARALLELS

Dio Chrysostom, Orations 50.3

I had mercy on the commoners . . . and did my best to ease their burdens . . . since also with *the body* we always heal the afflicted part and give more *care* to the feet than to the eyes, if the former is in pain and has been injured, while the latter are healthy.

1 Corinthians 13:1–7

If I speak with the tongues of men and of angels, but do not have love, I have become a noisy gong or a clanging cymbal. [2]If I have the gift of prophecy, and know all mysteries and all knowledge; and if I have all faith, so as to remove mountains, but do not have love, I am nothing. [3]And if I give all my possessions to feed the poor, and if I surrender my body to be burned, but do not have love, it profits me nothing. [4]Love is patient, love is kind and is not jealous; love does not brag and is not arrogant,

⁵does not act unbecomingly; it does not seek
its own, is not provoked, does not take into
account a wrong suffered, ⁶does not rejoice in
unrighteousness, but rejoices with the truth;
⁷bears all things, believes all things, hopes all
things, endures all things.

1 CORINTHIANS PARALLELS

1 Corinthians 1:4–5
I thank my God always concerning you for
the grace of God which was given you in
Christ Jesus, ⁵that in everything you were
enriched in Him, in all speech and *all
knowledge.*

1 Corinthians 2:1
And when I came to you, brethren, I did not
come with superiority of speech or of wisdom, proclaiming to you the testimony of
God.

1 Corinthians 4:1
Let a man regard us in this manner, as servants of Christ and stewards of the *mysteries* of God.

1 Corinthians 4:18–19
Now some have become *arrogant,* as though
I were not coming to you. ¹⁹But I will come
to you soon, if the Lord wills, and I shall
find out, not the words of those who are
arrogant but their power.

1 Corinthians 8:1–3
Now concerning things sacrificed to idols,
we know that we all have *knowledge.*
Knowledge makes *arrogant,* but *love* edifies.
²If anyone supposes that he knows anything,
he has not yet known as he ought to know;
³but if anyone loves God, he is known by
Him.

1 Corinthians 9:11–12
If we sowed spiritual things in you, is it too
much if we reap material things from you?
¹²If others share the right over you, do we
not more? Nevertheless, we did not use this
right, but we *endure all things* so that we
will cause no hindrance to the gospel of
Christ.

1 Corinthians 10:24
Let no one *seek* his *own good,* but that of his
neighbor.

1 Corinthians 12:8–10
For to one is given the word of wisdom
through the Spirit, and to another the word
of *knowledge* according to the same Spirit;
⁹to another *faith* by the same Spirit, and to
another *gifts* of healing by the one Spirit,
¹⁰and to another the effecting of miracles,
and to another *prophecy,* and to another the
distinguishing of spirits, to another various
kinds of *tongues,* and to another the interpretation of tongues.

1 Corinthians 14:1–2, 39–40
Pursue *love,* yet desire earnestly spiritual
gifts, but especially that you may *prophesy.*
²For one who *speaks* in a *tongue* does not
speak to men but to God; for no one understands, but in his spirit he speaks *mysteries.*
. . . ³⁹Therefore, my brethren, desire
earnestly to prophesy, and do not forbid to
speak in tongues. ⁴⁰But all things must be
done properly and in an orderly manner.

OTHER PAULINE PARALLELS

Romans 12:9–16
Let *love* be without hypocrisy. Abhor what is
evil; cling to what is good. ¹⁰Be devoted to
one another in brotherly love; give preference to one another in honor; ¹¹not lagging
behind in diligence, fervent in spirit, serving
the Lord; ¹²rejoicing in *hope,* persevering in
tribulation, devoted to prayer, ¹³contributing
to the needs of the saints, practicing hospitality. ¹⁴Bless those who persecute you; bless
and do not curse. ¹⁵*Rejoice* with those who
rejoice, and weep with those who weep.
¹⁶Be of the same mind toward one another;
do not be haughty in mind, but associate
with the lowly. Do not be wise in your own
estimation.

Ephesians 4:1–2
Therefore I, the prisoner of the Lord, implore
you to walk in a manner worthy of the calling with which you have been called, ²with
all humility and gentleness, with *patience,*
showing tolerance for one another in *love.*

Philippians 2:3–4
Do nothing from selfishness or empty conceit, but with humility of mind regard one
another as more important than yourselves;
⁴do not merely look out for your own per-
sonal interests, but also for the interests of
others.

Psalm 150:5

Praise Him with loud *cymbals*; Praise Him with resounding cymbals.

Proverbs 10:12

Hatred stirs up strife, But *love* covers all transgressions.

Daniel 3:26, 28

Then Shadrach, Meshach and Abed-nego came out of the midst of the fire. . . . ²⁸Nebuchadnezzar responded and said, "Blessed be the God of Shadrach, Meshach and Abed-nego, who has sent His angel and delivered His servants who put their trust in Him, violating the king's command, and yielded up their *bodies* so as not to serve or worship any god except their own God."

Matthew 17:20

"Because of the littleness of your faith; for truly I say to you, if you have *faith* the size of a mustard seed, you will say to this *mountain*, 'Move from here to there,' and it will *move*; and nothing will be impossible to you."

Matthew 19:21

"If you wish to be complete, go and sell your *possessions* and give *to the poor*, and you will have treasure in heaven; and come, follow Me."

1 Peter 1:22

Since you have in obedience to *the truth* purified your souls for a sincere *love* of the brethren, fervently love one another from the heart.

Wisdom of Solomon 3:1, 4, 9

But the souls of the righteous are in the hand of God, and no torment will ever touch them. . . . ⁴For though in the sight of others they were punished, their *hope* is full of immortality. . . . ⁹Those who trust in him will understand *truth*, and the faithful will abide with him in *love*, because grace and mercy are upon his holy ones, and he watches over his elect.

Testament of Job 48:1–3

Thus, when the one called Hemera arose, she wrapped around her own string just as her father said. ²And she took on another heart—no longer minded toward earthly things—³but she spoke ecstatically in the angelic dialect, sending up a hymn to God in accord with the hymnic style of the *angels*.

1 Corinthians 13:8–13

Love never fails; but if there are gifts of prophecy, they will be done away; if there are tongues, they will cease; if there is knowledge, it will be done away. ⁹For we know in part and we prophesy in part; ¹⁰but when the perfect comes, the partial will be done away. ¹¹When I was a child, I used to speak like a child, think like a child, reason like a child; when I became a man, I did away with childish things. ¹²For now we see in a mirror dimly, but then face to face; now I know in part, but then I will know fully just as I also have been fully known. ¹³But now faith, hope, love, abide these three; but the greatest of these is love.

1 Corinthians 1:4–5, 7–8

I thank my God always concerning you for the grace of God which was given you in Christ Jesus, ⁵that in everything you were enriched in Him, in all speech and all *knowledge* . . . ⁷so that you are not lacking in any *gift*, awaiting eagerly the revelation of our Lord Jesus Christ, ⁸who will also confirm you to the end, blameless in the day of our Lord Jesus Christ.

1 Corinthians 3:1–3

And I, brethren, could not speak to you as to spiritual men, but as to men of flesh, as to infants in Christ. ²I gave you milk to drink, not solid food; for you were not yet able to receive it. Indeed, even now you are not yet able, ³for you are still fleshly. For since there is jealousy and strife among you, are you not fleshly, and are you not walking like mere men?

1 Corinthians 4:5

Therefore do not go on passing judgment before the time, but wait until the Lord comes who will both bring to light the things hidden in the darkness and disclose the motives of men's hearts; and then each man's praise will come to him from God.

1 Corinthians 8:1–3

Now concerning things sacrificed to idols, we know that we all have *knowledge*. Knowledge makes arrogant, but *love* edifies. [2]If anyone supposes that he *knows* anything, he has not yet known as he ought to know; [3]but if anyone loves God, he is *known* by Him.

1 Corinthians 12:8–10

For to one is given the word of wisdom through the Spirit, and to another the word of *knowledge* according to the same Spirit; [9]to another *faith* by the same Spirit, and to another *gifts* of healing by the one Spirit, [10]and to another the effecting of miracles, and to another *prophecy*, and to another the distinguishing of spirits, to another various kinds of *tongues*, and to another the interpretation of tongues.

1 Corinthians 14:20

Brethren, do not be *children* in your *thinking*; yet in evil be infants, but in your thinking be mature.

1 Corinthians 14:39–40

Therefore, my brethren, desire earnestly to *prophesy*, and do not forbid to speak in *tongues*. [40]But all things must be done properly and in an orderly manner.

OTHER PAULINE PARALLELS

Romans 8:38–39

For I am convinced that neither death, nor life, nor angels, nor principalities, nor things present, nor things to come, nor powers, [39]nor height, nor depth, nor any other created thing, will be able to separate us from the *love* of God, which is in Christ Jesus our Lord.

2 Corinthians 5:6–7

Therefore, being always of good courage, and knowing that while we are at home in the body we are absent from the Lord— [7]for we walk by *faith*, not by sight.

Galatians 5:5–6

For we through the Spirit, by *faith*, are waiting for the *hope* of righteousness. [6]For in Christ Jesus neither circumcision nor uncir-

cumcision means anything, but faith working through *love*.

Colossians 1:3–5

We give thanks to God, the Father of our Lord Jesus Christ, praying always for you, [4]since we heard of your *faith* in Christ Jesus and the *love* which you have for all the saints; [5]because of the *hope* laid up for you in heaven, of which you previously heard in the word of truth, the gospel.

1 Thessalonians 1:2–3

We give thanks to God always for all of you, making mention of you in our prayers; [3]constantly bearing in mind your work of *faith* and labor of *love* and steadfastness of *hope* in our Lord Jesus Christ in the presence of our God and Father.

1 Thessalonians 5:8

But since we are of the day, let us be sober, having put on the breastplate of *faith* and *love*, and as a helmet, the *hope* of salvation.

OTHER BIBLICAL PARALLELS

Numbers 12:7–8

"Not so, with My servant Moses, He is faithful in all My household; [8]With him I speak mouth to mouth, Even openly, and not in dark sayings, And he beholds the form of the LORD. Why then were you not afraid To speak against My servant, against Moses?"

Hebrews 10:22–24

Let us draw near with a sincere heart in full assurance of *faith*, having our hearts sprinkled clean from an evil conscience and our bodies washed with pure water. [23]Let us hold fast the confession of our *hope* without wavering, for He who promised is faithful; [24]and let us consider how to stimulate one another to *love* and good deeds.

James 1:23–24

For if anyone is a hearer of the word and not a doer, he is like a man who looks at his natural face *in a mirror*; [24]for once he has looked at himself and gone away, he has immediately forgotten what kind of person he was.

1 John 3:2

Beloved, now we are *children* of God, and it has not appeared as yet what we will be. We know that when He appears, we will be like Him, because *we* will *see* Him just as He is.

1 Corinthians 14:1–12

Pursue love, yet desire earnestly spiritual gifts, but especially that you may prophesy. [2]For one who speaks in a tongue does not speak to men but to God; for no one understands, but in his spirit he speaks mysteries. [3]But one who prophesies speaks to men for edification and exhortation and consolation. [4]One who speaks in a tongue edifies himself; but one who prophesies edifies the church. [5]Now I wish that you all spoke in tongues, but even more that you would prophesy; and greater is one who prophesies than one who speaks in tongues, unless he interprets, so that the church may receive edifying. [6]But now, brethren, if I come to you speaking in tongues, what will I profit you unless I speak to you either by way of revelation or of knowledge or of prophecy or of teaching? [7]Yet even lifeless things, either flute or harp, in producing a sound, if they do not produce a distinction in the tones, how will it be known what is played on the flute or on the harp? [8]For if the bugle produces an indistinct sound, who will prepare himself for battle? [9]So also you, unless you utter by the tongue speech that is clear, how will it be known what is spoken? For you will be speaking into the air. [10]There are, perhaps, a great many kinds of languages in the world, and no kind is without meaning. [11]If then I do not know the meaning of the language, I will be to the one who speaks a barbarian, and the one who speaks will be a barbarian to me. [12]So also you, since you are zealous of spiritual gifts, seek to abound for the edification of the church.

1 CORINTHIANS PARALLELS

1 Corinthians 1:4–5
I thank my God always concerning you for the grace of God which was given you in Christ Jesus, [5]that in everything you were enriched in Him, in all speech and all *knowledge.*

1 Corinthians 2:1
And when I came to you, brethren, I did not come with superiority of speech or of wisdom, proclaiming to you the testimony of God.

1 Corinthians 4:1
Let a man regard us in this manner, as servants of Christ and stewards of the *mysteries* of God.

1 Corinthians 11:4–5
Every man who has something on his head while praying or *prophesying* disgraces his head. [5]But every woman who has her head uncovered while praying or prophesying disgraces her head, for she is one and the same as the woman whose head is shaved.

1 Corinthians 12:1, 8–10
Now concerning *spiritual gifts,* brethren, I do not want you to be unaware. . . . [8]For to one is given the word of wisdom through the Spirit, and to another the word of *knowledge* according to the same Spirit; [9]to another faith by the same Spirit, and to another gifts of healing by the one Spirit, [10]and to another the effecting of miracles, and to another *prophecy,* and to another the distinguishing of spirits, to another various kinds of *tongues,* and to another the *interpretation* of tongues.

1 Corinthians 12:28–13:2
And God has appointed in the church, first apostles, second prophets, third *teachers,* then miracles, then gifts of healings, helps, administrations, various kinds of tongues. [29]All are not apostles, are they? All are not prophets, are they? All are not teachers, are they? All are not workers of miracles, are they? [30]All do not have gifts of healings, do they? All do not *speak* with *tongues,* do they? All do not *interpret,* do they? [31]But earnestly desire the greater *gifts.* And I show you a still more excellent way. [13:1]If I speak with the tongues of men and of angels, but do not have *love,* I have become a noisy gong or a clanging cymbal. [2]If I have the gift of *prophecy,* and know all *mysteries* and all *knowledge;* and if I have all faith, so as to remove mountains, but do not have love, I am nothing.

1 Corinthians 14:26–27, 31, 39
What is the outcome then, brethren? When you assemble, each one has a psalm, has a *teaching,* has a *revelation,* has a tongue, has an *interpretation.* Let all things be done for *edification.* [27]If anyone *speaks in a tongue,* it should be by two or at the most three, and each in turn, and one must interpret; . . .

³¹For you can all *prophesy* one by one, so that all may learn and all may be *exhorted*; . . . ³⁹Therefore, my brethren, *desire earnestly* to prophesy, and do not forbid to speak in tongues.

OTHER PAULINE PARALLELS

Romans 15:1–2

Now we who are strong ought to bear the weaknesses of those without strength and not just please ourselves. ²Each of us is to please his neighbor for his good, to his *edification*.

Ephesians 4:29

Let no unwholesome word proceed from your mouth, but only such a word as is good for *edification* according to the need of the moment, so that it will give grace to those who hear.

1 Timothy 4:12–14

Let no one look down on your youthfulness, but rather in speech, conduct, *love*, faith and purity, show yourself an example of those who believe. ¹³Until I come, give attention to the public reading of Scripture, to *exhortation* and *teaching*. ¹⁴Do not neglect the *spiritual gift* within you, which was bestowed on you through *prophetic* utterance with the laying on of hands by the presbytery.

OTHER BIBLICAL PARALLELS

Numbers 10:9

"When you go to war in your land against the adversary who attacks you, then you shall sound an alarm with the trumpets, that you may be remembered before the LORD your God, and be saved from your enemies."

Numbers 11:29

But Moses said to him, "Are you jealous for my sake? Would that all the LORD's people were *prophets*, that the LORD would put His Spirit upon them!"

Mark 16:17

These signs will accompany those who have believed: in My name they will cast out demons, they will *speak* with new *tongues*.

Acts 19:5–6

When they heard this, they were baptized in the name of the Lord Jesus. ⁶And when Paul had laid his hands upon them, the Holy Spirit came on them, and they began *speaking* with *tongues* and *prophesying*.

NONCANONICAL PARALLELS

Plutarch, On the Obsolescence of Oracles *412A*

The oracular *prophet* there [at Mys], who had previously used the Aeolic dialect, on that occasion sided with the *barbarians* and uttered an oracle that no one present could *understand* except for the prophet himself.

1 Corinthians 14:13–19

Therefore let one who speaks in a tongue pray that he may interpret. ¹⁴For if I pray in a tongue, my spirit prays, but my mind is unfruitful. ¹⁵What is the outcome then? I will pray with the spirit and I will pray with the mind also; I will sing with the spirit and I will sing with the mind also. ¹⁶Otherwise if you bless in the spirit only, how will the one who fills the place of the ungifted say the "Amen" at your giving of thanks, since he does not know what you are saying? ¹⁷For you are giving thanks well enough, but the other person is not edified. ¹⁸I thank God, I speak in tongues more than you all; ¹⁹however, in the church I desire to speak five words with my mind so that I may instruct others also, rather than ten thousand words in a tongue.

1 CORINTHIANS PARALLELS

1 Corinthians 1:14

I thank God that I baptized none of you except Crispus and Gaius.

1 Corinthians 10:16

Is not the cup of blessing which we *bless* a sharing in the blood of Christ? Is not the bread which we break a sharing in the body of Christ?

1 Corinthians 10:30

If I partake with thankfulness, why am I slandered concerning that for which I *give thanks*?

1 Corinthians 12:7–10

But to each one is given the manifestation of the Spirit for the common good. [8]For to one is given the word of wisdom through the Spirit, and to another the word of knowledge according to the same Spirit; [9]to another faith by the same Spirit, and to another gifts of healing by the one Spirit, [10]and to another the effecting of miracles, and to another prophecy, and to another the distinguishing of spirits, to another various kinds of *tongues*, and to another the *interpretation* of tongues.

1 Corinthians 12:30

All do not have gifts of healings, do they? All do not *speak* with *tongues*, do they? All do not *interpret*, do they?

OTHER PAULINE PARALLELS

Romans 8:26

In the same way the Spirit also helps our weakness; for we do not know how to *pray* as we should, but the Spirit Himself intercedes for us with groanings too deep for words.

Ephesians 5:18–20

And do not get drunk with wine, for that is dissipation, but be filled with the Spirit, [19]speaking to one another in psalms and hymns and spiritual songs, *singing* and making melody with your heart to the Lord; [20]always *giving thanks* for all things in the name of our Lord Jesus Christ to God, even the Father.

OTHER BIBLICAL PARALLELS

Psalm 106:48

Blessed be the LORD, the God of Israel, From everlasting even to everlasting. And let all the people *say, "Amen."* Praise the LORD!

James 5:13

Is anyone among you suffering? Then he must *pray*. Is anyone cheerful? He is to *sing* praises.

Revelation 5:13–14

And every created thing which is in heaven and on the earth and under the earth and on the sea, and all things in them, I heard saying, "To Him who sits on the throne, and to the Lamb, be *blessing* and honor and glory and dominion forever and ever." [14]And the four living creatures kept *saying, "Amen."*

NONCANONICAL PARALLELS

Philo, Who Is the Heir of Divine Things? *265*

This is what usually happens to those of the prophetic office. *The mind* is evicted when *the* divine *spirit* arrives, but when it departs the mind returns to its tenancy. Mortal and immortal may not dwell together. Therefore the twilight of reason and the darkness that surrounds it produce ecstasy and inspired frenzy.

1 Corinthians 14:20–25

Brethren, do not be children in your thinking; yet in evil be infants, but in your thinking be mature. [21]In the Law it is written, "BY MEN OF STRANGE TONGUES AND BY THE LIPS OF STRANGERS I WILL SPEAK TO THIS PEOPLE, AND EVEN SO THEY WILL NOT LISTEN TO ME," says the Lord. [22]So then tongues are for a sign, not to those who believe but to unbelievers; but prophecy is for a sign, not to unbelievers but to those who believe. [23]Therefore if the whole church assembles together and all speak in tongues, and ungifted men or unbelievers enter, will they not say that you are mad? [24]But if all prophesy, and an unbeliever or an ungifted man enters, he is convicted by all, he is called to account by all; [25]the secrets of his heart are disclosed; and so he will fall on his face and worship God, declaring that God is certainly among you.

1 CORINTHIANS PARALLELS

1 Corinthians 2:6

Yet we do speak wisdom among those who are *mature*; a wisdom, however, not of this age nor of the rulers of this age, who are passing away.

1 Corinthians 3:1–3

· And I, brethren, could not speak to you as to spiritual men, but as to men of flesh, as to *infants* in Christ. [2]I gave you milk to drink, not solid food; for you were not yet able to receive it. Indeed, even now you are not yet able, [3]for you are still fleshly. For since there is jealousy and strife among you, are you not fleshly, and are you not walking like mere men?

1 Corinthians 4:5

Therefore do not go on passing judgment before the time, but wait until the Lord comes who will both bring to light the things hidden in the darkness and *disclose* the motives of men's *hearts*; and then each man's praise will come to him from God.

1 Corinthians 7:12–13

But to the rest I say, not the Lord, that if any brother has a wife who is an *unbeliever*, and she consents to live with him, he must not divorce her. [13]And a woman who has an unbelieving husband, and he consents to live with her, she must not send her husband away.

1 Corinthians 10:27

If one of the *unbelievers* invites you and you want to go, eat anything that is set before you without asking questions for conscience' sake.

1 Corinthians 11:20–21

Therefore when you meet *together*, it is not to eat the Lord's Supper, [21]for in your eating each one takes his own supper first; and one is hungry and another is drunk.

1 Corinthians 12:7–10

But to each one is given the manifestation of the Spirit for the common good. [8]For to one is given the word of wisdom through the Spirit, and to another the word of knowledge according to the same Spirit; [9]to another faith by the same Spirit, and to another gifts of healing by the one Spirit, [10]and to another the effecting of miracles, and to another *prophecy*, and to another the distinguishing of spirits, to another various kinds of *tongues*, and to another the interpretation of tongues.

1 Corinthians 13:11

When I was a child, I used to speak like a child, *think* like a *child*, reason like a child; when I became a man, I did away with childish things.

1 Corinthians 14:1, 4–5

Pursue love, yet desire earnestly spiritual gifts, but especially that you may *prophesy*. . . . [4]One who speaks in a tongue edifies himself; but one who prophesies edifies the church. [5]Now I wish that you all spoke in tongues, but even more that you would prophesy; and greater is one who prophesies than one who *speaks in tongues*, unless he interprets, so that the church may receive edifying.

OTHER PAULINE PARALLELS

Romans 16:19

For the report of your obedience has reached to all; therefore I am rejoicing over you, but I want you to be wise in what is good and innocent *in* what is *evil*.

2 Corinthians 12:12

The *signs* of a true apostle were performed among you with all perseverance, by signs and wonders and miracles.

Ephesians 4:14

As a result, we are no longer to be *children*, tossed here and there by waves and carried about by every wind of doctrine, by the trickery of men, by craftiness in deceitful scheming.

OTHER BIBLICAL PARALLELS

1 Kings 18:39

When all the people saw it, they *fell on* their *faces*; and they said, "The LORD, He is God; the LORD, He is God."

Isaiah 28:11–12

Indeed, He *will speak to this people* Through stammering *lips* and a foreign *tongue*, [12]He who said to them, "Here is rest, give rest to the weary," And, "Here is repose," but *they* would *not listen*.

Isaiah 45:14

"The products of Egypt and the merchandise of Cush And the Sabeans, men of stature, Will come over to you and will be yours; They will walk behind you, they will come over in chains And will bow down to you; They will make supplication to you: 'Surely, *God is* with *you*, and there is none else, No other God.'"

Zechariah 8:23

"In those days ten men from all the nations will grasp the garment of a Jew, saying, 'Let us go with you, for we have heard that *God is* with *you.*'"

Acts 2:3–4, 13

And there appeared to them tongues as of fire distributing themselves, and they rested on each one of them. [4]And they were all filled with the Holy Spirit and began to *speak* with other *tongues*, as the Spirit was giving them utterance. . . . [13]But others were mocking and saying, "They are full of sweet wine."

Acts 15:12

All the people kept silent, and they were listening to Barnabas and Paul as they were relating what *signs* and wonders God had done through them among the Gentiles.

Revelation 7:11

And all the angels were standing around the throne and around the elders and the four living creatures; and they *fell on* their *faces* before the throne and *worshiped God.*

1 Corinthians 14:26–33

What is the outcome then, brethren? When you assemble, each one has a psalm, has a teaching, has a revelation, has a tongue, has an interpretation. Let all things be done for edification. [27]If anyone speaks in a tongue, it should be by two or at the most three, and each in turn, and one must interpret; [28]but if there is no interpreter, he must keep silent in the church; and let him speak to himself and to God. [29]Let two or three prophets speak, and let the others pass judgment. [30]But if a revelation is made to another who is seated, the first one must keep silent. [31]For you can all prophesy one by one, so that all may learn and all may be exhorted; [32]and the spirits of prophets are subject to prophets; [33]for God is not a God of confusion but of peace, as in all the churches of the saints.

1 CORINTHIANS PARALLELS

1 Corinthians 10:23

All things are lawful, but not all things are profitable. All things are lawful, but not all things *edify.*

1 Corinthians 11:18

For, in the first place, when you come together as a *church,* I hear that divisions exist among you; and in part I believe it.

1 Corinthians 12:7–10

But to each one is given the manifestation of the Spirit for the common good. [8]For to one is given the word of wisdom through the Spirit, and to another the word of knowledge according to the same Spirit; [9]to another faith by the same Spirit, and to another gifts of healing by the one Spirit, [10]and to another the effecting of miracles, and to another *prophecy,* and to another the distinguishing of spirits, to another various kinds of *tongues,* and to another the *interpretation* of tongues.

1 Corinthians 12:28–29

And God has appointed *in the church,* first apostles, second *prophets,* third *teachers,* then miracles, then gifts of healings, helps, administrations, various kinds of *tongues.* [29]All are not apostles, are they? All are not prophets, are they? All are not teachers, are they? All are not workers of miracles, are they?

1 Corinthians 13:1–2

If I *speak* with the *tongues* of men and of angels, but do not have love, I have become a noisy gong or a clanging cymbal. [2]If I have the gift of *prophecy,* and know all mysteries and all knowledge; and if I have all faith, so as to remove mountains, but do not have love, I am nothing.

1 Corinthians 14:1–6

Pursue love, yet desire earnestly spiritual gifts, but especially that you may *prophesy.* [2]For one who *speaks in a tongue* does not speak to men but to God; for no one understands, but in his *spirit* he speaks mysteries. [3]But one who prophesies speaks to men for *edification* and *exhortation* and consolation. [4]One who speaks in a tongue edifies himself; but one who prophesies edifies the church. [5]Now I wish that you all spoke in tongues, but even more that you would prophesy; and greater is one who prophesies than one who speaks in tongues, unless he *interprets,* so that *the church* may receive edifying. [6]But now, brethren, if I come to you speaking in tongues, what will I profit you unless I speak to you either by way of *revelation* or of knowledge or of prophecy or of *teaching*?

OTHER PAULINE PARALLELS

Romans 14:19

So then we pursue the things which make for *peace* and the building up of one another.

2 Corinthians 13:11

Finally, brethren, rejoice, be made complete, be comforted, be like-minded, live in peace; and the *God of* love and *peace* will be with you.

Ephesians 4:11–13

And He gave some as apostles, and some as *prophets*, and some as evangelists, and some as pastors and *teachers*, [12]for the equipping of the saints for the work of service, to the building up of the body of Christ; [13]until we all attain to the unity of the faith, and of the knowledge of the Son of God, to a mature man, to the measure of the stature which belongs to the fullness of Christ.

Ephesians 5:18–19

And do not get drunk with wine, for that is dissipation, but be filled with the Spirit, [19]speaking to one another in *psalms* and hymns and spiritual songs, singing and making melody with your heart to the Lord.

Colossians 3:16

Let the word of Christ richly dwell within you, with all wisdom *teaching* and admonishing one another with *psalms* and hymns and spiritual songs, singing with thankfulness in your hearts to God.

1 Thessalonians 5:19–23

Do not quench the Spirit; [20]do not despise *prophetic* utterances. [21]But examine everything carefully; hold fast to that which is good; [22]abstain from every form of evil. [23]Now may the *God of peace* Himself sanctify you entirely; and may your spirit and soul and body be preserved complete, without blame at the coming of our Lord Jesus Christ.

OTHER BIBLICAL PARALLELS

Revelation 22:6

And he said to me, "These words are faithful and true"; and the Lord, the God of *the spirits of* the *prophets*, sent His angel to show to His bond-servants the things which must soon take place.

NONCANONICAL PARALLELS

The Rule of the Community *(1QS) 6.8–10*

This is the Rule for the session of the Many. Each one by his rank: the priests will sit down first, the elders next and the remainder of [9]all the people will sit down in order of rank. And following the same system they shall be questioned with regard to the *judgment* . . . so that each one can impart his wisdom [10]to the council. . . . No one should talk during the speech of his fellow brother before his brother has finished *speaking.*

Philo, Life of Moses *2.188*

Of the oracles, some are spoken from the very person of God through an *interpreter*, the divine *prophet*, others are declared through question and answer, and others are spoken from the person of Moses himself when inspired by God and carried outside himself.

1 Corinthians 14:34–40

The women are to keep silent in the churches; for they are not permitted to speak, but are to subject themselves, just as the Law also says. [35]If they desire to learn anything, let them ask their own husbands at home; for it is improper for a woman to speak in church. [36]Was it from you that the word of God first went forth? Or has it come to you only? [37]If anyone thinks he is a prophet or spiritual, let him recognize that the things which I write to you are the Lord's commandment. [38]But if anyone does not recognize this, he is not recognized. [39]Therefore, my brethren, desire earnestly to prophesy, and do not forbid to speak in tongues. [40]But all things must be done properly and in an orderly manner.

1 CORINTHIANS PARALLELS

1 Corinthians 2:14–15

But a natural man does not accept the things of the Spirit of God, for they are foolishness to him; and he cannot understand them, because they are spiritually appraised. [15]But he who is *spiritual* appraises all things, yet he himself is appraised by no one.

1 Corinthians 3:18

Let no man deceive himself. *If any* man among you *thinks* that *he is* wise in this age, he must become foolish, so that he may become wise.

1 Corinthians 7:4, 10, 17

The wife does not have authority over her own body, but the *husband* does; and likewise also the husband does not have authority over his own body, but the wife does. . . . [10]But to the married I give instructions, not I, but the Lord, that the wife should not leave her husband. . . .[17]Only, as the Lord has assigned to each one, as God has called each, in this manner let him walk. And so I direct *in* all *the churches.*

1 Corinthians 11:5, 7–11, 16

But every *woman* who has her head uncovered while praying or *prophesying* disgraces her head, for she is one and the same as the woman whose head is shaved. . . . [7]For a man ought not to have his head covered, since he is the image and glory of God; but the woman is the glory of man. [8]For man does not originate from woman, but woman from man; [9]for indeed man was not created for the woman's sake, but woman for the man's sake. [10]Therefore the woman ought to have a symbol of authority on her head, because of the angels. [11]However, in the Lord, neither is woman independent of man, nor is man independent of woman. . . . [16]But if one is inclined to be contentious, we have no other practice, nor have *the churches* of God.

1 Corinthians 12:28

And God has appointed in the church, first apostles, second *prophets*, third teachers, then miracles, then gifts of healings, helps, administrations, various kinds of *tongues.*

1 Corinthians 14:5–6

Now I wish that you all *spoke in tongues*, but even more that you would *prophesy*; and greater is one who prophesies than one who speaks in tongues, unless he interprets, so that the church may receive edifying. [6]But now, brethren, if I come to you speaking in tongues, what will I profit you unless I speak to you either by way of revelation or of knowledge or of prophecy or of teaching?

OTHER PAULINE PARALLELS

Galatians 6:3

For *if anyone thinks he is* something when he is nothing, he deceives himself.

Ephesians 5:22, 24

Wives, be *subject* to your *own husbands*, as to the Lord. . . . [24]But as the church is subject to Christ, so also the wives ought to be to their husbands in everything.

Colossians 3:18

Wives, be *subject* to your *husbands*, as is fitting in the Lord.

1 Timothy 2:11–12

A *woman* must quietly receive instruction with entire submissiveness. [12]But I do not allow a woman to teach or exercise authority over a man, but to remain quiet.

Titus 2:3–5

Older *women* likewise are to be reverent in their behavior, not malicious gossips nor enslaved to much wine, teaching what is good, [4]so that they may encourage the young women to love their husbands, to love their children, [5]to be sensible, pure, workers at home, kind, being *subject* to their *own husbands*, so that the word of God will not be dishonored.

OTHER BIBLICAL PARALLELS

Genesis 3:16

To the *woman* He said, "I will greatly multiply Your pain in childbirth, In pain you will bring forth children; Yet your desire will be for your *husband*, And he will rule over you."

Judges 4:4

Now Deborah, a *prophetess*, the wife of Lappidoth, was judging Israel at that time.

Luke 2:36

And there was a *prophetess*, Anna the daughter of Phanuel, of the tribe of Asher. She was advanced in years and had lived with her *husband* seven years after her marriage.

Acts 21:8–9

On the next day we left and came to Caesarea, and entering the house of Philip the evangelist, who was one of the seven, we stayed with him. [9]Now this man had four virgin daughters who were *prophetesses*.

1 Peter 3:1
In the same way, you wives, be submissive to your *own husbands* so that even if any of them are disobedient to the word, they may be won without a word by the behavior of their wives.

Revelation 2:18, 20
"And to the angel of the church in Thyatira write: '. . . [20]But I have this against you, that you tolerate the woman Jezebel, who calls herself a *prophetess*, and she teaches and leads My bond-servants astray so that they commit acts of immorality and eat things sacrificed to idols.'"

NONCANONICAL PARALLELS

Plutarch, Advice to Bride and Groom *142D*
For a woman must *speak* either to her *husband* or through her husband, without being annoyed if, like a flute player, she makes a finer sound with someone else's tongue.

1 Corinthians 15:1–11

Now I make known to you, brethren, the gospel which I preached to you, which also you received, in which also you stand, [2]by which also you are saved, if you hold fast the word which I preached to you, unless you believed in vain. [3]For I delivered to you as of first importance what I also received, that Christ died for our sins according to the Scriptures, [4]and that He was buried, and that He was raised on the third day according to the Scriptures, [5]and that He appeared to Cephas, then to the twelve. [6]After that He appeared to more than five hundred brethren at one time, most of whom remain until now, but some have fallen asleep; [7]then He appeared to James, then to all the apostles; [8]and last of all, as to one untimely born, He appeared to me also. [9]For I am the least of the apostles, and not fit to be called an apostle, because I persecuted the church of God. [10]But by the grace of God I am what I am, and His grace toward me did not prove vain; but I labored even more than all of them, yet not I, but the grace of God with me. [11]Whether then it was I or they, so we preach and so you believed.

1 CORINTHIANS PARALLELS

1 Corinthians 1:12
Now I mean this, that each one of you is saying, "I am of Paul," and "I of Apollos," and "I of *Cephas*," and "I of Christ."

1 Corinthians 1:21
For since in the wisdom of God the world through its wisdom did not come to know God, God was well-pleased through the foolishness of the message *preached* to *save* those who *believe*.

1 Corinthians 9:1
Am I not free? Am I not an *apostle*? Have I not seen Jesus our Lord? Are you not my work in the Lord?

1 Corinthians 11:23
For *I received* from the Lord that which *I* also *delivered to you*, that the Lord Jesus in the night in which He was betrayed took bread.

OTHER PAULINE PARALLELS

Romans 5:8
But God demonstrates His own love toward us, in that while we were yet *sinners, Christ died* for us.

Romans 6:4–5
Therefore we have been *buried* with Him through baptism into death, so that as Christ was *raised* from the dead through the glory of the Father, so we too might walk in newness of life. [5]For if we have become united with Him in the likeness of His death, certainly we shall also be in the likeness of His resurrection.

Galatians 1:3–4
Grace to you and peace from God our Father and the Lord Jesus Christ, [4]who gave Himself *for our sins* so that He might rescue us from this present evil age, according to the will of our God and Father.

Galatians 1:13, 15–16, 18–19
For you have heard of my former manner of life in Judaism, how I used to *persecute the church of God* beyond measure and tried to destroy it; . . .[15]But when God, who had set me apart even from my mother's womb and called me through *His grace*, was pleased

¹⁶to reveal His Son in me so that I might *preach* Him among the Gentiles, I did not immediately consult with flesh and blood. . . . ¹⁸Then three years later I went up to Jerusalem to become acquainted with *Cephas*, and stayed with him fifteen days. ¹⁹But I did not see any other of *the apostles* except *James*, the Lord's brother.

Ephesians 3:8

To me, *the* very *least* of all saints, this *grace* was given, to *preach* to the Gentiles the unfathomable riches of Christ.

Philippians 3:4, 6

If anyone else has a mind to put confidence in the flesh, I far more; . . . ⁶as to zeal, a *persecutor* of *the church*; as to the righteousness which is in the Law, found blameless.

1 Thessalonians 2:13

For this reason we also constantly thank God that when you received *the word* of God which you heard from us, you accepted it not as the word of men, but for what it really is, the word of God, which also performs its work in you who *believe*.

1 Timothy 1:13–14

I was formerly a blasphemer and a *persecutor* and a violent aggressor. Yet I was shown mercy because I acted ignorantly in unbelief; ¹⁴and the *grace* of our Lord was more than abundant, with the faith and love which are found in Christ Jesus.

OTHER BIBLICAL PARALLELS

Isaiah 53:5

But He was pierced through for our transgressions, He was crushed for our iniquities; The chastening for our well-being fell upon Him, And by His scourging we are healed.

Hosea 6:2

"He will revive us after two days; He will *raise* us up *on the third day*, That we may live before Him."

Matthew 16:21

From that time Jesus began to show His disciples that He must go to Jerusalem, and suffer many things from the elders and chief priests and scribes, and be killed, and be *raised* up *on the third day*.

Luke 24:33–34, 36

And they got up that very hour and returned to Jerusalem, and found gathered together the eleven and those who were with them, ³⁴saying, "The Lord has really risen and has *appeared* to Simon." . . .³⁶While they were telling these things, He Himself stood in their midst and said to them, "Peace be to you."

Acts 1:1–3

The first account I composed, Theophilus, about all that Jesus began to do and teach, ²until the day when He was taken up to heaven, after He had by the Holy Spirit given orders to *the apostles* whom He had chosen. ³To these He also presented Himself alive after His suffering, by many convincing proofs, *appearing* to them over a period of forty days and speaking of the things concerning the kingdom of God.

Acts 9:3–5

As he was traveling, it happened that he was approaching Damascus, and suddenly a light from heaven flashed around him; ⁴and he fell to the ground and heard a voice saying to him, "Saul, Saul, why are you *persecuting* Me?" ⁵And he said, "Who are You, Lord?" And He said, "I am Jesus whom you are persecuting."

Acts 10:40–41

"God *raised* Him up *on the third day* and granted that He become visible, ⁴¹not to all the people, but to witnesses who were chosen beforehand by God, that is, to us who ate and drank with Him after He arose from the dead."

Acts 26:22–23

"So, having obtained help from God, I stand to this day testifying both to small and great, stating nothing but what the Prophets and Moses said was going to take place; ²³that the Christ was to suffer, and that by reason of His resurrection from the dead He would be the first to proclaim light both to the Jewish people and to the Gentiles."

1 Corinthians 15:12–19

Now if Christ is preached, that He has been raised from the dead, how do some among you say that there is no resurrection of the dead?

¹³But if there is no resurrection of the dead, not even Christ has been raised; ¹⁴and if Christ has not been raised, then our preaching is vain, your faith also is vain. ¹⁵Moreover we are even found to be false witnesses of God, because we testified against God that He raised Christ, whom He did not raise, if in fact the dead are not raised. ¹⁶For if the dead are not raised, not even Christ has been raised; ¹⁷and if Christ has not been raised, your faith is worthless; you are still in your sins. ¹⁸Then those also who have fallen asleep in Christ have perished. ¹⁹If we have hoped in Christ in this life only, we are of all men most to be pitied.

1 CORINTHIANS PARALLELS

1 Corinthians 6:13–15

Food is for the stomach and the stomach is for food, but God will do away with both of them. Yet the body is not for immorality, but for the Lord, and the Lord is for the body. ¹⁴Now God has not only *raised* the Lord, but will also raise us up through His power. ¹⁵Do you not know that your bodies are members of Christ?

1 Corinthians 15:35, 42–44

But someone will say, "How are the dead *raised*? And with what kind of body do they come?" . . . ⁴²So also is the *resurrection of the dead*. It is sown a perishable body, it is raised an imperishable body; ⁴³it is sown in dishonor, it is raised in glory; it is sown in weakness, it is raised in power; ⁴⁴it is sown a natural body, it is raised a spiritual body. If there is a natural body, there is also a spiritual body.

OTHER PAULINE PARALLELS

Romans 4:23–25

Now not for his sake only was it written that it was credited to him, ²⁴but for our sake also, to whom it will be credited, as those who believe in Him who *raised* Jesus our Lord *from the dead*, ²⁵He who was delivered over because of our transgressions, and was raised because of our justification.

Romans 8:11

But if the Spirit of Him who *raised* Jesus *from the dead* dwells in you, He who raised Christ Jesus from the dead will also give life to your mortal bodies through His Spirit who dwells in you.

Philippians 3:9–11

. . . and may be found in Him, not having a righteousness of my own derived from the Law, but that which is through *faith* in Christ, the righteousness which comes from God on the basis of faith, ¹⁰that I may know Him and the power of His resurrection and the fellowship of His sufferings, being conformed to His death; ¹¹in order that I may attain to the *resurrection* from *the dead*.

1 Thessalonians 1:9–10

For they themselves report about us what kind of a reception we had with you, and how you turned to God from idols to serve a living and true God, ¹⁰and to wait for His Son from heaven, whom He *raised from the dead*, that is Jesus, who rescues us from the wrath to come.

1 Thessalonians 4:13–16

But we do not want you to be uninformed, brethren, about those who are asleep, so that you will not grieve as do the rest who have no *hope*. ¹⁴For if we believe that Jesus died and rose again, even so God will bring with Him *those who have fallen asleep* in Jesus. ¹⁵For this we say to you by the word of the Lord, that we who are alive and remain until the coming of the Lord, will not precede those who have fallen asleep. ¹⁶For the Lord Himself will descend from heaven with a shout, with the voice of the archangel and with the trumpet of God, and *the dead* in Christ will rise first.

2 Timothy 2:16–18

But avoid worldly and empty chatter, for it will lead to further ungodliness, ¹⁷and their talk will spread like gangrene. Among them are Hymenaeus and Philetus, ¹⁸men who have gone astray from the truth saying that the *resurrection* has already taken place, and they upset the *faith* of some.

OTHER BIBLICAL PARALLELS

Luke 20:34–38

"The sons of this age marry and are given in marriage, ³⁵but those who are considered worthy to attain to that age and the *resurrection* from *the dead*, neither marry nor are given in marriage; ³⁶for they cannot even die anymore, because they are like angels, and are sons of God, being sons of the resurrection. ³⁷But that *the dead* are *raised*, even Moses showed, in the passage about the burning bush, where he calls the Lord THE GOD OF ABRAHAM, AND THE GOD OF ISAAC, AND THE GOD OF JACOB. [38]Now He is not the God of the dead but of the living; for all live to Him."

Acts 2:24

"But God *raised* Him up again, putting an end to the agony of death, since it was impossible for Him to be held in its power."

Acts 17:18, 32

And also some of the Epicurean and Stoic philosophers were conversing with him. Some were saying, "What would this idle babbler wish to say?" Others, "He seems to be a proclaimer of strange deities,"—because he was *preaching* Jesus and the resurrection. . . . [32]Now when they heard of the *resurrection of the dead*, some began to sneer, but others said, "We shall hear you again concerning this."

Acts 23:8

For the Sadducees say that there is *no resurrection*, nor an angel, nor a spirit, but the Pharisees acknowledge them all.

Acts 26:6–8

"And now I am standing trial for the *hope* of the promise made by God to our fathers; [7]the promise to which our twelve tribes hope to attain, as they earnestly serve God night and day. And for this hope, O King, I am being accused by Jews. [8]Why is it considered incredible among you people if God does *raise the dead*?"

1 Peter 1:3

Blessed be the God and Father of our Lord Jesus Christ, who according to His great mercy has caused us to be born again to a living *hope* through the *resurrection* of Jesus Christ *from the dead*.

Revelation 14:13

And I heard a voice from heaven, saying, "Write, 'Blessed are *the dead* who die in the Lord from now on!'" "Yes," says the Spirit, "so that they may rest from their labors, for their deeds follow with them."

2 Baruch 21:10, 12–13

For you are the only Living One. . . . [12]You know where you have preserved the end of those who have sinned or the fulfillment of those who have proved themselves to be righteous. [13]For if *only this life* exists which everyone possesses here, nothing could be more bitter than this.

Mishnah Sanhedrin *10:1*

These are the ones who have no portion in the world to come: He who says, the *resurrection of the dead* is a teaching which does not derive from the Torah.

1 Corinthians 15:20–28

But now Christ has been raised from the dead, the first fruits of those who are asleep. [21]For since by a man came death, by a man also came the resurrection of the dead. [22]For as in Adam all die, so also in Christ all will be made alive. [23]But each in his own order: Christ the first fruits, after that those who are Christ's at His coming, [24]then comes the end, when He hands over the kingdom to the God and Father, when He has abolished all rule and all authority and power. [25]For He must reign until He has put all His enemies under His feet. [26]The last enemy that will be abolished is death. [27]For HE HAS PUT ALL THINGS IN SUBJECTION UNDER HIS FEET. But when He says, "All things are put in subjection," it is evident that He is excepted who put all things in subjection to Him. [28]When all things are subjected to Him, then the Son Himself also will be subjected to the One who subjected all things to Him, so that God may be all in all.

1 Corinthians 3:21–23

So then let no one boast in men. For *all things* belong to you, [22]whether Paul or Apollos or Cephas or the world or life or *death* or things present or things to come; all things belong to you, [23]and you belong to Christ; and Christ belongs to God.

1 Corinthians 6:13–15

Food is for the stomach and the stomach is for food, but God will do away with both of them. Yet the body is not for immorality, but for the Lord, and the Lord is for the body. [14]Now God has not only *raised* the Lord, but will also raise us up through His power. [15]Do you not know that your bodies are members of Christ?

1 Corinthians 15:3–4

For I delivered to you as of first importance what I also received, that Christ died for our sins according to the Scriptures, [4]and that He was buried, and that He was *raised* on the third day according to the Scriptures.

1 Corinthians 15:45, 50, 54

So also it is written, "The first MAN, *Adam*, BECAME A LIVING SOUL." The last Adam became a life-giving spirit. . . . [50]Now I say this, brethren, that flesh and blood cannot inherit *the kingdom* of God; nor does the perishable inherit the imperishable. . . . [54]But when this perishable will have put on the imperishable, and this mortal will have put on immortality, then will come about the saying that is written, "*DEATH* IS SWALLOWED UP in victory."

OTHER PAULINE PARALLELS

Romans 5:12, 14

Therefore, just as through one man sin entered into the world, and *death* through sin, and so death spread to all men, because all sinned. . . . [14]Nevertheless death reigned from *Adam* until Moses, even over those who had not sinned in the likeness of the offense of Adam, who is a type of Him who was to come.

Romans 8:34, 38–39

Christ Jesus is He who died, yes, rather who was *raised*, who is at the right hand of God, who also intercedes for us. . . . [38]For I am convinced that neither *death*, nor life, nor angels, nor principalities, nor things present, nor things to come, nor *powers*, [39]nor height, nor depth, nor any other created thing, will be able to separate us from the love of God, which is in Christ Jesus our Lord.

Ephesians 1:19–23

These are in accordance with the working of the strength of His might [20]which He brought about in Christ, when He *raised* Him *from the dead* and seated Him at His right hand in the heavenly places, [21]far above *all rule and authority and power* and dominion, and every name that is named, not only in this age but also in the one to come. [22]And *He put all things in subjection under His feet*, and gave Him as head over all things to the church, [23]which is His body, the fullness of Him who fills *all in all*.

Philippians 3:20–21

For our citizenship is in heaven, from which also we eagerly wait for a Savior, the Lord Jesus Christ; [21]who will transform the body of our humble state into conformity with the body of His glory, by the exertion of the power that He has even to *subject all things* to Himself.

Colossians 1:16, 18

For by Him *all things* were created, both in the heavens and on earth, visible and invisible, whether thrones or dominions or *rulers* or *authorities*—all things have been created through Him and for Him. . . . [18]He is also head of the body, the church; and He is the beginning, the firstborn from *the dead*, so that He Himself will come to have first place in everything.

Colossians 2:15

When He had disarmed the *rulers* and *authorities*, He made a public display of them, having triumphed over them through Him.

1 Thessalonians 4:15–17

For this we say to you by the word of the Lord, that we who are alive and remain until the *coming* of the Lord, will not precede those who have fallen *asleep*. [16]For the Lord Himself will descend from heaven with a shout, with the voice of the archangel and with the trumpet of God, and *the dead* in Christ will rise first. [17]Then we who are alive and remain will be caught up together with them in the clouds to meet the Lord in the air, and so we shall always be with the Lord.

2 Timothy 1:10

. . . but now has been revealed by the appearing of our Savior Christ Jesus, who *abolished death* and brought life and immortality to light through the gospel.

1 Corinthians 15:29–34

Psalm 8:4, 6

What is man that You take thought of him,
And the son of man that You care for him?
. . . [6]You make him to rule over the works of
Your hands; You have *put all things under
his feet.*

Psalm 110:1

The LORD says to my Lord: "Sit at My right
hand Until I make Your *enemies* a footstool
for Your *feet.*"

Daniel 7:13–14

"And behold, with the clouds of heaven One
like a Son of Man was *coming*, And He came
up to the Ancient of Days And was presented before Him. [14]And to Him was given
dominion, Glory and a *kingdom*, That all the
peoples, nations and men of every language
Might serve Him."

1 Peter 3:21–22

Corresponding to that, baptism now saves
you—not the removal of dirt from the flesh,
but an appeal to God for a good conscience—through *the resurrection* of Jesus
Christ, [22]who is at the right hand of God,
having gone into heaven, after angels and
authorities and powers had been *subjected to
Him.*

Revelation 20:13–14

And the sea gave up *the dead* which were in
it, and *death* and Hades gave up the dead
which were in them; and they were judged,
every one of them according to their deeds.
[14]Then death and Hades were thrown into
the lake of fire.

NONCANONICAL PARALLELS

2 Esdras (4 Ezra) *7:118–19*

O *Adam*, what have you done? For though it
was you who sinned, the fall was not yours
alone, but ours also who are your descendants. [119]For what good is it to us, if an
immortal time has been promised to us, but
we have done deeds that bring *death*?

Otherwise, what will those do who are baptized for the dead? If the dead are not raised at
all, why then are they baptized for them?
[30]Why are we also in danger every hour? [31]I
affirm, brethren, by the boasting in you which
I have in Christ Jesus our Lord, I die daily. [32]If
from human motives I fought with wild beasts
at Ephesus, what does it profit me? If the dead
are not raised, LET US EAT AND DRINK, FOR
TOMORROW WE DIE. [33]Do not be deceived:
"Bad company corrupts good morals."
[34]Become sober-minded as you ought, and
stop sinning; for some have no knowledge of
God. I speak this to your shame.

1 CORINTHIANS PARALLELS

1 Corinthians 1:4–5

I thank my God always concerning you for
the grace of God which was given you in
Christ Jesus, [5]that in everything you were
enriched in Him, in all speech and all
knowledge.

1 Corinthians 1:13–15

Has Christ been divided? Paul was not crucified for you, was he? Or were you *baptized*
in the name of Paul? [14]I thank God that I
baptized none of you except Crispus and
Gaius, [15]so that no one would say you were
baptized in my name.

1 Corinthians 4:9, 11–14

For, I think, God has exhibited us apostles
last of all, as men condemned to death;
because we have become a spectacle to the
world, both to angels and to men. . . . [11]To
this present hour we are both hungry and
thirsty, and are poorly clothed, and are
roughly treated, and are homeless; [12]and
we toil, working with our own hands; when
we are reviled, we bless; when we are persecuted, we endure; [13]when we are slandered, we try to conciliate; we have become
as the scum of the world, the dregs of all
things, even until now. [14]I do not write these
things to *shame* you, but to admonish you as
my beloved children.

1 Corinthians 6:5–6, 9

I say *this to your shame.* Is it so, that there is
not among you one wise man who will be
able to decide between his brethren, [6]but

brother goes to law with brother, and that before unbelievers? . . . [9]Or do you not know that the unrighteous will not inherit the kingdom of God? *Do not be deceived.*

1 Corinthians 15:12, 15

Now if Christ is preached, that He has been *raised* from *the dead*, how do some among you say that there is no resurrection of the dead? . . . [15]Moreover we are even found to be false witnesses of God, because we testified against God that He raised Christ, whom He did not raise, if in fact the dead are not raised.

1 Corinthians 16:8–9

But I will remain in *Ephesus* until Pentecost; [9]for a wide door for effective service has opened to me, and there are many adversaries.

OTHER PAULINE PARALLELS

2 Corinthians 1:8–9

For we do not want you to be unaware, brethren, of our affliction which came to us in Asia, that we were burdened excessively, beyond our strength, so that we despaired even of life; [9]indeed, we had the sentence of death within ourselves so that we would not trust in ourselves, but in God who *raises the dead.*

2 Corinthians 4:8–11

We are afflicted in every way, but not crushed; perplexed, but not despairing; [9]persecuted, but not forsaken; struck down, but not destroyed; [10]always carrying about in the body the *dying* of Jesus, so that the life of Jesus also may be manifested in our body. [11]For we who live are constantly being delivered over to death for Jesus' sake, so that the life of Jesus also may be manifested in our mortal flesh.

2 Corinthians 6:4–5, 9

But in everything commending ourselves as servants of God, in much endurance, in afflictions, in hardships, in distresses, [5]in beatings, in imprisonments, in tumults, in labors, in sleeplessness, in hunger, . . . [9]as unknown yet well-known, as *dying* yet behold, we live; as punished yet not put to death.

2 Corinthians 7:4

Great is my confidence in you; great is my *boasting* on your behalf. I am filled with comfort; I am overflowing with joy in all our affliction.

2 Corinthians 11:25–26

Three times I was beaten with rods, once I was stoned, three times I was shipwrecked, a night and a day I have spent in the deep. [26]I have been on frequent journeys, in *dangers* from rivers, dangers from robbers, dangers from my countrymen, dangers from the Gentiles, dangers in the city, dangers in the wilderness, dangers on the sea, dangers among false brethren.

1 Thessalonians 5:8

But since we are of the day, let us be *sober*, having put on the breastplate of faith and love, and as a helmet, the hope of salvation.

OTHER BIBLICAL PARALLELS

Isaiah 22:13

Instead, there is gaiety and gladness, Killing of cattle and slaughtering of sheep, Eating of meat and drinking of wine: "*Let us eat and drink, for tomorrow we* may *die.*"

Luke 12:19

"And I will say to my soul, 'Soul, you have many goods laid up for many years to come; take your ease, *eat, drink* and be merry.'"

NONCANONICAL PARALLELS

Wisdom of Solomon 2:1, 5–6

For they reasoned unsoundly, saying to themselves, "Short and sorrowful is our life, and there is no remedy when a life comes to its end, and no one has been known to return from Hades. . . . [5]For our allotted time is the passing of a shadow, and there is no return from our death, because it is sealed up and no one turns back. [6]Come, therefore, let us enjoy the good things that exist, and make use of the creation to the full as in youth."

2 Maccabees 12:44–45

For if he [Judas] were not expecting that those who had fallen would *rise* again, it would have been superfluous and foolish to pray for *the dead.* [45]But if he was looking to the splendid reward that is laid up for those who fall asleep in godliness, it was a holy and pious thought. Therefore he made atonement for the dead, so that they might be delivered from their sin.

Menander, Thais *fragment 218*
> Bad company corrupts good morals.

Lucian, The Runaways *23*
> Zeus: But off you go, Heracles, bearing Philosophy herself, as quickly as possible to the world. You will complete a thirteenth labor of no small magnitude should you eradicate such coarse and shameless *beasts* [i.e., the Cynic philosophers].

1 Corinthians 15:35–41

But someone will say, "How are the dead raised? And with what kind of body do they come?" [36]You fool! That which you sow does not come to life unless it dies; [37]and that which you sow, you do not sow the body which is to be, but a bare grain, perhaps of wheat or of something else. [38]But God gives it a body just as He wished, and to each of the seeds a body of its own. [39]All flesh is not the same flesh, but there is one flesh of men, and another flesh of beasts, and another flesh of birds, and another of fish. [40]There are also heavenly bodies and earthly bodies, but the glory of the heavenly is one, and the glory of the earthly is another. [41]There is one glory of the sun, and another glory of the moon, and another glory of the stars; for star differs from star in glory.

1 CORINTHIANS PARALLELS

1 Corinthians 6:13
> Food is for the stomach and the stomach is for food, but God will do away with both of them. Yet *the body* is not for immorality, but for the Lord, and the Lord is for the body.

1 Corinthians 12:18
> But now God has placed the members, each one of them, in *the body*, just as He desired.

1 Corinthians 15:12, 20
> Now if Christ is preached, that He has been *raised* from *the dead*, how do some among you say that there is no resurrection of the dead? . . . [20]But now Christ has been raised

from the dead, the first fruits of those who are asleep.

OTHER PAULINE PARALLELS

Romans 8:11
> But if the Spirit of Him who *raised* Jesus from the dead dwells in you, He who raised Christ Jesus from *the dead* will also give *life* to your mortal *bodies* through His Spirit who dwells in you.

Romans 8:23
> And not only this, but also we ourselves, having the first fruits of the Spirit, even we ourselves groan within ourselves, waiting eagerly for our adoption as sons, the redemption of our *body*.

OTHER BIBLICAL PARALLELS

Genesis 1:11, 16, 20, 24, 26
> Then God said, "Let the earth sprout vegetation: plants yielding *seed*, and fruit trees on the earth bearing fruit after their kind with seed in them"; and it was so. . . . [16]God made the two great lights, the greater light to govern the day, and the lesser light to govern the night; He made the *stars* also. . . . [20]Then God said, "Let the waters teem with swarms of living creatures, and let *birds* fly above the earth in the open expanse of the heavens." . . . [24]Then God said, "Let the earth bring forth living creatures after their kind: cattle and creeping things and *beasts* of the earth after their kind"; and it was so. . . . [26]Then God said, "Let Us make *man* in Our image, according to Our likeness."

Daniel 12:2–3
> "Many of those who sleep in the dust of the ground will awake, these to everlasting life, but the others to disgrace and everlasting contempt. [3]Those who have insight will shine brightly like the brightness of the expanse of heaven, and those who lead the many to righteousness, like the *stars* forever and ever."

Matthew 13:43
> "Then THE RIGHTEOUS WILL SHINE FORTH AS *THE SUN* in the kingdom of their Father."

John 12:24

"Truly, truly, I say to you, unless a *grain of wheat* falls into the earth and *dies*, it remains alone; but if it dies, it bears much fruit."

2 Baruch *49:1–51:3*

But further, I ask you, O Mighty One; . . . [2]In which shape will the living live in your day? Or how will remain their splendor which will be after that? [3]Will they, perhaps, take again this present form? . . . Or will you perhaps change these things which have been in the world, as also the world itself? [50:1]And he answered and said to me, . . . [2]For the earth will surely give back *the dead* at that time; it receives them now in order to keep them, not changing in their form. . . . [51:1]And it will happen after this day . . . the *glory* of those who have proved to be righteous will be changed. . . . [3] . . . Their splendor will then be glorified by transformations, and the shape of their face will be changed into the light of their beauty so that they may acquire the undying world which is promised to them.

Philo, Concerning Noah's Work as a Planter *12*

The stars are in heaven. Those who study philosophy say that these too are living beings, but of a kind composed entirely of intellect.

1 Corinthians 15:42–49

So also is the resurrection of the dead. It is sown a perishable body, it is raised an imperishable body; [43]it is sown in dishonor, it is raised in glory; it is sown in weakness, it is raised in power; [44]it is sown a natural body, it is raised a spiritual body. If there is a natural body, there is also a spiritual body. [45]So also it is written, "The first MAN, Adam, BECAME A LIVING SOUL." The last Adam became a life-giving spirit. [46]However, the spiritual is not first, but the natural; then the spiritual. [47]The first man is from the earth, earthy; the second man is from heaven. [48]As is the earthy, so also are those who are earthy; and as is the heavenly, so also are those who are heavenly. [49]Just as we have borne the image of the earthy, we will also bear the image of the heavenly.

1 Corinthians 2:14

But a *natural* man does not accept the things of the Spirit of God, for they are foolishness to him; and he cannot understand them, because they are *spiritually* appraised.

1 Corinthians 15:3–4, 12

For I delivered to you as of first importance what I also received, that Christ died for our sins according to the Scriptures, [4]and that He was buried, and that He was *raised* on the third day according to the Scriptures. . . . [12]Now if Christ is preached, that He has been raised from the dead, how do some among you say that there is no *resurrection of the dead*?

1 Corinthians 15:21–22

For since by a man came death, by a man also came *the resurrection of the dead.* [22]For as in *Adam* all die, so also in Christ all will be made alive.

Romans 5:14–15, 17

Nevertheless death reigned from *Adam* until Moses, even over those who had not sinned in the likeness of the offense of Adam, who is a type of Him who was to come. [15]But the free gift is not like the transgression. For if by the transgression of the one the many died, much more did the grace of God and the gift by the grace of the one Man, Jesus Christ, abound to the many. . . . [17]For if by the transgression of the one, death reigned through the one, much more those who receive the abundance of grace and of the gift of righteousness will reign in *life* through the One, Jesus Christ.

Romans 8:11, 29

But if the Spirit of Him who *raised* Jesus from *the dead* dwells in you, He who raised Christ Jesus from the dead will also give *life* to your mortal bodies through His Spirit who dwells in you. . . . [29]For those whom He foreknew, He also predestined to become conformed to *the image* of His Son, so that He would be the firstborn among many brethren.

2 Corinthians 3:18

But we all, with unveiled face, beholding as in a mirror the glory of the Lord, are being transformed into the same *image* from glory to *glory*, just as from the Lord, the Spirit.

2 Corinthians 4:3–4

And even if our gospel is veiled, it is veiled to those who are perishing, [4]in whose case the god of this world has blinded the minds of the unbelieving so that they might not see the light of the gospel of the *glory* of Christ, who is *the image* of God.

2 Corinthians 5:1

For we know that if the *earthly* tent which is our house is torn down, we have a building from God, a house not made with hands, eternal in the *heavens*.

Philippians 3:20–21

For our citizenship is in *heaven,* from which also we eagerly wait for a Savior, the Lord Jesus Christ; [21]who will transform the *body* of our humble state into conformity with the body of His *glory*, by the exertion of the *power* that He has even to subject all things to Himself.

Colossians 1:15–16

He is *the image* of the invisible God, the firstborn of all creation. [16]For by Him all things were created, both in the heavens and on earth, visible and invisible, whether thrones or dominions or rulers or authorities—all things have been created through Him and for Him.

Colossians 3:4, 9–10

When Christ, who is our *life,* is revealed, then you also will be revealed with Him in *glory.* . . . [9]Do not lie to one another, since you laid aside the old self with its evil practices, [10]and have put on the new self who is being renewed to a true knowledge according to *the image* of the One who created him.

Genesis 1:26

"Let Us make man in Our *image,* according to Our likeness; and let them rule over the fish of the sea and over the birds of the sky and over the cattle and over all the earth, and over every creeping thing that creeps on the earth."

Genesis 2:7

Then the LORD God formed man of dust from the ground, and breathed into his nostrils the breath of life; and *man became a living* being.

Genesis 3:19

"By the sweat of your face You will eat bread, Till you return to the ground, Because from it you were taken; For you are dust, And to dust you shall return."

Daniel 12:2–3

"Many of those who sleep in the dust of the ground will awake, these to everlasting life, but the others to disgrace and everlasting contempt. [3]Those who have insight will shine brightly like the brightness of the expanse of *heaven,* and those who lead the many to righteousness, like the stars forever and ever."

Wisdom of Solomon 2:23

God created us for incorruption, and made us in *the image* of his own eternity.

Wisdom of Solomon 9:14–15

For the reasoning of mortals is worthless, and our designs are likely to fail; [15]for a *perishable body* weighs down the soul, and this *earthy* tent burdens the thoughtful mind.

The Rule of the Community *(1QS) 4.20–23*

God will refine, with his truth, all man's deeds, and will purify for himself the configuration of man, ripping out all spirit of deceit from the innermost part [21]of his flesh. . . . [22] . . . For these are those selected by God for an everlasting covenant [23]and to them shall belong all the *glory* of *Adam.*

1 Corinthians 15:50–58

Now I say this, brethren, that flesh and blood cannot inherit the kingdom of God; nor does the perishable inherit the imperishable. [51]Behold, I tell you a mystery; we will not all sleep, but we will all be changed, [52]in a moment, in the twinkling of an eye, at the last trumpet; for the trumpet will sound, and the dead will be raised imperishable, and we will be changed. [53]For this perishable must put on the imperishable, and this mortal must put on immortality. ⁵⁴But when this perishable will have put on the imperishable, and this mortal will have put on immortality, then will come about the saying that is written, "DEATH IS SWALLOWED UP in victory. ⁵⁵O DEATH, WHERE IS YOUR VICTORY? O DEATH, WHERE IS YOUR STING?" ⁵⁶The sting of death is sin, and the power of sin is the law; ⁵⁷but thanks be to God, who gives us the victory through our Lord Jesus Christ. ⁵⁸Therefore, my beloved brethren, be steadfast, immovable, always abounding in the work of the Lord, knowing that your toil is not in vain in the Lord.

1 CORINTHIANS PARALLELS

1 Corinthians 6:9
Or do you not know that the unrighteous will *not inherit the kingdom of God*? Do not be deceived.

1 Corinthians 15:16, 21, 23–24, 26
For if *the dead* are not *raised*, not even Christ has been raised; . . . ²¹For since by a man came *death*, by a man also came the resurrection of the dead. . . . ²³But each in his own order: Christ the first fruits, after that those who are Christ's at His coming, ²⁴then comes the end, when He hands over *the kingdom* to the God and Father, when He has abolished all rule and all authority and power. . . . ²⁶The last enemy that will be abolished is death.

OTHER PAULINE PARALLELS

Romans 2:6–7
[God] WILL RENDER TO EACH PERSON ACCORDING TO HIS DEEDS: ⁷to those who by perseverance in doing good seek for glory and honor and *immortality*, eternal life.

Romans 5:12–13
Therefore, just as through one man *sin* entered into the world, and *death* through sin, and so death spread to all men, because all sinned— ¹³for until *the Law* sin was in the world, but sin is not imputed when there is no law.

Romans 7:9–10, 24–25
I was once alive apart from *the Law*; but when the commandment came, *sin* became alive and I died; ¹⁰and this commandment,

which was to result in life, proved to result in *death* for me; . . . ²⁴Wretched man that I am! Who will set me free from the body of this death? ²⁵Thanks be to God through Jesus Christ our Lord! So then, on the one hand I myself with my mind am serving the law of God, but on the other, with my flesh the law of sin.

2 Corinthians 5:4
For indeed while we are in this tent, we groan, being burdened, because we do not want to be unclothed but to be clothed, so that what is *mortal* will be *swallowed up* by life.

Philippians 3:20–21
For our citizenship is in heaven, from which also we eagerly wait for a Savior, the Lord Jesus Christ; ²¹who will transform the body of our humble state into conformity with the body of His glory, by the exertion of the power that He has even to subject all things to Himself.

1 Thessalonians 4:15–16
For this we say to you by the word of the Lord, that we who are alive and remain until the coming of the Lord, will not precede those who have fallen asleep. ¹⁶For the Lord Himself will descend from heaven with a shout, with the voice of the archangel and with *the trumpet* of God, and *the dead* in Christ *will rise* first.

2 Timothy 1:10
. . . but now has been revealed by the appearing of our Savior Christ Jesus, who abolished *death* and brought life and *immortality* to light through the gospel.

OTHER BIBLICAL PARALLELS

Isaiah 25:7–8
And on this mountain He will swallow up the covering which is over all peoples, Even the veil which is stretched over all nations. ⁸He will *swallow up death* for all time, And the Lord GOD will wipe tears away from all faces, And He will remove the reproach of His people from all the earth; For the LORD has spoken.

Isaiah 27:13
It will come about also in that day that a great *trumpet* will be blown, and those who

were perishing in the land of Assyria and who were scattered in the land of Egypt will come and worship the LORD in the holy mountain at Jerusalem.

Hosea 13:14

Shall I ransom them from the power of Sheol? Shall I redeem them from death? *O Death*, where are your thorns? O Sheol, *where is your sting?*

Matthew 24:31

"And He will send forth His angels with A GREAT *TRUMPET* and THEY WILL GATHER TOGETHER His elect from the four winds, from one end of the sky to the other."

John 3:5–6

Jesus answered, "Truly, truly, I say to you, unless one is born of water and the Spirit he cannot enter into *the kingdom of God*. ⁶That which is born of the flesh is *flesh*, and that which is born of the Spirit is spirit."

Hebrews 2:14–15

Therefore, since the children share in *flesh and blood*, He Himself likewise also partook of the same, that through death He might render powerless him who had the power of *death*, that is, the devil, ¹⁵and might free those who through fear of death were subject to slavery all their lives.

Revelation 21:3–4

"Behold, the tabernacle of God is among men, and He will dwell among them, and they shall be His people, and God Himself will be among them, ⁴and He will wipe away every tear from their eyes; and there will no longer be any *death*; there will no longer be any mourning, or crying, or pain; the first things have passed away."

NONCANONICAL PARALLELS

1 Enoch *62:15–16*

The righteous and elect ones shall rise from the earth. . . . They shall wear the garments of glory. ¹⁶These garments of yours shall become the garments of life from the Lord of the Spirits. Neither shall your garments wear out, nor your glory come to an end before the Lord of the Spirits.

2 Baruch *50:2; 51:1, 3*

For the earth will surely give back the dead at that time; it receives them now in order to keep them, not changing in their form. . . . ⁵¹:¹And it will happen after this day . . . the glory of those who have proved to be righteous will be *changed*. . . . ³ . . . Their splendor will then be glorified by transformations, and the shape of their face will be changed into the light of their beauty so that they may acquire the undying world which is promised to them.

1 Corinthians 16:1–12

Now concerning the collection for the saints, as I directed the churches of Galatia, so do you also. ²On the first day of every week each one of you is to put aside and save, as he may prosper, so that no collections be made when I come. ³When I arrive, whomever you may approve, I will send them with letters to carry your gift to Jerusalem; ⁴and if it is fitting for me to go also, they will go with me. ⁵But I will come to you after I go through Macedonia, for I am going through Macedonia; ⁶and perhaps I will stay with you, or even spend the winter, so that you may send me on my way wherever I may go. ⁷For I do not wish to see you now just in passing; for I hope to remain with you for some time, if the Lord permits. ⁸But I will remain in Ephesus until Pentecost; ⁹for a wide door for effective service has opened to me, and there are many adversaries. ¹⁰Now if Timothy comes, see that he is with you without cause to be afraid, for he is doing the Lord's work, as I also am. ¹¹So let no one despise him. But send him on his way in peace, so that he may come to me; for I expect him with the brethren. ¹²But concerning Apollos our brother, I encouraged him greatly to come to you with the brethren; and it was not at all his desire to come now, but he will come when he has opportunity.

1 CORINTHIANS PARALLELS

1 Corinthians 3:4–6

For when one says, "I am of Paul," and another, "I am of *Apollos*," are you not mere men? ⁵What then is Apollos? And what is Paul? Servants through whom you believed, even as the Lord gave *opportunity* to each one. [6]I planted, Apollos watered, but God was causing the growth.

Now these things, brethren, I have figuratively applied to myself and *Apollos* for your sakes, so that in us you may learn not to exceed what is written, so that no one of you will become arrogant in behalf of one against the other.

1 Corinthians 4:17, 19

For this reason I have sent to you *Timothy*, who is my beloved and faithful child in the Lord, and he will remind you of my ways which are in Christ, just as I teach everywhere in every church. . . . [19]But *I will come to you* soon, if the Lord wills, and I shall find out, not the words of those who are arrogant but their power.

OTHER PAULINE PARALLELS

Romans 15:25–26

But now, I am going to *Jerusalem* serving *the saints*. [26]For *Macedonia* and Achaia have been pleased to make a contribution for the poor among the saints in Jerusalem.

2 Corinthians 1:1

Paul, an apostle of Christ Jesus by the will of God, and *Timothy* our brother, To the church of God which is at Corinth . . .

2 Corinthians 1:15–16

In this confidence I intended at first to *come to you*, so that you might twice receive a blessing; [16]that is, to pass your way into *Macedonia*, and again from Macedonia to come to you, and by you to be helped on my journey to Judea.

2 Corinthians 8:1, 4, 10

Now, brethren, we wish to make known to you the grace of God which has been given in the churches of *Macedonia*, . . . [4]begging us with much urging for the favor of participation in the support of *the saints*. . . . [10]I give my opinion in this matter, for this is to your advantage, who were the first to begin a year ago not only to do this, but also to desire to do it.

2 Corinthians 8:18–20

We have sent along with him [Titus] the brother whose fame in the things of the gospel has spread through all the churches; [19]and not only this, but he has also been appointed by the churches to travel with us in this gracious work, which is being administered by us for the glory of the Lord Himself, and to show our readiness, [20]taking precaution so that no one will discredit us in our administration of this generous *gift*.

2 Corinthians 9:2, 5, 12

For I know your readiness, of which I boast about you to the Macedonians, namely, that Achaia has been prepared since last year, and your zeal has stirred up most of them. . . . [5]So I thought it necessary to urge the brethren that they would go on ahead to you and arrange beforehand your previously promised bountiful *gift*, so that the same would be ready as a bountiful gift and not affected by covetousness. . . . [12]For the ministry of this service is not only fully supplying the needs of *the saints*, but is also overflowing through many thanksgivings to God.

Galatians 2:9–10

Recognizing the grace that had been given to me, James and Cephas and John, who were reputed to be pillars, gave to me and Barnabas the right hand of fellowship, so that we might go to the Gentiles and they to the circumcised. [10]They only asked us to remember the poor—the very thing I also was eager to do.

1 Timothy 4:12

Let no one look down on your youthfulness, but rather in speech, conduct, love, faith and purity, show yourself an example of those who believe.

OTHER BIBLICAL PARALLELS

Acts 11:29–30

And in the proportion that any of the disciples had means, each of them determined to *send* a contribution for the relief of the brethren living in Judea. [30]And this they did, sending it in charge of Barnabas and Saul to the elders.

Acts 18:24–28

Now a Jew named *Apollos*, an Alexandrian by birth, an eloquent man, came to *Ephesus*; and he was mighty in the Scriptures. 25This man had been instructed in the way of the Lord; and being fervent in spirit, he was speaking and teaching accurately the things concerning Jesus, being acquainted only with the baptism of John; 26and he began to speak out boldly in the synagogue. But when Priscilla and Aquila heard him, they took him aside and explained to him the way of God more accurately. 27And when he wanted to go across to Achaia, the brethren *encouraged* him and wrote to the disciples to welcome him; and when he had arrived, he greatly helped those who had believed through grace, 28for he powerfully refuted the Jews in public, demonstrating by the Scriptures that Jesus was the Christ.

Acts 19:1, 8–10

It happened that while *Apollos* was at Corinth, Paul passed through the upper country and came to *Ephesus*, and found some disciples. . . . 8And he entered the synagogue and continued speaking out boldly for three months. . . . 9But when some were becoming hardened and disobedient, speaking evil of the Way before the people, he withdrew from them and took away the disciples, reasoning daily in the school of Tyrannus. 10This took place for two years, so that all who lived in Asia heard the word of the Lord, both Jews and Greeks.

Acts 19:21–22

Now after these things were finished, Paul purposed in the spirit to go to *Jerusalem* after he had passed *through Macedonia* and Achaia, saying, "After I have been there, I must also see Rome." 22And having sent into Macedonia two of those who ministered to him, *Timothy* and Erastus, he himself stayed in Asia for a while.

Acts 20:1–3, 7

After the uproar had ceased, Paul sent for the disciples, and when he had exhorted them and taken his leave of them, he left to go to Macedonia. 2When he had gone through those districts and had given them much exhortation, he came to Greece. 3And there he spent three months, and when a plot was formed against him by the Jews as he was about to set sail for Syria, he decided

to return *through Macedonia*. . . . 7On the *first day of* the *week*, when we were gathered together to break bread, Paul began talking to them, intending to leave the next day, and he prolonged his message until midnight.

1 Corinthians 16:13–24

Be on the alert, stand firm in the faith, act like men, be strong. 14Let all that you do be done in love. 15Now I urge you, brethren (you know the household of Stephanas, that they were the first fruits of Achaia, and that they have devoted themselves for ministry to the saints), 16that you also be in subjection to such men and to everyone who helps in the work and labors. 17I rejoice over the coming of Stephanas and Fortunatus and Achaicus, because they have supplied what was lacking on your part. 18For they have refreshed my spirit and yours. Therefore acknowledge such men. 19The churches of Asia greet you. Aquila and Prisca greet you heartily in the Lord, with the church that is in their house. 20All the brethren greet you. Greet one another with a holy kiss. 21The greeting is in my own hand—Paul. 22If anyone does not love the Lord, he is to be accursed. Maranatha. 23The grace of the Lord Jesus be with you. 24My love be with you all in Christ Jesus. Amen.

1 CORINTHIANS PARALLELS

1 Corinthians 1:16

Now I did baptize also *the household of Stephanas*; beyond that, I do not know whether I baptized any other.

1 Corinthians 11:26

For as often as you eat this bread and drink the cup, you proclaim the Lord's death until He comes.

1 Corinthians 12:3

Therefore I make known to you that no one speaking by the Spirit of God says, "Jesus is *accursed*"; and no one can say, "Jesus is Lord," except by the Holy Spirit.

1 Corinthians 13:13

But now *faith,* hope, *love,* abide these three; but the greatest of these is love.

Romans 16:3–5

Greet *Prisca* and *Aquila,* my fellow workers in Christ Jesus, [4]who for my life risked their own necks, to whom not only do I give thanks, but also all the churches of the Gentiles; [5]also greet *the church that is in their house.*

Romans 16:16, 20

Greet one another with a holy kiss. All the churches of Christ *greet you. . . .*[20]The God of peace will soon crush Satan under your feet. *The grace of* our *Lord Jesus be with you.*

Galatians 1:9

As we have said before, so I say again now, if any man is preaching to you a gospel contrary to what you received, *he is to be accursed!*

Galatians 6:11

See with what large letters I am writing to you with *my own hand.*

Ephesians 6:10

Finally, *be strong* in the Lord and in the strength of His might.

Philippians 2:29–30

Receive him [Epaphroditus] then in the Lord with all joy, and hold men like him in high regard; [30]because he came close to death for *the work* of Christ, risking his life to complete what was deficient in your service to me.

Philippians 4:1

Therefore, my beloved brethren whom I long to see, my joy and crown, in this way *stand firm* in the Lord, my beloved.

Colossians 4:18

I, *Paul,* write this *greeting* with *my own hand.* Remember my imprisonment. *Grace be with you.*

1 Thessalonians 5:6

So then let us not sleep as others do, but let us be *alert* and sober.

1 Thessalonians 5:12–13

But we request of you, brethren, that you appreciate those who diligently *labor* among you, and have charge over you in the Lord and give you instruction, [13]and that you

esteem them very highly in *love* because of their *work.*

1 Thessalonians 5:26, 28

Greet all the brethren *with a holy kiss. . . .*[28]*The grace of* our *Lord Jesus* Christ *be with you.*

2 Thessalonians 3:17–18

I, *Paul,* write this *greeting* with *my own hand,* and this is a distinguishing mark in every letter; this is the way I write. [18]*The grace of* our *Lord Jesus* Christ *be with you* all.

Philemon 7

For I have come to have much joy and comfort in your *love,* because the hearts of the saints have been *refreshed* through you, brother.

Psalm 31:23–24

O *love the* LORD, all you His godly ones! The LORD preserves the faithful And fully recompenses the proud doer. [24]*Be strong* and let your heart take courage, All you who hope in the LORD.

Acts 18:1–3

After these things he left Athens and went to Corinth. [2]And he found a Jew named *Aquila,* a native of Pontus, having recently come from Italy with his wife *Priscilla,* because Claudius had commanded all the Jews to leave Rome. He came to them, [3]and because he was of the same trade, he stayed with them and they were working, for by trade they were tent-makers.

Hebrews 13:17

Obey your leaders and submit to them, for they keep watch over your souls as those who will give an account. Let them do this with joy and not with grief, for this would be unprofitable for you.

1 Peter 5:14

Greet one another with a kiss of love. Peace be to you all who are in Christ.

Revelation 22:20–21

He who testifies to these things says, "Yes, I am coming quickly." Amen. Come, Lord Jesus. [21]*The grace of the Lord Jesus be with* all. *Amen.*

2 Corinthians

2 Corinthians 1:1–2

Paul, an apostle of Christ Jesus by the will of God, and Timothy our brother, To the church of God which is at Corinth with all the saints who are throughout Achaia: ²Grace to you and peace from God our Father and the Lord Jesus Christ.

2 CORINTHIANS PARALLELS

2 Corinthians 1:19

For the Son of God, Christ Jesus, who was preached among you by us—by me and Silvanus and *Timothy*—was not yes and no, but is yes in Him.

2 Corinthians 9:1–2

For it is superfluous for me to write to you about this ministry to the saints; ²for I know your readiness, of which I boast about you to the Macedonians, namely, that *Achaia* has been prepared since last year, and your zeal has stirred up most of them.

2 Corinthians 11:9–10

When I was present with you and was in need, I was not a burden to anyone; for when the brethren came from Macedonia they fully supplied my need, and in everything I kept myself from being a burden to you, and will continue to do so. ¹⁰As the truth of Christ is in me, this boasting of mine will not be stopped in the regions of *Achaia*.

OTHER PAULINE PARALLELS

1 Corinthians 1:1–3

Paul, called as *an apostle of Jesus Christ by the will of God,* and Sosthenes our brother,

²*To the church of God which is at Corinth,* to those who have been sanctified in Christ Jesus, *saints* by calling, with all who in every place call on the name of our Lord Jesus Christ, their Lord and ours: ³*Grace to you and peace from God our Father and the Lord Jesus Christ.*

1 Corinthians 4:17

For this reason I have sent to you *Timothy,* who is my beloved and faithful child in the Lord, and he will remind you of my ways which are in Christ, just as I teach everywhere in every church.

1 Corinthians 16:10–11, 15

Now if *Timothy* comes, see that he is with you without cause to be afraid, for he is doing the Lord's work, as I also am. ¹¹So let no one despise him. But send him on his way in peace, so that he may come to me; for I expect him with the brethren. . . . ¹⁵Now I urge you, brethren (you know the household of Stephanas, that they were the first fruits of *Achaia,* and that they have devoted themselves for ministry to *the saints*) . . .

Ephesians 1:1–2

Paul, an apostle of Christ Jesus by the will of God, To *the saints* who are at Ephesus and who are faithful in Christ Jesus: ²*Grace to you and peace from God our Father and the Lord Jesus Christ.*

Philippians 1:1–2

Paul and *Timothy,* bond-servants of Christ Jesus, To all *the saints* in Christ Jesus who are in Philippi, including the overseers and deacons: ²*Grace to you and peace from God our Father and the Lord Jesus Christ.*

Colossians 1:1–2

Paul, an apostle of Jesus Christ by the will of God, and Timothy our brother, ²*To the saints* and faithful brethren in Christ who are at Colossae: *Grace to you and peace from God our Father.*

2 Timothy 1:1–2

Paul, an apostle of Christ Jesus by the will of God, according to the promise of life in Christ Jesus, ²*To Timothy,* my beloved son: *Grace,* mercy and *peace from God* the *Father and Christ Jesus* our *Lord.*

OTHER BIBLICAL PARALLELS

Acts 16:1–3

Paul came also to Derbe and to Lystra. And a disciple was there, named *Timothy,* the son of a Jewish woman who was a believer, but his father was a Greek, ²and he was well spoken of by the brethren who were in Lystra and Iconium. ³Paul wanted this man to go with him; and he took him and circumcised him because of the Jews who were in those parts, for they all knew that his father was a Greek.

Acts 18:1–5, 12–13

After these things he left Athens and went to *Corinth.* ²And he found a Jew named Aquila, a native of Pontus, having recently come from Italy with his wife Priscilla, because Claudius had commanded all the Jews to leave Rome. He came to them, ³and because he was of the same trade, he stayed with them and they were working, for by trade they were tent-makers. ⁴And he was reasoning in the synagogue every Sabbath and trying to persuade Jews and Greeks. ⁵But when Silas and *Timothy* came down from Macedonia, *Paul* began devoting himself completely to the word, solemnly testifying to the Jews that Jesus was the Christ. . . . ¹²But while Gallio was proconsul of *Achaia,* the Jews with one accord rose up against Paul and brought him before the judgment seat, ¹³saying, "This man persuades men to worship God contrary to the law."

2 Corinthians 1:3–11

Blessed be the God and Father of our Lord Jesus Christ, the Father of mercies and God of all comfort, ⁴who comforts us in all our afflic-tion so that we will be able to comfort those who are in any affliction with the comfort with which we ourselves are comforted by God. ⁵For just as the sufferings of Christ are ours in abun-dance, so also our comfort is abundant through Christ. ⁶But if we are afflicted, it is for your comfort and salvation; or if we are com-forted, it is for your comfort, which is effective in the patient enduring of the same sufferings which we also suffer; ⁷and our hope for you is firmly grounded, knowing that as you are shar-ers of our sufferings, so also you are sharers of our comfort. ⁸For we do not want you to be unaware, brethren, of our affliction which came to us in Asia, that we were burdened exces-sively, beyond our strength, so that we despaired even of life; ⁹indeed, we had the sentence of death within ourselves so that we would not trust in ourselves, but in God who raises the dead; ¹⁰who delivered us from so great a peril of death, and will deliver us, He on whom we have set our hope. And He will yet deliver us, ¹¹you also joining in helping us through your prayers, so that thanks may be given by many persons on our behalf for the favor bestowed on us through the prayers of many.

2 CORINTHIANS PARALLELS

2 Corinthians 4:7–8, 10

But we have this treasure in earthen vessels, so that the surpassing greatness of the power will be of God and not from ourselves; ⁸we are *afflicted* in every way, but not crushed; perplexed, but not *despairing*; . . . ¹⁰always carrying about in the body the dying of Jesus, so that the life of Jesus also may be mani-fested in our body.

2 Corinthians 4:16–17

Therefore we do not lose heart, but though our outer man is decaying, yet our inner man is being renewed day by day. ¹⁷For momentary, light *affliction* is producing for us an eternal weight of glory far beyond all comparison.

2 Corinthians 6:3–4

. . . giving no cause for offense in anything, so that the ministry will not be discredited, ⁴but in everything commending ourselves as servants of God, in much *endurance,* in *afflictions,* in hardships, in distresses . . .

2 Corinthians 7:4–7

Great is my confidence in you; great is my boasting on your behalf. I am filled with *comfort*; I am overflowing with joy in all our *affliction.* [5]For even when we came into Macedonia our flesh had no rest, but we were afflicted on every side: conflicts without, fears within. [6]But God, who comforts the depressed, *comforted* us by the coming of Titus; [7]and not only by his coming, but also by the comfort with which he was comforted in you, as he reported to us your longing, your mourning, your zeal for me; so that I rejoiced even more.

2 Corinthians 11:23

Are they servants of Christ?—I speak as if insane—I more so; in far more labors, in far more imprisonments, beaten times without number, often in danger of *death.*

OTHER PAULINE PARALLELS

Romans 5:3

And not only this, but we also exult in our tribulations, knowing that tribulation brings about perseverance.

Romans 15:30–31

Now I urge you, brethren, by our Lord Jesus Christ and by the love of the Spirit, to strive together with me in *your prayers* to God for me, [31]that I may be rescued from those who are disobedient in Judea, and that my service for Jerusalem may prove acceptable to the saints.

1 Corinthians 15:32

If from human motives I fought with wild beasts at Ephesus, what does it profit me? If *the dead* are not *raised*, LET US EAT AND DRINK, FOR TOMORROW WE DIE.

Ephesians 1:3

Blessed be the God and Father of our Lord Jesus Christ, who has blessed us with every spiritual blessing in the heavenly places in Christ.

Philippians 1:19–20

For I know that this will turn out for my *deliverance* through *your prayers* and the provision of the Spirit of Jesus Christ, [20]according to my earnest expectation and *hope*, that I will not be put to shame in any-

thing, but that with all boldness, Christ will even now, as always, be exalted in my body, whether by life or by *death.*

Philippians 3:8, 10

More than that, I count all things to be loss in view of the surpassing value of knowing Christ Jesus my Lord, for whom I have suffered the loss of all things, and count them but rubbish so that I may gain Christ, . . . [10]that I may know Him and the power of His resurrection and the fellowship of His *sufferings*, being conformed to His *death.*

Colossians 1:24

Now I rejoice in my *sufferings* for your sake, and in my flesh I do my share on behalf of His body, which is the church, in filling up what is lacking in Christ's *afflictions.*

OTHER BIBLICAL PARALLELS

Psalm 56:13

For You have *delivered* my soul from *death*, Indeed my feet from stumbling, So that I may walk before God In the light of the living.

Isaiah 49:13

Shout for joy, O heavens! And rejoice, O earth! Break forth into joyful shouting, O mountains! For the Lord has *comforted* His people And will have compassion on His *afflicted.*

Acts 20:18–19

"You yourselves know, from the first day that I set foot in *Asia*, how I was with you the whole time, [19]serving the Lord with all humility and with tears and with trials which came upon me through the plots of the Jews."

1 Peter 1:3

Blessed be the God and Father of our Lord Jesus Christ, who according to His great *mercy* has caused us to be born again to a living *hope* through the resurrection of Jesus Christ from *the dead.*

1 Peter 4:13

But to the degree that you *share the sufferings of Christ*, keep on rejoicing, so that also at the revelation of His glory you may rejoice with exultation.

Qumran Hymns (1QH) 17[9].6–8, 13–14

As for me, from ruin to annihilation, from sickness to disease, from pains to tortures, [7]my soul reflects on your wonders; you, in your favor, have not rejected me, [8]from one moment to the next my soul delights in your bountiful *mercy.* . . . [13]In my troubles you *comfort* me. I delight in forgiveness, I console myself for former sin. [14]I know that there is *hope*, thanks to your kindness.

Letter to Epimachus (BGU 423)

I give *thanks* to the Lord Serapis because when I was in danger on the sea he saved me right away.

2 Corinthians 1:12–14

For our proud confidence is this: the testimony of our conscience, that in holiness and godly sincerity, not in fleshly wisdom but in the grace of God, we have conducted ourselves in the world, and especially toward you. [13]For we write nothing else to you than what you read and understand, and I hope you will understand until the end; [14]just as you also partially did understand us, that we are your reason to be proud as you also are ours, in the day of our Lord Jesus.

2 Corinthians 2:17

For we are not like many, peddling the word of God, but as from *sincerity*, but as from God, we speak in Christ in the sight of God.

2 Corinthians 5:11–12

Therefore, knowing the fear of the Lord, we persuade men, but we are made manifest to God; and *I hope* that we are made manifest also in your *consciences.* [12]We are not again commending ourselves to you but are giving you an occasion *to be proud* of us, so that you will have an answer for those who take pride in appearance and not in heart.

2 Corinthians 7:1

Therefore, having these promises, beloved, let us cleanse ourselves from all defilement of *flesh* and spirit, perfecting *holiness* in the fear of God.

2 Corinthians 8:24

Therefore openly before the churches, show them the proof of your love and of our reason for boasting about you.

2 Corinthians 10:2

I ask that when I am present I need not be bold with the *confidence* with which I propose to be courageous against some, who regard us as if we walked according to the *flesh.*

2 Corinthians 10:13, 15–17

But we will not boast beyond our measure, but within the measure of the sphere which God apportioned to us as a measure, to reach even as far as you, . . . [15]not boasting beyond our measure, that is, in other men's labors, but with the hope that as your faith grows, we will be, within our sphere, enlarged even more by you, [16]so as to preach the gospel even to the regions beyond you, and not to boast in what has been accomplished in the sphere of another. [17]But HE WHO BOASTS IS TO BOAST IN THE LORD.

2 Corinthians 12:18

I urged Titus to go, and I sent the brother with him. Titus did not take any advantage of you, did he? Did we not *conduct ourselves* in the same spirit and walk in the same steps?

Romans 9:1

I am telling the truth in Christ, I am not lying, my *conscience* testifies with me in the Holy Spirit.

1 Corinthians 1:7–8

You are not lacking in any gift, awaiting eagerly the revelation of our Lord Jesus Christ, [8]who will also confirm you to the end, blameless *in the day of our Lord Jesus* Christ.

1 Corinthians 1:20

Where is the wise man? Where is the scribe? Where is the debater of this age? Has not God made foolish the *wisdom* of *the world*?

1 Corinthians 3:10

According to *the grace of God* which was given to me, like a wise master builder I laid a foundation, and another is building on it. But each man must be careful how he builds on it.

1 Corinthians 13:12

For now we see in a mirror dimly, but then face to face; now I know *in part*, but then I will know fully just as I also have been fully known.

1 Corinthians 15:31

I affirm, brethren, by the boasting in you which I have in Christ Jesus our Lord, I die daily.

Ephesians 3:2–4

. . . if indeed you have heard of the stewardship of God's grace which was given to me for you; ³that by revelation there was made known to me the mystery, as I *wrote* before in brief. ⁴By referring to this, when *you read* you can *understand* my insight into the mystery of Christ.

Philippians 2:14–16

Do all things without grumbling or disputing; ¹⁵so that you will prove yourselves to be blameless and innocent, children of God above reproach in the midst of a crooked and perverse generation, among whom you appear as lights *in the world,* ¹⁶holding fast the word of life, so that *in the day* of Christ I will have reason to glory because I did not run in vain nor toil in vain.

OTHER BIBLICAL PARALLELS

Acts 24:14–16

"But this I admit to you, that according to the Way which they call a sect I do serve the God of our fathers, believing everything that is in accordance with the Law and that is written in the Prophets; ¹⁵having a hope in God, which these men cherish themselves, that there shall certainly be a resurrection of both the righteous and the wicked. ¹⁶In view of this, I also do my best to maintain always a blameless *conscience* both before God and before men."

James 3:14–15

But if you have bitter jealousy and selfish ambition in your heart, do not be arrogant and so lie against the truth. ¹⁵This *wisdom* is not that which comes down from above, but is earthly, natural, demonic.

2 Peter 3:15–16

Regard the patience of our Lord as salvation; just as also our beloved brother Paul, according to the *wisdom* given him, *wrote to you,* ¹⁶as also in all his letters, speaking in them of these things, in which are some things hard to *understand,* which the untaught and unstable distort, as they do also the rest of the Scriptures, to their own destruction.

2 Corinthians 1:15–22

In this confidence I intended at first to come to you, so that you might twice receive a blessing; ¹⁶that is, to pass your way into Macedonia, and again from Macedonia to come to you, and by you to be helped on my journey to Judea. ¹⁷Therefore, I was not vacillating when I intended to do this, was I? Or what I purpose, do I purpose according to the flesh, so that with me there will be yes, yes and no, no at the same time? ¹⁸But as God is faithful, our word to you is not yes and no. ¹⁹For the Son of God, Christ Jesus, who was preached among you by us—by me and Silvanus and Timothy—was not yes and no, but is yes in Him. ²⁰For as many as are the promises of God, in Him they are yes; therefore also through Him is our Amen to the glory of God through us. ²¹Now He who establishes us with you in Christ and anointed us is God, ²²who also sealed us and gave us the Spirit in our hearts as a pledge.

2 CORINTHIANS PARALLELS

2 Corinthians 1:1

Paul, an apostle of Christ Jesus by the will of God, and *Timothy* our brother, To the church of God which is at Corinth with all the saints who are throughout Achaia:

2 Corinthians 4:5

For we do not *preach* ourselves but Christ Jesus as Lord, and ourselves as your bondservants for Jesus' sake.

2 Corinthians 5:4–5

For indeed while we are in this tent, we groan, being burdened, because we do not want to be unclothed but to be clothed, so that what is mortal will be swallowed up by life. ⁵Now He who prepared us for this very purpose is God, who *gave* to *us the Spirit as a pledge.*

2 Corinthians 7:1

Therefore, having these *promises*, beloved, let us cleanse ourselves from all defilement of flesh and spirit, perfecting holiness in the fear of God.

2 Corinthians 8:1, 3–4, 18–19

Now, brethren, we wish to make known to you the grace of God which has been given in the churches of *Macedonia*. . . . [3]For I testify that according to their ability, and beyond their ability, they gave of their own accord, [4]begging us with much urging for the favor of participation in the support of the saints. . . . [18]We have sent along with him [Titus] the brother whose fame in the things of the gospel has spread through all the churches; [19]and not only this, but he has also been appointed by the churches to travel with us in this gracious work.

2 Corinthians 10:2

I ask that when I am present I need not be bold with the *confidence* with which I propose to be courageous against some, who regard us as if we walked *according to the flesh*.

2 Corinthians 13:1–2

This is the third time *I* am *coming to you*. EVERY FACT IS TO BE CONFIRMED BY THE TESTIMONY OF TWO OR THREE WITNESSES. [2]I have previously said when present the second time, and though now absent I say in advance to those who have sinned in the past and to all the rest as well, that if I come again I will not spare anyone.

OTHER PAULINE PARALLELS

1 Corinthians 1:9

God is faithful, through whom you were called into fellowship with His Son, Jesus Christ our Lord.

1 Corinthians 4:17, 19

For this reason I have sent to you *Timothy*, who is my beloved and faithful child in the Lord, and he will remind you of my ways which are in Christ, just as I teach everywhere in every church. . . . [19]But *I will come to you* soon, if the Lord wills, and I shall find out, not the words of those who are arrogant but their power.

1 Corinthians 16:3–7, 10

When I arrive, whomever you may approve, I will send them with letters to carry your gift to Jerusalem; [4]and if it is fitting for me to go also, they will go with me. [5]But *I will come to you* after I go through *Macedonia*, for I am going through Macedonia; [6]and perhaps I will stay with you, or even spend the winter, so that you may send me on my way wherever I may go. [7]For I do not wish to see you now just in passing; for I hope to remain with you for some time, if the Lord permits. . . . [10]Now if *Timothy* comes, see that he is with you without cause to be afraid, for he is doing the Lord's work, as I also am.

Ephesians 1:13

In Him, you also, after listening to the message of truth, the gospel of your salvation— having also believed, you were *sealed* in Him with *the* Holy *Spirit* of promise.

1 Thessalonians 1:1

Paul and *Silvanus* and *Timothy*, To the church of the Thessalonians in God the Father and the Lord Jesus Christ . . .

OTHER BIBLICAL PARALLELS

Deuteronomy 7:9

"Know therefore that the LORD your God, He is God, the *faithful God*, who keeps His covenant and His lovingkindness to a thousandth generation with those who love Him and keep His commandments."

Matthew 5:37

"But let your statement be, 'Yes, yes' or 'No, no'; anything beyond these is of evil."

Acts 18:1, 5

After these things he left Athens and went to Corinth. . . . [5]But when *Silas* and *Timothy* came down from *Macedonia*, Paul began devoting himself completely to the word, solemnly testifying to the Jews that Jesus was the Christ.

Acts 19:21

Now after these things were finished, Paul purposed in the spirit to go to Jerusalem after he had passed through *Macedonia* and Achaia, saying, "After I have been there, I must also see Rome."

James 5:12

But above all, my brethren, do not swear, either by heaven or by earth or with any other oath; but your *yes* is to be *yes*, and your *no, no,* so that you may not fall under judgment.

1 Peter 5:12

Through *Silvanus,* our faithful brother (for so I regard him), I have written to you briefly, exhorting and testifying that this is the true grace of God.

1 John 2:20

But you have an *anointing* from the Holy One, and you all know.

Revelation 3:14

To the angel of the church in Laodicea write: The *Amen,* the faithful and true Witness, the Beginning of the creation of God, says this . . .

Terence, The Eunuch *251–53*

Whatever they say I commend; if they turn around and say the opposite, I commend that as well. [252]He says *no,* I say *no*; he says *yes,* I say *yes.* In the end I commanded myself [253]to agree with them in everything.

2 Corinthians 1:23–2:4

But I call God as witness to my soul, that to spare you I did not come again to Corinth. [24]Not that we lord it over your faith, but are workers with you for your joy; for in your faith you are standing firm. [2:1]But I determined this for my own sake, that I would not come to you in sorrow again. [2]For if I cause you sorrow, who then makes me glad but the one whom I made sorrowful? [3]This is the very thing I wrote you, so that when I came, I would not have sorrow from those who ought to make me rejoice; having confidence in you all that my joy would be the joy of you all. [4]For out of much affliction and anguish of heart I wrote to you with many tears; not so that you would be made sorrowful, but that you might know the love which I have especially for you.

2 Corinthians 1:3–4

Blessed be the God and Father of our Lord Jesus Christ, the Father of mercies and God of all comfort, [4]who comforts us in all our *affliction* so that we will be able to comfort those who are in any affliction with the comfort with which we ourselves are comforted by God.

2 Corinthians 6:4, 9–10

. . . in everything commending ourselves as servants of God, in much endurance, in *afflictions,* in hardships, in distresses, . . . [9]as unknown yet well-known, as dying yet behold, we live; as punished yet not put to death, [10]as *sorrowful* yet always *rejoicing,* as poor yet making many rich, as having nothing yet possessing all things.

2 Corinthians 7:8–9

For though I *caused you sorrow* by my letter, I do not regret it; though I did regret it—for I see that that letter caused you sorrow, though only for a while— [9]I now *rejoice,* not that you were *made sorrowful,* but that you were made sorrowful to the point of repentance; for you were made sorrowful according to the will of God, so that you might not suffer loss in anything through us.

2 Corinthians 7:12–13

So although I *wrote to you,* it was not for the sake of the offender nor for the sake of the one offended, but that your earnestness on our behalf might be made known to you in the sight of God. [13]For this reason we have been comforted. And besides our comfort, we *rejoiced* even much more for the *joy* of Titus, because his spirit has been refreshed by you all.

2 Corinthians 12:14–15

Here for this third time I am ready to *come* to you, and I will not be a burden to you; for I do not seek what is yours, but you; for children are not responsible to save up for their parents, but parents for their children. [15]I will most gladly spend and be expended for your souls. If I *love* you more, am I to be loved less?

2 Corinthians 12:21–13:2

I am afraid that when I *come again* my God may humiliate me before you, and I may mourn over many of those who have sinned in the past and not repented of the impurity, immorality and sensuality which they have practiced. ^{13:1}This is the third time I am coming to you. EVERY FACT IS TO BE CONFIRMED BY THE TESTIMONY OF TWO OR THREE WITNESSES. ²I have previously said when present the second time, and though now absent I say in advance to those who have sinned in the past and to all the rest as well, that if I come again I will not *spare* anyone.

OTHER PAULINE PARALLELS

1 Corinthians 3:8–9
Now he who plants and he who waters are one; but each will receive his own reward according to his own labor. ⁹For we are God's fellow *workers*; you are God's field, God's building.

1 Corinthians 4:19, 21
But I will come to you soon, if the Lord wills, and I shall find out, not the words of those who are arrogant but their power. . . . ²¹What do you desire? Shall I *come* to you with a rod, or with *love* and a spirit of gentleness?

1 Corinthians 16:13
Be on the alert, *stand firm in* the *faith*, act like men, be strong.

Galatians 1:20
Now in what I am writing to you, I assure you before God that I am not lying.

Philippians 2:17–18
But even if I am being poured out as a drink offering upon the sacrifice and service of your faith, I *rejoice* and share my *joy* with you all. ¹⁸You too, I urge you, rejoice in the same way and share your joy with me.

1 Thessalonians 1:5
Our gospel did not come to you in word only, but also in power and in the Holy Spirit and with full conviction; just as you know what kind of men we proved to be among you for your sake.

1 Thessalonians 2:5–6
For we never came with flattering speech, as you know, nor with a pretext for greed— God is *witness*— ⁶nor did we seek glory from men, either from you or from others, even though as apostles of Christ we might have asserted our authority.

OTHER BIBLICAL PARALLELS

Jeremiah 42:5
Then they said to Jeremiah, "May the LORD be a true and faithful *witness* against us if we do not act in accordance with the whole message with which the LORD your God will send you to us."

Acts 20:29–31
"I know that after my departure savage wolves will come in among you, not sparing the flock; ³⁰and from among your own selves men will arise, speaking perverse things, to draw away the disciples after them. ³¹Therefore be on the alert, remembering that night and day for a period of three years I did not cease to admonish each one *with tears*."

Hebrews 12:11
All discipline for the moment seems not to be *joyful*, but *sorrowful*; yet to those who have been trained by it, afterwards it yields the peaceful fruit of righteousness.

1 Peter 5:1–3
Therefore, I exhort the elders among you, as your fellow elder and witness of the sufferings of Christ, and a partaker also of the glory that is to be revealed, ²shepherd the flock of God among you, exercising oversight not under compulsion, but voluntarily, according to the will of God; and not for sordid gain, but with eagerness; ³nor yet as *lording it over* those allotted to your charge, but proving to be examples to the flock.

2 Corinthians 2:5–13

But if any has caused sorrow, he has caused sorrow not to me, but in some degree—in order not to say too much—to all of you. ⁶Sufficient for such a one is this punishment which was inflicted by the majority, ⁷so that on the contrary you should rather forgive and comfort him, otherwise such a one might be overwhelmed by excessive sorrow. ⁸Wherefore I urge you to reaffirm your love for him. ⁹For to this end also I wrote, so that I might put you to the test, whether you are obedient in all things. [10]But one whom you forgive anything, I forgive also; for indeed what I have forgiven, if I have forgiven anything, I did it for your sakes in the presence of Christ, [11]so that no advantage would be taken of us by Satan, for we are not ignorant of his schemes. [12]Now when I came to Troas for the gospel of Christ and when a door was opened for me in the Lord, [13]I had no rest for my spirit, not finding Titus my brother; but taking my leave of them, I went on to Macedonia.

2 CORINTHIANS PARALLELS

2 Corinthians 1:3–4

Blessed be the God and Father of our Lord Jesus Christ, the Father of mercies and God of all comfort, [4]who comforts us in all our affliction so that we will be able to *comfort* those who are in any affliction with the comfort with which we ourselves are comforted by God.

2 Corinthians 7:5–9

For even when we came into *Macedonia* our flesh had *no rest*, but we were afflicted on every side: conflicts without, fears within. [6]But God, who *comforts* the depressed, comforted us by the coming of *Titus*; [7]and not only by his coming, but also by the comfort with which he was comforted in you, as he reported to us your longing, your mourning, your zeal for me; so that I rejoiced even more. [8]For though I *caused* you *sorrow* by my letter, I do not regret it; though I did regret it—for I see that that letter caused you sorrow, though only for a while— [9]I now rejoice, not that you were made sorrowful, but that you were made sorrowful to the point of repentance; for you were made sorrowful according to the will of God, so that you might not suffer loss in anything through us.

2 Corinthians 7:11–13, 15

For behold what earnestness this very thing, this godly *sorrow*, has produced in you: what vindication of yourselves, what indignation, what fear, what longing, what zeal, what avenging of wrong! In everything you demonstrated yourselves to be innocent in the matter. [12]So although I *wrote* to you, it was not for the sake of the offender nor for the sake of the one offended, but that your earnestness on our behalf might be made

known to you in the sight of God. [13]For this reason we have been *comforted*. And besides our comfort, we rejoiced even much more for the joy of *Titus*, because his spirit has been refreshed by you all. . . . [15]His affection abounds all the more toward you, as he remembers the *obedience* of you all, how you received him with fear and trembling.

2 Corinthians 8:23

As for *Titus*, he is my partner and fellow worker among you; as for our brethren, they are messengers of the churches, a glory to Christ.

2 Corinthians 10:5–6, 8

We are destroying speculations and every lofty thing raised up against the knowledge of God, and we are taking every thought captive to the *obedience* of Christ, [6]and we are ready to *punish* all disobedience, whenever your obedience is complete. . . . [8]For even if I boast somewhat further about our authority, which the Lord gave for building you up and not for destroying you, I will not be put to shame.

2 Corinthians 11:3

But I am afraid that, as the serpent deceived Eve by his craftiness, your minds will be led astray from the simplicity and purity of devotion to Christ.

2 Corinthians 11:13–14

For such men are false apostles, deceitful workers, disguising themselves as apostles of Christ. [14]No wonder, for even *Satan* disguises himself as an angel of light.

OTHER PAULINE PARALLELS

1 Corinthians 5:1–5

It is actually reported that there is immorality among you, and immorality of such a kind as does not exist even among the Gentiles, that someone has his father's wife. [2]You have become arrogant and have not mourned instead, so that the one who had done this deed would be removed from your midst. [3]For I, on my part, though absent in body but present in spirit, have already judged him who has so committed this, as though I were present. [4]In the name of our Lord Jesus, when you are assembled, and I with you in spirit, with the power of our Lord Jesus, [5]I have decided to deliver

195

such a one to *Satan* for the destruction of his flesh, so that his spirit may be saved in the day of the Lord Jesus.

1 Corinthians 16:5, 8–9

But I will come to you after I go through *Macedonia*, for I am going through Macedonia. . . . [8]But I will remain in Ephesus until Pentecost; [9]for *a* wide *door* for effective service has *opened* to me, and there are many adversaries.

Galatians 6:1

Brethren, even if anyone is caught in any trespass, you who are spiritual, restore such a one in a spirit of gentleness; each one looking to yourself, so that you too will not be tempted.

Colossians 3:12–14

So, as those who have been chosen of God, holy and beloved, put on a heart of compassion, kindness, humility, gentleness and patience; [13]bearing with one another, and *forgiving* each other, whoever has a complaint against anyone; just as the Lord forgave you, so also should you. [14]Beyond all these things put on *love*, which is the perfect bond of unity.

2 Thessalonians 3:14–15

If anyone does not obey our instruction in this letter, take special note of that person and do not associate with him, so that he will be put to shame. [15]Yet do not regard him as an enemy, but admonish him as a brother.

2 Timothy 4:13

When you come bring the cloak which I left at *Troas* with Carpus, and the books, especially the parchments.

OTHER BIBLICAL PARALLELS

Jeremiah 8:18

My *sorrow* is beyond healing, My heart is faint within me!

Luke 22:31

"Simon, Simon, behold, *Satan* has demanded permission to sift you like wheat."

Acts 16:7–11

After they came to Mysia, they were trying to go into Bithynia, and the Spirit of Jesus did not permit them; [8]and passing by Mysia, they came down to *Troas*. [9]A vision appeared to Paul in the night: a man of Macedonia was standing and appealing to him, and saying, "Come over to *Macedonia* and help us." [10]When he had seen the vision, immediately we sought to go into Macedonia, concluding that God had called us to preach *the gospel* to them. [11]So putting out to sea from Troas, we ran a straight course to Samothrace, and on the day following to Neapolis.

1 Peter 5:8

Be of sober spirit, be on the alert. Your adversary, the devil, prowls around like a roaring lion, seeking someone to devour.

2 Corinthians 2:14–17

But thanks be to God, who always leads us in triumph in Christ, and manifests through us the sweet aroma of the knowledge of Him in every place. [15]For we are a fragrance of Christ to God among those who are being saved and among those who are perishing; [16]to the one an aroma from death to death, to the other an aroma from life to life. And who is adequate for these things? [17]For we are not like many, peddling the word of God, but as from sincerity, but as from God, we speak in Christ in the sight of God.

2 CORINTHIANS PARALLELS

2 Corinthians 1:12

For our proud confidence is this: the testimony of our conscience, that in holiness and godly *sincerity*, not in fleshly wisdom but in the grace of God, we have conducted ourselves in the world, and especially toward you.

2 Corinthians 4:1–3

Therefore, since we have this ministry, as we received mercy, we do not lose heart, [2]but we have renounced the things hidden because of shame, not walking in craftiness or adulterating *the word of God*, but by the *manifestation* of truth commending ourselves to every man's conscience *in the sight of God.* [3]And even if our gospel is veiled, it is veiled to *those who are perishing.*

2 Corinthians 11:5–8

For I consider myself not in the least inferior to the most eminent apostles. [6]But even if I am unskilled in speech, yet I am not so in *knowledge*; in fact, in every way we have made this evident to you in all things. [7]Or did I commit a sin in humbling myself so that you might be exalted, because I preached the gospel of God to you without charge? [8]I robbed other churches by taking wages from them to serve you.

2 Corinthians 12:19

All this time you have been thinking that we are defending ourselves to you. Actually, it is *in the sight of God* that we have been *speaking in Christ*; and all for your upbuilding, beloved.

OTHER PAULINE PARALLELS

1 Corinthians 1:18

For the word of the cross is foolishness to *those who are perishing*, but to us *who are being saved* it is the power of God.

1 Corinthians 4:9

For, I think, God has exhibited us apostles last of all, as men condemned to death; because we have become a spectacle to the world, both to angels and to men.

1 Corinthians 5:8

Therefore let us celebrate the feast, not with old leaven, nor with the leaven of malice and wickedness, but with the unleavened bread of *sincerity* and truth.

1 Corinthians 15:57

Thanks be to God, who gives us the victory through our Lord Jesus Christ.

Ephesians 1:15–17

For this reason I too, having heard of the faith in the Lord Jesus which exists among you and your love for all the saints, [16]do not cease giving *thanks* for you, while making mention of you in my prayers; [17]that the God of our Lord Jesus Christ, the Father of glory, may give to you a spirit of wisdom and of revelation in *the knowledge of Him*.

Ephesians 5:2

Walk in love, just as Christ also loved you and gave Himself up for us, an offering and a sacrifice to God as a fragrant *aroma*.

Philippians 4:18

But I have received everything in full and have an abundance; I am amply supplied, having received from Epaphroditus what you have sent, a fragrant *aroma*, an acceptable sacrifice, well-pleasing to God.

Colossians 2:15

When He had disarmed the rulers and authorities, He made a public display of them, having *triumphed* over them through Him.

1 Thessalonians 1:8

For the word of the Lord has sounded forth from you, not only in Macedonia and Achaia, but also *in every place* your faith toward God has gone forth, so that we have no need to say anything.

OTHER BIBLICAL PARALLELS

Leviticus 1:9

"Its entrails, however, and its legs he shall wash with water. And the priest shall offer up in smoke all of it on the altar for a burnt offering, an offering by fire of a soothing *aroma* to the LORD."

Ezekiel 8:11

Standing in front of them were seventy elders of the house of Israel, with Jaazaniah the son of Shaphan standing among them, each man with his censer in his hand and the *fragrance* of the cloud of incense rising.

Ezekiel 20:41

"As a soothing *aroma* I will accept you when I bring you out from the peoples and gather you from the lands where you are scattered; and I will prove Myself holy among you in the sight of the nations."

NONCANONICAL PARALLELS

Sirach 24:1, 15

Wisdom praises herself, and tells of her glory in the midst of her people. . . . [15]Like cassia and camel's thorn I gave forth perfume, and like choice myrrh I spread my *fragrance*, like galbanum, onycha, and stacte, and like the odor of incense in the tent.

Plato, Protagoras 313C–D

And we must make sure that the sophists do not deceive us when touting their wares, like merchants and peddlers of ordinary food.... ᴰ ... Like them, those who deal in education, touring the cities and *peddling* their learning to anyone who will buy, vouch for whatever they have to sell, though it's likely that they do not know whether their wares are good for the soul or bad.

Appian, The Punic Wars *66*

The order [of the *triumph*], which they still continue to follow today, was as follows: ... trumpeters led the way and wagons full of spoil.... After them were white oxen, and after them elephants and all the Carthaginian and Numidian leaders who had been captured.... After this came a throng of incense-bearers, and after them the general himself on a chariot.

2 Corinthians 3:1–6

Are we beginning to commend ourselves again? Or do we need, as some, letters of commendation to you or from you? ²You are our letter, written in our hearts, known and read by all men; ³being manifested that you are a letter of Christ, cared for by us, written not with ink but with the Spirit of the living God, not on tablets of stone but on tablets of human hearts. ⁴Such confidence we have through Christ toward God. ⁵Not that we are adequate in ourselves to consider anything as coming from ourselves, but our adequacy is from God, ⁶who also made us adequate as servants of a new covenant, not of the letter but of the Spirit; for the letter kills, but the Spirit gives life.

2 CORINTHIANS PARALLELS

2 Corinthians 1:12

For our proud *confidence* is this: the testimony of our conscience, that in holiness and godly sincerity, not in fleshly wisdom but in the grace of God, we have conducted ourselves in the world, and especially toward you.

2 Corinthians 5:12

We are not again *commending ourselves* to you but are giving you an occasion to be proud of us, so that you will have an answer for those who take pride in appearance and not in *heart.*

2 Corinthians 6:4

... in everything *commending ourselves* as *servants* of God, in much endurance, in afflictions, in hardships, in distresses ...

2 Corinthians 10:12, 18

For we are not bold to class or compare ourselves with some of those who *commend* themselves; but when they measure themselves by themselves and compare themselves with themselves, they are without understanding.... ¹⁸For it is not he who commends himself that is approved, but he whom the Lord commends.

2 Corinthians 12:11–12

I have become foolish; you yourselves compelled me. Actually I should have been *commended* by you, for in no respect was I inferior to the most eminent apostles, even though I am a nobody. ¹²The signs of a true apostle were performed among you with all perseverance, by signs and wonders and miracles.

OTHER PAULINE PARALLELS

Romans 2:29

But he is a Jew who is one inwardly; and circumcision is that which is of the *heart,* by *the Spirit,* not by *the letter*; and his praise is not from men, but from God.

Romans 7:6

But now we have been released from the Law, having died to that by which we were bound, so that we serve in newness of *the Spirit* and not in oldness of *the letter.*

Romans 8:2

For the law of *the Spirit* of life in Christ Jesus has set you free from the law of sin and of death.

Romans 16:1–2

I *commend* to you our sister Phoebe, who is a servant of the church which is at Cenchrea; ²that you receive her in the Lord in a manner worthy of the saints, and that you help her in whatever matter she may have need of you; for she herself has also been a helper of many, and of myself as well.

1 Corinthians 9:2

If to others I am not an apostle, at least I am to you; for you are the seal of my apostleship in the Lord.

1 Corinthians 11:25

In the same way He took the cup also after supper, saying, "This cup is the *new covenant* in My blood; do this, as often as you drink it, in remembrance of Me."

1 Corinthians 16:3

When I arrive, whomever you may approve, I will send them with *letters* to carry your gift to Jerusalem.

1 Thessalonians 2:7

But we proved to be gentle among you, as a nursing mother tenderly *cares for* her own children.

Exodus 31:18

When He had finished speaking with him upon Mount Sinai, He gave Moses the two tablets of the testimony, *tablets of stone*, written by the finger of God.

Jeremiah 31:31, 33

"Behold, days are coming," declares the Lord, "when I will make *a new covenant* with the house of Israel and with the house of Judah" . . . ³³"But this is the covenant which I will make with the house of Israel after those days," declares the Lord, "I will put My law within them and on their *heart* I will *write* it; and I will be their God, and they shall be My people."

Proverbs 3:3

Do not let kindness and truth leave you; Bind them around your neck, *Write* them on the *tablet* of your *heart*.

Acts 18:27

And when he [Apollos] wanted to go across to Achaia, the brethren encouraged him and wrote to the disciples to welcome him; and when he had arrived, he greatly helped those who had believed through grace.

Hebrews 9:15

For this reason He is the mediator of a *new covenant*, so that, since a death has taken place for the redemption of the transgres-

sions that were committed under the first covenant, those who have been called may receive the promise of the eternal inheritance.

Cicero, Letters to His Friends *13.77.2*

I strongly *commend* to you M. Bolanus, a good and noble man possessed of every good quality and an old friend of mine. You would do me a favor if you endeavor to make him see that this recommendation has proven to be of assistance to him.

Epictetus, Discourses *2.3.1*

Diogenes spoke well to the man who asked for a *letter of commendation* from him. "That you are a person," he said, "he will know when he sees you. But whether you are good or bad he will know if he is experienced in distinguishing good things from bad. But if he is inexperienced at this, it will not matter if I write him ten thousand times."

2 Corinthians 3:7–11

But if the ministry of death, in letters engraved on stones, came with glory, so that the sons of Israel could not look intently at the face of Moses because of the glory of his face, fading as it was, ⁸how will the ministry of the Spirit fail to be even more with glory? ⁹For if the ministry of condemnation has glory, much more does the ministry of righteousness abound in glory. ¹⁰For indeed what had glory, in this case has no glory because of the glory that surpasses it. ¹¹For if that which fades away was with glory, much more that which remains is in glory.

2 Corinthians 4:3–6

And even if our gospel is veiled, it is veiled to those who are perishing, ⁴in whose case the god of this world has blinded the minds of the unbelieving so that they might not see the light of the gospel of the *glory* of Christ, who is the image of God. ⁵For we do not preach ourselves but Christ Jesus as Lord, and ourselves as your bond-servants for Jesus' sake. ⁶For God, who said, "Light shall shine out of darkness," is the One who has shone in our hearts to give the Light of the knowledge of the glory of God in *the face* of Christ.

2 Corinthians 5:18

Now all these things are from God, who reconciled us to Himself through Christ and gave us *the ministry* of reconciliation.

2 Corinthians 11:14–15

No wonder, for even Satan disguises himself as an angel of light. [15]Therefore it is not surprising if his servants also disguise themselves as servants of *righteousness*, whose end will be according to their deeds.

OTHER PAULINE PARALLELS

Romans 3:21

But now apart from the Law the *righteousness* of God has been manifested, being witnessed by the Law and the Prophets.

Romans 5:16–18

The gift is not like that which came through the one who sinned; for on the one hand the judgment arose from one transgression resulting in *condemnation*, but on the other hand the free gift arose from many transgressions resulting in justification. [17]For if by the transgression of the one, *death* reigned through the one, much more those who receive the abundance of grace and of the gift of *righteousness* will reign in life through the One, Jesus Christ. [18]So then as through one transgression there resulted condemnation to all men, even so through one act of righteousness there resulted justification of life to all men.

Romans 7:9–11

I was once alive apart from the Law; but when the commandment came, sin became alive and I died; [10]and this commandment, which was to result in life, proved to result in *death* for me; [11]for sin, taking an opportunity through the commandment, deceived me and through it killed me.

Romans 8:2

For the law of *the Spirit* of life in Christ Jesus has set you free from the law of sin and of *death*.

Romans 10:3–4

For not knowing about God's *righteousness* and seeking to establish their own, they did not subject themselves to the righteousness of God. [4]For Christ is the end of the law for righteousness to everyone who believes.

Galatians 3:19–22

Why the Law then? It was added because of transgressions, having been ordained through angels by the agency of a mediator, until the seed would come to whom the promise had been made. [20]Now a mediator is not for one party only; whereas God is only one. [21]Is the Law then contrary to the promises of God? May it never be! For if a law had been given which was able to impart life, then *righteousness* would indeed have been based on law. [22]But the Scripture has shut up everyone under sin, so that the promise by faith in Jesus Christ might be given to those who believe.

OTHER BIBLICAL PARALLELS

Exodus 24:16–17

The *glory* of the Lord rested on Mount Sinai, and the cloud covered it for six days; and on the seventh day He called to *Moses* from the midst of the cloud. [17]And to the eyes of *the sons of Israel* the appearance of the glory of the Lord was like a consuming fire on the mountain top.

Exodus 32:16

The tablets were God's work, and the writing was God's writing *engraved* on the tablets.

Exodus 34:29–32

It came about when *Moses* was coming down from Mount Sinai (and the two tablets of the testimony were in Moses' hand as he was coming down from the mountain), that Moses did not know that the skin of his *face* shone because of his speaking with Him. [30]So when Aaron and all *the sons of Israel* saw Moses, behold, the skin of his face shone, and they were afraid to come near him. [31]Then Moses called to them, and Aaron and all the rulers in the congregation returned to him; and Moses spoke to them. [32]Afterward all the sons of Israel came near, and he commanded them to do everything that the Lord had spoken to him on Mount Sinai.

2 Esdras (4 Ezra) 9:36–37

"For we who have received the law and sinned will perish, as well as our hearts that received it; ³⁷the law, however, does not perish but survives in its *glory*."

2 Corinthians 3:12–18

Therefore having such a hope, we use great boldness in our speech, ¹³and are not like Moses, who used to put a veil over his face so that the sons of Israel would not look intently at the end of what was fading away. ¹⁴But their minds were hardened; for until this very day at the reading of the old covenant the same veil remains unlifted, because it is removed in Christ. ¹⁵But to this day whenever Moses is read, a veil lies over their heart; ¹⁶but whenever a person turns to the Lord, the veil is taken away. ¹⁷Now the Lord is the Spirit, and where the Spirit of the Lord is, there is liberty. ¹⁸But we all, with unveiled face, beholding as in a mirror the glory of the Lord, are being transformed into the same image from glory to glory, just as from the Lord, the Spirit.

2 CORINTHIANS PARALLELS

2 Corinthians 1:9–10

Indeed, we had the sentence of death within ourselves so that we would not trust in ourselves, but in God who raises the dead; ¹⁰who delivered us from so great a peril of death, and will deliver us, He on whom we have set our *hope*.

2 Corinthians 5:4–5

For indeed while we are in this tent, we groan, being burdened, because we do not want to be unclothed but to be clothed, so that what is mortal will be swallowed up by life. ⁵Now He who prepared us for this very purpose is God, who gave to us *the Spirit* as a pledge.

2 Corinthians 10:1

Now I, Paul, myself urge you by the meekness and gentleness of Christ—I who am meek when face to face with you, but *bold* toward you when absent!

Romans 7:6

But now we have been released from the Law, having died to that by which we were bound, so that we serve in newness of *the Spirit* and not in *oldness* of the letter.

Romans 8:29–30

For those whom He foreknew, He also predestined to become conformed to *the image* of His Son, so that He would be the firstborn among many brethren; ³⁰and these whom He predestined, He also called; and these whom He called, He also justified; and these whom He justified, He also *glorified*.

Romans 11:7–8

What then? What Israel is seeking, it has not obtained, but those who were chosen obtained it, and the rest were *hardened*; ⁸just as it is written, "GOD GAVE THEM A SPIRIT OF STUPOR, EYES TO SEE NOT AND EARS TO HEAR NOT, DOWN TO *THIS VERY DAY*."

1 Corinthians 13:12

For now we see *in a mirror* dimly, but then face to *face*; now I know in part, but then I will know fully just as I also have been fully known.

1 Corinthians 15:45, 47, 49

So also it is written, "The first MAN, Adam, BECAME A LIVING SOUL." The last Adam became a life-giving spirit. . . . ⁴⁷The first man is from the earth, earthy; the second man is from heaven. . . . ⁴⁹Just as we have borne the image of the earthy, we will also bear *the image* of the heavenly.

Galatians 2:3–4

But not even Titus, who was with me, though he was a Greek, was compelled to be circumcised. ⁴But it was because of the false brethren secretly brought in, who had sneaked in to spy out our *liberty* which we have in Christ Jesus, in order to bring us into bondage.

Philippians 3:20–21

For our citizenship is in heaven, from which also we eagerly wait for a Savior, the Lord Jesus Christ; ²¹who will *transform* the body of our humble state into conformity with the body of His *glory*, by the exertion of the power that He has even to subject all things to Himself.

Colossians 3:9–10

Do not lie to one another, since you laid aside the old self with its evil practices, [10]and have put on the new self who is being renewed to a true knowledge according to *the image* of the One who created him.

1 Thessalonians 1:9

For they themselves report about us what kind of a reception we had with you, and how you *turned to* God from idols to serve a living and true God.

OTHER BIBLICAL PARALLELS

Exodus 34:33–35

When *Moses* had finished speaking with them, he *put a veil over his face*. [34]But whenever Moses went in before the LORD to speak with Him, he would take off the veil until he came out; and whenever he came out and spoke to *the sons of Israel* what he had been commanded, [35]the sons of Israel would see the face of Moses, that the skin of Moses' face shone. So Moses would replace the veil over his face until he went in to speak with Him.

Jeremiah 31:31–32

"Behold, days are coming," declares the LORD, "when I will make a new covenant with the house of Israel and with the house of Judah, [32]not like the *covenant* which I made with their fathers in the day I took them by the hand to bring them out of the land of Egypt, My covenant which they broke, although I was a husband to them."

Acts 11:21

And the hand of the Lord was with them, and a large number who believed *turned to* the Lord.

Acts 15:21

"For *Moses* from ancient generations has in every city those who preach him, since he is *read* in the synagogues every Sabbath."

Acts 19:8

And he [Paul] entered the synagogue and continued *speaking* out *boldly* for three months, reasoning and persuading them about the kingdom of God.

NONCANONICAL PARALLELS

Wisdom of Solomon 7:24–26

For wisdom is more mobile than any motion; because of her pureness she pervades and penetrates all things. [25]For she is a breath of the power of God, and a pure emanation of *the glory* of the Almighty; therefore nothing defiled gains entrance into her. [26]For she is a reflection of eternal light, a spotless *mirror* of the working of God, and an *image* of his goodness.

2 Baruch 51:3, 8

As for the *glory* of those who proved to be righteous, . . . their splendor will then be glorified by *transformations*, and the shape of their *face* will be changed into the light of their beauty so that they may acquire and receive the undying world which is promised to them. . . . [8]For they shall see that world which is now invisible to them, and they will see a time which is now hidden to them.

2 Corinthians 4:1–6

Therefore, since we have this ministry, as we received mercy, we do not lose heart, [2]but we have renounced the things hidden because of shame, not walking in craftiness or adulterating the word of God, but by the manifestation of truth commending ourselves to every man's conscience in the sight of God. [3]And even if our gospel is veiled, it is veiled to those who are perishing, [4]in whose case the god of this world has blinded the minds of the unbelieving so that they might not see the light of the gospel of the glory of Christ, who is the image of God. [5]For we do not preach ourselves but Christ Jesus as Lord, and ourselves as your bondservants for Jesus' sake. [6]For God, who said, "Light shall shine out of darkness," is the One who has shone in our hearts to give the Light of the knowledge of the glory of God in the face of Christ.

2 CORINTHIANS PARALLELS

2 Corinthians 1:12

For our proud confidence is this: the testimony of our *conscience*, that in holiness and godly sincerity, not in fleshly wisdom but in the grace of God, we have conducted ourselves in the world, and especially toward you.

2 Corinthians 2:15–17

For we are a fragrance of Christ to God among those who are being saved and among *those who are perishing*; [16]to the one an aroma from death to death, to the other an aroma from life to life. And who is adequate for these things? [17]For we are not like many, peddling *the word of God*, but as from sincerity, but as from God, we speak in Christ *in the sight of God*.

2 Corinthians 3:7–8

But if the ministry of death, in letters engraved on stones, came with *glory*, so that the sons of Israel could not look intently at the *face* of Moses because of the glory of his face, fading as it was, [8]how will the *ministry* of the Spirit fail to be even more with glory?

2 Corinthians 5:11–12

Therefore, knowing the fear of the Lord, we persuade men, but we are made *manifest* to God; and I hope that we are made manifest also in your *consciences*. [12]We are not again *commending ourselves* to you but are giving you an occasion to be proud of us, so that you will have an answer for those who take pride in appearance and not in heart.

2 Corinthians 11:3

But I am afraid that, as the serpent deceived Eve by his *craftiness*, your *minds* will be led astray from the simplicity and purity of devotion to Christ.

2 Corinthians 12:14, 16

Here for this third time I am ready to come to you, and I will not be a burden to you; for I do not seek what is yours, but you; for children are not responsible to save up for their parents, but parents for their children. . . . [16]But be that as it may, I did not burden you myself; nevertheless, *crafty* fellow that I am, I took you in by deceit.

OTHER PAULINE PARALLELS

Ephesians 2:1–2

And you were dead in your trespasses and sins, [2]in which you formerly walked according to the course of *this world*, according to the prince of the power of the air, of the spirit that is now working in the sons of disobedience.

Philippians 2:10–11

At the name of Jesus EVERY KNEE WILL BOW, of those who are in heaven and on earth and under the earth, [11]and that every tongue will confess that Jesus Christ is Lord, to *the glory of God* the Father.

Colossians 1:15

He is *the image of* the invisible *God*, the firstborn of all creation.

1 Thessalonians 2:3, 5

For our exhortation does not come from error or impurity or by way of deceit; . . . [5]For we never came with flattering speech, as you know, nor with a pretext for greed.

2 Timothy 1:9–11

. . . according to His own purpose and grace which was granted us in Christ Jesus from all eternity, [10]but now has been revealed by the appearing of our Savior Christ Jesus, who abolished death and brought life and immortality to *light* through *the gospel*, [11]for which I was appointed a preacher and an apostle and a teacher.

OTHER BIBLICAL PARALLELS

Genesis 1:3

Then God said, "Let there be *light*"; and there was light.

Genesis 1:27

God created man in His own image, in *the image of God* He created him; male and female He created them.

Isaiah 9:2

The people who walk in *darkness* Will see a great *light*; Those who live in a dark land, The light will *shine* on them.

Habakkuk 2:14

"For the earth will be filled With *the knowledge of the glory* of the LORD, As the waters cover the sea."

Acts 26:16–18

"For this purpose I have appeared to you, to appoint you a minister and a witness not only to the things which you have seen, but also to the things in which I will appear to you; [17]rescuing you from the Jewish people and from the Gentiles, to whom I am sending you, [18]to open their eyes so that they may turn from *darkness* to *light* and from the dominion of Satan to God, that they may receive forgiveness of sins and an inheritance among those who have been sanctified by faith in Me."

Hebrews 1:3

And He is the radiance of His *glory* and the exact representation of His nature, and upholds all things by the word of His power. When He had made purification of sins, He sat down at the right hand of the Majesty on high.

Testament of Judah 19:4–20:2

"The prince of error *blinded* me and I was ignorant—as a human being, as flesh, in my corrupt sins—until I learned of my own weakness after supposing myself to be invincible. [20:1]So understand, my children, that two spirits await an opportunity with humanity: the spirit of *truth* and the spirit of error. [2]In between is the *conscience* of the *mind* which inclines as it will."

Philo, On the Confusion of Tongues 97

For it is appropriate for those who entered into association with *knowledge* to desire to see The One Who Is, but, if they are unable to do so, to see at least his *image*, the most holy Word.

Lucian, Hermotimus 59

I for one do not agree with you in saying that philosophy and wine are similar, except in this alone, that philosophers sell their lessons as wine-merchants their wine—most of them *adulterating* and cheating and giving false measure.

2 Corinthians 4:7–12

But we have this treasure in earthen vessels, so that the surpassing greatness of the power will be of God and not from ourselves; [8]we are afflicted in every way, but not crushed; perplexed, but not despairing; [9]persecuted, but not forsaken; struck down, but not destroyed;

[10]always carrying about in the body the dying of Jesus, so that the life of Jesus also may be manifested in our body. [11]For we who live are constantly being delivered over to death for Jesus' sake, so that the life of Jesus also may be manifested in our mortal flesh. [12]So death works in us, but life in you.

2 Corinthians 1:3–5, 8

Blessed be the God and Father of our Lord Jesus Christ, the Father of mercies and God of all comfort, [4]who comforts us in all our *affliction* so that we will be able to comfort those who are in any affliction with the comfort with which we ourselves are comforted by God. [5]For just as the sufferings of Christ are ours in abundance, so also our comfort is abundant through Christ. . . . [8]For we do not want you to be unaware, brethren, of our affliction which came to us in Asia, that we were burdened excessively, beyond our strength, so that we *despaired* even of life.

2 Corinthians 6:4–5, 7–10

. . . in everything commending ourselves as servants of God, in much endurance, in *afflictions*, in hardships, in distresses, [5]in beatings, in imprisonments, in tumults, in labors, in sleeplessness, in hunger, . . . [7]in the word of truth, in *the power of God*; by the weapons of righteousness for the right hand and the left, [8]by glory and dishonor, by evil report and good report; regarded as deceivers and yet true; [9]as unknown yet well-known, as *dying* yet behold, we *live*; as punished yet not put to *death*, [10]as sorrowful yet always rejoicing, as poor yet making many rich, as having nothing yet possessing all things.

2 Corinthians 7:5

For even when we came into Macedonia our flesh had no rest, but we were *afflicted* on every side: conflicts without, fears within.

2 Corinthians 12:10

Therefore I am well content with weaknesses, with insults, with distresses, with *persecutions*, with difficulties, for Christ's sake; for when I am weak, then I am strong.

Romans 6:5

For if we have become united with Him in the likeness of His *death*, certainly we shall also be in the likeness of His resurrection.

Romans 8:35

Who will separate us from the love of Christ? Will tribulation, or distress, or *persecution*, or famine, or nakedness, or peril, or sword?

1 Corinthians 4:9, 11–13

For, I think, God has exhibited us apostles last of all, as men condemned to *death*; because we have become a spectacle to the world, both to angels and to men. . . . [11]To this present hour we are both hungry and thirsty, and are poorly clothed, and are roughly treated, and are homeless; [12]and we toil, working with our own hands; when we are reviled, we bless; when we are *persecuted*, we endure; [13]when we are slandered, we try to conciliate; we have become as the scum of the world, the dregs of all things, even until now.

Galatians 2:20

"I have been crucified with Christ; and it is no longer I who live, but Christ lives in me; and the *life* which I now live in the *flesh* I live by faith in the Son of God, who loved me and gave Himself up for me."

Galatians 6:17

From now on let no one cause trouble for me, for I bear on my *body* the brand-marks of Jesus.

Philippians 1:19–20

For I know that this will turn out for my deliverance through your prayers and the provision of the Spirit of Jesus Christ, [20]according to my earnest expectation and hope, that I will not be put to shame in anything, but that with all boldness, Christ will even now, as always, be exalted in my *body*, whether by *life* or by *death*.

Philippians 3:10–11

. . . that I may know Him and the *power* of His resurrection and the fellowship of His sufferings, being conformed to His *death*; [11]in order that I may attain to the resurrection from the dead.

Colossians 1:24

Now I rejoice in my sufferings for your sake, and in my *flesh* I do my share on behalf of His body, which is the church, in filling up what is lacking in Christ's *afflictions*.

Genesis 3:19

"By the sweat of your face You will eat bread, Till you return to the ground, Because from it you were taken; For you are dust, And to dust you shall return."

Job 10:9

"Remember now, that You have made me as clay; And would You turn me into dust again?"

Psalm 94:5

They *crush* Your people, O LORD, And *afflict* Your heritage.

Lamentations 4:2

The precious sons of Zion, Weighed against fine gold, How they are regarded as *earthen* jars, The work of a potter's hands!

Matthew 20:18

"Behold, we are going up to Jerusalem; and the Son of Man will be *delivered* to the chief priests and scribes, and they will condemn Him to *death*."

Qumran Hymns (1QH) 19[11].3

I give you thanks, my God, because you have done wonders with dust; with the creature of mud you have acted in an immeasurably very *powerful* way. And I, what am I?

Seneca, To Marcia *11.3*

The *body* is . . . a *vessel* that any shaking or tossing can break, . . . a body feeble and fragile, naked, . . . exposed to all of fortune's assaults.

Seneca, Moral Epistles *41.4*

If you see someone undaunted by perils, unimpaired by desires, happy in adversity, peaceful amid the storm, who views humanity from a higher vantage point and the gods from an equal one, will not a certain veneration for him come over you? Will you not say, "This condition is too great and lofty to believe it resembles the puny *body* in which it resides. Some divine *power* has descended on him"?

2 Corinthians 4:13–18

But having the same spirit of faith, according to what is written, I BELIEVED, THEREFORE I SPOKE, we also believe, therefore we also speak, ¹⁴knowing that He who raised the Lord Jesus will raise us also with Jesus and will present us with you. ¹⁵For all things are for your sakes, so that the grace which is spreading to more and more people may cause the giving of thanks to abound to the glory of God. ¹⁶Therefore we do not lose heart, but though our outer man is decaying, yet our inner man is being renewed day by day. ¹⁷For momentary, light affliction is producing for us an eternal weight of glory far beyond all comparison, ¹⁸while we look not at the things which are seen, but at the things which are not seen; for the things which are seen are temporal, but the things which are not seen are eternal.

2 CORINTHIANS PARALLELS

2 Corinthians 1:3–4
Blessed be the God and Father of our Lord Jesus Christ, the Father of mercies and God of all comfort, ⁴who comforts us in all our *affliction* so that we will be able to comfort those who are in any affliction with the comfort with which we ourselves are comforted by God.

2 Corinthians 1:9–12
Indeed, we had the sentence of death within ourselves so that we would not trust in ourselves, but in God who *raises* the dead; ¹⁰who delivered us from so great a peril of death, and will deliver us, He on whom we have set our hope. And He will yet deliver us, ¹¹you also joining in helping us through your prayers, so that *thanks* may be *given* by many persons on our behalf for the favor bestowed on us through the prayers of many. ¹²For our proud confidence is this: the testimony of our conscience, that in holiness and godly sincerity, not in fleshly wisdom but in *the grace* of God, we have conducted ourselves in the world, and especially toward you.

2 Corinthians 5:6–8
Therefore, being always of good courage, and knowing that while we are at home in the body we are absent from the Lord— ⁷for we walk by *faith*, not by sight— ⁸we are of good courage, I say, and prefer rather to be absent from the body and to be at home with the Lord.

2 Corinthians 9:11–12
You will be enriched in everything for all liberality, which through us is producing *thanksgiving* to God. ¹²For the ministry of this service is not only fully supplying the needs of the saints, but is also overflowing through many thanksgivings to God.

OTHER PAULINE PARALLELS

Romans 7:22–23
For I joyfully concur with the law of God in the *inner man*, ²³but I see a different law in the members of my body, waging war against the law of my mind and making me a prisoner of the law of sin which is in my members.

Romans 8:11
But if the Spirit of Him who *raised* Jesus from the dead dwells in you, He who raised Christ Jesus from the dead will also give life to your mortal bodies through His Spirit who dwells in you.

Romans 8:18, 24–25
For I consider that the sufferings of this present time are not worthy to be compared with the *glory* that is to be revealed to us. . . . ²⁴For in hope we have been saved, but hope that is *seen* is not hope; for who hopes for what he already sees? ²⁵But if we hope for what we do *not see*, with perseverance we wait eagerly for it.

Romans 12:2
And do not be conformed to this world, but be transformed by the *renewing* of your mind, so that you may prove what the will of God is, that which is good and acceptable and perfect.

1 Corinthians 2:9
Just as it is written, "*THINGS WHICH EYE HAS NOT SEEN AND EAR HAS NOT HEARD, AND which HAVE NOT ENTERED THE HEART OF MAN, ALL*

THAT GOD HAS PREPARED FOR
THOSE WHO LOVE HIM."

1 Corinthians 6:14
Now God has not only *raised the Lord*, but
will *also raise us* up through His power.

1 Corinthians 15:20–22
But now Christ has been *raised* from the
dead, the first fruits of those who are asleep.
[21]For since by a man came death, by a man
also came the resurrection of the dead. [22]For
as in Adam all die, so also in Christ all will
be made alive.

Ephesians 3:13–14, 16–17
Therefore I ask you *not* to *lose heart* at my
tribulations on your behalf, for they are your
glory. [14]For this reason I bow my knees
before the Father . . . [16]that He would grant
you, according to the riches of His glory, to
be strengthened with power through His
Spirit in the *inner man,* [17]so that Christ may
dwell in your hearts through *faith.*

Colossians 1:21–22
And although you were formerly alienated
and hostile in mind, engaged in evil deeds,
[22]yet He has now reconciled you in His
fleshly body through death, in order to *pre-*
sent you before Him holy and blameless and
beyond reproach.

2 Timothy 2:10
For this reason I endure all things for the
sake of those who are chosen, so that they
also may obtain the salvation which is in
Christ Jesus and with it *eternal glory.*

Psalm 116:8–10
For You have rescued my soul from death,
My eyes from tears, My feet from stumbling.
[9]I shall walk before the LORD In the land of
the living. [10]I *believed* when *I* said, "I am
greatly *afflicted.*"

Hebrews 11:1
Now *faith* is the assurance of things hoped
for, the conviction of things *not seen.*

2 Esdras (4 Ezra) 7:26–27
"For indeed the time will come, when the
signs that I have foretold to you will come to
pass, that the city that now is *not seen* shall
appear, and the land that now is hidden
shall be disclosed. [27]Everyone who has been
delivered from the evils that I have foretold
shall see my wonders."

2 Baruch 51:13–14, 16
For the first will receive the last, those
whom they expected; . . . [14]For they have
been saved from this world of *affliction* and
have put down the burden of anguishes. . . .
[16]For once they chose for themselves that
time which cannot pass away without afflictions. And they chose for themselves that
time of which the end is full of lamentations
and evils.

2 Corinthians 5:1–5

For we know that if the earthly tent which is our
house is torn down, we have a building from
God, a house not made with hands, eternal in
the heavens. [2]For indeed in this house we
groan, longing to be clothed with our dwelling
from heaven, [3]inasmuch as we, having put it
on, will not be found naked. [4]For indeed while
we are in this tent, we groan, being burdened,
because we do not want to be unclothed but to
be clothed, so that what is mortal will be swallowed up by life. [5]Now He who prepared us for
this very purpose is God, who gave to us the
Spirit as a pledge.

2 Corinthians 1:21–22
Now He who establishes us with you in
Christ and anointed us is God, [22]who also
sealed us and *gave us the Spirit* in our hearts
as a pledge.

2 Corinthians 4:7
But we have this treasure in *earthen* vessels,
so that the surpassing greatness of the
power will be of God and not from ourselves.

Romans 8:23

And not only this, but also we ourselves, having the first fruits of *the Spirit*, even *we* ourselves *groan* within ourselves, waiting eagerly for our adoption as sons, the redemption of our body.

1 Corinthians 15:42–44

So also is the resurrection of the dead. It is sown a perishable body, it is raised an imperishable body; [43]it is sown in dishonor, it is raised in glory; it is sown in weakness, it is raised in power; [44]it is sown a natural body, it is raised a spiritual body. If there is a natural body, there is also a spiritual body.

1 Corinthians 15:47, 49, 53

The first man is from the earth, *earthy*; the second man is from *heaven*. . . . [49]Just as we have borne the image of the earthy, we will also bear the image of the heavenly. . . . [53]For this perishable must *put on* the imperishable, and this *mortal* must put on immortality.

Galatians 3:27

For all of you who were baptized into Christ have *clothed* yourselves with Christ.

Ephesians 2:19–22

So then you are no longer strangers and aliens, but you are fellow citizens with the saints, and are of God's household, [20]having been built on the foundation of the apostles and prophets, Christ Jesus Himself being the corner stone, [21]in whom the whole *building*, being fitted together, is growing into a holy temple in the Lord, [22]in whom you also are being built together into a *dwelling* of God in *the Spirit*.

Philippians 3:20–21

For our citizenship is *in heaven*, from which also we eagerly wait for a Savior, the Lord Jesus Christ; [21]who will transform the body of our humble state into conformity with the body of His glory, by the exertion of the power that He has even to subject all things to Himself.

Mark 14:58

We heard Him say, "I will destroy this temple made with hands, and in three days I will build another *made without hands*."

Hebrews 9:11–12

But when Christ appeared as a high priest of the good things to come, He entered through the greater and more perfect tabernacle, *not made with hands*, that is to say, not of this creation; [12]and not through the blood of goats and calves, but through His own blood, He entered the holy place once for all, having obtained *eternal* redemption.

Hebrews 9:24

For Christ did *not* enter a holy place *made with hands*, a mere copy of the true one, but into *heaven* itself, now to appear in the presence of God for us.

2 Peter 1:13–14

I consider it right, as long as I am in this *earthly* dwelling, to stir you up by way of reminder, [14]knowing that the laying aside of my earthly *dwelling* is imminent, as also our Lord Jesus Christ has made clear to me.

Wisdom of Solomon 9:14–15

For the reasoning of mortals is worthless, and our designs are likely to fail; [15]for a perishable body weighs down the soul, and this *earthy tent* burdens the thoughtful mind.

1 Enoch 62:15–16

The righteous and elect ones shall rise from the earth. . . . They shall wear the garments of glory. [16]These garments of yours shall become the garments of *life* from the Lord of the Spirits. Neither shall your garments wear out, nor your glory come to an end before the Lord of the Spirits.

Qumran Hymns *(1QH) 15[7].4, 6–8*

The foundations of my *building* have crumbled, my bones have been disjointed. . . . [6]I give you thanks, Lord, because you have sustained me with your strength, [7]you have spread your holy *spirit* over me. . . . [8] . . . You placed me like a sturdy tower, like a high wall, you founded my building upon rock.

2 Corinthians 5:6–10

Therefore, being always of good courage, and knowing that while we are at home in the body we are absent from the Lord — [7]for we walk by faith, not by sight — [8]we are of good courage, I say, and prefer rather to be absent from the body and to be at home with the Lord. [9]Therefore we also have as our ambition, whether at home or absent, to be pleasing to Him. [10]For we must all appear before the judgment seat of Christ, so that each one may be recompensed for his deeds in the body, according to what he has done, whether good or bad.

2 CORINTHIANS PARALLELS

2 Corinthians 4:8–10

We are afflicted in every way, but not crushed; perplexed, but not despairing; [9]persecuted, but not forsaken; struck down, but not destroyed; [10]always carrying about in *the body* the dying of Jesus, so that the life of Jesus also may be manifested in our body.

2 Corinthians 4:13

But having the same spirit of *faith*, according to what is written, "I BELIEVED, THEREFORE I SPOKE," we also believe, therefore we also speak.

2 Corinthians 4:17–18

For momentary, light affliction is producing for us an eternal weight of glory far beyond all comparison, [18]while we look not at the things which are seen, but at the things which are not seen; for the things which are seen are temporal, but the things which are not seen are eternal.

OTHER PAULINE PARALLELS

Romans 8:23–25

And not only this, but also we ourselves, having the first fruits of the Spirit, even we ourselves groan within ourselves, waiting eagerly for our adoption as sons, the redemption of our *body*. [24]For in hope we have been saved, but hope that is seen is not hope; for who hopes for what he already sees? [25]But if we hope for what we do not see, with perseverance we wait eagerly for it.

Romans 14:10

But you, why do you judge your brother? Or you again, why do you regard your brother with contempt? For we will all stand *before the judgment seat* of God.

1 Corinthians 4:5

Therefore do not go on passing *judgment* before the time, but wait until the Lord comes who will both bring to light the things hidden in the darkness and disclose the motives of men's hearts; and then each man's praise will come to him from God.

1 Corinthians 13:12

For now we see in a mirror dimly, but then face to face; now I know in part, but then I will know fully just as I also have been fully known.

Ephesians 5:8–10

You were formerly darkness, but now you are Light in the Lord; *walk* as children of Light [9](for the fruit of the Light consists in all goodness and righteousness and truth), [10]trying to learn what is *pleasing* to the Lord.

Philippians 1:23–24

But I am hard-pressed from both directions, having the desire to depart and be with Christ, for that is very much better; [24]yet to remain on in the flesh is more necessary for your sake.

Colossians 1:9–10

For this reason also, since the day we heard of it, we have not ceased to pray for you and to ask that you may be filled with the knowledge of His will in all spiritual wisdom and understanding, [10]so that you will *walk* in a manner worthy of the Lord, to *please* Him in all respects, bearing fruit in every good work and increasing in the knowledge of God.

OTHER BIBLICAL PARALLELS

Psalm 31:23–24

O love the LORD, all you His godly ones! The LORD preserves the faithful And fully *recompenses* the proud doer. [24]Be strong and let your heart take *courage*, All you who hope in the LORD.

Isaiah 59:18

According to their *deeds*, so He will repay, Wrath to His adversaries, *recompense* to His enemies.

Matthew 25:31–32

"But when the Son of Man comes in His glory, and all the angels with Him, then He will sit on His glorious throne. ³²All the nations will be gathered before Him; and He will separate them from one another, as the shepherd separates the sheep from the goats."

Acts 10:42

"And He ordered us to preach to the people, and solemnly to testify that this is the One who has been appointed by God as *Judge* of the living and the dead."

Hebrews 11:1

Now *faith* is the assurance of things hoped for, the conviction of things not seen.

1 Peter 1:17

If you address as Father the One who impartially *judges* according to each one's work, conduct yourselves in fear during the time of your stay on earth.

Revelation 20:13

And the sea gave up the dead which were in it, and death and Hades gave up the dead which were in them; and they were *judged*, every one of them according to their *deeds*.

2 Corinthians 5:11–15

Therefore, knowing the fear of the Lord, we persuade men, but we are made manifest to God; and I hope that we are made manifest also in your consciences. ¹²We are not again commending ourselves to you but are giving you an occasion to be proud of us, so that you will have an answer for those who take pride in appearance and not in heart. ¹³For if we are beside ourselves, it is for God; if we are of sound mind, it is for you. ¹⁴For the love of Christ controls us, having concluded this, that one died for all, therefore all died; ¹⁵and He died for all, so that they who live might no longer live for themselves, but for Him who died and rose again on their behalf.

2 Corinthians 1:13–14

For we write nothing else to you than what you read and understand, and I hope you will understand until the end; ¹⁴just as you also partially did understand us, that we are your reason *to be proud* as you also are ours, in the day of our Lord Jesus.

2 Corinthians 3:1

Are we beginning to *commend ourselves* again? Or do we need, as some, letters of commendation to you or from you?

2 Corinthians 4:2

We have renounced the things hidden because of shame, not walking in craftiness or adulterating the word of God, but by the *manifestation* of truth *commending ourselves* to every man's *conscience* in the sight of God.

2 Corinthians 6:4

. . . in everything *commending ourselves* as servants of God, in much endurance, in afflictions, in hardships, in distresses . . .

2 Corinthians 7:1

Therefore, having these promises, beloved, let us cleanse ourselves from all defilement of flesh and spirit, perfecting holiness in the *fear* of God.

2 Corinthians 10:12, 18

For we are not bold to class or compare ourselves with some of those who *commend* themselves; but when they measure themselves by themselves and compare themselves with themselves, they are without understanding. . . . ¹⁸For it is not he who commends himself that is approved, but he whom the Lord commends.

2 Corinthians 11:12, 18

But what I am doing I will continue to do, so that I may cut off opportunity from those who desire an opportunity to be regarded just as we are in the matter about which they are boasting. . . . ¹⁸Since many boast according to the flesh, I will boast also.

2 Corinthians 11:23

Are they servants of Christ?—I speak as if insane—I more so; in far more labors, in far more imprisonments, beaten times without number, often in danger of death.

Romans 5:8

But God demonstrates His own *love* toward us, in that while we were yet sinners, Christ *died* for us.

Romans 6:8–11

Now if we have *died* with Christ, we believe that we shall also *live* with Him, [9]knowing that Christ, having been raised from the dead, is never to die again; death no longer is master over Him. [10]For the death that He died, He died to sin once for all; but the life that He lives, He lives to God. [11]Even so consider yourselves to be dead to sin, but alive to God in Christ Jesus.

Romans 7:4

Therefore, my brethren, you also were made to *die* to the Law through the body of Christ, so that you might be joined to another, to Him who was raised from the dead, in order that we might bear fruit for God.

Romans 14:7–9

For not one of us *lives* for himself, and not one *dies* for himself; [8]for if we live, we live for the Lord, or if we die, we die for the Lord; therefore whether we live or die, we are the Lord's. [9]For to this end Christ died and lived again, that He might be Lord both of the dead and of the living.

1 Corinthians 15:20–22

But now Christ has been raised from the dead, the first fruits of those who are asleep. [21]For since by a man came death, by a man also came the resurrection of the dead. [22]For as in Adam all *die*, so also in Christ all will be made *alive*.

Galatians 2:19–20

"For through the Law I *died* to the Law, so that I might *live* to God. [20]I have been crucified with Christ; and it is no longer I who live, but Christ lives in me; and the life which I now live in the flesh I live by faith in the Son of God, who *loved* me and gave Himself up for me."

OTHER BIBLICAL PARALLELS

1 Samuel 16:7

But the LORD said to Samuel, "Do not look at his appearance or at the height of his stature, because I have rejected him; for God sees not as man sees, for man looks at the outward *appearance*, but the LORD looks at the *heart*."

1 Peter 1:17

If you address as Father the One who impartially judges according to each one's work, conduct yourselves in *fear* during the time of your stay on earth.

NONCANONICAL PARALLELS

Sirach 1:30

Do not exalt yourself, or you may fall and bring dishonor upon yourself. The Lord will reveal your secrets and overthrow you before the whole congregation, because you did not come in *the fear of the Lord*, and your *heart* was full of deceit.

2 Corinthians 5:16–21

Therefore from now on we recognize no one according to the flesh; even though we have known Christ according to the flesh, yet now we know Him in this way no longer. [17]Therefore if anyone is in Christ, he is a new creature; the old things passed away; behold, new things have come. [18]Now all these things are from God, who reconciled us to Himself through Christ and gave us the ministry of reconciliation, [19]namely, that God was in Christ reconciling the world to Himself, not counting their trespasses against them, and He has committed to us the word of reconciliation. [20]Therefore, we are ambassadors for Christ, as though God were making an appeal through us; we beg you on behalf of Christ, be reconciled to God. [21]He made Him who knew no sin to be sin on our behalf, so that we might become the righteousness of God in Him.

2 CORINTHIANS PARALLELS

2 Corinthians 4:1–2

Therefore, since we have this *ministry*, as we received mercy, we do not lose heart, [2]but we have renounced the things hidden because of shame, not walking in craftiness or adulterating the word of God, but by the manifestation of truth commending ourselves to every man's conscience in the sight of God.

2 Corinthians 11:17–18

What I am saying, I am not saying as the Lord would, but as in foolishness, in this confidence of boasting. [18]Since many boast *according to the flesh*, I will boast also.

OTHER PAULINE PARALLELS

Romans 3:23–25

For all have sinned and fall short of the glory of God, [24]being justified as a gift by His grace through the redemption which is in Christ Jesus; [25]whom God displayed publicly as a propitiation in His blood through faith. This was to demonstrate His *righteousness*, because in the forbearance of God He passed over the *sins* previously committed.

Romans 5:9–10

Much more then, having now been justified by His blood, we shall be saved from the wrath of God through Him. [10]For if while we were enemies we were *reconciled* to God through the death of His Son, much more, having been reconciled, we shall be saved by His life.

Romans 8:3

For what the Law could not do, weak as it was through the flesh, God did: sending His own Son in the likeness of sinful *flesh* and as an offering for *sin*, He condemned sin in the flesh.

1 Corinthians 1:30

But by His doing you are in Christ Jesus, who became to us wisdom from God, and *righteousness* and sanctification, and redemption.

Galatians 3:13

Christ redeemed us from the curse of the Law, having become a curse for us—for it is written, "CURSED IS EVERYONE WHO HANGS ON A TREE."

Galatians 6:14–15

But may it never be that I would boast, except in the cross of our Lord Jesus Christ, through which the world has been crucified to me, and I to *the world.* [15]For neither is circumcision anything, nor uncircumcision, but a *new creation.*

Ephesians 1:7–8

In Him we have redemption through His blood, the forgiveness of our *trespasses*, according to the riches of His grace [8]which He lavished on us.

Ephesians 2:14–16

For He Himself is our peace, who made both groups into one and broke down the barrier of the dividing wall, [15]by abolishing in His *flesh* the enmity, which is the Law of commandments contained in ordinances, so that in Himself He might make the two into one new man, thus establishing peace, [16]and might *reconcile* them both in one body to God through the cross, by it having put to death the enmity.

Ephesians 6:19–20

Pray on my behalf, that utterance may be given to me in the opening of my mouth, to make known with boldness the mystery of the gospel, [20]for which I am an *ambassador* in chains; that in proclaiming it I may speak boldly, as I ought to speak.

Colossians 1:21–22

And although you were formerly alienated and hostile in mind, engaged in evil deeds, [22]yet He has now *reconciled* you in His *fleshly* body through death, in order to present you before Him holy and blameless and beyond reproach.

OTHER BIBLICAL PARALLELS

Isaiah 53:12

Therefore, I will allot Him a portion with the great, And He will divide the booty with the strong; Because He poured out Himself to death, And was numbered with the transgressors; Yet He Himself bore the *sin* of many, And interceded for the transgressors.

Isaiah 65:17

"For behold, I create *new* heavens and a new earth; And the former things will not be remembered or come to mind."

Hebrews 4:15

For we do not have a high priest who cannot sympathize with our weaknesses, but One who has been tempted in all things as we are, yet without *sin.*

1 Peter 2:21–22, 24

For you have been called for this purpose, since Christ also suffered for you, leaving you an example for you to follow in His steps, [22]WHO COMMITTED *NO SIN*, NOR WAS ANY DECEIT FOUND IN HIS MOUTH; . . . [24]and He Himself bore our sins in His body on the cross, so that we might die to sin and live to *righteousness*; for by His wounds you were healed.

1 John 3:5

You know that He appeared in order to take away sins; and in Him there is *no sin*.

Revelation 21:1, 5

Then I saw a new heaven and a new earth; for the first heaven and the first earth *passed away*, and there is no longer any sea. . . . [5]And He who sits on the throne said, "Behold, I am making all *things new*."

NONCANONICAL PARALLELS

2 Maccabees 7:32–33

"For we are suffering because of our own *sins*. [33]And if our living Lord is angry for a little while, to rebuke and discipline us, he will again be *reconciled* with his own servants."

Psalms of Solomon *17:32, 36*

And he will be a righteous king over them, taught by God. There will be no unrighteousness among them in his days, for all shall be holy, and their king shall be the Lord Messiah. . . . [36]And he himself (will be) free from *sin*, (in order) to rule a great people.

2 Corinthians 6:1–10

And working together with Him, we also urge you not to receive the grace of God in vain— [2]for He says, "AT THE ACCEPTABLE TIME I LISTENED TO YOU, AND ON THE DAY OF SALVATION I HELPED YOU." Behold, now is "THE ACCEPTABLE TIME," behold, now is "THE DAY OF SALVATION"— [3]giving no cause for offense in anything, so that the ministry will not be discredited, [4]but in everything commending ourselves as servants of God, in much endurance, in afflictions, in hardships, in distresses, [5]in beatings, in imprisonments, in tumults, in labors, in sleeplessness, in hunger, [6]in purity, in knowledge, in patience, in kindness, in the Holy Spirit, in genuine love, [7]in the word of truth, in the power of God; by the weapons of righteousness for the right hand and the left, [8]by glory and dishonor, by evil report and good report; regarded as deceivers and yet true; [9]as unknown yet well-known, as dying yet behold, we live; as punished yet not put to death, [10]as sorrowful yet always rejoicing, as poor yet making many rich, as having nothing yet possessing all things.

2 CORINTHIANS PARALLELS

2 Corinthians 1:8

For we do not want you to be unaware, brethren, of our *affliction* which came to us in Asia, that we were burdened excessively, beyond our strength, so that we despaired even of life.

2 Corinthians 3:1, 5–6

Are we beginning to *commend ourselves* again? Or do we need, as some, letters of commendation to you or from you? . . . [5]Not that we are adequate in ourselves to consider anything as coming from ourselves, but our adequacy is from God, [6]who also made us adequate as *servants* of a new covenant, not of the letter but of *the Spirit*; for the letter kills, but *the Spirit* gives life.

2 Corinthians 4:7–12

We have this treasure in earthen vessels, so that the surpassing greatness of *the power* will be of God and not from ourselves; [8]we are *afflicted* in every way, but not crushed; perplexed, but not despairing; [9]persecuted, but not forsaken; struck down, but not destroyed; [10]always carrying about in the body the *dying* of Jesus, so that the life of Jesus also may be manifested in our body. [11]For we who *live* are constantly being delivered over to *death* for Jesus' sake, so that the life of Jesus also may be manifested in our mortal flesh. [12]So death works in us, but life in you.

2 Corinthians 8:9

For you know the grace of our Lord Jesus Christ, that though He was rich, yet for your sake He became *poor*, so that you through His poverty might become *rich*.

2 Corinthians 10:3–4

For though we walk in the flesh, we do not war according to the flesh, [4]for the *weapons* of our warfare are not of the flesh, but divinely *powerful* for the destruction of fortresses.

2 Corinthians 11:23–27
Are they *servants* of Christ?—I speak as if insane—I more so; in far more *labors*, in far more *imprisonments, beaten* times without number, often in danger of *death.* [24]Five times I received from the Jews thirty-nine lashes. [25]Three times I was *beaten* with rods, once I was stoned, three times I was shipwrecked, a night and a day I have spent in the deep. [26]I have been on frequent journeys, in dangers from rivers, dangers from robbers, dangers from my countrymen, dangers from the Gentiles, dangers in the city, dangers in the wilderness, dangers on the sea, dangers among false brethren; [27]I have been in labor and *hardship*, through many *sleepless* nights, in *hunger* and thirst, often without food, in cold and exposure.

2 Corinthians 12:10
Therefore I am well content with weaknesses, with insults, with *distresses*, with persecutions, with difficulties, for Christ's sake; for when I am weak, then I am strong.

Romans 8:32, 35
He who did not spare His own Son, but delivered Him over for us all, how will He not also with Him freely give us *all things*? . . . [35]Who will separate us from the love of Christ? Will tribulation, or *distress*, or persecution, or famine, or nakedness, or peril, or sword?

1 Corinthians 2:4–5
My message and my preaching were not in persuasive words of wisdom, but in demonstration of *the Spirit* and of power, [5]so that your faith would not rest on the wisdom of men, but on *the power of God.*

1 Corinthians 4:10–13
We are fools for Christ's sake, but you are prudent in Christ; we are weak, but you are strong; you are distinguished, but we are *without honor.* [11]To this present hour we are both *hungry* and thirsty, and are poorly clothed, and are roughly treated, and are homeless; [12]and we toil, working with our own hands; when we are reviled, we bless;

when we are persecuted, we *endure;* [13]when we are slandered, we try to conciliate; we have become as the scum of the world, the dregs of all things, even until now.

1 Corinthians 10:32–33
Give *no offense* either to Jews or to Greeks or to the church of God; [33]just as I also please all men in all things, not seeking my own profit but the profit of the many, so that they may be saved.

1 Corinthians 15:1–2
Now I make known to you, brethren, the gospel which I preached to you, which also you received, in which also you stand, [2]by which also you are saved, if you hold fast the word which I preached to you, unless you believed *in vain.*

Galatians 5:22–23
But the fruit of *the Spirit* is *love,* joy, peace, *patience, kindness,* goodness, faithfulness, [23]gentleness, self-control; against such things there is no law.

Isaiah 49:8
Thus says the LORD, "In a favorable *time* I have answered You, And in a *day of salvation I* have *helped You;* And I will keep You and give You for a covenant of the people, To restore the land, to make them inherit the desolate heritages."

Psalm 118:17–18
I will not *die,* but *live,* And tell of the works of the LORD. [18]The LORD has disciplined me severely, But He has not given me over to *death.*

1 Enoch *103:9–10*
"Now to the righteous and kind ones during their lifetime: Do not say, 'In the days of our toil we have surely suffered *hardships* and have experienced every trouble. We have faced many evil things and have become consumed. We have *died* and become few, (characterized) by the littleness of our spirit. [10]We have been destroyed and we have found none whatsoever to help us with a word or otherwise. We have been tortured

and destroyed, and could not even hope to see life from one day to the other.'"

Philo, *On Moses 1.157*

For God, *possessing all things*, is in need of nothing. And the good person, though possessing *nothing* in the proper sense, not even himself, shares in the treasures of God, to the extent that this is possible.

Dio Chrysostom, Orations *8.15–16*

The noble man . . . fears none of his opponents . . . [16]but challenges them all one after another, struggling with *hunger* and cold, *enduring* thirst, and showing no softness even when he must bear whips, cuts, and burns. Hunger, exile, disrepute, and such things bring no terror to him.

2 Corinthians 6:11–13

Our mouth has spoken freely to you, O Corinthians, our heart is opened wide. [12]You are not restrained by us, but you are restrained in your own affections. [13]Now in a like exchange—I speak as to children—open wide to us also.

2 CORINTHIANS PARALLELS

2 Corinthians *1:12*

For our proud confidence is this: the testimony of our conscience, that in holiness and godly sincerity, not in fleshly wisdom but in the grace of God, we have conducted ourselves in the world, and especially toward you.

2 Corinthians *2:4*

For out of much affliction and anguish of *heart* I wrote to you with many tears; not so that you would be made sorrowful, but that you might know the love which I have especially for you.

2 Corinthians *7:2–3*

Make room for us in your hearts; we wronged no one, we corrupted no one, we took advantage of no one. [3]I do not speak to condemn you, for I have said before that you are in *our hearts* to die together and to live together.

2 Corinthians *7:14–15*

For if in anything I have boasted to him about you, I was not put to shame; but as we spoke all things to you in truth, so also our boasting before Titus proved to be the truth. [15]His *affection* abounds all the more toward you, as he remembers the obedience of you all, how you received him with fear and trembling.

2 Corinthians *12:14*

Here for this third time I am ready to come to you, and I will not be a burden to you; for I do not seek what is yours, but you; for *children* are not responsible to save up for their parents, but parents for their children.

OTHER PAULINE PARALLELS

1 Corinthians *4:14–15*

I do not write these things to shame you, but to admonish you as my beloved *children*. [15]For if you were to have countless tutors in Christ, yet you would not have many fathers, for in Christ Jesus I became your father through the gospel.

1 Thessalonians *2:7–8*

But we proved to be gentle among you, as a nursing mother tenderly cares for her own *children*. [8]Having so fond an affection for you, we were well-pleased to impart to you not only the gospel of God but also our own lives, because you had become very dear to us.

1 Thessalonians *2:10–11*

You are witnesses, and so is God, how devoutly and uprightly and blamelessly we behaved toward you believers; [11]just as you know how we were exhorting and encouraging and imploring each one of you as a father would his own *children*.

OTHER BIBLICAL PARALLELS

Psalm *119:32*

I shall run the way of Your commandments, For You will enlarge my *heart*.

Acts *16:14*

A woman named Lydia, from the city of Thyatira, a seller of purple fabrics, a worshiper of God, was listening; and the Lord *opened* her *heart* to respond to the things spoken by Paul.

2 Corinthians 6:14–7:1

Do not be bound together with unbelievers; for what partnership have righteousness and lawlessness, or what fellowship has light with darkness? [15]Or what harmony has Christ with Belial, or what has a believer in common with an unbeliever? [16]Or what agreement has the temple of God with idols? For we are the temple of the living God; just as God said, "I WILL DWELL IN THEM AND WALK AMONG THEM; AND I WILL BE THEIR GOD, AND THEY SHALL BE MY PEOPLE. [17]Therefore, COME OUT FROM THEIR MIDST AND BE SEPARATE," says the Lord. "AND DO NOT TOUCH WHAT IS UNCLEAN; And I will welcome you. [18]And I will be a father to you, And you shall be sons and daughters to Me," Says the Lord Almighty. [7:1]Therefore, having these promises, beloved, let us cleanse ourselves from all defilement of flesh and spirit, perfecting holiness in the fear of God.

2 CORINTHIANS PARALLELS

2 Corinthians 2:10–11
But one whom you forgive anything, I forgive also; for indeed what I have forgiven, if I have forgiven anything, I did it for your sakes in the presence of Christ, [11]so that no advantage would be taken of us by Satan, for we are not ignorant of his schemes.

2 Corinthians 4:3–4
And even if our gospel is veiled, it is veiled to those who are perishing, [4]in whose case the god of this world has blinded the minds of the *unbelieving* so that they might not see the *light* of the gospel of the glory of Christ, who is the image of God.

2 Corinthians 11:13–14
For such men are false apostles, deceitful workers, disguising themselves as apostles of Christ. [14]No wonder, for even Satan disguises himself as an angel of *light*.

OTHER PAULINE PARALLELS

1 Corinthians 3:16–17
Do you not know that you are a *temple of God* and that the Spirit of God *dwells* in you? [17]If any man destroys the temple of God, God will destroy him, for the temple of God is holy, and that is what you are.

1 Corinthians 5:9–10
I wrote you in my letter not to associate with immoral people; [10]I did not at all mean with the immoral people of this world, or with the covetous and swindlers, or with *idolaters*, for then you would have to go out of the world.

1 Corinthians 6:19
Or do you not know that your body is a *temple* of the Holy Spirit who is in you, whom you have from God, and that you are not your own?

1 Corinthians 7:12–13
But to the rest I say, not the Lord, that if any brother has a wife who is *an unbeliever*, and she consents to live with him, he must not divorce her. [13]And a woman who has an unbelieving husband, and he consents to live with her, she must not send her husband away.

1 Corinthians 10:21
You cannot drink the cup of the Lord and the cup of demons; you cannot partake of the table of the Lord and the table of demons.

Ephesians 2:19–22
So then you are no longer strangers and aliens, but you are fellow citizens with the saints, and are of God's household, [20]having been built on the foundation of the apostles and prophets, Christ Jesus Himself being the corner stone, [21]in whom the whole building, being fitted together, is growing into a holy *temple* in the Lord, [22]in whom you also are being built together into a *dwelling* of God in the Spirit.

Ephesians 5:6–8
Let no one deceive you with empty words, for because of these things the wrath of God comes upon the sons' of disobedience. [7]Therefore do not be partakers with them; [8]for you were formerly *darkness*, but now you are *Light* in the Lord; walk as children of Light.

OTHER BIBLICAL PARALLELS

Exodus 29:45–46
"I *will dwell* among the sons of Israel and *will be their God*. [46]They shall know that I am the LORD their God who brought them

out of the land of Egypt, that I might dwell among them; I am the LORD their God."

Leviticus 26:11–12

"Moreover, *I will* make My *dwelling* among you, and My soul will not reject you. [12]I will also *walk among* you and *be* your *God*, and you *shall be My people*."

2 Samuel 7:14

"*I will be a father to* him and he will *be a son to Me*; when he commits iniquity, I will correct him with the rod of men and the strokes of the sons of men."

Isaiah 52:11

Depart, depart, go *out from* there, *Touch* nothing *unclean*; Go *out* of the *midst* of her, purify yourselves, You who carry the vessels of the LORD.

Jeremiah 31:1

"At that time," declares the LORD, "I will be the God of all the families of Israel, and *they shall be My people*."

Ezekiel 37:23, 27

"They will no longer *defile* themselves with their *idols*, or with their detestable things, or with any of their transgressions; but I will deliver them from all their dwelling places in which they have sinned, and will *cleanse* them. And they will be My people, and I will be their God. . . . [27]My *dwelling* place also will be with them; *and I will be their God, and they* will *be My people*."

NONCANONICAL PARALLELS

Testament of Levi 19:1

"And now, my children, you have heard everything. Choose for yourselves *light* or *darkness*, the Law of the Lord or the works of Beliar."

The Damascus Document (CD) 6.14–15, 17

They are careful to act in accordance with the exact interpretation of the law for the age of wickedness: to *separate* themselves [15]from the sons of the pit, . . . [17] . . . to separate *unclean* from clean.

The War Scroll (1QM) 13.4–5, 7

Accursed be *Belial* in his malicious plan, may he be damned for his wicked rule. Accursed be all the spirits of his lot in his wicked plan, [5]may they be damned for their deeds of filthy *uncleanness*. For they are the lot of *darkness* and the lot of God is for everlasting *light*. . . . [7]You are the God of our fathers. . . . We are the people of your [inhe]ritance. You established a covenant with our fathers.

2 Corinthians 7:2–4

Make room for us in your hearts; we wronged no one, we corrupted no one, we took advantage of no one. [3]I do not speak to condemn you, for I have said before that you are in our hearts to die together and to live together. [4]Great is my confidence in you; great is my boasting on your behalf. I am filled with comfort; I am overflowing with joy in all our affliction.

2 CORINTHIANS PARALLELS

2 Corinthians 1:3–7

Blessed be the God and Father of our Lord Jesus Christ, the Father of mercies and God of all *comfort*, [4]who comforts us in all our *affliction* so that we will be able to comfort those who are in any affliction with the comfort with which we ourselves are comforted by God. [5]For just as the sufferings of Christ are ours in abundance, so also our comfort is abundant through Christ. [6]But if we are afflicted, it is for your comfort and salvation; or if we are comforted, it is for your comfort, which is effective in the patient enduring of the same sufferings which we also suffer; [7]and our hope for you is firmly grounded, knowing that as you are sharers of our sufferings, so also you are sharers of our comfort.

2 Corinthians 2:3

This is the very thing I wrote you, so that when I came, I would not have sorrow from those who ought to make me rejoice; having *confidence* in you all that my *joy* would be the joy of you all.

2 Corinthians 6:11–13

Our mouth has spoken freely to you, O Corinthians, our *heart* is opened wide. [12]You are not restrained by us, but you are restrained in your own affections. [13]Now in a like exchange—I speak as to children—open wide to us also.

2 Corinthians 7:14

For if in anything I have boasted to him about you, I was not put to shame; but as we spoke all things to you in truth, so also our *boasting* before Titus proved to be the truth.

2 Corinthians 8:24

Therefore openly before the churches, show them the proof of your love and of our reason for *boasting* about you.

2 Corinthians 10:15–16

. . . not *boasting* beyond our measure, that is, in other men's labors, but with the hope that as your faith grows, we will be, within our sphere, enlarged even more by you, [16]so as to preach the gospel even to the regions beyond you, and not to boast in what has been accomplished in the sphere of another.

2 Corinthians 12:16–18

But be that as it may, I did not burden you myself; nevertheless, crafty fellow that I am, I took you in by deceit. [17]Certainly I have not *taken advantage* of you through any of those whom I have sent to you, have I? [18]I urged Titus to go, and I sent the brother with him. Titus did not take any advantage of you, did he? Did we not conduct ourselves in the same spirit and walk in the same steps?

OTHER PAULINE PARALLELS

Romans 14:8

For if we *live*, we live for the Lord, or if we *die*, we die for the Lord; therefore whether we live or die, we are the Lord's.

Philippians 1:7

For it is only right for me to feel this way about you all, because I have you in my *heart*, since both in my imprisonment and in the defense and confirmation of the gospel, you all are partakers of grace with me.

2 Thessalonians 1:4

Therefore, we ourselves speak proudly of you among the churches of God for your perseverance and faith in the midst of all your persecutions and *afflictions* which you endure.

OTHER BIBLICAL PARALLELS

2 Samuel 15:21

But Ittai answered the king and said, "As the LORD lives, and as my lord the king lives, surely wherever my lord the king may be, whether for *death* or for *life*, there also your servant will be."

2 Corinthians 7:5–13a

For even when we came into Macedonia our flesh had no rest, but we were afflicted on every side: conflicts without, fears within. [6]But God, who comforts the depressed, comforted us by the coming of Titus; [7]and not only by his coming, but also by the comfort with which he was comforted in you, as he reported to us your longing, your mourning, your zeal for me; so that I rejoiced even more. [8]For though I caused you sorrow by my letter, I do not regret it; though I did regret it—for I see that that letter caused you sorrow, though only for a while— [9]I now rejoice, not that you were made sorrowful, but that you were made sorrowful to the point of repentance; for you were made sorrowful according to the will of God, so that you might not suffer loss in anything through us. [10]For the sorrow that is according to the will of God produces a repentance without regret, leading to salvation, but the sorrow of the world produces death. [11]For behold what earnestness this very thing, this godly sorrow, has produced in you: what vindication of yourselves, what indignation, what fear, what longing, what zeal, what avenging of wrong! In everything you demonstrated yourselves to be innocent in the matter. [12]So although I wrote to you, it was not for the sake of the offender nor for the sake of the one offended, but that your earnestness on our behalf might be made known to you in the sight of God. [13]For this reason we have been comforted.

2 CORINTHIANS PARALLELS

2 Corinthians 1:3–4

Blessed be the God and Father of our Lord Jesus Christ, the Father of mercies and God of all comfort, [4]who *comforts* us in all our *affliction* so that we will be able to comfort those who are in any affliction with the comfort with which we ourselves are comforted by God.

2 Corinthians 2:3–9

This is the very thing *I wrote you*, so that when I came, I would not have *sorrow* from those who ought to make me *rejoice*; having confidence in you all that my joy would be the joy of you all. [4]For out of much *affliction* and anguish of heart I wrote to you with many tears; not so that you would be *made sorrowful*, but that you might know the love which I have especially for you. [5]But if any has *caused sorrow*, he has caused sorrow not to me, but in some degree—in order not to say too much—to all of you. [6]Sufficient for such a one is this punishment which was inflicted by the majority, [7]so that on the contrary you should rather forgive and *comfort* him, otherwise such a one might be overwhelmed by excessive sorrow. [8]Wherefore I urge you to reaffirm your love for him. [9]For to this end also I wrote, so that I might put you to the test, whether you are obedient in all things.

2 Corinthians 2:12–13

Now when I came to Troas for the gospel of Christ and when a door was opened for me in the Lord, [13]I had *no rest* for my spirit, not finding *Titus* my brother; but taking my leave of them, I went on to *Macedonia*.

2 Corinthians 8:7

But just as you abound in everything, in faith and utterance and knowledge and in all *earnestness* and in the love we inspired in you, see that you abound in this gracious work also.

2 Corinthians 9:2

I know your readiness, of which I boast about you to the Macedonians, namely, that Achaia has been prepared since last year, and your *zeal* has stirred up most of them.

2 Corinthians 12:21

I am afraid that when I come again my God may humiliate me before you, and I may mourn over many of those who have sinned in the past and not *repented* of the impurity, immorality and sensuality which they have practiced.

OTHER PAULINE PARALLELS

Romans 16:19

For the report of your obedience has reached to all; therefore *I am rejoicing* over you, but I want you to be wise in what is good and *innocent* in what is evil.

1 Corinthians 16:5

But I will come to you after I go through *Macedonia*, for I am going through Macedonia.

Philippians 2:14–15

Do all things without grumbling or disputing; [15]so that you will prove yourselves to be blameless and *innocent*, children of God above reproach in the midst of a crooked and perverse generation.

2 Timothy 2:24–25

The Lord's bond-servant must not be quarrelsome, but be kind to all, able to teach, patient when wronged, [25]with gentleness correcting those who are in opposition, if perhaps God may grant them *repentance* leading to the knowledge of the truth.

OTHER BIBLICAL PARALLELS

Isaiah 49:13

Shout for joy, O heavens! And *rejoice*, O earth! Break forth into joyful shouting, O mountains! For the LORD has *comforted* His people And will have compassion on His *afflicted*.

Zephaniah 3:8

"Indeed, My decision is to gather nations, To assemble kingdoms, To pour out on them My *indignation*, All My burning anger; For all the earth will be devoured By the fire of My *zeal*."

Acts 11:18

When they heard this, they quieted down and glorified God, saying, "Well then, God has granted to the Gentiles also the *repentance* that leads to life."

Acts 16:7–10

After they came to Mysia, they were trying to go into Bithynia, and the Spirit of Jesus did not permit them; [8]and passing by Mysia, they came down to Troas. [9]A vision appeared to Paul in the night: a man of *Macedonia* was standing and appealing to him, and saying, "Come over to Macedonia and help us." [10]When he had seen the vision, immediately we sought to go into

Macedonia, concluding that God had called us to preach the gospel to them.

Acts 20:1

After the uproar had ceased, Paul sent for the disciples, and when he had exhorted them and taken his leave of them, he left to go to *Macedonia*.

NONCANONICAL PARALLELS

Testament of Gad 5:7

For according to God's truth, *repentance* destroys disobedience, puts darkness to flight, illumines the vision, furnishes knowledge for the soul, and guides the deliberative powers to *salvation*.

Plutarch, On Tranquility of Mind *476F*

For reason bears away the other *sorrows*, but *repentance* is caused by reason itself, the soul in its shame being vexed and punished by itself.

2 Corinthians 7:13b–16

And besides our comfort, we rejoiced even much more for the joy of Titus, because his spirit has been refreshed by you all. ¹⁴For if in anything I have boasted to him about you, I was not put to shame; but as we spoke all things to you in truth, so also our boasting before Titus proved to be the truth. ¹⁵His affection abounds all the more toward you, as he remembers the obedience of you all, how you received him with fear and trembling. ¹⁶I rejoice that in everything I have confidence in you.

2 CORINTHIANS PARALLELS

2 Corinthians 1:3–4

Blessed be the God and Father of our Lord Jesus Christ, the Father of mercies and God of all *comfort*, ⁴who comforts us in all our affliction so that we will be able to comfort those who are in any affliction with the comfort with which we ourselves are comforted by God.

2 Corinthians 1:13–14

For we write nothing else to you than what you read and understand, and I hope you will understand until the end; ¹⁴just as you

also partially did understand us, that we are your reason to be proud as you also are ours, in the day of our Lord Jesus.

2 Corinthians 2:3

This is the very thing I wrote you, so that when I came, I would not have sorrow from those who ought to make me *rejoice*; having *confidence in you* all that my *joy* would be the joy of you all.

2 Corinthians 2:9

For to this end also I wrote, so that I might put you to the test, whether you are *obedient* in all things.

2 Corinthians 2:13

I had no rest for my spirit, not finding *Titus* my brother; but taking my leave of them, I went on to Macedonia.

2 Corinthians 6:11–13

Our mouth has spoken freely to you, O Corinthians, our heart is opened wide. ¹²You are not restrained by us, but you are restrained in your own *affections*. ¹³Now in a like exchange—I speak as to children—open wide to us also.

2 Corinthians 8:16–17

But thanks be to God who puts the same earnestness on your behalf in the heart of *Titus*. ¹⁷For he not only accepted our appeal, but being himself very earnest, he has gone to you of his own accord.

2 Corinthians 8:23–24

As for *Titus*, he is my partner and fellow worker among you; as for our brethren, they are messengers of the churches, a glory to Christ. ²⁴Therefore openly before the churches, show them the proof of your love and of our reason for *boasting about you*.

2 Corinthians 9:2–4

For I know your readiness, of which *I boast about you* to the Macedonians, namely, that Achaia has been prepared since last year, and your zeal has stirred up most of them. ³But I have sent the brethren, in order that our boasting about you may not be made empty in this case, so that, as I was saying, you may be prepared; ⁴otherwise if any Macedonians come with me and find you unprepared, we—not to speak of you—will be *put to shame* by this *confidence*.

2 Corinthians 12:18

I urged *Titus* to go, and I sent the brother with him. Titus did not take any advantage of you, did he? Did we not conduct ourselves in the same spirit and walk in the same steps?

OTHER PAULINE PARALLELS

Romans 16:19

For the report of your *obedience* has reached to all; therefore I am *rejoicing* over you, but I want you to be wise in what is good and innocent in what is evil.

1 Corinthians 2:1, 3

And when I came to you, brethren, I did not come with superiority of speech or of wisdom, proclaiming to you the testimony of God. . . . [3]I was with you in weakness and in *fear* and in much *trembling.*

Philippians 2:12

So then, my beloved, just as you have always *obeyed*, not as in my presence only, but now much more in my absence, work out your salvation *with fear and trembling.*

1 Thessalonians 2:8

Having so fond an *affection* for you, we were well-pleased to impart to you not only the gospel of God but also our own lives, because you had become very dear to us.

2 Thessalonians 1:4

Therefore, we ourselves speak proudly of you among the churches of God for your perseverance and faith in the midst of all your persecutions and afflictions which you endure.

OTHER BIBLICAL PARALLELS

Psalm 2:11

Worship the LORD with reverence And rejoice *with trembling.*

2 Corinthians 8:1–6

Now, brethren, we wish to make known to you the grace of God which has been given in the churches of Macedonia, [2]that in a great ordeal of affliction their abundance of joy and their deep poverty overflowed in the wealth of their liberality. [3]For I testify that according to their ability, and beyond their ability, they gave of their own accord, [4]begging us with much urging for the favor of participation in the support of the saints, [5]and this, not as we had expected, but they first gave themselves to the Lord and to us by the will of God. [6]So we urged Titus that as he had previously made a beginning, so he would also complete in you this gracious work as well.

2 CORINTHIANS PARALLELS

2 Corinthians 1:3–4

Blessed be the God and Father of our Lord Jesus Christ, the Father of mercies and God of all comfort, [4]who comforts us in all our *affliction* so that we will be able to comfort those who are in any affliction with the comfort with which we ourselves are comforted by God.

2 Corinthians 2:13

I had no rest for my spirit, not finding *Titus* my brother; but taking my leave of them, I went on to *Macedonia.*

2 Corinthians 7:4

Great is my confidence in you; great is my boasting on your behalf. I am filled with comfort; I am overflowing with *joy* in all our *affliction.*

2 Corinthians 8:16–19

But thanks be to God who puts the same earnestness on your behalf in the heart of *Titus.* [17]For he not only accepted our appeal, but being himself very earnest, he has gone to you of his own accord. [18]We have sent along with him the brother whose fame in the things of the gospel has spread through all the churches; [19]and not only this, but he has also been appointed by the churches to travel with us in *this gracious work*, which is being administered by us for the glory of the Lord Himself, and to show our readiness.

2 Corinthians 8:23

As for *Titus*, he is my partner and fellow worker among you; as for our brethren, they are messengers of the churches, a glory to Christ.

2 Corinthians 9:1–2

For it is superfluous for me to write to you about this ministry to *the saints*; [2]for I know your readiness, of which I boast about you to the *Macedonians*, namely, that Achaia has been prepared since last year, and your zeal has stirred up most of them.

2 Corinthians 9:12–14

For the ministry of this service is not only fully supplying the needs of *the saints*, but is also overflowing through many thanksgivings to God. [13]Because of the proof given by this ministry, they will glorify God for your obedience to your confession of the gospel of Christ and for the *liberality* of your contribution to them and to all, [14]while they also, by prayer on your behalf, yearn for you because of the surpassing *grace of God* in you.

OTHER PAULINE PARALLELS

Romans 12:6, 8

Since we have gifts that differ according to *the grace given* to us, each of us is to exercise them accordingly: if prophecy, according to the proportion of his faith; . . . [8]or he who exhorts, in his exhortation; he who *gives*, with *liberality*; he who leads, with diligence; he who shows mercy, with cheerfulness.

Romans 15:25–27

Now, I am going to Jerusalem serving *the saints*. [26]For *Macedonia* and Achaia have been pleased to make a contribution for the poor among the saints in Jerusalem. [27]Yes, they were pleased to do so, and they are indebted to them. For if the Gentiles have shared in their spiritual things, they are indebted to minister to them also in material things.

Romans 15:30–31

Now I urge you, brethren, by our Lord Jesus Christ and by the love of the Spirit, to strive together with me in your prayers to God for me, [31]that I may be rescued from those who are disobedient in Judea, and that my service for Jerusalem may prove acceptable to *the saints*.

1 Corinthians 16:1–4

Now concerning the collection for *the saints*, as I directed the churches of Galatia, so do you also. [2]On the first day of every week each one of you is to put aside and save, as he may prosper, so that no collections be made when I come. [3]When I arrive,

whomever you may approve, I will send them with letters to carry your gift to Jerusalem; [4]and if it is fitting for me to go also, they will go with me.

Galatians 2:9–10

Recognizing *the grace* that had been *given* to me, James and Cephas and John, who were reputed to be pillars, gave to me and Barnabas the right hand of fellowship, so that we might go to the Gentiles and they to the circumcised. [10]They only asked us to remember the poor—the very thing I also was eager to do.

1 Thessalonians 1:6–7

You also became imitators of us and of the Lord, having received the word in much tribulation with the *joy* of the Holy Spirit, [7]so that you became an example to all the believers in *Macedonia* and in Achaia.

1 Thessalonians 3:2–3

We sent Timothy, our brother and God's fellow worker in the gospel of Christ, to strengthen and encourage you as to your faith, [3]so that no one would be disturbed by these *afflictions*; for you yourselves know that we have been destined for this.

OTHER BIBLICAL PARALLELS

Isaiah 60:5–7

"Then you will see and be radiant, And your heart will thrill and rejoice; Because the *abundance* of the sea will be turned to you, The *wealth* of the nations will come to you. [6]A multitude of camels will cover you; . . . They will bring gold and frankincense, And will bear good news of the praises of the LORD. [7]All the flocks of Kedar will be gathered together to you; . . . They will go up with acceptance on My altar, And I shall glorify My glorious house."

Mark 12:43–44

"Truly I say to you, this poor widow put in more than all the contributors to the treasury; [44]for they all put in out of their surplus, but she, out of her *poverty*, put in all she owned, all she had to live on."

Acts 11:27–30

Now at this time some prophets came down from Jerusalem to Antioch. [28]One of them named Agabus stood up and began to indicate by the Spirit that there would certainly be a great famine all over the world. And this took place in the reign of Claudius. [29]And in the proportion that any of the disciples had means, each of them determined to send a contribution for the relief of the brethren living in Judea. [30]And this they did, sending it in charge of Barnabas and Saul to the elders.

Acts 24:10, 17

When the governor had nodded for him to speak, Paul responded: "Knowing that for many years you have been a judge to this nation, I cheerfully make my defense. . . . [17]Now after several years I came to bring alms to my nation and to present offerings."

2 Corinthians 8:7–15

But just as you abound in everything, in faith and utterance and knowledge and in all earnestness and in the love we inspired in you, see that you abound in this gracious work also. [8]I am not speaking this as a command, but as proving through the earnestness of others the sincerity of your love also. [9]For you know the grace of our Lord Jesus Christ, that though He was rich, yet for your sake He became poor, so that you through His poverty might become rich. [10]I give my opinion in this matter, for this is to your advantage, who were the first to begin a year ago not only to do this, but also to desire to do it. [11]But now finish doing it also, so that just as there was the readiness to desire it, so there may be also the completion of it by your ability. [12]For if the readiness is present, it is acceptable according to what a person has, not according to what he does not have. [13]For this is not for the ease of others and for your affliction, but by way of equality— [14]at this present time your abundance being a supply for their need, so that their abundance also may become a supply for your need, that there may be equality; [15]as it is written, "HE WHO gathered MUCH DID NOT HAVE TOO MUCH, AND HE WHO gathered LITTLE HAD NO LACK."

2 CORINTHIANS PARALLELS

2 Corinthians 1:3–4

Blessed be the God and Father of our Lord Jesus Christ, the Father of mercies and God of all comfort, [4]who comforts us in all our *affliction* so that we will be able to comfort those who are in any affliction with the comfort with which we ourselves are comforted by God.

2 Corinthians 5:21

He made Him who knew no sin to be sin on our behalf, so that we might become the righteousness of God in Him.

2 Corinthians 6:4, 10

. . . in everything commending ourselves as servants of God, in much endurance, in *afflictions,* in hardships, in distresses, . . . [10]as sorrowful yet always rejoicing, as *poor* yet making many *rich*, as having nothing yet possessing all things.

2 Corinthians 9:1–2, 7–8, 12

For it is superfluous for me to write to you about this ministry to the saints; [2]for I know your *readiness*, of which I boast about you to the Macedonians, namely, that Achaia has been prepared since last *year*, and your zeal has stirred up most of them. . . . [7]Each one must do just as he has purposed in his heart, not grudgingly or under compulsion, for God loves a cheerful giver. [8]And God is able to make all *grace abound* to you, so that always having all sufficiency in everything, you may have an *abundance* for every good deed. . . . [12]For the ministry of this service is not only fully *supplying* the *needs* of the saints, but is also overflowing through many thanksgivings to God.

OTHER PAULINE PARALLELS

Romans 15:30–31

Now I urge you, brethren, by our Lord Jesus Christ and by the love of the Spirit, to strive together with me in your prayers to God for me, [31]that I may be rescued from those who are disobedient in Judea, and that my service for Jerusalem may prove *acceptable* to the saints.

1 Corinthians 1:4–5

I thank my God always concerning you for the *grace* of God which was given you in Christ Jesus, [5]that in everything you were *enriched* in Him, in all speech and all *knowledge,*

1 Corinthians 13:2–3

If I have the gift of prophecy, and know all mysteries and all *knowledge*; and if I have all faith, so as to remove mountains, but do not have *love*, I am nothing. ³And if I give all my possessions to feed the *poor*, and if I surrender my body to be burned, but do not have love, it profits me nothing.

1 Corinthians 16:1–2

Now concerning the collection for the saints, as I directed the churches of Galatia, so do you also. ²On the first day of every week each one of you is to put aside and save, as he may prosper, so that no collections be made when I come.

Galatians 2:9–10

Recognizing the *grace* that had been given to me, James and Cephas and John, who were reputed to be pillars, gave to me and Barnabas the right hand of fellowship, so that we might go to the Gentiles and they to the circumcised. ¹⁰They only asked us to remember the *poor*—the very thing I also was eager to do.

Philippians 2:5–8

Have this attitude in yourselves which was also in Christ Jesus, ⁶who, although He existed in the form of God, did not regard equality with God a thing to be grasped, ⁷but emptied Himself, taking the form of a bond-servant, and being made in the likeness of men. ⁸Being found in appearance as a man, He humbled Himself by becoming obedient to the point of death, even death on a cross.

OTHER BIBLICAL PARALLELS

Exodus 16:4, 18

Then the Lord said to Moses, "Behold, I will rain bread from heaven for you; and the people shall go out and gather a day's portion every day, that I may test them, whether or not they will walk in My instruction." . . . ¹⁸When they measured it with an omer, *he who* had *gathered much* had no excess, and *he who* had *gathered little had no lack*; every man gathered as much as he should eat.

Proverbs 3:27

Do not withhold good from those to whom it is due, When it is in your power to do it.

Matthew 20:26–28

"It is not this way among you, but whoever wishes to become great among you shall be your servant, ²⁷and whoever wishes to be first among you shall be your slave; ²⁸just as the Son of Man did not come to be served, but to serve, and to give His life a ransom for many."

Mark 12:43–44

"Truly I say to you, this *poor* widow put in more than all the contributors to the treasury; ⁴⁴for they all put in out of their surplus, but she, out of her *poverty*, put in all she owned, all she had to live on."

NONCANONICAL PARALLELS

Tobit 4:6–10

"To all those who practice righteousness ⁷give alms from your possessions, and do not let your eye begrudge the gift when you make it. Do not turn your face away from anyone who is *poor*, and the face of God will not be turned away from you. ⁸If you have many possessions, make your gift from them in proportion; if few, do not be afraid to give according to the little you have. ⁹So you will be laying up a good treasure for yourself against the day of necessity. ¹⁰For almsgiving delivers from death and keeps you from going into the Darkness."

Philo, Who Is the Heir of Divine Things? 145

One basic form of *equality* is the proportional, according to which a few things are held to be equal to many, and small things equal to those that are larger. Cities are accustomed to use this at certain times, when they direct each of the citizens to contribute an equal share from his possessions, not numerically equal of course, but in proportion to the assessment of each one's property.

2 Corinthians 8:16–24

But thanks be to God who puts the same earnestness on your behalf in the heart of Titus. ¹⁷For he not only accepted our appeal, but being himself very earnest, he has gone to you of his own accord. ¹⁸We have sent along with him the brother whose fame in the things of the gospel has spread through all the churches; [19]and not only this, but he has also been appointed by the churches to travel with us in this gracious work, which is being administered by us for the glory of the Lord Himself, and to show our readiness, [20]taking precaution so that no one will discredit us in our administration of this generous gift; [21]for we have regard for what is honorable, not only in the sight of the Lord, but also in the sight of men. [22]We have sent with them our brother, whom we have often tested and found diligent in many things, but now even more diligent because of his great confidence in you. [23]As for Titus, he is my partner and fellow worker among you; as for our brethren, they are messengers of the churches, a glory to Christ. [24]Therefore openly before the churches, show them the proof of your love and of our reason for boasting about you.

2 CORINTHIANS PARALLELS

2 Corinthians 2:13–14

I had no rest for my spirit, not finding *Titus* my brother; but taking my leave of them, I went on to Macedonia. [14]*But thanks be to God,* who always leads us in triumph in Christ, and manifests through us the sweet aroma of the knowledge of Him in every place.

2 Corinthians 6:3–4, 10

. . . giving no cause for offense in anything, so that the ministry will not be *discredited,* [4]but in everything commending ourselves as servants of God, in much endurance, in afflictions, in hardships, in distresses, . . . [10]as sorrowful yet always rejoicing, as poor yet making many rich, as having nothing yet possessing all things.

2 Corinthians 7:4

Great is my *confidence in you*; great is my *boasting* on your behalf. I am filled with comfort; I am overflowing with joy in all our affliction.

2 Corinthians 7:14

For if in anything I have *boasted* to him *about you*, I was not put to shame; but as we spoke all things to you in truth, so also our boasting before *Titus* proved to be the truth.

2 Corinthians 8:6

So we urged *Titus* that as he had previously made a beginning, so he would also complete in you *this gracious work* as well.

2 Corinthians 12:18

I urged *Titus* to go, and I sent *the brother* with him. Titus did not take any advantage of you, did he? Did we not conduct ourselves in the same spirit and walk in the same steps?

Romans 14:18–19

For he who in this way serves Christ is acceptable to God and approved by *men*. [19]So then we pursue the things which make for peace and the building up of one another.

1 Corinthians 12:28

And God has *appointed* in the church, first apostles, second prophets, third teachers, then miracles, then gifts of healings, helps, *administrations,* various kinds of tongues.

1 Corinthians 13:13

But now faith, hope, *love*, abide these three; but the greatest of these is love.

1 Corinthians 16:3–4, 14

When I arrive, whomever you may approve, I will send them with letters to carry your *gift* to Jerusalem; [4]and if it is fitting for me to go also, they will go with me. . . . [14]Let all that you do be done in *love*.

Philippians 2:25

But I thought it necessary to send to you Epaphroditus, my brother and *fellow worker* and fellow soldier, who is also your *messenger* and minister to my need.

Philippians 4:8

Finally, brethren, whatever is true, whatever is *honorable*, whatever is right, whatever is pure, whatever is lovely, whatever is of good repute, if there is any excellence and if anything worthy of praise, dwell on these things.

1 Timothy 3:10

These men must also first be *tested*; then let them serve as deacons if they are beyond reproach.

2 Timothy 2:15

Be *diligent* to present yourself approved to God as a workman who does not need to be ashamed, accurately handling the word of truth.

2 Corinthians 9:1–5

Deuteronomy 15:7–8

"If there is a poor man with you, one of your brothers, in any of your towns in your land which the LORD your God is giving you, you shall not harden your heart, nor close your hand from your poor brother; [8]but you shall freely open your hand to him, and shall *generously* lend him sufficient for his need in whatever he lacks."

Proverbs 3:3–4

Do not let kindness and truth leave you; Bind them around your neck, Write them on the tablet of your heart. [4]So you will find favor and good repute *In the sight of* God and *man.*

Acts 14:23

When they had *appointed* elders for them in every church, having prayed with fasting, they commended them to the Lord in whom they had believed.

Acts 20:1–4

After the uproar had ceased, Paul sent for the disciples, and when he had exhorted them and taken his leave of them, he left to go to Macedonia. [2]When he had gone through those districts and had given them much exhortation, he came to Greece. [3]And there he spent three months, and when a plot was formed against him by the Jews as he was about to set sail for Syria, he decided to return through Macedonia. [4]And he was accompanied by Sopater of Berea, the son of Pyrrhus, and by Aristarchus and Secundus of the Thessalonians, and Gaius of Derbe, and Timothy, and Tychicus and Trophimus of Asia.

NONCANONICAL PARALLELS

Philo, On the Special Laws *1.78*

In almost every city there are treasuries for the sacred contributions where the people routinely come and deposit their offerings. And at certain times envoys are *appointed* by merit to convey the sacred tribute.

For it is superfluous for me to write to you about this ministry to the saints; [2]for I know your readiness, of which I boast about you to the Macedonians, namely, that Achaia has been prepared since last year, and your zeal has stirred up most of them. [3]But I have sent the brethren, in order that our boasting about you may not be made empty in this case, so that, as I was saying, you may be prepared; [4]otherwise if any Macedonians come with me and find you unprepared, we—not to speak of you—will be put to shame by this confidence. [5]So I thought it necessary to urge the brethren that they would go on ahead to you and arrange beforehand your previously promised bountiful gift, so that the same would be ready as a bountiful gift and not affected by covetousness.

2 CORINTHIANS PARALLELS

2 Corinthians 1:1

Paul, an apostle of Christ Jesus by the will of God, and Timothy our brother, To the church of God which is at Corinth with all the saints who are throughout *Achaia* . . .

2 Corinthians 7:4

Great is my *confidence* in you; great is my *boasting* on your behalf. I am filled with comfort; I am overflowing with joy in all our affliction.

2 Corinthians 7:14

For if in anything I have *boasted* to him *about you,* I was not *put to shame*; but as we spoke all things to you in truth, so also our boasting before Titus proved to be the truth.

2 Corinthians 8:1, 3–4

Now, brethren, we wish to make known to you the grace of God which has been given in the churches of *Macedonia.* . . . [3]For I testify that according to their ability, and beyond their ability, they gave of their own accord, [4]begging us with much urging for the favor of participation in the support of *the saints.*

2 Corinthians 8:10–11

I give my opinion in this matter, for this is to your advantage, who were the first to begin a *year* ago not only to do this, but also to desire to do it. [11]But now finish doing it also, so that just as there was the *readiness* to desire it, so there may be also the completion of it by your ability.

2 Corinthians 12:17–18

Certainly I have not taken advantage of you through any of those whom I have sent to you, have I? [18]I urged Titus to go, and I sent the brother with him. Titus did not take any advantage of you, did he? Did we not conduct ourselves in the same spirit and walk in the same steps?

OTHER PAULINE PARALLELS

Romans 15:26–28

For *Macedonia* and *Achaia* have been pleased to make a contribution for the poor among *the saints* in Jerusalem. [27]Yes, they were pleased to do so, and they are indebted to them. For if the Gentiles have shared in their spiritual things, they are indebted to *minister* to them also in material things. [28]Therefore, when I have finished this, and have put my seal on this fruit of theirs, I will go on by way of you to Spain.

1 Corinthians 5:11

But actually, I wrote to you not to associate with any so-called brother if he is an immoral person, or *covetous*, or an idolater, or a reviler, or a drunkard, or a swindler—not even to eat with such a one.

1 Corinthians 16:1–2

Now concerning the collection for *the saints*, as I directed the churches of Galatia, so do you also. [2]On the first day of every week each one of you is to put aside and save, as he may prosper, so that no collections be made when I come.

Titus 2:13–14

Christ Jesus [14] . . . gave Himself for us to redeem us from every lawless deed, and to purify for Himself a people for His own possession, *zealous* for good deeds.

OTHER BIBLICAL PARALLELS

Acts 20:1–4

After the uproar had ceased, Paul sent for the disciples, and when he had exhorted them and taken his leave of them, he left to go to *Macedonia*. [2]When he had gone through those districts and had given them much exhortation, he came to Greece. [3]And there he spent three months, and when a plot was formed against him by the Jews as he was about to set sail for Syria, he decided to return through Macedonia. [4]And he was accompanied by Sopater of Berea, the son of Pyrrhus, and by Aristarchus and Secundus of the Thessalonians, and Gaius of Derbe, and Timothy, and Tychicus and Trophimus of Asia.

2 Corinthians 9:6–15

Now this I say, he who sows sparingly will also reap sparingly, and he who sows bountifully will also reap bountifully. [7]Each one must do just as he has purposed in his heart, not grudgingly or under compulsion, for God loves a cheerful giver. [8]And God is able to make all grace abound to you, so that always having all sufficiency in everything, you may have an abundance for every good deed; [9]as it is written, "HE SCATTERED ABROAD, HE GAVE TO THE POOR, HIS RIGHTEOUSNESS ENDURES FOREVER." [10]Now He who supplies seed to the sower and bread for food will supply and multiply your seed for sowing and increase the harvest of your righteousness; [11]you will be enriched in everything for all liberality, which through us is producing thanksgiving to God. [12]For the ministry of this service is not only fully supplying the needs of the saints, but is also overflowing through many thanksgivings to God. [13]Because of the proof given by this ministry, they will glorify God for your obedience to your confession of the gospel of Christ and for the liberality of your contribution to them and to all, [14]while they also, by prayer on your behalf, yearn for you because of the surpassing grace of God in you. [15]Thanks be to God for His indescribable gift!

2 CORINTHIANS PARALLELS

2 Corinthians 2:9

For to this end also I wrote, so that I might put you to the test, whether you are *obedient* in all things.

2 Corinthians 4:15

For all things are for your sakes, so that the grace which is spreading to more and more people may cause the *giving* of *thanks* to abound to the glory of God.

2 Corinthians 8:1–2

Now, brethren, we wish to make known to you *the grace of God* which has been given in the churches of Macedonia, [2]that in a great ordeal of affliction their *abundance* of joy and their deep poverty overflowed in the wealth of their *liberality.*

2 Corinthians 8:9

For you know the *grace* of our Lord Jesus Christ, that though He was rich, yet for your sake He became *poor*, so that you through His poverty might become *rich.*

2 Corinthians 8:13–14

For this is not for the ease of others and for your affliction, but by way of equality— [14]at this present time your *abundance* being a *supply* for their *need*, so that their abundance also may become a supply for your need, that there may be equality.

2 Corinthians 8:16

But *thanks be to God* who puts the same earnestness on your behalf in the heart of Titus.

OTHER PAULINE PARALLELS

Romans 12:6, 8

Since we have *gifts* that differ according to the *grace* given to us, each of us is to exercise them accordingly: if prophecy, according to the proportion of his faith; . . . [8]or he who exhorts, in his exhortation; he who *gives*, with *liberality*; he who leads, with diligence; he who shows mercy, with *cheerfulness.*

Romans 15:26–28

For Macedonia and Achaia have been pleased to make a *contribution* for *the poor* among *the saints* in Jerusalem. [27]Yes, they were pleased to do so, and they are indebted to them. For if the Gentiles have shared in their spiritual things, they are indebted to *minister* to them also in material things. [28]Therefore, when I have finished this, and have put my seal on this fruit of theirs, I will go on by way of you to Spain.

1 Corinthians 1:4–5

I thank my God always concerning you for *the grace of God* which was given you in Christ Jesus, [5]that in everything you were *enriched* in Him, in all speech and all knowledge,

Galatians 6:7, 9

Do not be deceived, God is not mocked; for whatever a man *sows*, this he will also *reap.* . . . [9]Let us not lose heart in doing good, for in due time we will reap if we do not grow weary.

Philemon 14

Without your consent I did not want to do anything, so that your goodness would not be, in effect, by *compulsion* but of your own free will.

OTHER BIBLICAL PARALLELS

Exodus 25:2

"Tell the sons of Israel to raise a *contribution* for Me; from every man whose *heart* moves him you shall raise My contribution."

Deuteronomy 15:7–8, 10

"If there is a *poor* man with you, one of your brothers, in any of your towns in your land which the LORD your God is giving you, you shall not harden your *heart*, nor close your hand from your poor brother; [8]but you shall freely open your hand to him, and shall generously lend him sufficient for his need in whatever he lacks. . . . [10]You shall generously *give* to him, and your heart shall not be grieved when you give to him, because for this thing the LORD your God will bless you in all your work and in all your undertakings."

Psalm 112:9

He has given freely *to the poor, His righteousness endures forever;* His horn will be exalted in honor.

Proverbs 11:24

There is one who *scatters*, and yet increases all the more, And there is one who withholds what is justly due, and yet it results only in want.

Isaiah 55:10

"For as the rain and the snow come down from heaven, And do not return there without watering the earth And making it bear and sprout, And furnishing *seed to the sower and bread* to the eater . . . "

Hosea 10:12
Sow with a view to *righteousness, Reap* in accordance with kindness; Break up your fallow ground, For it is time to seek the LORD Until He comes to rain righteousness on you.

Hebrews 10:23–24
Let us hold fast the *confession* of our hope without wavering, for He who promised is faithful; 24and let us consider how to stimulate one another to love and *good deeds.*

Testament of Job 11:2–3
And there were still others, at the time without resources and unable to invest in a thing, who came and entreated me, saying, "We beg you, may we also engage in this *service.* 3We own nothing, however. Show mercy on us and lend us money so we may leave for distant cities on business and be able to do *the poor* a service."

2 Corinthians 10:1–6

Now I, Paul, myself urge you by the meekness and gentleness of Christ—I who am meek when face to face with you, but bold toward you when absent! 2I ask that when I am present I need not be bold with the confidence with which I propose to be courageous against some, who regard us as if we walked according to the flesh. 3For though we walk in the flesh, we do not war according to the flesh, 4for the weapons of our warfare are not of the flesh, but divinely powerful for the destruction of fortresses. 5We are destroying speculations and every lofty thing raised up against the knowledge of God, and we are taking every thought captive to the obedience of Christ, 6and we are ready to punish all disobedience, whenever your obedience is complete.

2 Corinthians 1:12
For our proud *confidence* is this: the testimony of our conscience, that in holiness and godly sincerity, not in *fleshly* wisdom but in the grace of God, we have conducted ourselves in the world, and especially toward you.

2 Corinthians 2:7–9
On the contrary you should rather forgive and comfort him, otherwise such a one might be overwhelmed by excessive sorrow. 8Wherefore I urge you to reaffirm your love for him. 9For to this end also I wrote, so that I might put you to the test, whether you are *obedient* in all things.

2 Corinthians 5:16
Therefore from now on we recognize no one *according to the flesh*; even though we have known Christ according to the flesh, yet now we know Him in this way no longer.

2 Corinthians 6:1, 3–4, 6–7
And working together with Him, we also urge you not to receive the grace of God in vain, . . . 3giving no cause for offense in anything, so that the ministry will not be discredited, 4but in everything commending ourselves as servants of God, in much endurance, in afflictions, in hardships, in distresses, . . . 6in purity, in *knowledge*, in patience, in kindness, in the Holy Spirit, in genuine love, 7in the word of truth, in the *power* of God; by the *weapons* of righteousness for the right hand and the left.

2 Corinthians 11:5–6
For I consider myself not in the least inferior to the most eminent apostles. 6But even if I am unskilled in speech, yet I am not so in *knowledge*; in fact, in every way we have made this evident to you in all things.

2 Corinthians 11:21
To my shame I must say that we have been weak by comparison. But in whatever respect anyone else is bold—I speak in foolishness—I am just as *bold* myself.

2 Corinthians 13:10
For this reason I am writing these things while *absent*, so that when *present* I need not use severity, in accordance with the authority which the Lord gave me for building up and not for tearing down.

Romans 1:4–5

. . . Jesus Christ our Lord, [5]through whom we have received grace and apostleship to bring about the *obedience* of faith among all the Gentiles for His name's sake.

Romans 13:12

The night is almost gone, and the day is near. Therefore let us lay aside the deeds of darkness and put on the armor of light.

1 Corinthians 2:3–5

I was with you in weakness and in fear and in much trembling, [4]and my message and my preaching were not in persuasive words of wisdom, but in demonstration of the Spirit and of *power*, [5]so that your faith would not rest on the wisdom of men, but on the power of God.

1 Corinthians 4:19–20

But I will come to you soon, if the Lord wills, and I shall find out, not the words of those who are arrogant but their power. [20]For the kingdom of God does not consist in words but in *power*.

Ephesians 5:6

Let no one deceive you with empty words, for because of these things the wrath of God comes upon the sons of *disobedience*.

Ephesians 6:11–12

Put on the full armor of God, so that you will be able to stand firm against the schemes of the devil. [12]For our struggle is not against *flesh* and blood, but against the rulers, against the powers, against the world forces of this darkness, against the spiritual forces of wickedness in the heavenly places.

Colossians 2:8

See to it that no one *takes* you *captive* through philosophy and empty deception, according to the tradition of men, according to the elementary principles of the world, rather than according to Christ.

2 Timothy 2:23

But refuse foolish and ignorant *speculations*, knowing that they produce quarrels.

Proverbs 21:22

A wise man scales the city of the mighty And brings down the stronghold in which they trust.

Isaiah 2:12

For the Lord of hosts will have a day of reckoning Against everyone who is proud and lofty And against everyone who is lifted up, That he may be abased.

Amos 5:9

It is He who flashes forth with *destruction* upon the strong, So that destruction comes upon the *fortress*.

Matthew 11:29

"Take My yoke upon you and learn from Me, for I am *gentle* and humble in heart, and YOU WILL FIND REST FOR YOUR SOULS."

Philo, On the Confusion of Tongues *128–30*

Justice, the friend of virtue and enemy of vice, comes and destroys the cities which they [the children of Cain] built for the harassment of the soul. [129] . . . For the *fortress* erected by means of persuasive arguments is built solely to distract and alienate the mind from the honor owed to God. [130]But for the *destruction* of this fortress there stands ready and armed an attacker, an enemy of injustice.

2 Corinthians 10:7–11

You are looking at things as they are outwardly. If anyone is confident in himself that he is Christ's, let him consider this again within himself, that just as he is Christ's, so also are we. [8]For even if I boast somewhat further about our authority, which the Lord gave for building you up and not for destroying you, I will not be put to shame, [9]for I do not wish to seem as if I would terrify you by my letters. [10]For they say, "His letters are weighty and strong, but his personal presence is unimpressive and his speech contemptible." [11]Let such a person consider this, that what we are in word by letters when absent, such persons we are also in deed when present.

2 CORINTHIANS PARALLELS

2 Corinthians 5:12

We are not again commending ourselves to you but are giving you an occasion to be proud of us, so that you will have an answer for those who take pride in appearance and not in heart.

2 Corinthians 5:16

Therefore from now on we recognize no one according to the flesh; even though we have known Christ according to the flesh, yet now we know Him in this way no longer.

2 Corinthians 11:6

But even if I am unskilled in *speech*, yet I am not so in knowledge; in fact, in every way we have made this evident to you in all things.

2 Corinthians 11:16–17

Again I say, let no one think me foolish; but if you do, receive me even as foolish, so that I also may *boast* a little. [17]What I am saying, I am not saying as the Lord would, but as in foolishness, in this confidence of boasting.

2 Corinthians 11:20–21

For you tolerate it if anyone enslaves you, anyone devours you, anyone takes advantage of you, anyone exalts himself, anyone hits you in the face. [21]To my *shame* I must say that we have been weak by comparison.

2 Corinthians 12:6

For if I do wish to *boast* I will not be foolish, for I will be speaking the truth; but I refrain from this, so that no one will credit me with more than he sees in me or hears from me.

2 Corinthians 12:19–20

All this time you have been thinking that we are defending ourselves to you. Actually, it is in the sight of God that we have been speaking in Christ; and all for your *upbuilding*, beloved. [20]For I am afraid that perhaps when I come I may find you to be not what I wish and may be found by you to be not what you wish; that perhaps there will be strife, jealousy, angry tempers, disputes, slanders, gossip, arrogance, disturbances.

2 Corinthians 13:2–3

I have previously said when *present* the second time, and though now *absent* I say in advance to those who have sinned in the past and to all the rest as well, that if I come again I will not spare anyone, [3]since you are seeking for proof of the Christ who speaks in me, and who is not weak toward you, but mighty in you.

2 Corinthians 13:10

For this reason I am writing these things while *absent*, so that when *present* I need not use severity, in accordance with the *authority which the Lord gave* me for *building up and not for* tearing down.

OTHER PAULINE PARALLELS

1 Corinthians 2:1–4

And when I came to you, brethren, I did not come with superiority of *speech* or of wisdom, proclaiming to you the testimony of God. [2]For I determined to know nothing among you except Jesus Christ, and Him crucified. [3]I was with you in weakness and in fear and in much trembling, [4]and my message and my preaching were not in persuasive words of wisdom, but in demonstration of the Spirit and of power.

1 Corinthians 14:37

If anyone thinks he is a prophet or spiritual, let him recognize that the things which I write to you are the Lord's commandment.

Galatians 4:13–14

You know that it was because of a bodily illness that I preached the gospel to you the first time; [14]and that which was a trial to you in my bodily condition you did not despise or loathe, but you received me as an angel of God, as Christ Jesus Himself.

Ephesians 4:11–12

And He gave some as apostles, and some as prophets, and some as evangelists, and some as pastors and teachers, [12]for the equipping of the saints for the work of service, to the *building up* of the body of Christ.

1 Thessalonians 2:5–6

For we never came with flattering *speech*, as you know, nor with a pretext for greed—God is witness—[6]nor did we seek glory from men, either from you or from others, even though as apostles of Christ we might have asserted our *authority*.

Jeremiah 1:9–10

Then the LORD stretched out His hand and touched my mouth, and the LORD said to me, "Behold, I have put My words in your mouth. [10]See, I have appointed you this day over the nations and over the kingdoms, To pluck up and to break down, To *destroy* and to overthrow, To *build* and to plant."

Matthew 23:27–28

"Woe to you, scribes and Pharisees, hypocrites! For you are like whitewashed tombs which on the outside appear beautiful, but inside they are full of dead men's bones and all uncleanness. [28]So you, too, *outwardly* appear righteous to men, but inwardly you are full of hypocrisy and lawlessness."

2 Peter 3:15–16

Regard the patience of our Lord as salvation; just as also our beloved brother Paul, according to the wisdom given him, wrote to you, [16]as also in all his *letters*, speaking in them of these things, in which are some things hard to understand, which the untaught and unstable distort, as they do also the rest of the Scriptures, to their own destruction.

Epictetus, Discourses *3.22.86–88*

For him [the true Cynic] there is also need of a certain kind of body. Since if some ailing man steps forward, thin and pale, his testimony does not make the same impression. [87]For he must not merely prove to the uninitiated that it is possible to be a good and excellent man by exhibiting the things of the soul, . . . but he must also show this through his body. . . . [88]"Look," he says, "both I and my body are testimony for this."

2 Corinthians 10:12–18

For we are not bold to class or compare ourselves with some of those who commend themselves; but when they measure themselves by themselves and compare themselves with themselves, they are without understanding. [13]But we will not boast beyond our measure, but within the measure of the sphere which God apportioned to us as a measure, to reach even as far as you. [14]For we are not overextending ourselves, as if we did not reach to you, for we were the first to come even as far as you in the gospel of Christ; [15]not boasting beyond our measure, that is, in other men's labors, but with the hope that as your faith grows, we will be, within our sphere, enlarged even more by you, [16]so as to preach the gospel even to the regions beyond you, and not to boast in what has been accomplished in the sphere of another. [17]But HE WHO BOASTS IS TO BOAST IN THE LORD. [18]For it is not he who commends himself that is approved, but he whom the Lord commends.

2 Corinthians 3:1–2

Are we beginning to *commend* ourselves again? Or do we need, as some, letters of commendation to you or from you? [2]You are our letter, written in our hearts, known and read by all men.

2 Corinthians 5:12

We are not again *commending* ourselves to you but are giving you an occasion to be proud of us, so that you will have an answer for those who take pride in appearance and not in heart.

2 Corinthians 11:17–21

What I am saying, I am not saying as the Lord would, but as in foolishness, in this confidence of *boasting*. [18]Since many boast according to the flesh, I will boast also. [19]For you, being so wise, tolerate the foolish gladly. [20]For you tolerate it if anyone enslaves you, anyone devours you, anyone takes advantage of you, anyone exalts himself, anyone hits you in the face. [21]To my shame I must say that we have been weak by *comparison*. But in whatever respect anyone else is *bold*—I speak in foolishness—I am just as bold myself.

2 Corinthians 12:11

I have become foolish; you yourselves compelled me. Actually I should have been *commended* by you, for in no respect was I inferior to the most eminent apostles, even though I am a nobody.

2 Corinthians 13:7

Now we pray to God that you do no wrong; not that we ourselves may appear *approved*, but that you may do what is right, even though we may appear unapproved.

OTHER PAULINE PARALLELS

Romans 15:17–20

Therefore in Christ Jesus I have found reason for *boasting* in things pertaining to God. [18]For I will not presume to speak of anything except what Christ has accomplished through me, resulting in the obedience of the Gentiles by word and deed, [19]in the power of signs and wonders, in the power of the Spirit; so that from Jerusalem and round about as far as Illyricum I have fully preached *the gospel of Christ.* [20]And thus I aspired *to preach the gospel,* not where Christ was already named, so that I would not build on another man's foundation.

Romans 15:22–24

For this reason I have often been prevented from coming to you; [23]but now, with no further place for me in these *regions,* and since I have had for many years a longing to come to you [24]whenever I go to Spain—for I hope to see you in passing, and to be helped on my way there by you, when I have first enjoyed your company for a while.

1 Corinthians 1:26–27, 29–31

For consider your calling, brethren, that there were not many wise according to the flesh, not many mighty, not many noble; [27]but God has chosen the foolish things of the world to shame the wise, and God has chosen the weak things of the world to shame the things which are strong, . . . [29]so that no man may boast before God. [30]But by His doing you are in Christ Jesus, who became to us wisdom from God, and righteousness and sanctification, and redemption, [31]so that, just as it is written, "LET HIM *WHO BOASTS, BOAST IN THE LORD.*"

1 Corinthians 3:5–6

What then is Apollos? And what is Paul? Servants through whom you believed, even as the Lord gave opportunity to each one. [6]I planted, Apollos watered, but God was causing the *growth.*

Ephesians 4:7

But to each one of us grace was given according to the *measure* of Christ's gift.

1 Thessalonians 2:4

Just as we have been *approved* by God to be entrusted with the gospel, so we speak, not as pleasing men, but God who examines our hearts.

OTHER BIBLICAL PARALLELS

Jeremiah 9:23–24

"Let not a wise man boast of his wisdom, and let not the mighty man boast of his might, let not a rich man boast of his riches; [24]but let him *who boasts boast* of this, that he understands and knows Me, that I am *the* LORD who exercises lovingkindness, justice and righteousness on earth."

Acts 19:21

Now after these things were finished, Paul purposed in the Spirit to go to Jerusalem after he had passed through Macedonia and Achaia, saying, "After I have been there, I must also see Rome."

NONCANONICAL PARALLELS

Letter to Theon (P.Oxy. 18.2190)

When I informed Philoxenus of your opinion he agreed, saying that . . . this shortage of professors . . . was in the same condition as the city, but he said that Didymus . . . would be sailing down and would take more care than the others. . . . For they . . . have been looking until now for a cleverer teacher. . . . As for myself, if only I had found some decent teachers, I would pray never set eyes on Didymus, even from a distance—what makes me despair is that this fellow who used to be a mere provincial teacher sees fit to compete with the rest.

2 Corinthians 11:1–6

I wish that you would bear with me in a little foolishness; but indeed you are bearing with me. [2]For I am jealous for you with a godly jealousy; for I betrothed you to one husband, so that to Christ I might present you as a pure virgin. [3]But I am afraid that, as the serpent deceived Eve by his craftiness, your minds will be led astray from the simplicity and purity of devotion to Christ. ⁴For if one comes and preaches another Jesus whom we have not preached, or you receive a different spirit which you have not received, or a different gospel which you have not accepted, you bear this beautifully. ⁵For I consider myself not in the least inferior to the most eminent apostles. ⁶But even if I am unskilled in speech, yet I am not so in knowledge; in fact, in every way we have made this evident to you in all things.

2 CORINTHIANS PARALLELS

2 Corinthians 4:1–2

Therefore, since we have this ministry, as we received mercy, we do not lose heart, ²but we have renounced the things hidden because of shame, not walking in *craftiness* or adulterating the word of God, but by the manifestation of truth commending ourselves to every man's conscience in the sight of God.

2 Corinthians 10:5

We are destroying speculations and every lofty thing raised up against the *knowledge* of God, and we are taking every thought captive to the obedience of Christ.

2 Corinthians 10:10

For they say, "His letters are weighty and strong, but his personal presence is unimpressive and his *speech* contemptible."

2 Corinthians 11:13–14

For such men are false apostles, deceitful workers, disguising themselves as apostles of Christ. ¹⁴No wonder, for even Satan disguises himself as an angel of light.

2 Corinthians 11:16–19

Again I say, let no one think me foolish; but if you do, receive me even as foolish, so that I also may boast a little. ¹⁷What I am saying, I am not saying as the Lord would, but as in *foolishness*, in this confidence of boasting. ¹⁸Since many boast according to the flesh, I will boast also. ¹⁹For you, being so wise, tolerate the foolish gladly.

2 Corinthians 12:11

I have become *foolish*; you yourselves compelled me. Actually I should have been commended by you, for in no respect was I *inferior to the most eminent apostles*, even though I am a nobody.

2 Corinthians 12:14–16

Here for this third time I am ready to come to you, and I will not be a burden to you; for I do not seek what is yours, but you; for children are not responsible to save up for their parents, but parents for their children. ¹⁵I will most gladly spend and be expended for your souls. If I love you more, am I to be loved less? ¹⁶But be that as it may, I did not burden you myself; nevertheless, *crafty* fellow that I am, I took you in by *deceit*.

OTHER PAULINE PARALLELS

Romans 7:3–4

So then, if while her *husband* is living she is joined to another man, she shall be called an adulteress; but if her husband dies, she is free from the law, so that she is not an adulteress though she is joined to another man. ⁴Therefore, my brethren, you also were made to die to the Law through the body of Christ, so that you might be joined to another, to Him who was raised from the dead, in order that we might bear fruit for God.

Romans 8:15

For you have not received a *spirit* of slavery leading to fear again, but you have received a spirit of adoption as sons by which we cry out, "Abba! Father!"

1 Corinthians 1:17, 20

For Christ did not send me to baptize, but to *preach* the gospel, not in cleverness of *speech*, so that the cross of Christ would not be made void. . . . ²⁰Where is the wise man? Where is the scribe? Where is the debater of this age? Has not God made *foolish* the wisdom of the world?

Galatians 1:6–8

I am amazed that you are so quickly deserting Him who called you by the grace of Christ, for *a different gospel*; ⁷which is really not another; only there are some who are disturbing you and want to distort the gospel of Christ. ⁸But even if we, or an angel from heaven, should *preach* to you a gospel contrary to what we have *preached* to you, he is to be accursed!

Ephesians 5:25–27

Husbands, love your wives, just as Christ also loved the church and gave Himself up for her, [26]so that He might sanctify her, having cleansed her by the washing of water with the word, [27]that He might *present* to Himself the church in all her glory, having no spot or wrinkle or any such thing; but that she would be holy and blameless.

OTHER BIBLICAL PARALLELS

Genesis 3:13

Then the LORD God said to the woman, "What is this you have done?" And the woman said, "*The serpent deceived* me, and I ate."

Hosea 2:19–20

"I will *betroth* you to Me forever; Yes, I will betroth you to Me in righteousness and in justice, In lovingkindness and in compassion, [20]And I will betroth you to Me in faithfulness. Then you will know the LORD."

Matthew 25:1

"Then the kingdom of heaven will be comparable to ten *virgins*, who took their lamps and went out to meet the bridegroom."

Revelation 12:9

And the great dragon was thrown down, *the serpent* of old who is called the devil and Satan, who *deceives* the whole world; he was thrown down to the earth, and his angels were thrown down with him.

Revelation 19:7–8

"Let us rejoice and be glad and give the glory to Him, for the marriage of the Lamb has come and His bride has made herself ready." [8]It was given to her to clothe herself in fine linen, bright and clean; for the fine linen is the righteous acts of the saints.

NONCANONICAL PARALLELS

Apocalypse of Abraham 23:1, 10–11

Look again at the picture: Who is the one who seduced *Eve*, and what is the fruit of the tree? . . . [10]This is the world of men, this is Adam and this is their thought on earth, this is Eve. [11]And he who is between them is the impiety of their behavior unto perdition, Azazel himself.

Didache 11.1–2

So if anyone comes and teaches you all these things mentioned above, you shall receive him. [2]But if the teacher himself turns away and teaches a *different* teaching, destroying these things, you shall not listen to him.

2 Corinthians 11:7–11

Or did I commit a sin in humbling myself so that you might be exalted, because I preached the gospel of God to you without charge? [8]I robbed other churches by taking wages from them to serve you; [9]and when I was present with you and was in need, I was not a burden to anyone; for when the brethren came from Macedonia they fully supplied my need, and in everything I kept myself from being a burden to you, and will continue to do so. [10]As the truth of Christ is in me, this boasting of mine will not be stopped in the regions of Achaia. [11]Why? Because I do not love you? God knows I do!

2 CORINTHIANS PARALLELS

2 Corinthians 1:1

Paul, an apostle of Christ Jesus by the will of God, and Timothy our brother, To the church of God which is at Corinth with all the saints who are throughout *Achaia* . . .

2 Corinthians 2:17

For we are not like many, peddling the word of God, but as from sincerity, but as from God, we speak in Christ in the sight of God.

2 Corinthians 10:8

For even if I *boast* somewhat further about our authority, which the Lord gave for building you up and not for destroying you, I will not be put to shame.

2 Corinthians 11:30–31

If I have to *boast*, I will boast of what pertains to my weakness. [31]The God and Father of the Lord Jesus, He who is blessed forever, knows that I am not lying.

2 Corinthians 12:13–16

For in what respect were you treated as inferior to the rest of the churches, except that I myself did *not* become *a burden to you*? Forgive me this wrong! [14]Here for this third time I am ready to come to you, and I will not be a burden to you; for I do not seek what is yours, but you; for children are not responsible to save up for their parents, but parents for their children. [15]I will most gladly spend and be expended for your souls. If *I love you* more, am I to be loved less? [16]But be that as it may, I did not burden you myself; nevertheless, crafty fellow that I am, I took you in by deceit.

OTHER PAULINE PARALLELS

Romans 9:1

I am telling *the truth* in *Christ*, I am not lying, my conscience testifies with me in the Holy Spirit.

1 Corinthians 4:8, 10

You are already filled, you have already become rich, you have become kings without us; and indeed, I wish that you had. become kings so that we also might reign with you. . . . [10]We are fools for Christ's sake, but you are prudent in Christ; we are weak, but you are strong; you are distinguished, but we are without honor.

1 Corinthians 9:6, 11–12, 14–15, 18

Or do only Barnabas and I not have a right to refrain from working? . . . [11]If we sowed spiritual things in you, is it too much if we reap material things from you? [12]If others share the right over you, do we not more? Nevertheless, we did not use this right, but we endure all things so that we will cause no hindrance to the gospel of Christ. . . . [14]So also the Lord directed those who proclaim the gospel to get their living from the gospel. [15]But I have used none of these things. And I am not writing these things so that it will be done so in my case; for it would be better for me to die than have any man make my *boast* an empty one. . . . [18]What then is my reward? That, when *I preach the gospel*, I may offer the gospel *without charge*, so as not to make full use of my right in the gospel.

Philippians 4:12

I know how to get along with *humble* means, and I also know how to live in prosperity; in any and every circumstance I have learned the secret of being filled and going hungry, both of having abundance and suffering *need*.

Philippians 4:15

You yourselves also know, Philippians, that at the first *preaching* of *the gospel*, after I left *Macedonia*, no church shared with me in the matter of giving and receiving but you alone.

1 Thessalonians 2:9

For you recall, brethren, our labor and hardship, how working night and day so as *not* to be *a burden to* any of *you*, we proclaimed to you *the gospel of God*.

2 Thessalonians 3:7–9

For you yourselves know how you ought to follow our example, because we did not act in an undisciplined manner among you, [8]nor did we eat anyone's bread without paying for it, but with labor and hardship we kept working night and day so that we would *not* be *a burden to* any of *you*; [9]not because we do not have the right to this, but in order to offer ourselves as a model for you, so that you would follow our example.

1 Timothy 5:17–18

The elders who rule well are to be considered worthy of double honor, especially those who work hard at *preaching* and teaching. [18]For the Scripture says, "YOU SHALL NOT MUZZLE THE OX WHILE HE IS THRESHING," and "The laborer is worthy of his *wages*."

OTHER BIBLICAL PARALLELS

Acts 18:1–3, 5

After these things he left Athens and went to Corinth. [2]And he found a Jew named Aquila, a native of Pontus, having recently come from Italy with his wife Priscilla, because Claudius had commanded all the Jews to leave Rome. He came to them, [3]and because he was of the same trade, he stayed with them and they were working, for by trade they were tent-makers. . . . [5]But when Silas and Timothy *came* down *from Macedonia*, Paul began devoting himself completely to the word, solemnly testifying to the Jews that Jesus was the Christ.

Didache *11.12*

If someone says in the Spirit, "Give me money (or something else)," you shall not listen to him. But if he asks on behalf of others who are *in need,* let no one pass judgment on him.

2 Corinthians 11:12–15

But what I am doing I will continue to do, so that I may cut off opportunity from those who desire an opportunity to be regarded just as we are in the matter about which they are boasting. [13]For such men are false apostles, deceitful workers, disguising themselves as apostles of Christ. [14]No wonder, for even Satan disguises himself as an angel of light. [15]Therefore it is not surprising if his servants also disguise themselves as servants of righteousness, whose end will be according to their deeds.

2 CORINTHIANS PARALLELS

2 Corinthians 2:10–11

But one whom you forgive anything, I forgive also; for indeed what I have forgiven, if I have forgiven anything, I did it for your sakes in the presence of Christ, [11]so that no advantage would be taken of us by *Satan,* for we are not ignorant of his schemes.

2 Corinthians 4:3–4

And even if our gospel is veiled, it is veiled to those who are perishing, [4]in whose case the god of this world has blinded the minds of the unbelieving so that they might not see the *light* of the gospel of the glory of Christ, who is the image of God.

2 Corinthians 5:10

For we must all appear before the judgment seat of Christ, so that each one may be recompensed for his *deeds* in the body, according to what he has done, whether good or bad.

2 Corinthians 10:13, 15–16

But we will not *boast* beyond our measure, but within the measure of the sphere which God apportioned to us as a measure, to reach even as far as you, . . . [15]not boasting beyond our measure, that is, in other men's

labors, but with the hope that as your faith grows, we will be, within our sphere, enlarged even more by you, [16]so as to preach the gospel even to the regions beyond you, and not to boast in what has been accomplished in the sphere of another.

2 Corinthians 11:3, 5

But I am afraid that, as the serpent *deceived* Eve by his craftiness, your minds will be led astray from the simplicity and purity of devotion to Christ. . . . [5]For I consider myself not in the least inferior to the most eminent apostles.

2 Corinthians 12:1

Boasting is necessary, though it is not profitable; but I will go on to visions and revelations of the Lord.

2 Corinthians 12:11

I have become foolish; you yourselves compelled me. Actually I should have been commended by you, for in no respect was I inferior to the most eminent *apostles,* even though I am a nobody.

OTHER PAULINE PARALLELS

Galatians 1:6–8

I am amazed that you are so quickly deserting Him who called you by the grace of Christ, for a different gospel; [7]which is really not another; only there are some who are disturbing you and want to distort the gospel of Christ. [8]But even if we, or *an angel* from heaven, should preach to you a gospel contrary to what we have preached to you, he is to be accursed!

Galatians 2:3–5

But not even Titus, who was with me, though he was a Greek, was compelled to be circumcised. [4]But it was because of the *false* brethren secretly brought in, who had sneaked in to spy out our liberty which we have in Christ Jesus, in order to bring us into bondage. [5]But we did not yield in subjection to them for even an hour, so that the truth of the gospel would remain with you.

Philippians 1:15, 17

Some, to be sure, are preaching Christ even from envy and strife, but some also from good will; . . . [17]the former proclaim Christ out of selfish ambition rather than from pure motives, thinking to cause me distress in my imprisonment.

Philippians 3:18–19

For many walk, of whom I often told you, and now tell you even weeping, that they are enemies of the cross of Christ, [19]*whose end* is destruction, whose god is their appetite, and whose glory is in their shame, who set their minds on earthly things.

1 Timothy 4:1–2

But the Spirit explicitly says that in later times some will fall away from the faith, paying attention to *deceitful* spirits and doctrines of demons, [2]by means of the hypocrisy of liars seared in their own conscience as with a branding iron.

2 Timothy 3:13

But evil men and impostors will proceed from bad to worse, *deceiving* and being deceived.

Titus 1:10–11

For there are many rebellious men, empty talkers and *deceivers*, especially those of the circumcision, [11]who must be silenced because they are upsetting whole families, teaching things they should not teach for the sake of sordid gain.

OTHER BIBLICAL PARALLELS

Acts 20:29–30

"I know that after my departure savage wolves will come in among you, not sparing the flock; [30]and from among your own selves men will arise, speaking perverse things, to draw away the disciples after them."

2 Peter 2:1

But false prophets also arose among the people, just as there will also be *false* teachers among you, who will secretly introduce destructive heresies, even denying the Master who bought them, bringing swift destruction upon themselves.

1 John 3:10

By this the children of God and the children of the devil are obvious: anyone who does not practice *righteousness* is not of God, nor the one who does not love his brother.

Revelation 2:2

I know your *deeds* and your toil and perseverance, and that you cannot tolerate evil men, and you put to the test those who call themselves *apostles,* and they are not, and you found them to be *false.*

NONCANONICAL PARALLELS

Life of Adam and Eve [Apocalypse of Moses] 17:1

And immediately he suspended himself from the walls of Paradise about the time when the angels of God went up to worship. Then Satan came in the form of *an angel* and sang hymns to God as the angels.

2 Corinthians 11:16–21a

Again I say, let no one think me foolish; but if you do, receive me even as foolish, so that I also may boast a little. [17]What I am saying, I am not saying as the Lord would, but as in foolishness, in this confidence of boasting. [18]Since many boast according to the flesh, I will boast also. [19]For you, being so wise, tolerate the foolish gladly. [20]For you tolerate it if anyone enslaves you, anyone devours you, anyone takes advantage of you, anyone exalts himself, anyone hits you in the face. [21]To my shame I must say that we have been weak by comparison.

2 CORINTHIANS PARALLELS

2 Corinthians 5:16

Therefore from now on we recognize no one *according to the flesh*; even though we have known Christ according to the flesh, yet now we know Him in this way no longer.

2 Corinthians 7:2

Make room for us in your hearts; we wronged no one, we corrupted no one, we *took advantage* of no one.

2 Corinthians 10:2

I ask that when I am present I need not be bold with the *confidence* with which I propose to be courageous against some, who regard us as if we walked *according to the flesh.*

2 Corinthians 10:8–9

For even if I *boast* somewhat further about our authority, which the Lord gave for building you up and not for destroying you, I will not be put to *shame*, [9]for I do not wish to seem as if I would terrify you by my letters.

2 Corinthians 10:12–13

For we are not bold to class or *compare* ourselves with some of those who commend themselves; but when they measure themselves by themselves and compare themselves with themselves, they are without understanding. [13]But we will not *boast* beyond our measure, but within the measure of the sphere which God apportioned to us as a measure, to reach even as far as you.

2 Corinthians 11:1, 3–4

I wish that you would bear with me in a little *foolishness*; but indeed you are bearing with me. . . . [3]But I am afraid that, as the serpent deceived Eve by his craftiness, your minds will be led astray from the simplicity and purity of devotion to Christ. [4]For if one comes and preaches another Jesus whom we have not preached, or you receive a different spirit which you have not received, or a different gospel which you have not accepted, you bear this beautifully.

2 Corinthians 12:11

I have become *foolish*; you yourselves compelled me. Actually I should have been commended by you, for in no respect was I inferior to the most eminent apostles, even though I am a nobody.

2 Corinthians 12:17–18

Certainly I have not *taken advantage of you* through any of those whom I have sent to you, have I? [18]I urged Titus to go, and I sent the brother with him. Titus did not take any advantage of you, did he? Did we not conduct ourselves in the same spirit and walk in the same steps?

1 Corinthians 2:1, 3

And when I came to you, brethren, I did not come with superiority of speech or of wisdom, proclaiming to you the testimony of God. . . . [3]I was with you in *weakness* and in fear and in much trembling.

1 Corinthians 3:19–21

For the wisdom of this world is *foolishness* before God. For it is written, "He is THE ONE WHO CATCHES THE *WISE* IN THEIR CRAFTINESS"; [20]and again, "THE LORD KNOWS THE REASONINGS of the wise, THAT THEY ARE USELESS." [21]So then let no one *boast* in men.

1 Corinthians 4:10

We are *fools* for Christ's sake, but you are prudent in Christ; we are *weak*, but you are strong; you are distinguished, but we are without honor.

Galatians 2:3–4

But not even Titus, who was with me, though he was a Greek, was compelled to be circumcised. [4]But it was because of the false brethren secretly brought in, who had sneaked in to spy out our liberty which we have in Christ Jesus, in order to bring us into bondage.

Galatians 6:13

For those who are circumcised do not even keep the Law themselves, but they desire to have you circumcised so that they may *boast* in your flesh.

Psalm 53:4

Have the workers of wickedness no knowledge, Who eat up My people as though they ate bread And have not called upon God?

Livy, History of Rome 38.49.6

"I beseech you to indulge me in what follows, senators, if my speech is made overlong, not out of a desire to *boast* about myself, but by the need to defend myself against these charges."

2 Corinthians 11:21b–29

But in whatever respect anyone else is bold—I speak in foolishness—I am just as bold myself. [22]Are they Hebrews? So am I. Are they Israelites? So am I. Are they descendants of Abraham? So am I. [23]Are they servants of Christ?—I speak as if insane—I more so; in far more labors, in far more imprisonments, beaten times without number, often in danger of death. ²⁴Five times I received from the Jews thirty-nine lashes. ²⁵Three times I was beaten with rods, once I was stoned, three times I was shipwrecked, a night and a day I have spent in the deep. ²⁶I have been on frequent journeys, in dangers from rivers, dangers from robbers, dangers from my countrymen, dangers from the Gentiles, dangers in the city, dangers in the wilderness, dangers on the sea, dangers among false brethren; ²⁷I have been in labor and hardship, through many sleepless nights, in hunger and thirst, often without food, in cold and exposure. ²⁸Apart from such external things, there is the daily pressure on me of concern for all the churches. ²⁹Who is weak without my being weak? Who is led into sin without my intense concern?

2 CORINTHIANS PARALLELS

2 Corinthians 1:8–9

For we do not want you to be unaware, brethren, of our affliction which came to us in Asia, that we were burdened excessively, beyond our strength, so that we despaired even of life; ⁹indeed, we had the sentence of *death* within ourselves so that we would not trust in ourselves, but in God who raises the dead.

2 Corinthians 4:7–11

But we have this treasure in earthen vessels, so that the surpassing greatness of the power will be of God and not from ourselves; ⁸we are afflicted in every way, but not crushed; perplexed, but not despairing; ⁹persecuted, but not forsaken; struck down, but not destroyed; ¹⁰always carrying about in the body the dying of Jesus, so that the life of Jesus also may be manifested in our body. ¹¹For we who live are constantly being delivered over to *death* for Jesus' sake, so that the life of Jesus also may be manifested in our mortal flesh.

2 Corinthians 6:3–5, 8–10

. . . giving no cause for offense in anything, so that the ministry will not be discredited, ⁴but in everything commending ourselves as *servants* of God, in much endurance, in afflictions, in *hardships*, in distresses, ⁵in *beatings*, in *imprisonments*, in tumults, in *labors*, in *sleeplessness*, in *hunger*, . . . ⁸by glory and dishonor, by evil report and good

report; regarded as deceivers and yet true; ⁹as unknown yet well-known, as dying yet behold, we live; as punished yet not put to *death*, ¹⁰as sorrowful yet always rejoicing, as poor yet making many rich, as having nothing yet possessing all things.

2 Corinthians 10:2

I ask that when I am present I need not be *bold* with the confidence with which I propose to be courageous against some, who regard us as if we walked according to the flesh.

2 Corinthians 11:13

For such men are *false* apostles, deceitful workers, disguising themselves as apostles of Christ.

2 Corinthians 12:10

Therefore I am well content with weaknesses, with insults, with distresses, with persecutions, with difficulties, for Christ's sake; for when I am *weak*, then I am strong.

OTHER PAULINE PARALLELS

Romans 11:1

I say then, God has not rejected His people, has He? May it never be! For I too am an *Israelite*, a *descendant of Abraham*, of the tribe of Benjamin.

1 Corinthians 4:9–13

For, I think, God has exhibited us apostles last of all, as men condemned to *death*; because we have become a spectacle to the world, both to angels and to men. ¹⁰We are *fools* for Christ's sake, but you are prudent in Christ; we are *weak*, but you are strong; you are distinguished, but we are without honor. ¹¹To this present hour we are both *hungry* and *thirsty*, and are poorly clothed, and are roughly treated, and are homeless; ¹²and we toil, working with our own hands; when we are reviled, we bless; when we are persecuted, we endure; ¹³when we are slandered, we try to conciliate; we have become as the scum of the world, the dregs of all things, even until now.

1 Corinthians 9:22

To the *weak* I became weak, that I might win the weak; I have become all things to all men, so that I may by all means save some.

Galatians 2:4

But it was because of the *false brethren* secretly brought in, who had sneaked in to spy out our liberty which we have in Christ Jesus, in order to bring us into bondage.

Philippians 3:4–6

If anyone else has a mind to put confidence in the flesh, I far more: [5]circumcised the eighth day, of the nation of *Israel*, of the tribe of Benjamin, a Hebrew of *Hebrews*; as to the Law, a Pharisee; [6]as to zeal, a persecutor of the church; as to the righteousness which is in the Law, found blameless.

OTHER BIBLICAL PARALLELS

Deuteronomy 25:2–3

"Then it shall be if the wicked man deserves to be beaten, the judge shall then make him lie down and be beaten in his presence with the number of stripes according to his guilt. [3]He may beat him forty times but no more."

Acts 14:5–6

And when an attempt was made by both *the Gentiles* and *the Jews* with their rulers, to mistreat and to *stone* them, [6]they [Paul and Barnabas] became aware of it and fled to the cities of Lycaonia, Lystra and Derbe, and the surrounding region.

Acts 16:22–23

The crowd rose up together against them [Paul and Silas], and the chief magistrates tore their robes off them and proceeded to order them to be *beaten with rods*. [23]When they had struck them with many blows, they threw them into *prison*, commanding the jailer to guard them securely.

NONCANONICAL PARALLELS

Pliny the Elder, Natural History 7.45.147–49

So also in the case of the divine Augustus, . . . great turnings of the human lot can be discerned: . . . [148]his flight from the battle of Philippi when he was sick, . . . his *shipwreck* off of Sicily, . . . his fall from a tower in the Pannonian Wars, [149]all his troops' mutinies, all his critical illnesses, . . . the many plots against his life, . . . plague at Rome, famine in Italy . . .

Dio Chrysostom, Orations 8.15–16

The noble man . . . fears none of his opponents . . . [16]but challenges them all one after another, struggling with *hunger* and *cold*, enduring *thirst*, and showing no softness even when he must bear whips, cuts, and burns. Hunger, exile, disrepute, and such things bring no terror to him.

Plutarch, Caesar 29.2

The residents of Novum Comum . . . were stripped of citizenship, . . . and Marcellus, while he was consul, *beat with rods* one of their senators who had come to Rome, telling him moreover that he put these marks on him to show that he was not a Roman.

2 Corinthians 11:30–33

If I have to boast, I will boast of what pertains to my weakness. [31]The God and Father of the Lord Jesus, He who is blessed forever, knows that I am not lying. [32]In Damascus the ethnarch under Aretas the king was guarding the city of the Damascenes in order to seize me, [33]and I was let down in a basket through a window in the wall, and so escaped his hands.

2 CORINTHIANS PARALLELS

2 Corinthians 1:3

Blessed be *the God and Father of* our *Lord Jesus* Christ, the Father of mercies and God of all comfort.

2 Corinthians 10:13, 15–17

But we will not *boast* beyond our measure, but within the measure of the sphere which God apportioned to us as a measure, to reach even as far as you. . . . [15]not boasting beyond our measure, that is, in other men's labors, but with the hope that as your faith grows, we will be, within our sphere, enlarged even more by you, [16]so as to preach the gospel even to the regions beyond you, and not to boast in what has been accomplished in the sphere of another. [17]But HE WHO BOASTS IS TO BOAST IN THE LORD.

2 Corinthians 11:10–11

As the truth of Christ is in me, this *boasting* of mine will not be stopped in the regions of

Achaia. [11]Why? Because I do not love you? God knows I do!

2 Corinthians 11:16–18

Again I say, let no one think me foolish; but if you do, receive me even as foolish, so that I also may *boast* a little. [17]What I am saying, I am not saying as the Lord would, but as in foolishness, in this confidence of boasting. [18]Since many boast according to the flesh, I will boast also.

2 Corinthians 11:20–21

For you tolerate it if anyone enslaves you, anyone devours you, anyone takes advantage of you, anyone exalts himself, anyone hits you in the face. [21]To my shame I must say that we have been *weak* by comparison.

OTHER PAULINE PARALLELS

Romans 1:25

For they exchanged the truth of God for a lie, and worshiped and served the creature rather than the Creator, *who is blessed forever*. Amen.

Romans 9:4–5

. . . who are Israelites, to whom belongs the adoption as sons, and the glory and the covenants and the giving of the Law and the temple service and the promises, [5]whose are the fathers, and from whom is the Christ according to the flesh, who is over all, God *blessed forever*. Amen.

1 Corinthians 2:1, 3

And when I came to you, brethren, I did not come with superiority of speech or of wisdom, proclaiming to you the testimony of God. . . . [3]I was with you in *weakness* and in fear and in much trembling.

1 Corinthians 4:10

We are fools for Christ's sake, but you are prudent in Christ; we are *weak*, but you are strong; you are distinguished, but we are without honor.

Galatians 1:17–20

Nor did I go up to Jerusalem to those who were apostles before me; but I went away to Arabia, and returned once more to *Damascus*. [18]Then three years later I went up to Jerusalem to become acquainted with Cephas, and stayed with him fifteen days.

[19]But I did not see any other of the apostles except James, the Lord's brother. [20](Now in what I am writing to you, I assure you before God that *I am not lying*.)

OTHER BIBLICAL PARALLELS

Joshua 2:1–4, 15

Then Joshua the son of Nun sent two men as spies secretly from Shittim, saying, "Go, view the land, especially Jericho." So they went and came into the house of a harlot whose name was Rahab, and lodged there. [2]It was told the king of Jericho, saying, "Behold, men from the sons of Israel have come here tonight to search out the land." [3]And the king of Jericho sent word to Rahab, saying, "Bring out the men who have come to you, who have entered your house, for they have come to search out all the land." [4]But the woman had taken the two men and hidden them, and she said, "Yes, the men came to me, but I did not know where they were from." . . . [15]Then she *let* them *down* by a rope *through* the *window*, for her house was on the city *wall*, so that she was living on the wall.

1 Samuel 19:11–12

Then Saul sent messengers to David's house to watch him, in order to put him to death in the morning. But Michal, David's wife, told him, saying, "If you do not save your life tonight, tomorrow you will be put to death." [12]So Michal *let* David *down through a window*, and he went out and fled and *escaped*.

Matthew 10:23

But whenever they persecute you in one *city,* flee to the next; for truly I say to you, you will not finish going through the cities of Israel until the Son of Man comes.

Acts 9:22–25

But Saul kept increasing in strength and confounding the Jews who lived at *Damascus* by proving that this Jesus is the Christ. [23]When many days had elapsed, the Jews plotted together to do away with him, [24]but their plot became known to Saul. They were also watching the gates day and night so that they might put him to death; [25]but his disciples took him by night and *let* him *down* through an opening in *the wall*, lowering him in a large *basket*.

Plutarch, Aemilius Paulus *26.1, 4*

Gnaeus Octavius . . . anchored off Samothrace . . . and took measures to prevent him from *escaping* by sea. . . . [4]And Perseus suffered pitifully in *letting* himself *down* through a narrow *window* in the *wall*, together with his wife and little children, who were unfamiliar with hardships and wandering.

Epictetus, Discourses *2.1.35*

Rather *boast* as follows: " . . . Look how I do not fall into the things I would avoid. Bring on death and you would know; bring on troubles, bring on imprisonment, bring on disgrace, bring on condemnation."

2 Corinthians 12:1–6

Boasting is necessary, though it is not profitable; but I will go on to visions and revelations of the Lord. [2]I know a man in Christ who fourteen years ago—whether in the body I do not know, or out of the body I do not know, God knows—such a man was caught up to the third heaven. [3]And I know how such a man—whether in the body or apart from the body I do not know, God knows—[4]was caught up into Paradise and heard inexpressible words, which a man is not permitted to speak. [5]On behalf of such a man I will boast; but on my own behalf I will not boast, except in regard to my weaknesses. [6]For if I do wish to boast I will not be foolish, for I will be speaking the truth; but I refrain from this, so that no one will credit me with more than he sees in me or hears from me.

2 CORINTHIANS PARALLELS

2 Corinthians 4:7

But we have this treasure in earthen vessels, so that the surpassing greatness of the power will be of God and not from ourselves.

2 Corinthians 11:1

I wish that you would bear with me in a little *foolishness*; but indeed you are bearing with me.

2 Corinthians 11:16–18

Again I say, let no one think me *foolish*; but if you do, receive me even as foolish, so that I also may *boast* a little. [17]What I am saying,

I am not saying as the Lord would, but as in foolishness, in this confidence of boasting. [18]Since many boast according to the flesh, I will boast also.

2 Corinthians 12:11

I have become *foolish*; you yourselves compelled me. Actually I should have been commended by you, for in no respect was I inferior to the most eminent apostles, even though I am a nobody.

OTHER PAULINE PARALLELS

1 Corinthians 1:27–29

God has chosen the *foolish* things of the world to shame the wise, and God has chosen the *weak* things of the world to shame the things which are strong, [28]and the base things of the world and the despised God has chosen, the things that are not, so that He may nullify the things that are, [29]so that no man may *boast* before God.

1 Corinthians 2:1, 3

And when I came to you, brethren, I did not come with superiority of speech or of wisdom, proclaiming to you the testimony of God. . . . [3]I was with you in *weakness* and in fear and in much trembling.

1 Corinthians 14:6

But now, brethren, if I come to you speaking in tongues, what will I profit you unless I speak to you either by way of *revelation* or of knowledge or of prophecy or of teaching?

Galatians 1:11–12

For I would have you know, brethren, that the gospel which was preached by me is not according to man. [12]For I neither received it from man, nor was I taught it, but I received it through a *revelation* of Jesus Christ.

Galatians 2:1–2

Then after an interval of *fourteen years* I went up again to Jerusalem with Barnabas, taking Titus along also. [2]It was because of a *revelation* that I went up; and I submitted to them the gospel which I preach among the Gentiles, but I did so in private to those who were of reputation, for fear that I might be running, or had run, in vain.

Colossians 2:18

Let no one keep defrauding you of your prize by delighting in self-abasement and the worship of the angels, taking his stand on *visions* he has seen, inflated without cause by his fleshly mind.

1 Thessalonians 4:17

Then we who are alive and remain will be *caught up* together with them in the clouds to meet the Lord in the air, and so we shall always be with the Lord.

OTHER BIBLICAL PARALLELS

Genesis 5:24

Enoch walked with God; and he was not, for God took him.

2 Kings 2:11

As they were going along and talking, behold, there appeared a chariot of fire and horses of fire which separated the two of them. And Elijah went up by a whirlwind *to heaven.*

Ezekiel 8:3

He stretched out the form of a hand and caught me by a lock of my head; and the Spirit lifted me up between earth and *heaven* and brought me in the *visions* of God to Jerusalem, to the entrance of the north gate of the inner court, where the seat of the idol of jealousy, which provokes to jealousy, was located.

Daniel 12:4

"But as for you, Daniel, conceal these *words* and seal up the book until the end of time; many will go back and forth, and knowledge will increase."

Acts 26:13–14, 19–20

"At midday, O King, I saw on the way a light from *heaven,* brighter than the sun, shining all around me and those who were journeying with me. [14]And when we had all fallen to the ground, I heard a voice saying to me in the Hebrew dialect, 'Saul, Saul, why are you persecuting Me?' . . . [19]So, King Agrippa, I did not prove disobedient to the heavenly *vision,* [20]but kept declaring both to those of Damascus first, and also at Jerusalem and then throughout all the region of Judea, and even to the Gentiles, that they should repent and turn to God."

Revelation 10:4

When the seven peals of thunder had spoken, I was about to write; and I heard a voice from *heaven* saying, "Seal up the things which the seven peals of thunder have spoken and do not write them."

NONCANONICAL PARALLELS

1 Enoch 71:1

(Thus) it happened after this that my spirit passed out of sight and ascended into the *heavens.* And I saw the sons of the holy angels.

Testament of Levi 2:7–10

"And I entered the first heaven and saw there much water suspended. [8]And again I saw a second heaven much brighter and more lustrous. . . . [9] . . . And the angel said to me, 'Do not be amazed concerning this, for you shall see another *heaven* more lustrous and beyond compare. [10]And when you have mounted there, you shall stand near the Lord. You shall be his priest and you shall tell forth his mysteries.'"

Life of Adam and Eve [Apocalypse of Moses] 37:3–5

One of the six-winged seraphim came and carried Adam off, . . . [4] . . . and so the LORD of all, sitting on his throne, stretched out his hands and took Adam and handed him over to the archangel Michael, saying to him, [5]"Take him up into *Paradise,* to *the third heaven,* and leave (him) there until that great and fearful day which I am about to establish for the world."

2 Corinthians 12:7–10

Because of the surpassing greatness of the revelations, for this reason, to keep me from exalting myself, there was given me a thorn in the flesh, a messenger of Satan to torment me—to keep me from exalting myself! [8]Concerning this I implored the Lord three times that it might leave me. [9]And He has said to me, "My grace is sufficient for you, for power is perfected in weakness." Most gladly, therefore, I will rather boast about my weaknesses, so that the power of Christ may dwell in me. [10]Therefore I am well content with weaknesses, with insults, with distresses, with persecutions,

with difficulties, for Christ's sake; for when I am weak, then I am strong.

2 CORINTHIANS PARALLELS

2 Corinthians 4:7–9

But we have this treasure in earthen vessels, so that *the surpassing greatness* of the *power* will be of God and not from ourselves; [8]we are afflicted in every way, but not crushed; perplexed, but not despairing; [9]*persecuted*, but not forsaken; struck down, but not destroyed.

2 Corinthians 6:3–10

. . . giving no cause for offense in anything, so that the ministry will not be discredited, [4]but in everything commending ourselves as servants of God, in much endurance, in afflictions, in hardships, in *distresses*, [5]in beatings, in imprisonments, in tumults, in labors, in sleeplessness, in hunger, [6]in purity, in knowledge, in patience, in kindness, in the Holy Spirit, in genuine love, [7]in the word of truth, in the *power* of God; by the weapons of righteousness for the right hand and the left, [8]by glory and dishonor, by evil report and good report; regarded as deceivers and yet true; [9]as unknown yet well-known, as dying yet behold, we live; as punished yet not put to death, [10]as sorrowful yet always rejoicing, as poor yet making many rich, as having nothing yet possessing all things.

2 Corinthians 11:13–14

For such men are false apostles, deceitful workers, disguising themselves as apostles of Christ. [14]No wonder, for even *Satan* disguises himself as an angel of light.

2 Corinthians 11:20

For you tolerate it if anyone enslaves you, anyone devours you, anyone takes advantage of you, anyone *exalts* himself, anyone hits you in the face.

2 Corinthians 11:23–27, 29–30

Are they servants of Christ?—I speak as if insane—I more so; in far more labors, in far more imprisonments, beaten times without number, often in danger of death. [24]Five times I received from the Jews thirty-nine lashes. [25]Three times I was beaten with rods, once I was stoned, three times I was shipwrecked, a night and a day I have spent in the deep. [26]I have been on frequent journeys, in dangers from rivers, dangers from robbers, dangers from my countrymen, dangers from the Gentiles, dangers in the city, dangers in the wilderness, dangers on the sea, dangers among false brethren; [27]I have been in labor and hardship, through many sleepless nights, in hunger and thirst, often without food, in cold and exposure. . . . [29]Who is weak without my being *weak*? Who is led into sin without my intense concern? [30]If I have to *boast*, I will boast of what pertains to my *weakness*.

2 Corinthians 13:4

For indeed He was crucified because of *weakness*, yet He lives because of the *power* of God. For we also are *weak* in Him, yet we will live with Him because of the power of God directed toward you.

OTHER PAULINE PARALLELS

Romans 8:35, 37

Who will separate us from the love of Christ? Will tribulation, or *distress*, or *persecution*, or famine, or nakedness, or peril, or sword? . . . [37]But in all these things we overwhelmingly conquer through Him who loved us.

1 Corinthians 2:1, 3–5

And when I came to you, brethren, I did not come with superiority of speech or of wisdom, proclaiming to you the testimony of God. . . . [3]I was with you in *weakness* and in fear and in much trembling, [4]and my message and my preaching were not in persuasive words of wisdom, but in demonstration of the Spirit and of *power*, [5]so that your faith would not rest on the wisdom of men, but on the power of God.

1 Corinthians 4:9–13

For, I think, God has exhibited us apostles last of all, as men condemned to death; because we have become a spectacle to the world, both to angels and to men. [10]We are fools for Christ's sake, but you are prudent in Christ; we are *weak*, but you are *strong*; you are distinguished, but we are without honor. [11]To this present hour we are both hungry and thirsty, and are poorly clothed, and are roughly treated, and are homeless; [12]and we toil, working with our own hands; when we are reviled, we bless; when we are *persecuted*, we endure; [13]when we are slandered, we try to conciliate; we have become as the scum of the world, the dregs of all things, even until now.

1 Corinthians 15:42–43

So also is the resurrection of the dead. It is sown a perishable body, it is raised an imperishable body; [43]It is sown in dishonor, it is raised in glory. It is sown in *weakness*, it is raised in *power*.

Galatians 4:13–14

You know that it was because of a bodily illness that I preached the gospel to you the first time; [14]and that which was a trial to you in my bodily condition you did not despise or loathe, but you received me as an angel of God, as Christ Jesus Himself.

Galatians 6:17

From now on let no one cause trouble for me, for I bear on my body the brand-marks of Jesus.

Numbers 33:55

"But if you do not drive out the inhabitants of the land from before you, then it shall come about that those whom you let remain of them will become as pricks in your eyes and as *thorns* in your sides, and they will trouble you in the land in which you live."

Matthew 26:36, 39, 44

Then Jesus came with them to a place called Gethsemane, and said to His disciples, "Sit here while I go over there and pray." . . . [39]And He went a little beyond them, and fell on His face and prayed, saying, "My Father, if it is possible, let this cup pass from Me; yet not as I will, but as You will." . . . [44]And He left them again, and went away and prayed a *third time*, saying the same thing once more.

Revelation 12:7, 9

And there was war in heaven, Michael and his angels waging war with the dragon. The dragon and his angels waged war. . . . [9]And the great dragon was thrown down, the serpent of old who is called the devil and *Satan*, who deceives the whole world; he was thrown down to the earth, and his angels were thrown down with him.

Qumran Hymns *(1QH) 12[4].22–23*

And I, when I lean on you, I remain resolute and rise above those who scorn me, and my hands succeed against all who mock me; [23]for they do not value me, even though you exhibit your *power* in me and reveal yourself in me with your strength to enlighten them.

2 Corinthians 12:11–13

I have become foolish; you yourselves compelled me. Actually I should have been commended by you, for in no respect was I inferior to the most eminent apostles, even though I am a nobody. [12]The signs of a true apostle were performed among you with all perseverance, by signs and wonders and miracles. [13]For in what respect were you treated as inferior to the rest of the churches, except that I myself did not become a burden to you? Forgive me this wrong!

2 Corinthians 3:1–2

Are we beginning to *commend* ourselves again? Or do we need, as some, letters of commendation to you or from you? [2]You are our letter, written in our hearts, known and read by all men.

2 Corinthians 5:12

We are not again *commending* ourselves to you but are giving you an occasion to be proud of us, so that you will have an answer for those who take pride in appearance and not in heart.

2 Corinthians 7:2

Make room for us in your hearts; we wronged no one, we corrupted no one, we took advantage of no one.

2 Corinthians 11:1, 4–6

I wish that you would bear with me in a little *foolishness*; but indeed you are bearing with me. . . . [4]For if one comes and preaches another Jesus whom we have not preached, or you receive a different spirit which you have not received, or a different gospel which you have not accepted, you bear this beautifully. [5]For I consider myself not in the least *inferior to the most eminent apostles.* [6]But even if I am unskilled in speech, yet I am not so in knowledge; in fact, in every way we have made this evident to you in all things.

2 Corinthians 11:7–9

Or did I commit a sin in humbling myself so that you might be exalted, because I preached the gospel of God to you without charge? [8]I robbed other *churches* by taking wages from them to serve you; [9]and when I was present with you and was in need, I was not a burden to anyone; for when the brethren came from Macedonia they fully supplied my need, and in everything I kept myself from being *a burden to you*, and will continue to do so.

2 Corinthians 11:16–17, 19

Again I say, let no one think me *foolish*; but if you do, receive me even as foolish, so that I also may boast a little. [17]What I am saying, I am not saying as the Lord would, but as in foolishness, in this confidence of boasting. . . . [19]For you, being so wise, tolerate the foolish gladly.

2 Corinthians 12:6

For if I do wish to boast I will not be *foolish*, for I will be speaking the truth; but I refrain from this, so that no one will credit me with more than he sees in me or hears from me.

OTHER PAULINE PARALLELS

Romans 5:3–4

And not only this, but we also exult in our tribulations, knowing that tribulation brings about *perseverance*; [4]and perseverance, proven character; and proven character, hope.

Romans 15:18–19

For I will not presume to speak of anything except what Christ has accomplished through me, resulting in the obedience of the Gentiles by word and deed, [19]in the power of *signs and wonders*, in the power of the Spirit; so that from Jerusalem and round about as far as Illyricum I have fully preached the gospel of Christ.

1 Corinthians 1:20, 22

Where is the wise man? Where is the scribe? Where is the debater of this age? Has not God made *foolish* the wisdom of the world? . . . [22]For indeed Jews ask for *signs* and Greeks search for wisdom.

1 Corinthians 3:7

So then neither the one who plants nor the one who waters is anything, but God who causes the growth.

1 Corinthians 9:11–12, 18

If we sowed spiritual things in you, is it too much if we reap material things from you? [12]If others share the right over you, do we not more? Nevertheless, we did not use this right, but we endure all things so that we will cause no hindrance to the gospel of Christ. . . . [18]What then is my reward? That, when I preach the gospel, I may offer the gospel without charge, so as not to make full use of my right in the gospel.

1 Corinthians 12:7–10

But to each one is given the manifestation of the Spirit for the common good. [8]For to one is given the word of wisdom through the Spirit, and to another the word of knowledge according to the same Spirit; [9]to another faith by the same Spirit, and to another gifts of healing by the one Spirit, [10]and to another the effecting of *miracles*, and to another prophecy, and to another the distinguishing of spirits, to another various kinds of tongues, and to another the interpretation of tongues.

1 Corinthians 14:22

So then tongues are for a *sign*, not to those who believe but to unbelievers; but prophecy is for a sign, not to unbelievers but to those who believe.

1 Corinthians 15:9–10

For I am the least of the apostles, and not fit to be called an *apostle*, because I persecuted the church of God. [10]But by the grace of God I am what I am, and His grace toward me did not prove vain; but I labored even more than all of them, yet not I, but the grace of God with me.

John 4:48

"Unless you people see *signs and wonders*, you simply will not believe."

Acts 2:22

"Men of Israel, listen to these words: Jesus the Nazarene, a man attested to you by God with *miracles* and *wonders* and *signs* which God *performed* through Him in your midst, just as you yourselves know . . . ''

Acts 15:12

All the people kept silent, and they were listening to Barnabas and Paul as they were relating what *signs and wonders* God had done through them among the Gentiles.

Hebrews 2:3–4

After it was at the first spoken through the Lord, it was confirmed to us by those who heard, [4]God also testifying with them, both by *signs and wonders* and by various *miracles* and by gifts of the Holy Spirit according to His own will.

NONCANONICAL PARALLELS

Plutarch, On Inoffensive Self-Praise *539E*

Nevertheless, there are occasions where the statesman might take the risk of self-praise, as it is called, not for personal glory or gain, but when the situation requires that the *truth* be told about oneself.

2 Corinthians 12:14–18

Here for this third time I am ready to come to you, and I will not be a burden to you; for I do not seek what is yours, but you; for children are not responsible to save up for their parents, but parents for their children. [15]I will most gladly spend and be expended for your souls. If I love you more, am I to be loved less? [16]But be that as it may, I did not burden you myself; nevertheless, crafty fellow that I am, I took you in by deceit. [17]Certainly I have not taken advantage of you through any of those whom I have sent to you, have I? [18]I urged Titus to go, and I sent the brother with him. Titus did not take any advantage of you, did he? Did we not conduct ourselves in the same spirit and walk in the same steps?

2 Corinthians 1:15–16

In this confidence I intended at first *to come to you*, so that you might twice receive a blessing; [16]that is, to pass your way into Macedonia, and again from Macedonia to come to you, and by you to be helped on my journey to Judea.

2 Corinthians 2:4

For out of much affliction and anguish of heart I wrote to you with many tears; not so that you would be made sorrowful, but that you might know the *love* which I have especially for you.

2 Corinthians 4:2

We have renounced the things hidden because of shame, not *walking* in *craftiness* or adulterating the word of God, but by the manifestation of truth commending ourselves to every man's conscience in the sight of God.

2 Corinthians 7:2

Make room for us in your hearts; we wronged no one, we corrupted no one, we *took advantage* of no one.

2 Corinthians 8:16–20

But thanks be to God who puts the same earnestness on your behalf in the heart of *Titus*. [17]For he not only accepted our appeal, but being himself very earnest, he has gone to you of his own accord. [18]We have *sent* along *with him the brother* whose fame in the things of the gospel has spread through all the churches; [19]and not only this, but he has also been appointed by the churches to travel with us in this gracious work, which is being administered by us for the glory of the Lord Himself, and to show our readiness, [20]taking precaution so that no one will discredit us in our administration of this generous gift.

2 Corinthians 9:5

So I thought it necessary to urge the brethren that they would go on ahead to you and arrange beforehand your previously promised bountiful gift, so that the same would be ready as a bountiful gift and not affected by covetousness.

2 Corinthians 11:3

But I am afraid that, as the serpent *deceived* Eve by his *craftiness*, your minds will be led astray from the simplicity and purity of devotion to Christ.

2 Corinthians 11:7–11

Or did I commit a sin in humbling myself so that you might be exalted, because I preached the gospel of God to you without charge? [8]I robbed other churches by taking wages from them to serve you; [9]and when I was present with you and was in need, I was not a burden to anyone; for when the brethren came from Macedonia they fully supplied my need, and in everything I kept myself from being *a burden to you*, and will continue to do so. [10]As the truth of Christ is in me, this boasting of mine will not be stopped in the regions of Achaia. [11]Why? Because *I do not love you*? God knows I do!

2 Corinthians 11:13

For such men are false apostles, *deceitful* workers, disguising themselves as apostles of Christ.

2 Corinthians 11:20

For you tolerate it if anyone enslaves you, anyone devours you, anyone *takes advantage of you*, anyone exalts himself, anyone hits you in the face.

2 Corinthians 13:1–2

This is the *third time* I am *coming to you*. EVERY FACT IS TO BE CONFIRMED BY THE TESTIMONY OF TWO OR THREE WITNESSES. [2]I have previously said when present the second time, and though now absent I say in advance to those who have sinned in the past and to all the rest as well, that if I come again I will not spare anyone.

OTHER PAULINE PARALLELS

1 Corinthians 4:14–15

I do not write these things to shame you, but to admonish you as my beloved *children*. [15]For if you were to have countless tutors in Christ, yet you would not have many fathers, for in Christ Jesus I became your father through the gospel.

1 Corinthians 4:21

What do you desire? Shall *I come to you* with a rod, or with *love* and a spirit of gentleness?

Philippians 2:17

But even if I am being poured out as a drink offering upon the sacrifice and service of your faith, I rejoice and share my joy with you all.

1 Thessalonians 2:8–9

Having so fond an affection for you, we were well-pleased to impart to you not only the gospel of God but also our own lives, because you had become very dear to us. [9]For you recall, brethren, our labor and hardship, how working night and day so as *not* to be *a burden to* any of *you*, we proclaimed to you the gospel of God.

1 Timothy 5:4, 8

If any widow has *children* or grandchildren, they must first learn to practice piety in regard to their own family and to make some return to their *parents*; for this is acceptable in the sight of God. . . . [8]But if anyone does not provide for his own, and especially for those of his household, he has denied the faith and is worse than an unbeliever.

OTHER BIBLICAL PARALLELS

Proverbs 19:14

House and wealth are an inheritance from fathers, But a prudent wife is from the LORD.

Matthew 15:5–6

"But you say, 'Whoever says to his father or mother, "Whatever I have that would help you has been given to God," [6]he is not to honor his father or his mother.' And by this you invalidated the word of God for the sake of your tradition."

NONCANONICAL PARALLELS

Philo, On Moses 2.245

It is a law of nature that *children* inherit from their *parents*, not parents from their children.

All this time you have been thinking that we are defending ourselves to you. Actually, it is in the sight of God that we have been speaking in Christ; and all for your upbuilding, beloved. [20]For I am afraid that perhaps when I come I may find you to be not what I wish and may be found by you to be not what you wish; that perhaps there will be strife, jealousy, angry tempers, disputes, slanders, gossip, arrogance, disturbances; [21]I am afraid that when I come again my God may humiliate me before you, and I may mourn over many of those who have sinned in the past and not repented of the impurity, immorality and sensuality which they have practiced.

2 CORINTHIANS PARALLELS

2 Corinthians 2:1–4

But I determined this for my own sake, that I would not *come* to you in sorrow again. [2]For if I cause you sorrow, who then makes me glad but the one whom I made sorrowful? [3]This is the very thing I wrote you, so that when I came, I would not have sorrow from those who ought to make me rejoice; having confidence in you all that my joy would be the joy of you all. [4]For out of much affliction and anguish of heart I wrote to you with many tears; not so that you would be made sorrowful, but that you might know the love which I have especially for you.

2 Corinthians 2:17

For we are not like many, peddling the word of God, but as from sincerity, but as from God, *we speak in Christ in the sight of God.*

2 Corinthians 7:9–10

I now rejoice, not that you were made sorrowful, but that you were made sorrowful to the point of *repentance*; for you were made sorrowful according to the will of God, so that you might not suffer loss in anything through us. [10]For the sorrow that is according to the will of God produces a repentance without regret, leading to salvation, but the sorrow of the world produces death.

2 Corinthians 10:8

For even if I boast somewhat further about our authority, which the Lord gave for *building you up* and not for destroying you, I will not be put to shame.

2 Corinthians 13:10

For this reason I am writing these things while absent, so that when present I need not use severity, in accordance with the authority which the Lord gave me for *building up* and not for tearing down.

OTHER PAULINE PARALLELS

Romans 1:28–30

And just as they did not see fit to acknowledge God any longer, God gave them over to a depraved mind, to do those things which are not proper, [29]being filled with all unrighteousness, wickedness, greed, evil; full of envy, murder, *strife*, deceit, malice; they are *gossips*, [30]*slanderers*, haters of God, insolent, *arrogant*, boastful, inventors of evil, disobedient to parents.

Romans 13:13

Let us behave properly as in the day, not in carousing and drunkenness, not in sexual promiscuity and *sensuality*, not in *strife* and *jealousy*.

Romans 14:19

So then we pursue the things which make for peace and the *building up* of one another.

1 Corinthians 1:11

For I have been informed concerning you, my brethren, by Chloe's people, that there are quarrels among you.

1 Corinthians 3:3

For since there is *jealousy* and *strife* among you, are you not fleshly, and are you not walking like mere men?

1 Corinthians 4:18, 21

Now some have become *arrogant*, as though I were not coming to you. . . . [21]What do you desire? Shall I *come* to you with a rod, or with love and a spirit of gentleness?

1 Corinthians 5:1–2

It is actually reported that there is *immorality* among you, and immorality of such a kind as does not exist even among the Gentiles, that someone has his father's wife. [2]You have become *arrogant* and have not mourned instead, so that the one who had done this deed would be removed from your midst.

1 Corinthians 6:18

Flee *immorality*. Every other sin that a man commits is outside the body, but the immoral man *sins* against his own body.

1 Corinthians 9:3–4, 6

My *defense* to those who examine me is this: [4]Do we not have a right to eat and drink? . . . [6]Or do only Barnabas and I not have a right to refrain from working?

Galatians 5:19–21

Now the deeds of the flesh are evident, which are: *immorality, impurity, sensuality*, [20]idolatry, sorcery, enmities, *strife, jealousy*, outbursts of *anger, disputes*, dissensions, factions, [21]envying, drunkenness, carousing, and things like these, of which I forewarn you, just as I have forewarned you, that those who *practice* such things will not inherit the kingdom of God.

Ephesians 4:17, 19

So this I say, and affirm together with the Lord, that you walk no longer just as the Gentiles also walk, in the futility of their mind, . . . [19]and they, having become callous, have given themselves over to *sensuality* for the *practice* of every kind of *impurity* with greediness.

Ephesians 4:31

Let all bitterness and wrath and *anger* and clamor and *slander* be put away from you, along with all malice.

Colossians 3:5, 8

Therefore consider the members of your earthly body as dead to *immorality, impurity*, passion, evil desire, and greed, which amounts to idolatry. . . . [8]But now you also, put them all aside: *anger*, wrath, malice, *slander*, and abusive speech from your mouth.

James 3:14

But if you have bitter *jealousy* and selfish ambition in your heart, do not be *arrogant* and so lie against the truth.

1 Peter 2:1

Therefore, putting aside all malice and all deceit and hypocrisy and envy and all *slander* . . .

Livy, History of Rome *38.49.6*

"I beseech you to indulge me in what follows, senators, if my speech is made overlong, not out of a desire to boast about myself, but by the need to *defend* myself against these charges."

2 Corinthians 13:1–4

This is the third time I am coming to you. EVERY FACT IS TO BE CONFIRMED BY THE TESTIMONY OF TWO OR THREE WITNESSES. [2]I have previously said when present the second time, and though now absent I say in advance to those who have sinned in the past and to all the rest as well, that if I come again I will not spare anyone, [3]since you are seeking for proof of the Christ who speaks in me, and who is not weak toward you, but mighty in you. [4]For indeed He was crucified because of weakness, yet He lives because of the power of God. For we also are weak in Him, yet we will live with Him because of the power of God directed toward you.

2 Corinthians 1:15, 23

In this confidence I intended at first to *come to you*, so that you might twice receive a blessing. . . . [23]But I call God as witness to my soul, that to *spare* you I did not come again to Corinth.

2 Corinthians 2:1

But I determined this for my own sake, that I would not *come to you* in sorrow again.

2 Corinthians 4:7

But we have this treasure in earthen vessels, so that the surpassing greatness of *the power* will be *of God* and not from ourselves.

2 Corinthians 4:10–11

. . . always carrying about in the body the dying of Jesus, so that the life of Jesus also may be manifested in our body. [11]For we who *live* are constantly being delivered over to death for Jesus' sake, so that the life of Jesus also may be manifested in our mortal flesh.

2 Corinthians 10:1–4
Now I, Paul, myself urge you by the meekness and gentleness of Christ—I who am meek when face to face with you, but bold toward you when *absent!* [2]I ask that when I am *present* I need not be bold with the confidence with which I propose to be courageous against some, who regard us as if we walked according to the flesh. [3]For though we walk in the flesh, we do not war according to the flesh, [4]for the weapons of our warfare are not of the flesh, but divinely powerful for the destruction of fortresses.

2 Corinthians 10:10–11
For they say, "His letters are weighty and strong, but his personal presence is unimpressive and his speech contemptible." [11]Let such a person consider this, that what we are in word by letters when *absent*, such persons we are also in deed when *present*.

2 Corinthians 12:9
And He has said to me, "My grace is sufficient for you, for *power* is perfected in *weakness.*" Most gladly, therefore, I will rather boast about my weaknesses, so that the power of Christ may dwell in me.

2 Corinthians 12:14
Here for this *third time I am* ready to *come to you*, and I will not be a burden to you; for I do not seek what is yours, but you; for children are not responsible to save up for their parents, but parents for their children.

OTHER PAULINE PARALLELS

Romans 1:4
. . . who was declared the Son of God with *power* by the resurrection from the dead, according to the Spirit of holiness, Jesus Christ our Lord.

Romans 6:8–10
Now if we have died with Christ, we believe that we shall also *live with Him*, [9]knowing that Christ, having been raised from the dead, is never to die again; death no longer is master over Him. [10]For the death that He

died, He died to sin once for all; but the life that *He lives*, He lives to God.

Romans 15:18
For I will not presume to *speak* of anything except what Christ has accomplished through me, resulting in the obedience of the Gentiles by word and deed.

1 Corinthians 1:23–25
But we preach Christ *crucified*, to Jews a stumbling block and to Gentiles foolishness, [24]but to those who are the called, both Jews and Greeks, Christ *the power of God* and the wisdom of God. [25]Because the foolishness of God is wiser than men, and the *weakness* of God is stronger than men.

1 Corinthians 2:2–3
For I determined to know nothing among you except Jesus Christ, and Him *crucified*. [3]I was with you in *weakness* and in fear and in much trembling.

1 Corinthians 4:18–19
Now some have become arrogant, as though I were not *coming to you*. [19]But I will come to you soon, if the Lord wills, and I shall find out, not the words of those who are arrogant but their *power*.

1 Corinthians 6:14
Now God has not only raised the Lord, but will also raise us up through His *power*.

Philippians 2:6–8
Although He existed in the form of God, [Christ] did not regard equality with God a thing to be grasped, [7]but emptied Himself, taking the form of a bond-servant, and being made in the likeness of men. [8]Being found in appearance as a man, He humbled Himself by becoming obedient to the point of death, even death on a cross.

1 Timothy 5:19
Do not receive an accusation against an elder except on the basis of *two or three witnesses*.

OTHER BIBLICAL PARALLELS

Deuteronomy 19:15
"A single witness shall not rise up against a man on account of any iniquity or any *sin* which he has committed; on the evidence of *two or three witnesses* a matter shall be *confirmed.*"

"If your brother *sins*, go and show him his fault in private; if he listens to you, you have won your brother. [16]But if he does not listen to you, take one or two more with you, so that *BY THE* MOUTH OF *TWO OR THREE WITNESSES EVERY FACT* MAY BE *CONFIRMED*."

2 Corinthians 13:5–10

Test yourselves to see if you are in the faith; examine yourselves! Or do you not recognize this about yourselves, that Jesus Christ is in you—unless indeed you fail the test? [6]But I trust that you will realize that we ourselves do not fail the test. [7]Now we pray to God that you do no wrong; not that we ourselves may appear approved, but that you may do what is right, even though we may appear unapproved. [8]For we can do nothing against the truth, but only for the truth. [9]For we rejoice when we ourselves are weak but you are strong; this we also pray for, that you be made complete. [10]For this reason I am writing these things while absent, so that when present I need not use severity, in accordance with the authority which the Lord gave me for building up and not for tearing down.

2 CORINTHIANS PARALLELS

2 Corinthians 2:3

This is the very thing I wrote you, so that when I came, I would not have sorrow from those who ought to make me *rejoice*; having confidence in you all that my joy would be the joy of you all.

2 Corinthians 10:8–11

For even if I boast somewhat further about our *authority, which the Lord gave* for *building* you *up* and not for destroying you, I will not be put to shame, [9]for I do not wish to seem as if I would terrify you by my letters. [10]For they say, "His letters are weighty and *strong*, but his personal presence is unimpressive and his speech contemptible." [11]Let such a person consider this, that what we are in word by letters when *absent*, such persons we are also in deed when *present*.

2 Corinthians 10:18

For it is not he who commends himself that is *approved*, but he whom the Lord commends.

2 Corinthians 12:10

Therefore I am well content with weaknesses, with insults, with distresses, with persecutions, with difficulties, for Christ's sake; for when I am *weak*, then I am *strong*.

2 Corinthians 12:19

All this time you have been thinking that we are defending ourselves to you. Actually, it is in the sight of God that we have been speaking in Christ; and all for your *upbuilding*, beloved.

OTHER PAULINE PARALLELS

Romans 8:10

If *Christ is in you*, though the body is dead because of sin, yet the spirit is alive because of righteousness.

1 Corinthians 1:10

Now I exhort you, brethren, by the name of our Lord Jesus Christ, that you all agree and that there be no divisions among you, but *that you be made complete* in the same mind and in the same judgment.

1 Corinthians 4:10

We are fools for Christ's sake, but you are prudent in Christ; *we are weak, but you are strong*; you are distinguished, but we are without honor.

1 Corinthians 9:27

I discipline my body and make it my slave, so that, after I have preached to others, I myself will not be disqualified.

1 Corinthians 11:28

But a man must *examine* himself, and in so doing he is to eat of the bread and drink of the cup.

Galatians 6:1, 4

Brethren, even if anyone is caught in any trespass, you who are spiritual, restore such a one in a spirit of gentleness; each one looking to yourself, so that you too will not be tempted. . . . [4]But each one must *examine* his own work, and then he will have reason for boasting in regard to himself alone, and not in regard to another.

Colossians 1:26–28

. . . that is, the mystery which has been hidden from the past ages and generations, but has now been manifested to His saints, [27]to whom God willed to make known what is the riches of the glory of this mystery among the Gentiles, which is *Christ in you*, the hope of glory. [28]We proclaim Him, admonishing every man and teaching every man with all wisdom, so that we may present every man *complete* in Christ.

1 Thessalonians 3:9–10

For what thanks can we render to God for you in return for all the joy with which we *rejoice* before our God on your account, [10]as we night and day keep praying most earnestly that we may see your face, and may *complete* what is lacking in your *faith*?

Titus 1:13

This testimony is true. For this reason reprove them *severely* so that they may be *sound* in the *faith*.

Deuteronomy 12:2–3

"You shall utterly destroy all the places where the nations whom you shall dispossess serve their gods, on the high mountains and on the hills and under every green tree. [3]You shall *tear down* their altars and smash their sacred pillars and burn their Asherim with fire, and you shall cut down the engraved images of their gods and obliterate their name from that place."

Psalm 26:2

Examine me, O LORD, and try me; *Test* my mind and my heart.

Jeremiah 1:9–10

Then the LORD stretched out His hand and touched my mouth, and the LORD said to me, "Behold, I have put My words in your mouth. [10]See, I have appointed you this day over the nations and over the kingdoms, To pluck up and to break down, To destroy and to overthrow, To *build* and to plant."

Jeremiah 42:10

"If you will indeed stay in this land, then I will *build* you *up* and *not tear* you *down*, and I will plant you and not uproot you; for I will relent concerning the calamity that I have inflicted on you."

James 3:14

But if you have bitter jealousy and selfish ambition in your heart, do not be arrogant and so lie *against the truth*.

Sirach 4:25, 28

Never speak *against the truth*, but be ashamed of your ignorance. . . . [28]Fight to the death for truth, and the Lord God will fight for you.

Marcus Aurelius, Meditations 10.37

At every action carried out by someone else, be accustomed, as much as possible, to inquire within yourself: "What does he mean this to lead up to?" But begin [the inquiry] with yourself, *examine yourself* first.

2 Corinthians 13:11–14

Finally, brethren, rejoice, be made complete, be comforted, be like-minded, live in peace; and the God of love and peace will be with you. [12]Greet one another with a holy kiss. [13]All the saints greet you. [14]The grace of the Lord Jesus Christ, and the love of God, and the fellowship of the Holy Spirit, be with you all.

2 Corinthians 1:3–4

Blessed be the God and Father of our Lord Jesus Christ, the Father of mercies and God of all comfort, [4]who comforts us in all our affliction so that we will be able to comfort those who are in any affliction with the comfort with which we ourselves are *comforted* by God.

2 Corinthians 1:6

But if we are afflicted, it is for your comfort and salvation; or if we are *comforted*, it is for your comfort, which is effective in the patient enduring of the same sufferings which we also suffer.

2 Corinthians 2:3

This is the very thing I wrote you, so that when I came, I would not have sorrow from those who ought to make me *rejoice*; having confidence in you all that my joy would be the joy of you all.

Romans 12:15–16, 18

Rejoice with those who rejoice, and weep with those who weep. [16]Be of the same *mind* toward one another; do not be haughty in mind, but associate with the lowly. Do not be wise in your own estimation. . . . [18]If possible, so far as it depends on you, be at *peace* with all men.

Romans 15:5

Now may the God who gives perseverance and encouragement grant you to be of the same *mind* with one another according to Christ Jesus.

Romans 15:33

Now *the God of peace be with you* all. Amen.

Romans 16:16, 20

Greet one another with a holy kiss. All the churches of Christ *greet you.* . . . [20]*The God of peace* will soon crush Satan under your feet. *The grace of* our *Lord Jesus be with you.*

1 Corinthians 1:10

Now I exhort you, brethren, by the name of our Lord Jesus Christ, that you all agree and that there be no divisions among you, but that you *be made complete* in the same *mind* and in the same judgment.

1 Corinthians 16:19–24

The churches of Asia greet you. Aquila and Prisca greet you heartily in the Lord, with the church that is in their house. [20]*All* the brethren *greet you. Greet one another with a holy kiss.* [21]The greeting is in my own hand—Paul. [22]If anyone does not love the Lord, he is to be accursed. Maranatha. [23]*The grace of the Lord Jesus be with you.* [24]My love be with you all in Christ Jesus. Amen.

Ephesians 6:23–24

Peace be to the brethren, and *love* with faith, from God the Father and the Lord Jesus Christ. [24]*Grace be with all* those who love our Lord Jesus Christ with incorruptible love.

Philippians 2:1–2

Therefore if there is any encouragement in Christ, if there is any consolation of *love*, if there is any *fellowship of the Spirit*, if any affection and compassion, [2]make my joy complete by being of the same *mind*, maintaining the same love, united in spirit, intent on one purpose.

Philippians 3:1

Finally, my *brethren, rejoice* in the Lord. To write the same things again is no trouble to me, and it is a safeguard for you.

Philippians 4:21–23

Greet every saint in Christ Jesus. The brethren who are with me greet you. [22]*All the saints greet you*, especially those of Caesar's household. [23]*The grace of the Lord Jesus Christ be with* your spirit.

1 Thessalonians 5:23–28

Now may *the God of peace* Himself sanctify you entirely; and may your spirit and soul and body be preserved *complete*, without blame at the coming of our Lord Jesus Christ. [24]Faithful is He who calls you, and He also will bring it to pass. [25]Brethren, pray for us. [26]*Greet* all the brethren *with a holy kiss.* [27]I adjure you by the Lord to have this letter read to all the brethren. [28]*The grace of* our *Lord Jesus Christ be with you.*

1 Peter 5:14

Greet one another with a kiss of love. *Peace* be to you all who are in Christ.

Jude 20–21

But you, beloved, building yourselves up on your most holy faith, praying in *the Holy* Spirit, [21]keep yourselves in the *love* of God, waiting anxiously for the mercy of our Lord Jesus Christ to eternal life.

Testament of Dan 5:2–3

"Each of you speak truth clearly to his neighbor, and do not fall into pleasure and troublemaking, but be at peace, holding to *the God of peace*. Thus no conflict will overwhelm you. [3]Throughout all your life *love* the Lord, and one another with a true heart."

Galatians

Galatians 1:1–5

Paul, an apostle (not sent from men nor through the agency of man, but through Jesus Christ and God the Father, who raised Him from the dead), [2]and all the brethren who are with me, To the churches of Galatia: [3]Grace to you and peace from God our Father and the Lord Jesus Christ, [4]who gave Himself for our sins so that He might rescue us from this present evil age, according to the will of our God and Father, [5]to whom be the glory forevermore. Amen.

GALATIANS PARALLELS

Galatians 1:11–12, 15–16

For I would have you know, brethren, that the gospel which was preached by me is not according to man. [12]For I neither received it *from man*, nor was I taught it, but I received it through a revelation of Jesus Christ. . . . [15]But when God, who had set me apart even from my mother's womb and called me through His grace, was pleased [16]to reveal His Son in me so that I might preach Him among the Gentiles, I did not immediately consult with flesh and blood.

Galatians 2:20

"I have been crucified with Christ; and it is no longer I who live, but Christ lives in me; and the life which I now live in the flesh I live by faith in the Son of God, who loved me and *gave Himself* up for me."

OTHER PAULINE PARALLELS

Romans 1:1, 3–4, 7

Paul, a bond-servant of Christ Jesus, called as *an apostle*, set apart for the gospel of God . . . [3]concerning His Son, who was born of a descendant of David according to the flesh, [4]who was declared the Son of God with power by the resurrection from the dead, according to the Spirit of holiness, Jesus Christ our Lord; . . . [7]to all who are beloved of God in Rome, called as saints: *Grace to you and peace from God our Father and the Lord Jesus Christ.*

Romans 4:23–25

Now not for his sake only was it written that it was credited to him, [24]but for our sake also, to whom it will be credited, as those who believe in Him who *raised* Jesus our Lord *from the dead*, [25]He who was delivered over because of our transgressions, and was raised because of our justification.

1 Corinthians 1:1–3

Paul, called as *an apostle* of Jesus Christ by the will of God, and Sosthenes our brother, [2]*To the church* of God which is at Corinth, to those who have been sanctified in Christ Jesus, saints by calling, with all who in every place call on the name of our Lord Jesus Christ, their Lord and ours: [3]*Grace to you and peace from God our Father and the Lord Jesus Christ.*

1 Corinthians 16:1

Now concerning the collection for the saints, as I directed the *churches of Galatia*, so do you also.

Philippians 4:20

Now to *our God and Father be the glory forever* and ever. *Amen.*

Colossians 1:13–14

For He *rescued* us from the domain of darkness, and transferred us to the kingdom of

His beloved Son, [14]in whom we have redemption, the forgiveness of *sins*.

1 Timothy 2:5–6

For there is one God, and one mediator also between God and men, the man Christ Jesus, [6]who *gave Himself* as a ransom for all, the testimony given at the proper time.

Titus 2:13–14

Christ Jesus [14] . . . *gave Himself* for us to redeem us from every lawless deed, and to purify for Himself a people for His own possession, zealous for good deeds.

OTHER BIBLICAL PARALLELS

Acts 2:24

"But God *raised* Him up again, putting an end to the agony of death, since it was impossible for Him to be held in its power."

Acts 16:6

They [Paul, Silas, and Timothy] passed through the Phrygian and *Galatian* region, having been forbidden by the Holy Spirit to speak the word in Asia.

Acts 18:23

And having spent some time there, he [Paul] left and passed successively through the *Galatian* region and Phrygia, strengthening all the disciples.

1 Peter 1:1

Peter, *an apostle* of Jesus Christ, To those who reside as aliens, scattered throughout Pontus, *Galatia*, Cappadocia, Asia, and Bithynia . . .

1 Peter 2:24

He Himself bore *our sins* in His body on the cross, so that we might die to sin and live to righteousness; for by His wounds you were healed.

NONCANONICAL PARALLELS

2 Maccabees 7:37–38

"I, like my brothers, *give* up body and life for the laws of our ancestors, appealing to God to show mercy soon to our nation . . . [38]and through me and my brothers to bring to an end the wrath of the Almighty that has justly fallen on our whole nation."

2 Baruch 44:8–9

For that which is now is nothing. But that which is in the future will be very great. [9]For everything will pass away . . . and there will be no remembrance of the *present* time which is polluted by *evils*.

Galatians 1:6–10

I am amazed that you are so quickly deserting Him who called you by the grace of Christ, for a different gospel; [7]which is really not another; only there are some who are disturbing you and want to distort the gospel of Christ. [8]But even if we, or an angel from heaven, should preach to you a gospel contrary to what we have preached to you, he is to be accursed! [9]As we have said before, so I say again now, if any man is preaching to you a gospel contrary to what you received, he is to be accursed! [10]For am I now seeking the favor of men, or of God? Or am I striving to please men? If I were still trying to please men, I would not be a bond-servant of Christ.

GALATIANS PARALLELS

Galatians 2:7

But on the contrary, seeing that I had been entrusted with *the gospel* to the uncircumcised, just as Peter had been to the circumcised . . .

Galatians 5:7–10

You were running well; who hindered you from obeying the truth? [8]This persuasion did not come from Him who calls you. [9]A little leaven leavens the whole lump of dough. [10]I have confidence in you in the Lord that you will adopt no other view; but the one who is *disturbing you* will bear his judgment, whoever he is.

OTHER PAULINE PARALLELS

Romans 1:1

Paul, *a bond-servant of Christ* Jesus, called as an apostle, set apart for *the gospel* of God . . .

Romans 8:28

And we know that God causes all things to work together for good to those who love

God, to those who are *called* according to His purpose.

1 Corinthians 1:9

God is faithful, through whom you were *called* into fellowship with His Son, Jesus Christ our Lord.

1 Corinthians 10:32–33

Give no offense either to Jews or to Greeks or to the church of God; ³³just as I also *please* all *men* in all things, not seeking my own profit but the profit of the many, so that they may be saved.

1 Corinthians 16:22

If anyone does not love the Lord, *he is to be accursed*. Maranatha.

2 Corinthians 11:4, 14

For if one comes and *preaches* another Jesus whom we have not preached, or you receive a different spirit which you have not received, or *a different gospel* which you have not accepted, you bear this beautifully. . . . ¹⁴No wonder, for even Satan disguises himself as *an angel* of light.

Philippians 1:15–17

Some, to be sure, are *preaching* Christ even from envy and strife, but some also from good will; ¹⁶the latter do it out of love, knowing that I am appointed for the defense of *the gospel*; ¹⁷the former proclaim Christ out of selfish ambition rather than from pure motives, thinking to cause me distress in my imprisonment.

1 Thessalonians 2:3–4

For our exhortation does not come from error or impurity or by way of deceit; ⁴but just as we have been approved by God to be entrusted with *the gospel*, so we speak, not as *pleasing men*, but God who examines our hearts.

1 Thessalonians 2:10–13

You are witnesses, and so is God, how devoutly and uprightly and blamelessly we behaved toward you believers; ¹¹just as you know how we were exhorting and encouraging and imploring each one of you as a father would his own children, ¹²so that you would walk in a manner worthy of the God who *calls* you into His own kingdom and glory. ¹³For this reason we also constantly

thank God that when you received the word of God which you heard from us, you accepted it not as the word of men, but for what it really is, the word of God, which also performs its work in you who believe.

1 Timothy 6:3–4

If anyone advocates a *different* doctrine and does not agree with sound words, those of our Lord Jesus Christ, and with the doctrine conforming to godliness, ⁴he is conceited and understands nothing.

2 Timothy 1:8–9

Therefore do not be ashamed of the testimony of our Lord or of me His prisoner, but join with me in suffering for *the gospel* according to the power of God, ⁹who has saved us and *called* us with a holy calling, not according to our works, but according to His own purpose and *grace* which was granted us in Christ Jesus from all eternity.

Revelation 14:6–7

And I saw another *angel* flying in midheaven, having an eternal *gospel* to *preach* to those who live on the earth, and to every nation and tribe and tongue and people; ⁷and he said with a loud voice, "Fear God, and give Him glory, because the hour of His judgment has come; worship Him who made the heaven and the earth and sea and springs of waters."

NONCANONICAL PARALLELS

1 Enoch 1:2

And Enoch, the blessed and righteous man of the Lord, . . . said, "(This is) a holy vision from the heavens which the *angels* showed me; and I heard from them everything and I understood. . . . I speak about the elect ones and concerning them."

Galatians 1:11–17

For I would have you know, brethren, that the gospel which was preached by me is not according to man. ¹²For I neither received it from man, nor was I taught it, but I received it through a revelation of Jesus Christ. ¹³For you have heard of my former manner of life in Judaism, how I used to persecute the church of God beyond measure and tried to destroy it;

¹⁴and I was advancing in Judaism beyond many of my contemporaries among my countrymen, being more extremely zealous for my ancestral traditions. ¹⁵But when God, who had set me apart even from my mother's womb and called me through His grace, was pleased ¹⁶to reveal His Son in me so that I might preach Him among the Gentiles, I did not immediately consult with flesh and blood, ¹⁷nor did I go up to Jerusalem to those who were apostles before me; but I went away to Arabia, and returned once more to Damascus.

GALATIANS PARALLELS

Galatians 1:1

Paul, an *apostle* (not sent *from men* nor through the agency of man, but through Jesus Christ and God the Father, who raised Him from the dead) . . .

Galatians 2:2

It was because of *a revelation* that I went up; and I submitted to them *the gospel* which I *preach* among *the Gentiles*, but I did so in private to those who were of reputation, for fear that I might be running, or had run, in vain.

Galatians 4:25

Now this Hagar is Mount Sinai in *Arabia* and corresponds to the present *Jerusalem*, for she is in slavery with her children.

OTHER PAULINE PARALLELS

Romans 1:1, 3, 5

Paul, a bond-servant of Christ Jesus, *called* as an *apostle, set apart* for *the gospel* of God . . . ³concerning His Son, who was born of a descendant of David according to the flesh, . . . ⁵through whom we have received *grace* and apostleship to bring about the obedience of faith *among* all *the Gentiles* for His name's sake . . .

1 Corinthians 2:10

For to us God *revealed* them through the Spirit; for the Spirit searches all things, even the depths of God.

1 Corinthians 15:9

For I am the least of the *apostles*, and not fit to be called an apostle, because *I persecuted the church of God.*

2 Corinthians 11:32–33

In *Damascus* the ethnarch under Aretas the king was guarding the city of the Damascenes in order to seize me, ³³and I was let down in a basket through a window in the wall, and so escaped his hands.

Ephesians 3:1–3

For this reason I, Paul, the prisoner of Christ Jesus for the sake of you *Gentiles*— ²if indeed you have heard of the stewardship of God's *grace* which was given to me for you; ³that by *revelation* there was made known to me the mystery, as I wrote before in brief.

Philippians 3:4–6

If anyone else has a mind to put confidence in the flesh, I far more: ⁵circumcised the eighth day, of the nation of Israel, of the tribe of Benjamin, a Hebrew of Hebrews; as to the Law, a Pharisee; ⁶as to *zeal*, a *persecutor* of *the church*; as to the righteousness which is in the Law, found blameless.

1 Timothy 1:12–15

I thank Christ Jesus our Lord, who has strengthened me, because He considered me faithful, putting me into service, ¹³even though I was *formerly* a blasphemer and a *persecutor* and a violent aggressor. Yet I was shown mercy because I acted ignorantly in unbelief; ¹⁴and the *grace* of our Lord was more than abundant, with the faith and love which are found in Christ Jesus. ¹⁵It is a trustworthy statement, deserving full acceptance, that Christ Jesus came into the world to save sinners, among whom I am foremost of all.

Titus 1:1–3

Paul, a bond-servant of God and an *apostle* of Jesus Christ, for the faith of those chosen of God and the knowledge of the truth which is according to godliness, ²in the hope of eternal life, which God, who cannot lie, promised long ages ago, ³but at the proper time manifested, even His word, in the proclamation with which I was entrusted according to the commandment of God our Savior . . .

OTHER BIBLICAL PARALLELS

Isaiah 49:1

Listen to Me, O islands, And pay attention, you peoples from afar. The LORD *called Me from* the *womb*; From the body of My mother He named Me.

Jeremiah 1:5
"Before I formed you in the *womb* I knew you, And before you were born I consecrated you; I have appointed you a prophet to the nations."

Mark 7:3
For the Pharisees and all the Jews do not eat unless they carefully wash their hands, thus observing the *traditions* of the elders.

Acts 8:3
But Saul began ravaging *the church*, entering house after house, and dragging off men and women, he would put them in prison.

Acts 9:15, 19–20
But the Lord said to him [Ananias], "Go, for he is a chosen instrument of Mine, to bear My name before *the Gentiles* and kings and the sons of Israel." . . .[19] . . . Now for several days he was with the disciples who were at *Damascus,* [20]and immediately he began to proclaim Jesus in the synagogues, saying, "He is the Son of God."

Acts 22:3–4
"I am a Jew, born in Tarsus of Cilicia, but brought up in this city, educated under Gamaliel, strictly according to the law of our fathers, being *zealous* for God just as you all are today. [4]I *persecuted* this Way to the death, binding and putting both men and women into prisons."

NONCANONICAL PARALLELS

2 Maccabees 14:38
In former times, when there was no mingling with *the Gentiles,* he [Razis] had been accused of *Judaism,* and he had most *zealously* risked body and life for Judaism.

Galatians 1:18–24

Then three years later I went up to Jerusalem to become acquainted with Cephas, and stayed with him fifteen days. [19]But I did not see any other of the apostles except James, the Lord's brother. [20](Now in what I am writing to you, I assure you before God that I am not lying.) [21]Then I went into the regions of Syria and Cilicia. [22]I was still unknown by sight to the churches of Judea which were in Christ; [23]but only, they kept hearing, "He who once persecuted us is now preaching the faith which he once tried to destroy." [24]And they were glorifying God because of me.

GALATIANS PARALLELS

Galatians 2:11–12
But when *Cephas* came to Antioch, I opposed him to his face, because he stood condemned. [12]For prior to the coming of certain men from *James,* he used to eat with the Gentiles; but when they came, he began to withdraw and hold himself aloof, fearing the party of the circumcision.

Galatians 4:25–26, 29
Now this Hagar is Mount Sinai in Arabia and corresponds to the present *Jerusalem,* for she is in slavery with her children. [26]But the Jerusalem above is free; she is our mother. . . . [29]But as at that time he who was born according to the flesh *persecuted* him who was born according to the Spirit, so it is now also.

Galatians 5:11
But I, brethren, if I still preach circumcision, why am I still *persecuted*? Then the stumbling block of the cross has been abolished.

Galatians 6:12
Those who desire to make a good showing in the flesh try to compel you to be circumcised, simply so that they will not be *persecuted* for the cross of Christ.

OTHER PAULINE PARALLELS

Romans 15:18–19
For I will not presume to speak of anything except what Christ has accomplished through me, resulting in the obedience of the Gentiles by word and deed, [19]in the power of signs and wonders, in the power of the Spirit; so that from *Jerusalem* and round about as far as Illyricum I have fully *preached* the gospel of Christ.

1 Corinthians 9:5

Do we not have a right to take along a believing wife, even as the rest of *the apostles* and the *brothers of the Lord* and *Cephas*?

1 Corinthians 15:9

For I am the least of *the apostles*, and not fit to be called an apostle, because I *persecuted* the church of God.

2 Corinthians 11:31

The God and Father of the Lord Jesus, He who is blessed forever, knows that *I am not lying.*

Philippians 3:6

. . . as to zeal, a *persecutor* of the church; as to the righteousness which is in the Law, found blameless.

1 Thessalonians 2:14

For you, brethren, became imitators of *the churches* of God *in Christ* Jesus that are in *Judea,* for you also endured the same sufferings at the hands of your own countrymen, even as they did from the Jews.

1 Timothy 2:7

For this I was appointed a preacher and an apostle (I am telling the truth, *I am not lying*) as a teacher of the Gentiles in faith and truth.

OTHER BIBLICAL PARALLELS

Acts 9:19–21, 26–30

Now for several days he was with the disciples who were at Damascus, [20]and immediately he began to proclaim Jesus in the synagogues, saying, "He is the Son of God." [21]All those hearing him continued to be amazed, and were saying, "Is this not he who in Jerusalem *destroyed* those who called on this name, and who had come here for the purpose of bringing them bound before the chief priests?" . . . [26]When he came *to Jerusalem*, he was trying to associate with the disciples; but they were all afraid of him, not believing that he was a disciple. [27]But Barnabas took hold of him and brought him to *the apostles* and described to them how he had seen the Lord on the road, and that He had talked to him, and how at Damascus he had spoken out boldly in the name of Jesus. [28]And he was with them, moving about freely in Jerusalem, speaking out boldly in the name of the Lord. [29]And he was talking and arguing with the Hellenistic Jews; but they were attempting to put him to death. [30]But when the brethren learned of it, they brought him down to Caesarea and sent him away to Tarsus.

Acts 15:40–41

But Paul chose Silas and left, being committed by the brethren to the grace of the Lord. [41]And he was traveling through *Syria and Cilicia*, strengthening the churches.

Acts 21:39

But Paul said, "I am a Jew of Tarsus in *Cilicia*, a citizen of no insignificant city; and I beg you, allow me to speak to the people."

Galatians 2:1–10

Then after an interval of fourteen years I went up again to Jerusalem with Barnabas, taking Titus along also. [2]It was because of a revelation that I went up; and I submitted to them the gospel which I preach among the Gentiles, but I did so in private to those who were of reputation, for fear that I might be running, or had run, in vain. [3]But not even Titus, who was with me, though he was a Greek, was compelled to be circumcised. [4]But it was because of the false brethren secretly brought in, who had sneaked in to spy out our liberty which we have in Christ Jesus, in order to bring us into bondage. [5]But we did not yield in subjection to them for even an hour, so that the truth of the gospel would remain with you. [6]But from those who were of high reputation (what they were makes no difference to me; God shows no partiality)—well, those who were of reputation contributed nothing to me. [7]But on the contrary, seeing that I had been entrusted with the gospel to the uncircumcised, just as Peter had been to the circumcised [8](for He who effectually worked for Peter in his apostleship to the circumcised effectually worked for me also to the Gentiles), [9]and recognizing the grace that had been given to me, James and Cephas and John, who were reputed to be pillars, gave to me and Barnabas the right hand of fellowship, so that we might go to the Gentiles and they to the circumcised. [10]They only asked us to remember the poor—the very thing I also was eager to do.

Galatians 1:15–17

But when God, who had set me apart even from my mother's womb and called me through His *grace*, was pleased [16]to reveal His Son in me so that I might *preach* Him among *the Gentiles*, I did not immediately consult with flesh and blood, [17]nor did I go up to *Jerusalem* to those who were apostles before me.

Galatians 5:1, 6–7

It was for freedom that Christ set us free; therefore keep standing firm and do not be subject again to a yoke of slavery. . . . [6]For in Christ Jesus neither *circumcision* nor *uncircumcision* means anything, but faith working through love. [7]You were running well; who hindered you from obeying *the truth*?

Galatians 6:12

Those who desire to make a good showing in the flesh try to compel you to be *circumcised*, simply so that they will not be persecuted for the cross of Christ.

OTHER PAULINE PARALLELS

Romans 15:15–16, 25–26

But I have written very boldly to you on some points so as to remind you again, because of *the grace that* was *given me* from God, [16]to be a minister of Christ Jesus to *the Gentiles*, ministering as a priest *the gospel* of God, so that my offering of the Gentiles may become acceptable, sanctified by the Holy Spirit. . . . [25]But now, I am going to *Jerusalem* serving the saints. [26]For Macedonia and Achaia have been pleased to make a contribution for *the poor* among the saints in Jerusalem.

2 Corinthians 8:23

As for *Titus*, he is my partner and fellow worker among you.

Ephesians 2:19–20

So then you are no longer strangers and aliens, but you are fellow citizens with the saints, and are of God's household, [20]having been built on the foundation of the apostles and prophets, Christ Jesus Himself being the corner stone.

Ephesians 3:8

To me, the very least of all saints, this *grace* was *given,* to *preach* to *the Gentiles* the unfathomable riches of Christ.

Philippians 2:16

. . . holding fast the word of life, so that in the day of Christ I will have reason to glory because I did not *run in vain* nor toil in vain.

1 Thessalonians 2:4

Just as we have been approved by God to be *entrusted with the gospel*, so we speak, not as pleasing men, but God who examines our hearts.

OTHER BIBLICAL PARALLELS

Genesis 17:9–10

God said further to Abraham, . . . [10]"This is My covenant, which you shall keep, between Me and you and your descendants after you: every male among you shall be *circumcised*."

Deuteronomy 10:17

"For the LORD your God is the God of gods and the Lord of lords, the great, the mighty, and the awesome God who does *not show partiality* nor take a bribe."

Acts 11:29–30

And in the proportion that any of the disciples had means, each of them determined to send a contribution for the relief of the brethren living in Judea. [30]And this they did, sending it in charge of *Barnabas* and Saul to the elders.

Acts 15:1–2, 4–7, 13–14, 19–20, 22

Some men came down from Judea and began teaching the brethren, "Unless you are *circumcised* according to the custom of Moses, you cannot be saved." [2]And when Paul and *Barnabas* had great dissension and debate with them, the brethren determined that Paul and Barnabas and some others of them should go up to *Jerusalem* to the apostles and elders concerning this issue. . . . [4]When they arrived at Jerusalem, they were received by the church and the apostles and the elders, and they reported all that God had done with them. [5]But some of the sect of the Pharisees who had believed stood up, saying, "It is necessary to circumcise them and to direct them to observe the Law of

Moses." [6]The apostles and the elders came together to look into this matter. [7]After there had been much debate, *Peter* stood up and said to them, "Brethren, you know that in the early days God made a choice among you, that by my mouth *the Gentiles* would hear the word of *the gospel* and believe." . . . [13]After they had stopped speaking, *James* answered, saying, "Brethren, listen to me. [14]Simeon has related how God first concerned Himself about taking from among the Gentiles a people for His name. . . . [19]Therefore it is my judgment that we do not trouble those who are turning to God from among the Gentiles, [20]but that we write to them that they abstain from things contaminated by idols and from fornication and from what is strangled and from blood." . . . [22]Then it seemed good to the apostles and the elders, with the whole church, to choose men from among them to send to Antioch with Paul and Barnabas—Judas called Barsabbas, and Silas, leading men among the brethren.

2 Peter 2:1

But *false* prophets also arose among the people, just as there will also be false teachers among you, who will *secretly* introduce destructive heresies, even denying the Master who bought them, bringing swift destruction upon themselves.

NONCANONICAL PARALLELS

1 Maccabees 2:45–46, 48

Mattathias and his friends went around and tore down the altars; [46]they forcibly *circumcised* all the *uncircumcised* boys that they found within the borders of Israel. . . . [48]They rescued the law out of the hands of *the Gentiles* and kings, and they never let the sinner gain the upper hand.

Galatians 2:11–21

But when Cephas came to Antioch, I opposed him to his face, because he stood condemned. [12]For prior to the coming of certain men from James, he used to eat with the Gentiles; but when they came, he began to withdraw and hold himself aloof, fearing the party of the circumcision. [13]The rest of the Jews joined him in hypocrisy, with the result that even Barnabas

was carried away by their hypocrisy. [14]But when I saw that they were not straightforward about the truth of the gospel, I said to Cephas in the presence of all, "If you, being a Jew, live like the Gentiles and not like the Jews, how is it that you compel the Gentiles to live like Jews? [15]We are Jews by nature and not sinners from among the Gentiles; [16]nevertheless knowing that a man is not justified by the works of the Law but through faith in Christ Jesus, even we have believed in Christ Jesus, so that we may be justified by faith in Christ and not by the works of the Law; since by the works of the Law no flesh will be justified. [17]But if, while seeking to be justified in Christ, we ourselves have also been found sinners, is Christ then a minister of sin? May it never be! [18]For if I rebuild what I have once destroyed, I prove myself to be a transgressor. [19]For through the Law I died to the Law, so that I might live to God. [20]I have been crucified with Christ; and it is no longer I who live, but Christ lives in me; and the life which I now live in the flesh I live by faith in the Son of God, who loved me and gave Himself up for me. [21]I do not nullify the grace of God, for if righteousness comes through the Law, then Christ died needlessly."

GALATIANS PARALLELS

Galatians 1:3–4

Grace to you and peace from God our Father and the Lord Jesus Christ, [4]who *gave Himself* for our *sins* so that He might rescue us from this present evil age, according to the will of our God and Father.

Galatians 3:10–11

For as many as are of *the works of the Law* are under a curse; . . . [11]Now that no one is *justified* by the Law before God is evident; for, "THE RIGHTEOUS MAN SHALL LIVE BY *FAITH*."

Galatians 5:4, 24

You have been severed from Christ, you who are seeking to be *justified* by *law*; you have fallen from *grace*. . . . [24]Now those who belong to Christ Jesus have *crucified the flesh* with its passions and desires.

Galatians 6:14

But may it never be that I would boast, except in the cross of our Lord Jesus Christ, through which the world has been *crucified* to me, and I to the world.

Romans 3:5–6, 28

But if our unrighteousness demonstrates the *righteousness* of God, what shall we say? The God who inflicts wrath is not unrighteous, is He? (I am speaking in human terms.) [6]*May it never be!* For otherwise, how will God judge the world? . . . [28]For we maintain that a man is *justified* by *faith* apart from *works of the Law.*

Romans 6:6, 10–11

. . . knowing this, that our old self was *crucified* with Him, in order that our body of *sin* might be done away with, so that we would no longer be slaves to sin; . . . [10]For the death that He *died,* He died to sin once for all; but *the life* that He *lives,* He lives to God. [11]Even so consider yourselves to be dead to sin, but alive to God in Christ Jesus.

Romans 7:4

Therefore, my brethren, you also were made to *die to the Law* through the body of Christ, so that you might be joined to another, to Him who was raised from the dead, in order that we might bear fruit for God.

Romans 8:11

But if the Spirit of Him who raised Jesus from the dead dwells in you, He who raised Christ Jesus from the dead will also give *life* to your mortal bodies through His Spirit who dwells in you.

Romans 14:8

For if we live, we *live* for the Lord, or if we *die,* we die for the Lord; therefore whether we live or die, we are the Lord's.

Philippians 3:8–10

More than that, I count all things to be loss in view of the surpassing value of knowing Christ Jesus my Lord, for whom I have suffered the loss of all things, and count them but rubbish so that I may gain Christ, [9]and may be found in Him, not having a *righteousness* of my own derived from *the Law,* but that which is through *faith in Christ,* the righteousness which comes from God on the basis of faith, [10]that I may know Him and the power of His resurrection and the fellowship of His sufferings, being conformed to His death.

Titus 1:10

For there are many rebellious men, empty talkers and deceivers, especially those of *the circumcision.*

Acts 10:28

And he [Peter] said to them, "You yourselves know how unlawful it is for a man who is a *Jew* to associate with a foreigner or to visit him; and yet God has shown me that I should not call any man unholy or unclean."

Acts 11:2–3, 25–26

And when *Peter* came up to Jerusalem, those who were *circumcised* took issue with him, [3]saying, "You went to uncircumcised men and *ate* with them." . . . [25]And he [Barnabas] left for Tarsus to look for Saul; [26]and when he had found him, he brought him to *Antioch.* And for an entire year they met with the church and taught considerable numbers; and the disciples were first called Christians in Antioch.

Acts 13:1–3

Now there were at *Antioch,* in the church that was there, prophets and teachers: *Barnabas,* and Simeon who was called Niger, and Lucius of Cyrene, and Manaen who had been brought up with Herod the tetrarch, and Saul. [2]While they were ministering to the Lord and fasting, the Holy Spirit said, "Set apart for Me Barnabas and Saul for the work to which I have called them." [3]Then, when they had fasted and prayed and laid their hands on them, they sent them away.

Acts 15:13, 19–20

After they had stopped speaking, *James* answered, saying, ". . . [19] . . . It is my judgment that we do not trouble those who are turning to God from among *the Gentiles,* [20]but that we write to them that they abstain from things contaminated by idols and from fornication and from what is strangled and from blood."

Tobit 1:10–11

After I was carried away captive to Assyria and came as a captive to Nineveh, everyone of my kindred and my people ate the food of the Gentiles, [11]but I kept myself from *eating* the food of *the Gentiles.*

Jubilees *22:10, 16*

And he [Abraham] called Jacob and said, " . . . [16] . . . Separate yourself from *the gentiles,* and do not *eat* with them, and do not perform deeds like theirs."

Galatians 3:1–9

You foolish Galatians, who has bewitched you, before whose eyes Jesus Christ was publicly portrayed as crucified? [2]This is the only thing I want to find out from you: did you receive the Spirit by the works of the Law, or by hearing with faith? [3]Are you so foolish? Having begun by the Spirit, are you now being perfected by the flesh? [4]Did you suffer so many things in vain—if indeed it was in vain? [5]So then, does He who provides you with the Spirit and works miracles among you, do it by the works of the Law, or by hearing with faith? [6]Even so Abraham BELIEVED GOD, AND IT WAS RECKONED TO HIM AS RIGHTEOUSNESS. [7]Therefore, be sure that it is those who are of faith who are sons of Abraham. [8]The Scripture, foreseeing that God would justify the Gentiles by faith, preached the gospel beforehand to Abraham, saying, "ALL THE NATIONS WILL BE BLESSED IN YOU." [9]So then those who are of faith are blessed with Abraham, the believer.

GALATIANS PARALLELS

Galatians *4:6*

Because you are sons, God has sent forth *the Spirit* of His Son into our hearts, crying, "Abba! Father!"

Galatians *5:11, 16*

But I, brethren, if I still preach circumcision, why am I still persecuted? Then the stumbling block of the cross has been abolished. . . . [16]But I say, walk by *the Spirit,* and you will not carry out the desire of *the flesh.*

Galatians *6:12*

Those who desire to make a good showing in *the flesh* try to compel you to be circumcised, simply so that they will not be persecuted for the cross of Christ.

OTHER PAULINE PARALLELS

Romans *3:28*

For we maintain that a man is *justified* by *faith* apart from *works of the Law.*

Romans *4:2–3*

For if Abraham was *justified* by *works,* he has something to boast about, but not before God. [3]For what does the Scripture say? *"ABRAHAM BELIEVED GOD, AND IT WAS* CREDITED *TO HIM AS RIGHTEOUSNESS."*

Romans *4:9–12*

Is this *blessing* then on the circumcised, or on the uncircumcised also? . . . [10]How then was it credited? While he was circumcised, or uncircumcised? Not while circumcised, but while uncircumcised; [11]and he received the sign of circumcision, a seal of the *righteousness* of the *faith* which he had while uncircumcised, so that he might be the father of all who *believe* without being circumcised, that righteousness might be credited to them, [12]and the father of circumcision to those who not only are of the circumcision, but who also follow in the steps of the faith of our father *Abraham* which he had while uncircumcised.

Romans *4:16, 18*

For this reason it is by *faith,* in order that it may be in accordance with grace, so that the promise will be guaranteed to all the descendants, not only to those who are of *the Law,* but also to those who are of the faith of *Abraham,* who is the father of us all. . . .[18]In hope against hope he *believed,* so that he might become a father of many *nations* according to that which had been spoken, "SO SHALL YOUR DESCENDANTS BE."

Romans *10:17*

So *faith* comes from *hearing,* and hearing by the word of Christ.

1 Corinthians *2:1–2*

And when I came to you, brethren, I did not come with superiority of speech or of wisdom, proclaiming to you the testimony of God. [2]For I determined to know nothing among you except Jesus Christ, and Him *crucified.*

1 Corinthians 12:8–10

For to one is given the word of wisdom through *the Spirit*, and to another the word of knowledge according to the same Spirit; [9]to another *faith* by the same Spirit, and to another gifts of healing by the one Spirit, [10]and to another the effecting of *miracles*, and to another prophecy, and to another the distinguishing of spirits, to another various kinds of tongues, and to another the interpretation of tongues.

1 Corinthians 15:1–2

Now I make known to you, brethren, the gospel which I preached to you, which also you received, in which also you stand, [2]by which also you are saved, if you hold fast the word which I preached to you, unless you *believed in vain*.

OTHER BIBLICAL PARALLELS

Genesis 12:1, 3

Now the Lord said to *Abram*, ". . . [3]And I will bless those who bless you, And the one who curses you I will curse. And *in you all the* families of the earth *will be blessed*."

Genesis 15:6

Then he [Abram] *believed* in the Lord; *and* He *reckoned* it *to him as righteousness*.

Genesis 17:10–11

"This is My covenant, which you shall keep, between Me and you and your descendants after you: every male among you shall be circumcised. [11]And you shall be circumcised in *the flesh* of your foreskin, and it shall be the sign of the covenant between Me and you."

Acts 11:4, 17–18

But Peter began speaking, . . . [17]"Therefore if God gave to them the same gift as He gave to us also after *believing* in the Lord Jesus Christ, who was I that I could stand in God's way?" [18]When they heard this, they quieted down and glorified God, saying, "Well then, God has granted to *the Gentiles* also the repentance that leads to life."

James 2:22–24

You see that *faith* was working with his *works*, and as a result of the works, faith was *perfected*; [23]and the Scripture was fulfilled which says, "AND *ABRAHAM BELIEVED* GOD, AND IT WAS RECKONED TO HIM AS RIGHTEOUSNESS," and he was called the friend of God. [24]You see that a man is *justified* by works and not by faith alone.

NONCANONICAL PARALLELS

Sirach 44:20

He [Abraham] kept *the law* of the Most High, and entered into a covenant with him; he certified the covenant in his *flesh*, and when he was tested he proved faithful.

Mishnah Nedarim 3:11

Great is circumcision, for despite all the commandments which *Abraham* our father carried out, he was called complete and whole only when he had circumcised himself as it is said, "Walk before me and be *perfect*."

Galatians 3:10–18

For as many as are of the works of the Law are under a curse; for it is written, "CURSED IS EVERYONE WHO DOES NOT ABIDE BY ALL THINGS WRITTEN IN THE BOOK OF THE LAW, TO PERFORM THEM." [11]Now that no one is justified by the Law before God is evident; for, "THE RIGHTEOUS MAN SHALL LIVE BY FAITH." [12]However, the Law is not of faith; on the contrary, "HE WHO PRACTICES THEM SHALL LIVE BY THEM." [13]Christ redeemed us from the curse of the Law, having become a curse for us—for it is written, "CURSED IS EVERYONE WHO HANGS ON A TREE"— [14]in order that in Christ Jesus the blessing of Abraham might come to the Gentiles, so that we would receive the promise of the Spirit through faith. [15]Brethren, I speak in terms of human relations: even though it is only a man's covenant, yet when it has been ratified, no one sets it aside or adds conditions to it. [16]Now the promises were spoken to Abraham and to his seed. He does not say, "And to seeds," as referring to many, but rather to one, "And to your seed," that is, Christ. [17]What I am saying is this: the Law, which came four hundred and thirty years later, does not invalidate a covenant previously ratified by God, so as to nullify the promise. [18]For if the inheritance is based on law, it is no longer based on a promise; but God has granted it to Abraham by means of a promise.

Galatians 2:15–16

"We are Jews by nature and not sinners from among *the Gentiles*; [16]nevertheless knowing that a man is not *justified* by *the works of the Law* but through *faith* in Christ Jesus, even we have believed in Christ Jesus, so that we may be justified by faith in Christ and not by the works of the Law; since by the works of the Law no flesh will be justified."

Galatians 4:4–5

But when the fullness of the time came, God sent forth His Son, born of a woman, born under *the Law*, [5]so that He might *redeem* those who were under the Law, that we might receive the adoption as sons.

OTHER PAULINE PARALLELS

Romans 1:17

For in it the righteousness of God is revealed from faith to faith; as it is written, "BUT *THE RIGHTEOUS man* SHALL LIVE BY FAITH."

Romans 4:9, 13–18

Is this *blessing* then on the circumcised, or on the uncircumcised also? . . . [13]For *the promise* to *Abraham* or to his descendants that he would be heir of the world was not through *the Law*, but through the righteousness of *faith*. [14]For if those who are of the Law are heirs, faith is made void and the promise is nullified; [15]for the Law brings about wrath, but where there is no law, there also is no violation. [16]For this reason it is by faith, in order that it may be in accordance with grace, so that the promise will be guaranteed to all the descendants, not only to those who are of the Law, but also to those who are of the faith of Abraham, who is the father of us all, [17](as it is written, "A FATHER OF MANY NATIONS HAVE I MADE YOU") in the presence of Him whom he believed, even God, who gives life to the dead and calls into being that which does not exist. [18]In hope against hope he believed, so that he might become a father of many nations according to that which had been spoken, "SO SHALL YOUR DESCENDANTS BE."

2 Corinthians 5:21

He made Him who knew no sin to be sin on our behalf, so that we might become the righteousness of God in Him.

Ephesians 1:13–14

In Him, you also, after listening to the message of truth, the gospel of your salvation—having also believed, you were sealed in Him with *the* Holy *Spirit* of *promise*, [14]who is given as a pledge of our *inheritance*, with a view to the redemption of God's own possession, to the praise of His glory.

OTHER BIBLICAL PARALLELS

Genesis 17:19

But God said, "No, but Sarah your wife will bear you a son, and you shall call his name Isaac; and I will establish My *covenant* with him for an everlasting covenant for his descendants after him."

Genesis 22:17

"Indeed I will greatly *bless* you, and I will greatly multiply your *seed* as the stars of the heavens and as the sand which is on the seashore; and your seed shall possess the gate of their enemies."

Exodus 12:40

Now the time that the sons of Israel lived in Egypt was *four hundred and thirty years*.

Leviticus 18:5

"So you shall keep My statutes and My judgments, by which a man may *live* if he does *them*; I am the LORD."

Deuteronomy 21:23

"His corpse shall not hang all night on the tree, but you shall surely bury him on the same day (for he who is *hanged* is *accursed* of God), so that you do not defile your land which the LORD your God gives you as an inheritance."

Deuteronomy 27:26

"*Cursed is* he *who does not* confirm the words of this *law* by doing *them*."

Habakkuk 2:4

"Behold, as for the proud one, His soul is not right within him; But *the righteous* will *live by* his *faith*."

Acts 2:33

"Therefore having been exalted to the right hand of God, and having received from the Father *the promise* of *the* Holy *Spirit*, He has poured forth this which you both see and hear."

Hebrews 6:13–14

For when God made *the promise* to Abraham, since He could swear by no one greater, He swore by Himself, [14]saying, "I WILL SURELY BLESS YOU AND I WILL SURELY MULTIPLY YOU."

NONCANONICAL PARALLELS

2 Maccabees 2:17–18

It is God who has saved all his people, and has returned the *inheritance* to all, and the kingship and the priesthood to the consecration, [18]as he *promised* through the law.

Jubilees 16:16–18

Through Isaac a name and *seed* would be named for him [Abraham]. [17]And all of the seed of his sons would become nations. . . . But from the sons of Isaac one would become a holy seed and he would not be counted among the nations [18]because he would become the portion of the Most High.

Halakhic Letter (4QMMT) 106–8, 112–13

And we are aware that part of the *blessings* and *curses* have occurred [107]that are written in the b[ook of Mo]ses. And this is the end of days, when they will return in Israel [108]to the L[aw] . . . [112] . . . And also we have written to you [113]some of *the works* of the Torah which we think are good for you and your people.

Galatians 3:19–29

Why the Law then? It was added because of transgressions, having been ordained through angels by the agency of a mediator, until the seed would come to whom the promise had been made. [20]Now a mediator is not for one party only; whereas God is only one. [21]Is the Law then contrary to the promises of God? May it never be! For if a law had been given which was able to impart life, then righteousness would indeed have been based on law. [22]But the Scripture has shut up everyone under sin,

so that the promise by faith in Jesus Christ might be given to those who believe. [23]But before faith came, we were kept in custody under the law, being shut up to the faith which was later to be revealed. [24]Therefore the Law has become our tutor to lead us to Christ, so that we may be justified by faith. [25]But now that faith has come, we are no longer under a tutor. [26]For you are all sons of God through faith in Christ Jesus. [27]For all of you who were baptized into Christ have clothed yourselves with Christ. [28]There is neither Jew nor Greek, there is neither slave nor free man, there is neither male nor female; for you are all one in Christ Jesus. [29]And if you belong to Christ, then you are Abraham's descendants, heirs according to promise.

GALATIANS PARALLELS

Galatians 2:16, 19–20

"Nevertheless knowing that a man is not *justified* by the works of *the Law* but through *faith in Christ Jesus*, even we have *believed* in Christ Jesus, so that we may be justified by faith in Christ and not by the works of the Law; since by the works of the Law no flesh will be justified. . . . [19]For through the Law I died to the Law, so that I might live to God. [20]I have been crucified with Christ; and it is no longer I who live, but Christ lives in me; and the *life* which I now live in the flesh I live by faith in the Son of God, who loved me and gave Himself up for me."

OTHER PAULINE PARALLELS

Romans 4:13–14

For *the promise* to *Abraham* or to his *descendants* that he would be heir of the world was not through *the Law*, but through the *righteousness* of *faith*. [14]For if those who are of the Law are *heirs*, faith is made void and the promise is nullified.

Romans 5:20

The Law came in so that the *transgression* would increase; but where *sin* increased, grace abounded all the more.

Romans 7:7–10

What shall we say then? Is *the Law* sin? *May it never be!* On the contrary, I would not have come to know *sin* except through the Law; for I would not have known about coveting if the Law had not said, "YOU SHALL

NOT COVET." [8]But sin, taking opportunity through the commandment, produced in me coveting of every kind; for apart from the Law sin is dead. [9]I was once alive apart from the Law; but when the commandment came, sin became alive and I died; [10]and this commandment, which was to result in *life*, proved to result in death for me.

Romans 9:7–8

Nor are they all children because they are *Abraham's descendants*, but: "THROUGH ISAAC YOUR DESCENDANTS WILL BE NAMED." [8]That is, it is not the children of the flesh who are children of God, but the children of *the promise* are regarded as descendants.

Romans 11:32

For God has *shut up* all in disobedience so that He may show mercy to all.

1 Corinthians 12:13

For by one Spirit we were *all baptized* into one body, whether *Jews* or *Greeks*, whether *slaves* or *free*, and we were all made to drink of one Spirit.

Ephesians 2:15

. . . by abolishing in His flesh the enmity, which is *the Law* of commandments contained in ordinances, so that in Himself He might make the two into *one* new man, thus establishing peace.

Colossians 3:9–11

Do not lie to one another, since you laid aside the old self with its evil practices, [10]and have put on the new self who is being renewed to a true knowledge according to the image of the One who created him— [11]a renewal in which there is no distinction between *Greek* and *Jew*, circumcised and uncircumcised, barbarian, Scythian, *slave* and *freeman*, but Christ is *all*, and in all.

1 Timothy 2:5

For there is one God, and one *mediator* also between God and men, the man Christ Jesus.

OTHER BIBLICAL PARALLELS

Genesis 1:27

God created man in His own image, in the image of God He created him; *male* and *female* He created them.

Genesis 3:21

The LORD God made garments of skin for Adam and his wife, and *clothed* them.

Deuteronomy 6:4

"Hear, O Israel! The LORD is our *God*, the LORD *is one!*"

Deuteronomy 33:2

"The LORD came from Sinai, And dawned on them from Seir; He shone forth from Mount Paran, And He came from the midst of ten thousand holy ones; At His right hand there was flashing lightning for them."

Acts 7:52–53

"Which one of the prophets did your fathers not persecute? They killed those who had previously announced the coming of the Righteous One, whose betrayers and murderers you have now become; [53]you who received *the law* as *ordained* by *angels*, and yet did not keep it."

Hebrews 9:15

For this reason He is the *mediator* of a new covenant, so that, since a death has taken place for the redemption of the *transgressions* that were committed under the first covenant, those who have been called may receive *the promise* of the eternal inheritance.

NONCANONICAL PARALLELS

Josephus, Jewish Antiquities *15.136*

We have learned the noblest of our doctrines and the holiest of our laws through *angels* from God.

Aristotle, Nicomachean Ethics *3.12.8*

The part of us associated with desire should live under the command of reason just as a child should live under the command of a *tutor*.

Galatians 4:1–11

Now I say, as long as the heir is a child, he does not differ at all from a slave although he is owner of everything, [2]but he is under guardians and managers until the date set by the father. [3]So also we, while we were children, were held in bondage under the elemental things of the world. ⁴But when the fullness of the time came, God sent forth His Son, born of a woman, born under the Law, ⁵so that He might redeem those who were under the Law, that we might receive the adoption as sons. ⁶Because you are sons, God has sent forth the Spirit of His Son into our hearts, crying, "Abba! Father!" ⁷Therefore you are no longer a slave, but a son; and if a son, then an heir through God. ⁸However at that time, when you did not know God, you were slaves to those which by nature are no gods. ⁹But now that you have come to know God, or rather to be known by God, how is it that you turn back again to the weak and worthless elemental things, to which you desire to be enslaved all over again? ¹⁰You observe days and months and seasons and years. ¹¹I fear for you, that perhaps I have labored over you in vain.

GALATIANS PARALLELS

Galatians 2:2

It was because of a revelation that I went up; and I submitted to them the gospel which I preach among the Gentiles, but I did so in private to those who were of reputation, for fear that I might be running, or had run, *in vain.*

Galatians 3:13

Christ *redeemed* us from the curse of *the Law,* having become a curse for us—for it is written, "CURSED IS EVERYONE WHO HANGS ON A TREE."

Galatians 5:1

It was for freedom that Christ set us free; therefore keep standing firm and do not be subject *again* to a yoke of *slavery.*

OTHER PAULINE PARALLELS

Romans 6:16

Do you not know that when you present yourselves to someone as *slaves* for obedience, you are slaves of the one whom you obey, either of sin resulting in death, or of obedience resulting in righteousness?

Romans 8:3, 9, 15–17

For what *the Law* could not do, *weak* as it was through the flesh, God did: *sending His own Son* in the likeness of sinful flesh and as an offering for sin, He condemned sin in the

flesh. . . . ⁹However, you are not in the flesh but in the Spirit, if indeed the Spirit of God dwells in you. But if anyone does not have *the Spirit* of Christ, he does not belong to Him. . . .¹⁵For you have not received a spirit of *slavery* leading to fear again, but you have received a spirit of *adoption as sons* by which we *cry* out, "*Abba! Father!*" ¹⁶The Spirit Himself testifies with our spirit that we are *children* of God, ¹⁷and if children, *heirs* also, heirs of God and fellow heirs with Christ, if indeed we suffer with Him so that we may also be glorified with Him.

Romans 14:5

One person regards one *day* above another, another regards every day alike. Each person must be fully convinced in his own mind.

1 Corinthians 8:5–6

For even if there are so-called *gods* whether in heaven or on earth, as indeed there are many gods and many lords, ⁶yet for us there is but one God, the Father, from whom are all things and we exist for Him; and one Lord, Jesus Christ, by whom are all things, and we exist through Him.

1 Corinthians 12:2

You know that when you were pagans, you were led astray to the mute idols, however you were led.

Ephesians 1:8–10

. . . which He lavished on us. In all wisdom and insight ⁹He made known to us the mystery of His will, according to His kind intention which He purposed in Him ¹⁰with a view to an administration suitable to *the fullness of the times,* that is, the summing up of all things in Christ, things in the heavens and things on the earth.

Ephesians 2:12

Remember that you were at that time separate from Christ, excluded from the commonwealth of Israel, and strangers to the covenants of promise, having no hope and without God in the world.

Philippians 2:7–8

[Christ] emptied Himself, taking the form of a bond-servant, and being made in the likeness of men. ⁸Being found in appearance as a man, He humbled Himself by becoming obedient to the point of death, even death on a cross.

Colossians 2:8, 16, 20–21

See to it that no one takes you captive through philosophy and empty deception, according to the tradition of men, according to *the elementary* principles *of the world*, rather than according to Christ. . . . [16]Therefore no one is to act as your judge in regard to food or drink or in respect to a festival or a new moon or a Sabbath *day*. . . . [20]If you have died with Christ to the elementary principles of the world, why, as if you were living in the world, do you submit yourself to decrees, such as, [21]"Do not handle, do not taste, do not touch!"

OTHER BIBLICAL PARALLELS

Genesis 1:14

Then God said, "Let there be lights in the expanse of the heavens to separate the day from the night, and let them be for signs and for *seasons* and for *days* and *years*."

Isaiah 37:18–19

"Truly, O LORD, the kings of Assyria have devastated all the countries and their lands, [19]and have cast their gods into the fire, for they were *not gods* but the work of men's hands, wood and stone. So they have destroyed them."

Acts 16:6–7

They passed through the Phrygian and Galatian region, having been forbidden by the Holy Spirit to speak the word in Asia; [7]and after they came to Mysia, they were trying to go into Bithynia, and *the Spirit* of Jesus did not permit them.

1 John 4:9

By this the love of God was manifested in us, that *God* has *sent His* only begotten *Son* into the world so that we might live through Him.

NONCANONICAL PARALLELS

Wisdom of Solomon 13:1–2

All people who were ignorant of God were foolish by nature, . . . [2]but they supposed that either fire or wind or swift air, or the circle of the stars, or turbulent water, or the luminaries of heaven were the *gods* that rule the world.

1 Enoch 82:7–9

Uriel . . . has revealed to me . . . the luminaries, the *months*, the festivals, the *years*, and the *days*. [8]He has the power in the heaven . . . so that he may cause the light to shine over the people—sun, moon, and stars, and all the principalities of the heaven. . . . [9]These are the orders of the stars which set in their (respective) places *seasons*, festivals, and months.

Plato, Lysias 208B–C

And they [your parents] seem to regard a *slave* more highly than you, their son. . . . [C] . . . Do they allow you to be in charge of yourself or do they not entrust this to you either? Certainly not, he replied. So someone else is in charge over you? Yes, my tutor here. Isn't he a slave? But of course.

Galatians 4:12–20

I beg of you, brethren, become as I am, for I also have become as you are. You have done me no wrong; [13]but you know that it was because of a bodily illness that I preached the gospel to you the first time; [14]and that which was a trial to you in my bodily condition you did not despise or loathe, but you received me as an angel of God, as Christ Jesus Himself. [15]Where then is that sense of blessing you had? For I bear you witness that, if possible, you would have plucked out your eyes and given them to me. [16]So have I become your enemy by telling you the truth? [17]They eagerly seek you, not commendably, but they wish to shut you out so that you will seek them. [18]But it is good always to be eagerly sought in a commendable manner, and not only when I am present with you. [19]My children, with whom I am again in labor until Christ is formed in you— [20]but I could wish to be present with you now and to change my tone, for I am perplexed about you.

GALATIANS PARALLELS

Galatians 1:8

But even if we, or *an angel* from heaven, should *preach* to you a *gospel* contrary to what we have preached to you, he is to be accursed!

Galatians 2:5

But we did not yield in subjection to them for even an hour, so that *the truth* of *the gospel* would remain with you.

Galatians 3:13–14

Christ redeemed us from the curse of the Law, having become a curse for us—for it is written, "CURSED IS EVERYONE WHO HANGS ON A TREE"— [14]in order that in Christ Jesus the *blessing* of Abraham might come to the Gentiles, so that we would receive the promise of the Spirit through faith.

Galatians 5:7

You were running well; who hindered you from obeying *the truth*?

Galatians 6:17

From now on let no one cause trouble for me, for I bear on my *body* the brand-marks of Jesus.

OTHER PAULINE PARALLELS

Romans 8:22–23, 29

For we know that the whole creation groans and suffers the pains of childbirth together until now. [23]And not only this, but also we ourselves, having the first fruits of the Spirit, even we ourselves groan within ourselves, waiting eagerly for our adoption as sons, the redemption of our body. . . . [29]For those whom He foreknew, He also predestined to become conformed to the image of His Son, so that He would be the firstborn among many brethren.

1 Corinthians 4:14–16

I do not write these things to shame you, but to admonish you as my beloved *children*. [15]For if you were to have countless tutors in Christ, yet you would not have many fathers, for in Christ Jesus I became your father through *the gospel*. [16]Therefore I exhort you, be imitators of me.

1 Corinthians 9:20–21

To the Jews *I became as* a Jew, so that I might win Jews; to those who are under the Law, as under the Law though not being myself under the Law, so that I might win those who are under the Law; [21]to those who are without law, as without law, though not being without the law of God but under the law of Christ, so that I might win those who are without law.

2 Corinthians 3:18

But we all, with unveiled face, beholding as in a mirror the glory of the Lord, are being transformed into the same image from glory to glory, just as from the Lord, the Spirit.

2 Corinthians 10:2

I ask that when *I am present* I need not be bold with the confidence with which I propose to be courageous against some, who regard us as if we walked according to the flesh.

2 Corinthians 12:7

Because of the surpassing greatness of the revelations, for this reason, to keep me from exalting myself, there was given me a thorn in the flesh, a messenger of Satan to torment me—to keep me from exalting myself!

1 Thessalonians 2:7

But we proved to be gentle among you, as a nursing mother tenderly cares for her own *children*.

1 Thessalonians 2:13

For this reason we also constantly thank God that when you *received* the word of God which you heard from us, you accepted it not as the word of men, but for what it really is, the word of God, which also performs its work in you who believe.

OTHER BIBLICAL PARALLELS

Amos 5:10

They hate him who reproves in the gate, And they abhor him who speaks with integrity.

Matthew 10:40

"He who *receives* you receives Me, and he who receives Me receives Him who sent Me."

John 8:45

"But because I speak *the truth*, you do not believe Me."

Horace, Satires 2.5.32–36

"Publius, . . . [33]your virtue has made me your friend; [34]I know the complexities of the law, I can defend a case; [35]I will let someone *pluck out* my *eyes* sooner than have him [36]disgrace you or deprive you of a nutshell."

Galatians 4:21–5:1

Tell me, you who want to be under law, do you not listen to the law? [22]For it is written that Abraham had two sons, one by the bond-woman and one by the free woman. [23]But the son by the bondwoman was born according to the flesh, and the son by the free woman through the promise. [24]This is allegorically speaking, for these women are two covenants: one proceeding from Mount Sinai bearing children who are to be slaves; she is Hagar. [25]Now this Hagar is Mount Sinai in Arabia and corresponds to the present Jerusalem, for she is in slavery with her children. [26]But the Jerusalem above is free; she is our mother. [27]For it is written, "REJOICE, BARREN WOMAN WHO DOES NOT BEAR; BREAK FORTH AND SHOUT, YOU WHO ARE NOT IN LABOR; FOR MORE NUMEROUS ARE THE CHILDREN OF THE DESOLATE THAN OF THE ONE WHO HAS A HUSBAND." [28]And you brethren, like Isaac, are children of promise. [29]But as at that time he who was born according to the flesh persecuted him who was born according to the Spirit, so it is now also. [30]But what does the Scripture say? "CAST OUT THE BONDWOMAN AND HER SON, FOR THE SON OF THE BONDWOMAN SHALL NOT BE AN HEIR WITH THE SON OF THE FREE WOMAN." [31]So then, brethren, we are not children of a bondwoman, but of the free woman. [5:1]It was for freedom that Christ set us free; therefore keep standing firm and do not be subject again to a yoke of slavery.

GALATIANS PARALLELS

Galatians 2:1, 4–5

Then after an interval of fourteen years I went up again to *Jerusalem* with Barnabas, taking Titus along also. . . . [4]But it was because of the false brethren secretly brought in, who had sneaked in to spy out our liberty which we have in Christ Jesus, in order to bring us into bondage. [5]But we did not yield in subjection to them for even an hour, so that the truth of the gospel would remain with you.

Galatians 3:17, 23, 29

What I am saying is this: *the Law*, which came four hundred and thirty years later, does not invalidate a *covenant* previously ratified by God, so as to nullify *the promise.* . . . [23]But before faith came, we were kept in custody under the law, being shut up to the faith which was later to be revealed. . . . [29]And if you belong to Christ, then you are *Abraham's* descendants, *heirs* according to promise.

Galatians 4:3, 9

So also we, while we were *children*, were held in bondage under the elemental things of the world. . . . [9]But now that you have come to know God, or rather to be known by God, how is it that you turn back again to the weak and worthless elemental things, to which you desire to be *enslaved* all over again?

Galatians 5:13

For you were called to *freedom*, brethren; only do not turn your freedom into an opportunity for *the flesh*, but through love serve one another.

Galatians 6:12

Those who desire to make a good showing in *the flesh* try to compel you to be circumcised, simply so that they will not be *persecuted* for the cross of Christ.

OTHER PAULINE PARALLELS

Romans 8:15

For you have not received a spirit of *slavery* leading to fear again, but you have received a spirit of adoption as *sons* by which we cry out, "Abba! Father!"

Romans 9:6–9

But it is not as though the word of God has failed. For they are not all Israel who are descended from Israel; [7]nor are they all children because they are *Abraham's* descendants, but: "THROUGH *ISAAC* YOUR DESCENDANTS WILL BE NAMED." [8]That is, it is not the children of *the flesh* who are children of God, but the *children of the promise* are regarded as descendants.

9For this is the word of promise: "AT THIS TIME I WILL COME, AND SARAH SHALL HAVE A SON."

Genesis 17:19

"Sarah your wife will bear you a *son,* and you shall call his name *Isaac;* and I will establish My *covenant* with him for an everlasting covenant for his descendants after him."

Genesis 21:1–4, 9–12

Then the LORD took note of Sarah as He had said, and the LORD did for Sarah as He had *promised.* 2So Sarah conceived and bore a *son* to *Abraham* in his old age, at the appointed time of which God had spoken to him. 3Abraham called the name of his son who was born to him, whom Sarah bore to him, *Isaac.* 4Then Abraham circumcised his son Isaac when he was eight days old, as God had commanded him. . . . 9Now Sarah saw the son of *Hagar* the Egyptian, whom she had borne to Abraham, mocking. 10Therefore she said to Abraham, "Drive *out* this maid *and her son, for the son of* this maid *shall not be an heir with* my *son* Isaac." 11The matter distressed Abraham greatly because of his son. 12But God said to Abraham, "Do not be distressed because of the lad and your maid; whatever Sarah tells you, listen to her, for through Isaac your descendants shall be named."

Isaiah 54:1

"Shout for joy, O *barren* one, you *who* have *borne no* child; *Break forth* into joyful *shouting* and cry aloud, *you who* have *not* travailed; *For the* sons *of the desolate* one will be *more numerous Than* the sons *of the* married woman."

Acts 15:10

"Now therefore why do you put God to the test by placing upon the neck of the disciples *a yoke* which neither our fathers nor we have been able to bear?"

Hebrews 11:11

By faith even Sarah herself received ability to conceive, even beyond the proper time of life, since she considered Him faithful who had *promised.*

Hebrews 12:22

But you have come to Mount Zion and to the city of the living God, the heavenly *Jerusalem,* and to myriads of angels.

Revelation 21:2

And I saw the holy city, new *Jerusalem,* coming down out of heaven from God, made ready as a bride adorned for her husband.

Philo, On Abraham *99*

I also once heard certain natural philosophers not implausibly interpret the passage [Gen. 12:10–20] *allegorically,* the husband, they say, symbolically representing the excellent mind . . . while the wife is virtue, her name being in Chaldean Sarah but in Greek Queen, since nothing is more sovereign or preeminent than virtue.

Josephus, Jewish Antiquities *1.215*

At first Sarah felt affection for Ishmael . . . for he was being nurtured as a successor to the rule. But when she herself gave birth to *Isaac,* she did not deem it proper for him to be reared with Ishmael, who was older and able to cause him harm after their father had died.

Mishnah 'Abot *3:5*

From whoever accepts upon himself the *yoke* of Torah do they remove the yoke of the state and the yoke of hard labor.

Galatians 5:2–12

Behold I, Paul, say to you that if you receive circumcision, Christ will be of no benefit to you. 3And I testify again to every man who receives circumcision, that he is under obligation to keep the whole Law. 4You have been severed from Christ, you who are seeking to be justified by law; you have fallen from grace. 5For we through the Spirit, by faith, are waiting for the hope of righteousness. 6For in Christ Jesus neither circumcision nor uncircumcision means anything, but faith working through love. 7You were running well; who hindered you from obeying the truth? 8This persuasion did not come from Him who calls you. 9A little leaven leavens the whole lump of dough. [10]I have confidence in you in the Lord that you will adopt no other view; but the one who is disturbing you will bear his judgment, whoever he is. [11]But I, brethren, if I still preach circumcision, why am I still persecuted? Then the stumbling block of the cross has been abolished. [12]I wish that those who are troubling you would even mutilate themselves.

GALATIANS PARALLELS

Galatians 1:6–7

I am amazed that you are so quickly deserting *Him who called you* by the *grace* of Christ, for a different gospel; [7]which is really not another; only there are some who are *disturbing you* and want to distort the gospel of Christ.

Galatians 2:3–5, 7, 9

But not even Titus, who was with me, though he was a Greek, was compelled to be *circumcised*. [4]But it was because of the false brethren secretly brought in, who had sneaked in to spy out our liberty which we have in Christ Jesus, in order to bring us into bondage. [5]But we did not yield in subjection to them for even an hour, so that *the truth* of the gospel would remain with you. . . . [7]But on the contrary, seeing that I had been entrusted with the gospel to the *uncircumcised*, just as Peter had been to the circumcised, . . . [9]and recognizing the *grace* that had been given to me, James and Cephas and John, who were reputed to be pillars, gave to me and Barnabas the right hand of fellowship, so that we might go to the Gentiles and they to the circumcised.

Galatians 2:16

"Nevertheless knowing that a man is not *justified* by the works of *the Law* but through *faith* in Christ Jesus, even we have believed in Christ Jesus, so that we may be justified by faith in Christ and not by the works of the Law; since by the works of the Law no flesh will be justified."

Galatians 3:10

For as many as are of the works of *the Law* are under a curse; for it is written, "CURSED IS EVERYONE WHO DOES NOT ABIDE BY ALL THINGS WRITTEN IN THE BOOK OF THE LAW, TO PERFORM THEM."

Galatians 3:26–28

For you are all sons of God through *faith* in Christ Jesus. [27]For all of you who were baptized into Christ have clothed yourselves with Christ. [28]There is neither Jew nor Greek, there is neither slave nor free man, there is neither male nor female; for you are all one in Christ Jesus.

Galatians 5:22–23

But the fruit of *the Spirit* is *love*, joy, peace, patience, kindness, goodness, faithfulness, [23]gentleness, self-control; against such things there is no *law*.

Galatians 6:12, 15

Those who desire to make a good showing in the flesh try to compel you to be circumcised, simply so that they will not be *persecuted* for *the cross* of Christ. . . . [15]For neither is *circumcision* anything, nor *uncircumcision*, but a new creation.

OTHER PAULINE PARALLELS

Romans 2:25

For indeed *circumcision* is of value if you practice *the Law*; but if you are a transgressor of the Law, your circumcision has become *uncircumcision*.

Romans 8:23–24, 28

And not only this, but also we ourselves, having the first fruits of *the Spirit*, even we ourselves groan within ourselves, waiting eagerly for our adoption as sons, the redemption of our body. [24]For in *hope* we have been saved, but hope that is seen is not hope; for who hopes for what he already sees? . . . [28]And we know that God causes all things to work together for good to those who *love* God, to those who are *called* according to His purpose.

Romans 9:30–31

What shall we say then? That Gentiles, who did not pursue *righteousness*, attained righteousness, even the righteousness which is by *faith*; [31]but Israel, pursuing a *law* of righteousness, did not arrive at that law.

1 Corinthians 1:23

We preach Christ crucified, to Jews a *stumbling block* and to Gentiles foolishness.

1 Corinthians 5:6–7

Your boasting is not good. Do you not know that *a little leaven leavens the whole lump of dough*? ⁷Clean out the old leaven so that you may be a new lump, just as you are in fact unleavened. For Christ our Passover also has been sacrificed.

1 Corinthians 7:19–20

Circumcision is nothing, and *uncircumcision* is nothing, but what matters is the keeping of the commandments of God. ²⁰Each man must remain in that condition in which he was *called*.

Philippians 3:2

Beware of the dogs, beware of the evil workers, beware of the false *circumcision*.

OTHER BIBLICAL PARALLELS

Leviticus 2:11

"No grain offering, which you bring to the LORD, shall be made with *leaven*, for you shall not offer up in smoke any leaven or any honey as an offering by fire to the LORD."

Deuteronomy 23:1

"No one who is emasculated or has his male organ cut off shall enter the assembly of the LORD."

Esther 8:17

In each and every province and in each and every city, wherever the king's commandment and his decree arrived, there was gladness and joy for the Jews, a feast and a holiday. And many among the peoples of the land became Jews, for the dread of the Jews had fallen on them.

Acts 15:1

Some men came down from Judea and began teaching the brethren, "Unless you are *circumcised* according to the custom of Moses, you cannot be saved."

NONCANONICAL PARALLELS

Catullus, Poems 63.1–6, 8–9

Attis had hastened across towering seas on a raft. ²Eagerly setting his swift foot in the Phrygian grove, ³he entered the goddess's dark, forest-encircled domain ⁴and there was attacked by insanity's goad. Blinded by passion, ⁵he lightened the weight of his loins

with a sharp fragment of flint. . . . ⁶ . . . Lacking the male . . . , ⁸she excitedly took in her white hands a petite tambourine, ⁹Cybele's horn, tool of your sacrosanct rituals, mother.

Galatians 5:13–21

For you were called to freedom, brethren; only do not turn your freedom into an opportunity for the flesh, but through love serve one another. ¹⁴For the whole Law is fulfilled in one word, in the statement, "YOU SHALL LOVE YOUR NEIGHBOR AS YOURSELF." ¹⁵But if you bite and devour one another, take care that you are not consumed by one another. ¹⁶But I say, walk by the Spirit, and you will not carry out the desire of the flesh. ¹⁷For the flesh sets its desire against the Spirit, and the Spirit against the flesh; for these are in opposition to one another, so that you may not do the things that you please. ¹⁸But if you are led by the Spirit, you are not under the Law. ¹⁹Now the deeds of the flesh are evident, which are: immorality, impurity, sensuality, ²⁰idolatry, sorcery, enmities, strife, jealousy, outbursts of anger, disputes, dissensions, factions, ²¹envying, drunkenness, carousing, and things like these, of which I forewarn you, just as I have forewarned you, that those who practice such things will not inherit the kingdom of God.

GALATIANS PARALLELS

Galatians 3:18, 23

For if the inheritance is based on law, it is no longer based on a promise; but God has granted it to Abraham by means of a promise. . . . ²³But before faith came, we were kept in custody under *the law*, being shut up to the faith which was later to be revealed.

Galatians 5:1

It was for *freedom* that Christ set us free; therefore keep standing firm and do not be subject again to a yoke of slavery.

Galatians 6:2

Bear one another's burdens, and thereby *fulfill the law* of Christ.

Romans 1:29–31

. . . being filled with all unrighteousness, wickedness, greed, evil; full of *envy*, murder, *strife*, deceit, malice; they are gossips, [30]slanderers, haters of God, insolent, arrogant, boastful, inventors of evil, disobedient to parents, [31]without understanding, untrustworthy, unloving, unmerciful.

Romans 7:15, 18

For what I am doing, I do not understand; for I am *not* practicing what I would like to *do*, but I am doing the very thing I hate. . . . [18]For I know that nothing good dwells in me, that is, in my *flesh*; for the willing is present in me, but the doing of the good is not.

Romans 8:3–4, 14

For what *the Law* could not do, weak as it was through *the flesh*, God did: sending His own Son in the likeness of sinful flesh and as an offering for sin, He condemned sin in the flesh, [4]so that the requirement of the Law might be *fulfilled* in us, who do not *walk* according to the flesh but according to *the Spirit*. . . . [14]For all who are being *led by the Spirit* of God, these are sons of God.

Romans 13:8–10

Owe nothing to anyone except to *love one another*; for he who loves his neighbor has *fulfilled the law*. [9]For this, "YOU SHALL NOT COMMIT ADULTERY, YOU SHALL NOT MURDER, YOU SHALL NOT STEAL, YOU SHALL NOT COVET," and if there is any other commandment, it is summed up in this saying, *"YOU SHALL LOVE YOUR NEIGHBOR AS YOURSELF."* [10]Love does no wrong to a neighbor; therefore love is the fulfillment of the law.

Romans 13:13–14

Let us behave properly as in the day, not in *carousing* and *drunkenness*, not in sexual promiscuity and *sensuality*, not in *strife* and *jealousy*. [14]But put on the Lord Jesus Christ, and make no provision for *the flesh* in regard to its lusts.

1 Corinthians 6:9–10

Or do you not know that the unrighteous *will not inherit the kingdom of God*? Do not be deceived; neither fornicators, nor *idol-aters*, nor adulterers, nor effeminate, nor homosexuals, [10]nor thieves, nor the covetous, nor *drunkards*, nor revilers, nor swindlers, will inherit the kingdom of God.

1 Corinthians 9:19

For though I am *free* from all men, I have made myself a slave to all, so that I may win more.

2 Corinthians 12:20

For I am afraid that perhaps when I come I may find you to be not what I wish and may be found by you to be not what you wish; that perhaps there will be *strife, jealousy, angry* tempers, *disputes*, slanders, gossip, arrogance, disturbances.

Colossians 3:5–8

Therefore consider the members of your earthly body as dead to *immorality, impurity*, passion, evil *desire*, and greed, which amounts to *idolatry*. [6]For it is because of these things that the wrath of God will come upon the sons of disobedience, [7]and in them you also once *walked*, when you were living in them. [8]But now you also, put them all aside: *anger*, wrath, malice, slander, and abusive speech from your mouth.

Leviticus 19:18

"You shall not take vengeance, nor bear any grudge against the sons of your people, but *you shall love your neighbor as yourself.*"

Matthew 22:37–40

And He said to him, "'YOU SHALL LOVE THE LORD YOUR GOD WITH ALL YOUR HEART, AND WITH ALL YOUR SOUL, AND WITH ALL YOUR MIND.' [38]This is the great and foremost commandment. [39]The second is like it, 'YOU SHALL LOVE YOUR NEIGHBOR AS YOURSELF.' [40]On these two commandments depend *the whole Law* and the Prophets."

Mark 7:21–22

"For from within, out of the heart of men, proceed the evil thoughts, fornications, thefts, murders, adulteries, [22]deeds of coveting and wickedness, as well as deceit, *sensuality, envy*, slander, pride and foolishness."

James 2:8

If, however, you are *fulfilling* the royal *law* according to the Scripture, "*YOU SHALL LOVE YOUR NEIGHBOR AS YOURSELF*," you are doing well.

1 Peter 2:16

Act as free men, and do not use your *freedom* as a covering for evil, but use it as bondslaves of God.

1 Peter 4:3

For the time already past is sufficient for you to have carried out the *desire* of the Gentiles, having pursued a course of *sensuality*, lusts, *drunkenness*, *carousing*, drinking parties and abominable *idolatries*.

4 Maccabees 1:26–27

In the soul it [pleasure] is boastfulness, covetousness, thirst for honor, rivalry, and malice; ²⁷in the body, indiscriminate eating, gluttony, and solitary gormandizing.

Galatians 5:22–26

But the fruit of the Spirit is love, joy, peace, patience, kindness, goodness, faithfulness, ²³gentleness, self-control; against such things there is no law. ²⁴Now those who belong to Christ Jesus have crucified the flesh with its passions and desires. ²⁵If we live by the Spirit, let us also walk by the Spirit. ²⁶Let us not become boastful, challenging one another, envying one another.

GALATIANS PARALLELS

Galatians 2:19–20

"For through the Law I died to the Law, so that I might live to God. ²⁰I have been *crucified* with Christ; and it is no longer I who *live*, but Christ lives in me; and the life which I now live in *the flesh* I live by faith in the Son of God, who loved me and gave Himself up for me."

Galatians 5:6

For in Christ Jesus neither circumcision nor uncircumcision means anything, but faith working through *love*.

Galatians 6:14

But may it never be that I would *boast*, except in the cross of our Lord Jesus Christ, through which the world has been *crucified* to me, and I to the world.

OTHER PAULINE PARALLELS

Romans 6:5–6

For if we have become united with Him in the likeness of His death, certainly we shall also be in the likeness of His resurrection, ⁶knowing this, that our old self was *crucified* with Him, in order that our body of sin might be done away with, so that we would no longer be slaves to sin.

Romans 7:5

For while we were in *the flesh*, the sinful *passions*, which were aroused by the Law, were at work in the members of our body to bear *fruit* for death.

Romans 8:3–4

Sending His own Son in the likeness of sinful flesh and as an offering for sin, He condemned sin in *the flesh*, ⁴so that the requirement of the Law might be fulfilled in us, who do not *walk* according to the flesh but according to *the Spirit*.

Romans 8:9, 13

However, you are not in *the flesh* but in *the Spirit*, if indeed the Spirit of God dwells in you. But if anyone does not have the Spirit of Christ, he does not *belong* to Him. . . . ¹³For if you are living according to the flesh, you must die; but if by the Spirit you are putting to death the deeds of the body, you will live.

1 Corinthians 13:4

Love is *patient*, love is *kind* and is not jealous; love does not brag and is not arrogant.

2 Corinthians 6:4, 6

. . . in everything commending ourselves as servants of God, in much endurance, in afflictions, in hardships, in distresses, . . . ⁶in purity, in knowledge, in *patience*, in *kindness*, in *the* Holy *Spirit*, in genuine *love*.

Ephesians 2:3

Among them we too all formerly lived in the lusts of our flesh, indulging the *desires* of the *flesh* and of the mind, and were by nature children of wrath, even as the rest.

Ephesians 4:1–3
Therefore I, the prisoner of the Lord, implore you to *walk* in a manner worthy of the calling with which you have been called, [2]with all humility and *gentleness*, with *patience*, showing tolerance for one another in *love*, [3]being diligent to preserve the unity of *the Spirit* in the bond of *peace*.

Philippians 2:2
Make my *joy* complete by being of the same mind, maintaining the same *love*, united in spirit, intent on one purpose.

Colossians 3:5, 12
Therefore consider the members of your earthly body as dead to immorality, impurity, *passion*, evil *desire*, and greed, which amounts to idolatry. . . . [12]So, as those who have been chosen of God, holy and beloved, put on a heart of compassion, *kindness*, humility, *gentleness* and *patience*.

1 Timothy 6:11
But flee from these things, you man of God, and pursue righteousness, godliness, faith, *love*, perseverance and *gentleness*.

2 Timothy 2:22
Now flee from youthful lusts and pursue righteousness, faith, *love* and *peace*, with those who call on the Lord from a pure heart.

Titus 3:1–3
Remind them to be subject to rulers, to authorities, to be obedient, to be ready for every good deed, [2]to malign no one, to be *peaceable, gentle*, showing every consideration for all men. [3]For we also once were foolish ourselves, disobedient, deceived, enslaved to various lusts and pleasures, spending our life in malice and *envy*, hateful, hating one another.

OTHER BIBLICAL PARALLELS

1 Peter 2:1–2
Therefore, putting aside all malice and all deceit and hypocrisy and *envy* and all slander, [2]like newborn babies, long for the pure milk of the word, so that by it you may grow in respect to salvation.

2 Peter 1:5–7
Now for this very reason also, applying all diligence, in your faith supply moral excellence, and in your moral excellence, knowledge, [6]and in your knowledge, *self-control*, and in your self-control, perseverance, and in your perseverance, godliness, [7]and in your godliness, brotherly *kindness*, and in your brotherly kindness, *love*.

NONCANONICAL PARALLELS

Philo, On the Virtues 182
Proselytes become at once sensible, *self-controlled*, modest, *gentle, kind*, humane, reverent, just, high-minded, lovers of truth, superior to the *desire* for possessions and pleasure.

Galatians 6:1–10

Brethren, even if anyone is caught in any trespass, you who are spiritual, restore such a one in a spirit of gentleness; each one looking to yourself, so that you too will not be tempted. [2]Bear one another's burdens, and thereby fulfill the law of Christ. [3]For if anyone thinks he is something when he is nothing, he deceives himself. [4]But each one must examine his own work, and then he will have reason for boasting in regard to himself alone, and not in regard to another. [5]For each one will bear his own load. [6]The one who is taught the word is to share all good things with the one who teaches him. [7]Do not be deceived, God is not mocked; for whatever a man sows, this he will also reap. [8]For the one who sows to his own flesh will from the flesh reap corruption, but the one who sows to the Spirit will from the Spirit reap eternal life. [9]Let us not lose heart in doing good, for in due time we will reap if we do not grow weary. [10]So then, while we have opportunity, let us do good to all people, and especially to those who are of the household of the faith.

GALATIANS PARALLELS

Galatians 3:3
Are you so foolish? Having begun by *the Spirit*, are you now being perfected by *the flesh*?

Galatians 5:14, 16

For the whole Law is *fulfilled* in one word, in the statement, "YOU SHALL LOVE YOUR NEIGHBOR AS YOURSELF." . . . [16]But I say, walk by *the Spirit*, and you will not carry out the desire of *the flesh*.

OTHER PAULINE PARALLELS

Romans 8:2, 6–7, 11

For *the law of* the Spirit of life in *Christ* Jesus has set you free from the law of sin and of death. . . . [6]For the mind set on *the flesh* is death, but the mind set on *the Spirit* is life and peace, [7]because the mind set on the flesh is hostile toward God; for it does not subject itself to the law of God, for it is not even able to do so. . . . [11]But if the Spirit of Him who raised Jesus from the dead dwells in you, He who raised Christ Jesus from the dead will also give life to your mortal bodies through His Spirit who dwells in you.

Romans 15:2

Each of us is to please his neighbor for his *good,* to his edification.

Romans 15:17

Therefore in Christ Jesus I have found reason for *boasting* in things pertaining to God.

1 Corinthians 3:18

Let no man *deceive himself. If any* man among you *thinks* that *he is* wise in this age, he must become foolish, so that he may become wise.

1 Corinthians 6:9

Or do you not know that the unrighteous will not inherit the kingdom of God? *Do not be deceived.*

1 Corinthians 9:14

So also the Lord directed those who proclaim the gospel to get their living from the gospel.

1 Corinthians 15:42

So also is the resurrection of the dead. It is *sown* a perishable body, it is raised an imperishable body.

2 Corinthians 2:5–7

But if any has caused sorrow, he has caused sorrow not to me, but in some degree—in order not to say too much—to all of you. [6]Sufficient for such a one is this punishment which was inflicted by the majority, [7]so that on the contrary you should rather forgive and comfort him, otherwise such a one might be overwhelmed by excessive sorrow.

2 Corinthians 13:5

Test yourselves to see if you are in the faith; *examine* yourselves! Or do you not recognize this about yourselves, that Jesus Christ is in you—unless indeed you fail the test?

2 Thessalonians 3:13–15

But as for you, brethren, *do not grow weary* of *doing good.* [14]If anyone does not obey our instruction in this letter, take special note of that person and do not associate with him, so that he will be put to shame. [15]Yet do not regard him as an enemy, but admonish him as a brother.

1 Timothy 3:15

In case I am delayed, I write so that you will know how one ought to conduct himself in *the household* of God, which is the church of the living God, the pillar and support of the truth.

OTHER BIBLICAL PARALLELS

Proverbs 3:27

Do not withhold *good* from those to whom it is due, When it is in your power to do it.

Proverbs 22:8

He who *sows* iniquity will *reap* vanity, And the rod of his fury will perish.

Matthew 5:16–17

"Let your light shine before men in such a way that they may see your *good* works, and glorify your Father who is in heaven. [17]Do not think that I came to abolish *the Law* or the Prophets; I did not come to abolish but to *fulfill.*"

Matthew 18:15

"If your brother sins, go and show him his fault in private; if he listens to you, you have won your brother."

James 4:11

Do not speak against one another, brethren. He who speaks against a brother or judges his brother, speaks against *the law* and judges the law; but if you judge the law, you are not a doer of the law but a judge of it.

James 5:19–20

My brethren, if any among you strays from the truth and one turns him back, [20]let him know that he who turns a sinner from the error of his way will save his soul from death and will cover a multitude of sins.

NONCANONICAL PARALLELS

Testament of Levi 13:6

Sow good things in your souls and you will find them in your lives. For if you sow evil, you will *reap* every trouble and tribulation.

Menander, Sentences 534

Consider all the *burdens* borne by your friends to be yours as well.

Galatians 6:11–18

See with what large letters I am writing to you with my own hand. [12]Those who desire to make a good showing in the flesh try to compel you to be circumcised, simply so that they will not be persecuted for the cross of Christ. [13]For those who are circumcised do not even keep the Law themselves, but they desire to have you circumcised so that they may boast in your flesh. [14]But may it never be that I would boast, except in the cross of our Lord Jesus Christ, through which the world has been crucified to me, and I to the world. [15]For neither is circumcision anything, nor uncircumcision, but a new creation. [16]And those who will walk by this rule, peace and mercy be upon them, and upon the Israel of God. [17]From now on let no one cause trouble for me, for I bear on my body the brand-marks of Jesus. [18]The grace of our Lord Jesus Christ be with your spirit, brethren. Amen.

GALATIANS PARALLELS

Galatians 2:3–5, 12

But not even Titus, who was with me, though he was a Greek, was compelled to be *circumcised*. [4]But it was because of the false brethren secretly brought in, who had sneaked in to spy out our liberty which we have in Christ Jesus, in order to bring us into bondage. [5]But we did not yield in sub-

jection to them for even an hour, so that the truth of the gospel would remain with you. . . . [12]For prior to the coming of certain men from James, he [Cephas] used to eat with the Gentiles; but when they came, he began to withdraw and hold himself aloof, fearing the party of the circumcision.

Galatians 2:19–20

"For through the Law I died to *the Law*, so that I might live to God. [20]I have been *crucified* with Christ; and it is no longer I who live, but Christ lives in me; and the life which I now live in *the flesh* I live by faith in the Son of God, who loved me and gave Himself up for me."

Galatians 3:1

You foolish Galatians, who has bewitched you, before whose eyes Jesus Christ was publicly portrayed as *crucified*?

Galatians 4:29

But as at that time he who was born according to *the flesh persecuted* him who was born according to the Spirit, so it is now also.

Galatians 5:3, 6, 11

And I testify again to every man who receives circumcision, that he is under obligation to *keep the* whole *Law.* . . . [6]For in Christ Jesus *neither circumcision nor uncircumcision* means anything, but faith working through love. . . . [11]But I, brethren, if I still preach circumcision, why am I still *persecuted*? Then the stumbling block of *the cross* has been abolished.

Galatians 5:24

Now those who belong to Christ Jesus have *crucified the flesh* with its passions and desires.

OTHER PAULINE PARALLELS

Romans 2:23–25

You who *boast* in *the Law*, through your breaking the Law, do you dishonor God? [24]For "THE NAME OF GOD IS BLASPHEMED AMONG THE GENTILES BECAUSE OF YOU," just as it is written. [25]For indeed *circumcision* is of value if you practice the Law; but if you are a transgressor of the Law, your circumcision has become *uncircumcision*.

Romans 2:28–29

For he is not a Jew who is one outwardly, nor is circumcision that which is outward in *the flesh.* [29]But he is a Jew who is one inwardly; and circumcision is that which is of the heart, by the Spirit, not by the letter; and his praise is not from men, but from God.

Romans 6:6

. . . knowing this, that our old self was *crucified* with Him, in order that our body of sin might be done away with, so that we would no longer be slaves to sin.

Romans 15:17

Therefore in Christ Jesus I have found reason for *boasting* in things pertaining to God.

1 Corinthians 7:19

Circumcision is nothing, and *uncircumcision* is nothing, but what matters is the keeping of the commandments of God.

2 Corinthians 4:8–10

We are afflicted in every way, but not crushed; perplexed, but not despairing; [9]*persecuted*, but not forsaken; struck down, but not destroyed; [10]always carrying about in the *body* the dying *of Jesus*, so that the life of Jesus also may be manifested in our body.

2 Corinthians 5:17

Therefore if anyone is in Christ, he is *a new creature*; the old things passed away; behold, new things have come.

Philippians 3:2–3

Beware of the dogs, beware of the evil workers, beware of the false *circumcision*; [3]for we are the true circumcision, who worship in the Spirit of God and glory in Christ Jesus and put no confidence in *the flesh.*

Philippians 4:23

The grace of the *Lord Jesus Christ be with your spirit.*

2 Thessalonians 3:17

I, Paul, *write* this greeting *with my own hand,* and this is a distinguishing mark in every letter; this is the way I write.

NONCANONICAL PARALLELS

3 Maccabees 2:27–29

[King Ptolemy] proposed to inflict public disgrace on the Jewish community, and he set up a stone on the tower in the courtyard with this inscription: [28]"None of those who do not sacrifice shall enter their sanctuaries, and all Jews shall be subjected to a registration involving poll tax and to the status of slaves. Those who object to this are to be taken by force and put to death; [29]those who are registered are also to be *branded* on their *bodies* by fire with the ivy-leaf symbol of Dionysus, and they shall also be reduced to their former limited status."

Ephesians

Ephesians 1:1–2

Paul, an apostle of Christ Jesus by the will of God, To the saints who are at Ephesus and who are faithful in Christ Jesus: [2]Grace to you and peace from God our Father and the Lord Jesus Christ.

EPHESIANS PARALLELS

Ephesians 2:14–19

For He Himself is our *peace*, who made both groups into one and broke down the barrier of the dividing wall, [15]by abolishing in His flesh the enmity, which is the Law of commandments contained in ordinances, so that in Himself He might make the two into one new man, thus establishing peace, [16]and might reconcile them both in one body to God through the cross, by it having put to death the enmity. [17]AND HE CAME AND PREACHED PEACE TO YOU WHO WERE FAR AWAY, AND PEACE TO THOSE WHO WERE NEAR; [18]for through Him we both have our access in one Spirit to the *Father.* [19]So then you are no longer strangers and aliens, but you are fellow citizens with *the saints*, and are of God's household.

Ephesians 4:1–3

Therefore I, the prisoner of the Lord, implore you to walk in a manner worthy of the calling with which you have been called, [2]with all humility and gentleness, with patience, showing tolerance for one another in love, [3]being diligent to preserve the unity of the Spirit in the bond of *peace.*

Ephesians 6:23–24

Peace be to the brethren, and love with faith, from *God* the *Father and the Lord Jesus Christ.* [24]*Grace* be with all those who love our Lord Jesus Christ with incorruptible love.

OTHER PAULINE PARALLELS

Romans 1:1, 7

Paul, a bond-servant of Christ Jesus, called as *an apostle*, set apart for the gospel of God, . . . [7]to all who are beloved of God in Rome, called as *saints: Grace to you and peace from God our Father and the Lord Jesus Christ.*

1 Corinthians 15:32

If from human motives I fought with wild beasts at *Ephesus*, what does it profit me? If the dead are not raised, LET US EAT AND DRINK, FOR TOMORROW WE DIE.

1 Corinthians 16:8–9

But I will remain in *Ephesus* until Pentecost; [9]for a wide door for effective service has opened to me, and there are many adversaries.

2 Corinthians 1:1–2

Paul, an apostle of Christ Jesus by the will of God, and Timothy our brother, To the church of God which is at Corinth with all *the saints* who are throughout Achaia: [2]*Grace to you and peace from God our Father and the Lord Jesus Christ.*

Colossians 1:1–2

Paul, an apostle of Jesus Christ *by the will of God*, and Timothy our brother, [2]*To the saints* and *faithful* brethren *in Christ* who are at Colossae: *Grace to you and peace from God our Father.*

As I urged you upon my departure for Macedonia, remain on at *Ephesus* so that you may instruct certain men not to teach strange doctrines.

OTHER BIBLICAL PARALLELS

Acts 19:1, 8–10

It happened that while Apollos was at Corinth, *Paul* passed through the upper country and came to *Ephesus*, and found some disciples. . . . [8]And he entered the synagogue and continued speaking out boldly for three months, reasoning and persuading them about the kingdom of God. [9]But when some were becoming hardened and disobedient, speaking evil of the Way before the people, he withdrew from them and took away the disciples, reasoning daily in the school of Tyrannus. [10]This took place for two years, so that all who lived in Asia heard the word of the Lord, both Jews and Greeks.

Revelation 2:1–3

"To the angel of the church in *Ephesus* write: The One who holds the seven stars in His right hand, the One who walks among the seven golden lampstands, says this: [2]'I know your deeds and your toil and perseverance, and that you cannot tolerate evil men, and you put to the test those who call themselves *apostles*, and they are not, and you found them to be false; [3]and you have perseverance and have endured for My name's sake, and have not grown weary.'"

Ephesians 1:3–14

Blessed be the God and Father of our Lord Jesus Christ, who has blessed us with every spiritual blessing in the heavenly places in Christ, [4]just as He chose us in Him before the foundation of the world, that we would be holy and blameless before Him. In love [5]He predestined us to adoption as sons through Jesus Christ to Himself, according to the kind intention of His will, [6]to the praise of the glory of His grace, which He freely bestowed on us in the Beloved. [7]In Him we have redemption through His blood, the forgiveness of our trespasses, according to the riches of His grace [8]which He lavished on us. In all wisdom and insight [9]He made known to us the mystery of His will, according to His kind intention which He purposed in Him [10]with a view to an administration suitable to the fullness of the times, that is, the summing up of all things in Christ, things in the heavens and things on the earth. In Him [11]also we have obtained an inheritance, having been predestined according to His purpose who works all things after the counsel of His will, [12]to the end that we who were the first to hope in Christ would be to the praise of His glory. [13]In Him, you also, after listening to the message of truth, the gospel of your salvation—having also believed, you were sealed in Him with the Holy Spirit of promise, [14]who is given as a pledge of our inheritance, with a view to the redemption of God's own possession, to the praise of His glory.

EPHESIANS PARALLELS

Ephesians 2:4–7

But God, being rich in mercy, because of His great *love* with which He loved us, [5]even when we were dead in our transgressions, made us alive together with Christ (by grace you have been saved), [6]and raised us up with Him, and seated us with Him *in the heavenly places in Christ* Jesus, [7]so that in the ages to come He might show the surpassing *riches of His grace* in kindness toward us in Christ Jesus.

Ephesians 3:4–6, 10–11

By referring to this, when you read you can understand my insight into the *mystery* of Christ, [5]which in other generations was not *made known* to the sons of men, as it has now been revealed to His holy apostles and prophets in *the Spirit*; [6]to be specific, that the Gentiles are fellow *heirs* and fellow members of the body, and fellow partakers of the *promise* in Christ Jesus through *the gospel*, . . . [10]so that the manifold *wisdom* of God might now be made known through the church to the rulers and the authorities *in the heavenly places*. [11]This was in accordance with the eternal *purpose* which He carried out in Christ Jesus our Lord.

Ephesians 4:30, 32

Do not grieve *the Holy Spirit* of God, by whom you were *sealed* for the day of *redemption*. . . . [32]Be kind to one another, tender-hearted, forgiving each other, just as God in Christ also has *forgiven* you.

Romans 3:23–25

For all have sinned and fall short of the *glory* of God, [24]being justified as a gift by *His grace* through the *redemption* which is in Christ Jesus; [25]whom God displayed publicly as a propitiation in *His blood* through faith. This was to demonstrate His righteousness, because in the forbearance of God He passed over the sins previously committed.

Romans 8:23, 28–30

And not only this, but also we ourselves, having the first fruits of *the Spirit,* even we ourselves groan within ourselves, waiting eagerly for our *adoption as sons*, the *redemption* of our body. . . . [28]And we know that God causes all things to work together for good to those who *love* God, to those who are called *according to His purpose.* [29]For those whom He foreknew, He also *predestined* to become conformed to the image of His Son, so that He would be the firstborn among many brethren; [30]and these whom He predestined, He also called; and these whom He called, He also justified; and these whom He justified, He also glorified.

2 Corinthians 1:3

Blessed be the God and Father of our Lord Jesus Christ, the Father of mercies and God of all comfort.

2 Corinthians 1:21–22

Now He who establishes us with you in Christ and anointed us is God, [22]who also *sealed* us and gave us *the Spirit* in our hearts as a *pledge.*

Galatians 4:4–5

But when *the fullness of the time* came, God sent forth His Son, born of a woman, born under the Law, [5]so that He might *redeem* those who were under the Law, that we might receive the *adoption as sons.*

Colossians 1:12–16

. . . giving thanks to the *Father*, who has qualified us to share in the *inheritance* of the saints in Light. [13]For He rescued us from the domain of darkness, and transferred us to the kingdom of His *beloved* Son, [14]in whom we have *redemption*, the *forgiveness* of sins. [15]He is the image of the invisible God, the firstborn of all creation. [16]For by Him *all things* were created, both *in the heavens and on earth*, visible and invisible, whether thrones or dominions or rulers or authorities all things have been created through Him and for Him.

Colossians 1:19–22

For it was the Father's good pleasure for all *the fullness* to dwell in Him, [20]and through Him to reconcile *all things* to Himself, having made peace through the *blood* of His cross; through Him, I say, whether *things on earth or things in heaven.* [21]And although you were formerly alienated and hostile in mind, engaged in evil deeds, [22]yet He has now reconciled you in His fleshly body through death, in order to present you *before Him holy and blameless* and beyond reproach.

Colossians 1:25–28

. . . so that I might fully carry out the preaching of the word of God, [26]that is, the *mystery* which has been hidden from the past ages and generations, but has now been manifested to His saints, [27]to whom God willed to *make known* what is the *riches* of the *glory* of this mystery among the Gentiles, which is Christ in you, the *hope* of glory. [28]We proclaim Him, admonishing every man and teaching every man with all *wisdom.*

2 Thessalonians 2:13

But we should always give thanks to God for you, brethren beloved by the Lord, because God has *chosen* you from the beginning for *salvation* through sanctification by the Spirit and faith in the *truth.*

OTHER BIBLICAL PARALLELS

Acts 20:32

"And now I commend you to God and to the word of *His grace*, which is able to build you up and to give you the *inheritance* among all those who are sanctified."

Hebrews 9:15

For this reason He is the mediator of a new covenant, so that, since a death has taken place for the *redemption* of the transgressions that were committed under the first covenant, those who have been called may receive the *promise* of the eternal *inheritance.*

Joseph and Aseneth 8:10–11

Lord God of my father Israel . . . who gave life to *all (things)* and called (them) from the darkness to the light, . . . *bless* this virgin, [11]and renew her by your spirit, . . . and make her alive again by your life, . . . and number her among your people, that you have *chosen* before all (things) came into being, and let her enter your rest which you have prepared for your chosen ones, and live in your eternal life for ever (and) ever.

4QSapiential Work A[c] (4Q417) fragment 1 1.10–11

[Consider the *mystery* of] [11]existence and take the offspring of *salvation* and know who will *inherit glory* and injustice.

Ephesians 1:15–23

For this reason I too, having heard of the faith in the Lord Jesus which exists among you and your love for all the saints, [16]do not cease giving thanks for you, while making mention of you in my prayers; [17]that the God of our Lord Jesus Christ, the Father of glory, may give to you a spirit of wisdom and of revelation in the knowledge of Him. [18]I pray that the eyes of your heart may be enlightened, so that you will know what is the hope of His calling, what are the riches of the glory of His inheritance in the saints, [19]and what is the surpassing greatness of His power toward us who believe. These are in accordance with the working of the strength of His might [20]which He brought about in Christ, when He raised Him from the dead and seated Him at His right hand in the heavenly places, [21]far above all rule and authority and power and dominion, and every name that is named, not only in this age but also in the one to come. [22]And He put all things in subjection under His feet, and gave Him as head over all things to the church, [23]which is His body, the fullness of Him who fills all in all.

EPHESIANS PARALLELS

Ephesians 3:6–10

The Gentiles are fellow *heirs* and fellow members of the *body,* and fellow partakers of the promise in Christ Jesus through the gospel, [7]of which I was made a minister, according to the gift of God's grace which

was given to me according to the working of *His power.* [8]To me, the very least of all saints, this grace was given, to preach to the Gentiles the unfathomable *riches* of Christ, [9]and to bring to light what is the administration of the mystery which for ages has been hidden in God who created all things; [10]so that the manifold *wisdom* of God might now be made known through *the church* to the *rulers* and the *authorities in the heavenly places.*

Ephesians 4:9–10

Now this expression, "He ascended," what does it mean except that He also had descended into the lower parts of the earth? [10]He who descended is Himself also He who ascended far above all *the heavens,* so that He might *fill all things.*

Ephesians 4:15–16

Speaking the truth in *love,* we are to grow up in all aspects into Him who is the *head,* even Christ, [16]from whom the whole *body,* being fitted and held together by what every joint supplies, according to the proper working of each individual part, causes the growth of the body for the building up of itself in love.

Ephesians 6:10, 12

Finally, be strong in the Lord and in *the strength of His might.* . . . [12]For our struggle is not against flesh and blood, but against the *rulers,* against the *powers,* against the world forces of this darkness, against the spiritual forces of wickedness *in the heavenly places.*

OTHER PAULINE PARALLELS

Romans 1:8–9

First, I *thank* my God through Jesus Christ for you all, because *your faith* is being proclaimed throughout the whole world. [9]For God, whom I serve in my spirit in the preaching of the gospel of His Son, is my witness as to how *unceasingly* I make mention of you.

1 Corinthians 15:23–24

But each in his own order: Christ the first fruits, after that those who are Christ's at His coming, [24]then comes the end, when He hands over the kingdom to the God and

Father, when He has abolished *all rule and all authority and power.*

Philippians 2:9–10 ·

For this reason also, God highly exalted Him, and bestowed on Him the name which is *above every name,* [10]so that at the name of Jesus EVERY KNEE WILL BOW, of those who are *in heaven* and on earth and under the earth.

Colossians 1:3–4

We *give thanks* to God, the Father of our Lord Jesus Christ, *praying* always for you, [4]since we *heard of your faith* in Christ Jesus and the *love* which you have *for all the saints.*

Colossians 1:9, 11–12

For this reason also, since the day we heard of it, we have *not ceased* to *pray* for you and to ask that you may be filled with the *knowledge* of His will in all spiritual *wisdom* and understanding, . . . [11]strengthened with all *power,* according to His glorious *might,* for the attaining of all steadfastness and patience; joyously [12]*giving thanks* to the Father, who has qualified us to share in the *inheritance* of *the saints* in Light.

Colossians 1:16, 18–19

For by Him *all things* were created, both *in the heavens* and on earth, visible and invisible, whether thrones or *dominions* or *rulers* or *authorities*—all things have been created through Him and for Him. . . . [18]He is also *head* of the *body, the church*; and He is the beginning, the firstborn *from the dead,* so that He Himself will come to have first place in everything. [19]For it was the Father's good pleasure for all *the fullness* to dwell in Him.

Colossians 1:26–27

. . . that is, the mystery which has been hidden from the past ages and generations, but has now been manifested to His *saints,* [27]to whom God willed to make known what is *the riches of the glory* of this mystery among the Gentiles, which is Christ in you, the *hope* of glory.

Colossians 2:1–3

For I want you to know how great a struggle I have on your behalf and for those who are at Laodicea, and for all those who have

not personally seen my face, [2]that their *hearts* may be encouraged, having been knit together in *love,* and attaining to all the wealth that comes from the full assurance of understanding, resulting in a true knowledge of God's mystery, that is, Christ Himself, [3]in whom are hidden all the treasures of *wisdom* and *knowledge.*

Colossians 3:1

Therefore if you have been *raised* up with Christ, keep seeking the things above, where Christ is, *seated at* the *right hand* of God.

OTHER BIBLICAL PARALLELS

Psalm 8:4, 6

What is man that You take thought of him, And the son of man that You care for him? . . . [6]You make him to rule over the works of Your hands; You have *put all things under his feet.*

Psalm 110:1

The LORD says to my Lord: "*Sit at* My *right hand* Until I make Your enemies a footstool for Your feet."

Isaiah 11:2

The Spirit of the LORD will rest on Him, The *spirit of wisdom* and understanding, The spirit of counsel and strength, The spirit of *knowledge* and the fear of the LORD.

NONCANONICAL PARALLELS

1 Enoch 49:2–3

The Elect One stands before the Lord of the Spirits; his *glory* is forever and ever and his *power* is unto all generations. [3]In him dwells the *spirit of wisdom,* . . . the spirit of *knowledge* and strength.

Philo, On Moses *2.238*

All things have been *filled* all the way through by his [God's] own beneficent *power.*

Ephesians 2:1–10

And you were dead in your trespasses and sins, [2]in which you formerly walked according to the course of this world, according to the

prince of the power of the air, of the spirit that is now working in the sons of disobedience. [3]Among them we too all formerly lived in the lusts of our flesh, indulging the desires of the flesh and of the mind, and were by nature children of wrath, even as the rest. [4]But God, being rich in mercy, because of His great love with which He loved us, [5]even when we were dead in our transgressions, made us alive together with Christ (by grace you have been saved), [6]and raised us up with Him, and seated us with Him in the heavenly places in Christ Jesus, [7]so that in the ages to come He might show the surpassing riches of His grace in kindness toward us in Christ Jesus. [8]For by grace you have been saved through faith; and that not of yourselves, it is the gift of God; [9]not as a result of works, so that no one may boast. [10]For we are His workmanship, created in Christ Jesus for good works, which God prepared beforehand so that we would walk in them.

EPHESIANS PARALLELS

Ephesians 1:3, 7–8

Blessed be the God and Father of our Lord Jesus Christ, who has blessed us with every spiritual blessing *in the heavenly places* in Christ. . . . [7]In Him we have redemption through His blood, the forgiveness of our *trespasses*, according to *the riches of His grace* [8]which He lavished on us.

Ephesians 4:17–18

So this I say, and affirm together with the Lord, that you *walk* no longer just as the Gentiles also walk, in the futility of their *mind* [18]being darkened in their understanding, excluded from the life of God because of the ignorance that is in them, because of the hardness of their heart.

Ephesians 4:20–24

But you did not learn Christ in this way, [21]if indeed you have heard Him and have been taught in Him, just as truth is in Jesus, [22]that, in reference to your *former* manner of life, you lay aside the old self, which is being corrupted in accordance with the *lusts* of deceit, [23]and that you be renewed in the spirit of your *mind*, [24]and put on the new self, which in the likeness of God has been created in righteousness and holiness of the truth.

Ephesians 5:6, 8

Let no one deceive you with empty words, for because of these things the *wrath* of God comes upon *the sons of disobedience*. . . . [8]For you were *formerly* darkness, but now you are Light in the Lord; *walk* as children of Light.

Ephesians 6:12

For our struggle is not against flesh and blood, but against the rulers, against *the powers*, against the world forces of this darkness, against the spiritual forces of wickedness *in the heavenly places*.

OTHER PAULINE PARALLELS

Romans 3:23–24, 27

For all have *sinned* and fall short of the glory of God, [24]being justified as a *gift* by His *grace* through the redemption which is in Christ Jesus; . . . [27]Where then is *boasting*? It is excluded. By what kind of law? Of *works*? No, but by a law of *faith*.

Romans 9:22–24

What if God, although willing to demonstrate His *wrath* and to make His power known, endured with much patience vessels of wrath prepared for destruction? [23]And He did so to make known *the riches* of His glory upon vessels of *mercy*, which He *prepared beforehand* for glory, [24]even us, whom He also called, not from among Jews only, but also from among Gentiles.

Galatians 5:16

But I say, *walk* by the Spirit, and you will not carry out *the desire of the flesh*.

Colossians 1:21–22

And although you were *formerly* alienated and hostile in mind, engaged in evil deeds, [22]yet He has now reconciled you in His fleshly body through death, in order to present you before Him holy and blameless and beyond reproach.

Colossians 2:6

Therefore as you have received Christ Jesus the Lord, so *walk* in Him.

Colossians 2:12–13

. . . having been buried with Him in baptism, in which you were also *raised up with Him* through *faith* in the working of God, who raised Him from the dead. [13]When you were *dead in* your *transgressions* and the uncircumcision of your *flesh*, He *made* you *alive together with Him*, having forgiven us all our transgressions.

Colossians 3:1

Therefore if you have been *raised up with* Christ, keep seeking the things above, where Christ is, seated at the right hand of God.

2 Timothy 1:8–9

Join with me in suffering for the gospel according to the power of God, [9]who has *saved* us and called us with a holy calling, not according to our *works*, but according to His own purpose and *grace* which was granted us in Christ Jesus from all eternity.

Titus 3:3–5

For we also once were foolish ourselves, *disobedient*, deceived, enslaved to various *lusts* and pleasures, spending our life in malice and envy, hateful, hating one another. [4]But when the *kindness* of God our Savior and *His love* for mankind appeared, [5]He *saved* us, not on the basis of deeds which we have done in righteousness, but according to His *mercy*, by the washing of regeneration and renewing by the Holy Spirit.

OTHER BIBLICAL PARALLELS

John 12:31

"Now judgment is upon *this world*; now the ruler of this world will be cast out."

Acts 15:7, 11

After there had been much debate, Peter stood up and said to them, "Brethren, you know that in the early days God made a choice among you, that by my mouth the Gentiles would hear the word of the gospel and believe.... [11]But we believe that we are *saved* through the *grace* of the Lord Jesus, in the same way as they also are."

1 Peter 1:14–15

As obedient children, do not be conformed to the *former lusts* which were yours in your ignorance, [15]but like the Holy One who called you, be holy yourselves also in all your behavior.

NONCANONICAL PARALLELS

2 Enoch *[J] 29:4–5*

"But one from the order of the archangels deviated, together with the division that was under his authority. He thought up the impossible idea, that he might place his throne higher than the clouds . . . and that he might become equal to my power. [5]And I hurled him from the height, together with his angels. And he was flying around in *the air*, above the Bottomless."

Ephesians 2:11–16

Therefore remember that formerly you, the Gentiles in the flesh, who are called "Uncircumcision" by the so-called "Circumcision," which is performed in the flesh by human hands— [12]remember that you were at that time separate from Christ, excluded from the commonwealth of Israel, and strangers to the covenants of promise, having no hope and without God in the world. [13]But now in Christ Jesus you who formerly were far off have been brought near by the blood of Christ. [14]For He Himself is our peace, who made both groups into one and broke down the barrier of the dividing wall, [15]by abolishing in His flesh the enmity, which is the Law of commandments contained in ordinances, so that in Himself He might make the two into one new man, thus establishing peace, [16]and might reconcile them both in one body to God through the cross, by it having put to death the enmity.

EPHESIANS PARALLELS

Ephesians 3:4–6

By referring to this, when you read you can understand my insight into the mystery of Christ, [5]which in other generations was not made known to the sons of men, as it has now been revealed to His holy apostles and prophets in the Spirit; [6]to be specific, that *the Gentiles* are fellow heirs and fellow members of the *body*, and fellow partakers of the *promise* in Christ Jesus through the gospel.

Ephesians 4:1, 3

Walk in a manner worthy of the calling with which you have been called, . . . [3]being diligent to preserve the unity of the Spirit in the bond of *peace.*

Ephesians 4:17–18

So this I say, and affirm together with the Lord, that you walk no longer just as *the Gentiles* also walk, in the futility of their mind, [18]being darkened in their understanding, *excluded* from the life of God because of the ignorance that is in them, because of the hardness of their heart.

Ephesians 4:22–24

. . . that, in reference to your *former* manner of life, you lay aside the old self, which is being corrupted in accordance with the lusts of deceit, [23]and that you be renewed in the spirit of your mind, [24]and put on the *new* self, which in the likeness of God has been created in righteousness and holiness of the truth.

Ephesians 5:8

You were *formerly* darkness, but now you are Light in the Lord; walk as children of Light.

OTHER PAULINE PARALLELS

Romans 2:28–29

For he is not a Jew who is one outwardly, nor is *circumcision* that which is outward in *the flesh.* [29]But he is a Jew who is one inwardly; and circumcision is that which is of the heart, by the Spirit, not by the letter; and his praise is not from men, but from God.

Romans 9:3–4

. . . my brethren, my kinsmen according to *the flesh,* [4]who are *Israelites,* to whom belongs the adoption as sons, and the glory and the *covenants* and the giving of *the Law* and the temple service and the *promises.*

2 Corinthians 5:18–19

Now all these things are from God, who *reconciled* us to Himself through Christ and gave us the ministry of reconciliation, [19]namely, that God was in Christ reconciling the world to Himself, not counting their trespasses against them, and He has committed to us the word of reconciliation.

Galatians 4:8

However *at that time,* when you did not know God, you were slaves to those which by nature are no gods.

Galatians 6:15

For neither is *circumcision* anything, nor *uncircumcision,* but a *new* creation.

Colossians 1:19–22

For it was the Father's good pleasure for all the fullness to dwell in Him, [20]and through Him to *reconcile* all things to Himself, having made *peace* through *the blood* of His *cross;* through Him, I say, whether things on earth or things in heaven. [21]And although you were *formerly* alienated and hostile in mind, engaged in evil deeds, [22]yet He has now reconciled you in His fleshly *body* through death, in order to present you before Him holy and blameless and beyond reproach.

Colossians 2:13–14

When you were dead in your transgressions and the *uncircumcision* of your *flesh,* He made you alive together with Him, having forgiven us all our transgressions, [14]having canceled out the certificate of debt consisting of decrees against us, which was hostile to us; and He has taken it out of the way, having nailed it to *the cross.*

Colossians 3:9–11

Do not lie to one another, since you laid aside the old self with its evil practices, [10]and have put on the *new* self who is being renewed to a true knowledge according to the image of the One who created him— [11]a renewal in which there is no distinction between Greek and Jew, *circumcised* and *uncircumcised,* barbarian, Scythian, slave and freeman, but Christ is all, and in all.

1 Thessalonians 4:13

But we do not want you to be uninformed, brethren, about those who are asleep, so that you will not grieve as do the rest who *have no hope.*

OTHER BIBLICAL PARALLELS

1 Kings 2:3

"Keep the charge of the LORD your God, to walk in His ways, to keep His statutes, His *commandments,* His *ordinances,* and His testimonies, according to what is written in *the Law* of Moses, that you may succeed in all that you do and wherever you turn."

Micah 5:4–5
And He will arise and shepherd His flock In the strength of the LORD, In the majesty of the name of the LORD His God. And they will remain, Because at that time He will be great To the ends of the earth. [5]This One will be *our peace.*

Acts 2:39
"For the *promise* is for you and your children and for all who are *far off,* as many as the Lord our God will call to Himself."

Letter of Aristeas *139, 142*
In his wisdom the legislator . . . surrounded us with unbroken palisades and iron *walls* to prevent our mixing with any of the other peoples in any matter, being thus kept pure in body and soul, preserved from false beliefs. . . . [142]So . . . he hedged us in on all sides with strict observances connected with meat and drink and touch and hearing and sight, after the manner of *the Law.*

Josephus, The Jewish War *5.193*
Around the second court of the temple went a stone *wall* of separation, three cubits high and very elegantly made. On it stood at regular intervals slabs, some in Greek letters, others in Latin, declaring the law of purity, that no foreigner was allowed to enter the holy place.

Ephesians 2:17–22

AND HE CAME AND PREACHED PEACE TO YOU WHO WERE FAR AWAY, AND PEACE TO THOSE WHO WERE NEAR; [18]for through Him we both have our access in one Spirit to the Father. [19]So then you are no longer strangers and aliens, but you are fellow citizens with the saints, and are of God's household, [20]having been built on the foundation of the apostles and prophets, Christ Jesus Himself being the corner stone, [21]in whom the whole building, being fitted together, is growing into a holy temple in the Lord, [22]in whom you also are being built together into a dwelling of God in the Spirit.

Ephesians 3:11–12
This was in accordance with the eternal purpose which He carried out in Christ Jesus our Lord, [12]in whom we have boldness and confident *access* through faith in Him.

Ephesians 3:14–17
For this reason I bow my knees before *the Father,* [15]from whom every family in heaven and on earth derives its name, [16]that He would grant you, according to the riches of His glory, to be strengthened with power through His *Spirit* in the inner man, [17]so that Christ may *dwell* in your hearts through faith; and that you, being rooted and grounded in love . . .

Ephesians 4:11–12
And He gave some as *apostles,* and some as prophets, and some as evangelists, and some as pastors and teachers, [12]for the equipping of the saints for the work of service, to the *building* up of the body of Christ.

Romans 5:1–2
Therefore, having been justified by faith, we have *peace* with God through our Lord Jesus Christ, [2]through whom also we have obtained our introduction by faith into this grace in which we stand; and we exult in hope of the glory of God.

1 Corinthians 3:11, 16–17
For no man can lay a *foundation* other than the one which is laid, which is Jesus Christ. . . . [16]Do you not know that you are *a temple* of God and that *the Spirit* of God *dwells* in you? [17]If any man destroys the temple of God, God will destroy him, for the temple of God is *holy,* and that is what you are.

2 Corinthians 6:16
Or what agreement has the temple of God with idols? For we are the *temple* of the living God; just as God said, "I WILL *DWELL* IN THEM AND WALK AMONG THEM; AND I WILL BE THEIR GOD, AND THEY SHALL BE MY PEOPLE."

Philippians 3:20
For our *citizenship* is in heaven, from which also we eagerly wait for a Savior, the Lord Jesus Christ.

Colossians 2:6–7
Therefore as you have received Christ Jesus the Lord, so walk in Him, [7]having been firmly rooted and now being *built* up in Him and established in your faith, just as you were instructed, and overflowing with gratitude.

Colossians 2:19
. . . and not holding fast to the head, from whom the entire body, being supplied and held together by the joints and ligaments, *grows* with a growth which is from God.

1 Timothy 3:15
In case I am delayed, I write so that you will know how one ought to conduct himself in the *household of God*, which is the church of the living God, the pillar and support of the truth.

OTHER BIBLICAL PARALLELS

Psalm 118:22
The stone which the builders rejected Has become the chief *corner stone.*

Isaiah 28:16
Therefore thus says the Lord GOD, "Behold, I am laying in Zion a stone, a tested stone, A costly *cornerstone* for the *foundation*, firmly placed. He who believes in it will not be disturbed."

Isaiah 57:18–19
"I have seen his ways, but I will heal him; I will lead him and restore comfort to him and to his mourners, [19]Creating the praise of the lips. *Peace, peace to* him *who* is *far* and *to* him *who* is *near*," Says the LORD, "and I will heal him."

John 14:23
Jesus answered and said to him, "If anyone loves Me, he will keep My word; and My Father will love him, and We will come to him and make Our abode with him."

Hebrews 3:6
Christ was faithful as a Son over His *house*—whose house we are, if we hold fast

our confidence and the boast of our hope firm until the end.

1 Peter 2:4–6
And coming to Him as to a living stone which has been rejected by men, but is choice and precious in the sight of God, [5]you also, as living stones, are being *built* up as a spiritual *house* for a *holy* priesthood, to offer up spiritual sacrifices acceptable to God through Jesus Christ. [6]For this is contained in Scripture: "BEHOLD, I LAY IN ZION A CHOICE STONE, A PRECIOUS *COR-NER stone*, AND HE WHO BELIEVES IN HIM WILL NOT BE DISAPPOINTED."

NONCANONICAL PARALLELS

The Rule of the Community *(1QS) 8.5–7*
The Community council shall be founded on truth, like an everlasting plantation, a *holy house* for Israel and the *foundation* of the holy of [6]holies for Aaron, true witnesses for the judgment and chosen by the will (of God) to atone for the earth and to render [7]the wicked their retribution. It [the Community] will be the tested rampart, the precious *cornerstone.*

Ephesians 3:1–7

For this reason I, Paul, the prisoner of Christ Jesus for the sake of you Gentiles— [2]if indeed you have heard of the stewardship of God's grace which was given to me for you; [3]that by revelation there was made known to me the mystery, as I wrote before in brief. [4]By referring to this, when you read you can understand my insight into the mystery of Christ, [5]which in other generations was not made known to the sons of men, as it has now been revealed to His holy apostles and prophets in the Spirit; [6]to be specific, that the Gentiles are fellow heirs and fellow members of the body, and fellow partakers of the promise in Christ Jesus through the gospel, [7]of which I was made a minister, according to the gift of God's grace which was given to me according to the working of His power.

EPHESIANS PARALLELS

Ephesians 1:9–11, 13–14
He *made known* to us the *mystery* of His will, according to His kind intention which

He purposed in Him [10]with a view to an administration suitable to the fullness of the times, that is, the summing up of all things in Christ, things in the heavens and things on the earth. In Him [11]also we have obtained an *inheritance*, having been predestined according to His purpose who works all things after the counsel of His will. . . . [13]In Him, you also, after listening to the message of truth, *the gospel* of your salvation—having also believed, you were sealed in Him with the Holy Spirit of *promise*, [14]who is given as a pledge of our inheritance, with a view to the redemption of God's own possession, to the praise of His glory.

Ephesians 4:1
Therefore *I, the prisoner* of the Lord, implore you to walk in a manner worthy of the calling with which you have been called.

Ephesians 6:19–20
Pray on my behalf, that utterance may be given to me in the opening of my mouth, to make known with boldness the *mystery* of *the gospel*, [20]for which I am an ambassador in chains; that in proclaiming it I may speak boldly, as I ought to speak.

OTHER PAULINE PARALLELS

Romans 12:4–5
For just as we have many *members* in one *body* and all the members do not have the same function, [5]so we, who are many, are one body in Christ, and individually members one of another.

Romans 15:15–16
But I have written very boldly to you on some points so as to remind you again, because of the *grace* that was *given me* from God, [16]to be *a minister* of Christ Jesus to *the Gentiles*, ministering as a priest *the gospel* of God, so that my offering of the Gentiles may become acceptable, sanctified by the Holy Spirit.

Romans 16:25–26
Now to Him who is able to establish you according to my *gospel* and the preaching of Jesus Christ, according to the *revelation* of the *mystery* which has been kept secret for long ages past, [26]but now is manifested, and by the Scriptures of the *prophets,* according

to the commandment of the eternal God, has been *made known* to all the nations, leading to obedience of faith . . .

1 Corinthians 9:16–17
For if I preach *the gospel*, I have nothing to boast of, for I am under compulsion; for woe is me if I do not preach the gospel. [17]For if I do this voluntarily, I have a reward; but if against my will, I have a *stewardship* entrusted to me.

Galatians 1:11–12
For I would have you know, brethren, that *the gospel* which was preached by me is not according to man. [12]For I neither received it from man, nor was I taught it, but I received it through a *revelation* of Jesus Christ.

Galatians 3:28–29
There is neither Jew nor Greek, there is neither slave nor free man, there is neither male nor female; for you are all one in Christ Jesus. [29]And if you belong to Christ, then you are Abraham's descendants, *heirs* according to *promise.*

Philippians 1:7
For it is only right for me to feel this way about you all, because I have you in my heart, since both in my *imprisonment* and in the defense and confirmation of *the gospel*, you all are *partakers* of *grace* with me.

Colossians 1:23–27, 29
. . . if indeed you continue in the faith firmly established and steadfast, and not moved away from the hope of *the gospel* that you have heard, which was proclaimed in all creation under heaven, and of which *I, Paul*, was made a minister. [24]Now I rejoice in my sufferings for your sake, and in my flesh I do my share on behalf of His *body*, which is the church, in filling up what is lacking in Christ's afflictions. [25]Of this church *I was made a minister* according to the *stewardship* from God bestowed on me for your benefit, so that I might fully carry out the preaching of the word of God, [26]that is, the *mystery* which has been hidden from the past ages and *generations*, but has now been manifested to His saints, [27]to whom God willed to make known what is the riches of the glory of this mystery among *the Gentiles*, which is Christ in you, the hope of glory. . . . [29]For this purpose also I labor, striving

according to *His power*, which mightily *works* within me.

Colossians 4:3

. . . praying at the same time for us as well, that God will open up to us a door for the word, so that we may speak forth *the mystery of Christ*, for which I have also been *imprisoned*.

2 Timothy 1:8

Therefore do not be ashamed of the testimony of our Lord or of me His *prisoner*, but join with me in suffering for *the gospel* according to the *power* of God.

Philemon 1

Paul, a *prisoner* of Christ Jesus, and Timothy our brother, To Philemon our beloved brother and fellow worker . . .

Qumran Hymns (1QH) 20[12].11–13

And I, the Instructor, have known you, my God, [12]through *the spirit* which you gave to me, and I have listened loyally to your wonderful secret through your holy spirit. [13]You have opened within me knowledge of the *mystery* of your wisdom, the source of your *power*.

Ephesians 3:8–13

To me, the very least of all saints, this grace was given, to preach to the Gentiles the unfathomable riches of Christ, [9]and to bring to light what is the administration of the mystery which for ages has been hidden in God who created all things; [10]so that the manifold wisdom of God might now be made known through the church to the rulers and the authorities in the heavenly places. [11]This was in accordance with the eternal purpose which He carried out in Christ Jesus our Lord, [12]in whom we have boldness and confident access through faith in Him. [13]Therefore I ask you not to lose heart at my tribulations on your behalf, for they are your glory.

Ephesians 1:7–8

In Him we have redemption through His blood, the forgiveness of our trespasses, according to the *riches* of His *grace* [8]which He lavished on us.

Ephesians 1:9–11

He *made known* to us the *mystery* of His will, according to His kind intention which He purposed in Him [10]with a view to an *administration* suitable to the fullness of the times, that is, the summing up of *all things* in Christ, things *in the heavens* and things on the earth. In Him [11]also we have obtained an inheritance, having been predestined according to His *purpose* who works all things after the counsel of His will.

Ephesians 1:18–22

I pray that the eyes of your heart may be enlightened, so that you will know what is the hope of His calling, what are the *riches* of the *glory* of His inheritance in the *saints,* [19]and what is the surpassing greatness of His power toward us who believe. These are in accordance with the working of the strength of His might [20]which He brought about in Christ, when He raised Him from the dead and seated Him at His right hand *in the heavenly places,* [21]far above all *rule* and *authority* and power and dominion, and every name that is named, not only in this age but also in the one to come. [22]And He put all things in subjection under His feet, and gave Him as head over *all things* to *the church*.

Ephesians 2:17–18

AND HE CAME AND *PREACHED* PEACE TO YOU WHO WERE FAR AWAY, AND PEACE TO THOSE WHO WERE NEAR; [18]for through Him we both have our *access* in one Spirit to the Father.

Ephesians 6:12

For our struggle is not against flesh and blood, but against the *rulers*, against the powers, against the world forces of this darkness, against the spiritual forces of wickedness *in the heavenly places*.

Ephesians 6:19

Pray on my behalf, that utterance may be given to me in the opening of my mouth, to make known with *boldness* the *mystery* of the gospel.

OTHER PAULINE PARALLELS

1 Corinthians 2:7
We speak God's *wisdom* in a *mystery*, the *hidden* wisdom which God predestined before the *ages* to our *glory*.

1 Corinthians 15:9
For I am *the least* of the apostles, and not fit to be called an apostle, because I persecuted *the church* of God.

2 Corinthians 4:1–2
Therefore, since we have this ministry, as we received mercy, we do *not lose heart,* [2]but we have renounced the things hidden because of shame, not walking in craftiness or adulterating the word of God, but by the manifestation of truth commending ourselves to every man's conscience in the sight of God.

Galatians 1:15–16
But when God, who had set me apart even from my mother's womb and called me through His *grace,* was pleased [16]to reveal His Son in me so that I might *preach* Him among *the Gentiles,* I did not immediately consult with flesh and blood.

Colossians 1:24–28
Now I rejoice in my sufferings for your sake, and in my flesh I do my share on behalf of His body, which is *the church,* in filling up what is lacking in Christ's afflictions. [25]Of this church I was made a minister according to the stewardship from God bestowed on me for your benefit, so that I might fully carry out the *preaching* of the word of God, [26]that is, the *mystery* which has been *hidden* from the past *ages* and generations, but has now been manifested to His *saints,* [27]to whom God willed to *make known* what is the *riches* of the glory of this mystery among *the Gentiles,* which is Christ in you, the hope of *glory.* [28]We proclaim Him, admonishing every man and teaching every man with all *wisdom,* so that we may present every man complete in Christ.

1 Timothy 1:12–14
I thank Christ Jesus our Lord, who has strengthened me, because He considered me faithful, putting me into service, [13]even though I was formerly a blasphemer and a persecutor and a violent aggressor. Yet I was shown mercy because I acted ignorantly in unbelief; [14]and the *grace* of our Lord was more than abundant, with the *faith* and love which are found in Christ Jesus.

2 Timothy 2:10
For this reason I endure all things for the sake of those who are chosen, so that they also may obtain the salvation which is in Christ Jesus and with it eternal *glory.*

OTHER BIBLICAL PARALLELS

Acts 9:15
But the Lord said to him, "Go, for he is a chosen instrument of Mine, to bear My name before *the Gentiles* and kings and the sons of Israel."

Hebrews 4:16
Therefore let us draw near with *confidence* to the throne of grace, so that we may receive mercy and find *grace* to help in time of need.

1 Peter 1:10–12
As to this salvation, the prophets who prophesied of the *grace* that would come to you made careful searches and inquiries, [11]seeking to know what person or time the Spirit of Christ within them was indicating as He predicted the sufferings of Christ and the glories to follow. [12]It was revealed to them that they were not serving themselves, but you, in these things which now have been announced to you through those who *preached* the gospel to you by the Holy Spirit sent from heaven—things into which angels long to look.

NONCANONICAL PARALLELS

2 Enoch [J] 24:3
For not even to my angels have I explained my secrets, nor related to them their origin, nor my endlessness ⟨and inconceivableness⟩, as I devise the creatures, as I am *making* them *known* to you today.

Qumran Hymns (1QH) 9[1].10, 13–14, 21, 24
You have stretched out the heavens for your *glory.* Everything . . . according to your

approval: powerful spirits, according to their laws. . . . [13] . . . You have *created* the earth with your strength, [14]seas and deeps, . . . you have founded them with your *wisdom*. . . . [21]These things I know through your knowledge, for you opened my ears to wondrous *mysteries*, . . . [24] . . . all the incessant periods, in the eras of the number of everlasting years in all in their predetermined times, and nothing will be *hidden*.

Ephesians 3:14–21

For this reason I bow my knees before the Father, [15]from whom every family in heaven and on earth derives its name, [16]that He would grant you, according to the riches of His glory, to be strengthened with power through His Spirit in the inner man, [17]so that Christ may dwell in your hearts through faith; and that you, being rooted and grounded in love, [18]may be able to comprehend with all the saints what is the breadth and length and height and depth, [19]and to know the love of Christ which surpasses knowledge, that you may be filled up to all the fullness of God. [20]Now to Him who is able to do far more abundantly beyond all that we ask or think, according to the power that works within us, [21]to Him be the glory in the church and in Christ Jesus to all generations forever and ever. Amen.

EPHESIANS PARALLELS

Ephesians 1:15–19

For this reason I too, having heard of the *faith* in the Lord Jesus which exists among you and your *love* for all *the saints*, [16]do not cease giving thanks for you, while making mention of you in my prayers; [17]that the God of our Lord Jesus Christ, *the Father* of glory, may give to you a spirit of wisdom and of revelation in the *knowledge* of Him. [18]I pray that the eyes of your heart may be enlightened, so that you will know what is the hope of His calling, what are *the riches of* the *glory* of His inheritance in the saints, [19]and what is the surpassing greatness of His *power* toward us who believe.

Ephesians 1:22–23

And He put all things in subjection under His feet, and gave Him as head over all things to *the church*, [23]which is His body, the *fullness* of Him who fills all in all.

Ephesians 2:19, 21–22

So then you are no longer strangers and aliens, but you are fellow citizens with *the saints*, and are of God's household, . . . [21]in whom the whole building, being fitted together, is growing into a holy temple in the Lord, [22]in whom you also are being built together into a *dwelling* of God in the *Spirit*.

Ephesians 3:6–7

The Gentiles are fellow heirs and fellow members of the body, and fellow partakers of the promise in Christ Jesus through the gospel, [7]of which I was made a minister, according to the gift of God's grace which was given to me according to the *working* of His *power*.

OTHER PAULINE PARALLELS

Romans 8:9

However, you are not in the flesh but in the *Spirit*, if indeed the Spirit of God *dwells* in you. But if anyone does not have the Spirit of Christ, he does not belong to Him.

Romans 8:38–39

For I am convinced that neither death, nor life, nor angels, nor principalities, nor things present, nor things to come, nor powers, [39]nor *height*, nor *depth*, nor any other created thing, will be able to separate us from the *love* of God, which is in Christ Jesus our Lord.

Romans 11:36

For from Him and through Him and to Him are all things. *To Him be the glory forever. Amen.*

2 Corinthians 4:16

Therefore we do not lose heart, but though our outer man is decaying, yet our *inner man* is being renewed day by day.

Galatians 1:3–5

Grace to you and peace from God our Father and the Lord Jesus Christ, [4]who gave Himself for our sins so that He might rescue us from this present evil age, according to the will of our God and Father, [5]to whom *be the glory forevermore. Amen.*

Colossians 1:9, 11

For this reason also, since the day we heard of it, we have not ceased to pray for you and to ask *that you may be filled* with the *knowledge* of His will in all spiritual wisdom and understanding, . . . [11]*strengthened with* all *power*, according to His glorious might, for the attaining of all steadfastness and patience.

Colossians 1:27–29

. . . to whom God willed to make known what is *the riches of* the *glory* of this mystery among the Gentiles, which is Christ in you, the hope of glory. [28]We proclaim Him, admonishing every man and teaching every man with all wisdom, so that we may present every man complete in Christ. [29]For this purpose also I labor, striving according to His *power*, which mightily *works* within me.

Colossians 2:1–2

For I want you to know how great a struggle I have on your behalf and for those who are at Laodicea, and for all those who have not personally seen my face, [2]that their *hearts* may be encouraged, having been knit together in *love*, and attaining to all the wealth that comes from the full assurance of understanding, resulting in a true *knowledge* of God's mystery, that is, Christ Himself.

Colossians 2:6–7, 9–10

Therefore as you have received Christ Jesus the Lord, so walk in Him, [7]having been firmly *rooted* and now being built up in Him and established in your *faith*, just as you were instructed, and overflowing with gratitude. . . . [9]For in Him all the *fullness* of Deity dwells in bodily form, [10]and in Him you have been made complete, and He is the head over all rule and authority.

1 Timothy 1:17

Now to the King eternal, immortal, invisible, the only God, be honor and *glory forever and ever. Amen.*

OTHER BIBLICAL PARALLELS

Job 11:7–9

"Can you discover the *depths* of God? Can you discover the limits of the Almighty? [8]They are *high* as the heavens, what can you do? Deeper than Sheol, what can you *know*? [9]Its measure is *longer* than the earth And *broader* than the sea."

Psalm 147:4

He counts the number of the stars; He gives *names* to all of them.

NONCANONICAL PARALLELS

Sirach 1:3

The *height* of heaven, the *breadth* of the earth, the abyss, and wisdom—who can search them out?

Philo, On the Special Laws 2.165

There is one whom all agree, Greeks as well as barbarians, in acknowledging as the supreme *Father*, of both gods and mortals, and as the Creator of the entire cosmos.

Calling on the Living God (PGM 4.959–72)

I call upon you, the living god, [960]fiery, invisible begetter of light, . . . give your *strength*, rouse your daimon, [965]enter into this fire, fill it with a divine *spirit*, and show me your might. Let there be opened for me the house of the all-powerful god. . . . [970]Let there be light, *breadth*, *depth*, *length*, *height*, brightness, and let him who is inside shine through.

Ephesians 4:1–6

Therefore I, the prisoner of the Lord, implore you to walk in a manner worthy of the calling with which you have been called, [2]with all humility and gentleness, with patience, showing tolerance for one another in love, [3]being diligent to preserve the unity of the Spirit in the bond of peace. [4]There is one body and one Spirit, just as also you were called in one hope of your calling; [5]one Lord, one faith, one baptism, [6]one God and Father of all who is over all and through all and in all.

EPHESIANS PARALLELS

Ephesians 1:18

I pray that the eyes of your heart may be enlightened, so that you will know what is the *hope of* His *calling*, what are the riches of the glory of His inheritance in the saints.

Ephesians 2:14–16, 18

For He Himself is our *peace*, who made both groups into one and broke down the barrier of the dividing wall, [15]by abolishing in His flesh the enmity, which is the Law of commandments contained in ordinances, so that in Himself He might make the two into one new man, thus establishing peace, [16]and might reconcile them both in *one body* to God through the cross, by it having put to death the enmity. . . . [18]For through Him we both have our access in *one Spirit* to the Father.

Ephesians 3:1

For this reason *I*, Paul, *the prisoner* of Christ Jesus for the sake of you Gentiles . . .

OTHER PAULINE PARALLELS

Romans 8:28

And we know that God causes all things to work together for good to those who love God, to those who are *called* according to His purpose.

Romans 11:36

For from Him and *through* Him and to Him are *all* things. To Him be the glory forever. Amen.

1 Corinthians 7:17

Only, as the Lord has assigned to each one, as God has *called* each, in this manner let him *walk*. And so I direct in all the churches.

1 Corinthians 8:6

Yet for us there is but *one God*, the *Father*, from whom are *all* things and we exist for Him; and *one Lord*, Jesus Christ, by whom are all things, and we exist *through* Him.

1 Corinthians 12:12–13

For even as the body is one and yet has many members, and all the members of the body, though they are many, are *one body*, so also is Christ. [13]For by *one Spirit* we were all baptized into one body, whether Jews or Greeks, whether slaves or free, and we were all made to drink of one Spirit.

1 Corinthians 15:28

When all things are subjected to Him, then the Son Himself also will be subjected to the

One who subjected all things to Him, so that *God* may be *all in all*.

2 Corinthians 13:11

Finally, brethren, rejoice, be made complete, be comforted, be like-minded, live in *peace*; and the God of *love* and peace will be with you.

Galatians 5:22

But the fruit of the Spirit is *love*, joy, *peace*, *patience*, kindness, goodness, faithfulness.

Philippians 1:27

Only conduct yourselves *in a manner worthy* of the gospel of Christ, so that whether I come and see you or remain absent, I will hear of you that you are standing firm in *one spirit*, with one mind striving together for the *faith* of the gospel.

Colossians 1:9–10

For this reason also, since the day we heard of it, we have not ceased to pray for you and to ask that you may be filled with the knowledge of His will in all spiritual wisdom and understanding, [10]so that you will *walk in a manner worthy* of the Lord, to please Him in all respects, bearing fruit in every good work and increasing in the knowledge of God.

Colossians 3:12–15

So, as those who have been chosen of God, holy and beloved, put on a heart of compassion, kindness, *humility, gentleness* and *patience*; [13]bearing with one another, and forgiving each other, whoever has a complaint against anyone; just as the Lord forgave you, so also should you. [14]Beyond all these things put on *love*, which is the perfect *bond* of *unity*. [15]Let the *peace* of Christ rule in your hearts, to which indeed you were *called* in *one body*; and be thankful.

1 Thessalonians 2:11–12

You know how we were exhorting and encouraging and imploring each one of you as a father would his own children, [12]so that you would *walk in a manner worthy* of the God who *calls* you into His own kingdom and glory.

2 Thessalonians 1:11

To this end also we pray for you always, that our God will count you *worthy* of your *call-*

ing, and fulfill every desire for goodness and the work of faith with power.

1 Timothy 2:5–6

For there is *one God,* and one mediator also between God and men, the man Christ Jesus, [6]who gave Himself as a ransom for all, the testimony given at the proper time.

OTHER BIBLICAL PARALLELS

Malachi 2:10

Do we not all have *one father*? Has not *one God* created us? Why do we deal treacherously each against his brother so as to profane the covenant of our fathers?

NONCANONICAL PARALLELS

2 Baruch 48:23–24

We are all a people of the Name; [24]we, who received one Law from the *One.* And that Law that is among us will help us, and that excellent wisdom which is in us will support us.

Philo, On the Virtues 35

The highest and greatest source of their [the Jews'] unanimity is their belief that there is *one God,* through which, as from a fountain, they feel a *love* for one another.

Ephesians 4:7–16

But to each one of us grace was given according to the measure of Christ's gift. [8]Therefore it says, "WHEN HE ASCENDED ON HIGH, HE LED CAPTIVE A HOST OF CAPTIVES, AND HE GAVE GIFTS TO MEN." [9](Now this expression, "He ascended," what does it mean except that He also had descended into the lower parts of the earth? [10]He who descended is Himself also He who ascended far above all the heavens, so that He might fill all things.) [11]And He gave some as apostles, and some as prophets, and some as evangelists, and some as pastors and teachers, [12]for the equipping of the saints for the work of service, to the building up of the body of Christ; [13]until we all attain to the unity of the faith, and of the knowledge of the Son of God, to a mature man, to the measure of the stature which belongs to the fullness of Christ. [14]As a result, we are no longer to be children, tossed here and there by waves and carried

about by every wind of doctrine, by the trickery of men, by craftiness in deceitful scheming; [15]but speaking the truth in love, we are to grow up in all aspects into Him who is the head, even Christ, [16]from whom the whole body, being fitted and held together by what every joint supplies, according to the proper working of each individual part, causes the growth of the body for the building up of itself in love.

EPHESIANS PARALLELS

Ephesians 1:22–23

And He put all things in subjection under His feet, and gave Him as *head* over all things to the church, [23]which is His *body,* the *fullness* of Him who *fills all* in all.

Ephesians 2:20–22

. . . Christ Jesus Himself being the corner stone, [21]in whom the whole building, *being fitted together,* is *growing* into a holy temple in the Lord, [22]in whom you also are being *built* together into a dwelling of God in the Spirit.

Ephesians 3:17–19

. . . and that you, being rooted and grounded in *love,* [18]may be able to comprehend with all *the saints* what is the breadth and length and height and depth, [19]and to know the love of Christ which surpasses *knowledge,* that you may be filled up to all the *fullness* of God.

Ephesians 6:11

Put on the full armor of God, so that you will be able to stand firm against the *schemes* of the devil.

OTHER PAULINE PARALLELS

Romans 10:6–7

But the righteousness based on faith speaks as follows: "DO NOT SAY IN YOUR HEART, 'WHO WILL *ASCEND* INTO HEAVEN?' (that is, to bring Christ down), [7]or 'WHO WILL *DESCEND* INTO THE ABYSS?' (that is, to bring Christ up from the dead)."

Romans 12:3–7

For through the grace given to me I say to everyone among you not to think more highly of himself than he ought to think; but to think so as to have sound judgment, as

God has allotted to each a *measure* of faith. [4]For just as we have many members in one *body* and all the members do not have the same function, [5]so we, who are many, are one body in Christ, and *individually* members one of another. [6]Since we have *gifts* that differ according to the *grace* given to us, each of us is to exercise them accordingly: if *prophecy*, according to the proportion of his faith; [7]if service, in his serving; or he who *teaches*, in his teaching.

1 Corinthians 12:4–5, 7, 11

Now there are varieties of *gifts*, but the same Spirit. [5]And there are varieties of ministries, and the same Lord. . . . [7]But to each one is given the manifestation of the Spirit for the common good. . . . [11]But one and the same Spirit works all these things, distributing to each one *individually* just as He wills.

1 Corinthians 12:27–28

Now you are *Christ's body*, and *individually* members of it. [28]And God has appointed in the church, first *apostles*, second *prophets*, third *teachers*, then miracles, then *gifts* of healings, helps, administrations, various kinds of tongues.

1 Corinthians 14:20

Brethren, do not be *children* in your thinking; yet in evil be infants, but in your thinking be *mature*.

Colossians 1:18

He is also *head* of the *body*, the church; and He is the beginning, the firstborn from the dead, so that He Himself will come to have first place in everything.

Colossians 2:19

. . . and not holding fast to the *head*, from whom the entire *body*, being *supplied* and *held together* by the *joints* and ligaments, grows with a *growth* which is from God.

OTHER BIBLICAL PARALLELS

Psalm 68:18

You have *ascended on high*, You have *led captive* Your *captives*; You have received *gifts* among *men*, Even among the rebellious also, that the LORD God may dwell there.

Matthew 12:40

"Just as JONAH WAS THREE DAYS AND THREE NIGHTS IN THE BELLY OF THE SEA MONSTER, so will the Son of Man be three days and three nights in the heart of *the earth*."

Acts 1:11

They also said, "Men of Galilee, why do you stand looking into the sky? This Jesus, who has been taken up from you into *heaven*, will come in just the same way as you have watched Him go into heaven."

1 Peter 3:18–19

For Christ also died for sins once for all, the just for the unjust, so that He might bring us to God, having been put to death in the flesh, but made alive in the spirit; [19]in which also He went and made proclamation to the spirits now in prison.

Jude 12–13

These are the men who are hidden reefs in your love feasts when they feast with you without fear, caring for themselves; clouds without water, carried along by *winds*; autumn trees without fruit, doubly dead, uprooted; [13]wild *waves* of the sea, casting up their own shame like foam; wandering stars, for whom the black darkness has been reserved forever.

NONCANONICAL PARALLELS

Philo, On Rewards and Punishments *125*

The one who is excellent, whether an individual or a people, will be the *head* of the human race, and all others will be like limbs of a *body* drawing life from the powers that are in the head and top.

Philo, Questions and Answers on Genesis *4.29*

[A human being] is not wont to be divinely inspired at all times; rather, after being inspired for some time he then goes and returns to himself. . . . And this is what is said of the prophet [Moses]: his *descent* and *ascent* reveal the swift turning and change of his thoughts.

So this I say, and affirm together with the Lord, that you walk no longer just as the Gentiles also walk, in the futility of their mind, [18]being darkened in their understanding, excluded from the life of God because of the ignorance that is in them, because of the hardness of their heart; [19]and they, having become callous, have given themselves over to sensuality for the practice of every kind of impurity with greediness. [20]But you did not learn Christ in this way, [21]if indeed you have heard Him and have been taught in Him, just as truth is in Jesus, [22]that, in reference to your former manner of life, you lay aside the old self, which is being corrupted in accordance with the lusts of deceit, [23]and that you be renewed in the spirit of your mind, [24]and put on the new self, which in the likeness of God has been created in righteousness and holiness of the truth.

EPHESIANS PARALLELS

Ephesians 2:1–3

And you were dead in your trespasses and sins, [2]in which you *formerly walked* according to the course of this world, according to the prince of the power of the air, of the spirit that is now working in the sons of disobedience. [3]Among them we too all formerly lived in the *lusts* of our flesh, indulging the desires of the flesh and of the *mind*, and were by nature children of wrath, even as the rest.

Ephesians 2:11–12, 14–15

Therefore remember that *formerly* you, *the Gentiles* in the flesh, who are called "Uncircumcision" by the so-called "Circumcision," which is performed in the flesh by human hands— [12]remember that you were at that time separate from Christ, *excluded* from the commonwealth of Israel, and strangers to the covenants of promise, having no hope and without God in the world. . . . [14]For He Himself is our peace, who made both groups into one and broke down the barrier of the dividing wall, [15]by abolishing in His flesh the enmity, which is the Law of commandments contained in ordinances, so that in Himself He might make the two into one *new* man, thus establishing peace.

Romans 1:21, 24

For even though they knew God, they did not honor Him as God or give thanks, but they became *futile* in their speculations, and their foolish *heart* was *darkened*. . . . [24]Therefore God gave them over in the *lusts* of their hearts to *impurity*, so that their bodies would be dishonored among them.

Romans 6:6

. . . knowing this, that our *old self* was crucified with Him, in order that our body of sin might be done away with, so that we would no longer be slaves to sin.

Romans 12:2

And do not be conformed to this world, but be transformed by the *renewing* of *your mind*, so that you may prove what the will of God is, that which is good and acceptable and perfect.

Romans 13:14

But *put on* the Lord Jesus Christ, and make no provision for the flesh in regard to its *lusts*.

Galatians 3:27

For all of you who were baptized into Christ have clothed yourselves with Christ.

Colossians 1:21–22

And although you were *formerly* alienated and hostile in *mind*, engaged in evil deeds, [22]yet He has now reconciled you in His fleshly body through death, in order to present you before Him *holy* and blameless and beyond reproach.

Colossians 3:5–10

Therefore consider the members of your earthly body as dead to immorality, *impurity*, passion, evil desire, and *greed*, which amounts to idolatry. [6]For it is because of these things that the wrath of God will come upon the sons of disobedience, [7]and in them you also once *walked*, when you were living in them. [8]But now you also, put them all aside: anger, wrath, malice, slander, and abusive speech from your mouth. [9]Do not lie to one another, since you *laid aside the old self* with its evil practices, [10]and have *put on the new self* who is being *renewed* to a true knowledge according to the image of the One who *created* him.

OTHER BIBLICAL PARALLELS

Genesis 1:26

Then God said, "Let Us make man in Our image, according to Our *likeness*; and let them rule over the fish of the sea and over the birds of the sky and over the cattle and over all the earth, and over every creeping thing that creeps on the earth."

1 Peter 1:18–19

. . . knowing that you were not redeemed with perishable things like silver or gold from your *futile* way of *life* inherited from your forefathers, [19]but with precious blood, as of a lamb unblemished and spotless, the blood of Christ.

2 Peter 1:3–4

His divine power has granted to us everything pertaining to *life* and godliness, through the true knowledge of Him who called us by His own glory and excellence. [4]For by these He has granted to us His precious and magnificent promises, so that by them you may become partakers of the divine nature, having escaped the *corruption* that is in the world by *lust*.

NONCANONICAL PARALLELS

Wisdom of Solomon 13:1

For all people who were *ignorant* of God were foolish by nature; and they were unable from the good things that are seen to know the one who exists.

Wisdom of Solomon 14:12, 24–26

For the idea of making idols was . . . the *corruption* of *life*. . . . [24]They no longer keep either their lives or their marriages pure, but they either treacherously kill one another, or grieve one another by adultery, [25]and all is a raging riot of blood and murder, theft and *deceit*, corruption, faithlessness, tumult, perjury, [26]confusion over what is good, forgetfulness of favors, defiling of souls, sexual perversion, disorder in marriages, adultery, and debauchery.

Sibylline Oracles 3:36–39

Alas for a race which rejoices in blood, a crafty and evil race [37]of impious and false double-tongued men and immoral [38]adulterous idol-worshippers who plot *deceit*. [39]There is wickedness in their *hearts*, a frenzy raging within.

Testament of Gad 5:7–8

According to God's *truth*, repentance destroys disobedience, puts *darkness* to flight, illumines the vision, furnishes knowledge for the soul, and guides the deliberative powers to salvation. [8]What it has not *learned* from human agency, it understands through repentance.

Philo, On the Confusion of Tongues 31

For it was said to him [Moses], "You, stand here with me," in order that he should take off doubt and uncertainty . . . and *put on* faith.

Ephesians 4:25–5:2

Therefore, laying aside falsehood, SPEAK TRUTH EACH ONE of you WITH HIS NEIGHBOR, for we are members of one another. [26]BE ANGRY, AND yet DO NOT SIN; do not let the sun go down on your anger, [27]and do not give the devil an opportunity. [28]He who steals must steal no longer; but rather he must labor, performing with his own hands what is good, so that he will have something to share with one who has need. [29]Let no unwholesome word proceed from your mouth, but only such a word as is good for edification according to the need of the moment, so that it will give grace to those who hear. [30]Do not grieve the Holy Spirit of God, by whom you were sealed for the day of redemption. [31]Let all bitterness and wrath and anger and clamor and slander be put away from you, along with all malice. [32]Be kind to one another, tender-hearted, forgiving each other, just as God in Christ also has forgiven you. [5:1]Therefore be imitators of God, as beloved children; [2]and walk in love, just as Christ also loved you and gave Himself up for us, an offering and a sacrifice to God as a fragrant aroma.

EPHESIANS PARALLELS

Ephesians 1:13

In Him, you also, after listening to the message of *truth*, the gospel of your salvation—

having also believed, you were *sealed* in Him with *the Holy Spirit* of promise.

Ephesians 2:1–2

And you were dead in your trespasses and *sins,* [2]in which you formerly walked according to the course of this world, according to the prince of the power of the air, of the spirit that is now working in the sons of disobedience.

Ephesians 5:25

Husbands, *love* your wives, *just as Christ also loved* the church *and gave Himself up* for her.

Ephesians 6:11

Put on the full armor of God, so that you will be able to stand firm against the schemes of *the devil.*

OTHER PAULINE PARALLELS

Romans 8:3

For what the Law could not do, weak as it was through the flesh, God did: sending His own Son in the likeness of sinful flesh and as an *offering* for sin, He condemned *sin* in the flesh.

Romans 12:5

So we, who are many, are one body in Christ, and individually *members one of another.*

Galatians 2:20

"I have been crucified with Christ; and it is no longer I who live, but Christ lives in me; and the life which I now live in the flesh I live by faith in the Son of God, who *loved* me and *gave Himself up* for me."

Colossians 3:8–9

But now you also, put them all aside: *anger, wrath, malice, slander,* and abusive speech *from your mouth.* [9]Do not lie to one another, since you *laid aside* the old self with its evil practices.

Colossians 3:12–14

So, as those who have been chosen of God, holy and beloved, put on a heart of compassion, *kindness,* humility, gentleness and patience; [13]bearing with one another, and *forgiving each other,* whoever has a complaint against anyone; *just as* the Lord *for-*

gave you, so also should you. [14]Beyond all these things put on *love,* which is the perfect bond of unity.

Colossians 4:6

Let your speech always be with *grace,* as though seasoned with salt, so that you will know how you should respond to each person.

1 Thessalonians 4:11–12

Make it your ambition to lead a quiet life and attend to your own business and work *with* your *hands,* just as we commanded you, [12]so that you will behave properly toward outsiders and not be in any need.

OTHER BIBLICAL PARALLELS

Exodus 29:18

"You shall offer up in smoke the whole ram on the altar; it is a burnt *offering* to the LORD: it is a soothing *aroma,* an offering by fire to the LORD."

Leviticus 19:11

"You shall not *steal,* nor deal *falsely,* nor lie to one another."

Psalm 4:4

Tremble, and *do not sin;* Meditate in your heart upon your bed, and be still.

Isaiah 63:10

But they rebelled And *grieved His Holy Spirit;* Therefore He turned Himself to become their enemy, He fought against them.

Zechariah 8:16

These are the things which you should do: *speak* the *truth* to one another; judge with truth and judgment for peace in your gates.

John 13:34

"A new commandment I give to you, that you *love* one another, even as I have *loved you,* that you also love one another."

Hebrews 10:10–12

By this will we have been sanctified through the *offering* of the body of Jesus Christ once for all. [11]Every priest stands daily ministering and offering time after time the same sacrifices, which can never take away sins; [12]but He, having offered one *sacrifice* for sins for all time, SAT DOWN AT THE RIGHT HAND OF GOD.

1 Peter 2:1–2

Therefore, putting aside all *malice* and all deceit and hypocrisy and envy and all *slander*, [2]like newborn babies, long for the pure milk of the word, so that by it you may grow in respect to salvation.

NONCANONICAL PARALLELS

Testament of Zebulon 7:2

"Therefore, my children, on the basis of God's caring for you, without discrimination be compassionate and merciful to all. Provide for every person with a *kind* heart."

Testament of Dan 5:1–2

"Avoid *wrath*, and hate lying, in order that the Lord may dwell among you, and Beliar may flee from you. [2]Each of you *speak truth* clearly to *his neighbor*."

Philo, On the Virtues 168

Each person should *imitate God* to the extent that this can be done, leaving nothing undone that might foster such assimilation as is possible.

Ephesians 5:3–14

But immorality or any impurity or greed must not even be named among you, as is proper among saints; [4]and there must be no filthiness and silly talk, or coarse jesting, which are not fitting, but rather giving of thanks. [5]For this you know with certainty, that no immoral or impure person or covetous man, who is an idolater, has an inheritance in the kingdom of Christ and God. [6]Let no one deceive you with empty words, for because of these things the wrath of God comes upon the sons of disobedience. [7]Therefore do not be partakers with them; [8]for you were formerly darkness, but now you are Light in the Lord; walk as children of Light [9](for the fruit of the Light consists in all goodness and righteousness and truth), [10]trying to learn what is pleasing to the Lord. [11]Do not participate in the unfruitful deeds of darkness, but instead even expose them; [12]for it is disgraceful even to speak of the things which are done by them in secret. [13]But all things become visible when they are exposed by the light, for everything that becomes visible is light. [14]For this reason it says, "Awake, sleeper, And arise from the dead, And Christ will shine on you."

EPHESIANS PARALLELS

Ephesians 2:1–2

And you were dead in your trespasses and sins, [2]in which you *formerly walked* according to the course of this world, according to the prince of the power of the air, of the spirit that is now working in *the sons of disobedience.*

Ephesians 4:17–19

So this I say, and affirm together with the Lord, that you walk no longer just as the Gentiles also *walk*, in the futility of their mind, [18]being *darkened* in their understanding, excluded from the life of God because of the ignorance that is in them, because of the hardness of their heart; [19]and they, having become callous, have given themselves over to sensuality for the practice of every kind of *impurity* with *greediness.*

OTHER PAULINE PARALLELS

Romans 13:11–13

Do this, knowing the time, that it is already the hour for you to *awaken* from *sleep*; for now salvation is nearer to us than when we believed. [12]The night is almost gone, and the day is near. Therefore let us lay aside the *deeds of darkness* and put on the armor of *light.* [13]Let us behave properly as in the day, not in carousing and drunkenness, not in sexual promiscuity and sensuality, not in strife and jealousy.

1 Corinthians 6:9–11

Or do you not know that the unrighteous will not *inherit the kingdom of God*? Do not be *deceived*; neither fornicators, nor *idolaters*, nor adulterers, nor effeminate, nor homosexuals, [10]nor thieves, nor the *covetous*, nor drunkards, nor revilers, nor swindlers, will inherit the kingdom of God. [11]Such were some of you; but you were washed, but you were sanctified, but you were justified in the name of the Lord Jesus Christ and in the Spirit of our God.

Galatians 5:19–21

Now the deeds of the flesh are evident, which are: *immorality, impurity,* sensuality, [20]*idolatry,* sorcery, enmities, strife, jealousy, outbursts of anger, disputes, dissensions, factions, [21]envying, drunkenness, carousing, and things like these, of which I forewarn you, just as I have forewarned you, that those who practice such things will not *inherit the kingdom of God.*

Colossians 1:12–13

. . . *giving thanks* to the Father, who has qualified us to share in the *inheritance* of the saints in *Light.* [13]For He rescued us from the domain of *darkness,* and transferred us to *the kingdom* of His beloved Son.

Colossians 3:5–8

Therefore consider the members of your earthly body as dead to *immorality, impurity,* passion, evil desire, and *greed,* which amounts to *idolatry.* [6]For it is because of these things that *the wrath of God* will come upon *the sons of disobedience,* [7]and in them you also once *walked,* when you were living in them. [8]But now you also, put them all aside: anger, wrath, malice, slander, and abusive speech from your mouth.

Colossians 3:17

Whatever you do in word or deed, do all in the name of the Lord Jesus, *giving thanks* through Him to God the Father.

1 Thessalonians 5:4–6

But you, brethren, are not in *darkness,* that the day would overtake you like a thief; [5]for you are all sons of *light* and sons of day. We are not of night nor of darkness; [6]so then let us not sleep as others do, but let us be alert and sober.

OTHER BIBLICAL PARALLELS

Proverbs 16:7

When a man's ways are *pleasing to the* LORD, He makes even his enemies to be at peace with him.

Isaiah 26:19

Your *dead* will live; Their corpses will *rise.* You who lie in the dust, *awake* and shout for joy, For your dew is as the dew of the dawn, And the earth will give birth to the departed spirits.

John 3:20–21

"For everyone who does evil hates the *Light,* and does not come to the Light for fear that his *deeds* will be *exposed.* [21]But he who practices the *truth* comes to the Light, so that his deeds may be manifested as having been wrought in God."

John 12:35–36

"For a little while longer the *Light* is among you. *Walk* while you have the Light, so that *darkness* will not overtake you; he who walks in the darkness does not know where he goes. [36]While you have the Light, believe in the Light, so that you may become sons of Light."

Acts 26:16–18

"But get up and stand on your feet; for this purpose I have appeared to you, to appoint you a minister and a witness not only to the things which you have seen, but also to the things in which I will appear to you; [17]rescuing you from the Jewish people and from the Gentiles, to whom I am sending you, [18]to open their eyes so that they may turn from *darkness* to *light* and from the dominion of Satan to God, that they may receive forgiveness of sins and an *inheritance* among those who have been sanctified by faith in Me."

NONCANONICAL PARALLELS

Testament of Levi 18:2, 4, 10–11; 19:1

"And then the Lord will raise up a new priest. . . . [4]This one will *shine* forth like the sun in the earth. . . . [10]And he shall open the gates of paradise, . . . [11]and he will grant to the *saints* to eat of the tree of life. . . . [19:1]And now, my children, you have heard everything. Choose for yourselves *light* or *darkness,* the Law of the Lord or the works of Beliar."

The Rule of the Community *(1QS) 1.1–2, 5–6, 9–10*

. . . [book of the Rul]e of the Community: in order to [2]seek God . . . [5]and to become attached to all good works; to bring about truth, justice and uprightness [6]on earth and not to walk in the stubbornness of a guilty heart and of lecherous eyes, . . . [9] . . . in order to love all the sons of *light* . . . [10] . . . and to detest all the sons of *darkness* . . .

EPHESIANS 5:3–14

The Rule of the Community *(1QS) 3.20–21*

In the hand of the Prince of Lights is dominion over all the sons of justice; they walk on paths of *light*. And in the hand of the Angel [21]of Darkness is total dominion over the sons of deceit; they walk on paths of *darkness*.

Ephesians 5:15–21

Therefore be careful how you walk, not as unwise men but as wise, [16]making the most of your time, because the days are evil. [17]So then do not be foolish, but understand what the will of the Lord is. [18]And do not get drunk with wine, for that is dissipation, but be filled with the Spirit, [19]speaking to one another in psalms and hymns and spiritual songs, singing and making melody with your heart to the Lord; [20]always giving thanks for all things in the name of our Lord Jesus Christ to God, even the Father; [21]and be subject to one another in the fear of Christ.

EPHESIANS PARALLELS

Ephesians 1:15–17

For this reason I too, having heard of the faith in the Lord Jesus which exists among you and your love for all the saints, [16]do not cease *giving thanks* for you, while making mention of you in my prayers; [17]that the God of our Lord Jesus Christ, *the Father* of glory, may give to you a spirit of *wisdom* and of revelation in the knowledge of Him.

Ephesians 4:17

So this I say, and affirm together with the Lord, that you *walk* no longer just as the Gentiles also walk, in the futility of their mind.

Ephesians 6:13

Therefore, take up the full armor of God, so that you will be able to resist in *the evil day*, and having done everything, to stand firm.

OTHER PAULINE PARALLELS

Romans 13:13

Let us behave properly as in the day, not in carousing and *drunkenness*, not in sexual promiscuity and sensuality, not in strife and jealousy.

1 Corinthians 2:14

But a natural man does not accept the things of *the Spirit* of God, for they are *foolishness* to him; and he cannot *understand* them, because they are spiritually appraised.

1 Corinthians 14:26

What is the outcome then, brethren? When you assemble, each one has a *psalm*, has a teaching, has a revelation, has a tongue, has an interpretation. Let all things be done for edification.

Galatians 1:3–4

Grace to you and peace from God our Father and the Lord Jesus Christ, [4]who gave Himself for our sins so that He might rescue us from this present *evil* age, according to *the will* of our God and Father.

Galatians 5:13

For you were called to freedom, brethren; only do not turn your freedom into an opportunity for the flesh, but through love serve *one another*.

Colossians 3:16–17

Let the word of Christ richly dwell within you, with all *wisdom* teaching and admonishing *one another* with *psalms and hymns and spiritual songs, singing* with thankfulness in your *hearts* to God. [17]Whatever you do in word or deed, do all *in the name of* the *Lord Jesus, giving thanks* through Him to *God the Father*.

Colossians 4:5

Conduct yourselves with *wisdom* toward outsiders, *making the most* of the opportunity.

1 Thessalonians 5:16–19

Rejoice always; [17]pray without ceasing; [18]in everything *give thanks*; for this is God's will for you in Christ Jesus. [19]Do not quench *the Spirit*.

OTHER BIBLICAL PARALLELS

Proverbs 20:1

Wine is a mocker, strong drink a brawler, And whoever is intoxicated by it is not *wise*.

Amos 5:13

Therefore at such a time the prudent person keeps silent, for it is an *evil* time.

Luke 1:15

"For he will be great in the sight of the Lord; and he will drink no *wine* or liquor, and he will be *filled with the* Holy *Spirit* while yet in his mother's womb."

Luke 21:34

"Be on guard, so that your *hearts* will not be weighted down with *dissipation* and *drunkenness* and the worries of life, and that day will not come on you suddenly like a trap."

Acts 2:15–17

"For these men are not *drunk*, as you suppose, for it is only the third hour of the day; [16]but this is what was spoken of through the prophet Joel: [17]'AND IT SHALL BE IN THE LAST *DAYS*,' God says, 'THAT I WILL POUR FORTH OF MY *SPIRIT* ON ALL MANKIND; AND YOUR SONS AND YOUR DAUGHTERS SHALL PROPHESY, AND YOUR YOUNG MEN SHALL SEE VISIONS, AND YOUR OLD MEN SHALL DREAM DREAMS.'"

NONCANONICAL PARALLELS

Testament of Judah *14:1*

"Do not be *drunk with wine*, because wine perverts the mind from truth, arouses the impulses of desire, and leads the eyes into the path of error."

Testament of Judah *16:1*

"Take care to be temperate with *wine*, my children, for there are in it four evil spirits: desire, heated passion, debauchery, and sordid greed."

The Rule of the Community *(1QS) 10.21–23*

I shall not retain Belial within my *heart*. From my mouth no vulgarity shall be heard [22]or wicked deceptions. . . . [23] . . . With *hymns* shall I open my mouth and my tongue will ever number the just acts of God.

Ephesians 5:22–33

Wives, be subject to your own husbands, as to the Lord. [23]For the husband is the head of the wife, as Christ also is the head of the church, He Himself being the Savior of the body. [24]But as the church is subject to Christ, so also the wives ought to be to their husbands in everything. [25]Husbands, love your wives, just as Christ also loved the church and gave Himself up for her, [26]so that He might sanctify her, having cleansed her by the washing of water with the word, [27]that He might present to Himself the church in all her glory, having no spot or wrinkle or any such thing; but that she would be holy and blameless. [28]So husbands ought also to love their own wives as their own bodies. He who loves his own wife loves himself; [29]for no one ever hated his own flesh, but nourishes and cherishes it, just as Christ also does the church, [30]because we are members of His body. [31]FOR THIS REASON A MAN SHALL LEAVE HIS FATHER AND MOTHER AND SHALL BE JOINED TO HIS WIFE, AND THE TWO SHALL BECOME ONE FLESH. [32]This mystery is great; but I am speaking with reference to Christ and the church. [33]Nevertheless, each individual among you also is to love his own wife even as himself, and the wife must see to it that she respects her husband.

EPHESIANS PARALLELS

Ephesians 1:3–4

Blessed be the God and Father of our Lord Jesus Christ, who has blessed us with every spiritual blessing in the heavenly places in Christ, [4]just as He chose us in Him before the foundation of the world, that we would be *holy and blameless* before Him.

Ephesians 1:22–23

And He put all things in *subjection* under His feet, and gave Him as *head* over all things to *the church*, [23]which is His *body*, the fullness of Him who fills all in all.

Ephesians 4:15–16

Speaking the truth in *love*, we are to grow up in all aspects into Him who is the *head*, even Christ, [16]from whom the whole *body*, being fitted and held together by what every joint supplies, according to the proper working of each individual part, causes the growth of the body for the building up of itself in love.

Ephesians 5:2

Walk in *love, just as Christ also loved you* and *gave Himself up* for us, an offering and a sacrifice to God as a fragrant aroma.

1 Corinthians 6:11

Such were some of you; but you were *washed*, but you were *sanctified*, but you were justified in the name of the Lord Jesus Christ and in the Spirit of our God.

1 Corinthians 11:3

But I want you to understand that Christ is *the head* of every man, and the man is the head of a woman, and God is the head of Christ.

1 Corinthians 12:27

Now you are Christ's *body*, and individually *members* of it.

2 Corinthians 11:2

For I am jealous for you with a godly jealousy; for I betrothed you to one *husband*, so that to Christ I might *present* you as a pure virgin.

Galatians 2:20

"I have been crucified with Christ; and it is no longer I who live, but Christ lives in me; and the life which I now live in the flesh I live by faith in the Son of God, who *loved* me and *gave Himself up* for me."

Colossians 3:18–19

Wives, be subject to your husbands, as is fitting in *the Lord.* [19]*Husbands, love your wives* and do not be embittered against them.

Titus 2:3–5

Older women likewise are to be reverent in their behavior, not malicious gossips nor enslaved to much wine, teaching what is good, [4]so that they may encourage the young women to *love* their husbands, to love their children, [5]to be sensible, pure, workers at home, kind, *being subject to* their *own husbands*, so that *the word* of God will not be dishonored.

Titus 2:13–14

. . . looking for the blessed hope and the appearing of the glory of our great God and *Savior*, Christ Jesus, [14]who *gave Himself* for us to redeem us from every lawless deed, and to purify for Himself a people for His own possession, zealous for good deeds.

Genesis 2:24

For this reason a man shall leave his father and his mother, and be joined to his wife; and they shall become one flesh.

Leviticus 19:18

"You shall not take vengeance, nor bear any grudge against the sons of your people, but you shall *love* your neighbor *as* yourself; I am the LORD."

1 Peter 3:1, 7

In the same way, you *wives*, be submissive *to your own husbands* so that even if any of them are disobedient to *the word,* they may be won without a word by the behavior of their wives. . . . [7]You husbands in the same way, live with your wives in an understanding way, as with someone weaker, since she is a woman; and show her honor as a fellow heir of the grace of life, so that your prayers will not be hindered.

Pseudo-Phocylides, Sentences *195–97*

Love your wife: for what is sweeter and better [196]than when a wife is lovingly disposed to her husband into old age [197]and husband to his wife, and strife does not split them asunder?

Josephus, Against Apion *2.201*

"The woman is inferior [the Law says] in all things." Therefore let her be obedient, though not for any insolence, but so that she may be directed. For God gave control to the *husband.* And he must have relations with his spouse alone; (even) to try with another man's wife is unholy.

Plutarch, Advice to Bride and Groom *142E*

A *husband* must rule his *wife*, not like a master over his property, but like the soul over the *body*, with sympathy and joined together in goodwill.

Ephesians 6:1–9

Children, obey your parents in the Lord, for this is right. [2]HONOR YOUR FATHER AND MOTHER (which is the first commandment with a promise), [3]SO THAT IT MAY BE WELL WITH YOU, AND THAT YOU MAY LIVE LONG ON THE EARTH. [4]Fathers, do not provoke your children to anger, but bring them up in the discipline and instruction of the Lord. [5]Slaves, be obedient to those who are your masters according to the flesh, with fear and trembling, in the sincerity of your heart, as to Christ; [6]not by way of eye-service, as men-pleasers, but as slaves of Christ, doing the will of God from the heart. [7]With good will render service, as to the Lord, and not to men, [8]knowing that whatever good thing each one does, this he will receive back from the Lord, whether slave or free. [9]And masters, do the same things to them, and give up threatening, knowing that both their Master and yours is in heaven, and there is no partiality with Him.

EPHESIANS PARALLELS

Ephesians 4:26–27

BE ANGRY, AND yet DO NOT SIN; do not let the sun go down on your *anger*, [27]and do not give the devil an opportunity.

OTHER PAULINE PARALLELS

Romans 2:9–11

There will be tribulation and distress for every soul of man who does evil, of the Jew first and also of the Greek, [10]but glory and honor and peace to everyone who does *good*, to the Jew first and also to the Greek. [11]For *there is no partiality with God.*

1 Corinthians 7:22–23

For he who was called in the Lord while a *slave*, is the Lord's freedman; likewise he who was called while *free*, is *Christ's slave.* [23]You were bought with a price; do not become slaves of men.

Colossians 3:20–4:1

Children, be *obedient* to *your parents* in all things, for this is well-pleasing to the Lord. [21]*Fathers*, do not exasperate your children, so that they will not lose heart. [22]*Slaves*, in all things *obey those who are your masters* on earth, not with external *service*, as those who merely *please men*, but with *sincerity of heart*, *fearing* the Lord. [23]Whatever you do, do your work heartily, *as* for *the Lord* rather than for *men*, [24]*knowing that from the Lord* you *will receive* the reward of the inheritance. It is the Lord Christ whom you serve.

[25]For he who does wrong will receive the consequences of the wrong which he has done, and that *without partiality.* [4:1]*Masters*, grant to your *slaves* justice and fairness, *knowing that* you too have a *Master in heaven.*

1 Timothy 6:1–2

All who are under the yoke as *slaves* are to regard their own *masters* as worthy of all *honor* so that the name of God and our doctrine will not be spoken against. [2]Those who have believers as their masters must not be disrespectful to them because they are brethren, but must *serve* them all the more, because those who partake of the benefit are believers and beloved.

Titus 2:9–10

Urge *bondslaves* to be subject to their own *masters* in everything, to be well-pleasing, not argumentative, [10]not pilfering, but showing all good faith so that they will adorn the doctrine of God our Savior in every respect.

OTHER BIBLICAL PARALLELS

Leviticus 25:39, 42–43

"If a countryman of yours becomes so poor with regard to you that he sells himself to you, you shall not subject him to a slave's *service.* . . . [42]For they are My servants whom I brought out from the land of Egypt; they are not to be sold in a *slave* sale. [43]You shall not rule over him with severity, but are to revere your God."

Deuteronomy 5:16

"*Honor your father and* your *mother*, as the LORD your God has commanded you, that your days may be prolonged and that it may go *well with you* on the land which the LORD your God gives you."

Deuteronomy 10:17

"For the LORD your God is the God of gods and the Lord of lords, the great, the mighty, and the awesome God who does *not* show *partiality* nor take a bribe."

Proverbs 3:11–12

My son, do not reject the *discipline of the* LORD Or loathe His reproof, [12]For whom the LORD loves He reproves, Even as a *father* corrects the son in whom he delights.

Proverbs 22:6

Train up a *child* in the way he should go, Even when he is old he will not depart from it.

Proverbs 23:22

Listen to *your father* who begot you, And do not despise *your mother* when she is old.

Hebrews 12:9, 11

Furthermore, we had earthly *fathers* to *discipline* us, and we respected them; shall we not much rather be subject to the Father of spirits, and *live*? . . . [11]All discipline for the moment seems not to be joyful, but sorrowful; yet to those who have been trained by it, afterwards it yields the peaceful fruit of righteousness.

1 Peter 2:18

Servants, be submissive to *your masters* with all respect, not only to those who are good and gentle, but also to those who are unreasonable.

NONCANONICAL PARALLELS

Sirach 7:20

Do not abuse *slaves* who work faithfully, or hired laborers who devote themselves to their task.

Philo, On the Decalogue *167*

And many more commandments are prescribed [by the Law], to the young on making a return to the elderly, to the old on taking care of the young, to subjects on obedience to their rulers, to rulers on benefiting their subjects, . . . to servants on devotion in *service*, to *masters* on showing gentleness and kindness, through which inequality is moderated.

Xenophon, Memorabilia *2.1.16*

Let us consider this as well, how *masters* treat such *slaves*. Do they not *discipline* them with hunger so there is no desire in them? Do they not prevent them from stealing by locking up anything that might be taken? Do they not stop them from escaping with chains? Do they not force the laziness out of them with blows?

Pseudo-Plutarch, On the Education of Children *8F*

Children should be led to the finest of practices with guidance and reason, and on no

account with blows or injury. For it is apparent that the latter are appropriate for *slaves* rather than the free.

Ephesians 6:10–17

Finally, be strong in the Lord and in the strength of His might. [11]Put on the full armor of God, so that you will be able to stand firm against the schemes of the devil. [12]For our struggle is not against flesh and blood, but against the rulers, against the powers, against the world forces of this darkness, against the spiritual forces of wickedness in the heavenly places. [13]Therefore, take up the full armor of God, so that you will be able to resist in the evil day, and having done everything, to stand firm. [14]Stand firm therefore, HAVING GIRDED YOUR LOINS WITH TRUTH, and HAVING PUT ON THE BREASTPLATE OF RIGHTEOUSNESS, [15]and having shod YOUR FEET WITH THE PREPARATION OF THE GOSPEL OF PEACE; [16]in addition to all, taking up the shield of faith with which you will be able to extinguish all the flaming arrows of the evil one. [17]And take THE HELMET OF SALVATION, and the sword of the Spirit, which is the word of God.

EPHESIANS PARALLELS

Ephesians 1:18–21

I pray that the eyes of your heart may be enlightened, so that you will know what is the hope of His calling, what are the riches of the glory of His inheritance in the saints, [19]and what is the surpassing greatness of His power toward us who believe. These are in accordance with the working of *the strength of His might* [20]which He brought about in Christ, when He raised Him from the dead and seated Him at His right hand *in the heavenly places,* [21]far above all *rule* and authority and *power* and dominion, and every name that is named, not only in this age but also in the one to come.

Ephesians 2:1–2

And you were dead in your trespasses and sins, [2]in which you formerly walked according to the course of this world, according to the prince of *the power* of the air, of the spirit that is now working in the sons of disobedience.

Ephesians 2:17–18

AND HE CAME AND PREACHED *PEACE* TO YOU WHO WERE FAR AWAY, AND PEACE TO THOSE WHO WERE NEAR; [18]for through Him we both have our access in one Spirit to the Father.

Ephesians 3:8–10

To me, the very least of all saints, this grace was given, to preach to the Gentiles the unfathomable riches of Christ, [9]and to bring to light what is the administration of the mystery which for ages has been hidden in God who created all things; [10]so that the manifold wisdom of God might now be made known through the church to the *rulers* and the authorities *in the heavenly places.*

Ephesians 5:6–8, 11

Let no one deceive you with empty words, for because of these things the wrath of God comes upon the sons of disobedience. [7]Therefore do not be partakers with them; [8]for you were formerly *darkness*, but now you are Light in the Lord; walk as children of Light. . . . [11]Do not participate in the unfruitful deeds of darkness, but instead even expose them.

OTHER PAULINE PARALLELS

Romans 13:12

The night is almost gone, and the day is near. Therefore let us lay aside the deeds of *darkness* and *put on the armor* of light.

Colossians 1:13–14

For He rescued us from the domain of *darkness*, and transferred us to the kingdom of His beloved Son, [14]in whom we have redemption, the forgiveness of sins.

Colossians 2:13–15

He made you alive together with Him, having forgiven us all our transgressions, [14]having canceled out the certificate of debt consisting of decrees against us, which was hostile to us; and He has taken it out of the way, having nailed it to the cross. [15]When He had disarmed the *rulers* and authorities, He made a public display of them, having triumphed over them through Him.

1 Thessalonians 5:8

But since we are of the day, let us be sober, having put on the *breastplate* of *faith* and love, and as a *helmet*, the hope of *salvation*.

OTHER BIBLICAL PARALLELS

Job 29:14

"I *put on righteousness*, and it clothed me; My justice was like a robe and a turban."

Isaiah 11:4–5

But with righteousness He will judge the poor, And decide with fairness for the afflicted of the earth; And He will strike the earth with the rod of His mouth, And with the breath of His lips He will slay the *wicked.* [5]Also *righteousness* will be the belt about His *loins*, And *faithfulness* the belt about His waist.

Isaiah 49:2

He has made My mouth like a sharp *sword*, In the shadow of His hand He has concealed Me; And He has also made Me a select *arrow,* He has hidden Me in His quiver.

Isaiah 52:7

How lovely on the mountains Are the *feet* of him who brings good news, Who announces *peace* And brings good news of happiness, Who announces salvation, And says to Zion, "Your God reigns!"

Isaiah 59:17

He *put on righteousness* like a *breastplate*, And *a helmet of salvation* on His head; And He put on garments of vengeance for clothing And wrapped Himself with zeal as a mantle.

Hebrews 4:12

For *the word of God* is living and active and sharper than any two-edged *sword*, and piercing as far as the division of soul and spirit, of both joints and marrow, and able to judge the thoughts and intentions of the heart.

James 4:7

Submit therefore to God. *Resist the devil and he will flee from you.*

Wisdom of Solomon 5:17–20

The Lord will take his zeal as his whole *armor*, and will arm all creation to repel his enemies; [18]he will *put on righteousness* as a *breastplate*, and wear impartial justice as a *helmet*; [19]he will take holiness as an invincible *shield*, [20]and sharpen stern wrath for a *sword*, and creation will join with him to fight against his frenzied foes.

Pseudo-Philo, Biblical Antiquities *36.2*

And as soon as Gideon heard these words, he *put on* the spirit of the Lord and was *strengthened* and said to the three hundred men, "Rise up, let each one of you gird on his sword. . . ." And he drew near and began to fight, and they blew the trumpets and cried out together . . . , "The *sword* of the Lord is upon us."

The War Scroll *(1QM) 15.2–4, 7, 13–14*

All those who [are ready] for the war shall go and camp opposite the king of the Kittim and opposite all the army [3]of Belial, assembled with him for the day [of extermination] by God's *sword*. [4]The High Priest . . . [7] . . . will begin speaking and say: "*Be strong* and valiant. . . . [13] . . . The God of Israel is raising his hand with his marvellous power [14] . . . against all the *wicked spirits*."

Ephesians 6:18–24

With all prayer and petition pray at all times in the Spirit, and with this in view, be on the alert with all perseverance and petition for all the saints, [19]and pray on my behalf, that utterance may be given to me in the opening of my mouth, to make known with boldness the mystery of the gospel, [20]for which I am an ambassador in chains; that in proclaiming it I may speak boldly, as I ought to speak. [21]But that you also may know about my circumstances, how I am doing, Tychicus, the beloved brother and faithful minister in the Lord, will make everything known to you. [22]I have sent him to you for this very purpose, so that you may know about us, and that he may comfort your hearts. [23]Peace be to the brethren, and love with faith, from God the Father and the Lord Jesus Christ. [24]Grace be with all those who love our Lord Jesus Christ with incorruptible love.

Ephesians 3:1–3

For this reason I, Paul, the prisoner of Christ Jesus for the sake of you Gentiles— [2]if indeed you have heard of the stewardship of God's grace which was given to me for you; [3]that by revelation there was made known to me the *mystery*, as I wrote before in brief.

Ephesians 3:8–9

To me, the very least of all saints, this grace was given, to preach to the Gentiles the unfathomable riches of Christ, [9]and to bring to light what is the administration of the *mystery* which for ages has been hidden in God who created all things.

Romans 8:26–27

In the same way *the Spirit* also helps our weakness; for we do not know how to *pray* as we should, but the Spirit Himself intercedes for us with groanings too deep for words; [27]and He who searches the *hearts* knows what the mind of the Spirit is, because He intercedes for *the saints* according to the will of God.

1 Corinthians 4:17

For this reason I *have sent to you* Timothy, who is my *beloved* and *faithful* child in the Lord, and he will remind you of my ways which are in Christ, just as I teach everywhere in every church.

2 Corinthians 5:20

Therefore, we are *ambassadors* for Christ, as though God were making an appeal through us; we beg you on behalf of Christ, be reconciled to God.

Philippians 4:6

Be anxious for nothing, but in everything by *prayer* and supplication with thanksgiving let your requests be made known to God.

Colossians 4:2–4

Devote yourselves to *prayer*, keeping *alert* in it with an attitude of thanksgiving; [3]praying at the same time for us as well, that God will open up to us a door for the word, so that we may speak forth the *mystery* of Christ, for which I have also been imprisoned; [4]that I may make it clear in the way *I ought to speak.*

Colossians 4:7–9

As to all my affairs, *Tychicus,* our *beloved brother and faithful* servant and fellow bond-servant *in the Lord,* will bring you information. [8]For *I have sent him to you for this very purpose, that you may know about* our circumstances *and that he may* encourage *your hearts;* [9]and with him Onesimus, our *faithful* and beloved brother, who is one of your number. They will inform you about the whole situation here.

Colossians 4:18

I, Paul, write this greeting with my own hand. Remember my imprisonment. *Grace be with* you.

1 Thessalonians 2:2

After we had already suffered and been mistreated in Philippi, as you know, we had the *boldness* in our God to *speak* to you the *gospel* of God amid much opposition.

1 Thessalonians 5:16–19

Rejoice always; [17]*pray* without ceasing; [18]in everything give thanks; for this is God's will for you in Christ Jesus. [19]Do not quench *the Spirit.*

1 Thessalonians 5:23, 25, 28

Now may the God of *peace* Himself sanctify you entirely; and may your spirit and soul and body be preserved complete, without blame at the coming of our Lord Jesus Christ. . . . [25]Brethren, *pray* for us. . . . [28]The *grace* of our Lord Jesus Christ *be with* you.

2 Timothy 2:8–10

Remember Jesus Christ, risen from the dead, descendant of David, according to my *gospel,* [9]for which I suffer hardship even to imprisonment as a criminal; but the word of God is not imprisoned. [10]For this reason I endure all things for the sake of those who are chosen, so that they also may obtain the salvation which is in Christ Jesus and with it eternal glory.

2 Timothy 4:12

But *Tychicus I have sent* to Ephesus.

Titus 3:12

When *I send* Artemas or *Tychicus* to you, make every effort to come to me at Nicopolis, for I have decided to spend the winter there.

Philemon 8–9

Therefore, though I have enough confidence in Christ to order you to do what is proper, [9]yet for love's sake I rather appeal to you—since I am such a person as Paul, the aged, and now also a prisoner of Christ Jesus.

OTHER BIBLICAL PARALLELS

Acts 14:3

Therefore they [Paul and Barnabas] spent a long time there speaking *boldly* with reliance upon the Lord, who was testifying to the word of His grace, granting that signs and wonders be done by their hands.

Acts 20:2–4

He [Paul] came to Greece. [3]And there he spent three months, and when a plot was formed against him by the Jews as he was about to set sail for Syria, he decided to return through Macedonia. [4]And he was accompanied by Sopater of Berea, the son of Pyrrhus, and by Aristarchus and Secundus of the Thessalonians, and Gaius of Derbe, and Timothy, and *Tychicus* and Trophimus of Asia.

Acts 28:16–17, 20, 30–31

When we entered Rome, Paul was allowed to stay by himself, with the soldier who was guarding him. [17]After three days Paul called together those who were the leading men of the Jews, and when they came together, he began saying to them, "Brethren, though I had done nothing against our people or the customs of our fathers, yet I was delivered as a prisoner from Jerusalem into the hands of the Romans. . . . [20]For this reason, therefore, I requested to see you and to speak with you, for I am wearing this *chain* for the sake of the hope of Israel." . . . [30]And he stayed two full years in his own rented quarters and was welcoming all who came to him, [31]preaching the kingdom of God and teaching concerning the Lord Jesus Christ with all openness, unhindered.

Philippians

Philippians 1:1–2

Paul and Timothy, bond-servants of Christ Jesus, To all the saints in Christ Jesus who are in Philippi, including the overseers and deacons: ²Grace to you and peace from God our Father and the Lord Jesus Christ.

PHILIPPIANS PARALLELS

Philippians 2:19, 22

But I hope in the Lord Jesus to send *Timothy* to you shortly, so that I also may be encouraged when I learn of your condition. . . . ²²But you know of his proven worth, that he served with me in the furtherance of the gospel like a child serving his father.

Philippians 4:9

The things you have learned and received and heard and seen in me, practice these things, and the God of *peace* will be with you.

Philippians 4:23

The *grace* of *the Lord Jesus Christ* be with your spirit.

OTHER PAULINE PARALLELS

Romans 1:1, 7

Paul, a *bond-servant of Christ Jesus*, called as an apostle, set apart for the gospel of God, . . . ⁷*to all* who are beloved of God in Rome, called as *saints*: *Grace to you and peace from God our Father and the Lord Jesus Christ.*

2 Corinthians 1:1–2

Paul, an apostle of Christ Jesus by the will of God, and *Timothy* our brother, To the church of God which is at Corinth with *all the saints* who are throughout Achaia:

²*Grace to you and peace from God our Father and the Lord Jesus Christ.*

Galatians 1:10

For am I now seeking the favor of men, or of God? Or am I striving to please men? If I were still trying to please men, I would not be a *bond-servant of Christ*.

Colossians 1:1–2

Paul, an apostle of Jesus Christ by the will of God, and *Timothy* our brother, ²*To the saints* and faithful brethren in Christ who are at Colossae: *Grace to you and peace from God our Father.*

1 Thessalonians 2:1–2

For you yourselves know, brethren, that our coming to you was not in vain, ²but after we had already suffered and been mistreated in *Philippi*, as you know, we had the boldness in our God to speak to you the gospel of God amid much opposition.

1 Timothy 3:1–2, 8–10

It is a trustworthy statement: if any man aspires to the office of *overseer*, it is a fine work he desires to do. ²An overseer, then, must be above reproach, the husband of one wife, temperate, prudent, respectable, hospitable, able to teach. . . . ⁸*Deacons* likewise must be men of dignity, not double-tongued, or addicted to much wine or fond of sordid gain, ⁹but holding to the mystery of the faith with a clear conscience. ¹⁰These men must also first be tested; then let them serve as deacons if they are beyond reproach.

Philemon 1–3

Paul, a prisoner of Christ Jesus, and *Timothy* our brother, To Philemon our beloved brother and fellow worker, [2]and to Apphia our sister, and to Archippus our fellow soldier, and to the church in your house: [3]*Grace to you and peace from God our Father and the Lord Jesus Christ.*

Acts 16:1–3

Paul came also to Derbe and to Lystra. And a disciple was there, named *Timothy*, the son of a Jewish woman who was a believer, but his father was a Greek, [2]and he was well spoken of by the brethren who were in Lystra and Iconium. [3]Paul wanted this man to go with him; and he took him and circumcised him because of the Jews who were in those parts, for they all knew that his father was a Greek.

Acts 16:11–12, 16–19, 22–23

So putting out to sea from Troas, we ran a straight course to Samothrace, and on the day following to Neapolis; [12]and from there to *Philippi*, which is a leading city of the district of Macedonia, a Roman colony; and we were staying in this city for some days. . . . [16]It happened that as we were going to the place of prayer, a slave-girl having a spirit of divination met us, who was bringing her masters much profit by fortune-telling. [17]Following after *Paul* and us, she kept crying out, saying, "These men are *bond-servants* of the Most High God, who are proclaiming to you the way of salvation." [18]She continued doing this for many days. But Paul was greatly annoyed, and turned and said to the spirit, "I command you in the name of Jesus Christ to come out of her!" And it came out at that very moment. [19]But when her masters saw that their hope of profit was gone, they seized Paul and Silas and dragged them into the market place before the authorities. . . . [22]The crowd rose up together against them, and the chief magistrates tore their robes off them and proceeded to order them to be beaten with rods. [23]When they had struck them with many blows, they threw them into prison, commanding the jailer to guard them securely.

Josephus, Jewish Antiquities *10.53*

He [Josiah] also appointed certain judges and *overseers* who were to superintend the dealings of each person, putting justice above all else.

Philippians 1:3–11

I thank my God in all my remembrance of you, [4]always offering prayer with joy in my every prayer for you all, [5]in view of your participation in the gospel from the first day until now. [6]For I am confident of this very thing, that He who began a good work in you will perfect it until the day of Christ Jesus. [7]For it is only right for me to feel this way about you all, because I have you in my heart, since both in my imprisonment and in the defense and confirmation of the gospel, you all are partakers of grace with me. [8]For God is my witness, how I long for you all with the affection of Christ Jesus. [9]And this I pray, that your love may abound still more and more in real knowledge and all discernment, [10]so that you may approve the things that are excellent, in order to be sincere and blameless until the day of Christ; [11]having been filled with the fruit of righteousness which comes through Jesus Christ, to the glory and praise of God.

Philippians 1:25–26

Convinced of this, I know that I will remain and continue with you all for your progress and *joy* in the faith, [26]so that your proud *confidence* in me may abound in Christ Jesus through my coming to you again.

Philippians 2:12–13, 16–18

So then, my beloved, just as you have always obeyed, not as in my presence only, but now much more in my absence, work out your salvation with fear and trembling; [13]for it is God who is at work in you, both to will and to work for His good pleasure. . . . [16]holding fast the word of life, so that in *the day of Christ* I will have reason to glory because I did not run in vain nor toil in vain. [17]But even if I am being poured out as a drink offering upon the sacrifice and service of your faith, I rejoice and share my *joy* with you all. [18]You too, I urge you, rejoice in the same way and share your joy with me.

Philippians 3:8–9

More than that, I count all things to be loss in view of the surpassing value of knowing Christ Jesus my Lord, for whom I have suffered the loss of all things, and count them but rubbish so that I may gain Christ, [9]and may be found in Him, not having a *righteousness* of my own derived from the Law, but that which is through faith in Christ, the righteousness which comes from God on the basis of faith.

Philippians 3:12

Not that I have already obtained it or have already become *perfect*, but I press on so that I may lay hold of that for which also I was laid hold of by Christ Jesus.

Philippians 4:1

Therefore, my beloved brethren whom *I long* to see, my *joy* and crown, in this way stand firm in the Lord, my beloved.

Philippians 4:8

Finally, brethren, whatever is true, whatever is honorable, whatever is right, whatever is pure, whatever is lovely, whatever is of good repute, if there is any *excellence* and if anything worthy of praise, dwell on these things.

OTHER PAULINE PARALLELS

Romans 1:8–9, 11

First, *I thank my God* through Jesus Christ for you all, because your faith is being proclaimed throughout the whole world. [9]For God, whom I serve in my spirit in the preaching of *the gospel* of His Son, *is my witness* as to how unceasingly I make mention of you. . . . [11]For *I long* to see you so that I may impart some spiritual gift to you, that you may be established.

1 Corinthians 1:7–8

You are not lacking in any gift, awaiting eagerly the revelation of our Lord Jesus Christ, [8]who will also confirm you to the end, *blameless* in *the day of* our Lord Jesus Christ.

2 Corinthians 6:3–5

. . . giving no cause for offense in anything, so that the ministry will not be discredited, [4]but in everything commending ourselves as servants of God, in much endurance, in afflictions, in hardships, in distresses, [5]in beatings, in *imprisonments*, in tumults, in labors, in sleeplessness, in hunger.

2 Corinthians 7:4

Great is my *confidence* in you; great is my boasting on your behalf. I am filled with comfort; I am overflowing with *joy* in all our affliction.

Ephesians 4:1–2

Therefore I, the *prisoner* of the Lord, implore you to walk in a manner worthy of the calling with which you have been called, [2]with all humility and gentleness, with patience, showing tolerance for one another in *love*.

Colossians 1:3

We give *thanks* to *God*, the Father of our Lord Jesus Christ, *praying always* for you.

Colossians 1:9–10

For this reason also, since the *day* we heard of it, we have not ceased to *pray* for you and to ask that you may be filled with the *knowledge* of His will in all spiritual wisdom and understanding, [10]so that you will walk in a manner worthy of the Lord, to please Him in all respects, bearing *fruit* in every *good* work and increasing in the knowledge of God.

1 Thessalonians 3:12

May the Lord cause you to increase and *abound* in *love* for one another, and for all people, just as we also do for you.

2 Timothy 1:8

Therefore do not be ashamed of the testimony of our Lord or of me His *prisoner*, but join with me in suffering for *the gospel* according to the power of God.

Philemon 9

Yet for love's sake I rather appeal to you— since I am such a person as Paul, the aged, and now also a *prisoner* of Christ Jesus.

James 3:18

And the seed whose *fruit* is *righteousness* is sown in peace by those who make peace.

NONCANONICAL PARALLELS

4QSongs of the Sabbath Sacrifice[d] *(4Q403 [4QShirShabb[d]]) 1.38–40*

Give *thanks*, all the divinities of majesty, to the king of majesty; . . . [39]And they make his *knowledge* acceptable . . . when his powerful hand returns for the judgment of reward. Chant to the powerful God . . . [40] . . . so that it is [a melody] with the *joy* of God.

Philippians 1:12–18a

Now I want you to know, brethren, that my circumstances have turned out for the greater progress of the gospel, [13]so that my imprisonment in the cause of Christ has become well known throughout the whole praetorian guard and to everyone else, [14]and that most of the brethren, trusting in the Lord because of my imprisonment, have far more courage to speak the word of God without fear. [15]Some, to be sure, are preaching Christ even from envy and strife, but some also from good will; [16]the latter do it out of love, knowing that I am appointed for the defense of the gospel; [17]the former proclaim Christ out of selfish ambition rather than from pure motives, thinking to cause me distress in my imprisonment. [18]What then? Only that in every way, whether in pretense or in truth, Christ is proclaimed; and in this I rejoice.

PHILIPPIANS PARALLELS

Philippians 2:3

Do nothing from *selfishness* or empty conceit, but with humility of mind regard one another as more important than yourselves.

Philippians 2:17

But even if I am being poured out as a drink offering upon the sacrifice and service of your faith, *I rejoice* and share my joy with you all.

Philippians 4:10

But *I rejoiced* in the Lord greatly, that now at last you have revived your concern for me; indeed, you were concerned before, but you lacked opportunity.

Philippians 4:22

All the saints greet you, especially those of Caesar's household.

OTHER PAULINE PARALLELS

Romans 16:17–18

Now I urge you, brethren, keep your eye on those who cause dissensions and hindrances contrary to the teaching which you learned, and turn away from them. [18]For such men are slaves, not of our Lord Christ but of their own appetites; and by their smooth and flattering speech they deceive the hearts of the unsuspecting.

1 Corinthians 15:9–11

For I am the least of the apostles, and not fit to be called an apostle, because I persecuted the church of God. [10]But by the grace of God I am what I am, and His grace toward me did not prove vain; but I labored even more than all of them, yet not I, but the grace of God with me. [11]Whether then it was I or they, so we *preach* and so you believed.

2 Corinthians 6:3–5

. . . giving no cause for offense in anything, so that the ministry will not be discredited, [4]but in everything commending ourselves as servants of God, in much endurance, in afflictions, in hardships, in *distresses*, [5]in beatings, in *imprisonments*, in tumults, in labors, in sleeplessness, in hunger.

2 Corinthians 11:13

For such men are false apostles, deceitful workers, disguising themselves as apostles of Christ.

Galatians 1:6–7

I am amazed that you are so quickly deserting Him who called you by the grace of Christ, for a different gospel; [7]which is really not another; only there are some who are disturbing you and want to distort *the gospel* of Christ.

Ephesians 6:19–20

Pray on my behalf, that utterance may be given to me in the opening of my mouth, to make known with boldness the mystery of *the gospel,* ²⁰for which I am an ambassador in chains; that in *proclaiming* it I may speak boldly, as I ought to speak.

Colossians 1:28

We *proclaim* Him, admonishing every man and teaching every man with all wisdom, so that we may present every man complete in Christ.

Colossians 2:1

For *I want you to know* how great a struggle I have on your behalf and for those who are at Laodicea, and for all those who have not personally seen my face.

Colossians 4:3

. . . praying at the same time for us as well, that God will open up to us a door for *the word,* so that we may speak forth the mystery of Christ, for which I have also been *imprisoned.*

2 Thessalonians 3:1–2

Finally, brethren, pray for us that *the word* of the Lord will spread rapidly and be glorified, just as it did also with you; ²and that we will be rescued from perverse and evil men; for not all have faith.

1 Timothy 6:3–5

If anyone advocates a different doctrine and does not agree with sound words, those of our Lord Jesus Christ, and with the doctrine conforming to godliness, ⁴he is conceited and understands nothing; but he has a morbid interest in controversial questions and disputes about words, out of which arise *envy, strife,* abusive language, evil suspicions, ⁵and constant friction between men of depraved mind and deprived of the *truth,* who suppose that godliness is a means of gain.

2 Timothy 2:8–9

Remember Jesus Christ, risen from the dead, descendant of David, according to my *gospel,* ⁹for which I suffer hardship even to *imprisonment* as a criminal; but *the word of God* is not imprisoned.

Philemon 10, 13

I appeal to you for my child Onesimus, whom I have begotten in my *imprisonment,* . . . ¹³whom I wished to keep with me, so that on your behalf he might minister to me in my imprisonment for *the gospel.*

OTHER BIBLICAL PARALLELS

Luke 21:12–13

"But before all these things, they will lay their hands on you and will persecute you, delivering you to the synagogues and *prisons,* bringing you before kings and governors for My name's sake. ¹³It will lead to an opportunity for your testimony."

Acts 4:31

And when they had prayed, the place where they had gathered together was shaken, and they were all filled with the Holy Spirit and began *to speak the word of God* with boldness.

Acts 23:31, 33–35

So the soldiers, in accordance with their orders, took Paul and brought him by night to Antipatris. . . . ³³When these had come to Caesarea and delivered the letter to the governor, they also presented Paul to him. ³⁴When he had read it, he asked from what province he was, and when he learned that he was from Cilicia, ³⁵he said, "I will give you a hearing after your accusers arrive also," giving orders for him to be kept in Herod's *Praetorium.*

Philippians 1:18b–26

Yes, and I will rejoice, ¹⁹for I know that this will turn out for my deliverance through your prayers and the provision of the Spirit of Jesus Christ, ²⁰according to my earnest expectation and hope, that I will not be put to shame in anything, but that with all boldness, Christ will even now, as always, be exalted in my body, whether by life or by death. ²¹For to me, to live is Christ and to die is gain. ²²But if I am to live on in the flesh, this will mean fruitful labor for me; and I do not know which to choose. ²³But I am hard-pressed from both directions, having the desire to depart and be with Christ, for that is very much better; ²⁴yet to remain on in the flesh is more necessary for your sake.

²⁵Convinced of this, I know that I will remain and continue with you all for your progress and joy in the faith, ²⁶so that your proud confidence in me may abound in Christ Jesus through my coming to you again.

PHILIPPIANS PARALLELS

Philippians 2:17

But even if I am being poured out as a drink offering upon the sacrifice and service of your faith, *I rejoice* and share my *joy* with you all.

Philippians 3:9–11

. . . and may be found in Him, not having a righteousness of my own derived from the Law, but that which is through faith in Christ, the righteousness which comes from God on the basis of faith, ¹⁰that I may know Him and the power of His resurrection and the fellowship of His sufferings, being conformed to His *death*; ¹¹in order that I may attain to the resurrection from the dead.

Philippians 3:20–21

For our citizenship is in heaven, from which also we eagerly wait for a Savior, the Lord Jesus Christ; ²¹who will transform the *body* of our humble state into conformity with the body of His glory, by the exertion of the power that He has even to subject all things to Himself.

OTHER PAULINE PARALLELS

Romans 14:7–8

For not one of us lives for himself, and not one dies for himself; ⁸for if we live, we *live* for the Lord, or if we die, we *die* for the Lord; therefore whether we live or die, we are the Lord's.

1 Corinthians 6:20

For you have been bought with a price: therefore glorify God in your *body*.

2 Corinthians 1:9–11

Indeed, we had the sentence of *death* within ourselves so that we would not trust in ourselves, but in God who raises the dead; ¹⁰who *delivered* us from so great a peril of death, and will deliver us, He on whom we have set our *hope*. And He will yet deliver us, ¹¹you also joining in helping us *through your prayers*, so that thanks may be given by many persons on our behalf for the favor bestowed on us through the prayers of many.

2 Corinthians 4:8–12

We are afflicted in every way, but not crushed; perplexed, but not despairing; ⁹persecuted, but not forsaken; struck down, but not destroyed; ¹⁰always carrying about in the body the dying of Jesus, so that the life of Jesus also may be manifested in our *body*. ¹¹For we who live are constantly being delivered over to death for Jesus' sake, so that the *life* of Jesus also may be manifested in our mortal *flesh*. ¹²So *death* works in us, but life in you.

2 Corinthians 5:6–9

Therefore, being always of good courage, and knowing that while we are at home in the *body* we are absent from the Lord— ⁷for we walk by faith, not by sight— ⁸we are of good courage, I say, and prefer rather to be absent from the body and to be at home with the Lord. ⁹Therefore we also have as our ambition, whether at home or absent, to be pleasing to Him.

Galatians 2:20

I have been crucified with Christ; and it is no longer I who live, but Christ lives in me; and the life which I now *live in the flesh* I live by faith in the Son of God, who loved me and gave Himself up for me.

Galatians 6:17

From now on let no one cause trouble for me, for I bear on my *body* the brand-marks of Jesus.

Ephesians 6:19–20

Pray on my behalf, that utterance may be given to me in the opening of my mouth, to make known with *boldness* the mystery of the gospel, ²⁰for which I am an ambassador in chains; that in proclaiming it I may speak boldly, as I ought to speak.

OTHER BIBLICAL PARALLELS

Job 13:16, 18

"This also will be my salvation, For a godless man may not come before His presence. . . . ¹⁸Behold now, I have prepared my case; I know that I will be vindicated."

Acts 16:7

After they [Paul, Silas, and Timothy] came to Mysia, they were trying to go into Bithynia, and *the Spirit of Jesus* did not permit them.

1 Peter 4:15–16

Make sure that none of you suffers as a murderer, or thief, or evildoer, or a troublesome meddler; [16]but if anyone suffers as a Christian, he is not to be *ashamed*, but is to glorify God in this name.

NONCANONICAL PARALLELS

Plato, Apology 41C–D

But you, members of the jury, must also be hopeful regarding death and keep this one thing in mind, [D]that a good man incurs evil neither in *life* nor in *death*, and that his affairs are not neglected by the gods. . . . And it is clear to me that it was *better* for me to die now and escape from troubles. . . . So I am in no way angry with those who have convicted or accused me.

Plato, Phaedo 62C

So put this way, it is not unreasonable that one must not kill himself until a god sends some necessity to do so upon him, such as that now put upon us.

Philippians 1:27–30

Only conduct yourselves in a manner worthy of the gospel of Christ, so that whether I come and see you or remain absent, I will hear of you that you are standing firm in one spirit, with one mind striving together for the faith of the gospel; [28]in no way alarmed by your opponents—which is a sign of destruction for them, but of salvation for you, and that too, from God. [29]For to you it has been granted for Christ's sake, not only to believe in Him, but also to suffer for His sake, [30]experiencing the same conflict which you saw in me, and now hear to be in me.

PHILIPPIANS PARALLELS

Philippians 2:12

So then, my beloved, just as you have always obeyed, not as in my presence only,

but now much more in my *absence*, work out your *salvation* with fear and trembling.

Philippians 3:18–19

For many walk, of whom I often told you, and now tell you even weeping, that they are enemies of the cross of Christ, [19]whose end is *destruction*, whose god is their appetite, and whose glory is in their shame, who set their minds on earthly things.

Philippians 4:1, 3

Therefore, my beloved brethren whom I long to see, my joy and crown, in this way *stand firm* in the Lord, my beloved. . . . [3]Indeed, true companion, I ask you also to help these women who have shared my struggle in the cause of *the gospel*, together with Clement also and the rest of my fellow workers, whose names are in the book of life.

OTHER PAULINE PARALLELS

2 Corinthians 1:5

For just as the *sufferings* of Christ are ours in abundance, so also our comfort is abundant through Christ.

2 Corinthians 1:24

Not that we lord it over your faith, but are workers with you for your joy; for in your *faith* you are *standing firm*.

2 Corinthians 7:5

For even when we came into Macedonia our flesh had no rest, but we were afflicted on every side: *conflicts* without, fears within.

Galatians 4:17–18

They eagerly seek you, not commendably, but they wish to shut you out so that you will seek them. [18]But it is good always to be eagerly sought in a commendable manner, and not only when I am present with you.

Ephesians 4:1–6

Therefore I, the prisoner of the Lord, implore you to walk *in a manner worthy* of the calling with which you have been called, [2]with all humility and gentleness, with patience, showing tolerance for one another in love, [3]being diligent to preserve the unity of the Spirit in the bond of peace. [4]There is one body and *one Spirit*, just as also you were called in one hope of your calling; [5]one Lord, one faith, one baptism, [6]one God and Father of all who is over all and through all and in all.

Colossians 1:9–10

For this reason also, since the day we heard of it, we have not ceased to pray for you and to ask that you may be filled with the knowledge of His will in all spiritual wisdom and understanding, [10]so that you will walk *in a manner worthy* of the Lord, to please Him in all respects, bearing fruit in every good work and increasing in the knowledge of God.

Colossians 1:22–23

He has now reconciled you in His fleshly body through death, in order to present you before Him holy and blameless and beyond reproach— [23]if indeed you continue in *the faith* firmly established and steadfast, and not moved away from the hope of *the gospel* that you have heard, which was proclaimed in all creation under heaven, and of which I, Paul, was made a minister.

Colossians 2:4–5

I say this so that no one will delude you with persuasive argument. [5]For even though I am *absent* in body, nevertheless I am with you in spirit, rejoicing to see your good discipline and the stability of your *faith* in Christ.

1 Thessalonians 2:2

After we had already *suffered* and been mistreated in Philippi, as you know, we had the boldness in our God to speak to you *the gospel* of God amid much opposition.

1 Thessalonians 2:11–12

You know how we were exhorting and encouraging and imploring each one of you as a father would his own children, [12]so that you would walk *in a manner worthy* of the God who calls you into His own kingdom and glory.

2 Thessalonians 1:4–5

Therefore, we ourselves speak proudly of you among the churches of God for your perseverance and *faith* in the midst of all your persecutions and afflictions which you endure. [5]This is a plain indication of God's righteous judgment so that you will be con-sidered *worthy* of the kingdom of God, for which indeed you are *suffering.*

2 Timothy 2:24–25

The Lord's bond-servant must not be quarrelsome, but be kind to all, able to teach, patient when wronged, [25]with gentleness correcting those who are in opposition, if perhaps God may grant them repentance leading to the knowledge of the truth.

OTHER BIBLICAL PARALLELS

Psalm 37:38–40

But transgressors will be altogether destroyed; The posterity of the wicked will be cut off. [39]But the *salvation* of the righteous is from the LORD; He is their strength in time of trouble. [40]The LORD helps them and delivers them; He delivers them from the wicked and saves them, Because they take refuge in Him.

Matthew 24:3–6, 10–11

As He was sitting on the Mount of Olives, the disciples came to Him privately, saying, "Tell us, when will these things happen, and what will be the *sign* of Your coming, and of the end of the age?" [4]And Jesus answered and said to them, "See to it that no one misleads you. [5]For many will come in My name, saying, 'I am the Christ,' and will mislead many. [6]You will be hearing of wars and rumors of wars. See that you are not frightened, for those things must take place, but that is not yet the end. . . . [10]At that time many will fall away and will betray one another and hate one another. [11]Many false prophets will arise and will mislead many."

Jude 3–4

Beloved, while I was making every effort to write you about our common *salvation*, I felt the necessity to write to you appealing that you contend earnestly *for the faith* which was once for all handed down to the saints. [4]For certain persons have crept in unnoticed, those who were long beforehand marked out for this condemnation, ungodly persons who turn the grace of our God into licentiousness and deny our only Master and Lord, Jesus Christ.

When asked, "What is a friend?" He [Aristotle] replied, *"One mind* dwelling in two bodies."

Philippians 2:1–4

Therefore if there is any encouragement in Christ, if there is any consolation of love, if there is any fellowship of the Spirit, if any affection and compassion, [2]make my joy complete by being of the same mind, maintaining the same love, united in spirit, intent on one purpose. [3]Do nothing from selfishness or empty conceit, but with humility of mind regard one another as more important than yourselves; [4]do not merely look out for your own personal interests, but also for the interests of others.

PHILIPPIANS PARALLELS

Philippians 1:4
. . . always offering prayer with *joy* in my every prayer for you all.

Philippians 1:8–9
For God is my witness, how I long for you all with the *affection* of Christ Jesus. [9]And this I pray, that your *love* may abound still more and more in real knowledge and all discernment.

Philippians 1:15–17
Some, to be sure, are preaching Christ even from envy and strife, but some also from good will; [16]the latter do it out of *love,* knowing that I am appointed for the defense of the gospel; [17]the former proclaim Christ out of *selfish* ambition rather than from pure motives, thinking to cause me distress in my imprisonment.

Philippians 2:20–21
For I have no one else of kindred *spirit* who will genuinely be concerned for your welfare. [21]For they all seek after their *own interests,* not those of Christ Jesus.

Philippians 4:1–2
Therefore, my beloved brethren whom I long to see, my *joy* and crown, in this way

stand firm in the Lord, my beloved. [2]I urge Euodia and I urge Syntyche to live in harmony in the Lord.

OTHER PAULINE PARALLELS

Romans 12:9–10, 16
Let *love* be without hypocrisy. Abhor what is evil; cling to what is good. [10]Be devoted to one another in brotherly love; give preference to one another in honor. . . . [16]*Be of the same mind* toward one another; do not be haughty in mind, but associate with the lowly. Do not be wise in your own estimation.

Romans 15:1–3
Now we who are strong ought to bear the weaknesses of those without strength and not just please ourselves. [2]Each of us is to please his neighbor for his good, to his edification. [3]For even Christ did not please Himself; but as it is written, "THE REPROACHES OF THOSE WHO REPROACHED YOU FELL ON ME."

1 Corinthians 2:16
For WHO HAS KNOWN THE MIND OF THE LORD, THAT HE WILL INSTRUCT HIM? But we have the *mind* of Christ.

1 Corinthians 10:24
Let no one seek his own good, but that of his neighbor.

Galatians 5:22, 26
But the fruit of *the Spirit* is *love, joy,* peace, patience, kindness, goodness, faithfulness. . . . [26]Let us not become boastful, challenging one another, envying one another.

Ephesians 4:1–3
Therefore I, the prisoner of the Lord, implore you to walk in a manner worthy of the calling with which you have been called, [2]with all *humility* and gentleness, with patience, showing tolerance for one another in *love,* [3]being diligent to preserve the *unity of the Spirit* in the bond of peace.

Ephesians 5:21
Be subject to one another in the fear of Christ.

Colossians 3:12
So, as those who have been chosen of God, holy and beloved, put on a heart

of *compassion*, kindness, *humility*, gentleness and patience.

1 Timothy 6:17
Instruct those who are rich in this present world not to be *conceited* or to fix their hope on the uncertainty of riches, but on God, who richly supplies us with all things to enjoy.

NONCANONICAL PARALLELS

The Rule of the Community *(1QS) 2.24–25*
For all shall be in a single Community of truth, of proper meekness, of compassionate *love* and upright purpose, [25]towards each other in the holy council, associates of an everlasting society.

Mishnah 'Abot *4:12*
The honor owing to your disciple should be as precious to you as yours. And the honor owing to your fellow should be like the reverence owing to your master.

Philippians 2:5–11

Have this attitude in yourselves which was also in Christ Jesus, [6]who, although He existed in the form of God, did not regard equality with God a thing to be grasped, [7]but emptied Himself, taking the form of a bond-servant, and being made in the likeness of men. [8]Being found in appearance as a man, He humbled Himself by becoming obedient to the point of death, even death on a cross. [9]For this reason also, God highly exalted Him, and bestowed on Him the name which is above every name, [10]so that at the name of Jesus EVERY KNEE WILL BOW, of those who are in heaven and on earth and under the earth, [11]and that every tongue will confess that Jesus Christ is Lord, to the glory of God the Father.

PHILIPPIANS PARALLELS

Philippians 3:8–10
More than that, I count all things to be loss in view of the surpassing value of knowing Christ Jesus my Lord, for whom I have suffered the loss of all things, and count them but rubbish so that I may gain Christ, [9]and may be found in Him, not having a righteousness of my own derived from the Law,

but that which is through faith in Christ, the righteousness which comes from God on the basis of faith, [10]that I may know Him and the power of His resurrection and the fellowship of His sufferings, being conformed to His *death*.

Philippians 3:15–16
Let us therefore, as many as are perfect, *have this attitude*; and if in anything you have a different attitude, God will reveal that also to you; [16]however, let us keep living by that same standard to which we have attained.

Philippians 3:18–19
For many walk, of whom I often told you, and now tell you even weeping, that they are enemies of the *cross* of Christ, [19]whose end is destruction, whose god is their appetite, and whose *glory* is in their shame, who set their minds on earthly things.

OTHER PAULINE PARALLELS

Romans 5:19
For as through the one man's disobedience the many were made sinners, even so through the *obedience* of the One the many will be made righteous.

Romans 8:3
For what the Law could not do, weak as it was through the flesh, God did: sending His own Son in the *likeness* of sinful flesh and as an offering for sin, He condemned sin in the flesh.

Romans 10:8–9
But what does it say? "THE WORD IS NEAR YOU, in your mouth and in your heart"—that is, the word of faith which we are preaching, [9]that if you *confess* with your mouth *Jesus* as *Lord*, and believe in your heart that God raised Him from the dead, you will be saved.

2 Corinthians 4:3–4
And even if our gospel is veiled, it is veiled to those who are perishing, [4]in whose case the god of this world has blinded the minds of the unbelieving so that they might not see the light of the gospel of the *glory* of Christ, who is the image of God.

2 Corinthians 8:9

For you know the grace of our Lord Jesus Christ, that though He was rich, yet for your sake He became poor, so that you through His poverty might become rich.

2 Corinthians 13:4

For indeed He was crucified because of weakness, yet He lives because of the power of God. For we also are weak in Him, yet we will live with Him because of the power of God directed toward you.

Ephesians 1:19–21

These are in accordance with the working of the strength of His might [20]which He brought about in Christ, when He raised Him from the dead and seated Him at His right hand in the heavenly places, [21]far *above* all rule and authority and power and dominion, and *every name* that is named, not only in this age but also in the one to come.

Colossians 1:15–16, 20

He is the image of the invisible God, the firstborn of all creation. [16]For by Him all things were created, both in the heavens and on earth, visible and invisible, whether thrones or dominions or rulers or authorities—all things have been created through Him and for Him. . . . [20]and through Him to reconcile all things to Himself, having made peace through the blood of His *cross*; through Him, I say, whether things *on earth* or things *in heaven*.

1 Timothy 3:16

By common *confession,* great is the mystery of godliness: He who was revealed in the flesh, Was vindicated in the Spirit, Seen by angels, Proclaimed among the nations, Believed on in the world, Taken up in *glory.*

OTHER BIBLICAL PARALLELS

Isaiah 45:23

"I have sworn by Myself, The word has gone forth from My mouth in righteousness And will not turn back, That to Me *every knee will bow, every tongue* will swear allegiance."

Isaiah 52:13–14

Behold, My *servant* will prosper, He will be high and lifted up and greatly *exalted.* [14]Just as many were astonished at you, My people,

So His *appearance* was marred more than any *man,* And His form more than the sons of men.

Isaiah 53:11–12

As a result of the anguish of His soul, He will see it and be satisfied; By His knowledge the Righteous One, My *Servant,* will justify the many, As He will bear their iniquities. [12]Therefore, I will allot Him a portion with the great, And He will divide the booty with the strong; Because He poured out Himself to *death,* And was numbered with the transgressors; Yet He Himself bore the sin of many, And interceded for the transgressors.

John 10:17–18

"For this reason the Father loves Me, because I lay down My life so that I may take it again. [18]No one has taken it away from Me, but I lay it down on My own initiative. I have authority to lay it down, and I have authority to take it up again. This commandment I received from My Father."

Hebrews 2:9

But we do see Him who was made for a little while lower than the angels, namely, Jesus, because of the suffering of *death* crowned with *glory* and honor, so that by the grace of God He might taste death for everyone.

Hebrews 5:8

Although He was a Son, He learned *obedience* from the things which He suffered.

Hebrews 12:2

. . . fixing our eyes on Jesus, the author and perfecter of faith, who for the joy set before Him endured the *cross*, despising the shame, and has sat down at the right hand of the throne of God.

NONCANONICAL PARALLELS

Pliny the Younger, Epistles *10.96*

They [the Christians] were accustomed to gather on a fixed day before dawn and sing responsively among themselves a hymn to Christ as to a god.

Philippians 2:12–18

So then, my beloved, just as you have always obeyed, not as in my presence only, but now much more in my absence, work out your salvation with fear and trembling; [13]for it is God who is at work in you, both to will and to work for His good pleasure. [14]Do all things without grumbling or disputing; [15]so that you will prove yourselves to be blameless and innocent, children of God above reproach in the midst of a crooked and perverse generation, among whom you appear as lights in the world, [16]holding fast the word of life, so that in the day of Christ I will have reason to glory because I did not run in vain nor toil in vain. [17]But even if I am being poured out as a drink offering upon the sacrifice and service of your faith, I rejoice and share my joy with you all. [18]You too, I urge you, rejoice in the same way and share your joy with me.

PHILIPPIANS PARALLELS

Philippians 1:9–10
And this I pray, that your love may abound still more and more in real knowledge and all discernment, [10]so that you may approve the things that are excellent, in order to be sincere and *blameless* until *the day of Christ.*

Philippians 1:18–19
What then? Only that in every way, whether in pretense or in truth, Christ is proclaimed; and in this *I rejoice.* Yes, and I will rejoice, [19]for I know that this will turn out for my deliverance through your prayers and the provision of the Spirit of Jesus Christ.

Philippians 1:25, 27–28
Convinced of this, I know that I will remain and continue with you all for your progress and *joy* in the *faith.* . . . [27]Only conduct yourselves in a manner worthy of the gospel of Christ, so that whether I come and see you or remain *absent,* I will hear of you that you are standing firm in one spirit, with one mind striving together for the faith of the gospel; [28]in no way alarmed by your opponents—which is a sign of destruction for them, but of *salvation* for you, and that too, from God.

Philippians 4:4
Rejoice in the Lord always; again I will say, rejoice!

Philippians 4:18
But I have received everything in full and have an abundance; I am amply supplied, having received from Epaphroditus what you have sent, a fragrant aroma, an acceptable *sacrifice,* well-pleasing to God.

OTHER PAULINE PARALLELS

1 Corinthians 1:7–8
You are not lacking in any gift, awaiting eagerly the revelation of our Lord Jesus Christ, [8]who will also confirm you to the end, *blameless* in *the day of* our Lord Jesus Christ.

1 Corinthians 10:9–11
Nor let us try the Lord, as some of them did, and were destroyed by the serpents. [10]Nor *grumble,* as some of them did, and were destroyed by the destroyer. [11]Now these things happened to them as an example, and they were written for our instruction, upon whom the ends of the ages have come.

1 Corinthians 12:6–7
There are varieties of effects, but the same *God who works* all things in all persons. [7]But to each one is given the manifestation of the Spirit for the common good.

2 Corinthians 1:13–14
For we write nothing else to you than what you read and understand, and I hope you will understand until the end; [14]just as you also partially did understand us, that we are your reason to be proud as you also are ours, in *the day* of our Lord Jesus.

2 Corinthians 7:13, 15
And besides our comfort, we *rejoiced* even much more for the *joy* of Titus, because his spirit has been refreshed by you all. . . . [15]His affection abounds all the more toward you, as he remembers the *obedience* of you all, how you received him *with fear and trembling.*

Ephesians 5:1–2, 8
Therefore be imitators of God, as *beloved children;* [2]and walk in love, just as Christ also loved you and gave Himself up for us,

an *offering* and a *sacrifice* to God as a fragrant aroma. . . . [8]You were formerly darkness, but now you are *Light* in the Lord; walk as children of Light.

Colossians 2:5

For even though I am *absent* in body, nevertheless I am with you in spirit, *rejoicing* to see your good discipline and the stability of *your faith* in Christ.

1 Thessalonians 3:5

For this reason, when I could endure it no longer, I also sent to find out about your *faith*, for fear that the tempter might have tempted you, and our labor would be *in vain*.

1 Thessalonians 5:23

Now may the God of peace Himself sanctify you entirely; and may your spirit and soul and body be preserved complete, *without blame* at the coming of our Lord Jesus Christ.

2 Timothy 4:6

For *I am* already *being poured out as a drink offering*, and the time of my departure has come.

OTHER BIBLICAL PARALLELS

Numbers 28:3, 7

"This is the offering by fire which you shall offer to the LORD: two male lambs one year old without defect as a continual burnt offering every day. . . . [7]Then the drink offering with it shall be a fourth of a hin for each lamb, in the holy place you shall *pour out a drink offering* of strong drink to the LORD."

Deuteronomy 32:5

"They have acted corruptly toward Him, They are not His *children*, because of their defect; But are a *perverse* and *crooked generation*."

Daniel 12:3

"Those who have insight will shine brightly like the brightness of the expanse of heaven, and those who lead the many to righteousness, like the stars forever and ever."

Matthew 5:14

"You are the *light* of *the world*. A city set on a hill cannot be hidden."

Acts 2:40

And with many other words he [Peter] solemnly testified and kept on exhorting them, saying, "Be saved from this *perverse generation!*"

Philippians 2:19–30

But I hope in the Lord Jesus to send Timothy to you shortly, so that I also may be encouraged when I learn of your condition. [20]For I have no one else of kindred spirit who will genuinely be concerned for your welfare. [21]For they all seek after their own interests, not those of Christ Jesus. [22]But you know of his proven worth, that he served with me in the furtherance of the gospel like a child serving his father. [23]Therefore I hope to send him immediately, as soon as I see how things go with me; [24]and I trust in the Lord that I myself also will be coming shortly. [25]But I thought it necessary to send to you Epaphroditus, my brother and fellow worker and fellow soldier, who is also your messenger and minister to my need; [26]because he was longing for you all and was distressed because you had heard that he was sick. [27]For indeed he was sick to the point of death, but God had mercy on him, and not on him only but also on me, so that I would not have sorrow upon sorrow. [28]Therefore I have sent him all the more eagerly so that when you see him again you may rejoice and I may be less concerned about you. [29]Receive him then in the Lord with all joy, and hold men like him in high regard; [30]because he came close to death for the work of Christ, risking his life to complete what was deficient in your service to me.

PHILIPPIANS PARALLELS

Philippians 1:1

Paul and *Timothy*, bond-servants of Christ Jesus, To all the saints in Christ Jesus who are in Philippi, including the overseers and deacons . . .

Philippians 1:15, 17

Some, to be sure, are preaching Christ even from envy and strife, but some also from good will; . . . [17]the former proclaim Christ out of selfish ambition rather than from pure motives, thinking to cause me *distress* in my imprisonment.

Philippians 1:27

Only conduct yourselves in a manner worthy of *the gospel* of Christ, so that whether *I come* and see you or remain absent, I will hear of you that you are standing firm in one spirit, with one mind striving together for the faith of the gospel.

Philippians 2:4–5

Do not merely look out for your *own* personal *interests*, but also for the interests of others. [5]Have this attitude in yourselves which was also in Christ Jesus . . .

Philippians 4:1–4

Therefore, my beloved brethren whom I *long* to see, my *joy* and crown, in this way stand firm in the Lord, my beloved. [2]I urge Euodia and I urge Syntyche to live in harmony in the Lord. [3]Indeed, true companion, I ask you also to help these women who have shared my struggle in the cause of the *gospel*, together with Clement also and the rest of my *fellow workers*, whose names are in the book of life. [4]*Rejoice* in the Lord always; again I will say, rejoice!

Philippians 4:10, 18

But I *rejoiced* in the Lord greatly, that now at last you have revived your *concern* for me; indeed, you were concerned before, but you lacked opportunity. . . . [18]But I have received everything in full and have an abundance; I am amply supplied, having received from *Epaphroditus* what you have sent, a fragrant aroma, an acceptable sacrifice, well-pleasing to God.

OTHER PAULINE PARALLELS

Romans 16:1–4

I commend to you our sister Phoebe, who is a servant of the church which is at Cenchrea; [2]that you *receive* her *in the Lord* in a manner worthy of the saints, and that you help her in whatever matter she may have need of you; for she herself has also been a helper of many, and of myself as well. [3]Greet Prisca and Aquila, my *fellow workers* in Christ Jesus, [4]who for my life *risked* their own necks, to whom not only do I give thanks, but also all the churches of the Gentiles.

1 Corinthians 4:17

For this reason I have *sent* to you *Timothy*, who is my beloved and faithful *child* in the Lord, and he will remind you of my ways which are in Christ, just as I teach everywhere in every church.

1 Corinthians 16:10

Now if *Timothy* comes, see that he is with you without cause to be afraid, for he is doing the Lord's work, as I also am.

2 Corinthians 1:3–4

Blessed be the God and Father of our Lord Jesus Christ, the Father of mercies and God of all comfort, [4]who comforts us in all our affliction so that we will be able to comfort those who are in any affliction with the comfort with which we ourselves are comforted by God.

2 Corinthians 8:23

As for Titus, he is my partner and *fellow worker* among you; as for our brethren, they are *messengers* of the churches, a glory to Christ.

1 Thessalonians 3:1–2, 6–7

Therefore when we could endure it no longer, we thought it best to be left behind at Athens alone, [2]and we *sent Timothy*, our brother and God's *fellow worker* in the *gospel* of Christ, to strengthen and encourage you as to your faith. . . . [6]But now that Timothy has come to us from you, and has brought us good news of your faith and love, and that you always think kindly of us, longing to see us just as we also long to see you, [7]for this reason, brethren, in all our *distress* and affliction we were comforted about you through your faith.

2 Timothy 1:2

To *Timothy*, my beloved son: Grace, mercy and peace from God the Father and Christ Jesus our Lord.

Philemon 1–2

Paul, a prisoner of Christ Jesus, and *Timothy* our brother, To Philemon our beloved brother and *fellow worker*, [2]and to Apphia our sister, and to Archippus our *fellow soldier*, and to the church in your house . . .

Philemon 12–13

I have *sent* him back to you in person, that is, sending my very heart, [13]whom I wished to keep with me, so that on your behalf he might *minister* to me in my imprisonment for *the gospel.*

Acts 16:1–3

Paul came also to Derbe and to Lystra. And a disciple was there, named *Timothy,* the son of a Jewish woman who was a believer, but his father was a Greek, [2]and he was well spoken of by the brethren who were in Lystra and Iconium. [3]Paul wanted this man to go with him; and he took him and circumcised him because of the Jews who were in those parts, for they all knew that his father was a Greek.

Acts 19:21–22

Now after these things were finished, Paul purposed in the spirit to go to Jerusalem after he had passed through Macedonia and Achaia, saying, "After I have been there, I must also see Rome." [22]And having *sent* into Macedonia two of those who *ministered* to him, *Timothy* and Erastus, he himself stayed in Asia for a while.

Philippians 3:1–6

Finally, my brethren, rejoice in the Lord. To write the same things again is no trouble to me, and it is a safeguard for you. [2]Beware of the dogs, beware of the evil workers, beware of the false circumcision; [3]for we are the true circumcision, who worship in the Spirit of God and glory in Christ Jesus and put no confidence in the flesh, [4]although I myself might have confidence even in the flesh. If anyone else has a mind to put confidence in the flesh, I far more: [5]circumcised the eighth day, of the nation of Israel, of the tribe of Benjamin, a Hebrew of Hebrews; as to the Law, a Pharisee; [6]as to zeal, a persecutor of the church; as to the righteousness which is in the Law, found blameless.

Philippians 1:27–28

Only conduct yourselves in a manner worthy of the gospel of Christ, so that whether I come and see you or remain absent, I will hear of you that you are standing firm in one spirit, with one mind striving together for the faith of the gospel; [28]in no way alarmed by your opponents—which is a sign of destruction for them, but of salvation for you, and that too, from God.

Philippians 4:4

Rejoice in the Lord always; again I will say, rejoice!

Romans 2:28–29

For he is not a Jew who is one outwardly, nor is *circumcision* that which is outward in *the flesh.* [29]But he is a Jew who is one inwardly; and circumcision is that which is of the heart, by *the Spirit,* not by the letter; and his praise is not from men, but from God.

Romans 11:1

I say then, God has not rejected His people, has He? May it never be! For I too am an *Israelite,* a descendant of Abraham, *of the tribe of Benjamin.*

1 Corinthians 15:9

For I am the least of the apostles, and not fit to be called an apostle, because I *persecuted the church* of God.

2 Corinthians 11:13, 21–22

For such men are *false* apostles, deceitful *workers,* disguising themselves as apostles of Christ. . . . [21]To my shame I must say that we have been weak by comparison. But in whatever respect anyone else is bold—I speak in foolishness—I am just as bold myself. [22]Are they *Hebrews*? So am I. Are they *Israelites*? So am I. Are they descendants of Abraham? So am I.

Galatians 1:13–14

For you have heard of my former manner of life in Judaism, how I used to *persecute the church* of God beyond measure and tried to destroy it; [14]and I was advancing in Judaism beyond many of my contemporaries among my countrymen, being more extremely *zealous* for my ancestral traditions.

Galatians 5:11–12

But I, brethren, if I still preach *circumcision*, why am I still *persecuted*? Then the stumbling block of the cross has been abolished. [12]I wish that those who are troubling you would even mutilate themselves.

Galatians 6:12, 15

Those who desire to make a good showing in *the flesh* try to compel you to be circumcised, simply so that they will not be *persecuted* for the cross of Christ. . . . [15]For neither is *circumcision* anything, nor uncircumcision, but a new creation.

Ephesians 2:11–12

Therefore remember that formerly you, the Gentiles in *the flesh*, who are called "Uncircumcision" by the so-called "*Circumcision*," which is performed in the flesh by human hands— [12]remember that you were at that time separate from Christ, excluded from the commonwealth of *Israel*, and strangers to the covenants of promise, having no hope and without God in the world.

Colossians 2:11–12

In Him you were also circumcised with a *circumcision* made without hands, in the removal of the body of *the flesh* by the circumcision of Christ; [12]having been buried with Him in baptism, in which you were also raised up with Him through faith in the working of God, who raised Him from the dead.

OTHER BIBLICAL PARALLELS

Leviticus 12:2–3

"When a woman gives birth and bears a male child, then she shall be unclean for seven days, as in the days of her menstruation she shall be unclean. [3]On *the eighth day the flesh* of his foreskin shall be *circumcised*."

Deuteronomy 30:6

"Moreover the LORD your God will *circumcise* your heart and the heart of your descendants, to love the LORD your God with all your heart and with all your soul, so that you may live."

Psalm 22:16

For *dogs* have surrounded me; A band of evildoers has encompassed me; They pierced my hands and my feet.

Psalm 119:1

How blessed are those whose way is *blameless*, Who walk in *the law* of the LORD.

Matthew 7:15

"*Beware* of the *false* prophets, who come to you in sheep's clothing, but inwardly are ravenous wolves."

Mark 7:26–27

Now the woman was a Gentile, of the Syrophoenician race. And she kept asking Him to cast the demon out of her daughter. [27]And He was saying to her, "Let the children be satisfied first, for it is not good to take the children's bread and throw it to the *dogs*."

John 4:24

"God is spirit, and those who worship Him must *worship in spirit* and truth."

Acts 22:3–4

"I am a Jew, born in Tarsus of Cilicia, but brought up in this city, educated under Gamaliel, strictly according to *the law* of our fathers, being *zealous* for God just as you all are today. [4]I *persecuted* this Way to the death, binding and putting both men and women into prisons."

Acts 23:6

But perceiving that one group were Sadducees and the other Pharisees, Paul began crying out in the Council, "Brethren, I am *a Pharisee*, a son of Pharisees; I am on trial for the hope and resurrection of the dead!"

NONCANONICAL PARALLELS

The Rule of the Community (1QS) 5.4–6

No-one should walk in the stubbornness of his heart in order to go astray. . . . [5] . . . Instead he should *circumcise* in the Community the foreskin of his tendency and of his stiff neck in order to lay a foundation of truth for *Israel*, for the Community of the eternal [6]covenant.

Mishnah Bekhorot 5:6

He who slaughters a cow and sold it and it becomes known that it is terefah [forbidden], . . . if [the buyers] sold it to gentiles or tossed it to the *dogs*, they return to [the seller] the value of the terefah.

But whatever things were gain to me, those things I have counted as loss for the sake of Christ. [8]More than that, I count all things to be loss in view of the surpassing value of knowing Christ Jesus my Lord, for whom I have suffered the loss of all things, and count them but rubbish so that I may gain Christ, [9]and may be found in Him, not having a righteousness of my own derived from the Law, but that which is through faith in Christ, the righteousness which comes from God on the basis of faith, [10]that I may know Him and the power of His resurrection and the fellowship of His sufferings, being conformed to His death; [11]in order that I may attain to the resurrection from the dead. [12]Not that I have already obtained it or have already become perfect, but I press on so that I may lay hold of that for which also I was laid hold of by Christ Jesus. [13]Brethren, I do not regard myself as having laid hold of it yet; but one thing I do: forgetting what lies behind and reaching forward to what lies ahead, [14]I press on toward the goal for the prize of the upward call of God in Christ Jesus. [15]Let us therefore, as many as are perfect, have this attitude; and if in anything you have a different attitude, God will reveal that also to you; [16]however, let us keep living by that same standard to which we have attained.

PHILIPPIANS PARALLELS

Philippians 1:10–11

. . . so that you may approve the things that are excellent, in order to be sincere and blameless until the day of Christ; [11]having been filled with the fruit of *righteousness* which comes through Jesus Christ, to the glory and praise of God.

Philippians 1:20

. . . according to my earnest expectation and hope, that I will not be put to shame in anything, but that with all boldness, Christ will even now, as always, be exalted in my body, whether by life or by *death.*

Philippians 2:17

But even if I am being poured out as a drink offering upon the sacrifice and service of your *faith,* I rejoice and share my joy with you all.

OTHER PAULINE PARALLELS

Romans 3:21–22

But now apart from *the Law* the righteousness of God has been manifested, being witnessed by *the Law* and the Prophets, [22]even the *righteousness* of God through *faith* in Jesus Christ for all those who believe; for there is no distinction.

Romans 6:5–6

For if we have become united with Him in the likeness of *His death,* certainly we shall also be in the likeness of His *resurrection,* [6]knowing this, that our old self was crucified with Him, in order that our body of sin might be done away with, so that we would no longer be slaves to sin.

Romans 8:16–17

The Spirit Himself testifies with our spirit that we are children of God, [17]and if children, heirs also, heirs of God and fellow heirs with Christ, if indeed we *suffer* with Him so that we may also be glorified with Him.

Romans 10:3–4

For not knowing about God's *righteousness* and seeking to establish their own, they did not subject themselves to the righteousness of God. [4]For Christ is the end of *the law* for righteousness to everyone who believes.

1 Corinthians 2:2

For I determined to *know* nothing among you except Jesus *Christ,* and Him crucified.

1 Corinthians 9:24

Do you not know that those who run in a race all run, but only one receives *the prize*? Run in such a way that you may win.

1 Corinthians 15:20–23

But now Christ has been raised from the dead, the first fruits of those who are asleep. [21]For since by a man came death, by a man also came *the resurrection* of *the dead.* [22]For as in Adam all die, so also in Christ all will be made alive. [23]But each in his own order: Christ the first fruits, after that those who are Christ's at His coming.

1 Corinthians 15:42–43

So also is *the resurrection* of *the dead.* It is sown a perishable body, it is raised an imperishable body; [43]it is sown in dishonor, it is raised in glory; it is sown in weakness, it is raised in *power*.

2 Corinthians 4:10–12

. . . always carrying about in the body the dying of Jesus, so that the life of Jesus also may be manifested in our body. [11]For we who live are constantly being delivered over to death for Jesus' sake, so that the life of Jesus also may be manifested in our mortal flesh. [12]So *death* works in us, but life in you.

Colossians 1:24

Now I rejoice in my *sufferings* for your sake, and in my flesh I do my share on behalf of His body, which is the church, in filling up what is lacking in Christ's afflictions.

1 Thessalonians 5:23–24

Now may the God of peace Himself sanctify you entirely; and may your spirit and soul and body be preserved complete, without blame at the coming of our Lord Jesus Christ. [24]Faithful is He who *calls* you, and He also will bring it to pass.

2 Timothy 4:7

I have fought the good fight, I have finished the course, I have kept the *faith*.

OTHER BIBLICAL PARALLELS

Jeremiah 9:24

"Let him who boasts boast of this, that he understands and *knows* Me, that I am the LORD who exercises lovingkindness, justice and *righteousness* on earth; for I delight in these things."

Hebrews 3:1

Therefore, holy brethren, partakers of a heavenly *calling*, consider Jesus, the Apostle and High Priest of our confession.

Hebrews 12:1

Therefore, since we have so great a cloud of witnesses surrounding us, let us also lay aside every encumbrance and the sin which so easily entangles us, and let us run with endurance the race that is set before us.

NONCANONICAL PARALLELS

Philo, On Noah's Work as a Planter *23*

For this reason those who are constantly insatiate for wisdom and knowledge are said in the oracles to have been *called upward*. For it is proper that those who have been "down-breathed" by him [God] should be called upward to the divine.

Philippians 3:17–21

Brethren, join in following my example, and observe those who walk according to the pattern you have in us. [18]For many walk, of whom I often told you, and now tell you even weeping, that they are enemies of the cross of Christ, [19]whose end is destruction, whose god is their appetite, and whose glory is in their shame, who set their minds on earthly things. [20]For our citizenship is in heaven, from which also we eagerly wait for a Savior, the Lord Jesus Christ; [21]who will transform the body of our humble state into conformity with the body of His glory, by the exertion of the power that He has even to subject all things to Himself.

PHILIPPIANS PARALLELS

Philippians 1:27–28

Only conduct yourselves in a manner worthy of the gospel of Christ, so that whether I come and see you or remain absent, I will hear of you that you are standing firm in one spirit, with one mind striving together for the faith of the gospel; [28]in no way alarmed by your opponents—which is a sign of *destruction* for them, but of salvation for you, and that too, from God.

Philippians 3:2

Beware of the dogs, beware of the evil workers, beware of the false circumcision.

OTHER PAULINE PARALLELS

Romans 8:23, 29

And not only this, but also we ourselves, having the first fruits of the Spirit, even we ourselves groan within ourselves, *waiting eagerly* for our adoption as sons, the redemption of our *body*. . . . [29]For those whom He foreknew, He also predestined to become *conformed* to the image of His Son, so that He would be the firstborn among many brethren.

Romans 16:18

For such men are slaves, not of our Lord Christ but of their own *appetites*; and by their smooth and flattering speech they deceive the hearts of the unsuspecting.

1 Corinthians 11:1

Be imitators of me, just as I also am of Christ.

1 Corinthians 15:28

When *all things* are *subjected* to Him, then the Son Himself also will be subjected to the One who subjected all things to Him, so that God may be all in all.

1 Corinthians 15:42–43

So also is the resurrection of the dead. It is sown a perishable *body*, it is raised an imperishable body; [43]it is sown in dishonor, it is raised in *glory*; it is sown in weakness, it is raised in *power*.

2 Corinthians 3:18

But we all, with unveiled face, beholding as in a mirror the glory of the Lord, are being *transformed* into the same image from *glory* to glory, just as from the Lord, the Spirit.

2 Corinthians 5:4

For indeed while we are in this tent, we groan, being burdened, because we do not want to be unclothed but to be clothed, so that what is mortal will be swallowed up by life.

2 Corinthians 11:13

For such men are false apostles, deceitful workers, disguising themselves as apostles of Christ.

Ephesians 1:22–23

And He put *all things* in *subjection* under His feet, and gave Him as head over all things to the church, [23]which is His *body*, the fullness of Him who fills all in all.

Ephesians 2:19

So then you are no longer strangers and aliens, but you are fellow *citizens* with the saints, and are of God's household.

Colossians 3:1–2

Therefore if you have been raised up with Christ, keep seeking the things above, where Christ is, seated at the right hand of God. [2]Set your *mind* on the things above, not on the things that are on *earth*.

1 Thessalonians 1:6

You also became imitators of us and of the Lord, having received the word in much tribulation with the joy of the Holy Spirit.

1 Thessalonians 4:1

Finally then, *brethren*, we request and exhort you in the Lord Jesus, that as you received from us instruction as to how you ought to *walk* and please God (just as you actually do walk), that you excel still more.

2 Thessalonians 3:7

For you yourselves know how you ought to *follow* our *example*, because we did not act in an undisciplined manner among you.

Titus 2:11–13

For the grace of God has appeared, bringing salvation to all men, [12]instructing us to deny ungodliness and worldly desires and to live sensibly, righteously and godly in the present age, [13]looking for the blessed hope and the appearing of the *glory* of our great God and *Savior*, Christ Jesus.

OTHER BIBLICAL PARALLELS

Numbers 24:20

And he [Balaam] looked at Amalek and took up his discourse and said, "Amalek was the first of the nations, But his *end* shall be *destruction.*"

Hebrews 12:22–23

But you have come to Mount Zion and to the city of the living God, the heavenly Jerusalem, and to myriads of angels, [23]to the general assembly and church of the first-born who are enrolled *in heaven*, and to God, the Judge of all, and to the spirits of the righteous made perfect.

1 Peter 5:1–3

Therefore, I exhort the elders among you, as your fellow elder and witness of the sufferings of Christ, and a partaker also of the *glory* that is to be revealed, [2]shepherd the flock of God among you, exercising oversight not under compulsion, but voluntarily, according to the will of God; and not for sordid gain, but with eagerness; [3]nor yet as lording it over those allotted to your charge, but proving to be *examples* to the flock.

Philo, On the Confusion of Tongues 78
To them [the wise] the *heavenly* region, in which their *citizenship* lies, is their native land, while the *earthly* region in which they have become sojourners is regarded as a foreign place.

Philippians 4:1–9

Therefore, my beloved brethren whom I long to see, my joy and crown, in this way stand firm in the Lord, my beloved. [2]I urge Euodia and I urge Syntyche to live in harmony in the Lord. [3]Indeed, true companion, I ask you also to help these women who have shared my struggle in the cause of the gospel, together with Clement also and the rest of my fellow workers, whose names are in the book of life. [4]Rejoice in the Lord always; again I will say, rejoice! [5]Let your gentle spirit be known to all men. The Lord is near. [6]Be anxious for nothing, but in everything by prayer and supplication with thanksgiving let your requests be made known to God. [7]And the peace of God, which surpasses all comprehension, will guard your hearts and your minds in Christ Jesus. [8]Finally, brethren, whatever is true, whatever is honorable, whatever is right, whatever is pure, whatever is lovely, whatever is of good repute, if there is any excellence and if anything worthy of praise, dwell on these things. [9]The things you have learned and received and heard and seen in me, practice these things, and the God of peace will be with you.

Philippians 1:8–10
For God is my witness, how *I long* for you all with the affection of Christ Jesus. [9]And this I *pray,* that your love may abound still more and more in real knowledge and all discernment, [10]so that you may approve the things that are *excellent,* in order to be sincere and blameless until the day of Christ.

Philippians 1:18–19
What then? Only that in every way, whether in pretense or in truth, Christ is proclaimed; and in this I *rejoice.* Yes, and I will rejoice, [19]for I know that this will turn out for my deliverance through your *prayers* and the provision of the Spirit of Jesus Christ.

Philippians 1:27
Only conduct yourselves in a manner worthy of *the gospel* of Christ, so that whether I come and see you or remain absent, I will hear of you that you are *standing firm* in one spirit, with one mind striving together for the faith of the gospel.

Philippians 2:17–18
But even if I am being poured out as a drink offering upon the sacrifice and service of your faith, I *rejoice* and share my *joy* with you all. [18]You too, I urge you, rejoice in the same way and share your joy with me.

Philippians 2:25
But I thought it necessary to send to you Epaphroditus, my brother and *fellow worker* and fellow soldier, who is also your messenger and minister to my need.

Romans 12:17
Never pay back evil for evil to anyone. Respect *what is right* in the sight of all men.

Romans 15:33
Now *the God of peace be with you* all. Amen.

2 Corinthians 13:11
Finally, brethren, *rejoice,* be made complete, be comforted, be like-minded, live in peace; and *the God of* love and *peace will be with you.*

Colossians 4:2
Devote yourselves to *prayer,* keeping alert in it with an attitude of *thanksgiving.*

1 Thessalonians 2:19
For who is our hope or *joy* or *crown* of exultation? Is it not even you, in the presence of our Lord Jesus at His coming?

1 Thessalonians 5:23
Now may *the God of peace* Himself sanctify you entirely; and may your spirit and soul

and body be preserved complete, without blame at the coming of our Lord Jesus Christ.

2 Timothy 1:13

Retain the standard of sound words which you have *heard* from me, in the faith and love which are in Christ Jesus.

2 Timothy 3:14

You, however, continue in *the things you have learned* and become convinced of, knowing from whom you have learned them.

Titus 3:1–2

Remind them to be subject to rulers, to authorities, to be obedient, to be ready for every good deed, [2]to malign no one, to be peaceable, *gentle*, showing every consideration for *all men*.

OTHER BIBLICAL PARALLELS

Daniel 12:1

"Now at that time Michael, the great prince who stands guard over the sons of your people, will arise. And there will be a time of distress such as never occurred since there was a nation until that time; and at that time your people, everyone who is found written in *the book*, will be rescued."

James 5:8

You too be patient; strengthen your hearts, for the coming of *the Lord is near*.

1 Peter 2:12

Keep your behavior *excellent* among the Gentiles, so that in the thing in which they slander you as evildoers, they may because of your good deeds, as they observe them, glorify God in the day of visitation.

1 Peter 5:6–7

Therefore humble yourselves under the mighty hand of God, that He may exalt you at the proper time, [7]casting all your *anxiety* on Him, because He cares for you.

Revelation 3:5

He who overcomes will thus be clothed in white garments; and I will not erase his *name* from *the book of life*, and I will confess his name before My Father and before His angels.

NONCANONICAL PARALLELS

1 Enoch *47:2–3*

There shall be days when all the holy ones who dwell in the heaven above shall dwell (together). And with one voice they shall *supplicate* and *pray*. . . . [3]In those days, I saw him—the Antecedent of Time, while he was sitting upon the throne of his glory, and *the books* of the living ones were open before him.

The Rule of the Community *(1QS) 4.3–6*

[The spirit of light] is a spirit of meekness, of patience, generous compassion, eternal goodness, . . . [4] . . . of knowledge in all the plans of action, of enthusiasm for the decrees of justice, . . . [5] . . . of magnificent *purity*, . . . [6] . . . of prudence in respect of *the truth*.

Philippians 4:10–20

But I rejoiced in the Lord greatly, that now at last you have revived your concern for me; indeed, you were concerned before, but you lacked opportunity. [11]Not that I speak from want, for I have learned to be content in whatever circumstances I am. [12]I know how to get along with humble means, and I also know how to live in prosperity; in any and every circumstance I have learned the secret of being filled and going hungry, both of having abundance and suffering need. [13]I can do all things through Him who strengthens me. [14]Nevertheless, you have done well to share with me in my affliction. [15]You yourselves also know, Philippians, that at the first preaching of the gospel, after I left Macedonia, no church shared with me in the matter of giving and receiving but you alone; [16]for even in Thessalonica you sent a gift more than once for my needs. [17]Not that I seek the gift itself, but I seek for the profit which increases to your account. [18]But I have received everything in full and have an abundance; I am amply supplied, having received from Epaphroditus what you have sent, a fragrant aroma, an acceptable sacrifice, well-pleasing to God. [19]And my God will supply all your needs according to His riches in glory in Christ Jesus. [20]Now to our God and Father be the glory forever and ever. Amen.

Philippians 1:3–5

I thank my God in all my remembrance of you, ⁴always offering prayer with joy in my every prayer for you all, ⁵in view of your participation in *the gospel* from the first day until now.

Philippians 2:17

But even if I am being poured out as a drink offering upon the *sacrifice* and service of your faith, *I rejoice* and share my joy with you all.

Philippians 2:25, 30

But I thought it necessary to send to you *Epaphroditus*, my brother and fellow worker and fellow soldier, who is also your messenger and minister to my *need*; . . . ³⁰because he came close to death for the work of Christ, risking his life to complete what was deficient in your service to me.

OTHER PAULINE PARALLELS

Romans 12:1

Therefore I urge you, brethren, by the mercies of God, to present your bodies a living and holy *sacrifice, acceptable* to God, which is your spiritual service of worship.

Romans 16:27

To the only wise God, through Jesus Christ, *be the glory forever. Amen.*

1 Corinthians 9:11, 14

If we sowed spiritual things in you, is it too much if we reap material things from you? . . . ¹⁴So also the Lord directed those who proclaim *the gospel* to get their living from the gospel.

2 Corinthians 6:3–4

. . . giving no cause for offense in anything, so that the ministry will not be discredited, ⁴but in everything commending ourselves as servants of God, in much endurance, in *afflictions*, in hardships, in distresses.

2 Corinthians 11:7–9

Or did I commit a sin in humbling myself so that you might be exalted, because I *preached the gospel* of God to you without charge? ⁸I robbed other churches by taking wages from them to serve you; ⁹and when I was present with you and was in *need*, I was

not a burden to anyone; for when the brethren came from *Macedonia* they fully *supplied* my need, and in everything I kept myself from being a burden to you, and will continue to do so.

2 Corinthians 11:27

I have been in labor and hardship, through many sleepless nights, in *hunger* and thirst, often without food, in cold and exposure.

Ephesians 5:2

Walk in love, just as Christ also loved you and gave Himself up for us, an offering and a *sacrifice* to God as *a fragrant aroma.*

1 Thessalonians 2:1–2, 9

For you yourselves know, brethren, that our coming to you was not in vain, ²but after we had already suffered and been mistreated in *Philippi*, as you know, we had the boldness in our God to speak to you *the gospel* of God amid much opposition. . . . ⁹For you recall, brethren, our labor and hardship, how working night and day so as not to be a burden to any of you, we proclaimed to you the gospel of God.

1 Timothy 6:6–8

But godliness actually is a means of great gain when accompanied by contentment. ⁷For we have brought nothing into the world, so we cannot take anything out of it either. ⁸If we have food and covering, with these we shall be *content.*

OTHER BIBLICAL PARALLELS

Exodus 29:18

"You shall offer up in smoke the whole ram on the altar; it is a burnt offering to the LORD: it is a soothing *aroma*, an offering by fire to the LORD."

Leviticus 22:29

"When you sacrifice a *sacrifice* of thanksgiving to the LORD, you shall sacrifice it so that you may be *accepted*."

Acts 16:11–12

So putting out to sea from Troas, we ran a straight course to Samothrace, and on the day following to Neapolis; ¹²and from there to *Philippi*, which is a leading city of the district of *Macedonia*, a Roman colony; and we were staying in this city for some days.

Acts 17:1

Now when they [Paul and Silas] had traveled through Amphipolis and Apollonia, they came to *Thessalonica*, where there was a synagogue of the Jews.

Hebrews 10:32–33

But remember the former days, when, after being enlightened, you endured a great conflict of sufferings, [33]partly by being made a public spectacle through reproaches and tribulations, and partly by becoming *sharers* with those who were so treated.

Hebrews 13:5

Make sure that your character is free from the love of money, being *content* with what you have; for He Himself has said, "I WILL NEVER DESERT YOU, NOR WILL I EVER FORSAKE YOU."

NONCANONICAL PARALLELS

Letter to Dionysius the Physician (P.Mert. 1.12)

(I will) dispense with writing to you with a great show of thanks, for it is to those who are not friends that one must give thanks in words.

Philippians 4:21–23

Greet every saint in Christ Jesus. The brethren who are with me greet you. [22]All the saints greet you, especially those of Caesar's household. [23]The grace of the Lord Jesus Christ be with your spirit.

PHILIPPIANS PARALLELS

Philippians 1:1–2

Paul and Timothy, bond-servants of Christ Jesus, To *all the saints* in Christ Jesus who are in Philippi, including the overseers and deacons: [2]*Grace* to you and peace from God our Father and the Lord Jesus Christ.

Philippians 1:12–14

Now I want you to know, brethren, that my circumstances have turned out for the greater progress of the gospel, [13]so that my imprisonment in the cause of Christ has become well known throughout the whole praetorian guard and to everyone else, [14]and that most of the brethren, trusting in the

Lord because of my imprisonment, have far more courage to speak the word of God without fear.

OTHER PAULINE PARALLELS

1 Corinthians 16:20, 23–24

All *the brethren greet you. Greet* one another with a holy kiss. . . . [23]*The grace of the Lord Jesus* be with you. [24]My love be with you all in Christ Jesus. Amen.

2 Corinthians 13:12–14

Greet one another with a holy kiss. [13]*All the saints greet you.* [14]*The grace of the Lord Jesus Christ*, and the love of God, and the fellowship of the Holy Spirit, *be with* you all.

Galatians 6:18

The grace of our *Lord Jesus Christ be with your spirit*, brethren. Amen.

1 Thessalonians 5:26–28

Greet all *the brethren* with a holy kiss. [27]I adjure you by the Lord to have this letter read to all the brethren. [28]*The grace of our Lord Jesus Christ* be with you.

2 Timothy 4:19, 22

Greet Prisca and Aquila, and the household of Onesiphorus. . . . [22]The Lord be *with your spirit. Grace* be with you.

Philemon 23–25

Epaphras, my fellow prisoner in Christ Jesus, *greets you,* [24]as do Mark, Aristarchus, Demas, Luke, my fellow workers. [25]*The grace of the Lord Jesus Christ be with your spirit.*

OTHER BIBLICAL PARALLELS

2 Peter 3:18

Grow in the *grace* and knowledge of our Lord and Savior Jesus Christ. To Him be the glory, both now and to the day of eternity. Amen.

2 John 3

Grace, mercy and peace will be with us, from God the Father and from Jesus Christ, the Son of the Father, in truth and love.

Revelation 22:21

The grace of the Lord Jesus be with all. Amen.

Colossians

Colossians 1:1–2

Paul, an apostle of Jesus Christ by the will of God, and Timothy our brother, [2]To the saints and faithful brethren in Christ who are at Colossae: Grace to you and peace from God our Father.

COLOSSIANS PARALLELS

Colossians 1:19–20

For it was the Father's good pleasure for all the fullness to dwell in Him, [20]and through Him to reconcile all things to Himself, having made *peace* through the blood of His cross; through Him, I say, whether things on earth or things in heaven.

Colossians 1:25–27

Of this church I was made a minister according to the stewardship from God bestowed on me for your benefit, so that I might fully carry out the preaching of the word of God, [26]that is, the mystery which has been hidden from the past ages and generations, but has now been manifested to His *saints*, [27]to whom God willed to make known what is the riches of the glory of this mystery among the Gentiles, which is Christ in you, the hope of glory.

Colossians 3:15

Let the *peace* of Christ rule in your hearts, to which indeed you were called in one body; and be thankful.

Colossians 4:12

Epaphras, who is one of your number, a bondslave of Jesus Christ, sends you his greetings, always laboring earnestly for you in his prayers, that you may stand perfect and fully assured in all *the will of God.*

Colossians 4:16, 18

When this letter is read among you, have it also read in the church of the Laodiceans; and you, for your part read my letter that is coming from Laodicea. . . . [18]I, *Paul*, write this greeting with my own hand. Remember my imprisonment. *Grace* be with *you.*

OTHER PAULINE PARALLELS

2 Corinthians 1:1–2

Paul, an apostle of Christ Jesus by the will of God, and Timothy our brother, To the church of God which is at Corinth with all *the saints* who are throughout Achaia: [2]*Grace to you and peace from God our Father* and the Lord Jesus Christ.

Ephesians 1:1–2

Paul, an apostle of Christ Jesus by the will of God, To the saints who are at Ephesus and who are *faithful in Christ* Jesus: [2]*Grace to you and peace from God our Father* and the Lord Jesus Christ.

Philippians 1:1–2

Paul and *Timothy,* bond-servants of Christ Jesus, *To all the saints in Christ* Jesus who are in Philippi, including the overseers and deacons: [2]*Grace to you and peace from God our Father* and the Lord Jesus Christ.

1 Thessalonians 1:1

Paul and Silvanus and *Timothy,* To the church of the Thessalonians in God the Father and the Lord Jesus Christ: *Grace to you and peace.*

Acts 2:8–10

"And how is it that we each hear them in our own language to which we were born? [9]Parthians and Medes and Elamites, and residents of Mesopotamia, Judea and Cappadocia, Pontus and Asia, [10]Phrygia and Pamphylia, Egypt and the districts of Libya around Cyrene, and visitors from Rome, both Jews and proselytes . . . "

Acts 16:1–3

Paul came also to Derbe and to Lystra. And a disciple was there, named *Timothy*, the son of a Jewish woman who was a believer, but his father was a Greek, [2]and he was well spoken of by the brethren who were in Lystra and Iconium. [3]Paul wanted this man to go with him; and he took him and circumcised him because of the Jews who were in those parts, for they all knew that his father was a Greek.

Acts 18:22–23

When he [Paul] had landed at Caesarea, he went up and greeted the church, and went down to Antioch. [23]And having spent some time there, he left and passed successively through the Galatian region and Phrygia, strengthening all the disciples.

NONCANONICAL PARALLELS

Josephus, Jewish Antiquities *12.148–49*

"King Antiochus to Zeuxis, his father, greetings. [149]When I heard about the insurgents in Lydia and Phrygia, . . . I decided to relocate 2,000 Jewish households with their effects from Mesopotamia and Babylonia to the fortresses and most essential places there."

Colossians 1:3–8

We give thanks to God, the Father of our Lord Jesus Christ, praying always for you, [4]since we heard of your faith in Christ Jesus and the love which you have for all the saints; [5]because of the hope laid up for you in heaven, of which you previously heard in the word of truth, the gospel [6]which has come to you, just as in all the world also it is constantly bearing fruit and

increasing, even as it has been doing in you also since the day you heard of it and understood the grace of God in truth; [7]just as you learned it from Epaphras, our beloved fellow bond-servant, who is a faithful servant of Christ on our behalf, [8]and he also informed us of your love in the Spirit.

COLOSSIANS PARALLELS

Colossians 1:19–20

For it was the Father's good pleasure for all the fullness to dwell in Him, [20]and through Him to reconcile all things to Himself, having made peace through the blood of His cross; through Him, I say, whether things on earth or things *in heaven.*

Colossians 1:23

. . . if indeed you continue in the *faith* firmly established and steadfast, and not moved away from the *hope* of *the gospel* that you have *heard*, which was proclaimed in all creation under heaven, and of which I, Paul, was made a minister.

Colossians 4:12

Epaphras, who is one of your number, a bondslave of Jesus Christ, sends you his greetings, always laboring earnestly for you in his *prayers,* that you may stand perfect and fully assured in all the will of God.

OTHER PAULINE PARALLELS

Romans 1:8

First, I *thank* my *God* through Jesus Christ for you all, because your *faith* is being proclaimed throughout *the* whole *world.*

Romans 7:4

Therefore, my brethren, you also were made to die to the Law through the body of Christ, so that you might be joined to another, to Him who was raised from the dead, in order that we might *bear fruit* for God.

Romans 15:5–6

Now may the God who gives perseverance and encouragement grant you to be of the same mind with one another according to Christ Jesus, [6]so that with one accord you may with one voice glorify the *God* and *Father of our Lord Jesus Christ.*

Romans 15:30

Now I urge you, brethren, by our Lord Jesus Christ and by the *love* of *the Spirit*, to strive together with me in your *prayers* to God for me.

1 Corinthians 13:13

But now *faith, hope, love*, abide these three; but the greatest of these is love.

2 Corinthians 1:3

Blessed be the *God* and *Father of our Lord Jesus Christ*, the Father of mercies and God of all comfort.

Ephesians 1:13, 15–18

In Him, you also, after listening to the message of *truth, the gospel* of your salvation— having also believed, you were sealed in Him with *the* Holy *Spirit* of promise. . . . [15]For this reason I too, having *heard* of the *faith* in the Lord Jesus which exists among you and your *love for all the saints*, [16]do not cease *giving thanks* for you, while making mention of you in my prayers; [17]that the God of our Lord Jesus Christ, the Father of glory, may give to you a spirit of wisdom and of revelation in the knowledge of Him. [18]I *pray* that the eyes of your heart may be enlightened, so that you will know what is the *hope* of His calling, what are the riches of the glory of His inheritance in the saints.

Ephesians 4:20–21

But you did not *learn* Christ in this way, [21]if indeed you have *heard* Him and have been taught in Him, just as *truth* is in Jesus.

1 Thessalonians 1:2–3

We give thanks to God always for all of you, making mention of you in our *prayers*; [3]constantly bearing in mind your work of *faith* and labor of *love* and steadfastness of *hope* in our Lord Jesus Christ in the presence of our God and Father.

1 Timothy 3:16

By common confession, great is the mystery of godliness: He who was revealed in the flesh, Was vindicated in *the Spirit*, Seen by angels, Proclaimed among the nations, Believed on in *the world*, Taken up in glory.

Philemon 4–5

I *thank* my *God always*, making mention of you in my *prayers*, [5]because I *hear* of your *love* and of the *faith* which you have toward the Lord Jesus and toward *all the saints*.

Philemon 23

Epaphras, my fellow prisoner in Christ Jesus, greets you.

OTHER BIBLICAL PARALLELS

Mark 4:20

"And those are the ones on whom seed was sown on the good soil; and they *hear the word* and accept it and *bear fruit*, thirty, sixty, and a hundredfold."

Acts 1:7–8

"It is not for you to know times or epochs which the Father has fixed by His own authority; [8]but you will receive power when the Holy Spirit has come upon you; and you shall be My witnesses both in Jerusalem, and in all Judea and Samaria, and even to the remotest part of the earth."

James 1:18

In the exercise of His will He brought us forth by *the word of truth*, so that we would be a kind of first *fruits* among His creatures.

1 Peter 1:3–5

Blessed be the *God* and *Father of our Lord Jesus Christ*, who according to His great mercy has caused us to be born again to a living *hope* through the resurrection of Jesus Christ from the dead, [4]to obtain an inheritance which is imperishable and undefiled and will not fade away, reserved *in heaven* for you, [5]who are protected by the power of God through *faith* for a salvation ready to be revealed in the last time.

NONCANONICAL PARALLELS

2 Maccabees 9:19–21

"To his worthy Jewish citizens, Antiochus their king and general sends hearty greetings and good wishes for their health and prosperity. [20]If you and your children are well and your affairs are as you wish, I am glad. As my *hope* is *in heaven*, [21]I remember with affection your esteem and goodwill."

For this reason also, since the day we heard of it, we have not ceased to pray for you and to ask that you may be filled with the knowledge of His will in all spiritual wisdom and understanding, [10]so that you will walk in a manner worthy of the Lord, to please Him in all respects, bearing fruit in every good work and increasing in the knowledge of God; [11]strengthened with all power, according to His glorious might, for the attaining of all steadfastness and patience; joyously [12]giving thanks to the Father, who has qualified us to share in the inheritance of the saints in Light. [13]For He rescued us from the domain of darkness, and transferred us to the kingdom of His beloved Son, [14]in whom we have redemption, the forgiveness of sins.

COLOSSIANS PARALLELS

Colossians 2:1–3

For I want you to know how great a struggle I have on your behalf and for those who are at Laodicea, and for all those who have not personally seen my face, [2]that their hearts may be encouraged, having been knit together in love, and attaining to all the wealth that comes from the full assurance of *understanding*, resulting in a true *knowledge* of God's mystery, that is, Christ Himself, [3]in whom are hidden all the treasures of *wisdom* and knowledge.

Colossians 2:6–7

Therefore as you have received Christ Jesus the Lord, so *walk* in Him, [7]having been firmly rooted and now being built up in Him and established in your faith, just as you were instructed, and overflowing with gratitude.

Colossians 2:13

When you were dead in your transgressions and the uncircumcision of your flesh, He made you alive together with Him, having *forgiven* us all our transgressions.

Colossians 3:12, 17

So, as those who have been chosen of God, holy and beloved, put on a heart of compassion, kindness, humility, gentleness and *patience*. . . . [17]Whatever you do in word or deed, do all in the name of the Lord Jesus, *giving thanks* through Him to God the Father.

OTHER PAULINE PARALLELS

Romans 3:23–25

For all have sinned and fall short of the glory of God, [24]being justified as a gift by His grace through the *redemption* which is in Christ Jesus; [25]whom God displayed publicly as a propitiation in His blood through faith. This was to demonstrate His righteousness, because in the forbearance of God He passed over the *sins* previously committed.

Galatians 1:3–4

The Lord Jesus Christ [4] . . . gave Himself for our *sins* so that He might *rescue* us from this present evil age, according to the *will* of our God and Father.

Ephesians 1:7–11, 13–14

In Him we have *redemption* through His blood, the *forgiveness* of our trespasses, according to the riches of His grace [8]which He lavished on us. In all *wisdom* and insight [9]He made known to us the mystery of *His will*, according to His kind intention which He purposed in Him. . . . [10] . . . In Him [11]also we have obtained an *inheritance*, having been predestined according to His purpose who works all things after the counsel of His will. . . . [13]In Him, you also, after listening to the message of truth, the gospel of your salvation—having also believed, you were sealed in Him with the Holy Spirit of promise, [14]who is given as a pledge of our inheritance, with a view to the redemption of God's own possession, to the praise of His glory.

Ephesians 1:15–20

For this reason I too, having *heard* of the faith in the Lord Jesus which exists among you and your love for all *the saints*, [16]do not cease *giving thanks* for you, while making mention of you in my prayers; [17]that the God of our Lord Jesus Christ, the Father of glory, may give to you a spirit of *wisdom* and of revelation in the *knowledge* of Him. [18]I *pray* that the eyes of your heart may be enlightened, so that you will know what is the hope of His calling, what are the riches of the glory of His *inheritance* in *the saints*, [19]and what is the surpassing greatness of His *power* toward us who believe. These are in accordance with the working of the strength of His *might* [20]which He brought about in Christ.

Ephesians 3:14–17
For this reason I bow my knees before the Father, [15]from whom every family in heaven and on earth derives its name, [16]that He would grant you, according to the riches of His glory, to be *strengthened with power* through His Spirit in the inner man, [17]so that Christ may dwell in your hearts through faith.

Ephesians 4:1–2
Therefore I, the prisoner of the Lord, implore you to *walk in a manner worthy* of the calling with which you have been called, [2]with all humility and gentleness, with *patience*, showing tolerance for one another in love.

Ephesians 5:8–10
You were formerly *darkness*, but now you are *Light* in the Lord; *walk* as children of Light [9](for the *fruit* of the Light consists in all goodness and righteousness and truth), [10]trying to learn what is *pleasing* to the Lord.

1 Thessalonians 2:11–12
You know how we were exhorting and encouraging and imploring each one of you as a father would his own children, [12]so that you would *walk in a manner worthy* of the God who calls you into His own *kingdom* and glory.

1 Thessalonians 5:4–5
But you, brethren, are not in *darkness*, that the day would overtake you like a thief; [5]for you are all sons of *light* and sons of day. We are not of night nor of darkness.

OTHER BIBLICAL PARALLELS

Psalm 95:2
Let us come before His presence with *thanksgiving*, Let us shout *joyfully* to Him with psalms.

Acts 26:16–18
"But get up and stand on your feet; for this purpose I have appeared to you, to appoint you a minister and a witness not only to the things which you have seen, but also to the things in which I will appear to you; [17]rescuing you from the Jewish people and from the Gentiles, to whom I am sending you, [18]to open their eyes so that they may turn from *darkness* to *light* and from the dominion of Satan to God, that they may receive *forgiveness of sins* and an *inheritance* among those who have been sanctified by faith in Me."

NONCANONICAL PARALLELS

Sirach 39:6
If the great Lord is willing, he will be *filled* with the spirit of *understanding*; he will pour forth words of *wisdom* of his own and *give thanks* to the Lord in prayer.

4 Maccabees 18:3
Therefore those who gave over their bodies in suffering for the sake of religion were not only admired by mortals, but also were deemed worthy to *share* in a divine *inheritance*.

2 Baruch 48:50
For surely, as you endured much labor in the short time in which you live in this passing world, so you will receive great *light* in that world which has no end.

Colossians 1:15–20

He is the image of the invisible God, the first-born of all creation. [16]For by Him all things were created, both in the heavens and on earth, visible and invisible, whether thrones or dominions or rulers or authorities—all things have been created through Him and for Him. [17]He is before all things, and in Him all things hold together. [18]He is also head of the body, the church; and He is the beginning, the first-born from the dead, so that He Himself will come to have first place in everything. [19]For it was the Father's good pleasure for all the full-ness to dwell in Him, [20]and through Him to reconcile all things to Himself, having made peace through the blood of His cross; through Him, I say, whether things on earth or things in heaven.

Colossians 2:9–10, 14–15

For in Him *all the fullness* of Deity *dwells* in bodily form, [10]and in Him you have been made complete, and He is the *head* over all rule and authority; . . . [14]having canceled out the certificate of debt consisting of decrees against us, which was hostile to us; and He has taken it out of the way, having nailed it to the *cross.* [15]When He had disarmed the *rulers* and *authorities*, He made a public display of them, having triumphed over them through Him.

Colossians 2:18–19

Let no one keep defrauding you of your prize by delighting in self-abasement and the worship of the angels, taking his stand on visions he has seen, inflated without cause by his fleshly mind, [19]and not holding fast to the *head*, from whom *the* entire *body*, being supplied and held together by the joints and ligaments, grows with a growth which is from God.

Colossians 3:9–10

Do not lie to one another, since you laid aside the old self with its evil practices, [10]and have put on the new self who is being renewed to a true knowledge according to *the image* of the One who *created* him.

OTHER PAULINE PARALLELS

Romans 11:33, 36

Oh, the depth of the riches both of the wisdom and knowledge of God! . . . [36]For from Him and *through Him* and to Him are *all things*. To Him be the glory forever. Amen.

1 Corinthians 8:5–6

For even if there are so-called gods whether *in heaven* or *on earth*, as indeed there are many gods and many lords, [6]yet for us there is but one God, the Father, from whom are *all things* and we exist for Him; and one Lord, Jesus Christ, by whom are all things, and we exist *through Him.*

1 Corinthians 12:12

For even as *the body* is one and yet has many members, and all the members of the body, though they are many, are one body, so also is Christ.

1 Corinthians 15:20, 23–24

But now Christ has been raised *from the dead*, the first fruits of those who are asleep. . . . [23]But each in his own order: Christ the first fruits, after that those who are Christ's at His coming, [24]then comes the end, when He hands over the kingdom to the God and Father, when He has abolished all *rule* and all *authority* and power.

2 Corinthians 4:3–4

And even if our gospel is veiled, it is veiled to those who are perishing, [4]in whose case the god of this world has blinded the minds of the unbelieving so that they might not see the light of the gospel of the glory of Christ, who is *the image of God.*

Ephesians 1:9–10

He made known to us the mystery of His will, according to His kind intention which He purposed in Him [10]with a view to an administration suitable to the fullness of the times, that is, the summing up of *all things* in Christ, things *in the heavens and* things *on the earth.*

Ephesians 1:19–23

These are in accordance with the working of the strength of His might [20]which He brought about in Christ, when He raised Him *from the dead* and seated Him at His right hand in the *heavenly* places, [21]far above all *rule* and *authority* and power and *dominion*, and every name that is named, not only in this age but also in the one to come. [22]And He put *all things* in subjection under His feet, and gave Him as *head* over all things to *the church*, [23]which is His *body*, *the fullness* of Him who fills all in all.

Ephesians 2:13–16

But now in Christ Jesus you who formerly were far off have been brought near by *the blood* of Christ. [14]For He Himself is our *peace*, who made both groups into one and broke down the barrier of the dividing wall, [15]by abolishing in His flesh the enmity, which is the Law of commandments contained in ordinances, so that in Himself He might make the two into one new man, thus establishing *peace*, [16]and might *reconcile* them both in one *body* to God through the *cross*, by it having put to death the enmity.

Philippians 2:5–6

Have this attitude in yourselves which was also in Christ Jesus, [6]who, although He existed in the form of God, did not regard equality with God a thing to be grasped.

OTHER BIBLICAL PARALLELS

Proverbs 8:12, 22–23, 27, 29–30

"I, wisdom, dwell with prudence, And I find knowledge and discretion. . . . [22]The Lord possessed me at *the beginning* of His way, Before His works of old. [23]From everlasting I was established. . . . [27]When He established *the heavens*, I was there, When He inscribed a circle on the face of the deep, . . . [29]When He set for the sea its boundary So that the water would not transgress His command, When He marked out the foundations of the earth; [30]Then I was beside Him, as a master workman; And I was daily His delight, Rejoicing always before Him."

John 1:1, 3, 16

In *the beginning* was the Word, and the Word was with God, and the Word was God. . . . [3]*All things* came into being through *Him*. . . . [16]For of His *fullness* we have all received, and grace upon grace.

NONCANONICAL PARALLELS

Wisdom of Solomon 1:6–7

For wisdom is a kindly spirit, but will not free blasphemers from the guilt of their words; because God is witness of their inmost feelings, and a true observer of their hearts, and a hearer of their tongues. [7]Because the spirit of the Lord has filled the world, and that which *holds all things together* knows what is said . . .

Wisdom of Solomon 7:24–26

For wisdom is more mobile than any motion; because of her pureness she pervades and penetrates *all things*. [25]For she is a breath of the power of God, and a pure emanation of the glory of the Almighty; therefore nothing defiled gains entrance into her. [26]For she is a reflection of eternal light, a spotless mirror of the working of God, and an *image* of his goodness.

Calling on the Good Daimon (PGM 21.1–8)

Hear me, lord, whose secret name is unspeakable, . . . you of whom the sun . . .

and the moon . . . [5]are tireless eyes, . . . you of whom *heaven* is the *head*, air the *body*, *earth* the feet, the water around you, ocean. You are the Good Daimon, the lord.

Orphic Hymn (quoted in Eusebius, Preparation for the Gospel 3.9.2)

Zeus was the *first*, Zeus last, the lord of lightning, Zeus head, Zeus center, *all things* are from Zeus. . . . Zeus the firm foundation of *earth* and starry *heaven*; Zeus preeminent, Zeus alone first cause of all things.

Colossians 1:21–29

And although you were formerly alienated and hostile in mind, engaged in evil deeds, [22]yet He has now reconciled you in His fleshly body through death, in order to present you before Him holy and blameless and beyond reproach— [23]if indeed you continue in the faith firmly established and steadfast, and not moved away from the hope of the gospel that you have heard, which was proclaimed in all creation under heaven, and of which I, Paul, was made a minister. [24]Now I rejoice in my sufferings for your sake, and in my flesh I do my share on behalf of His body, which is the church, in filling up what is lacking in Christ's afflictions. [25]Of this church I was made a minister according to the stewardship from God bestowed on me for your benefit, so that I might fully carry out the preaching of the word of God, [26]that is, the mystery which has been hidden from the past ages and generations, but has now been manifested to His saints, [27]to whom God willed to make known what is the riches of the glory of this mystery among the Gentiles, which is Christ in you, the hope of glory. [28]We proclaim Him, admonishing every man and teaching every man with all wisdom, so that we may present every man complete in Christ. [29]For this purpose also I labor, striving according to His power, which mightily works within me.

COLOSSIANS PARALLELS

Colossians 1:5–6

. . . because of the *hope* laid up for you in heaven, of which you previously *heard* in the *word* of truth, *the gospel* [6]which has come to you, just as in all the world also it is constantly bearing fruit and increasing, even as it has been doing in you also since the day you heard of it and understood the grace of God in truth.

Colossians 3:16

Let *the word* of Christ richly dwell within you, *with all wisdom teaching* and *admonishing* one another with psalms and hymns and spiritual songs, singing with thankfulness in your hearts to God.

Colossians 4:3–4

. . . praying at the same time for us as well, that God will open up to us a door for the word, so that we may speak forth the *mystery* of Christ, for which I have also been imprisoned; [4]that I may make it clear in the way I ought to speak.

OTHER PAULINE PARALLELS

Romans 5:1–3

Therefore, having been justified by *faith*, we have peace with God through our Lord Jesus Christ, [2]through whom also we have obtained our introduction by *faith* into this grace in which we stand; and we exult in *hope* of the *glory* of God. [3]And not only this, but we also exult in our tribulations, knowing that tribulation brings about perseverance.

Romans 5:10

For if while we were enemies we were *reconciled* to God *through* the *death* of His Son, much more, having been reconciled, we shall be saved by His life.

Romans 15:15–16

But I have written very boldly to you on some points so as to remind you again, because of the grace that was given me from God, [16]to be *a minister* of Christ Jesus to *the Gentiles.*

1 Corinthians 2:4–7

My message and my *preaching* were not in persuasive words of wisdom, but in demonstration of the Spirit and of power, [5]so that your *faith* would not rest on the wisdom of men, but on the *power* of God. [6]Yet we do speak *wisdom* among those who are mature; a wisdom, however, not of this age nor of the rulers of this age, who are passing away; [7]but we speak God's wisdom in a *mystery*, the *hidden* wisdom which God predestined before the *ages* to our *glory.*

2 Corinthians 4:10–11

. . . always carrying about in the *body* the dying of Jesus, so that the life of Jesus also may be manifested in our body. [11]For we who live are constantly being delivered over to *death* for Jesus' sake, so that the life of Jesus also may be manifested in our mortal *flesh.*

2 Corinthians 5:18–19

Now all these things are from God, who *reconciled* us to Himself through Christ and gave us the ministry of reconciliation, [19]namely, that God was in Christ reconciling the world to Himself, not counting their trespasses against them, and He has committed to us the word of reconciliation.

Ephesians 2:11–12, 15–16

Therefore remember that *formerly* you, *the Gentiles* in the flesh, who are called "Uncircumcision" by the so-called "Circumcision," which is performed in the flesh by human hands— [12]remember that you were at that time separate from Christ, excluded from the commonwealth of Israel, and strangers to the covenants of promise, having no *hope* and without God in the world. . . . [15]by abolishing in His flesh the enmity, which is the Law of commandments contained in ordinances, so that in Himself He might make the two into one new man, thus establishing peace, [16]and might *reconcile* them both in one *body* to God through the cross, by it having put to *death* the enmity.

Ephesians 3:1–9

For this reason *I, Paul,* the prisoner of Christ Jesus for the sake of you Gentiles— [2]if indeed you have heard of the *stewardship* of God's grace which was given to me for you; [3]that by revelation there was made known to me *the mystery*, as I wrote before in brief. [4]By referring to this, when you read you can understand my insight into the mystery of Christ, [5]which in other *generations* was not *made known* to the sons of men, as it has now been revealed to His holy apostles and prophets in the Spirit; [6]to be specific, that *the Gentiles* are fellow heirs and fellow members of the *body*, and fellow partakers of the promise in Christ Jesus through *the gospel,* [7]*of which I was made a minister,* according to the gift of God's grace which was given to me according to the working of His *power.* [8]To me, the very least of all *saints*, this grace was given, to *preach* to the Gentiles the unfathomable *riches* of Christ, [9]and to bring to light what is the administration of the mystery which for *ages* has been *hidden* in God who created all things.

Ephesians 5:27
. . . that He might *present* to Himself the *church* in all her *glory*, having no spot or wrinkle or any such thing; but that she would be *holy and blameless*.

Philippians 3:10
. . . that I may know Him and the *power* of His resurrection and the fellowship of His *sufferings*, being conformed to His *death*.

OTHER BIBLICAL PARALLELS

Acts 9:15–16
But the Lord said to him [Ananias], "Go, for he is a chosen instrument of Mine, to bear My name before *the Gentiles* and kings and the sons of Israel; [16]for I will show him how much he must *suffer* for My name's sake."

NONCANONICAL PARALLELS

2 Esdras (4 Ezra) *4:33–37*
Then I answered and said, "How long? When will these things be? Why are our years few and evil?" [34]He [Uriel] answered me and said, "Do not be in a greater hurry than the Most High. You, indeed, are in a hurry for yourself, but the Highest is in a hurry on behalf of many. [35]Did not the souls of the righteous in their chambers ask about these matters, saying, 'How long are we to remain here? And when will the harvest of our reward come?' [36]And the archangel Jeremiel answered and said, 'When the number of those like yourselves is completed; for he has weighed the age in the balance, [37]and measured the times by measure, and numbered the times by number; and he will not move or arouse them until that measure is *fulfilled*.'"

Colossians 2:1–7

For I want you to know how great a struggle I have on your behalf and for those who are at Laodicea, and for all those who have not personally seen my face, [2]that their hearts may be encouraged, having been knit together in love, and attaining to all the wealth that comes from the full assurance of understanding, resulting in a true knowledge of God's mystery, that is, Christ Himself, [3]in whom are hidden all the treasures of wisdom and knowledge. [4]I say this so that no one will delude you with persuasive argument. [5]For even though I am absent in body, nevertheless I am with you in spirit, rejoicing to see your good discipline and the stability of your faith in Christ. [6]Therefore as you have received Christ Jesus the Lord, so walk in Him, [7]having been firmly rooted and now being built up in Him and established in your faith, just as you were instructed, and overflowing with gratitude.

COLOSSIANS PARALLELS

Colossians 1:9–10
For this reason also, since the day we heard of it, we have not ceased to pray for you and to ask that you may be filled with the *knowledge* of His will in all spiritual *wisdom* and *understanding*, [10]so that you will *walk* in a manner worthy of the Lord, to please Him in all respects, bearing fruit in every good work and increasing in the knowledge of God.

Colossians 4:7–8
As to all my affairs, Tychicus, our beloved brother and faithful servant and fellow bond-servant in the Lord, will bring you information. [8]For I have sent him to you for this very purpose, that you may know about our circumstances and that he may *encourage* your *hearts*.

Colossians 4:15–16
Greet the brethren who are in *Laodicea* and also Nympha and the church that is in her house. [16]When this letter is read among you, have it also read in the church of the Laodiceans; and you, for your part read my letter that is coming from Laodicea.

OTHER PAULINE PARALLELS

Romans 16:19
For the report of your obedience has reached to all; therefore I am *rejoicing* over you, but I want you to be wise in what is good and innocent in what is evil.

1 Corinthians 2:4–7

My message and my preaching were not in *persuasive* words of wisdom, but in demonstration of the Spirit and of power, [5]so that your *faith* would not rest on the wisdom of men, but on the power of God. [6]Yet we do speak *wisdom* among those who are mature; a wisdom, however, not of this age nor of the rulers of this age, who are passing away; [7]but we speak God's wisdom in a *mystery*, the *hidden* wisdom which God predestined before the ages to our glory.

1 Corinthians 3:10–11

According to the grace of God which was given to me, like a wise master builder I laid a foundation, and another is building on it. But each man must be careful how he *builds* on it. [11]For no man can lay a foundation other than the one which is laid, which is Jesus Christ.

1 Corinthians 5:3

For I, on my part, *though absent in body* but present *in spirit*, have already judged him who has so committed this, as though I were present.

Ephesians 2:19–22

So then you are no longer strangers and aliens, but you are fellow citizens with the saints, and are of God's household, [20]having been *built* on the foundation of the apostles and prophets, Christ Jesus Himself being the corner stone, [21]in whom the whole building, being fitted together, is growing into a holy temple in the Lord, [22]in whom you also are being built together into a dwelling of God in the Spirit.

Ephesians 3:14–19

For this reason I bow my knees before the Father, [15]from whom every family in heaven and on earth derives its name, [16]that He would grant you, according to the riches of His glory, to be strengthened with power through His Spirit in the inner man, [17]so that Christ may dwell in your *hearts* through *faith*; and that you, being *rooted* and grounded in *love*, [18]may be able to comprehend with all the saints what is the breadth and length and height and depth, [19]and to know the love of Christ which surpasses *knowledge*, that you may be filled up to all the fullness of God.

Ephesians 5:6

Let no one deceive you with empty words, for because of these things the wrath of God comes upon the sons of disobedience.

1 Thessalonians 4:1

Finally then, brethren, we request and exhort you in the Lord Jesus, that as you *received* from us *instruction* as to how you ought to *walk* and please God (just as you actually do walk), that you excel still more.

2 Thessalonians 2:15

So then, brethren, stand *firm* and hold to the traditions which you were taught, whether by word of mouth or by letter from us.

2 Timothy 1:7

For God has not given us a spirit of timidity, but of power and *love* and *discipline*.

OTHER BIBLICAL PARALLELS

Proverbs 2:3–5

For if you cry for discernment, Lift your voice for *understanding*; [4]If you seek her as silver And search for her as for *hidden treasures*; [5]Then you will discern the fear of the LORD And discover the *knowledge* of God.

Isaiah 11:2

The Spirit of the LORD will rest on Him, The spirit of *wisdom* and *understanding*, The spirit of counsel and strength, The spirit of *knowledge* and the fear of the LORD.

Jude 20–21

But you, beloved, *building* yourselves *up* on your most holy *faith*, praying in the Holy Spirit, [21]keep yourselves in the *love* of God, waiting anxiously for the mercy of our Lord Jesus Christ to eternal life.

Revelation 1:10–11

I was in the Spirit on the Lord's day, and I heard behind me a loud voice like the sound of a trumpet, [11]saying, "Write in a book what you see, and send it to the seven churches: to Ephesus and to Smyrna and to Pergamum and to Thyatira and to Sardis and to Philadelphia and to *Laodicea*."

2 Baruch 54:12–13
Who is able to imitate your miracles, O God, or who understands your deep thoughts of life? [13]For with your counsel you reign over all creation . . . and have established the whole fountain of light with yourself, and you have prepared under your throne the *treasures of wisdom*.

Colossians 2:8–15

See to it that no one takes you captive through philosophy and empty deception, according to the tradition of men, according to the elementary principles of the world, rather than according to Christ. [9]For in Him all the fullness of Deity dwells in bodily form, [10]and in Him you have been made complete, and He is the head over all rule and authority; [11]and in Him you were also circumcised with a circumcision made without hands, in the removal of the body of the flesh by the circumcision of Christ; [12]having been buried with Him in baptism, in which you were also raised up with Him through faith in the working of God, who raised Him from the dead. [13]When you were dead in your transgressions and the uncircumcision of your flesh, He made you alive together with Him, having forgiven us all our transgressions, [14]having canceled out the certificate of debt consisting of decrees against us, which was hostile to us; and He has taken it out of the way, having nailed it to the cross. [15]When He had disarmed the rulers and authorities, He made a public display of them, having triumphed over them through Him.

COLOSSIANS PARALLELS

Colossians 1:13–14, 16, 18–20
For He rescued us from the domain of darkness, and transferred us to the kingdom of His beloved Son, [14]in whom we have redemption, the *forgiveness* of sins. . . . [16]For by Him all things were created, both in the heavens and on earth, visible and invisible, whether thrones or dominions or *rulers* or *authorities*—all things have been created *through Him* and for Him. . . . [18]He is also *head* of the body, the church; and He is the beginning, the firstborn *from the dead*, so that He Himself will come to have first

place in everything. [19]For it was the Father's good pleasure for all *the fullness* to *dwell* in Him, [20]and through Him to reconcile all things to Himself, having made peace through the blood of His *cross*; through Him, I say, whether things on earth or things in heaven.

Colossians 3:1, 5
Therefore if you have been *raised up* with Christ, keep seeking the things above, where Christ is, seated at the right hand of God. . . . [5]Therefore consider the members of your earthly *body* as dead to immorality, impurity, passion, evil desire, and greed, which amounts to idolatry.

OTHER PAULINE PARALLELS

Romans 2:25, 29
For indeed *circumcision* is of value if you practice the Law; but if you are a *transgressor* of the Law, your circumcision has become *uncircumcision*. . . . [29]But he is a Jew who is one inwardly; and circumcision is that which is of the heart, by the Spirit, not by the letter; and his praise is not from men, but from God.

Romans 6:4
Therefore we have been *buried with Him* through *baptism* into death, so that as Christ was *raised from the dead* through the glory of the Father, so we too might walk in newness of life.

Romans 7:4
Therefore, my brethren, you also were made to die to the Law through the body of Christ, so that you might be joined to another, to Him who was *raised from the dead*, in order that we might bear fruit for God.

1 Corinthians 6:14
Now God has not only *raised* the Lord, but will also *raise* us *up* through His power.

1 Corinthians 15:23–24
But each in his own order: Christ the first fruits, after that those who are Christ's at His coming, [24]then comes the end, when He hands over the kingdom to the God and Father, when He has abolished *all rule and* all *authority* and power.

Galatians 4:3–5

So also we, while we were children, were held in bondage under *the elemental* things *of the world.* ⁴But when the fullness of the time came, God sent forth His Son, born of a woman, born under the Law, ⁵so that He might redeem those who were under the Law, that we might receive the adoption as sons.

Galatians 5:24

Now those who belong to Christ Jesus have crucified *the flesh* with its passions and desires.

Ephesians 2:4–6

But God, being rich in mercy, because of His great love with which He loved us, ⁵even when we *were dead in* our *transgressions, made* us *alive together with* Christ (by grace you have been saved), ⁶and *raised* us *up with Him,* and seated us with Him in the heavenly places in Christ Jesus.

Ephesians 2:11

Therefore remember that formerly you, the Gentiles in *the flesh,* who are called *"Uncircumcision"* by the so-called *"Circumcision,"* which is performed in the flesh by human *hands . . .*

Ephesians 3:8–10

To me, the very least of all saints, this grace was given, to preach to the Gentiles the unfathomable riches of Christ, ⁹and to bring to light what is the administration of the mystery which for ages has been hidden in God who created all things; ¹⁰so that the manifold wisdom of God might now be made known through the church to *the rulers and* the *authorities* in the heavenly places.

Ephesians 5:6

Let no one deceive you with *empty* words, for because of these things the wrath of God comes upon the sons of disobedience.

Philippians 3:3

We are the true *circumcision,* who worship in the Spirit of God and glory in Christ Jesus and put no confidence in *the flesh.*

Mark 7:5–6, 8

The Pharisees and the scribes asked Him, "Why do Your disciples not walk according to the tradition of the elders, but eat their bread with impure hands?" ⁶And He said to them, "Rightly did Isaiah prophesy of you hypocrites. . . . ⁸Neglecting the commandment of God, you hold to *the tradition of men."*

Revelation 20:12

And I saw the dead, the great and the small, standing before the throne, and books were opened; and another book was opened, which is the book of life; and the dead were judged from the things which were written in the books, according to their deeds.

1 Enoch 108:7

For some of (these things) were written and sealed above in heaven so that the angels may read them (the things that are written) and know that which is about to befall the sinners.

Apocalypse of Zephaniah 3:8–9

Also the angels of the accuser who is upon the earth, they also write down all of the sins of men upon their manuscript. ⁹They also sit at the gate of heaven. They tell the accuser and he writes them upon his manuscript so that he might accuse them when they come out of the world (and) down there.

Testament of Solomon 8:1–4

When I, Solomon, saw them, I was amazed and asked them, "Who are you?" ²They replied, "We are heavenly bodies, *rulers* of this *world* of darkness: . . . ³ . . . *Deception,* . . . Strife, . . . Fate, . . . Distress, . . . Error, . . . Power, . . . ⁴ . . . The Worst. Our stars in heaven look small, but we are named like gods."

Colossians 2:16–23

Therefore no one is to act as your judge in regard to food or drink or in respect to a festival or a new moon or a Sabbath day— ¹⁷things which are a mere shadow of what is to come;

but the substance belongs to Christ. [18]Let no one keep defrauding you of your prize by delighting in self-abasement and the worship of the angels, taking his stand on visions he has seen, inflated without cause by his fleshly mind, [19]and not holding fast to the head, from whom the entire body, being supplied and held together by the joints and ligaments, grows with a growth which is from God. [20]If you have died with Christ to the elementary principles of the world, why, as if you were living in the world, do you submit yourself to decrees, such as, [21]"Do not handle, do not taste, do not touch!" [22](which all refer to things destined to perish with use)—in accordance with the commandments and teachings of men? [23]These are matters which have, to be sure, the appearance of wisdom in self-made religion and self-abasement and severe treatment of the body, but are of no value against fleshly indulgence.

COLOSSIANS PARALLELS

Colossians 1:9

For this reason also, since the day we heard of it, we have not ceased to pray for you and to ask that you may be filled with the knowledge of His will in all spiritual *wisdom* and understanding.

Colossians 1:18

He is also *head* of *the body*, the church; and He is the beginning, the firstborn from the dead, so that He Himself will come to have first place in everything.

OTHER PAULINE PARALLELS

Romans 14:3, 5, 20

The one who eats is not to regard with contempt the one who does not eat, and the one who does not eat is not to *judge* the one who eats, for God has accepted him. . . . [5]One person regards one *day* above another, another regards every day alike. Each person must be fully convinced in his own *mind*. . . . [20]Do not tear down the work of God for the sake of *food*. All things indeed are clean, but they are evil for the man who eats and gives offense.

1 Corinthians 2:4-5

My message and my preaching were not in persuasive words of *wisdom*, but in demonstration of the Spirit and of power, [5]so that

your faith would not rest on the wisdom of men, but on the power of God.

Galatians 4:8-10

However at that time, when you did not know God, you were slaves to those which by nature are no gods. [9]But now that you have come to know God, or rather to be known by God, how is it that you turn back again to the weak and worthless *elemental* things, to which you desire to be enslaved all over again? [10]You observe *days* and months and seasons and years.

Ephesians 4:14-16

As a result, we are no longer to be children, tossed here and there by waves and carried about by every wind of doctrine, by the trickery of men, by craftiness in deceitful scheming; [15]but speaking the truth in love, we are to *grow* up in all aspects into Him who is *the head*, even Christ, [16]*from whom the* whole *body, being* fitted *and held together by* what every *joint supplies*, according to the proper working of each individual part, causes the *growth* of the body for the building up of itself in love.

1 Timothy 4:1-3

But the Spirit explicitly says that in later times some will fall away from the faith, paying attention to deceitful spirits and doctrines of demons, [2]by means of the hypocrisy of liars seared in their own conscience as with a branding iron, [3]men who forbid marriage and advocate abstaining from *foods* which God has created to be gratefully shared in by those who believe and know the truth.

Titus 1:13-14

For this reason reprove them severely so that they may be sound in the faith, [14]not paying attention to Jewish myths and *commandments of men* who turn away from the truth.

OTHER BIBLICAL PARALLELS

Leviticus 7:21

"When anyone *touches* anything unclean, whether human uncleanness, or an unclean animal, or any unclean detestable thing, and eats of the flesh of the sacrifice of peace offerings which belong to the LORD, that person shall be cut off from his people."

COLOSSIANS 2:16–23

They are to stand every morning to thank and to praise the LORD, and likewise at evening, [31]and to offer all burnt offerings to the LORD, on the *sabbaths*, the *new moons* and the fixed *festivals* in the number set by the ordinance concerning them, continually before the LORD.

Zechariah 10:2

For the teraphim speak iniquity, And the diviners *see* lying *visions* And tell false dreams; They comfort in vain. Therefore the people wander like sheep, They are afflicted, because there is no shepherd.

Hebrews 9:8–10

The Holy Spirit is signifying this, that the way into the holy place has not yet been disclosed while the outer tabernacle is still standing, [9]which is a symbol for the present time. Accordingly both gifts and sacrifices are offered which cannot make the worshiper perfect in conscience, [10]since they relate only to *food* and *drink* and various washings, regulations for *the body* imposed until a time of reformation.

Hebrews 10:1

For the Law, since it has only a *shadow of* the good things *to come* and not the very form of things, can never, by the same sacrifices which they offer continually year by year, make perfect those who draw near.

NONCANONICAL PARALLELS

1 Enoch *71:1, 11*

(Thus) it happened after this that my spirit passed out of sight and ascended into the heavens. And I saw the sons of the holy *angels* walking upon the flame of fire. . . . [11] . . . Then I cried with a great voice by the spirit of the power, blessing, glorifying, and extolling.

Apocalypse of Abraham *17:1–4, 7*

And while he was still speaking, behold the fire coming toward us round about, and a voice was in the fire like a voice of many waters. . . . [2]And the *angel* knelt down with me and worshiped. [3]And I wanted to fall face down on the earth. . . . [4]And he said, "Only *worship*, Abraham, and recite the song which I taught you." . . . [7]And I recited, and he himself recited the song.

Letter of Aristeas *139, 142*

In his *wisdom* the legislator . . . surrounded us with unbroken palisades and iron walls to prevent our mixing with any of the other peoples in any matter, being thus kept pure in *body* and soul, preserved from false beliefs. . . . [142]So . . . he hedged us in on all sides with strict observances connected with meat and *drink* and *touch* and hearing and sight, after the manner of the Law.

1QRule of the Blessings *(1Q28b [1QSb]) 4.24–26*

You shall be [25]like an angel of the face in the holy residence for the glory of the God of the Hosts. . . . You shall be around, serving in the temple of the [26]kingdom, sharing the lot with the *angels* of the face.

Colossians 3:1–4

Therefore if you have been raised up with Christ, keep seeking the things above, where Christ is, seated at the right hand of God. [2]Set your mind on the things above, not on the things that are on earth. [3]For you have died and your life is hidden with Christ in God. [4]When Christ, who is our life, is revealed, then you also will be revealed with Him in glory.

COLOSSIANS PARALLELS

Colossians 1:25–27

Of this church I was made a minister according to the stewardship from God bestowed on me for your benefit, so that I might fully carry out the preaching of the word of God, [26]that is, the mystery which has been *hidden* from the past ages and generations, but has now been manifested to His saints, [27]to whom God willed to make known what is the riches of the *glory* of this mystery among the Gentiles, which is Christ in you, the hope of glory.

Colossians 2:11–12

In Him you were also circumcised with a circumcision made without hands, in the removal of the body of the flesh by the circumcision of Christ; [12]having been buried with Him in baptism, in which you were also *raised up* with Him through faith in the working of God, who raised Him from the dead.

Romans 8:19

For the anxious longing of the creation waits eagerly for the *revealing* of the sons of God.

Romans 12:2

And do not be conformed to this world, but be transformed by the renewing of your *mind*, so that you may prove what the will of God is, that which is good and acceptable and perfect.

1 Corinthians 15:40, 47–49

There are also heavenly bodies and earthly bodies, but the *glory* of the heavenly is one, and the glory of the earthly is another. . . . [47]The first man is from the *earth*, earthy; the second man is from heaven. [48]As is the earthy, so also are those who are earthy; and as is the heavenly, so also are those who are heavenly. [49]Just as we have borne the image of the earthy, we will also bear the image of the heavenly.

2 Corinthians 4:16–18

Therefore we do not lose heart, but though our outer man is decaying, yet our inner man is being renewed day by day. [17]For momentary, light affliction is producing for us an eternal weight of *glory* far beyond all comparison, [18]while we look not at the things which are seen, but at the things which are not seen; for the things which are seen are temporal, but the things which are not seen are eternal.

2 Corinthians 5:2

For indeed in this house we groan, longing to be clothed with our dwelling from heaven.

Galatians 2:19–20

"For through the Law I *died* to the Law, so that I might live to God. [20]I have been crucified with Christ; and it is no longer I who live, but Christ lives in me; and the *life* which I now live in the flesh I live by faith in the Son of God, who loved me and gave Himself up for me."

Ephesians 1:19–20

These are in accordance with the working of the strength of His might [20]which He brought about in Christ, when He *raised* Him from the dead and *seated* Him *at* His *right hand* in the heavenly places.

Philippians 3:18–21

For many walk, of whom I often told you, and now tell you even weeping, that they are enemies of the cross of Christ, [19]whose end is destruction, whose god is their appetite, and whose glory is in their shame, who *set* their *minds on earthly things.* [20]For our citizenship is in heaven, from which also we eagerly wait for a Savior, the Lord Jesus Christ; [21]who will transform the body of our humble state into conformity with the body of His *glory*, by the exertion of the power that He has even to subject all things to Himself.

OTHER BIBLICAL PARALLELS

Psalm 110:1

The LORD says to my Lord: "*Sit at* My *right hand* Until I make Your enemies a footstool for Your feet."

Matthew 16:23

But He turned and said to Peter, "Get behind Me, Satan! You are a stumbling block to Me; for you are not *setting your mind on* God's interests, but man's."

Hebrews 1:3

And He is the radiance of His *glory* and the exact representation of His nature, and upholds all things by the word of His power. When He had made purification of sins, He *sat* down *at the right hand* of the Majesty on high.

1 John 3:2

Beloved, now we are children of God, and it has not appeared as yet what we will be. We know that when He appears, we will be like Him, because we will see Him just as He is.

NONCANONICAL PARALLELS

2 Esdras (4 Ezra) 7:26–28

"For indeed the time will come, when the signs that I have foretold to you will come to pass, that the city that now is not seen shall appear, and the land that now is *hidden* shall be disclosed. [27]Everyone who has been delivered from the evils that I have foretold shall see my wonders. [28]For my son the Messiah shall be *revealed* with those who are with him, and those who remain shall rejoice four hundred years."

Colossians 3:5–11

Therefore consider the members of your earthly body as dead to immorality, impurity, passion, evil desire, and greed, which amounts to idolatry. [6]For it is because of these things that the wrath of God will come upon the sons of disobedience, [7]and in them you also once walked, when you were living in them. [8]But now you also, put them all aside: anger, wrath, malice, slander, and abusive speech from your mouth. [9]Do not lie to one another, since you laid aside the old self with its evil practices, [10]and have put on the new self who is being renewed to a true knowledge according to the image of the One who created him— [11]a renewal in which there is no distinction between Greek and Jew, circumcised and uncircumcised, barbarian, Scythian, slave and freeman, but Christ is all, and in all.

COLOSSIANS PARALLELS

Colossians 1:9–10
For this reason also, since the day we heard of it, we have not ceased to pray for you and to ask that you may be filled with the *knowledge* of His will in all spiritual wisdom and understanding, [10]so that you will *walk* in a manner worthy of the Lord, to please Him in all respects, bearing fruit in every good work and increasing in the knowledge of God.

Colossians 1:15
He is *the image* of the invisible God, the firstborn of all creation.

Colossians 2:20
If you have died with Christ to the elementary principles of the world, why, as if you were *living in* the world, do you submit yourself to decrees?

OTHER PAULINE PARALLELS

Romans 1:18, 24, 26, 29–31
For *the wrath of God* is revealed from heaven against all ungodliness and unrighteousness of men who suppress the truth in unrighteousness. . . . [24]Therefore God gave

them over in the lusts of their hearts to *impurity*, so that their *bodies* would be dishonored among them. . . . [26]For this reason God gave them over to degrading *passions*, . . . [29]being filled with all unrighteousness, wickedness, *greed, evil*; full of envy, murder, strife, deceit, *malice*; they are gossips, [30]*slanderers*, haters of God, insolent, arrogant, boastful, inventors of evil, disobedient to parents, [31]without understanding, untrustworthy, unloving, unmerciful.

Romans 6:6, 19
. . . knowing this, that our *old self* was crucified with Him, in order that our *body* of sin might be done away with, so that we would no longer be slaves to sin; . . . [19]For just as you presented your *members* as slaves to *impurity* and to lawlessness, resulting in further lawlessness, so now present your members as slaves to righteousness, resulting in sanctification.

Romans 8:29
For those whom He foreknew, He also predestined to become conformed to *the image* of His Son, so that He would be the firstborn among many brethren.

Romans 10:12
For *there is no distinction between Jew* and *Greek*; for the same Lord is Lord of all, abounding in riches for all who call on Him.

Romans 12:2
And do not be conformed to this world, but be transformed by the *renewing* of your mind, so that you may prove what the will of God is, that which is good and acceptable and perfect.

Romans 13:13–14
Let us behave properly as in the day, not in carousing and drunkenness, not in sexual promiscuity and sensuality, not in strife and jealousy. [14]But *put on* the Lord Jesus Christ, and make no provision for the flesh in regard to its lusts.

1 Corinthians 12:13
For by one Spirit we were all baptized into one body, whether *Jews* or *Greeks*, whether *slaves* or *free*, and we were all made to drink of one Spirit.

2 Corinthians 3:18

But we all, with unveiled face, beholding as in a mirror the glory of the Lord, are being transformed into the same *image* from glory to glory, just as from the Lord, the Spirit.

2 Corinthians 4:16

Therefore we do not lose heart, but though our outer man is decaying, yet our inner man is being *renewed* day by day.

Galatians 3:27–28

For all of you who were baptized into Christ have clothed yourselves with Christ. [28]There is neither *Jew* nor *Greek*, there is neither *slave* nor *free man*, there is neither male nor female; for you are *all* one in Christ Jesus.

Galatians 5:19–21

Now the deeds of the flesh are evident, which are: *immorality, impurity,* sensuality, [20]*idolatry,* sorcery, enmities, strife, jealousy, outbursts of *anger,* disputes, dissensions, factions, [21]envying, drunkenness, carousing, and things like these.

Ephesians 2:1–3

And you were *dead* in your trespasses and sins, [2]in which you formerly *walked* according to the course of this world, according to the prince of the power of the air, of the spirit that is now working in *the sons of disobedience.* [3]Among them we too all formerly *lived* in the lusts of our flesh, indulging the *desires* of the flesh and of the mind, and were by nature children of *wrath,* even as the rest.

Ephesians 4:22–25, 31

. . . that, in reference to your former manner of life, *you lay aside the old self,* which is being corrupted in accordance with the lusts of deceit, [23] and that you be *renewed* in the spirit of your mind, [24]and *put on the new self,* which in the likeness of God has been *created* in righteousness and holiness of the truth. [25]Therefore, *laying aside* falsehood, SPEAK TRUTH EACH ONE of you WITH HIS NEIGHBOR, for we are members of one another. . . . [31]Let all bitterness and *wrath* and *anger* and clamor and *slander* be put away from you, along with all *malice.*

Ephesians 5:3–6

But *immorality* or any *impurity* or *greed* must not even be named among you, as is proper among saints; [4]and there must be no filthiness and silly talk, or coarse jesting, which are not fitting, but rather giving of thanks. [5]For this you know with certainty, that no immoral or impure person or covetous man, who is an *idolater,* has an inheritance in the kingdom of Christ and God. [6]Let no one deceive you with empty words, for because of these things *the wrath of God comes upon the sons of disobedience.*

OTHER BIBLICAL PARALLELS

Genesis 1:27

God *created* man in His own image, in *the image* of God He created him; male and female He created them.

NONCANONICAL PARALLELS

3 Maccabees 7:5

They also led them [the Jews] out with harsh treatment as slaves, or rather as traitors, and, girding themselves with a cruelty more savage than that of *Scythian* custom, they tried without any inquiry or examination to put them to death.

Colossians 3:12–17

So, as those who have been chosen of God, holy and beloved, put on a heart of compassion, kindness, humility, gentleness and patience; [13]bearing with one another, and forgiving each other, whoever has a complaint against anyone; just as the Lord forgave you, so also should you. [14]Beyond all these things put on love, which is the perfect bond of unity. [15]Let the peace of Christ rule in your hearts, to which indeed you were called in one body; and be thankful. [16]Let the word of Christ richly dwell within you, with all wisdom teaching and admonishing one another with psalms and hymns and spiritual songs, singing with thankfulness in your hearts to God. [17]Whatever you do in word or deed, do all in the name of the Lord Jesus, giving thanks through Him to God the Father.

Colossians 1:9–14

For this reason also, since the day we heard of it, we have not ceased to pray for you and to ask that you may be filled with the knowledge of His will in all spiritual *wisdom* and understanding, [10]so that you will walk in a manner worthy of the Lord, to please Him in all respects, bearing fruit in every good work and increasing in the knowledge of God; [11]strengthened with all power, according to His glorious might, for the attaining of all steadfastness and *patience*; joyously [12]*giving thanks to the Father,* who has qualified us to share in the inheritance of the saints in Light. [13]For He rescued us from the domain of darkness, and transferred us to the kingdom of His beloved Son, [14]in whom we have redemption, the *forgiveness* of sins.

Colossians 1:19–22

For it was the Father's good pleasure for all the fullness to dwell in Him, [20]and through Him to reconcile all things to Himself, having made *peace* through the blood of His cross; through Him, I say, whether things on earth or things in heaven. [21]And although you were formerly alienated and hostile in mind, engaged in evil deeds, [22]yet He has now reconciled you in His fleshly *body* through death, in order to present you before Him *holy* and blameless and beyond reproach.

Colossians 1:28

We proclaim Him, *admonishing* every man and *teaching* every man *with all wisdom,* so that we may present every man complete in Christ.

Romans 10:17

So faith comes from hearing, and hearing by *the word of Christ.*

1 Corinthians 14:26

What is the outcome then, brethren? When you assemble, each one has a *psalm,* has a *teaching,* has a revelation, has a tongue, has an interpretation. Let all things be done for edification.

Galatians 5:22–23

But the fruit of the Spirit is *love,* joy, *peace, patience, kindness,* goodness, faithfulness, [23]*gentleness,* self-control; against such things there is no law.

Ephesians 4:1–4

Therefore I, the prisoner of the Lord, implore you to walk in a manner worthy of the calling with which you have been called, [2]with all *humility* and *gentleness,* with *patience,* showing tolerance for one another in *love,* [3]being diligent to preserve the *unity* of the Spirit in the *bond* of *peace.* [4]There is *one body* and one Spirit, just as also *you were called* in one hope of your calling.

Ephesians 4:32

Be *kind* to one another, tender-hearted, *forgiving each other, just as* God in Christ also has *forgiven you.*

Ephesians 5:18–20

And do not get drunk with wine, for that is dissipation, but be filled with the Spirit, [19]speaking to one another in *psalms and hymns and spiritual songs, singing* and making melody with your *heart* to the Lord; [20]always *giving thanks* for all things *in the name of* our *Lord Jesus* Christ to God, even the Father.

Philippians 2:1–3

Therefore if there is any encouragement in Christ, if there is any consolation of *love,* if there is any fellowship of the Spirit, if any affection and *compassion,* [2]make my joy complete by being of the same mind, maintaining the same love, *united* in spirit, intent on one purpose. [3]Do nothing from selfishness or empty conceit, but with *humility* of mind regard one another as more important than yourselves.

Philippians 4:7

And the *peace* of God, which surpasses all comprehension, will guard your *hearts* and your minds in Christ Jesus.

1 Thessalonians 5:8

But since we are of the day, let us be sober, having *put on* the breastplate of faith and *love,* and as a helmet, the hope of salvation.

Matthew 6:14

"For if you *forgive* others for their transgressions, your heavenly Father will also *forgive you.*"

John 14:27

"*Peace* I leave with you; My peace I give to you; not as the world gives do I give to you. Do not let your *heart* be troubled, nor let it be fearful."

Acts 16:25

But about midnight Paul and Silas were praying and *singing hymns* of praise to God, and the prisoners were listening to them.

1 Peter 2:9

But you are A *CHOSEN* RACE, A royal PRIESTHOOD, A *HOLY* NATION, A PEOPLE FOR God's OWN POSSESSION, so that you may proclaim the excellencies of Him who has *called* you out of darkness into His marvelous light.

NONCANONICAL PARALLELS

Sirach 51:11

I will praise your name continually, and will *sing hymns* of *thanksgiving.*

Testament of Zebulon 7:2–3

"You, therefore, my children, on the basis of God's caring for you, without discrimination be *compassionate* and merciful to all. Provide for every person with a *kind heart.* [3]If at any time you do not have anything to give to the one who is in need, be compassionate and merciful in your inner self."

Testament of Gad 6:1, 3

"Now, my children, each of you *love* your brother. Drive hatred out of your *hearts.* . . . [3]Love one another from the heart, therefore, and if anyone sins against you, speak to him in *peace.* . . . If anyone confesses and repents, *forgive* him."

Colossians 3:18–4:1

Wives, be subject to your husbands, as is fitting in the Lord. [19]Husbands, love your wives and do not be embittered against them. [20]Chil-dren, be obedient to your parents in all things, for this is well-pleasing to the Lord. [21]Fathers, do not exasperate your children, so that they will not lose heart. [22]Slaves, in all things obey those who are your masters on earth, not with external service, as those who merely please men, but with sincerity of heart, fearing the Lord. [23]Whatever you do, do your work heartily, as for the Lord rather than for men, [24]knowing that from the Lord you will receive the reward of the inheritance. It is the Lord Christ whom you serve. [25]For he who does wrong will receive the consequences of the wrong which he has done, and that without partiality. [4:1]Masters, grant to your slaves justice and fairness, knowing that you too have a Master in heaven.

COLOSSIANS PARALLELS

Colossians 1:11–12

. . . joyously [12]giving thanks to the Father, who has qualified us to share in the *inheritance* of the saints in Light.

Colossians 1:19–20

For it was the Father's good pleasure for all the fullness to dwell in Him, [20]and through Him to reconcile all things to Himself, having made peace through the blood of His cross; through Him, I say, whether things *on earth* or things *in heaven.*

Colossians 2:1–2

For I want you to know how great a struggle I have on your behalf and for those who are at Laodicea, and for all those who have not personally seen my face, [2]that their hearts may be encouraged, having been knit together in *love*, and attaining to all the wealth that comes from the full assurance of understanding.

OTHER PAULINE PARALLELS

Romans 2:9–11

There will be tribulation and distress for every soul of man who does evil, of the Jew first and also of the Greek, [10]but glory and honor and peace to everyone who does good, to the Jew first and also to the Greek. [11]For there is no *partiality* with God.

Ephesians 5:21–23

Be subject to one another in the fear of Christ. [22]*Wives, be subject to your* own *husbands, as* to *the Lord.* [23]For the husband is the head of the wife, as Christ also is the head of the church, He Himself being the Savior of the body.

Ephesians 5:25–27

Husbands, love your wives, just as Christ also loved the church and gave Himself up for her, [26]so that He might sanctify her, having cleansed her by the washing of water with the word, [27]that He might present to Himself the church in all her glory, having no spot or wrinkle or any such thing; but that she would be holy and blameless.

Ephesians 6:1–3

Children, obey *your parents* in the Lord, for this is right. [2]HONOR YOUR FATHER AND MOTHER (which is the first commandment with a promise), [3]SO THAT IT MAY BE WELL WITH YOU, AND THAT YOU MAY LIVE LONG ON THE EARTH.

Ephesians 6:5–9

Slaves, be *obedient* to *those who are your masters* according to the flesh, with *fear* and trembling, in the *sincerity of* your *heart,* as to Christ; [6]not by way of *eyeservice,* as *menpleasers,* but as slaves of Christ, doing the will of God from the heart. [7]With good will render service, *as to the Lord,* and not to *men,* [8]*knowing that* whatever good thing each one does, this he *will receive* back *from the Lord,* whether slave or free. [9]And *masters,* do the same things to them, and give up threatening, knowing that both their *Master* and yours is *in heaven,* and there is no *partiality* with Him.

1 Timothy 6:1

All who are under the yoke as *slaves* are to regard their own *masters* as worthy of all honor so that the name of God and our doctrine will not be spoken against.

Titus 2:3–5

Older women likewise are to be reverent in their behavior, not malicious gossips nor enslaved to much wine, teaching what is good, [4]so that they may encourage the young women to *love* their husbands, to love their children, [5]to be sensible, pure, workers at home, kind, *being subject to* their own *husbands,* so that the word of God will not be dishonored.

Titus 2:9–10

Urge *bondslaves* to be subject to their own *masters* in everything, to be well-pleasing, not argumentative, [10]not pilfering, but showing all good faith so that they will adorn the doctrine of God our Savior in every respect.

Philemon 10, 15–16

I appeal to you for my child Onesimus, whom I have begotten in my imprisonment. . . . [15]For perhaps he was for this reason separated from you for a while, that you would have him back forever, [16]no longer as a *slave,* but more than a slave, a beloved brother, especially to me, but how much more to you, both in the flesh and in the Lord.

OTHER BIBLICAL PARALLELS

Leviticus 25:39–40, 43

"If a countryman of yours becomes so poor with regard to you that he sells himself to you, you shall not subject him to a *slave's* service. [40]He shall be with you as a hired man, as if he were a sojourner; he shall *serve* with you until the year of jubilee. . . . [43]You shall not rule over him with severity, but are to revere your God."

1 Peter 2:18–19

Servants, be submissive to *your masters* with all respect, not only to those who are good and gentle, but also to those who are unreasonable. [19]For this finds favor, if for the sake of conscience toward God a person bears up under sorrows when suffering unjustly.

1 Peter 3:1,7

In the same way, you *wives,* be submissive to *your* own *husbands* so that even if any of them are disobedient to the word, they may be won without a word by the behavior of their wives. . . . [7]You *husbands* in the same way, live with *your wives* in an understanding way, as with someone weaker, since she is a woman; and show her honor as a fellow heir of the grace of life, so that your prayers will not be hindered.

NONCANONICAL PARALLELS

Aristotle, Politics 1.2.1

The primary and smallest parts of the

household are *master* and *slave, husband* and *wife, father* and *children.*

Xenophon, Memorabilia *2.1.16*

Let us consider this as well, how *masters* treat such *slaves.* Do they not discipline them with hunger so there is no desire in them? Do they not prevent them from stealing by locking up anything that might be taken? Do they not stop them from escaping with chains? Do they not force the laziness out of them with blows?

Seneca, On Mercy *1.18*

To rule *slaves* with moderation is commendable. Even with purchased slaves one should consider not how much he can be made to suffer without retaliating, but how much you are allowed to inflict by natural *fairness* and *justice.*

Colossians 4:2–9

Devote yourselves to prayer, keeping alert in it with an attitude of thanksgiving; ³praying at the same time for us as well, that God will open up to us a door for the word, so that we may speak forth the mystery of Christ, for which I have also been imprisoned; ⁴that I may make it clear in the way I ought to speak. ⁵Conduct yourselves with wisdom toward outsiders, making the most of the opportunity. ⁶Let your speech always be with grace, as though seasoned with salt, so that you will know how you should respond to each person. ⁷As to all my affairs, Tychicus, our beloved brother and faithful servant and fellow bond-servant in the Lord, will bring you information. ⁸For I have sent him to you for this very purpose, that you may know about our circumstances and that he may encourage your hearts; ⁹and with him Onesimus, our faithful and beloved brother, who is one of your number. They will inform you about the whole situation here.

COLOSSIANS PARALLELS

Colossians 1:11–12

. . . strengthened with all power, according to His glorious might, for the attaining of all steadfastness and patience; joyously ¹²*giving thanks* to the Father, who has qualified us to share in the inheritance of the saints in Light.

Colossians 1:24–26, 28

Now I rejoice in my sufferings for your sake, and in my flesh I do my share on behalf of His body, which is the church, in filling up what is lacking in Christ's afflictions. ²⁵Of this church I was made a minister according to the stewardship from God bestowed on me for your benefit, so that I might fully carry out the preaching of *the word* of God, ²⁶that is, *the mystery* which has been hidden from the past ages and generations, but has now been manifested to His saints. . . . ²⁸We proclaim Him, admonishing every man and teaching every man with all *wisdom,* so that we may present every man complete in Christ.

Colossians 2:1–2

For I want you to know how great a struggle I have on your behalf and for those who are at Laodicea, and for all those who have not personally seen my face, ²that their *hearts* may be *encouraged,* having been knit together in love, and attaining to all the wealth that comes from the full assurance of understanding, resulting in a true knowledge of God's *mystery,* that is, Christ Himself.

OTHER PAULINE PARALLELS

Ephesians 3:1–4

For this reason I, Paul, the *prisoner* of Christ Jesus for the sake of you Gentiles — ²if indeed you have heard of the stewardship of God's grace which was given to me for you; ³that by revelation there was made known to me the mystery, as I wrote before in brief. ⁴By referring to this, when you read you can understand my insight into *the mystery of Christ* . . .

Ephesians 4:29

Let no unwholesome word proceed from your mouth, but only such a word as is good for edification according to the need of the moment, so that it will give *grace* to those who hear.

Ephesians 5:15–16

Therefore be careful how you walk, not as unwise men but as *wise,* ¹⁶*making the most* of your time, because the days are evil.

Ephesians 6:18–22

With all *prayer* and petition pray at all times in the Spirit, and with this in view, be on the *alert* with all perseverance and petition for all the saints, [19]and *pray* on my behalf, that utterance may be given to me in the opening of my mouth, to make known with boldness the *mystery* of the gospel, [20]for which I am an ambassador in chains; that in proclaiming it I may *speak* boldly, as *I ought to speak.* [21]But that you also may know about my *circumstances*, how I am doing, *Tychicus*, the *beloved brother and faithful* minister *in the Lord*, will make everything known to you. [22]*I have sent him to you for this very purpose*, so *that you may know about* us, *and that he may* comfort *your hearts.*

Philippians 4:6

Be anxious for nothing, but in everything by *prayer* and supplication with *thanksgiving* let your requests be made known to God.

1 Thessalonians 4:10–12

But we urge you, brethren, to excel still more, [11]and to make it your ambition to lead a quiet life and attend to your own business and work with your hands, just as we commanded you, [12]so that you will behave properly *toward outsiders* and not be in any need.

2 Thessalonians 3:1

Finally, brethren, *pray for us* that *the word* of the Lord will spread rapidly and be glorified, just as it did also with you.

2 Timothy 4:12

But *Tychicus I have sent* to Ephesus.

Philemon 1–2

Paul, a prisoner of Christ Jesus, and Timothy our brother, To Philemon our beloved brother and fellow worker, [2]and to Apphia our sister, and to Archippus our fellow soldier, and to the church in your house . . .

Philemon 10

I appeal to you for my child *Onesimus*, whom I have begotten in my *imprisonment.*

OTHER BIBLICAL PARALLELS

Exodus 30:34–36

"Take for yourself spices, stacte and onycha and galbanum, spices with pure frankincense; there shall be an equal part of each.

[35]With it you shall make incense, a perfume, the work of a perfumer, *salted*, pure, and holy. [36]You shall beat some of it very fine, and put part of it before the testimony in the tent of meeting where I will meet with you."

Mark 9:50

"*Salt* is good; but if the salt becomes unsalty, with what will you make it salty again? Have salt in yourselves, and be at peace with one another."

Acts 14:27

When they had arrived and gathered the church together, they began to report all things that God had done with them and how He had *opened a door* of faith to the Gentiles.

Acts 20:4

And he was accompanied by Sopater of Berea, the son of Pyrrhus, and by Aristarchus and Secundus of the Thessalonians, and Gaius of Derbe, and Timothy, and *Tychicus* and Trophimus of Asia.

1 Peter 3:15

Sanctify Christ as Lord in your hearts, always being ready to make a defense to everyone who asks you to give an account for the hope that is in you, yet with gentleness and reverence.

NONCANONICAL PARALLELS

Letter to Zenon (P.Col. 3.6)

Anything else remaining you can learn from the one who carries this letter to you. For he is no stranger to us.

Colossians 4:10–18

Aristarchus, my fellow prisoner, sends you his greetings; and also Barnabas's cousin Mark (about whom you received instructions; if he comes to you, welcome him); [11]and also Jesus who is called Justus; these are the only fellow workers for the kingdom of God who are from the circumcision, and they have proved to be an encouragement to me. [12]Epaphras, who is one of your number, a bondslave of Jesus Christ, sends you his greetings, always laboring earnestly for you in his prayers, that you may stand perfect and fully assured in all the will of God. [13]For I testify for him that he has a deep concern for you and for those who are in Laodicea and Hierapolis. [14]Luke, the beloved physician, sends you his greetings, and also Demas. [15]Greet the brethren who are in Laodicea and also Nympha and the church that is in her house. [16]When this letter is read among you, have it also read in the church of the Laodiceans; and you, for your part read my letter that is coming from Laodicea. [17]Say to Archippus, "Take heed to the ministry which you have received in the Lord, that you may fulfill it." [18]I, Paul, write this greeting with my own hand. Remember my imprisonment. Grace be with you.

COLOSSIANS PARALLELS

Colossians 1:5–8

. . . because of the hope laid up for you in heaven, of which you previously heard in the word of truth, the gospel [6]which has come to you, just as in all the world also it is constantly bearing fruit and increasing, even as it has been doing in you also since the day you heard of it and understood the grace of God in truth; [7]just as you learned it from *Epaphras*, our beloved fellow bond-servant, who is a faithful servant of Christ on our behalf, [8]and he also informed us of your love in the Spirit.

Colossians 1:13–14

For He rescued us from the domain of darkness, and transferred us to *the kingdom* of His beloved Son, [14]in whom we have redemption, the forgiveness of sins.

Colossians 2:1

For I want you to know how great a struggle I have on your behalf and for those who are at *Laodicea*, and for all those who have not personally seen my face.

OTHER PAULINE PARALLELS

Romans 12:2

And do not be conformed to this world, but be transformed by the renewing of your mind, so that you may prove what *the will of God* is, that which is good and acceptable and *perfect*.

Romans 14:10

But you, why do you judge your brother? Or you again, why do you regard your brother

with contempt? For we will all *stand* before the judgment seat of God.

1 Corinthians 16:21

The *greeting* is in *my own hand—Paul*.

Galatians 2:12

For prior to the coming of certain men from James, he used to eat with the Gentiles; but when they came, he began to withdraw and hold himself aloof, fearing the party of *the circumcision*.

Galatians 6:11

See with what large letters I am writing to you *with my own hand*.

1 Thessalonians 5:26–27

Greet all *the brethren* with a holy kiss. [27]I adjure you by the Lord to *have this letter read* to all the brethren.

2 Thessalonians 3:17

I, *Paul, write this greeting with my own hand*, and this is a distinguishing mark in every letter; this is the way I write.

2 Timothy 4:10–11

Demas, having loved this present world, has deserted me and gone to Thessalonica; Crescens has gone to Galatia, Titus to Dalmatia. [11]Only *Luke* is with me. Pick up *Mark* and bring him with you, for he is useful to me for service.

Philemon 1–2

Paul, a *prisoner* of Christ Jesus, and Timothy our brother, To Philemon our beloved brother and *fellow worker*, [2]and to Apphia our sister, and to *Archippus* our fellow soldier, and to the church in your house . . .

Philemon 19

I, Paul, am *writing* this *with my own hand*, I will repay it.

Philemon 23–24

Epaphras, my fellow prisoner in Christ Jesus, *greets you*, [24]as do *Mark, Aristarchus, Demas, Luke*, my *fellow workers*.

OTHER BIBLICAL PARALLELS

Acts 12:25

And *Barnabas* and Saul returned from Jerusalem when they had fulfilled their mission, taking along with them John, who was also called *Mark*.

Acts 15:37–39

Barnabas wanted to take John, called *Mark*, along with them also. [38]But Paul kept insisting that they should not take him along who had deserted them in Pamphylia and had not gone with them to the work. [39]And there occurred such a sharp disagreement that they separated from one another, and Barnabas took Mark with him and sailed away to Cyprus.

Acts 20:4

And he was accompanied by Sopater of Berea, the son of Pyrrhus, and by *Aristarchus* and Secundus of the Thessalonians, and Gaius of Derbe, and Timothy, and Tychicus and Trophimus of Asia.

Acts 27:2

And embarking in an Adramyttian ship, which was about to sail to the regions along the coast of Asia, we put out to sea accompanied by *Aristarchus*, a Macedonian of Thessalonica.

Revelation 3:14–17, 19

"To the angel of the church in *Laodicea* write, . . . [15]'I know your deeds, that you are neither cold nor hot; I wish that you were cold or hot. [16]So because you are lukewarm, and neither hot nor cold, I will spit you out of My mouth. [17]Because you say, "I am rich, and have become wealthy, and have need of nothing," and you do not know that you are wretched and miserable and poor and blind and naked . . . [19]Those whom I love, I reprove and discipline; therefore be zealous and repent.'"

NONCANONICAL PARALLELS

Cicero, Letters to Atticus *11.2*

To whomever you think right, please send *letters* in my name—you know my friends. If they look for my seal or *handwriting*, say that I have forgone these on account of the sentries.

1 Thessalonians

1 Thessalonians 1:1–5

Paul and Silvanus and Timothy, To the church of the Thessalonians in God the Father and the Lord Jesus Christ: Grace to you and peace. ²We give thanks to God always for all of you, making mention of you in our prayers; ³constantly bearing in mind your work of faith and labor of love and steadfastness of hope in our Lord Jesus Christ in the presence of our God and Father, ⁴knowing, brethren beloved by God, His choice of you; ⁵for our gospel did not come to you in word only, but also in power and in the Holy Spirit and with full conviction; just as you know what kind of men we proved to be among you for your sake.

1 THESSALONIANS PARALLELS

1 Thessalonians 2:5–7

For we never came with flattering speech, as you know, nor with a pretext for greed— God is witness— ⁶nor did we seek glory from men, either from you or from others, even though as apostles of Christ we might have asserted our authority. ⁷But *we proved to be* gentle among you, as a nursing mother tenderly cares for her own children.

1 Thessalonians 2:13

For this reason we also constantly *thank God* that when you received the word of God which you heard from us, you accepted it not as the *word* of men, but for what it really is, the word of God, which also performs its *work* in you who believe.

1 Thessalonians 3:2, 6

We sent *Timothy*, our brother and God's fellow worker in the *gospel* of Christ, to strengthen and encourage you as to your faith. . . . ⁶But now that Timothy has come to us from you, and has brought us good news of your *faith* and *love*, and that you always think kindly of us, longing to see us just as we also long to see you . . .

1 Thessalonians 5:8

But since we are of the day, let us be sober, having put on the breastplate of *faith* and *love*, and as a helmet, the *hope* of salvation.

OTHER PAULINE PARALLELS

Romans 1:1, 7–10

Paul, a bond-servant of Christ Jesus, called as an apostle, set apart for the *gospel* of God, . . . ⁷to all who are *beloved of God* in Rome, called as saints: *Grace to you and peace* from God our Father and the Lord Jesus Christ. ⁸First, I *thank* my *God* through Jesus Christ for you all, because your *faith* is being proclaimed throughout the whole world. ⁹For God, whom I serve in my spirit in the preaching of the *gospel* of His Son, is my witness as to how unceasingly I *make mention of you*, ¹⁰always in my *prayers* making request, if perhaps now at last by the will of God I may succeed in coming to you.

1 Corinthians 2:1, 4

And when I came to you, brethren, I *did not come* with superiority of speech or of wisdom, proclaiming to you the testimony of God. . . . ⁴And my message and my preaching were not in persuasive *words* of wisdom, but in demonstration of *the Spirit* and of *power*.

1 Corinthians 13:13

But now *faith, hope, love,* abide these three; but the greatest of these is love.

2 Corinthians 1:1–2

Paul, an apostle of Christ Jesus by the will of God, and *Timothy* our brother, *To the church* of God which is at Corinth with all the saints who are throughout Achaia: [2]*Grace to you and peace* from God our Father and the Lord Jesus Christ.

2 Corinthians 1:19

For the Son of God, Christ Jesus, who was preached among you by us—by me and *Silvanus* and *Timothy*—was not yes and no, but is yes in Him.

Ephesians 1:3–4

Blessed be the God and Father of our Lord Jesus Christ, who has blessed us with every spiritual blessing in the heavenly places in Christ, [4]just as He *chose* us in Him before the foundation of the world, that we would be holy and blameless before Him.

Colossians 1:3–5

We give thanks to God, the Father of our Lord Jesus Christ, *praying* always for you, [4]since we heard of your *faith* in Christ Jesus and the *love* which you have for all the saints; [5]because of the *hope* laid up for you in heaven, of which you previously heard in the word of truth, the *gospel*.

2 Thessalonians 1:1–3

Paul and Silvanus and Timothy, To the church of the Thessalonians in God our *Father and the Lord Jesus Christ*: [2]*Grace to you and peace* from God the Father and the Lord Jesus Christ. [3]*We ought always to give thanks to God for you, brethren*, as is only fitting, because your *faith* is greatly enlarged, and the *love* of each one of you toward one another grows ever greater.

2 Thessalonians 1:11

To this end also we *pray* for you always, that our God will count you worthy of your calling, and fulfill every desire for goodness and the *work of faith* with *power*.

2 Thessalonians 2:13–14

But *we should always give thanks to God for you, brethren beloved* by the Lord, because God has *chosen* you from the beginning for salvation through sanctification by *the Spirit* and faith in the truth. [14]It was for this He called you through *our gospel*, that you may gain the glory of our Lord Jesus Christ.

Isaiah 14:1

When the LORD will have compassion on Jacob and again *choose* Israel, and settle them in their own land, then strangers will join them and attach themselves to the house of Jacob.

Isaiah 41:8–9

"But you, Israel, My servant, Jacob whom I have *chosen*, Descendant of Abraham My friend, [9]You whom I have taken from the ends of the earth, And called from its remotest parts And said to you, 'You are My servant, I have chosen you and not rejected you.'"

Acts 16:1

Paul came also to Derbe and to Lystra. And a disciple was there, named *Timothy*, the son of a Jewish woman who was a believer, but his father was a Greek.

Acts 17:1–2, 4

Now when they had traveled through Amphipolis and Apollonia, they came to *Thessalonica*, where there was a synagogue of the Jews. [2]And according to *Paul's* custom, he went to them, and for three Sabbaths reasoned with them from the Scriptures. . . . [4]And some of them were persuaded and joined Paul and *Silas*, along with a large number of the God-fearing Greeks and a number of the leading women.

Seneca, Moral Epistles 52.8

Let us choose [for our teachers] not those who pour out *words* with the greatest alacrity, turning commonplaces and putting on private sideshows, but those who instruct us with their lives, who tell us what to do and show us what to do, who instruct us in what to avoid and are never discovered doing what they had told us to flee.

1 Thessalonians 1:6–10

You also became imitators of us and of the Lord, having received the word in much tribulation with the joy of the Holy Spirit, [7]so that you became an example to all the believers in

Macedonia and in Achaia. ⁸For the word of the Lord has sounded forth from you, not only in Macedonia and Achaia, but also in every place your faith toward God has gone forth, so that we have no need to say anything. ⁹For they themselves report about us what kind of a reception we had with you, and how you turned to God from idols to serve a living and true God, ¹⁰and to wait for His Son from heaven, whom He raised from the dead, that is Jesus, who rescues us from the wrath to come.

1 THESSALONIANS PARALLELS

1 Thessalonians 2:14–16

For you, brethren, became *imitators* of the churches of God in Christ Jesus that are in Judea, for you also endured the same sufferings at the hands of your own countrymen, even as they did from the Jews, ¹⁵who both killed the Lord Jesus and the prophets, and drove us out. They are not pleasing to God, but hostile to all men, ¹⁶hindering us from speaking to the Gentiles so that they may be saved; with the result that they always fill up the measure of their sins. But *wrath* has come upon them to the utmost.

1 Thessalonians 3:4

For indeed when we were with you, we kept telling you in advance that we were going to suffer affliction; and so it came to pass, as you know.

1 Thessalonians 4:9–10

Now as to the love of the brethren, you have no need for anyone to write to you, for you yourselves are taught by God to love one another; ¹⁰for indeed you do practice it toward all the brethren who are in all *Macedonia*.

1 Thessalonians 5:9

For God has not destined us for *wrath*, but for obtaining salvation through our Lord Jesus Christ.

OTHER PAULINE PARALLELS

Romans 1:8

First, I thank my God through Jesus Christ for you all, because your *faith* is being proclaimed throughout the whole world.

Romans 5:3–5

And not only this, but we also exult in our tribulations, knowing that *tribulation* brings about perseverance; ⁴and perseverance, proven character; and proven character, hope; ⁵and hope does not disappoint, because the love of God has been poured out within our hearts through *the Holy Spirit* who was given to us.

Romans 5:9

Much more then, having now been justified by His blood, we shall be saved from the *wrath* of God through Him.

Romans 10:8–9

But what does it say? "THE WORD IS NEAR YOU, in your mouth and in your heart"—that is, *the word* of *faith* which we are preaching, ⁹that if you confess with your mouth Jesus as Lord, and believe in your heart that God *raised* Him *from the dead*, you will be saved.

1 Corinthians 11:1

Be *imitators* of me, just as I also am of Christ.

1 Corinthians 12:2

You know that when you were pagans, you were led astray to the mute *idols*, however you were led.

Galatians 1:3–4

Grace to you and peace from God our Father and the Lord Jesus Christ, ⁴who gave Himself for our sins so that He might *rescue* us from this present evil age, according to the will of our God and Father.

Philippians 3:17

Brethren, join in following my example, and observe those who walk according to the pattern you have in us.

Philippians 3:20

For our citizenship is in *heaven*, from which also we eagerly *wait* for a Savior, the Lord Jesus Christ.

Colossians 1:13–14

For He *rescued* us from the domain of darkness, and transferred us to the kingdom of His beloved Son, ¹⁴in whom we have redemption, the forgiveness of sins.

2 Thessalonians 3:1

Finally, brethren, pray for us that *the word of the Lord* will spread rapidly and be glorified, just as it did also with you.

Isaiah 45:22

"*Turn to* Me and be saved, all the ends of the earth; For I am God, and there is no other."

Jeremiah 10:10

But the LORD is the *true God*; He is the *living God* and the everlasting King. At His *wrath* the earth quakes, And the nations cannot endure His indignation.

Acts 13:52

And the disciples were continually filled with *joy* and with *the Holy Spirit*.

Acts 17:1–3, 5

Now when they had traveled through Amphipolis and Apollonia, they came to Thessalonica, where there was a synagogue of the Jews. ²And according to Paul's custom, he went to them, and for three Sabbaths reasoned with them from the Scriptures, ³explaining and giving evidence that the Christ had to suffer and *rise* again *from the dead*, and saying, "This Jesus whom I am proclaiming to you is the Christ." . . . ⁵But the Jews, becoming jealous and taking along some wicked men from the market place, formed a mob and set the city in an uproar; and attacking the house of Jason, they were seeking to bring them out to the people.

Acts 26:19–20

So, King Agrippa, I did not prove disobedient to the heavenly vision, ²⁰but kept declaring both to those of Damascus first, and also at Jerusalem and then throughout all the region of Judea, and even to the Gentiles, that they should repent and *turn to God*, performing deeds appropriate to repentance.

Sibylline Oracles 3:545–48, 556–57

Greece, why do you rely on mortal leaders ⁵⁴⁶who are not able to flee the end of death? ⁵⁴⁷To what purpose do you give vain gifts to the dead ⁵⁴⁸and sacrifice to *idols*? . . . ⁵⁵⁶But

when the *wrath* of the great God comes upon you, ⁵⁵⁷then indeed you will recognize the face of the great God.

Joseph and Aseneth 11:10–11

But I have heard many saying that the God of the Hebrews is *a true God*, and *a living God*. . . . ¹¹Therefore I will take courage too and *turn* to him, and take refuge with him, and confess all my sins to him.

1 Thessalonians 2:1–8

For you yourselves know, brethren, that our coming to you was not in vain, ²but after we had already suffered and been mistreated in Philippi, as you know, we had the boldness in our God to speak to you the gospel of God amid much opposition. ³For our exhortation does not come from error or impurity or by way of deceit; ⁴but just as we have been approved by God to be entrusted with the gospel, so we speak, not as pleasing men, but God who examines our hearts. ⁵For we never came with flattering speech, as you know, nor with a pretext for greed—God is witness— ⁶nor did we seek glory from men, either from you or from others, even though as apostles of Christ we might have asserted our authority. ⁷But we proved to be gentle among you, as a nursing mother tenderly cares for her own children. ⁸Having so fond an affection for you, we were well-pleased to impart to you not only the gospel of God but also our own lives, because you had become very dear to us.

1 Thessalonians 1:5

Our gospel did not *come to you* in word only, but also in power and in the Holy Spirit and with full conviction.

1 Thessalonians 3:4–5

For indeed when we were with you, we kept telling you in advance that we were going to *suffer* affliction; and so it came to pass, *as you know*. ⁵For this reason, when I could endure it no longer, I also sent to find out about your faith, for fear that the tempter might have tempted you, and our labor would be *in vain*.

1 Thessalonians 4:1

Finally then, brethren, we request and *exhort* you in the Lord Jesus, that as you received from us instruction as to how you ought to walk and please God (just as you actually do walk), that you excel still more.

OTHER PAULINE PARALLELS

Romans 1:9

For *God*, whom I serve in my spirit in the preaching of the gospel of His Son, is my *witness* as to how unceasingly I make mention of you.

Romans 16:18

For such men are slaves, not of our Lord Christ but of their own appetites; and by their smooth and *flattering speech* they *deceive* the hearts of the unsuspecting.

1 Corinthians 2:1–3

And when I *came to you*, brethren, I did not come with superiority of *speech* or of wisdom, proclaiming to you the testimony of God. ²For I determined to know nothing among you except Jesus Christ, and Him crucified. ³I was with you in weakness and in fear and in much trembling.

2 Corinthians 2:17

For we are not like many, peddling the word of God, but as from sincerity, but as from God, we *speak* in Christ in the sight of God.

2 Corinthians 4:1–2

Therefore, since we have this ministry, as we received mercy, we do not lose heart, ²but we have renounced the things hidden because of shame, not walking in craftiness or adulterating the word of God, but by the manifestation of truth commending ourselves to every man's conscience in the sight of God.

2 Corinthians 11:6–7

But even if I am unskilled in *speech*, yet I am not so in knowledge; in fact, in every way we have made this evident to you in all things. ⁷Or did I commit a sin in humbling myself so that you might be exalted, because I preached *the gospel of God* to you without charge?

Galatians 1:10

For am I now seeking the favor of men, or of God? Or am I striving to *please men*? If I were still trying to please men, I would not be a bond-servant of Christ.

Galatians 2:7

But on the contrary, seeing that I had been *entrusted with the gospel* to the uncircumcised, just as Peter had been to the circumcised . . .

Galatians 4:19

My *children*, with whom I am again in labor until Christ is formed in you . . .

Ephesians 6:19–20

Pray on my behalf, that utterance may be given to me in the opening of my mouth, to make known with *boldness* the mystery of *the gospel*, ²⁰for which I am an ambassador in chains; that in proclaiming it I may *speak* boldly, as I ought to speak.

OTHER BIBLICAL PARALLELS

Jeremiah 12:3

But You know me, O LORD; You see me; And You *examine* my *heart's* attitude toward You.

Acts 16:11–12, 19, 22–23

So putting out to sea from Troas, we ran a straight course to Samothrace, and on the day following to Neapolis; ¹²and from there to *Philippi*, which is a leading city of the district of Macedonia, a Roman colony; and we were staying in this city for some days. . . . ¹⁹But when her masters saw that their hope of profit was gone, they seized Paul and Silas and dragged them into the market place before the authorities. . . . ²²The crowd rose up together against them, and the chief magistrates tore their robes off them and proceeded to order them to be beaten with rods. ²³When they had struck them with many blows, they threw them into prison, commanding the jailer to guard them securely.

Acts 17:1, 5, 10

Now when they had traveled through Amphipolis and Apollonia, they came to Thessalonica, where there was a synagogue of the Jews. . . . ⁵But the Jews, becoming jealous and taking along some wicked men from the market place, formed a mob and set the city in an uproar. . . . [10]The brethren immediately sent Paul and Silas away by night to Berea.

1 Peter 5:2

Shepherd the flock of God among you, exercising oversight not under compulsion, but voluntarily, according to the will of God; and not for sordid gain, but with eagerness.

2 Peter 2:2–3

Many will follow their sensuality, and because of them the way of the truth will be maligned; [3]and in their *greed* they will exploit you with false words; their judgment from long ago is not idle, and their destruction is not asleep.

Dio Chrysostom, Orations *32.11*

But to find a man who plainly and without guile *speaks* his mind with *boldness*, making no false pretensions for the sake of *glory* or gain, but out of goodwill and a concern for others stands ready, if necessary, to submit to ridicule and to the disorder and the uproar of the crowd—to find such a man as that is not easy.

Plutarch, How to Tell a Flatterer from a Friend *69B–C*

So, then, the circumstances of the unfortunate do not call for frank speech and moral pronouncements, but require *gentleness* and support. [C]For when *children* fall down, their nurses do not run up and revile them, but they take them up and wash them and set them right, and then afterwards they reprove and punish them.

1 Thessalonians 2:9–12

For you recall, brethren, our labor and hardship, how working night and day so as not to be a burden to any of you, we proclaimed to you the gospel of God. [10]You are witnesses, and so is God, how devoutly and uprightly and blamelessly we behaved toward you believers; [11]just as you know how we were exhorting and encouraging and imploring each one of you as a father would his own children, [12]so that you would walk in a manner worthy of the God who calls you into His own kingdom and glory.

1 Thessalonians 1:5

Our *gospel* did not come to you in word only, but also in power and in the Holy Spirit and with full conviction; just *as you know* what kind of men we proved to be among you for your sake.

1 Thessalonians 3:2

We sent Timothy, our brother and God's fellow worker in *the gospel* of Christ, to strengthen and *encourage* you as to your faith.

1 Thessalonians 4:1, 7

Finally then, brethren, we request and *exhort* you in the Lord Jesus, that as you received from us instruction as to how you ought to *walk* and please God (just as you actually do walk), that you excel still more. . . . [7]For God has not *called* us for the purpose of impurity, but in sanctification.

1 Thessalonians 5:24

Faithful is He who *calls* you, and He also will bring it to pass.

1 Corinthians 4:11–12, 14–15

To this present hour we are both hungry and thirsty, and are poorly clothed, and are roughly treated, and are homeless; [12]and we toil, *working* with our own hands; when we are reviled, we bless; when we are persecuted, we endure; . . . [14]I do not write these things to shame you, but to admonish you as my beloved *children*. [15]For if you were to have countless tutors in Christ, yet you would not have many fathers, for in Christ Jesus I became your *father* through *the gospel.*

1 Corinthians 9:12, 14, 18

If others share the right over you, do we not more? Nevertheless, we did not use this right, but we endure all things so that we will cause no hindrance to the gospel of Christ. . . . [14]So also the Lord directed those who *proclaim the gospel* to get their living from the gospel. . . . [18]What then is my reward? That, when I preach the gospel, I may offer the gospel without charge, so as not to make full use of my right in the gospel.

2 Corinthians 1:12

For our proud confidence is this: the testimony of our conscience, that in holiness and godly sincerity, not in fleshly wisdom but in the grace of God, we have conducted ourselves in the world, and especially toward you.

2 Corinthians 11:8–9

I robbed other churches by taking wages from them to serve you; [9]and when I was present with you and was in need, I was *not a burden* to anyone; for when the brethren came from Macedonia they fully supplied my need, and in everything I kept myself from being a burden to you, and will continue to do so.

2 Corinthians 11:27

I have been in *labor and hardship*, through many sleepless nights, in hunger and thirst, often without food, in cold and exposure.

Ephesians 4:1–2

Therefore I, the prisoner of the Lord, *implore* you to *walk in a manner worthy* of the calling with which you have been *called*, [2]with all humility and gentleness, with patience, showing tolerance for one another in love.

Philippians 4:15–16

You yourselves also know, Philippians, that at the first preaching of the gospel, after I left Macedonia, no church shared with me in the matter of giving and receiving but you alone; [16]for even in Thessalonica you sent a gift more than once for my needs.

2 Thessalonians 1:5

This is a plain indication of God's righteous judgment so that you will be considered *worthy* of the *kingdom* of God, for which indeed you are suffering.

2 Thessalonians 2:14

It was for this He *called* you through our gospel, that you may gain the *glory* of our Lord Jesus Christ.

2 Thessalonians 3:7–10

For you yourselves know how you ought to follow our example, because we did not act in an undisciplined manner among you, [8]nor did we eat anyone's bread without paying for it, but with *labor and hardship* we

kept *working night and day* so that we would *not be a burden to any of you*; [9]not because we do not have the right to this, but in order to offer ourselves as a model for you, so that you would follow our example. [10]For even when we were with you, we used to give you this order: if anyone is not willing to work, then he is not to eat, either.

Titus 1:7–8

For the overseer must be above reproach as God's steward, not self-willed, not quick-tempered, not addicted to wine, not pugnacious, not fond of sordid gain, [8]but hospitable, loving what is good, sensible, just, *devout*, self-controlled.

Isaiah 45:3–4

"I will give you the treasures of darkness And hidden wealth of secret places, So that you may know that it is I, The LORD, the God of Israel, who *calls* you by your name. [4]For the sake of Jacob My servant, And Israel My chosen one, I have also called you by your name; I have given you a title of honor Though you have not known Me."

Acts 18:2–3

And he found a Jew named Aquila, a native of Pontus, having recently come from Italy with his wife Priscilla, because Claudius had commanded all the Jews to leave Rome. He came to them, [3]and because he was of the same trade, he stayed with them and they were *working*, for by trade they were tent-makers.

1 Peter 5:10

After you have suffered for a little while, the God of all grace, who *called* you to His eternal *glory* in Christ, will Himself perfect, confirm, strengthen and establish you.

Philo, On the Life of Moses *1.328*

And they bore this admonition calmly, as lawful sons of a very well-disposed *father*, for they knew that he [Moses] was not bullying them on the basis of his authority, but taking care of them and honoring righteousness and equality.

Musonius Rufus, fragment 11

Now it seems to me that the young people would gain more not by meeting with their teacher in a city or hearing him deliver lectures, but by watching him *working* in the fields and in this work demonstrating the lesson being instructed, that one must toil and suffer *hardships* with one's body rather than depend on someone else for food.

1 Thessalonians 2:13–20

For this reason we also constantly thank God that when you received the word of God which you heard from us, you accepted it not as the word of men, but for what it really is, the word of God, which also performs its work in you who believe. ¹⁴For you, brethren, became imitators of the churches of God in Christ Jesus that are in Judea, for you also endured the same sufferings at the hands of your own countrymen, even as they did from the Jews, ¹⁵who both killed the Lord Jesus and the prophets, and drove us out. They are not pleasing to God, but hostile to all men, ¹⁶hindering us from speaking to the Gentiles so that they may be saved; with the result that they always fill up the measure of their sins. But wrath has come upon them to the utmost. ¹⁷But we, brethren, having been taken away from you for a short while—in person, ·not in spirit—were all the more eager with great desire to see your face. ¹⁸For we wanted to come to you—I, Paul, more than once—and yet Satan hindered us. ¹⁹For who is our hope or joy or crown of exultation? Is it not even you, in the presence of our Lord Jesus at His coming? ²⁰For you are our glory and joy.

1 THESSALONIANS PARALLELS

1 Thessalonians 1:2, 5–6, 10

We give *thanks* to *God* always for all of you, making mention of you in our prayers; . . . ⁵for our gospel did not come to you in word only, but also in power and in the Holy Spirit and with full conviction; just as you know what kind of men we proved to be among you for your sake. ⁶You also became *imitators* of us and of the Lord, having *received the word* in much tribulation with the *joy* of the Holy Spirit, . . . ¹⁰and . . . wait for His Son from heaven, whom He raised from the dead, that is Jesus, who rescues us from the *wrath* to come.

1 Thessalonians 3:9–10, 13

For what *thanks* can we render to *God* for you in return for all the *joy* with which we rejoice before our God on your account, ¹⁰as we night and day keep praying most earnestly that we may *see your face*, and may complete what is lacking in your faith? . . . ¹³so that He may establish your hearts without blame in holiness before our God and Father at the *coming* of our Lord Jesus with all His saints.

OTHER PAULINE PARALLELS

Romans 1:11, 13

For I long to *see you* so that I may impart some spiritual gift to you, that you may be established; . . . ¹³I do not want you to be unaware, brethren, that often I have planned *to come to you* (and have been prevented so far) so that I may obtain some fruit among you also, even as among the rest of *the Gentiles*.

1 Corinthians 5:3

For I, on my part, though absent in body but present *in spirit*, have already judged him who has so committed this, as though I were present.

Galatians 1:11–12

For I would have you know, brethren, that the gospel which was preached by me is not according to *man*. ¹²For I neither received it from man, nor was I taught it, but I received it through a revelation of Jesus Christ.

Galatians 1:22–23

I was still unknown by sight to *the churches of Judea* which were in Christ; ²³but only, they kept hearing, "He who once persecuted us is now preaching the faith which he once tried to destroy."

Philippians 1:27

Only conduct yourselves in a manner worthy of the gospel of Christ, so that whether I *come* and *see you* or remain absent, I will hear of you that you are standing firm in one spirit, with one mind striving together for the faith of the gospel.

Philippians 4:1

Therefore, my beloved brethren whom I long *to see*, my *joy* and *crown*, in this way stand firm in the Lord, my beloved.

2 Thessalonians 1:3–4

We ought always to give *thanks* to *God* for you, brethren, as is only fitting, because your faith is greatly enlarged, and the love of each one of you toward one another grows ever greater; [4]therefore, we ourselves speak proudly of you among the churches of God for your perseverance and faith in the midst of all your persecutions and afflictions which you *endure*.

2 Chronicles 36:15–16

The Lord, the God of their fathers, sent word to them again and again by His messengers, because He had compassion on His people and on His dwelling place; [16]but they continually mocked the messengers of God, despised His words and scoffed at His *prophets*, until the *wrath* of the Lord arose against His people, until there was no remedy.

Matthew 23:31–32

"So you testify against yourselves, that you are sons of those who murdered the *prophets*. [32]*Fill up*, then, *the measure* of the guilt of your fathers."

Acts 7:52

"Which one of the *prophets* did your fathers not persecute? They *killed* those who had previously announced the coming of the Righteous One, whose betrayers and murderers you have now become."

Acts 8:1

Saul was in hearty agreement with putting him to death. And on that day a great persecution began against the church in Jerusalem, and they were all scattered throughout the regions of *Judea* and Samaria, except the apostles.

Acts 13:48, 50

When *the Gentiles* heard this, they began rejoicing and glorifying *the word* of the Lord; and as many as had been appointed to eternal life *believed*. . . . [50]But *the Jews* incited the devout women of prominence

and the leading men of the city, and instigated a persecution against Paul and Barnabas, and *drove* them *out* of their district.

Acts 17:1, 5–6

Now when they had traveled through Amphipolis and Apollonia, they came to Thessalonica, where there was a synagogue of *the Jews*. . . . [5]But the Jews, becoming jealous and taking along some wicked men from the market place, formed a mob and set the city in an uproar; and attacking the house of Jason, they were seeking to bring them out to the people. [6]When they did not find them, they began dragging Jason and some brethren before the city authorities, shouting, "These men who have upset the world have come here also."

Acts 17:13

But when *the Jews* of Thessalonica found out that *the word of God* had been proclaimed by Paul in Berea also, they came there as well, agitating and stirring up the crowds.

2 Maccabees 6:14

For in the case of the other nations the Lord waits patiently to punish them until they have reached the full *measure of their sins*; but he does not deal in this way with us.

Pseudo-Demetrius, Epistolary Types *1*

Even if I happen to be separated from you for a long time, I suffer this in body only.

1 Thessalonians 3:1–5

Therefore when we could endure it no longer, we thought it best to be left behind at Athens alone, [2]and we sent Timothy, our brother and God's fellow worker in the gospel of Christ, to strengthen and encourage you as to your faith, [3]so that no one would be disturbed by these afflictions; for you yourselves know that we have been destined for this. [4]For indeed when we were with you, we kept telling you in advance that we were going to suffer affliction; and so it came to pass, as you know. [5]For this reason, when I could endure it no longer, I also sent to find out about your faith, for fear that the tempter might have tempted you, and our labor would be in vain.

1 Thessalonians 1:1

Paul and Silvanus and *Timothy*, To the church of the Thessalonians in God the Father and the Lord Jesus Christ: Grace to you and peace.

1 Thessalonians 1:6–8

You also became imitators of us and of the Lord, having received the word in much tribulation with the joy of the Holy Spirit, [7]so that you became an example to all the believers in Macedonia and in Achaia. [8]For the word of the Lord has sounded forth from you, not only in Macedonia and Achaia, but also in every place your *faith* toward God has gone forth, so that we have no need to say anything.

1 Thessalonians 2:1–2

For you yourselves know, brethren, that our coming to you was not *in vain*, [2]but after we had already *suffered* and been mistreated in Philippi, as you know, we had the boldness in our God to speak to you *the gospel* of God amid much opposition.

1 Thessalonians 5:9

For God has not *destined* us for wrath, but for obtaining salvation through our Lord Jesus Christ . . .

OTHER PAULINE PARALLELS

1 Corinthians 3:9

For we are *God's fellow workers*; you are God's field, God's building.

1 Corinthians 4:17

For this reason I have *sent* to you *Timothy*, who is my beloved and faithful child in the Lord, and he will remind you of my ways which are in Christ, just as I teach everywhere in every church.

2 Corinthians 6:1

And working together with Him, we also urge you not to receive the grace of God *in vain*.

Philippians 2:14–16

Do all things without grumbling or disputing; [15]so that you will prove yourselves to be blameless and innocent, children of God above reproach in the midst of a crooked and perverse generation, among whom you appear as lights in the world, [16]holding fast the word of life, so that in the day of Christ I will have reason to glory because I did not run in vain nor toil *in vain*.

Philippians 2:19–20

But I hope in the Lord Jesus to *send Timothy* to you shortly, so that I also may be encouraged when I learn of your condition. [20]For I have no one else of kindred spirit who will genuinely be concerned for your welfare.

Philippians 2:25

But I thought it necessary to *send* to you Epaphroditus, my *brother* and *fellow worker* and fellow soldier, who is also your messenger and minister to my need.

Colossians 4:7–8

As to all my affairs, Tychicus, our beloved *brother* and faithful servant and fellow bond-servant in the Lord, will bring you information. [8]For I have *sent* him to you for this very purpose, that you may know about our circumstances and that he may *encourage* your hearts.

2 Thessalonians 1:3–4

We ought always to give thanks to God for you, brethren, as is only fitting, because your faith is greatly enlarged, and the love of each one of you toward one another grows ever greater; [4]therefore, we ourselves speak proudly of you among the churches of God for your perseverance and *faith* in the midst of all your persecutions and *afflictions* which you endure.

2 Thessalonians 2:1–2

Now we request you, brethren, with regard to the coming of our Lord Jesus Christ and our gathering together to Him, [2]that you not be quickly shaken from your composure or be *disturbed* either by a spirit or a message or a letter as if from us, to the effect that the day of the Lord has come.

OTHER BIBLICAL PARALLELS

Matthew 4:3

And *the tempter* came and said to Him, "If You are the Son of God, command that these stones become bread."

Acts 14:21–22

After they [Paul and Barnabas] had preached *the gospel* to that city and had made many disciples, they returned to Lystra and to Iconium and to Antioch, ²²*strengthening* the souls of the disciples, *encouraging* them to continue in the *faith*, and saying, "Through many tribulations we must enter the kingdom of God."

Acts 16:1–3

Paul came also to Derbe and to Lystra. And a disciple was there, named *Timothy*, the son of a Jewish woman who was a believer, but his father was a Greek, ²and he was well spoken of by the brethren who were in Lystra and Iconium. ³Paul wanted this man to go with him; and he took him and circumcised him because of the Jews who were in those parts, for they all knew that his father was a Greek.

Acts 17:13–16

But when the Jews of Thessalonica found out that the word of God had been proclaimed by Paul in Berea also, they came there as well, agitating and stirring up the crowds. ¹⁴Then immediately the brethren sent Paul out to go as far as the sea; and Silas and *Timothy* remained there. ¹⁵Now those who escorted Paul brought him as far as *Athens*; and receiving a command for Silas and Timothy to come to him as soon as possible, they left. ¹⁶Now while Paul was waiting for them at Athens, his spirit was being provoked within him as he was observing the city full of idols.

NONCANONICAL PARALLELS

2 Esdras (4 Ezra) 13:23

The one who brings the peril at that time will protect those who fall into peril, who have works and *faith* toward the Almighty.

2 Esdras (6 Ezra) 16:74–75

Listen, my elect ones, says the Lord; the days of tribulation are at hand, but I will deliver you from them. ⁷⁵Do not fear or doubt, for God is your guide.

1 Thessalonians 3:6–13

But now that Timothy has come to us from you, and has brought us good news of your faith and love, and that you always think kindly of us, longing to see us just as we also long to see you, ⁷for this reason, brethren, in all our distress and affliction we were comforted about you through your faith; ⁸for now we really live, if you stand firm in the Lord. ⁹For what thanks can we render to God for you in return for all the joy with which we rejoice before our God on your account, ¹⁰as we night and day keep praying most earnestly that we may see your face, and may complete what is lacking in your faith? ¹¹Now may our God and Father Himself and Jesus our Lord direct our way to you; ¹²and may the Lord cause you to increase and abound in love for one another, and for all people, just as we also do for you; ¹³so that He may establish your hearts without blame in holiness before our God and Father at the coming of our Lord Jesus with all His saints.

1 THESSALONIANS PARALLELS

1 Thessalonians 1:2–3

We give *thanks* to God always *for* all of *you*, making mention of you in our *prayers*; ³constantly bearing in mind your work of *faith* and labor of *love* and steadfastness of hope in our Lord Jesus Christ in the presence of our God and Father.

1 Thessalonians 2:17, 19

But we, brethren, having been taken away from you for a short while—in person, not in spirit—were all the more eager with great desire to *see your face*. . . . ¹⁹For who is our hope or *joy* or crown of exultation? Is it not even you, in the presence of our Lord Jesus at His *coming*?

1 Thessalonians 4:9–10

Now as to the love of the brethren, you have no need for anyone to write to you, for you yourselves are taught by God to *love one another*; ¹⁰for indeed you do practice it toward all the brethren who are in all Macedonia. But we urge you, brethren, to excel still more.

1 Thessalonians 4:15

For this we say to you by the word of the Lord, that we who are alive and remain until *the coming of* the *Lord*, will not precede those who have fallen asleep.

1 Thessalonians 5:23

Now may the God of peace Himself sanctify you entirely; and may your spirit and soul and body be preserved complete, *without blame* at *the coming of our Lord Jesus* Christ.

1 Corinthians 1:7–8

You are not lacking in any gift, awaiting eagerly the revelation of our Lord Jesus Christ, [8]who will also confirm you to the end, *blameless* in the day of our Lord Jesus Christ.

2 Corinthians 1:3–4

Blessed be the God and Father of our Lord Jesus Christ, the Father of mercies and God of all comfort, [4]who *comforts* us in all our *affliction* so that we will be able to comfort those who are in any affliction with the comfort with which we ourselves are comforted by God.

2 Corinthians 7:6–7

But God, who comforts the depressed, *comforted* us by the coming of Titus; [7]and not only by his coming, but also by the comfort with which he was comforted in you, as he reported to us your *longing*, your mourning, your zeal for me; so that I *rejoiced* even more.

Philippians 1:9

And this I *pray,* that your *love* may *abound* still more and more in real knowledge and all discernment.

Philippians 2:15

. . . so that you will prove yourselves to be *blameless* and innocent, children of God above reproach in the midst of a crooked and perverse generation, among whom you appear as lights in the world.

Philippians 4:1

Therefore, my beloved brethren whom I *long to see,* my *joy* and crown, in this way *stand firm* in the Lord, my beloved.

2 Thessalonians 1:3–4

We ought always to give *thanks* to *God* for *you,* brethren, as is only fitting, because your faith is greatly enlarged, and the *love* of each one of you toward *one another* grows ever greater; [4]therefore, we ourselves speak proudly of you among the churches of God for your perseverance and *faith* in the midst of all your persecutions and *afflictions* which you endure.

2 Thessalonians 1:9–10

These will pay the penalty of eternal destruction, away from the presence of the Lord and from the glory of His power, [10]when He comes to be glorified in *His saints* on that day, and to be marveled at among all who have believed—for our testimony to you was believed.

2 Thessalonians 2:16–17

Now may our Lord Jesus Christ Himself and *God our Father,* who has loved us and given us eternal *comfort* and good hope by grace, [17]comfort and strengthen *your hearts* in every good work and word.

2 Thessalonians 3:5

May the *Lord* direct *your hearts* into the *love* of God and into the steadfastness of Christ.

2 Timothy 1:3

I *thank God,* whom I serve with a clear conscience the way my forefathers did, as I constantly remember you in my *prayers night and day.*

Isaiah 49:13

Shout for *joy,* O heavens! And *rejoice,* O earth! Break forth into joyful shouting, O mountains! For the LORD has *comforted* His people And will have compassion on His *afflicted.*

Acts 17:15

Now those who escorted Paul brought him as far as Athens; and receiving a command for Silas and *Timothy* to come to him as soon as possible, they left.

Acts 18:1, 5

After these things he left Athens and went to Corinth. . . . [5]But when Silas and *Timothy* came down from Macedonia, Paul began devoting himself completely to the word, solemnly testifying to the Jews that Jesus was the Christ.

James 5:8

You too be patient; strengthen *your hearts*, for *the coming of* the Lord is near.

Letter to Aphrodous (P.Mich. 3.203)

If you want even a little to *see* me, I do so greatly and *pray* daily to the gods that they may soon give me an opportunity to come.

1 Thessalonians 4:1–8

Finally then, brethren, we request and exhort you in the Lord Jesus, that as you received from us instruction as to how you ought to walk and please God (just as you actually do walk), that you excel still more. [2]For you know what commandments we gave you by the authority of the Lord Jesus. [3]For this is the will of God, your sanctification; that is, that you abstain from sexual immorality; [4]that each of you know how to possess his own vessel in sanctification and honor, [5]not in lustful passion, like the Gentiles who do not know God; [6]and that no man transgress and defraud his brother in the matter because the Lord is the avenger in all these things, just as we also told you before and solemnly warned you. [7]For God has not called us for the purpose of impurity, but in sanctification. [8]So, he who rejects this is not rejecting man but the God who gives His Holy Spirit to you.

1 Thessalonians 2:3, 6

For our *exhortation* does not come from error or *impurity* or by way of deceit; . . . [6]nor did we seek glory from men, either from you or from others, even though as apostles of Christ we might have asserted our *authority*.

1 Thessalonians 2:11–13

You know how we were *exhorting* and encouraging and imploring each one of you as a father would his own children, [12]so that you would *walk* in a manner worthy of the God who *calls* you into His own kingdom and glory. [13]For this reason we also constantly thank God that when you *received* the word of God which you heard from us, you accepted it not as the word of men, but

for what it really is, the word of God, which also performs its work in you who believe.

1 Thessalonians 5:23–24

Now may the God of peace Himself *sanctify* you entirely; and may your spirit and soul and body be preserved complete, without blame at the coming of our Lord Jesus Christ. [24]Faithful is He who *calls* you, and He also will bring it to pass.

1 Corinthians 5:1

It is actually reported that there is *immorality* among you, and immorality of such a kind as does not exist even among *the Gentiles*, that someone has his father's wife.

1 Corinthians 6:8–11

On the contrary, you yourselves wrong and *defraud*. You do this even to your brethren. [9]Or do you not know that the unrighteous will not inherit the kingdom of God? Do not be deceived; neither fornicators, nor idolaters, nor adulterers, nor effeminate, nor homosexuals, [10]nor thieves, nor the covetous, nor drunkards, nor revilers, nor swindlers, will inherit the kingdom of God. [11]Such were some of you; but you were washed, but you were *sanctified*, but you were justified in the name of the Lord Jesus Christ and in the *Spirit* of our God.

1 Corinthians 6:18–19

Flee *immorality*. Every other sin that a man commits is outside the body, but the immoral man sins against his own body. [19]Or do you not know that your body is a temple of the *Holy Spirit* who is in you, whom you have from God, and that you are not your own?

1 Corinthians 7:2

But because of *immoralities*, each man is to have his own wife, and each woman is to have her own husband.

1 Corinthians 7:19

Circumcision is nothing, and uncircumcision is nothing, but what matters is the keeping of the *commandments* of God.

2 Corinthians 4:7

But we have this treasure in earthen *vessels*, so that the surpassing greatness of the power will be of God and not from ourselves.

Galatians 5:19

Now the deeds of the flesh are evident, which are: *immorality, impurity,* sensuality . . .

Colossians 2:6–7

Therefore as you have *received* Christ Jesus the Lord, so *walk* in Him, [7]having been firmly rooted and now being built up in Him and established in your faith, just as you were *instructed*, and overflowing with gratitude.

2 Thessalonians 1:6, 8

For after all it is only just for God to repay with affliction those who afflict you, . . . [8]dealing out retribution to those *who do not know God* and to those who do not obey the gospel of our Lord Jesus.

2 Thessalonians 2:13–14

But we should always give thanks to God for you, brethren beloved by the Lord, because God has chosen you from the beginning for salvation through *sanctification* by the *Spirit* and faith in the truth. [14]It was for this He *called* you through our gospel, that you may gain the glory of our Lord Jesus Christ.

2 Thessalonians 3:4

We have confidence in the Lord concerning you, that you are doing and will continue to do what we command.

OTHER BIBLICAL PARALLELS

Psalm 79:6

Pour out Your wrath upon the nations which *do not know* You, And upon the kingdoms which do not call upon Your name.

Luke 10:16

"The one who listens to you listens to Me, and the one who *rejects* you rejects Me; and he who rejects Me rejects the One who sent Me."

Acts 15:19–20

"Therefore it is my judgment that we do not trouble those who are turning to God from among *the Gentiles,* [20]but that we write to them that they abstain from things contami-

nated by idols and from fornication and from what is strangled and from blood."

1 Peter 3:7

You husbands in the same way, live with your wives in an understanding way, as with someone weaker, since she is a woman; and show her *honor* as a fellow heir of the grace of life, so that your prayers will not be hindered.

NONCANONICAL PARALLELS

Testament of Reuben 4:5–6, 8–9

So then, my children, observe all the things that I command you [6]and do not sin, for the sin of promiscuity is the pitfall of life. . . . [8]You heard how Joseph protected himself from a woman and purified his mind from all [9]promiscuity: He found favor before God and men.

Seneca, Moral Epistles *5.1*

That you study diligently and, disregarding all else, work to become better every day I approve and celebrate. Not only do I *exhort* you to persist in this, I even implore you to do so.

1 Thessalonians 4:9–12

Now as to the love of the brethren, you have no need for anyone to write to you, for you yourselves are taught by God to love one another; [10]for indeed you do practice it toward all the brethren who are in all Macedonia. But we urge you, brethren, to excel still more, [11]and to make it your ambition to lead a quiet life and attend to your own business and work with your hands, just as we commanded you, [12]so that you will behave properly toward outsiders and not be in any need.

1 THESSALONIANS PARALLELS

1 Thessalonians 1:6–7

You also became imitators of us and of the Lord, having received the word in much tribulation with the joy of the Holy Spirit, [7]so that you became an example to all the believers in *Macedonia* and in Achaia.

1 Thessalonians 2:9

For you recall, brethren, our labor and hardship, how *working* night and day so as not to be a burden to any of you, we proclaimed to you the gospel of God.

1 Thessalonians 3:11–12

Now may our God and Father Himself and Jesus our Lord direct our way to you; [12]and may the Lord cause you to increase and abound in *love* for *one another*, and for all people, just as we also do for you.

1 Thessalonians 5:1

Now as to the times and the epochs, brethren, *you have no need* of anything to be *written to you.*

OTHER PAULINE PARALLELS

Romans 12:10

Be devoted to one another in *brotherly love*; give preference to one another in honor.

1 Corinthians 4:12

We toil, *working with* our own *hands*; when we are reviled, we bless; when we are persecuted, we endure.

2 Corinthians 9:1

For it is superfluous for me *to write to you* about this ministry to the saints.

Ephesians 4:28

He who steals must steal no longer; but rather he must labor, performing *with* his own *hands* what is good, so that he will have something to share with one who has *need.*

Colossians 4:5

Conduct yourselves with wisdom toward *outsiders*, making the most of the opportunity.

2 Thessalonians 3:6–12

Now we command you, brethren, in the name of our Lord Jesus Christ, that you keep away from every brother who leads an unruly life and not according to the tradition which you received from us. [7]For you yourselves know how you ought to follow our example, because we did not act in an undisciplined manner among you, [8]nor did we eat anyone's bread without paying for it, but with labor and hardship we kept working night and day so that we would not be a burden to any of you; [9]not because we do not have the right to this, but in order to offer ourselves as a model for you, so that you would follow our example. [10]For even when we were with you, we used to give you this order: if anyone is not willing to *work*, then he is not to eat, either. [11]For we hear that some among you are leading an undisciplined life, doing no work at all, but acting like busybodies. [12]Now such persons we *command* and exhort in the Lord Jesus Christ to work in *quiet* fashion and eat their own bread.

1 Timothy 2:1–2

First of all, then, I *urge* that entreaties and prayers, petitions and thanksgivings, be made on behalf of all men, [2]for kings and all who are in authority, so that we may lead a tranquil and *quiet life* in all godliness and dignity.

OTHER BIBLICAL PARALLELS

Isaiah 54:13

"All your sons will be *taught* of the LORD; And the well-being of your sons will be great."

Jeremiah 31:33–34

"But this is the covenant which I will make with the house of Israel after those days," declares the LORD, "I will put My law within them and on their heart I will write it; and I will be their God, and they shall be My people. [34]They will not *teach* again, each man his neighbor and each man his brother, saying, 'Know the LORD,' for they will all know Me, from the least of them to the greatest of them," declares the LORD, "for I will forgive their iniquity, and their sin I will remember no more."

John 6:45

"It is written in the prophets, 'AND THEY SHALL ALL BE *TAUGHT* OF *GOD*.' Everyone who has heard and learned from the Father, comes to Me."

John 13:34

"A new commandment I give to you, that you *love one another*, even as I have loved you, that you also love one another."

Acts 18:2–3

And he found a Jew named Aquila, a native of Pontus, having recently come from Italy with his wife Priscilla, because Claudius had commanded all the Jews to leave Rome. He came to them, ³and because he was of the same trade, he stayed with them and they were *working*, for by trade they were tent-makers.

1 Peter 1:22

Since you have in obedience to the truth purified your souls for a sincere *love of the brethren*, fervently *love one another* from the heart.

1 Peter 4:15

Make sure that none of you suffers as a murderer, or thief, or evildoer, or a troublesome meddler.

1 John 2:27

As for you, the anointing which you received from Him abides in you, and *you have no need* for anyone to teach you; but as His anointing teaches you about all things, and is true and is not a lie, and just as it has *taught* you, you abide in Him.

NONCANONICAL PARALLELS

Plato, Republic *496D–E*

Taking all these things into consideration, he [the philosopher] remains *quiet* and minds his own affairs and . . . ᴱis satisfied if he can somehow live his life free from injustice and impious acts.

Cicero, Letters to His Friends *1.4.3*

Of my fondness for you I do not believe any mention need be made in this letter.

1 Thessalonians 4:13–18

But we do not want you to be uninformed, brethren, about those who are asleep, so that you will not grieve as do the rest who have no hope. ¹⁴For if we believe that Jesus died and rose again, even so God will bring with Him those who have fallen asleep in Jesus. ¹⁵For this we say to you by the word of the Lord, that we who are alive and remain until the coming of the Lord, will not precede those who have fallen asleep. ¹⁶For the Lord Himself will

descend from heaven with a shout, with the voice of the archangel and with the trumpet of God, and the dead in Christ will rise first. ¹⁷Then we who are alive and remain will be caught up together with them in the clouds to meet the Lord in the air, and so we shall always be with the Lord. ¹⁸Therefore comfort one another with these words.

1 THESSALONIANS PARALLELS

1 Thessalonians 1:8–10

For *the word of the Lord* has sounded forth from you, not only in Macedonia and Achaia, but also in every place your faith toward God has gone forth, so that we have no need to say anything. ⁹For they themselves report about us what kind of a reception we had with you, and how you turned to God from idols to serve a living and true God, ¹⁰and to wait for His Son *from heaven*, whom He *raised* from the dead, that is Jesus, who rescues us from the wrath to come.

1 Thessalonians 2:19

For who is our *hope* or joy or crown of exultation? Is it not even you, in the presence of our Lord Jesus at His *coming*?

1 Thessalonians 5:9–10

For God has not destined us for wrath, but for obtaining salvation through our Lord Jesus Christ, ¹⁰who *died* for us, so that whether we are awake or *asleep*, we will live together with Him.

1 Thessalonians 5:23

Now may the God of peace Himself sanctify you entirely; and may your spirit and soul and body be preserved complete, without blame at *the coming of* our *Lord* Jesus Christ.

OTHER PAULINE PARALLELS

Romans 14:9

For to this end Christ *died* and lived again, that He might be Lord both of *the dead* and of the *living*.

1 Corinthians 15:16–18, 20, 23–24

For if *the dead* are not raised, not even Christ has been raised; ¹⁷and if Christ has not been raised, your faith is worthless; you are still in your sins. ¹⁸Then *those* also *who have fallen asleep in* Christ have perished.

... [20]But now Christ has been raised from the dead, the first fruits of those who are asleep. ... [23]But each in his own order: Christ the first fruits, after that those who are Christ's at His *coming*, [24]then comes the end, when He hands over the kingdom to the God and Father, when He has abolished all rule and all authority and power.

1 Corinthians 15:51–52

Behold, I tell you a mystery; we will not all *sleep*, but we will all be changed, [52]in a moment, in the twinkling of an eye, at the last trumpet; for *the trumpet* will sound, and *the dead* will be raised imperishable, and we will be changed.

2 Corinthians 5:15

He died for all, so that they who live might no longer live for themselves, but for Him who *died and rose again* on their behalf.

2 Corinthians 12:2

I know a man in Christ who fourteen years ago—whether in the body I do not know, or out of the body I do not know, God knows—such a man was *caught up* to the third *heaven*.

Ephesians 2:12

Remember that you were at that time separate from Christ, excluded from the commonwealth of Israel, and strangers to the covenants of promise, having *no hope* and without God in the world.

2 Thessalonians 1:7

... and to give relief to you who are afflicted and to us as well when the Lord Jesus will be revealed *from heaven* with His mighty *angels* in flaming fire.

2 Thessalonians 2:1–2

Now we request you, brethren, with regard to *the coming of* our *Lord* Jesus Christ and our gathering together to Him, [2]that you not be quickly shaken from your composure or be disturbed either by a spirit or a message or a letter as if from us, to the effect that the day of the Lord has come.

OTHER BIBLICAL PARALLELS

Exodus 19:16–18

So it came about on the third day, when it was morning, that there were thunder and

lightning flashes and a thick *cloud* upon the mountain and a very loud *trumpet* sound, so that all the people who were in the camp trembled. [17]And Moses brought the people out of the camp to *meet* God, and they stood at the foot of the mountain. [18]Now Mount Sinai was all in smoke because the LORD *descended* upon it in fire; and its smoke ascended like the smoke of a furnace, and the whole mountain quaked violently.

Zechariah 9:14, 16

Then the LORD will appear over them, And His arrow will go forth like lightning; And the Lord GOD will blow *the trumpet*, And will march in the storm winds of the south. ... [16]And the LORD their God will save them in that day As the flock of His people; For they are as the stones of a crown, Sparkling in His land.

Matthew 24:30–31

"And then the sign of the Son of Man will appear in the sky, and then all the tribes of the earth will mourn, and they will see the SON OF MAN *COMING* ON THE *CLOUDS* OF THE SKY with power and great glory. [31]And He will send forth His *angels* with A GREAT *TRUMPET* and THEY WILL GATHER TOGETHER His elect from the four winds, from one end of the sky to the other."

Revelation 8:2

And I saw the seven *angels* who stand before God, and seven *trumpets* were given to them.

NONCANONICAL PARALLELS

Wisdom of Solomon 3:18–19

If they die young, they will have *no hope* and no consolation on the day of judgment. [19]For the end of an unrighteous generation is grievous.

2 Esdras (4 Ezra) 6:23–26

"*The trumpet* shall sound aloud, and when all hear it, they shall suddenly be terrified. [24]At that time friends shall make war on friends like enemies, the earth and those who inhabit it shall be terrified, and the springs of the fountains shall stand still, so that for three hours they shall not flow. [25]It shall be that whoever *remains* after all that I have foretold to you shall be saved and shall see my salvation and the end of my world. [26]And they shall see those who were taken up, who from their birth have not tasted death; and the heart of the earth's inhabitants shall be changed and converted to a different spirit."

1 Thessalonians 5:1–5a

Now as to the times and the epochs, brethren, you have no need of anything to be written to you. [2]For you yourselves know full well that the day of the Lord will come just like a thief in the night. [3]While they are saying, "Peace and safety!" then destruction will come upon them suddenly like labor pains upon a woman with child, and they will not escape. [4]But you, brethren, are not in darkness, that the day would overtake you like a thief; [5]for you are all sons of light and sons of day.

1 THESSALONIANS PARALLELS

1 Thessalonians 3:13
. . . so that He may establish your hearts without blame in holiness before our God and Father at the coming of our Lord Jesus with all His saints.

1 Thessalonians 4:9
Now as to the love of the brethren, you have *no need* for anyone to *write to you*, for you yourselves are taught by God to love one another.

OTHER PAULINE PARALLELS

Romans 8:22
For we know that the whole creation groans and suffers the *pains* of *childbirth* together until now.

Romans 13:12–13
The *night* is almost gone, and the *day* is near. Therefore let us lay aside the deeds of *darkness* and put on the armor of *light*. [13]Let us behave properly as in the day, not in carousing and drunkenness, not in sexual promiscuity and sensuality, not in strife and jealousy.

2 Corinthians 4:4, 6
. . . in whose case the god of this world has blinded the minds of the unbelieving so that

they might not see the *light* of the gospel of the glory of Christ, who is the image of God. . . . [6]For God, who said, "Light shall shine out of *darkness*," is the One who has shone in our hearts to give the Light of the knowledge of the glory of God in the face of Christ.

Ephesians 5:8
You were formerly *darkness*, but now you are Light in the Lord; walk as children of *Light*.

2 Thessalonians 1:9–10
These will pay the penalty of eternal *destruction*, away from the presence of the Lord and from the glory of His power, [10]when He comes to be glorified in His saints on that *day*, and to be marveled at among all who have believed—for our testimony to you was believed.

OTHER BIBLICAL PARALLELS

Isaiah 13:6, 8
Wail, for *the day of the* LORD is near! It will come as *destruction* from the Almighty. . . . [8]They will be terrified, *Pains* and anguish will take hold of them; They will writhe like a *woman* in *labor*, They will look at one another in astonishment, Their faces aflame.

Jeremiah 6:14
"They have healed the brokenness of My people superficially, *Saying, 'Peace*, peace,' But there is no peace."

Jeremiah 11:11
"Behold I am bringing disaster on them which they will *not* be able to *escape*; though they will cry to Me, yet I will not listen to them."

Amos 5:20
Will not *the day of the* LORD be *darkness* instead of *light*, Even gloom with no brightness in it?

Matthew 24:7–8, 42–43
"For nation will rise against nation, and kingdom against kingdom, and in various places there will be famines and earthquakes. [8]But all these things are merely the beginning of birth pangs. . . . [42]Therefore be on the alert, for you do not know which *day* your Lord is coming. [43]But be sure of this,

that if the head of the house had known at what time of the *night* the *thief* was coming, he would have been on the alert and would not have allowed his house to be broken into."

John 12:35–36
"For a little while longer the Light is among you. Walk while you have the Light, so that *darkness* will not overtake you; he who walks in the darkness does not know where he goes. [36]While you have the Light, believe in the Light, so that you may become *sons of Light*."

Acts 1:6–7
So when they had come together, they were asking Him, saying, "Lord, is it at this time You are restoring the kingdom to Israel?" [7]He said to them, "It is not for you to know *times* or *epochs* which the Father has fixed by His own authority."

Acts 26:16–18
"But get up and stand on your feet; for this purpose I have appeared to you, to appoint you a minister and a witness not only to the things which you have seen, but also to the things in which I will appear to you; [17]rescuing you from the Jewish people and from the Gentiles, to whom I am sending you, [18]to open their eyes so that they may turn from *darkness* to *light* and from the dominion of Satan to God, that they may receive forgiveness of sins and an inheritance among those who have been sanctified by faith in Me."

2 Peter 3:10
But *the day of the Lord will come like a thief*, in which the heavens will pass away with a roar and the elements will be destroyed with intense heat, and the earth and its works will be burned up.

Revelation 3:3
"So remember what you have received and heard; and keep it, and repent. Therefore if you do not wake up, I will *come like a thief*, and you will not know at what hour I will come to you."

2 Esdras (6 Ezra) 16:38–39
Just as a pregnant *woman*, in the ninth month when the time of her delivery draws

near, has great *pains* around her womb for two or three hours beforehand, but when the *child* comes forth from the womb, there will not be a moment's delay, [39]so the calamities will not delay in coming upon the earth, and the world will groan, and pains will seize it on every side.

1 Enoch 62:3–4
On the *day* of judgment, all the kings . . . shall see and recognize him – how he sits on the throne of his glory, and righteousness is judged before him. . . . [4]Then *pain* shall come upon them as on a *woman* in travail with birth pangs.

The Rule of the Community (1QS) 3.20–21, 24–25
And in the hand of the Angel [21]of Darkness is total dominion over the sons of deceit; they walk on paths of *darkness*. . . . [24] . . . However, the God of Israel and the angel of his truth assist all [25]the *sons of light*.

1 Thessalonians 5:5b–11

We are not of night nor of darkness; [6]so then let us not sleep as others do, but let us be alert and sober. [7]For those who sleep do their sleeping at night, and those who get drunk get drunk at night. [8]But since we are of the day, let us be sober, having put on the breastplate of faith and love, and as a helmet, the hope of salvation. [9]For God has not destined us for wrath, but for obtaining salvation through our Lord Jesus Christ, [10]who died for us, so that whether we are awake or asleep, we will live together with Him. [11]Therefore encourage one another and build up one another, just as you also are doing.

1 Thessalonians 1:2–3
We give thanks to God always for all of you, making mention of you in our prayers; [3]constantly bearing in mind your work of *faith* and labor of *love* and steadfastness of *hope* in our Lord Jesus Christ in the presence of our God and Father.

1 Thessalonians 1:9–10
For they themselves report about us what kind of a reception we had with you, and how you turned to God from idols to serve

a living and true God, [10]and to wait for His Son from heaven, whom He raised from the dead, that is Jesus, who rescues us from the *wrath* to come.

1 Thessalonians 2:11

You know how we were exhorting and *encouraging* and imploring each one of you as a father would his own children.

1 Thessalonians 3:3

. . . so that no one would be disturbed by these afflictions; for you yourselves know that we have been *destined* for this.

1 Thessalonians 4:14, 17–18

For if we believe that Jesus *died* and rose again, even so God will bring with Him those who have fallen *asleep* in Jesus. . . . [17]Then we who are alive and remain will be caught up together with them in the clouds to meet the Lord in the air, and so we shall always be with the Lord. [18]Therefore comfort *one another* with these words.

OTHER PAULINE PARALLELS

Romans 5:8–9

But God demonstrates His own love toward us, in that while we were yet sinners, Christ *died for us*. [9]Much more then, having now been justified by His blood, we shall be saved from the *wrath* of God through Him.

Romans 13:11–13

Do this, knowing the time, that it is already the hour for you to awaken from *sleep*; for now *salvation* is nearer to us than when we believed. [12]The *night* is almost gone, and the *day* is near. Therefore let us lay aside the deeds of *darkness* and *put on* the armor of light. [13]Let us behave properly as in the day, not in carousing and *drunkenness*, not in sexual promiscuity and sensuality, not in strife and jealousy.

Romans 14:7–8, 19

For not one of us lives for himself, and not one dies for himself; [8]for if we live, we *live* for the Lord, or if we die, we die for the Lord; therefore whether we live or die, we are the Lord's. . . . [19]So then we pursue the things which make for peace and the *building up* of *one another*.

1 Corinthians 4:5

Therefore do not go on passing judgment before the time, but wait until the Lord comes who will both bring to light the things hidden in the *darkness* and disclose the motives of men's hearts; and then each man's praise will come to him from God.

1 Corinthians 13:13

But now *faith, hope, love*, abide these three; but the greatest of these is love.

Galatians 2:20

I have been crucified with Christ; and it is no longer I who live, but Christ lives in me; and the life which I now *live* in the flesh I live by *faith* in the Son of God, who loved me and gave Himself up for me.

Ephesians 6:12–14, 17

For our struggle is not against flesh and blood, but against the rulers, against the powers, against the world forces of this *darkness*, against the spiritual forces of wickedness in the heavenly places. [13]Therefore, take up the full armor of God, so that you will be able to resist in the evil day, and having done everything, to stand firm. [14]Stand firm therefore, HAVING GIRDED YOUR LOINS WITH TRUTH, and HAVING *PUT ON THE BREASTPLATE* OF RIGHTEOUSNESS. . . . [17]And take THE *HELMET* OF *SALVATION*, and the sword of the Spirit, which is the word of God.

2 Thessalonians 2:13

But we should always give thanks to God for you, brethren beloved by the Lord, because God has chosen you from the beginning for *salvation* through sanctification by the Spirit and *faith* in the truth.

2 Timothy 4:5

But you, be *sober* in all things, endure hardship, do the work of an evangelist, fulfill your ministry.

OTHER BIBLICAL PARALLELS

Isaiah 59:17

He *put on* righteousness like a *breastplate*, And a *helmet* of *salvation* on His head; And He put on garments of vengeance for clothing And wrapped Himself with zeal as a mantle.

Matthew 24:42

"Therefore be on the *alert*, for you do not know which day your Lord is coming."

Luke 21:34, 36

"Be on guard, so that your hearts will not be weighted down with dissipation and *drunkenness* and the worries of life, and that day will not come on you suddenly like a trap; . . . [36]But keep on the *alert* at all times, praying that you may have strength to escape all these things that are about to take place, and to stand before the Son of Man."

Hebrews 3:13

But *encourage one another* day after day, as long as it is still called "Today," so that none of you will be hardened by the deceitfulness of sin.

1 Peter 1:13

Therefore, prepare your minds for action, keep *sober* in spirit, fix your *hope* completely on the grace to be brought to you at the revelation of Jesus Christ.

NONCANONICAL PARALLELS

Wisdom of Solomon 5:17–18

The Lord will take his zeal as his whole armor, and will arm all creation to repel his enemies; [18]he will put on righteousness as a *breastplate*, and wear impartial justice as a *helmet*.

1 Thessalonians 5:12–22

But we request of you, brethren, that you appreciate those who diligently labor among you, and have charge over you in the Lord and give you instruction, [13]and that you esteem them very highly in love because of their work. Live in peace with one another. [14]We urge you, brethren, admonish the unruly, encourage the fainthearted, help the weak, be patient with everyone. [15]See that no one repays another with evil for evil, but always seek after that which is good for one another and for all people. [16]Rejoice always; [17]pray without ceasing; [18]in everything give thanks; for this is God's will for you in Christ Jesus. [19]Do not quench the Spirit; [20]do not despise prophetic utterances. [21]But examine everything carefully; hold fast to that which is good; [22]abstain from every form of evil.

1 THESSALONIANS PARALLELS

1 Thessalonians 1:2

We *give thanks* to God always for all of you, making mention of you in our *prayers*.

1 Thessalonians 2:11

You know how we were exhorting and *encouraging* and imploring each one of you as a father would his own children.

1 Thessalonians 3:12

May the Lord cause you to increase and abound in *love* for *one another, and for all people,* just as we also do for you.

1 Thessalonians 4:1

Finally then, brethren, *we request* and exhort you in the Lord Jesus, that as you received from us *instruction* as to how you ought to walk and please God (just as you actually do walk), that you excel still more.

OTHER PAULINE PARALLELS

Romans 12:9, 11–12, 17–18, 21

Let *love* be without hypocrisy. Abhor what is *evil*; cling to what is *good*, . . . [11]not lagging behind in diligence, fervent in *spirit*, serving the Lord; [12]*rejoicing* in hope, persevering in tribulation, devoted to *prayer.* . . . [17]Never pay back *evil for evil* to anyone. Respect what is right in the sight of all men. [18]If possible, so far as it depends on you, be at *peace* with all men. . . . [21]Do not be overcome by evil, but overcome evil with good.

Romans 15:1

Now we who are strong ought to bear the *weaknesses* of those without strength and not just please ourselves.

1 Corinthians 14:29, 31

Let two or three *prophets* speak, and let the others pass judgment. . . . [31]For you can all prophesy one by one, so that all may learn and all may be exhorted.

1 Corinthians 16:16, 18

. . . that you also be in subjection to such men and to everyone who helps in the *work* and *labors.* . . . [18]For they have refreshed my spirit and yours. Therefore acknowledge such men.

Galatians 6:6, 10

The one who is taught the word is to share all good things with the one who teaches him. . . . [10]So then, while we have opportunity, let us do *good* to *all people*, and especially to those who are of the household of the faith.

Ephesians 6:18

With all prayer and petition *pray* at all times in *the Spirit,* and with this in view, be on the alert with all perseverance and petition for all the saints.

Philippians 4:4, 6

Rejoice in the Lord *always*; again I will say, rejoice! . . . [6]Be anxious for nothing, but in everything by *prayer* and supplication with *thanksgiving* let your requests be made known to God.

2 Thessalonians 3:6

Now we command you, brethren, in the name of our Lord Jesus Christ, that you keep away from every brother who leads an *unruly* life and not according to the tradition which you received from us.

2 Thessalonians 3:13–15

But as for you, brethren, do not grow weary of doing *good*. [14]If anyone does not obey our *instruction* in this letter, take special note of that person and do not associate with him, so that he will be put to shame. [15]Yet do not regard him as an enemy, but *admonish* him as a brother.

1 Timothy 5:17

The elders who rule well are to be considered worthy of double honor, especially those who *work* hard at preaching and teaching.

OTHER BIBLICAL PARALLELS

Proverbs 20:22

Do not say, "I will *repay evil*"; Wait for the LORD, and He will save you.

Isaiah 35:4

Say to those with anxious heart, "Take courage, fear not. Behold, your God will come with vengeance; The recompense of God will come, But He will save you."

Acts 20:35

"In everything I showed you that by *working* hard in this manner you must *help the weak* and remember the words of the Lord Jesus, that He Himself said, 'It is more blessed to give than to receive.'"

Hebrews 12:14

Pursue *peace* with all men, and the sanctification without which no one will see the Lord.

Hebrews 13:17

Obey your leaders and submit to them, for they keep watch over your souls as those who will give an account. Let them do this with joy and not with grief, for this would be unprofitable for you.

1 Peter 3:8–9

To sum up, all of you be harmonious, sympathetic, brotherly, kindhearted, and humble in spirit; [9]not returning *evil for evil* or insult for insult, but giving a blessing instead; for you were called for the very purpose that you might inherit a blessing.

NONCANONICAL PARALLELS

Didache *11.8*

Not everyone who is speaking in *the Spirit* is a *prophet*, but only if their conduct is the Lord's. So from their conduct the false prophet and the prophet will be known.

1 Thessalonians 5:23–28

Now may the God of peace Himself sanctify you entirely; and may your spirit and soul and body be preserved complete, without blame at the coming of our Lord Jesus Christ. [24]Faithful is He who calls you, and He also will bring it to pass. [25]Brethren, pray for us. [26]Greet all the brethren with a holy kiss. [27]I adjure you by the Lord to have this letter read to all the brethren. [28]The grace of our Lord Jesus Christ be with you.

1 THESSALONIANS PARALLELS

1 Thessalonians 2:11–12

You know how we were exhorting and encouraging and imploring each one of you as a father would his own children, [12]so that you would walk in a manner worthy of the God who *calls you* into His own kingdom and glory.

1 Thessalonians 2:19

For who is our hope or joy or crown of exultation? Is it not even you, in the presence of our Lord Jesus at His *coming*?

1 Thessalonians 3:12–13

May the Lord cause you to increase and abound in love for one another, and for all people, just as we also do for you; [13]so that He may establish your hearts *without blame* in holiness before our God and Father at *the coming of our Lord Jesus* with all His saints.

1 Thessalonians 4:3

For this is the will of God, your *sanctification*; that is, that you abstain from sexual immorality.

OTHER PAULINE PARALLELS

Romans 15:30, 33

Now I urge you, brethren, by our Lord Jesus Christ and by the love of the Spirit, to strive together with me in your *prayers* to God for me. . . . [33]Now *the God of peace* be with you all. Amen.

Romans 16:16, 20

Greet one another *with a holy kiss.* All the churches of Christ greet you. . . . [20]*The God of peace* will soon crush Satan under your feet. *The grace of our Lord Jesus be with you.*

1 Corinthians 1:7–9

You are not lacking in any gift, awaiting eagerly the revelation of our Lord Jesus Christ, [8]who will also confirm you to the end, *blameless* in the day of our Lord Jesus Christ. [9]God is *faithful*, through whom you were *called* into fellowship with His Son, Jesus Christ our Lord.

1 Corinthians 16:20

All the brethren greet you. *Greet* one another *with a holy kiss.*

2 Corinthians 13:11–12

Finally, brethren, rejoice, be made *complete*, be comforted, be like-minded, live in peace; and *the God of* love and *peace* will be with you. [12]*Greet* one another *with a holy kiss.*

Philippians 1:9–10

And this I pray, that your love may abound still more and more in real knowledge and all discernment, [10]so that you may approve the things that are excellent, in order to be sincere and *blameless* until the day of Christ.

Colossians 4:3

. . . *praying* at the same time *for us* as well, that God will open up to us a door for the word, so that we may speak forth the mystery of Christ, for which I have also been imprisoned.

Colossians 4:16

When *this letter* is read among you, *have* it also *read* in the church of the Laodiceans; and you, for your part read my letter that is coming from Laodicea.

2 Thessalonians 3:1–3

Finally, *brethren, pray for us* that the word of the Lord will spread rapidly and be glorified, just as it did also with you; [2]and that we will be rescued from perverse and evil men; for not all have faith. [3]But the Lord is *faithful*, and He will strengthen and protect you from the evil one.

2 Thessalonians 3:16, 18

Now may the Lord of *peace* Himself continually grant you peace in every circumstance. The Lord be with you all! . . . [18]*The grace of our Lord Jesus Christ be with you* all.

OTHER BIBLICAL PARALLELS

Deuteronomy 7:9

"Know therefore that the LORD your God, He is God, the *faithful* God, who keeps His covenant and His lovingkindness to a thousandth generation with those who love Him and keep His commandments."

Isaiah 45:3

"I will give you the treasures of darkness And hidden wealth of secret places, So that you may know that it is I, The LORD, the God of Israel, who *calls* you by your name."

Isaiah 48:12

"Listen to Me, O Jacob, even Israel whom I *called*; I am He, I am the first, I am also the last."

Isaiah 49:7

Thus says the LORD, the Redeemer of Israel and its Holy One, To the despised One, To the One abhorred by the nation, To the Servant of rulers, "Kings will see and arise, Princes will also bow down, Because of the LORD who is *faithful*, the Holy One of Israel who has chosen You."

Hebrews 4:12

For the word of God is living and active and sharper than any two-edged sword, and piercing as far as the division of *soul* and *spirit*, of both joints and marrow, and able to judge the thoughts and intentions of the heart.

Hebrews 13:18

Pray for us, for we are sure that we have a good conscience, desiring to conduct ourselves honorably in all things.

2 Peter 3:14–15

Therefore, beloved, since you look for these things, be diligent to be found by Him in peace, spotless and *blameless*, [15]and regard the patience of our Lord as salvation.

2 Thessalonians

2 Thessalonians 1:1–4

Paul and Silvanus and Timothy, To the church of the Thessalonians in God our Father and the Lord Jesus Christ: ²Grace to you and peace from God the Father and the Lord Jesus Christ. ³We ought always to give thanks to God for you, brethren, as is only fitting, because your faith is greatly enlarged, and the love of each one of you toward one another grows ever greater; ⁴therefore, we ourselves speak proudly of you among the churches of God for your perseverance and faith in the midst of all your persecutions and afflictions which you endure.

2 THESSALONIANS PARALLELS

2 Thessalonians 2:13
> But *we* should *always give thanks to God for you, brethren* beloved by the Lord, because God has chosen you from the beginning for salvation through sanctification by the Spirit and *faith* in the truth.

2 Thessalonians 3:5
> May the Lord direct your hearts into the *love* of God and into the steadfastness of Christ.

2 Thessalonians 3:16
> Now may the Lord of peace Himself continually grant you *peace* in every circumstance.

OTHER PAULINE PARALLELS

Romans 1:1, 7
> *Paul*, a bond-servant of Christ Jesus, called as an apostle, set apart for the gospel of God, . . . ⁷to all who are beloved of God in Rome, called as saints: *Grace to you and peace from God our Father and the Lord Jesus Christ.*

Romans 5:3–4
> And not only this, but we also exult in our tribulations, knowing that tribulation brings about *perseverance*; ⁴and perseverance, proven character; and proven character, hope.

1 Corinthians 4:12
> We toil, working with our own hands; when we are reviled, we bless; when we are *persecuted*, we *endure*.

2 Corinthians 1:19
> For the Son of God, Christ Jesus, who was preached among you by us—by me and *Silvanus and Timothy*—was not yes and no, but is yes in Him.

2 Corinthians 7:4
> Great is my confidence in you; great is my boasting on your behalf. I am filled with comfort; I am overflowing with joy in all our *affliction*.

2 Corinthians 8:24
> Therefore openly before *the churches*, show them the proof of your *love* and of our reason for boasting about you.

Colossians 1:1–4
> *Paul*, an apostle of Jesus Christ by the will of God, and *Timothy* our brother, ²To the saints and faithful brethren in Christ who are at Colossae: *Grace to you and peace from God our Father.* ³*We give thanks to God*, the Father of our Lord Jesus Christ, praying always for you, ⁴since we heard of your *faith*

in Christ Jesus and the *love* which you have for all the saints.

1 Thessalonians 1:1–3

Paul and Silvanus and Timothy, *To the church of the Thessalonians in God* the *Father and the Lord Jesus Christ*: *Grace to you and peace.* [2]*We give thanks to God always for* all of *you*, making mention of you in our prayers; [3]constantly bearing in mind your work of *faith* and labor of *love* and steadfastness of hope in our Lord Jesus Christ in the presence of our God and Father.

1 Thessalonians 1:8

For the word of the Lord has sounded forth from you, not only in Macedonia and Achaia, but also in every place your *faith* toward God has gone forth, so that we have no need to say anything.

1 Thessalonians 2:13–14

For this reason *we* also constantly *thank God* that when you received the word of God which you heard from us, you accepted it not as the word of men, but for what it really is, the word of God, which also performs its work in you who believe. [14]For you, brethren, became imitators of the churches of God in Christ Jesus that are in Judea, for you also *endured* the same sufferings at the hands of your own countrymen, even as they did from the Jews.

1 Thessalonians 3:2–4

We sent *Timothy*, our brother and God's fellow worker in the gospel of Christ, to strengthen and encourage you as to your *faith*, [3]so that no one would be disturbed by these *afflictions*; for you yourselves know that we have been destined for this. [4]For indeed when we were with you, we kept telling you in advance that we were going to suffer affliction; and so it came to pass, as you know.

1 Thessalonians 3:6–8

But now that *Timothy* has come to us from you, and has brought us good news of your *faith* and *love*, and that you always think kindly of us, longing to see us just as we also long to see you, [7]for this reason, brethren, in all our distress and *affliction* we were comforted about you through your faith; [8]for now we really live, if you stand firm in the Lord.

1 Thessalonians 3:12

May the Lord cause you to increase and abound in *love* for *one another*, and for all people, just as we also do for you.

Mark 4:16–17

"In a similar way these are the ones on whom seed was sown on the rocky places, who, when they hear the word, immediately receive it with joy; [17]and they have no firm root in themselves, but are only temporary; then, when *affliction* or *persecution* arises because of the word, immediately they fall away."

Acts 16:1

Paul came also to Derbe and to Lystra. And a disciple was there, named *Timothy*, the son of a Jewish woman who was a believer, but his father was a Greek.

Acts 17:1–2, 4

Now when they had traveled through Amphipolis and Apollonia, they came to *Thessalonica*, where there was a synagogue of the Jews. [2]And according to *Paul's* custom, he went to them, and for three Sabbaths reasoned with them from the Scriptures. . . . [4]And some of them were persuaded and joined Paul and *Silas*, along with a large number of the God-fearing Greeks and a number of the leading women.

Revelation 13:10

If anyone is destined for captivity, to captivity he goes; if anyone kills with the sword, with the sword he must be killed. Here is the *perseverance* and the *faith* of the saints.

2 Thessalonians 1:5–12

This is a plain indication of God's righteous judgment so that you will be considered worthy of the kingdom of God, for which indeed you are suffering. [6]For after all it is only just for God to repay with affliction those who afflict you, [7]and to give relief to you who are afflicted and to us as well when the Lord Jesus will be revealed from heaven with His mighty angels in flaming fire, [8]dealing out retribution to those who do not know God and to those who do not obey the gospel of our Lord Jesus.

⁹These will pay the penalty of eternal destruction, away from the presence of the Lord and from the glory of His power, ¹⁰when He comes to be glorified in His saints on that day, and to be marveled at among all who have believed—for our testimony to you was believed. ¹¹To this end also we pray for you always, that our God will count you worthy of your calling, and fulfill every desire for goodness and the work of faith with power, ¹²so that the name of our Lord Jesus will be glorified in you, and you in Him, according to the grace of our God and the Lord Jesus Christ.

2 THESSALONIANS PARALLELS

2 Thessalonians 2:14

It was for this He *called* you through our *gospel,* that you may gain the *glory* of our Lord Jesus Christ.

2 Thessalonians 3:1–3

Finally, brethren, pray for us that the word of the Lord will spread rapidly and be *glorified,* just as it did also with you; ²and that we will be rescued from perverse and evil men; for not all have *faith.* ³But the Lord is faithful, and He will strengthen and protect you from the evil one.

OTHER PAULINE PARALLELS

1 Corinthians 3:13

Each man's work will become evident; for the *day* will show it because it is to be *revealed* with *fire,* and the fire itself will test the quality of each man's work.

Philippians 1:27–28

Only conduct yourselves in a manner *worthy* of *the gospel* of Christ, so that whether I come and see you or remain absent, I will hear of you that you are standing firm in one spirit, with one mind striving together for the *faith* of the gospel; ²⁸in no way alarmed by your opponents—which is a sign of *destruction* for them, but of salvation for you, and that too, from God.

1 Thessalonians 1:2–3

We give thanks to God always for all of you, making mention of you in our *prayers*; ³constantly bearing in mind your *work of faith* and labor of love and steadfastness of hope in our Lord Jesus Christ in the presence of our God and Father.

1 Thessalonians 2:11–12

You know how we were exhorting and encouraging and imploring each one of you as a father would his own children, ¹²so that you would walk in a manner *worthy* of the God who *calls you* into His own *kingdom* and *glory.*

1 Thessalonians 3:2–4

We sent Timothy, our brother and God's fellow worker in *the gospel* of Christ, to strengthen and encourage you as to your *faith,* ³so that no one would be disturbed by these afflictions; for you yourselves know that we have been destined for this. ⁴For indeed when we were with you, we kept telling you in advance that we were going to suffer *affliction*; and so it came to pass, as you know.

1 Thessalonians 4:16

For the Lord Himself will descend *from heaven* with a shout, with the voice of the *archangel* and with the trumpet of God, and the dead in Christ will rise first.

1 Thessalonians 5:3

While they are saying, "Peace and safety!" then *destruction* will come upon them suddenly like labor pains upon a woman with child, and they will not escape.

OTHER BIBLICAL PARALLELS

Deuteronomy 32:35

"Vengeance is Mine, and *retribution*, In due time their foot will slip; For the *day* of their calamity is near, And the impending things are hastening upon them."

Isaiah 66:15–16

For behold, the LORD will come in *fire* And His chariots like the whirlwind, To render His anger with fury, And His rebuke with flames of fire. ¹⁶For the LORD will execute *judgment* by fire And by His sword on all flesh, And those slain by the LORD will be many.

Jeremiah 10:25

Pour out Your wrath on the nations that *do not know* You And on the families that do not call Your name; For they have devoured Jacob; They have devoured him and consumed him And have laid waste his habitation.

Obadiah 15

"For the *day* of the LORD draws near on all the nations. As you have done, it will be done to you. Your dealings will return on your own head."

1 Peter 4:16–17

If anyone *suffers* as a Christian, he is not to be ashamed, but is to *glorify* God in this *name.* [17]For it is time for *judgment* to begin with the household of God; and if it begins with us first, what will be the outcome for *those who do not obey the gospel* of God?

2 Peter 3:7

But by His word the present heavens and earth are being reserved for *fire*, kept for the *day* of *judgment* and *destruction* of ungodly men.

Revelation 18:1–2, 4, 6

After these things I saw another *angel* coming down *from heaven*, having great authority, and the earth was illumined with his *glory.* [2]And he cried out with a mighty voice, saying, "Fallen, fallen is Babylon the great! . . . " [4]I heard another voice from heaven, saying, " . . . [6]*Pay* her back even as she has paid, and give back to her double according to her deeds; in the cup which she has mixed, mix twice as much for her."

2 Esdras (4 Ezra) *11:40, 44–46*

"You, the fourth that has come, have conquered all the beasts that have gone before; and you have held sway over the world with great terror, and over all the earth with grievous oppression; . . . [44]The Most High has looked at his times; now they have ended, and his ages have reached completion. [45]Therefore you, eagle, will surely disappear . . . [46]so that the whole earth, freed from your violence, may be refreshed and relieved, and may hope for the *judgment* and mercy of him who made it."

1 Enoch 62:10–11

But the Lord of the Spirits himself will cause them to be frantic, so that they shall rush and depart from his *presence.* . . . [11]So he will deliver them to the *angels* for punishments in order that vengeance shall be executed on them—oppressors of his children and his elect ones.

The Rule of the Community (1QS) 4.11–13

And the visitation [12]of those who walk in it [the spirit of deceit] will be for a glut of punishments at the hands of all the *angels* of *destruction*, for *eternal* damnation for the scorching wrath of the God of revenge, for permanent error and shame [13]without end with the humiliation of destruction by the *fire* of the dark regions.

2 Thessalonians 2:1–5

Now we request you, brethren, with regard to the coming of our Lord Jesus Christ and our gathering together to Him, [2]that you not be quickly shaken from your composure or be disturbed either by a spirit or a message or a letter as if from us, to the effect that the day of the Lord has come. [3]Let no one in any way deceive you, for it will not come unless the apostasy comes first, and the man of lawlessness is revealed, the son of destruction, [4]who opposes and exalts himself above every so–called god or object of worship, so that he takes his seat in the temple of God, displaying himself as being God. [5]Do you not remember that while I was still with you, I was telling you these things?

2 Thessalonians 2:15

So then, brethren, stand firm and hold to the traditions which you were taught, whether by word of mouth or by *letter from us.*

2 Thessalonians 3:17

I, Paul, write this greeting with my own hand, and this is a distinguishing mark in every *letter*; this is the way I write.

1 Thessalonians 3:2–3

We sent Timothy, our brother and God's fellow worker in the gospel of Christ, to strengthen and encourage you as to your faith, [3]so that no one would be *disturbed* by these afflictions; for you yourselves know that we have been destined for this.

1 Thessalonians 4:15–17

For this we say to you by the word of the Lord, that we who are alive and remain until *the coming of* the Lord, will not precede those who have fallen asleep. [16]For the Lord Himself will descend from heaven with a shout, with the voice of the archangel and with the trumpet of God, and the dead in Christ will rise first. [17]Then we who are alive and remain will be caught up *together* with them in the clouds to meet the Lord in the air, and so we shall always be with the Lord.

1 Thessalonians 5:2

For you yourselves know full well that *the day of the Lord* will come just like a thief in the night.

1 Thessalonians 5:19–20

Do not quench the Spirit; [20]do not despise prophetic utterances.

1 Timothy 4:1

But the Spirit explicitly says that in later times some will fall away from the faith, paying attention to deceitful *spirits* and doctrines of demons.

OTHER BIBLICAL PARALLELS

Psalm 89:22

"The enemy will not *deceive* him, Nor the son of wickedness afflict him."

Ezekiel 28:2

"Son of man, say to the leader of Tyre, 'Thus says the Lord GOD, "Because your heart is lifted up And you have said, 'I am a *god*, I sit in the *seat* of gods In the heart of the seas'; Yet you are a man and not God, Although you make your heart like the heart of God." '"

Daniel 8:23–25

"A king will arise, Insolent and skilled in intrigue. [24]His power will be mighty, but not by his own power, And he will destroy to an extraordinary degree And prosper and perform his will; He will destroy mighty men and the holy people. [25]And through his shrewdness He will cause *deceit* to succeed by his influence; And he will magnify himself in his heart, And he will destroy many while they are at ease. He will even *oppose* the Prince of princes, But he will be broken without human agency."

Daniel 9:26–27

"Then after the sixty-two weeks the Messiah will be cut off and have nothing, and the people of the prince who is to come will destroy the city and the sanctuary. And its end will come with a flood; even to the end there will be war; desolations are determined. [27]And he will make a firm covenant with the many for one week, but in the middle of the week he will put a stop to sacrifice and grain offering; and on the wing of abominations will come one who makes desolate, even until a complete *destruction*, one that is decreed, is poured out on the one who makes desolate."

Daniel 11:36

"Then the king will do as he pleases, and he will *exalt* and magnify *himself above every god* and will speak monstrous things against the God of gods; and he will prosper until the indignation is finished, for that which is decreed will be done."

Joel 2:1

Blow a trumpet in Zion, And sound an alarm on My holy mountain! Let all the inhabitants of the land tremble, For *the day of the* LORD is coming; Surely it is near.

Matthew 24:10–12, 23–24

"At that time many will fall away and will betray one another and hate one another. [11]Many false prophets will arise and will mislead many. [12]Because *lawlessness* is increased, most people's love will grow cold. . . . [23]Then if anyone says to you, 'Behold, here is the Christ,' or 'There He is,' do not believe him. [24]For false Christs and false prophets will arise and will show great signs and wonders, so as to mislead, if possible, even the elect."

Mark 13:27

"And then He will send forth the angels, and will *gather together* His elect from the four winds, from the farthest end of the earth to the farthest end of heaven."

1 John 4:1

Beloved, do not believe every *spirit*, but test the spirits to see whether they are from God, because many false prophets have gone out into the world.

And the beast which I saw was like a leopard, and his feet were like those of a bear, and his mouth like the mouth of a lion. And the dragon gave him his power and his throne and great authority. ³I saw one of his heads as if it had been slain, and his fatal wound was healed. And the whole earth was amazed and followed after the beast; ⁴they *worshiped* the dragon because he gave his authority to the beast; and they worshiped the beast.

NONCANONICAL PARALLELS

Sibylline Oracles *3:63–70*

Then Beliar will come from the *Sebastenoi* [line of Augustus] ⁶⁴and he will raise up the height of mountains, he will raise up the sea, ⁶⁵the great fiery sun and shining moon, ⁶⁶and he will raise up the dead, and perform many signs ⁶⁷for men. But they will not be effective in him. ⁶⁸But he will, indeed, also lead men astray, and he will lead astray ⁶⁹many faithful, chosen Hebrews, and also other *lawless* men ⁷⁰who have not yet listened to the word of God.

1QpHabakkuk Pesher *(1QpHab) 2.1–6*

[The interpretation of the word concerns] the traitors with *the Man* of ²Lies, since they do not [believe in the words of the] Teacher of Righteousness from the mouth of ³God; (and it concerns) the traito[rs of the] new [covenant] since they did not ⁴believe in the covenant of God [and dishonored] his holy name. ⁵Likewise: The interpretation of the word [concerns the trai]tors in the ⁶last days.

2 Thessalonians 2:6–12

And you know what restrains him now, so that in his time he will be revealed. ⁷For the mystery of lawlessness is already at work; only he who now restrains will do so until he is taken out of the way. ⁸Then that lawless one will be revealed whom the Lord will slay with the breath of His mouth and bring to an end by the appearance of His coming; ⁹that is, the one whose coming is in accord with the activity of Satan, with all power and signs and false wonders, ¹⁰and with all the deception of wickedness for those who perish, because they did not receive the love of the truth so as to be saved. ¹¹For this reason God will send upon them a deluding influence so that they will believe what is false, ¹²in order that they all may be judged who did not believe the truth, but took pleasure in wickedness.

2 THESSALONIANS PARALLELS

2 Thessalonians 1:6–8

For after all it is only just for God to repay with affliction those who afflict you, ⁷and to give relief to you who are afflicted and to us as well when the Lord Jesus will be *revealed* from heaven with His mighty angels in flaming fire, ⁸dealing out retribution to those who do not know God and to those who do not obey the gospel of our Lord Jesus.

OTHER PAULINE PARALLELS

Romans 1:28–29

And just as they did not see fit to acknowledge God any longer, God gave them over to a depraved mind, to do those things which are not proper, ²⁹being filled with all unrighteousness, *wickedness*, greed, evil; full of envy, murder, strife, deceit, malice.

1 Thessalonians 4:15

For this we say to you by the word of the Lord, that we who are alive and remain until the *coming* of the Lord, will not precede those who have fallen asleep.

1 Thessalonians 5:1–4, 9

Now as to the times and the epochs, brethren, you have no need of anything to be written to you. ²For you yourselves know full well that the day of the Lord will come just like a thief in the night. ³While they are saying, "Peace and safety!" then destruction will come upon them suddenly like labor pains upon a woman with child, and they will not escape. ⁴But you, brethren, are not in darkness, that the day would overtake you like a thief. . . . ⁹For God has not destined us for wrath, but for obtaining salvation through our Lord Jesus Christ.

1 Timothy 2:3–4

This is good and acceptable in the sight of God our Savior, ⁴who desires all men to be *saved* and to come to the knowledge of *the truth.*

Isaiah 11:4

But with righteousness He will judge the poor, And decide with fairness for the afflicted of the earth; And He will strike the earth with the rod of *His mouth*, And *with the breath* of His lips He *will slay* the wicked.

Matthew 24:11–12, 24

"Many *false* prophets will arise and will mislead many. [12]Because *lawlessness* is increased, most people's love will grow cold. . . . [24]For false Christs and false prophets will arise and will show great *signs* and *wonders*, so as to mislead, if possible, even the elect."

1 John 4:3

Every spirit that does not confess Jesus is not from God; this is the spirit of the antichrist, of which you have heard that it is *coming*, and now it is already in the world.

Revelation 7:2–3

And I saw another angel ascending from the rising of the sun, having the seal of the living God; and he cried out with a loud voice to the four angels to whom it was granted to harm the earth and the sea, [3]saying, "Do not harm the earth or the sea or the trees until we have sealed the bond-servants of our God on their foreheads."

Revelation 9:13–15

Then the sixth angel sounded, and I heard a voice from the four horns of the golden altar which is before God, [14]one saying to the sixth angel who had the trumpet, "Release the four angels who are bound at the great river Euphrates." [15]And the four angels, who had been prepared for the hour and day and month and year, were released, so that they would kill a third of mankind.

Revelation 13:2, 11–14

And the beast which I saw was like a leopard, and his feet were like those of a bear, and his mouth like the mouth of a lion. And the dragon gave him his *power* and his throne and great authority. . . . [11]Then I saw another beast coming up out of the earth; and he had two horns like a lamb and he spoke as a dragon. [12]He exercises all the authority of the first beast in his presence.

And he makes the earth and those who dwell in it to worship the first beast, whose fatal wound was healed. [13]He performs great *signs*, so that he even makes fire come down out of heaven to the earth in the presence of men. [14]And he *deceives* those who dwell on the earth.

Revelation 17:4–7

The woman was clothed in purple and scarlet, and adorned with gold and precious stones and pearls, having in her hand a gold cup full of abominations and of the unclean things of her immorality, [5]and on her forehead a name was written, a mystery, "BABYLON THE GREAT. . . ." [6]And I saw the woman drunk with the blood of the saints, and with the blood of the witnesses of Jesus. When I saw her, I wondered greatly. [7]And the angel said to me, "Why do you wonder? I will tell you *the mystery* of the woman and of the beast that carries her."

Revelation 19:15

From *His mouth* comes a sharp sword, so that with it He may strike down the nations, and He will rule them with a rod of iron; and He treads the wine press of the fierce wrath of God, the Almighty.

Revelation 20:1–3

Then I saw an angel coming down from heaven, holding the key of the abyss and a great chain in his hand. [2]And he laid hold of the dragon, the serpent of old, who is the devil and *Satan*, and bound him for a thousand years; [3]and he threw him into the abyss, and shut it and sealed it over him, so that he would not *deceive* the nations any longer, until the thousand years were completed; after these things he must be released for a short time.

2 Esdras (4 Ezra) 13:3, 8–10

As I kept looking the wind made something like the figure of a man come up out of the heart of the sea. And I saw that this man flew with the clouds of heaven. . . . [8]After this I looked and saw that all who had gathered together against him . . . were filled with fear. . . . [9]When he saw the onrush of the approaching multitude, he neither lifted his hand nor held a spear or any weapon of war; [10]but I saw only how he sent forth from *his mouth* something like a stream of fire, and from his lips a flaming *breath*, and from his tongue he shot forth a storm of sparks.

Sibylline Oracles *3:63–74*

Then Beliar will come from the *Sebastenoi* [line of Augustus] [64]and he will raise up the height of mountains, he will raise up the sea, [65]the great fiery sun and shining moon, [66]and he will raise up the dead, and perform many *signs* [67]for men. But they will not be effective in him. [68]But he will, indeed, also lead men astray, and he will lead astray [69]many faithful, chosen Hebrews, and also other *lawless* men [70]who have not yet listened to the word of God. [71]But whenever the threats of the great God draws nigh [72]and a burning power comes through the sea to land [73]it will also burn Beliar and all overbearing men, [74]as many as put faith in him.

2 Thessalonians 2:13–17

But we should always give thanks to God for you, brethren beloved by the Lord, because God has chosen you from the beginning for salvation through sanctification by the Spirit and faith in the truth. [14]It was for this He called you through our gospel, that you may gain the glory of our Lord Jesus Christ. [15]So then, brethren, stand firm and hold to the traditions which you were taught, whether by word of mouth or by letter from us. [16]Now may our Lord Jesus Christ Himself and God our Father, who has loved us and given us eternal comfort and good hope by grace, [17]comfort and strengthen your hearts in every good work and word.

2 THESSALONIANS PARALLELS

2 Thessalonians 1:3

We ought *always* to *give thanks to God for you, brethren*, as is only fitting, because your *faith* is greatly enlarged, and the love of each one of you toward one another grows ever greater.

2 Thessalonians 1:8

. . . dealing out retribution to those who do not know God and to those who do not obey the *gospel* of our Lord Jesus.

2 Thessalonians 2:1–2

Now we request you, brethren, with regard to the coming of our Lord Jesus Christ and our gathering together to Him, [2]that you not be quickly shaken from your composure or be disturbed either by a spirit or a message or a *letter* as if *from us*, to the effect that the day of the Lord has come.

2 Thessalonians 3:6

Now we command you, brethren, in the name of our Lord Jesus Christ, that you keep away from every brother who leads an unruly life and not according to the *tradition* which you received from us.

OTHER PAULINE PARALLELS

Romans 8:30

These whom He predestined, He also *called*; and these whom He called, He also justified; and these whom He justified, He also *glorified*.

1 Corinthians 11:2

Now I praise you because you remember me in everything and *hold* firmly *to the traditions*, just as I delivered them to you.

2 Corinthians 1:3–4

Blessed be the God and Father of our Lord Jesus Christ, the Father of mercies and God of all comfort, [4]who *comforts* us in all our affliction so that we will be able to comfort those who are in any affliction with the comfort with which we ourselves are comforted by God.

2 Corinthians 9:8

And God is able to make all *grace* abound to you, so that always having all sufficiency in everything, you may have an abundance for every *good* deed.

Ephesians 1:3–4

Blessed be the God and Father of our Lord Jesus Christ, who has blessed us with every spiritual blessing in the heavenly places in Christ, [4]just as He *chose* us in Him before the foundation of the world, that we would be holy and blameless before Him.

1 Thessalonians 1:2, 4

We give thanks to God always for all of *you*, making mention of you in our prayers, . . .

[4]knowing, *brethren beloved* by God, His *choice* of you.

1 Thessalonians 2:11–12

You know how we were exhorting and encouraging and imploring each one of you as a father would his own children, [12]so that you would walk in a manner worthy of the God who *calls* you into His own kingdom and *glory*.

1 Thessalonians 3:8

Now we really live, if you *stand firm* in the Lord.

1 Thessalonians 3:11–13

Now may our God and *Father* Himself and *Jesus our Lord* direct our way to you; [12]and may the Lord cause you to increase and abound in love for one another, and for all people, just as we also do for you; [13]so that He may establish your *hearts* without blame in holiness before our God and Father at the coming of our Lord Jesus with all His saints.

1 Thessalonians 4:7–8

For God has not *called* us for the purpose of impurity, but in *sanctification*. [8]So, he who rejects this is not rejecting man but the God who gives His Holy *Spirit* to you.

1 Thessalonians 5:9

For God has not destined us for wrath, but for obtaining *salvation* through our Lord Jesus Christ.

OTHER BIBLICAL PARALLELS

Deuteronomy 10:15

"Yet on your fathers did the LORD set His affection to *love* them, and He *chose* their descendants after them, even you above all peoples, as it is this day."

Deuteronomy 33:12

"May the *beloved* of *the* LORD dwell in security by Him, Who shields him all the day, And he dwells between His shoulders."

Isaiah 43:1, 7

"Do not fear, for I have redeemed you; I have *called* you by name; you are Mine! . . . [7]Everyone who is called by My name, And whom I have created for My *glory*, Whom I have formed, even whom I have made."

Isaiah 49:13

Shout for joy, O heavens! And rejoice, O earth! Break forth into joyful shouting, O mountains! For the LORD has *comforted* His people And will have compassion on His afflicted.

1 Peter 5:10, 12

After you have suffered for a little while, the God of all *grace*, who *called* you to His eternal *glory* in Christ, will Himself perfect, confirm, strengthen and establish you. . . . [12]Through Silvanus, our faithful brother (for so I regard him), I have written to you briefly, exhorting and testifying that this is the true grace of God. *Stand firm* in it!

2 Thessalonians 3:1–5

Finally, brethren, pray for us that the word of the Lord will spread rapidly and be glorified, just as it did also with you; [2]and that we will be rescued from perverse and evil men; for not all have faith. [3]But the Lord is faithful, and He will strengthen and protect you from the evil one. [4]We have confidence in the Lord concerning you, that you are doing and will continue to do what we command. [5]May the Lord direct your hearts into the love of God and into the steadfastness of Christ.

2 THESSALONIANS PARALLELS

2 Thessalonians 1:11–12

To this end also we *pray* for you always, that our God will count you worthy of your calling, and fulfill every desire for goodness and the work of *faith* with power, [12]so that the name of our Lord Jesus will be *glorified* in you, and you in Him, according to the grace of our God and the Lord Jesus Christ.

2 Thessalonians 2:8–10

Then that lawless one will be revealed whom the Lord will slay with the breath of His mouth and bring to an end by the appearance of His coming; [9]that is, the one whose coming is in accord with the activity of Satan, with all power and signs and false wonders, [10]and with all the deception of wickedness for those who perish, because they did not receive the love of the truth so as to be saved.

Romans 15:30–31

Now I urge you, brethren, by our Lord Jesus Christ and by the *love* of the Spirit, to strive together with me in your *prayers* to God for me, [31]that I may be *rescued* from those who are disobedient in Judea, and that my service for Jerusalem may prove acceptable to the saints.

1 Corinthians 1:7–9

You are not lacking in any gift, awaiting eagerly the revelation of our Lord Jesus Christ, [8]who will also confirm you to the end, blameless in the day of our Lord Jesus Christ. [9]God is *faithful*, through whom you were called into fellowship with His Son, Jesus Christ our Lord.

1 Corinthians 10:13

No temptation has overtaken you but such as is common to man; and God is *faithful*, who will not allow you to be tempted beyond what you are able, but with the temptation will provide the way of escape also, so that you will be able to endure it.

2 Corinthians 2:3

This is the very thing I wrote you, so that when I came, I would not have sorrow from those who ought to make me rejoice; having *confidence* in you all that my joy would be the joy of you all.

Philippians 2:14–15

Do all things without grumbling or disputing; [15]so that you will prove yourselves to be blameless and innocent, children of God above reproach in the midst of a crooked and *perverse* generation, among whom you appear as lights in the world.

Colossians 4:3

. . . *praying* at the same time *for us* as well, that God will open up to us a door for *the word*, so that we may speak forth the mystery of Christ, for which I have also been imprisoned.

1 Thessalonians 1:2–3

We give thanks to God always for all of you, making mention of you in our *prayers*; [3]constantly bearing in mind your work of *faith* and labor of *love* and *steadfastness* of hope

in our Lord Jesus Christ in the presence of our God and Father.

1 Thessalonians 1:8

For *the word of the Lord* has sounded forth from you, not only in Macedonia and Achaia, but also in every place your *faith* toward God has gone forth, so that we have no need to say anything.

1 Thessalonians 4:1–2

Finally then, brethren, we request and exhort you in the Lord Jesus, that as you received from us instruction as to how you ought to walk and please God (just as you actually do walk), that you excel still more. [2]For you know what *commandments* we gave you by the authority of the Lord Jesus.

1 Thessalonians 5:24–25

Faithful is He who calls you, and He also will bring it to pass. [25]*Brethren, pray for us.*

2 Timothy 4:17

But the Lord stood with me and *strengthened* me, so that through me the proclamation might be fully accomplished, and that all the Gentiles might hear; and I was *rescued* out of the lion's mouth.

Deuteronomy 7:9

"Know therefore that the LORD your God, He is God, the *faithful* God, who keeps His covenant and His lovingkindness to a thousandth generation with those who *love* Him and keep His commandments."

Deuteronomy 32:20

"Then He said, 'I will hide My face from them, I will see what their end shall be; For they are a *perverse* generation, Sons in whom is no faithfulness.'"

1 Chronicles 29:18

"O LORD, the God of Abraham, Isaac and Israel, our fathers, preserve this forever in the intentions of the heart of Your people, and *direct* their *heart* to You."

Psalm 121:7

The LORD will *protect* you from all *evil*; He will keep your soul.

Psalm 147:15

He sends forth His command to the earth; His *word* runs very swiftly.

Proverbs 2:10–12

For wisdom will enter your heart And knowledge will be pleasant to your soul; [11]Discretion will guard you, Understanding will watch over you, [12]To deliver you from the way of *evil*, From the man who speaks *perverse* things.

Matthew 6:13

"And do not lead us into temptation, but deliver us from *evil*."

2 Thessalonians 3:6–13

Now we command you, brethren, in the name of our Lord Jesus Christ, that you keep away from every brother who leads an unruly life and not according to the tradition which you received from us. [7]For you yourselves know how you ought to follow our example, because we did not act in an undisciplined manner among you, [8]nor did we eat anyone's bread without paying for it, but with labor and hardship we kept working night and day so that we would not be a burden to any of you; [9]not because we do not have the right to this, but in order to offer ourselves as a model for you, so that you would follow our example. [10]For even when we were with you, we used to give you this order: if anyone is not willing to work, then he is not to eat, either. [11]For we hear that some among you are leading an undisciplined life, doing no work at all, but acting like busybodies. [12]Now such persons we command and exhort in the Lord Jesus Christ to work in quiet fashion and eat their own bread. [13]But as for you, brethren, do not grow weary of doing good.

2 THESSALONIANS PARALLELS

2 Thessalonians 2:15

So then, brethren, stand firm and hold to the *traditions* which you were taught, whether by word of mouth or by letter from us.

OTHER PAULINE PARALLELS

Romans 16:17

Now I urge you, brethren, keep your eye on those who cause dissensions and hin-

drances contrary to the teaching which you learned, and turn away from them.

1 Corinthians 4:11–12

To this present hour we are both hungry and thirsty, and are poorly clothed, and are roughly treated, and are homeless; [12]and we toil, *working* with our own hands; when we are reviled, we bless; when we are persecuted, we endure.

1 Corinthians 5:11

But actually, I wrote to you not to associate with any so-called brother if he is an immoral person, or covetous, or an idolater, or a reviler, or a drunkard, or a swindler— not even to eat with such a one.

1 Corinthians 9:4, 12

Do we not have a right to *eat* and drink? . . . [12]If others share the *right* over you, do we not more? Nevertheless, we did not use this right, but we endure all things so that we will cause no hindrance to the gospel of Christ.

1 Corinthians 11:1–2

Be imitators of me, just as I also am of Christ. [2]Now I praise you because you remember me in everything and hold firmly to the *traditions*, just as I delivered them to you.

2 Corinthians 11:7–9

Or did I commit a sin in humbling myself so that you might be exalted, because I preached the gospel of God to you without charge? [8]I robbed other churches by taking wages from them to serve you; [9]and when I was present with you and was in need, I was *not a burden to anyone*; for when the brethren came from Macedonia they fully supplied my need, and in everything I kept myself from being a burden to you, and will continue to do so.

Galatians 6:9

Let us not lose heart in *doing good*, for in due time we will reap if we do not grow weary.

Ephesians 4:28

He who steals must steal no longer; but rather he must *labor*, performing with his own hands what is *good*, so that he will have something to share with one who has need.

Philippians 3:17

Brethren, join in *following* my *example*, and observe those who walk according to the pattern you have in us.

Philippians 4:9

The things you have learned and *received* and heard and seen in me, practice these things, and the God of peace will be with you.

1 Thessalonians 1:6

You also became imitators of us and of the Lord, having *received* the word in much tribulation with the joy of the Holy Spirit.

1 Thessalonians 2:9

For you recall, brethren, our *labor and hardship*, how *working night and day so* as *not to be a burden to any of you*, we proclaimed to you the gospel of God.

1 Thessalonians 4:10–12

But we urge you, brethren, to excel still more, [11]and to make it your ambition to lead a *quiet* life and attend to your own business and *work* with your hands, just as we *commanded* you, [12]so that you will behave properly toward outsiders and not be in any need.

1 Thessalonians 5:12, 14

But we request of you, brethren, that you appreciate those who diligently *labor* among you, and have charge over you in the Lord and give you instruction. . . . [14]We urge you, brethren, admonish the *unruly*, encourage the fainthearted, help the weak, be patient with everyone.

1 Timothy 2:1–2

First of all, then, I urge that entreaties and prayers, petitions and thanksgivings, be made on behalf of all men, [2]for kings and all who are in authority, so that we may lead a tranquil and *quiet* life in all godliness and dignity.

1 Timothy 5:11, 13

But refuse to put younger widows on the list, for when they feel sensual desires in disregard of Christ, they want to get married. . . . [13]At the same time they also learn to be idle, as they go around from house to house; and not merely idle, but also gossips and *busybodies*, talking about things not proper to mention.

Acts 18:2–3

And he found a Jew named Aquila, a native of Pontus, having recently come from Italy with his wife Priscilla, because Claudius had commanded all the Jews to leave Rome. He came to them, [3]and because he was of the same trade, he stayed with them and they were *working*, for by trade they were tent-makers.

1 Peter 4:15

Make sure that none of you suffers as a murderer, or thief, or evildoer, or a troublesome meddler.

Pseudo-Phocylides, Sentences *153–54, 156–57*

Work with much *labor* so that you can live from your own means; [154]for every man who's idle lives off thieving hands. [. . .] [156]You should not eat refuse from the meal of another's table, [157]but you should live life from your own means without disgrace.

Josephus, Against Apion *2.291*

The laws . . . teach not impiety but the most genuine piety, summon[ing] us not to meanness but to share our possessions; they are the enemies of injustice, attentive to righteousness; they evict sloth and extravagance, teaching us to be self-sufficient and industrious.

2 Thessalonians 3:14–18

If anyone does not obey our instruction in this letter, take special note of that person and do not associate with him, so that he will be put to shame. [15]Yet do not regard him as an enemy, but admonish him as a brother. [16]Now may the Lord of peace Himself continually grant you peace in every circumstance. The Lord be with you all! [17]I, Paul, write this greeting with my own hand, and this is a distinguishing mark in every letter; this is the way I write. [18]The grace of our Lord Jesus Christ be with you all.

2 Thessalonians 1:2
Grace to you and *peace* from God the Father and the Lord Jesus Christ.

2 Thessalonians 2:2
... that you not be quickly shaken from your composure or be disturbed either by a spirit or a message or a *letter* as if from us, to the effect that the day of the Lord has come.

2 Thessalonians 2:15
So then, brethren, stand firm and hold to the traditions which you were taught, whether by word of mouth or by *letter* from us.

Romans 15:14
And concerning you, my brethren, I myself also am convinced that you yourselves are full of goodness, filled with all knowledge and able also to *admonish* one another.

Romans 16:17, 20
Now I urge you, brethren, keep your eye on those who cause dissensions and hindrances contrary to the teaching which you learned, and turn away from them.... [20]The God of *peace* will soon crush Satan under your feet. *The grace of our Lord Jesus be with you.*

1 Corinthians 5:9, 11
I wrote you in my *letter* not to *associate* with immoral people.... [11]But actually, I wrote to you not to associate with any so-called brother if he is an immoral person, or covetous, or an idolater, or a reviler, or a drunkard, or a swindler—not even to eat with such a one.

1 Corinthians 16:21
The *greeting* is in *my own hand—Paul.*

Galatians 6:1
Brethren, even if anyone is caught in any trespass, you who are spiritual, restore such a one in a spirit of gentleness; each one looking to yourself, so that you too will not be tempted.

Galatians 6:11
See with what large letters I am *writing* to you *with my own hand.*

Philippians 3:17–18
Brethren, join in following my example, and observe those who walk according to the pattern you have in us. [18]For many walk, of whom I often told you, and now tell you even weeping, that they are *enemies* of the cross of Christ.

Colossians 4:18
I, Paul, write this greeting with my own hand. Remember my imprisonment. *Grace be with you.*

1 Thessalonians 5:14
We urge you, brethren, *admonish* the unruly, encourage the fainthearted, help the weak, be patient with everyone.

1 Thessalonians 5:23, 28
Now may the God of *peace* Himself sanctify you entirely; and may your spirit and soul and body be preserved complete, without blame at the coming of our Lord Jesus Christ. ... [28]*The grace of our Lord Jesus Christ be with you.*

Titus 3:10
Reject a factious man after a first and second warning.

Philemon 19
I, Paul, am *writing* this *with my own hand,* I will repay it.

Matthew 18:15–17
"If your *brother* sins, go and show him his fault in private; if he listens to you, you have won your brother. [16]But if he does not listen to you, take one or two more with you, so that BY THE MOUTH OF TWO OR THREE WITNESSES EVERY FACT MAY BE CONFIRMED. [17]If he refuses to listen to them, tell it to the church; and if he refuses to listen even to the church, let him be to you as a Gentile and a tax collector."

The Rule of the Community *(1QS) 8.21–25*
All who enter the council of holiness of those walking along the path of perfection as has been commanded, anyone of them [22]who breaks one word of the law of Moses impertinently or through carelessness will

be banished from the Community council [23]and shall not go back again; none of the men of holiness should *associate* with his goods or his advice on any [24]matter. However if he acted through oversight he should be excluded from pure food and from the council and the regulation applied to him: [25]"He cannot judge anyone and no one should ask his advice for two whole years."

Cicero, Letters to Atticus *11.2*

To whomever you think right, please send *letters* in my name – you know my friends. If they look for my seal or *handwriting,* say that I have forgone these on account of the sentries.

1 Timothy

Paul, an apostle of Christ Jesus according to the commandment of God our Savior, and of Christ Jesus, who is our hope, [2]To Timothy, my true child in the faith: Grace, mercy and peace from God the Father and Christ Jesus our Lord. [3]As I urged you upon my departure for Macedonia, remain on at Ephesus so that you may instruct certain men not to teach strange doctrines, [4]nor to pay attention to myths and endless genealogies, which give rise to mere speculation rather than furthering the administration of God which is by faith. [5]But the goal of our instruction is love from a pure heart and a good conscience and a sincere faith. [6]For some men, straying from these things, have turned aside to fruitless discussion, [7]wanting to be teachers of the Law, even though they do not understand either what they are saying or the matters about which they make confident assertions.

1 TIMOTHY PARALLELS

1 Timothy 1:18–19

This command I entrust to you, *Timothy*, my son, in accordance with the prophecies previously made concerning you, that by them you fight the good fight, [19]keeping *faith* and *a good conscience*, which some have rejected and suffered shipwreck in regard to their faith.

1 Timothy 4:7, 10

But have nothing to do with worldly fables fit only for old women. On the other hand, discipline yourself for the purpose of godliness. . . . [10]For it is for this we labor and strive, because we have fixed our *hope* on the living God, who is the *Savior* of all men, especially of believers.

1 Timothy 6:3–5

If anyone advocates a different *doctrine* and does not agree with sound words, those of our Lord Jesus Christ, and with the doctrine conforming to godliness, [4]he is conceited and *understands* nothing; but he has a morbid interest in controversial questions and disputes about words, out of which arise envy, strife, abusive language, evil suspicions, [5]and constant friction between men of depraved mind and deprived of the truth, who suppose that godliness is a means of gain.

1 Timothy 6:20–21

O *Timothy*, guard what has been entrusted to you, avoiding worldly and empty chatter and the opposing arguments of what is falsely called "knowledge"— [21]which some have professed and thus gone *astray* from the *faith. Grace* be with you.

OTHER PAULINE PARALLELS

1 Corinthians 4:17

For this reason I have sent to you *Timothy*, who is my beloved and faithful *child* in the Lord, and he will remind you of my ways which are in Christ, just as I *teach* everywhere in every church.

Ephesians 1:1–2

Paul, an apostle of Christ Jesus by the will of God, To the saints who are at *Ephesus* and who are faithful in Christ Jesus: [2]*Grace* to you and *peace from God* our *Father* and the Lord Jesus Christ.

2 Timothy 1:1–2, 5

Paul, *an apostle of Christ Jesus* by the will of God, according to the promise of life in Christ Jesus, [2]*To Timothy,* my beloved son: *Grace, mercy and peace from God the Father and Christ Jesus our Lord. . . .* [5]For I am mindful of the *sincere faith* within you, which first dwelt in your grandmother Lois and your mother Eunice, and I am sure that it is in you as well.

2 Timothy 2:17–18

Among them are Hymenaeus and Philetus, [18]men who have gone *astray* from the truth saying that the resurrection has already taken place, and they upset the *faith* of some.

2 Timothy 2:22–23

Now flee from youthful lusts and pursue righteousness, *faith, love* and *peace,* with those who call on the Lord from *a pure heart.* [23]But refuse foolish and ignorant *speculations,* knowing that they produce quarrels.

2 Timothy 4:3–4

For the time will come when they will not endure sound *doctrine;* but wanting to have their ears tickled, they will accumulate for themselves *teachers* in accordance to their own desires, [4]and will turn away their ears from the truth and will *turn aside* to *myths.*

Titus 1:1–4

Paul, a bond-servant of God and *an apostle* of Jesus Christ, for the *faith* of those chosen of God and the knowledge of the truth which is according to godliness, [2]in the *hope* of eternal life, which God, who cannot lie, promised long ages ago, [3]but at the proper time manifested, even His word, in the proclamation with which I was entrusted *according to the commandment of God our Savior,* [4]To Titus, *my true child* in a common *faith: Grace* and *peace from God the Father and Christ Jesus our Savior.*

Titus 1:10–11, 13–14

For there are many rebellious men, empty talkers and deceivers, especially those of the circumcision, [11]who must be silenced because they are upsetting whole families, teaching things they should not *teach* for the sake of sordid gain. . . . [13] . . . For this reason reprove them severely so that they may be sound in the *faith,* [14]not paying attention to Jewish *myths* and *commandments* of men who turn away from the truth.

Titus 3:9

But avoid foolish controversies and *genealogies* and strife and disputes about *the Law,* for they are unprofitable and worthless.

OTHER BIBLICAL PARALLELS

Isaiah 43:3, 11

"For I am the LORD your God, The Holy One of Israel, your *Savior;* . . . [11]I, even I, am the LORD, And there is no savior besides Me."

Acts 16:1

Paul came also to Derbe and to Lystra. And a disciple was there, named *Timothy,* the son of a Jewish woman who was a believer, but his father was a Greek.

Acts 19:1, 21–22; 20:1

It happened that while Apollos was at Corinth, *Paul* passed through the upper country and came to *Ephesus,* and found some disciples. . . . [21]Now after these things were finished, Paul purposed in the spirit to go to Jerusalem after he had passed through *Macedonia* and Achaia, saying, "After I have been there, I must also see Rome." [22]And having sent into Macedonia two of those who ministered to him, *Timothy* and Erastus, he himself stayed in Asia for a while. . . . [20:1]After the uproar had ceased, Paul sent for the disciples, and when he had exhorted them and taken his leave of them, he left to go to Macedonia.

2 Peter 1:16

For we did not follow cleverly devised tales when we made known to you the power and coming of our Lord Jesus Christ, but we were eyewitnesses of His majesty.

NONCANONICAL PARALLELS

Philo, On Moses 2.45–47

The most holy books . . . [46]have an historical part as well as a second part, which is concerned with commands and prohibitions. . . . [47]The historical part is then further divided into the account of the world's creation and the *genealogies,* which concern both the punishment of the impious and the honoring of the righteous.

1 Timothy 1:8–11

But we know that the Law is good, if one uses it lawfully, [9]realizing the fact that law is not made for a righteous person, but for those who are lawless and rebellious, for the ungodly and sinners, for the unholy and profane, for those who kill their fathers or mothers, for murderers [10]and immoral men and homosexuals and kidnappers and liars and perjurers, and whatever else is contrary to sound teaching, [11]according to the glorious gospel of the blessed God, with which I have been entrusted.

1 TIMOTHY PARALLELS

1 Timothy 4:6

In pointing out these things to the brethren, you will be a good servant of Christ Jesus, constantly nourished on the words of the faith and of the *sound* doctrine which you have been following.

1 Timothy 6:3–4

If anyone advocates a different doctrine and does not agree with *sound* words, those of our Lord Jesus Christ, and with the doctrine conforming to godliness, [4]he is conceited and understands nothing; but he has a morbid interest in controversial questions and disputes about words, out of which arise envy, strife, abusive language, evil suspicions . . .

OTHER PAULINE PARALLELS

Romans 1:27–30

In the same way also the men abandoned the natural function of the woman and burned in their desire toward one another, men with men committing indecent acts and receiving in their own persons the due penalty of their error. [28]And just as they did not see fit to acknowledge God any longer, God gave them over to a depraved mind, to do those things which are not proper, [29]being filled with all unrighteousness, wickedness, greed, evil; full of envy, *murder*, strife, deceit, malice; they are gossips, [30]slanderers, haters of God, insolent, arrogant, boastful, inventors of evil, disobedient to parents.

Romans 7:12–13

So then, *the Law* is holy, and the commandment is holy and righteous and *good*. [13]Therefore did that which is good become a cause of death for me? May it never be! Rather it was sin, in order that it might be shown to be sin by effecting my death through that which is good, so that through the commandment sin would become utterly sinful.

1 Corinthians 6:9–10

Or do you not know that the unrighteous will not inherit the kingdom of God? Do not be deceived; neither fornicators, nor idolaters, nor adulterers, nor effeminate, nor *homosexuals*, [10]nor thieves, nor the covetous, nor drunkards, nor revilers, nor swindlers, will inherit the kingdom of God.

Galatians 2:7

But on the contrary, seeing that *I had been entrusted with the gospel* to the uncircumcised, just as Peter had been to the circumcised. . . .

Galatians 3:19

Why *the Law* then? It was added because of transgressions, having been ordained through angels by the agency of a mediator, until the seed would come to whom the promise had been made.

1 Thessalonians 2:3–4

For our exhortation does not come from error or impurity or by way of deceit; [4]but just as we have been approved by God to be *entrusted with the gospel*, so we speak, not as pleasing men, but God who examines our hearts.

2 Timothy 1:13

Retain the standard of *sound* words which you have heard from me, in the faith and love which are in Christ Jesus.

2 Timothy 4:3

For the time will come when they will not endure *sound* doctrine; but wanting to have their ears tickled, they will accumulate for themselves teachers in accordance to their own desires.

Titus 1:2–3

. . . in the hope of eternal life, which God, who cannot lie, promised long ages ago, [3]but at the proper time manifested, even His word, in the proclamation with which *I was entrusted* according to the commandment of God our Savior.

Titus 1:7, 9–10

For the overseer must be above reproach as God's steward, . . . ⁹holding fast the faithful word which is in accordance with the teaching, so that he will be able both to exhort in *sound* doctrine and to refute those who contradict. ¹⁰For there are many *rebellious* men, empty talkers and deceivers, especially those of the circumcision.

Titus 2:1

But as for you, speak the things which are fitting for *sound* doctrine.

Exodus 20:12–13, 16

"Honor your *father* and your *mother*, that your days may be prolonged in the land which the Lᴏʀᴅ your God gives you. ¹³You shall not *murder*. . . . ¹⁶You shall not bear false witness against your neighbor."

Exodus 21:16

"He who *kidnaps* a man, whether he sells him or he is found in his possession, shall surely be put to death."

Leviticus 18:22

"You shall not lie with a male as one lies with a female; it is an abomination."

Jude 14–15

It was also about these men that Enoch, in the seventh generation from Adam, prophesied, saying, "Behold, the Lord came with many thousands of His holy ones, ¹⁵to execute judgment upon all, and to convict all the ungodly of all their ungodly deeds which they have done in an ungodly way, and of all the harsh things which *ungodly sinners* have spoken against Him."

Revelation 21:8

"But for the cowardly and unbelieving and abominable and *murderers* and *immoral* persons and sorcerers and idolaters and all *liars*, their part will be in the lake that burns with fire and brimstone, which is the second death."

Sirach 41:8

Woe to you, the *ungodly*, who have forsaken *the law* of the Most High God!

1 Timothy 1:12–17

I thank Christ Jesus our Lord, who has strengthened me, because He considered me faithful, putting me into service, ¹³even though I was formerly a blasphemer and a persecutor and a violent aggressor. Yet I was shown mercy because I acted ignorantly in unbelief; ¹⁴and the grace of our Lord was more than abundant, with the faith and love which are found in Christ Jesus. ¹⁵It is a trustworthy statement, deserving full acceptance, that Christ Jesus came into the world to save sinners, among whom I am foremost of all. ¹⁶Yet for this reason I found mercy, so that in me as the foremost, Jesus Christ might demonstrate His perfect patience as an example for those who would believe in Him for eternal life. ¹⁷Now to the King eternal, immortal, invisible, the only God, be honor and glory forever and ever. Amen.

1 Timothy 4:9–10

It is a trustworthy statement deserving full acceptance. ¹⁰For it is for this we labor and strive, because we have fixed our hope on the living God, who is the Savior of all men, especially of believers.

1 Timothy 6:12

Fight the good fight of *faith*; take hold of the *eternal life* to which you were called, and you made the good confession in the presence of many witnesses.

1 Timothy 6:15–16

He who is the blessed and only Sovereign, *the King* of kings and Lord of lords, ¹⁶who alone possesses *immortality* and dwells in unapproachable light, whom no man has seen or can see. To Him be *honor* and *eternal* dominion! *Amen.*

Romans 9:22

What if God, although willing to *demonstrate* His wrath and to make His power known, endured with much *patience* vessels of wrath prepared for destruction?

Romans 11:36

For from Him and through Him and to Him are all things. To Him be the *glory forever. Amen.*

Romans 16:27

To the only wise God, through Jesus Christ, be the *glory forever. Amen.*

1 Corinthians 1:4

I thank my God always concerning you for the *grace* of God which was given you in Christ Jesus.

1 Corinthians 15:9

For I am the least of the apostles, and not fit to be called an apostle, because I *persecuted* the church of God.

Galatians 1:13–16

For you have heard of my former manner of life in Judaism, how I used to *persecute* the church of God beyond measure and tried to destroy it; [14]and I was advancing in Judaism beyond many of my contemporaries among my countrymen, being more extremely zealous for my ancestral traditions. [15]But when God, who had set me apart even from my mother's womb and called me through His *grace*, was pleased [16]to reveal His Son in me so that I might preach Him among the Gentiles, I did not immediately consult with flesh and blood.

Ephesians 3:8

To me, the very least of all saints, this *grace* was given, to preach to the Gentiles the unfathomable riches of Christ.

Philippians 3:4, 6

If anyone else has a mind to put confidence in the flesh, I far more: . . . [6]as to zeal, a *persecutor* of the church; as to the righteousness which is in the Law, found blameless.

2 Timothy 1:13

Retain the standard of sound words which you have heard from me, in *the faith and love which are in Christ Jesus.*

2 Timothy 4:17

But the Lord stood with me and *strengthened* me, so that through me the proclama-tion might be fully accomplished, and that all the Gentiles might hear; and I was res-cued out of the lion's mouth.

Titus 3:5

He *saved* us, not on the basis of deeds which we have done in righteousness, but accord-ing to His *mercy*, by the washing of regener-ation and renewing by the Holy Spirit.

OTHER BIBLICAL PARALLELS

Luke 19:10

"For the Son of Man has come to seek and to *save* that which was lost."

Acts 3:12, 17

But when Peter saw this, he replied to the people, "Men of Israel . . . [17]And now, brethren, I know that you acted in *igno-rance*, just as your rulers did also."

Acts 8:3

But Saul began ravaging the church, enter-ing house after house, and dragging off men and women, he would put them in prison.

Acts 9:4–5

He fell to the ground and heard a voice say-ing to him, "Saul, Saul, why are you *perse-cuting* Me?" [5]And he said, "Who are You, Lord?" And He said, "I am Jesus whom you are persecuting."

Acts 9:15–16

But the Lord said to him [Ananias], "Go, for he is a chosen instrument of Mine, to bear My name before the Gentiles and kings and the sons of Israel; [16]for I will show him how much he must suffer for My name's sake."

Acts 26:1, 11

Then Paul stretched out his hand and pro-ceeded to make his defense: " . . . [11]And as I punished them often in all the synagogues, I tried to force them to *blaspheme*; and being furiously enraged at them, I kept pur-suing them even to foreign cities."

NONCANONICAL PARALLELS

2 Baruch *21:10*

For you are the only Living One, the *Immor-tal* One and the Inscrutable One.

1 Timothy 1:18–20

This command I entrust to you, Timothy, my son, in accordance with the prophecies previously made concerning you, that by them you fight the good fight, ¹⁹keeping faith and a good conscience, which some have rejected and suffered shipwreck in regard to their faith. ²⁰Among these are Hymenaeus and Alexander, whom I have handed over to Satan, so that they will be taught not to blaspheme.

1 TIMOTHY PARALLELS

1 Timothy 1:2
> To *Timothy*, my true child in the *faith*: Grace, mercy and peace from God the Father and Christ Jesus our Lord.

1 Timothy 1:5
> But the goal of our instruction is love from a pure heart and *a good conscience* and a sincere *faith*.

1 Timothy 4:14
> Do not neglect the spiritual gift within you, which was bestowed on you through *prophetic* utterance with the laying on of hands by the presbytery.

1 Timothy 6:12
> *Fight the good fight* of faith; take hold of the eternal life to which you were called, and you made the good confession in the presence of many witnesses.

1 Timothy 6:20–21
> O *Timothy*, guard what has been *entrusted to you*, avoiding worldly and empty chatter and the opposing arguments of what is falsely called "knowledge"— ²¹which some have professed and thus gone astray from the *faith*. Grace be with you.

OTHER PAULINE PARALLELS

1 Corinthians 5:5
> I have decided to deliver such a one to *Satan* for the destruction of his flesh, so that his spirit may be saved in the day of the Lord Jesus.

2 Corinthians 10:3–4
> For though we walk in the flesh, we do not war according to the flesh, ⁴for the weapons of our warfare are not of the flesh, but divinely powerful for the destruction of fortresses.

Ephesians 6:11
> Put on the full armor of God, so that you will be able to stand firm against the schemes of the devil.

2 Timothy 2:16–18
> But avoid worldly and empty chatter, for it will lead to further ungodliness, ¹⁷and their talk will spread like gangrene. Among them are *Hymenaeus* and Philetus, ¹⁸men who have gone astray from the truth saying that the resurrection has already taken place, and they upset the *faith* of some.

2 Timothy 4:7
> I have *fought the good fight*, I have finished the course, I have *kept* the *faith*.

2 Timothy 4:14
> *Alexander* the coppersmith did me much harm; the Lord will repay him according to his deeds.

Titus 3:10–11
> Reject a factious man after a first and second warning, ¹¹knowing that such a man is perverted and is sinning, being self-condemned.

OTHER BIBLICAL PARALLELS

Job 2:6–7
> So the LORD said to *Satan*, "Behold, he is in your power, only spare his life." ⁷Then Satan went out from the presence of the LORD and smote Job with sore boils from the sole of his foot to the crown of his head.

Acts 19:28–34
> When they heard this and were filled with rage, they began crying out, saying, "Great is Artemis of the Ephesians!" ²⁹The city was filled with the confusion, and they rushed with one accord into the theater, dragging along Gaius and Aristarchus, Paul's traveling companions from Macedonia. ³⁰And when Paul wanted to go into the assembly, the disciples would not let him. ³¹Also some of the Asiarchs who were friends of his sent to him and repeatedly urged him not to venture into the theater. ³²So then, some were shouting one thing and some another, for

the assembly was in confusion and the majority did not know for what reason they had come together. [33]Some of the crowd concluded it was *Alexander*, since the Jews had put him forward; and having motioned with his hand, Alexander was intending to make a defense to the assembly. [34]But when they recognized that he was a Jew, a single outcry arose from them all as they shouted for about two hours, "Great is Artemis of the Ephesians!"

4 Maccabees 9:23–24
"Do not leave your post in my struggle or renounce our courageous family ties. [24]*Fight* the sacred and noble battle for religion. Thereby the just Providence of our ancestors may become merciful to our nation and take vengeance on the accursed tyrant."

1 Timothy 2:1–7

First of all, then, I urge that entreaties and prayers, petitions and thanksgivings, be made on behalf of all men, [2]for kings and all who are in authority, so that we may lead a tranquil and quiet life in all godliness and dignity. [3]This is good and acceptable in the sight of God our Savior, [4]who desires all men to be saved and to come to the knowledge of the truth. [5]For there is one God, and one mediator also between God and men, the man Christ Jesus, [6]who gave Himself as a ransom for all, the testimony given at the proper time. [7]For this I was appointed a preacher and an apostle (I am telling the truth, I am not lying) as a teacher of the Gentiles in faith and truth.

1 Timothy 1:15
It is a trustworthy statement, deserving full acceptance, that Christ Jesus came into the world to *save* sinners, among whom I am foremost of all.

1 Timothy 4:8–10
For bodily discipline is only of little profit, but *godliness* is profitable for all things, since it holds promise for the present life and also for the life to come. [9]It is a trustworthy statement deserving full acceptance.

[10]For it is for this we labor and strive, because we have fixed our hope on the living God, who is the *Savior* of *all men*, especially of believers.

Romans 1:4–5
. . . Jesus Christ our Lord, [5]through whom we have received grace and *apostleship* to bring about the obedience of faith among all *the Gentiles* for His name's sake.

Romans 9:1–2
I am telling the truth in Christ, *I am not lying*, my conscience testifies with me in the Holy Spirit, [2]that I have great sorrow and unceasing grief in my heart.

Romans 13:1
Every person is to be in subjection to the governing authorities. For there is no *authority* except from God, and those which exist are established by God.

1 Corinthians 8:5–6
For even if there are so-called gods whether in heaven or on earth, as indeed there are many gods and many lords, [6]yet for us there is but *one God*, the Father, from whom are all things and we exist for Him; and one Lord, Jesus Christ, by whom are all things, and we exist through Him.

Galatians 1:3–4
. . . the Lord Jesus Christ, [4]*who gave Himself* for our sins so that He might rescue us from this present evil age, according to the will of our God and Father.

Ephesians 4:4–6
There is one body and one Spirit, just as also you were called in one hope of your calling; [5]one Lord, one faith, one baptism, [6]*one God* and Father of all who is over all and through all and in all.

Ephesians 6:18
With all *prayer* and *petition* pray at all times in the Spirit, and with this in view, be on the alert with all perseverance and petition for all the saints.

1 Thessalonians 4:10–12
But we urge you, brethren, to excel still more, [11]and to make it your ambition to *lead*

a quiet life and attend to your own business and work with your hands, just as we commanded you, [12]so that you will behave properly toward outsiders and not be in any need.

2 Timothy 1:10–11

. . . but now has been revealed by the appearing of our *Savior* Christ Jesus, who abolished death and brought life and immortality to light through the gospel, [11]for which *I was appointed a preacher and an apostle* and *a teacher*.

Titus 1:1–3

Paul, a bond-servant of God and *an apostle* of Jesus Christ, for the *faith* of those chosen of God and *the knowledge of the truth* which is according to *godliness,* [2]in the hope of eternal life, which God, who cannot lie, promised long ages ago, [3]but *at the proper time* manifested, even His word, in the proclamation with which I was entrusted according to the commandment of *God our Savior* . . .

Titus 2:11–14

For the grace of God has appeared, bringing salvation to *all men,* [12]instructing us to deny ungodliness and worldly desires and to live sensibly, righteously and *godly* in the present age, [13]looking for the blessed hope and the appearing of the glory of our great God and *Savior,* Christ Jesus, [14]who *gave Himself* for us to redeem us from every lawless deed, and to purify for Himself a people for His own possession, zealous for good deeds.

Titus 3:1

Remind them to be subject to rulers, to *authorities,* to be obedient, to be ready for every good deed.

Deuteronomy 6:4

"Hear, O Israel! The LORD is our *God,* the LORD is *one!*"

Matthew 20:28

"The Son of Man did not come to be served, but to serve, and to *give* His life *a ransom* for many."

Hebrews 9:15

For this reason He is the *mediator* of a new covenant, so that, since a death has taken place for the redemption of the transgressions that were committed under the first covenant, those who have been called may receive the promise of the eternal inheritance.

1 Peter 2:17

Honor all people, love the brotherhood, fear God, honor the *king.*

4 Maccabees 17:20–22

These, then, who have been consecrated for the sake of God, are honored, not only with this honor, but also by the fact that because of them our enemies did not rule over our nation, [21]the tyrant was punished, and the homeland purified—they having become, as it were, a *ransom* for the sin of our nation. [22]And through the blood of those devout ones and their death as an atoning sacrifice, divine Providence preserved Israel that previously had been mistreated.

Testament of Dan 6:2

"Draw near to God and to the angel who intercedes for you, because he is the *mediator* between God and men for the peace of Israel. He shall stand in opposition to the kingdom of the enemy."

Philo, Flaccus 49

In every part of the inhabited world the reverence of the Jews towards the Augustan house is based, as is evident to all, in our *prayer* houses, and if these are destroyed from our midst what other place or means is left for showing such honor?

1 Timothy 2:8–15

Therefore I want the men in every place to pray, lifting up holy hands, without wrath and dissension. [9]Likewise, I want women to adorn themselves with proper clothing, modestly and discreetly, not with braided hair and gold or pearls or costly garments, [10]but rather by means of good works, as is proper for women making a claim to godliness. [11]A woman must quietly receive instruction with entire submissiveness. [12]But I do not allow a woman to teach or exercise authority over a man, but to remain quiet. [13]For it was Adam who was first created, and then Eve. [14]And it was not Adam who was deceived, but the woman being deceived, fell into transgression. [15]But women will be preserved through the bearing of children if they continue in faith and love and sanctity with self-restraint.

1 TIMOTHY PARALLELS

1 Timothy 4:1–3

But the Spirit explicitly says that in later times some will fall away from the *faith,* paying attention to deceitful spirits and doctrines of demons, [2]by means of the hypocrisy of liars seared in their own conscience as with a branding iron, [3]men who forbid marriage and advocate abstaining from foods which God has created to be gratefully shared in by those who believe and know the truth.

1 Timothy 5:9–10, 14

A widow is to be put on the list only if she is not less than sixty years old, having been the wife of one man, [10]having a reputation for *good works*; and if she has brought up children, if she has shown hospitality to strangers, if she has washed the saints' feet, if she has assisted those in distress, and if she has devoted herself to every good work. . . . [14]Therefore, I want younger widows to get married, *bear children,* keep house, and give the enemy no occasion for reproach.

OTHER PAULINE PARALLELS

Romans 5:12–14

Therefore, just as through one man sin entered into the world, and death through sin, and so death spread to all men, because all sinned—[13]for until the Law sin was in the world, but sin is not imputed when there is no law. [14]Nevertheless death reigned from *Adam* until Moses, even over those who had not sinned in the likeness of the offense of Adam, who is a type of Him who was to come.

1 Corinthians 7:8

But I say to the unmarried and to widows that it is good for them if they remain even as I.

1 Corinthians 11:8–10

For man does not originate from woman, but woman from man; [9]for indeed man was not *created* for the woman's sake, but woman for the man's sake. [10]Therefore the woman ought to have a symbol of *authority* on her head, because of the angels.

1 Corinthians 14:34–35

The women are to keep silent in the churches; for they are not permitted to speak, but are to subject themselves, just as the Law also says. [35]If they desire to learn anything, let them ask their own husbands at home; for it is improper for a woman to speak in church.

1 Corinthians 15:22

For as in *Adam* all die, so also in Christ all will be made alive.

2 Corinthians 11:3

But I am afraid that, as the serpent *deceived* Eve by his craftiness, your minds will be led astray from the simplicity and purity of devotion to Christ.

Ephesians 5:22

Wives, be subject to your own husbands, as to the Lord.

2 Timothy 1:5

For I am mindful of the sincere *faith* within you, which first dwelt in your grandmother Lois and your mother Eunice, and I am sure that it is in you as well.

2 Timothy 3:5–7, 13

Avoid such men as these. [6]For among them are those who enter into households and captivate weak women weighed down with sins, led on by various impulses, [7]always learning and never able to come to the knowledge of the truth. . . . [13]But evil men and impostors will proceed from bad to worse, deceiving and *being deceived.*

Titus 2:3–5

Older women likewise are to be reverent in their behavior, not malicious gossips nor enslaved to much wine, teaching what is good, [4]so that they may encourage the young women to love their husbands, to love their *children*, [5]to be sensible, pure, workers at home, kind, being subject to their own husbands, so that the word of God will not be dishonored.

Genesis 2:22

The LORD God fashioned into a woman the rib which He had taken from the man, and brought her to the man.

Genesis 3:13, 16

Then the LORD God said to the woman, "What is this you have done?" And the woman said, "The serpent *deceived* me, and I ate." . . . [16]To the woman He said, "I will greatly multiply Your pain in childbirth, In pain you will bring forth *children*; Yet your desire will be for your husband, And he will rule over you."

Psalm 141:2

May my *prayer* be counted as incense before You; The *lifting up* of my *hands* as the evening offering.

Malachi 1:11

"For from the rising of the sun even to its setting, My name will be great among the nations, and *in every place* incense is going to be offered to My name, and a grain offering that is pure; for My name will be great among the nations."

1 Peter 3:1–6

In the same way, you wives, be *submissive* to your own husbands so that even if any of them are disobedient to the word, they may be won without a word by the behavior of their wives, [2]as they observe your chaste and respectful behavior. [3]Your adornment must not be merely external—*braiding the hair*, and wearing *gold* jewelry, or putting on dresses; [4]but let it be the hidden person of the heart, with the imperishable quality of a gentle and *quiet* spirit, which is precious in the sight of God. [5]For in this way in former times the holy women also, who hoped in God, used to *adorn themselves*, being submissive to their own husbands; [6]just as Sarah obeyed Abraham, calling him lord, and you have become her children if you do what is right without being frightened by any fear.

Sirach 25:24–25

From a woman sin had its beginning, and because of her we all die. [25]Allow no outlet

to water, and no boldness of speech to an evil wife.

Testament of Reuben 5:5

Accordingly, my children, flee from promiscuity, and order your wives and your daughters not to *adorn* their heads and their appearances so as to *deceive* men's sound minds.

1 Timothy 3:1–7

It is a trustworthy statement: if any man aspires to the office of overseer, it is a fine work he desires to do. [2]An overseer, then, must be above reproach, the husband of one wife, temperate, prudent, respectable, hospitable, able to teach, [3]not addicted to wine or pugnacious, but gentle, peaceable, free from the love of money. [4]He must be one who manages his own household well, keeping his children under control with all dignity [5](but if a man does not know how to manage his own household, how will he take care of the church of God?), [6]and not a new convert, so that he will not become conceited and fall into the condemnation incurred by the devil. [7]And he must have a good reputation with those outside the church, so that he will not fall into reproach and the snare of the devil.

1 Timothy 3:15

In case I am delayed, I write so that you will know how one ought to conduct himself in the *household* of God, which is the church of the living God, the pillar and support of the truth.

1 Timothy 5:9–10

A widow is to be put on the list only if she is not less than sixty years old, having been the wife *of one* man, [10]having a *reputation* for good works; and if she has brought up *children*, if she has shown *hospitality* to strangers, if she has washed the saints' feet, if she has assisted those in distress, and if she has devoted herself to every good work.

1 Timothy 6:3–4

If anyone advocates a different doctrine and does not agree with sound words, those of our Lord Jesus Christ, and with the doctrine conforming to godliness, [4]he is *conceited* and understands nothing; but he has a morbid interest in controversial questions and disputes about words, out of which arise envy, strife, abusive language, evil suspicions.

1 Timothy 6:10

For *the love of money* is a root of all sorts of evil, and some by longing for it have wandered away from the faith and pierced themselves with many griefs.

OTHER PAULINE PARALLELS

Philippians 1:1

Paul and Timothy, bond-servants of Christ Jesus, To all the saints in Christ Jesus who are in Philippi, including the *overseers* and deacons . . .

Colossians 4:5

Conduct yourselves with wisdom toward *outsiders*, making the most of the opportunity.

1 Thessalonians 4:11–12

Make it your ambition to lead a quiet life and attend to your own business and work with your hands, just as we commanded you, [12]so that you will behave properly toward *outsiders* and not be in any need.

2 Timothy 2:24–26

The Lord's bond-servant must not be quarrelsome, but be kind to all, *able to teach,* patient when wronged, [25]with *gentleness* correcting those who are in opposition, if perhaps God may grant them repentance leading to the knowledge of the truth, [26]and they may come to their senses and escape from *the snare of the devil,* having been held captive by him to do his will.

2 Timothy 3:2–4

For men will be lovers of self, *lovers of money,* boastful, arrogant, revilers, disobedient to parents, ungrateful, unholy, [3]unloving, irreconcilable, malicious gossips, without self-control, brutal, haters of good, [4]treacherous, reckless, *conceited,* lovers of pleasure rather than lovers of God.

Titus 1:5–9

For this reason I left you in Crete, that you would set in order what remains and appoint elders in every city as I directed you, [6]namely, if any man is *above reproach, the husband of one wife,* having *children* who believe, not accused of dissipation or rebellion. [7]For the *overseer* must be above *reproach* as God's steward, not self-willed, not quick-tempered, *not addicted to wine,* not *pugnacious,* not fond of sordid gain, [8]but *hospitable,* loving what is good, sensible, just, devout, self-controlled, [9]holding fast the faithful word which is in accordance with the *teaching,* so that he will be able both to exhort in sound doctrine and to refute those who contradict.

Titus 2:2

Older men are to be *temperate,* dignified, sensible, sound in faith, in love, in perseverance.

Titus 3:1–2

Remind them to be subject to rulers, to authorities, to be obedient, to be ready for every good deed, [2]to malign no one, to be *peaceable, gentle,* showing every consideration for all men.

Titus 3:8

This is *a trustworthy statement;* and concerning these things I want you to speak confidently, so that those who have believed God will be careful to engage in good deeds. These things are good and profitable for men.

OTHER BIBLICAL PARALLELS

Acts 20:28

Be on guard for yourselves and for all the flock, among which the Holy Spirit has made you *overseers,* to shepherd *the church* of God which He purchased with His own blood.

Hebrews 13:2–5

Do not neglect to show *hospitality* to strangers, for by this some have entertained angels without knowing it. [3]Remember the prisoners, as though in prison with them, and those who are ill-treated, since you yourselves also are in the body. [4]Marriage is to be held in honor among all, and the marriage bed is to be undefiled; for fornicators and adulterers God will judge. [5]Make sure that your character is free from *the love of money,* being content with what you have.

Isocrates, To Demonicus 35

Whenever you are planning to ask someone for advice about your affairs, first see how he has *managed* his own; for one who has made bad decisions regarding the affairs of *his own household* will never give good advice regarding the affairs of others.

Plutarch, Advice to Bride and Groom 144C

Anyone who plans to set the state and the forum and his friends in good order must do the same first with *his own household.*

Onosander, On Choosing a General 1

We must choose a general, not because of noble birth as priests are chosen, nor because of wealth as the superintendents of the gymnasia, but because he is *prudent,* self-restrained, vigilant, frugal, hard-working, alert, free from avarice, neither too young nor too old, preferably a father of *children,* able to speak well, of good *repute.*

1 Timothy 3:8–13

Deacons likewise must be men of dignity, not double-tongued, or addicted to much wine or fond of sordid gain, [9]but holding to the mystery of the faith with a clear conscience. [10]These men must also first be tested; then let them serve as deacons if they are beyond reproach. [11]Women must likewise be dignified, not malicious gossips, but temperate, faithful in all things. [12]Deacons must be husbands of only one wife, and good managers of their children and their own households. [13]For those who have served well as deacons obtain for themselves a high standing and great confidence in the faith that is in Christ Jesus.

1 TIMOTHY PARALLELS

1 Timothy 1:5

But the goal of our instruction is love from a pure heart and a good *conscience* and a sincere *faith.*

1 Timothy 5:13

At the same time they also learn to be idle, as they go around from house to house; and not merely idle, but also *gossips* and busybodies, talking about things not proper to mention.

1 Timothy 5:22–23

Do not lay hands upon anyone too hastily and thereby share responsibility for the sins of others; keep yourself free from sin. [23]No longer drink water exclusively, but use a little *wine* for the sake of your stomach and your frequent ailments.

1 Timothy 6:3–5

If anyone advocates a different doctrine, . . . [4]he is conceited and understands nothing; but he has a morbid interest in controversial questions and disputes about words, out of which arise envy, strife, abusive language, evil suspicions, [5]and constant friction between men of depraved mind and deprived of the truth, who suppose that godliness is a means of *gain.*

OTHER PAULINE PARALLELS

Philippians 1:1

Paul and Timothy, bond-servants of Christ Jesus, To all the saints in Christ Jesus who are in Philippi, including the overseers and *deacons.*

2 Timothy 1:3

I thank God, whom I serve *with a clear conscience* the way my forefathers did, as I constantly remember you in my prayers night and day.

2 Timothy 3:2–3

For men will be lovers of self, lovers of money, boastful, arrogant, revilers, disobedient to parents, ungrateful, unholy, [3]unloving, irreconcilable, *malicious gossips,* without self-control, brutal, haters of good.

Titus 1:6–7

. . . namely, if any man is above *reproach,* the *husband of one wife,* having *children* who believe, not accused of dissipation or rebellion. [7]For the overseer must be above reproach as God's steward, not self-willed, not quick-tempered, not *addicted to wine,* not pugnacious, not *fond of sordid gain.*

Titus 2:3

Older women likewise are to be reverent in their behavior, *not malicious gossips* nor enslaved to *much wine,* teaching what is good.

Hebrews 13:18

Pray for us, for we are sure that we have a good *conscience*, desiring to conduct ourselves honorably in all things.

1 Peter 5:1–2

Therefore, I exhort the elders among you, as your fellow elder and witness of the sufferings of Christ, and a partaker also of the glory that is to be revealed, [2]shepherd the flock of God among you, exercising oversight not under compulsion, but voluntarily, according to the will of God; and not for *sordid gain*, but with eagerness.

NONCANONICAL PARALLELS

The Damascus Document (CD) 12.6–8

He is not to stretch out his hand to shed the blood of one of the gentiles [7]for the sake of riches and *gain*. Neither should he take any of his riches, so that they do not [8]blaspheme.

1 Timothy 3:14–16

I am writing these things to you, hoping to come to you before long; [15]but in case I am delayed, I write so that you will know how one ought to conduct himself in the household of God, which is the church of the living God, the pillar and support of the truth. [16]By common confession, great is the mystery of godliness: He who was revealed in the flesh, Was vindicated in the Spirit, Seen by angels, Proclaimed among the nations, Believed on in the world, Taken up in glory.

1 TIMOTHY PARALLELS

1 Timothy 3:4–5

He must be one who manages his own *household* well, keeping his children under control with all dignity [5](but if a man does not know how to manage his own household, how will he take care of *the church of God*?).

1 Timothy 4:7–8, 10

On the other hand, discipline yourself for the purpose of *godliness*; [8]for bodily discipline is only of little profit, but godliness is profitable for all things, since it holds prom-

ise for the present life and also for the life to come. . . . [10]For it is for this we labor and strive, because we have fixed our hope on *the living God*, who is the Savior of all men, especially of believers.

1 Timothy 4:13

Until *I come*, give attention to the public reading of Scripture, to exhortation and teaching.

OTHER PAULINE PARALLELS

Romans 1:1, 3–5

Paul, a bond-servant of Christ Jesus, called as an apostle, set apart for the gospel of God, . . . [3]concerning His Son, who was born of a descendant of David according to *the flesh*, [4]who was declared the Son of God with power by the resurrection from the dead, according to *the Spirit* of holiness, Jesus Christ our Lord, [5]through whom we have received grace and apostleship to bring about the obedience of faith among all the Gentiles for His name's sake.

Romans 1:13

I do not want you to be unaware, brethren, that often I have planned *to come to you* (and have been prevented so far) so that I may obtain some fruit among you also, even as among the rest of the Gentiles.

Romans 16:25–26

Now to Him who is able to establish you according to my gospel and the preaching of Jesus Christ, according to the revelation of the *mystery* which has been kept secret for long ages past, [26]but now is manifested, and by the Scriptures of the prophets, according to the commandment of the eternal God, has been made known to all *the nations*, leading to obedience of faith.

2 Corinthians 13:10

For this reason *I am writing these things* while absent, so that when present I need not use severity, in accordance with the authority which the Lord gave me for building up and not for tearing down.

Galatians 2:9

Recognizing the grace that had been given to me, James and Cephas and John, who were reputed to be *pillars*, gave to me and Barnabas the right hand of fellowship, so that we might go to the Gentiles and they to the circumcised.

Ephesians 2:19–22

So then you are no longer strangers and aliens, but you are fellow citizens with the saints, and are of *God's household,* [20]having been built on the foundation of the apostles and prophets, Christ Jesus Himself being the corner stone, [21]in whom the whole building, being fitted together, is growing into a holy temple in the Lord, [22]in whom you also are being built together into a dwelling of God in *the Spirit.*

Colossians 1:23

. . . if indeed you continue in the faith firmly established and steadfast, and not moved away from the hope of the gospel that you have heard, which was *proclaimed* in all creation under heaven, and of which I, Paul, was made a minister.

1 Thessalonians 2:18

For we wanted *to come to you*—I, Paul, more than once—and yet Satan hindered us.

2 Timothy 1:9–10

. . . who has saved us and called us with a holy calling, not according to our works, but according to His own purpose and grace which was granted us in Christ Jesus from all eternity, [10]but now has been *revealed* by the appearing of our Savior Christ Jesus, who abolished death and brought life and immortality to light through the gospel.

OTHER BIBLICAL PARALLELS

Jeremiah 1:18

"Now behold, I have made you today as a fortified city and as a *pillar* of iron and as walls of bronze against the whole land, to the kings of Judah, to its princes, to its priests and to the people of the land."

Luke 24:22–23

"But also some women among us amazed us. When they were at the tomb early in the morning, [23]and did not find His body, they came, saying that they had also seen a vision of *angels* who said that He was alive."

Acts 1:9–11

And after He had said these things, He was lifted up while they were looking on, and a cloud received Him out of their sight. [10]And as they were gazing intently into the sky while He was going, behold, two men in white clothing stood beside them. [11]They also said, "Men of Galilee, why do you stand looking into the sky? This Jesus, who has been *taken up* from you into heaven, will come in just the same way as you have watched Him go into heaven."

Hebrews 3:6

Christ was faithful as a Son over His *house*—whose house we are, if we hold fast our confidence and the boast of our hope firm until the end.

1 Peter 2:5

You also, as living stones, are being built up as a spiritual *house* for a holy priesthood, to offer up spiritual sacrifices acceptable to God through Jesus Christ.

1 Peter 3:18

For Christ also died for sins once for all, the just for the unjust, so that He might bring us to God, having been put to death in *the flesh,* but made alive in *the spirit.*

1 Peter 4:17

For it is time for judgment to begin with *the household of God*; and if it begins with us first, what will be the outcome for those who do not obey the gospel of God?

1 Timothy 4:1–5

But the Spirit explicitly says that in later times some will fall away from the faith, paying attention to deceitful spirits and doctrines of demons, [2]by means of the hypocrisy of liars seared in their own conscience as with a branding iron, [3]men who forbid marriage and advocate abstaining from foods which God has created to be gratefully shared in by those who believe and know the truth. [4]For everything created by God is good, and nothing is to be rejected if it is received with gratitude; [5]for it is sanctified by means of the word of God and prayer.

1 TIMOTHY PARALLELS

1 Timothy 1:3, 5

As I urged you upon my departure for Macedonia, remain on at Ephesus so that you may instruct certain men not to teach strange *doctrines*. . . . [5]But the goal of our instruction is love from a pure heart and a good *conscience* and a sincere *faith*.

1 Timothy 1:8–10

But we know that the Law is good, if one uses it lawfully, [9]realizing the fact that law is not made for a righteous person, but for those who are lawless and rebellious . . . [10]and immoral men and homosexuals and kidnappers and *liars* and perjurers, and whatever else is contrary to sound teaching.

1 Timothy 6:17

Instruct those who are rich in this present world not to be conceited or to fix their hope on the uncertainty of riches, but on God, who richly supplies us with all things to enjoy.

OTHER PAULINE PARALLELS

Romans 14:2–3, 6

One person has *faith* that he may eat all things, but he who is weak eats vegetables only. [3]The one who eats is not to regard with contempt the one who does not eat, and the one who does not eat is not to judge the one who eats, for God has accepted him. . . . [6]He who observes the day, observes it for the Lord, and he who eats, does so for the Lord, for he gives thanks to God; and he who eats not, for the Lord he does not eat, and gives thanks to God.

Romans 14:14

I know and am convinced in the Lord Jesus that nothing is unclean in itself; but to him who thinks anything to be unclean, to him it is unclean.

1 Corinthians 7:8–9

But I say to the unmarried and to widows that it is good for them if they remain even as I. [9]But if they do not have self-control, let them *marry*; for it is better to marry than to burn with passion.

1 Corinthians 10:25–30

Eat anything that is sold in the meat market without asking questions for *conscience'* sake; [26]FOR THE EARTH IS THE LORD'S, AND ALL IT CONTAINS. [27]If one of the unbelievers invites you and you want to go, eat anything that is set before you without asking questions for conscience' sake. [28]But if anyone says to you, "This is meat sacrificed to idols," do not eat it, for the sake of the one who informed you, and for conscience' sake; [29]I mean not your own conscience, but the other man's; for why is my freedom judged by another's conscience? [30]If I partake with thankfulness, why am I slandered concerning that for which I give thanks?

2 Corinthians 11:13–14

For such men are false apostles, *deceitful* workers, disguising themselves as apostles of Christ. [14]No wonder, for even Satan disguises himself as an angel of light.

Colossians 2:16

Therefore no one is to act as your judge in regard to *food* or drink or in respect to a festival or a new moon or a Sabbath day.

2 Thessalonians 2:2–3

. . . that you not be quickly shaken from your composure or be disturbed either by a *spirit* or a message or a letter as if from us, to the effect that the day of the Lord has come. [3]Let no one in any way *deceive* you, for it will not come unless the apostasy comes first.

2 Timothy 3:1–2, 5–7

But realize this, that in the last days difficult times will come. [2]For men will be lovers of self, lovers of money, boastful, arrogant, revilers, disobedient to parents, ungrateful, unholy, . . . [5]holding to a form of godliness, although they have denied its power; Avoid such men as these. [6]For among them are those who enter into households and captivate weak women weighed down with sins, led on by various impulses, [7]always learning and never able to come to the knowledge of *the truth*.

2 Timothy 4:3–4

For the time will come when they will not endure sound *doctrine*; but wanting to have their ears tickled, they will accumulate for themselves teachers in accordance to their own desires, [4]and will turn away their ears from *the truth* and will turn aside to myths.

Titus 1:15

To the pure, all things are pure; but to those who are defiled and unbelieving, nothing is pure, but both their mind and their *conscience* are defiled.

OTHER BIBLICAL PARALLELS

Genesis 1:29
"Behold, I have given you every plant yielding seed that is on the surface of all the earth, and every tree which has fruit yielding seed; it shall be *food* for you."

Genesis 1:31
God saw all that He had made, and behold, it was very *good*.

Genesis 9:3
"Every moving thing that is alive shall be *food* for you; I give all to you, as I gave the green plant."

Acts 20:29–30
"I know that after my departure savage wolves will come in among you, not sparing the flock; [30]and from among your own selves men will arise, speaking perverse things, to draw away the disciples after them."

2 Peter 2:1–2
But false prophets also arose among the people, just as there will also be false teachers among you, who will secretly introduce destructive heresies, even denying the Master who bought them, bringing swift destruction upon themselves. [2]Many will follow their sensuality, and because of them the way of *the truth* will be maligned.

NONCANONICAL PARALLELS

The Acts of Paul and Thecla *5–6, 23, 25*
(Concerning) *the word of God* about abstinence and the resurrection, Paul said, " . . . [6] . . . Blessed are the bodies of the virgins, for they shall be well pleasing to God and shall not lose the reward of their chastity. . . ." . . . [23]And Paul was fasting with Onesiphorus and his wife and his children. . . . And Paul, having taken off his cloak, said, "Go, my child, sell this and buy some loaves and bring them." . . . [25] . . . And they had five loaves and vegetables and water, and they rejoiced in the holy works of Christ.

In pointing out these things to the brethren, you will be a good servant of Christ Jesus, constantly nourished on the words of the faith and of the sound doctrine which you have been following. [7]But have nothing to do with worldly fables fit only for old women. On the other hand, discipline yourself for the purpose of godliness; [8]for bodily discipline is only of little profit, but godliness is profitable for all things, since it holds promise for the present life and also for the life to come. [9]It is a trustworthy statement deserving full acceptance. [10]For it is for this we labor and strive, because we have fixed our hope on the living God, who is the Savior of all men, especially of believers.

1 TIMOTHY PARALLELS

1 Timothy 1:1, 3–4
Paul, an apostle of Christ Jesus according to the commandment of God our *Savior*, and of Christ Jesus, who is our *hope*. . . . [3]As I urged you upon my departure for Macedonia, remain on at Ephesus so that you may instruct certain men not to teach strange *doctrines*, [4]nor to pay attention to myths and endless genealogies, which give rise to mere speculation rather than furthering the administration of God which is by *faith*.

1 Timothy 1:15
It is a trustworthy statement, deserving full acceptance, that Christ Jesus came into the world to save sinners, among whom I am foremost of all.

1 Timothy 2:1–4
First of all, then, I urge that entreaties and prayers, petitions and thanksgivings, be made on behalf of all men, [2]for kings and all who are in authority, so that we may lead a tranquil and quiet life in all *godliness* and dignity. [3]This is good and acceptable in the sight of God our *Savior*, [4]who desires *all men* to be saved and to come to the knowledge of the truth.

1 Timothy 3:15
In case I am delayed, I write so that you will know how one ought to conduct himself in the household of God, which is the church of *the living God*, the pillar and support of the truth.

If anyone advocates a different *doctrine* and does not agree with *sound* words, those of our Lord Jesus Christ, and with the doctrine conforming to *godliness*, [4]he is conceited and understands nothing; but he has a morbid interest in controversial questions and disputes about words, out of which arise envy, strife, abusive language, evil suspicions, [5]and constant friction between men of depraved mind and deprived of the truth, who suppose that godliness is a means of gain. [6]But godliness actually is a means of great gain when accompanied by contentment.

OTHER PAULINE PARALLELS

2 Corinthians 1:9–10

Indeed, we had the sentence of death within ourselves so that we would not trust in ourselves, but in God who raises the dead; [10]who delivered us from so great a peril of death, and will deliver us, He on whom we have set our *hope.*

Colossians 2:5

For even though I am absent in body, nevertheless I am with you in spirit, rejoicing to see your good *discipline* and the stability of your *faith* in Christ.

Colossians 2:23

These are matters which have, to be sure, the appearance of wisdom in self-made religion and self-abasement and severe treatment of the *body*, but are of no value against fleshly indulgence.

2 Timothy 1:7

For God has not given us a spirit of timidity, but of power and love and *discipline.*

2 Timothy 2:16

But avoid *worldly* and empty chatter, for it will lead to further ungodliness.

2 Timothy 3:10–11

Now you *followed* my teaching, conduct, purpose, *faith*, patience, love, perseverance, [11]persecutions, and sufferings.

2 Timothy 4:3–4

For the time will come when they will not endure *sound doctrine*; but wanting to have their ears tickled, they will accumulate for themselves teachers in accordance to their own desires, [4]and will turn away their ears from the truth and will turn aside to myths.

Titus 1:7, 9

For the overseer must be above reproach as God's steward, . . . [9]holding fast the faithful word which is in accordance with the teaching, so that he will be able both to exhort in *sound doctrine* and to refute those who contradict.

Titus 2:11–13

For the grace of God has appeared, bringing salvation to *all men*, [12]instructing us to deny ungodliness and *worldly* desires and to live sensibly, righteously and *godly* in the *present* age, [13]looking for the blessed *hope* and the appearing of the glory of our great God and Savior, Christ Jesus.

OTHER BIBLICAL PARALLELS

1 Samuel 2:9

"He keeps the feet of His *godly* ones, But the wicked ones are silenced in darkness; For not by might shall a man prevail."

Proverbs 23:12

Apply your heart to *discipline* And your ears to words of knowledge.

Isaiah 43:11

"I, even I, am the LORD, And there is no *savior* besides Me."

John 4:42

"It is no longer because of what you said that we believe, for we have heard for ourselves and know that this One is indeed *the Savior* of the world."

1 Timothy 4:11–16

Prescribe and teach these things. [12]Let no one look down on your youthfulness, but rather in speech, conduct, love, faith and purity, show yourself an example of those who believe. [13]Until I come, give attention to the public reading of Scripture, to exhortation and teaching. [14]Do not neglect the spiritual gift within you, which was bestowed on you through prophetic utterance with the laying on of hands by the presbytery. [15]Take pains with these things; be absorbed in them, so that

your progress will be evident to all. [16]Pay close attention to yourself and to your teaching; persevere in these things, for as you do this you will ensure salvation both for yourself and for those who hear you.

1 TIMOTHY PARALLELS

1 Timothy 1:18–19

This command I entrust to you, Timothy, my son, in accordance with the *prophecies* previously made concerning you, that by them you fight the good fight, [19]keeping *faith* and a good conscience.

1 Timothy 3:14

I am writing these things to you, hoping to *come* to you before long.

1 Timothy 5:22

Do not *lay hands* upon anyone too hastily and thereby share responsibility for the sins of others; keep yourself free from sin.

OTHER PAULINE PARALLELS

1 Corinthians 12:4, 8–10

Now there are varieties of *gifts*, but the same Spirit. . . . [8]For to one is given the word of wisdom through the Spirit, and to another the word of knowledge according to the same Spirit; [9]to another faith by the same Spirit, and to another gifts of healing by the one Spirit, [10]and to another the effecting of miracles, and to another prophecy, and to another the distinguishing of spirits, to another various kinds of tongues, and to another the interpretation of tongues.

Galatians 5:22–23

But the fruit of the Spirit is *love*, joy, peace, patience, kindness, goodness, *faithfulness*, [23]gentleness, self-control; against such things there is no law.

Philippians 1:25

Convinced of this, I know that I will remain and continue with you all for your *progress* and joy in the *faith*.

Philippians 3:17

Brethren, join in following my *example*, and observe those who walk according to the pattern you have in us.

2 Timothy 1:6

For this reason I remind you to kindle afresh the *gift* of God which is in you through *the laying on of* my *hands*.

2 Timothy 3:10–11

Now you followed my *teaching, conduct, purpose, faith*, patience, *love, perseverance*, [11]persecutions, and sufferings.

2 Timothy 3:14–17

You, however, continue in the things you have learned and become convinced of, knowing from whom you have learned them, [15]and that from childhood you have known the sacred writings which are able to give you the wisdom that leads to *salvation* through *faith* which is in Christ Jesus. [16]All *Scripture* is inspired by God and profitable for *teaching*, for reproof, for correction, for training in righteousness; [17]so that the man of God may be adequate, equipped for every good work.

2 Timothy 4:1–2

I solemnly charge you in the presence of God and of Christ Jesus, who is to judge the living and the dead, and by His appearing and His kingdom: [2]preach the word; be ready in season and out of season; reprove, rebuke, *exhort*, with great patience and instruction.

Titus 2:7–8

In all things *show yourself* to be *an example* of good deeds, with *purity* in doctrine, dignified, [8]sound in *speech* which is beyond reproach, so that the opponent will be put to shame, having nothing bad to say about us.

Titus 2:15

These things speak and *exhort* and reprove with all authority. Let no one disregard you.

OTHER BIBLICAL PARALLELS

Numbers 27:18–20

So the LORD said to Moses, "Take Joshua the son of Nun, a man in whom is the Spirit, and *lay* your *hand on* him; [19]and have him stand before Eleazar the priest and before all the congregation, and commission him in their sight. [20]You shall put some of your authority on him, in order that all the congregation of the sons of Israel may obey him."

Deuteronomy 31:9–12

So Moses wrote this law and gave it to the priests, the sons of Levi who carried the ark of the covenant of the LORD, and to all the elders of Israel. [10]Then Moses commanded them, saying, "At the end of every seven years, at the time of the year of remission of debts, at the Feast of Booths, [11]when all Israel comes to appear before the LORD your God at the place which He will choose, you shall *read* this law in front of all Israel in their hearing. [12]Assemble the people, the men and the women and children and the alien who is in your town, so that they may *hear* and learn and fear the LORD your God, and be careful to observe all the words of this law."

Acts 6:6

And these they brought before the apostles; and after praying, they *laid* their *hands on* them.

Acts 13:2–3

While they were ministering to the Lord and fasting, the Holy Spirit said, "Set apart for Me Barnabas and Saul for the work to which I have called them." [3]Then, when they had fasted and prayed and *laid* their *hands on* them, they sent them away.

1 Peter 5:1–3

Therefore, I exhort the elders among you, . . . [2]shepherd the flock of God among you, exercising oversight not under compulsion, but voluntarily, according to the will of God; and not for sordid gain, but with eagerness; [3]nor yet as lording it over those allotted to your charge, but proving to be *examples* to the flock.

1 Timothy 5:1–8

Do not sharply rebuke an older man, but rather appeal to him as a father, to the younger men as brothers, [2]the older women as mothers, and the younger women as sisters, in all purity. [3]Honor widows who are widows indeed; [4]but if any widow has children or grandchildren, they must first learn to practice piety in regard to their own family and to make some return to their parents; for this is acceptable in the sight of God. [5]Now she who is a widow indeed and who has been left alone, has fixed her hope on God and continues in entreaties and prayers night and day. [6]But she who gives herself to wanton pleasure is dead even while she lives. [7]Prescribe these things as well, so that they may be above reproach. [8]But if anyone does not provide for his own, and especially for those of his household, he has denied the faith and is worse than an unbeliever.

1 TIMOTHY PARALLELS

1 Timothy 2:1–4

First of all, then, I urge that entreaties and *prayers,* petitions and thanksgivings, be made on behalf of all men, [2]for kings and all who are in authority, so that we may lead a tranquil and quiet life in all godliness and dignity. [3]This is good and *acceptable in the sight of God* our Savior, [4]who desires all men to be saved and to come to the knowledge of the truth.

1 Timothy 3:2, 4–6

An overseer, then, must be *above reproach,* the husband of one wife, temperate, prudent, respectable, hospitable, able to teach. . . . [4]He must be one who manages his own *household* well, keeping his *children* under control with all dignity [5](but if a man does not know how to manage his own household, how will he take care of the church of God?), [6]and not a new convert, so that he will not become conceited and fall into the condemnation incurred by the devil.

1 Timothy 4:7–8

But have nothing to do with worldly fables fit only for *old women.* On the other hand, discipline yourself for the purpose of godliness; [8]for bodily discipline is only of little profit, but godliness is profitable for all things, since it holds promise for the present life and also for the life to come.

1 Timothy 5:17–18

The elders who rule well are to be considered worthy of double *honor,* especially those who work hard at preaching and teaching. [18]For the Scripture says, "YOU SHALL NOT MUZZLE THE OX WHILE HE IS THRESHING," and "The laborer is worthy of his wages."

1 Corinthians 7:34

The woman who is unmarried, and the virgin, is concerned about the things of the Lord, that she may be holy both in body and spirit; but one who is married is concerned about the things of the world, how she may please her husband.

Ephesians 6:1–3

Children, obey your *parents* in the Lord, for this is right. [2]HONOR YOUR FATHER AND MOTHER (which is the first commandment with a promise), [3]SO THAT IT MAY BE WELL WITH YOU, AND THAT YOU MAY LIVE LONG ON THE EARTH.

2 Timothy 2:12

If we endure, we will also reign with Him; If we *deny* Him, He also will deny us.

Titus 2:2–7

Older men are to be temperate, dignified, sensible, sound in faith, in love, in perseverance. [3]*Older women* likewise are to be reverent in their behavior, not malicious gossips nor enslaved to much wine, teaching what is good, [4]so that they may encourage the *young women* to love their husbands, to love their children, [5]to be sensible, pure, workers at home, kind, being subject to their own husbands, so that the word of God will not be dishonored. [6]Likewise urge the *young men* to be sensible; [7]in all things show yourself to be an example of good deeds, with purity in doctrine, dignified.

OTHER BIBLICAL PARALLELS

Exodus 20:12

"*Honor* your father and your mother, that your days may be prolonged in the land which the LORD your God gives you."

Deuteronomy 24:17–21

"You shall not pervert the justice due an alien or an orphan, nor take a *widow's* garment in pledge. [18]But you shall remember that you were a slave in Egypt, and that the LORD your God redeemed you from there; therefore I am commanding you to do this thing. [19]When you reap your harvest in your field and have forgotten a sheaf in the field, you shall not go back to get it; it shall be for the alien, for the orphan, and for the widow,

in order that the LORD your God may bless you in all the work of your hands. [20]When you beat your olive tree, you shall not go over the boughs again; it shall be for the alien, for the orphan, and for the widow. [21]When you gather the grapes of your vineyard, you shall not go over it again; it shall be for the alien, for the orphan, and for the widow."

Deuteronomy 26:12

"When you have finished paying all the tithe of your increase in the third year, the year of tithing, then you shall give it to the Levite, to the stranger, to the orphan and to the *widow*, that they may eat in your towns and be satisfied."

Deuteronomy 27:19

"Cursed is he who distorts the justice due an alien, orphan, and *widow*. And all the people shall say, 'Amen.'"

Ruth 4:5

Then Boaz said, "On the day you buy the field from the hand of Naomi, you must also acquire Ruth the Moabitess, the *widow* of the deceased, in order to raise up the name of the deceased on his inheritance."

Luke 2:36–37

And there was a prophetess, Anna the daughter of Phanuel, of the tribe of Asher. She was advanced in years and had lived with her husband seven years after her marriage, [37]and then as a *widow* to the age of eighty-four. She never left the temple, serving *night and day* with fastings and *prayers*.

Acts 6:1

Now at this time while the disciples were increasing in number, a complaint arose on the part of the Hellenistic Jews against the native Hebrews, because their *widows* were being overlooked in the daily serving of food.

1 Peter 5:5

You *younger men*, likewise, be subject to your elders; and all of you, clothe yourselves with humility toward one another, for GOD IS OPPOSED TO THE PROUD, BUT GIVES GRACE TO THE HUMBLE.

Judith 8:4–6

Judith remained as a *widow* for three years and four months [5]at home where she set up a tent for herself on the roof of her house. She put sackcloth around her waist and dressed in widow's clothing. [6]She fasted all the days of her widowhood, except the day before the sabbath and the sabbath itself, the day before the new moon and the day of the new moon, and the festivals and days of rejoicing of the house of Israel.

1 Timothy 5:9–16

A widow is to be put on the list only if she is not less than sixty years old, having been the wife of one man, [10]having a reputation for good works; and if she has brought up children, if she has shown hospitality to strangers, if she has washed the saints' feet, if she has assisted those in distress, and if she has devoted herself to every good work. [11]But refuse to put younger widows on the list, for when they feel sensual desires in disregard of Christ, they want to get married, [12]thus incurring condemnation, because they have set aside their previous pledge. [13]At the same time they also learn to be idle, as they go around from house to house; and not merely idle, but also gossips and busybodies, talking about things not proper to mention. [14]Therefore, I want younger widows to get married, bear children, keep house, and give the enemy no occasion for reproach; [15]for some have already turned aside to follow Satan. [16]If any woman who is a believer has dependent widows, she must assist them and the church must not be burdened, so that it may assist those who are widows indeed.

1 Timothy 1:6–7, 20

For some men, straying from these things, have *turned aside* to fruitless discussion, [7]wanting to be teachers of the Law, even though they do not understand either what they are saying or the matters about which they make confident assertions. . . . [20]Among these are Hymenaeus and Alexander, whom I have handed over to *Satan*, so that they will be taught not to blaspheme.

Likewise, I want women to adorn themselves with proper clothing, modestly and discreetly, not with braided hair and gold or pearls or costly garments, [10]but rather by means of *good works*, as is proper for women making a claim to godliness. . . . [15]But women will be preserved through the *bearing of children* if they continue in faith and love and sanctity with self-restraint.

1 Timothy 3:2–4, 7, 11

An overseer, then, must be above reproach, the husband *of one* wife, temperate, prudent, respectable, *hospitable*, able to teach, [3]not addicted to wine or pugnacious, but gentle, peaceable, free from the love of money. [4]He must be one who manages his own *household* well, keeping his *children* under control with all dignity. . . . [7]And he must have a good *reputation* with those outside the church, so that he will not fall into *reproach* and the snare of the devil. . . . [11]Women must likewise be dignified, not malicious *gossips*, but temperate, faithful in all things.

1 Timothy 4:1–3

But the Spirit explicitly says that in later times some will fall away from the faith, paying attention to deceitful spirits and doctrines of demons, [2]by means of the hypocrisy of liars seared in their own conscience as with a branding iron, [3]men who forbid *marriage* and advocate abstaining from foods which God has created to be gratefully shared in by those who believe and know the truth.

Romans 12:10–13

Be devoted to one another in brotherly love; give preference to one another in honor; [11]not lagging behind in diligence, fervent in spirit, serving the Lord; [12]rejoicing in hope, persevering in tribulation, devoted to prayer, [13]contributing to the needs of *the saints*, practicing *hospitality*.

1 Corinthians 7:8–9

But I say to the unmarried and to *widows* that it is good for them if they remain even as I. [9]But if they do not have self-control, let them *marry*; for it is better to marry than to burn with passion.

1 Corinthians 7:39–40

A wife is bound as long as her husband lives; but if her husband is dead, she is free to be *married* to whom she wishes, only in the Lord. [40]But in my opinion she is happier if she remains as she is; and I think that I also have the Spirit of God.

2 Thessalonians 3:11

For we hear that some among you are leading an undisciplined life, doing no work at all, but acting like *busybodies*.

2 Timothy 3:1–7

But realize this, that in the last days difficult times will come. [2]For men will be lovers of self, lovers of money, boastful, arrogant, revilers, disobedient to parents, ungrateful, unholy, [3]unloving, irreconcilable, malicious *gossips*, without self-control, brutal, haters of good, [4]treacherous, reckless, conceited, lovers of pleasure rather than lovers of God, [5]holding to a form of godliness, although they have denied its power; Avoid such men as these. [6]For among them are those who enter into households and captivate weak women weighed down with sins, led on by various impulses, [7]always learning and never able to come to the knowledge of the truth.

2 Timothy 4:3–4

For the time will come when they will not endure sound doctrine; but wanting to have their ears tickled, they will accumulate for themselves teachers in accordance to their own *desires,* [4]and will turn away their ears from the truth and will *turn aside* to myths.

Titus 1:10–11

For there are many rebellious men, empty talkers and deceivers, especially those of the circumcision, [11]who must be silenced because they are upsetting whole families, teaching things they should not teach for the sake of sordid gain.

Titus 2:3–5

Older women likewise are to be reverent in their behavior, not malicious *gossips* nor enslaved to much wine, teaching what is good, [4]so that they may encourage the young women to love their husbands, to love their *children,* [5]to be sensible, pure, workers at home, kind, being subject to their own hus-

bands, so that the word of God will not be dishonored.

Deuteronomy 11:26–28

"See, I am setting before you today a blessing and a curse: [27]the blessing, if you listen to the commandments of the LORD your God, which I am commanding you today; [28]and the curse, if you do not listen to the commandments of the LORD your God, but *turn aside* from the way which I am commanding you today, by following other gods which you have not known."

1 Kings 17:8–9

Then the word of the LORD came to him [Elijah], saying, [9]"Arise, go to Zarephath, which belongs to Sidon, and stay there; behold, I have commanded a *widow* there to provide for you."

John 13:14

"If I then, the Lord and the Teacher, washed your feet, you also ought to *wash* one another's *feet.*"

Acts 9:36, 39

Now in Joppa there was a disciple named Tabitha (which translated in Greek is called Dorcas); this woman was abounding with deeds of kindness and charity which she continually did. . . . [39]So Peter arose and went with them. When he arrived, they brought him into the upper room; and all the *widows* stood beside him, weeping and showing all the tunics and garments that Dorcas used to make while she was with them.

Hebrews 13:2

Do not neglect to *show hospitality to strangers*, for by this some have entertained angels without knowing it.

1 Timothy 5:17–25

The elders who rule well are to be considered worthy of double honor, especially those who work hard at preaching and teaching. [18]For the Scripture says, "YOU SHALL NOT MUZZLE THE OX WHILE HE IS THRESHING," and "The laborer is worthy of his wages." ¹⁹Do not receive an accusation against an elder except on the basis of two or three witnesses. ²⁰Those who continue in sin, rebuke in the presence of all, so that the rest also will be fearful of sinning. ²¹I solemnly charge you in the presence of God and of Christ Jesus and of His chosen angels, to maintain these principles without bias, doing nothing in a spirit of partiality. ²²Do not lay hands upon anyone too hastily and thereby share responsibility for the sins of others; keep yourself free from sin. ²³No longer drink water exclusively, but use a little wine for the sake of your stomach and your frequent ailments. ²⁴The sins of some men are quite evident, going before them to judgment; for others, their sins follow after. ²⁵Likewise also, deeds that are good are quite evident, and those which are otherwise cannot be concealed.

1 TIMOTHY PARALLELS

1 Timothy 3:8–10
Deacons likewise must be men of dignity, not double-tongued, or addicted to much *wine* or fond of sordid gain, ⁹but holding to the mystery of the faith with a clear conscience. ¹⁰These men must also first be tested; then let them serve as deacons if they are beyond reproach.

1 Timothy 4:14
Do not neglect the spiritual gift within you, which was bestowed on you through prophetic utterance with the *laying* on of *hands* by the presbytery.

1 Timothy 5:3
Honor widows who are widows indeed.

1 Timothy 6:13–14
I *charge you in the presence of God*, who gives life to all things, and of Christ Jesus, who testified the good confession before Pontius Pilate, ¹⁴that you keep the commandment without stain or reproach until the appearing of our Lord Jesus Christ.

OTHER PAULINE PARALLELS

1 Corinthians 9:9, 14
For it is written in the Law of Moses, "*YOU SHALL NOT MUZZLE THE OX WHILE HE IS THRESHING.*" God is not concerned

about oxen, is He? . . . ¹⁴So also the Lord directed those who proclaim the gospel to get their living from the gospel.

1 Thessalonians 5:12–13
But we request of you, brethren, that you appreciate those who diligently *labor* among you, and have charge over you in the Lord and give you instruction, ¹³and that you esteem them very highly in love because of their *work*. Live in peace with one another.

2 Timothy 1:6
For this reason I remind you to kindle afresh the gift of God which is in you through the *laying* on of my *hands*.

2 Timothy 4:1–2
I solemnly *charge you in the presence of God and of Christ Jesus*, who is to judge the living and the dead, and by His appearing and His kingdom: ²*preach* the word; be ready in season and out of season; reprove, *rebuke*, exhort, with great patience and instruction.

Titus 1:5–7, 9
For this reason I left you in Crete, that you would set in order what remains and appoint *elders* in every city as I directed you, ⁶namely, if any man is above reproach, the husband of one wife, having children who believe, not accused of dissipation or rebellion. ⁷For the overseer must be above reproach as God's steward, . . . ⁹holding fast the faithful word which is in accordance with the *teaching*, so that he will be able both to exhort in sound doctrine and to refute those who contradict.

OTHER BIBLICAL PARALLELS

Deuteronomy 19:15
"A single witness shall not rise up against a man on account of any iniquity or any *sin* which he has committed; on the evidence of *two or three witnesses* a matter shall be confirmed."

Deuteronomy 25:4
"*You shall not muzzle the ox while he is threshing.*"

Proverbs 31:6
Give strong drink to him who is perishing, And *wine* to him whose life is bitter.

Daniel 1:8, 11–12

But Daniel made up his mind that he would not defile himself with the king's choice food or with the *wine* which he drank; so he sought permission from the commander of the officials that he might not defile himself. . . . [11]But Daniel said to the overseer, . . . [12]"Please test your servants for ten days, and let us be given some vegetables to eat and *water* to *drink*."

Matthew 18:15–17

"If your brother *sins,* go and show him his fault in private; if he listens to you, you have won your brother. [16]But if he does not listen to you, take one or two more with you, so that BY THE MOUTH OF *TWO OR THREE WITNESSES* EVERY FACT MAY BE CONFIRMED. [17]If he refuses to listen to them, tell it to the church; and if he refuses to listen even to the church, let him be to you as a Gentile and a tax collector."

Luke 10:2, 5–7

And He was saying to them, "The harvest is plentiful, but the laborers are few; therefore beseech the Lord of the harvest to send out laborers into His harvest. . . . [5]Whatever house you enter, first say, 'Peace be to this house.' [6]If a man of peace is there, your peace will rest on him; but if not, it will return to you. [7]Stay in that house, eating and drinking what they give you; for *the laborer is worthy of his wages.* Do not keep moving from house to house."

Acts 13:2–3

While they were ministering to the Lord and fasting, the Holy Spirit said, "Set apart for Me Barnabas and Saul for the *work* to which I have called them." [3]Then, when they had fasted and prayed and *laid* their *hands* on them, they sent them away.

Revelation 14:13

And I heard a voice from heaven, saying, "Write, 'Blessed are the dead who die in the Lord from now on!'" "Yes," says the Spirit, "so that they may rest from their labors, for their deeds *follow* with them."

Sirach 20:1–3

There is a *rebuke* that is untimely, and there is the person who is wise enough to keep

silent. [2]How much better it is to rebuke than to fume! [3]And the one who admits his fault will be kept from failure.

1 Timothy 6:1–2

All who are under the yoke as slaves are to regard their own masters as worthy of all honor so that the name of God and our doctrine will not be spoken against. [2]Those who have believers as their masters must not be disrespectful to them because they are brethren, but must serve them all the more, because those who partake of the benefit are believers and beloved. Teach and preach these principles.

1 Timothy 1:3

As I urged you upon my departure for Macedonia, remain on at Ephesus so that you may instruct certain men not to teach strange *doctrines.*

1 Timothy 3:2, 7

An overseer, then, must be above reproach, the husband of one wife, temperate, prudent, respectable, hospitable, able to *teach.* . . . [7]And he must have a good reputation with those outside the church, so that he will not fall into reproach and the snare of the devil.

1 Timothy 4:10–12

For it is for this we labor and strive, because we have fixed our hope on the living God, who is the Savior of all men, especially of *believers.* [11]Prescribe and *teach* these things. [12]Let no one look down on your youthfulness, but rather in speech, conduct, love, faith and purity, show yourself an example of those who believe.

1 Timothy 5:3–4

Honor widows who are widows indeed; [4]but if any widow has children or grandchildren, they must first learn to practice piety in regard to their own family and to make some return to their parents; for this is acceptable in the sight of God.

1 Corinthians 7:21–24

Were you called while a *slave*? Do not worry about it; but if you are able also to become free, rather do that. [22]For he who was called in the Lord while a slave, is the Lord's freedman; likewise he who was called while free, is Christ's slave. [23]You were bought with a price; do not become slaves of men. [24]Brethren, each one is to remain with God in that condition in which he was called.

Ephesians 6:5–8

Slaves, be obedient to those who are your *masters* according to the flesh, with fear and trembling, in the sincerity of your heart, as to Christ; [6]not by way of eyeservice, as menpleasers, but as slaves of Christ, doing the will of God from the heart. [7]With good will render service, as to the Lord, and not to men, [8]knowing that whatever good thing each one does, this he will receive back from the Lord, whether slave or free.

Colossians 3:22–25

Slaves, in all things obey those who are your *masters* on earth, not with external service, as those who merely please men, but with sincerity of heart, fearing the Lord. [23]Whatever you do, do your work heartily, as for the Lord rather than for men, [24]knowing that from the Lord you will receive the reward of the inheritance. It is the Lord Christ whom you *serve*. [25]For he who does wrong will receive the consequences of the wrong which he has done, and that without partiality.

Titus 2:3–5

Older women likewise are to be reverent in their behavior, not malicious gossips nor enslaved to much wine, *teaching* what is good, [4]so that they may encourage the young women to love their husbands, to love their children, [5]to be sensible, pure, workers at home, kind, being subject to their own husbands, so that the word of God will not be dishonored.

Titus 2:9–10

Urge *bondslaves* to be subject to their own *masters* in everything, to be well-pleasing, not argumentative, [10]not pilfering, but show-

ing all good faith so that they will adorn the *doctrine* of God our Savior in every respect.

Philemon 15–16

For perhaps he was for this reason separated from you for a while, that you would have him back forever, [16]no longer as a *slave*, but more than a slave, a *beloved brother*, especially to me, but how much more to you, both in the flesh and in the Lord.

Exodus 21:2

"If you buy a Hebrew *slave*, he shall *serve* for six years; but on the seventh he shall go out as a free man without payment."

Leviticus 25:44

"As for your male and female *slaves* whom you may have—you may acquire male and female slaves from the pagan nations that are around you."

1 Peter 2:18–20

Servants, be submissive to your *masters* with all respect, not only to those who are good and gentle, but also to those who are unreasonable. [19]For this finds favor, if for the sake of conscience toward God a person bears up under sorrows when suffering unjustly. [20]For what credit is there if, when you sin and are harshly treated, you endure it with patience? But if when you do what is right and suffer for it you patiently endure it, this finds favor with God.

Philo, On the Decalogue 167

And many more commandments are prescribed [by the Law], to the young on making a return to the elderly, to the old on taking care of the young, to subjects on obedience to their rulers, to rulers on benefiting their subjects, . . . to servants on devotion in service, to *masters* on showing gentleness and kindness, through which inequality is moderated.

Aristotle, Oeconomica 1.5.2

Let our relationship with *slaves* be such that they do not offend us and we do not grieve them.

If anyone advocates a different doctrine and does not agree with sound words, those of our Lord Jesus Christ, and with the doctrine conforming to godliness, [4]he is conceited and understands nothing; but he has a morbid interest in controversial questions and disputes about words, out of which arise envy, strife, abusive language, evil suspicions, [5]and constant friction between men of depraved mind and deprived of the truth, who suppose that godliness is a means of gain. [6]But godliness actually is a means of great gain when accompanied by contentment. [7]For we have brought nothing into the world, so we cannot take anything out of it either. [8]If we have food and covering, with these we shall be content. [9]But those who want to get rich fall into temptation and a snare and many foolish and harmful desires which plunge men into ruin and destruction. [10]For the love of money is a root of all sorts of evil, and some by longing for it have wandered away from the faith and pierced themselves with many griefs.

1 TIMOTHY PARALLELS

1 Timothy 1:3–4, 6–7

As I urged you upon my departure for Macedonia, remain on at Ephesus so that you may instruct certain men not to teach strange *doctrines*, [4]nor to pay attention to myths and endless genealogies, which give rise to mere speculation rather than furthering the administration of God which is by faith. . . . [6]For some men, straying from these things, have turned aside to fruitless discussion, [7]wanting to be teachers of the Law, even though they do not *understand* either what they are saying or the matters about which they make confident assertions.

1 Timothy 3:2–3, 6–7

An overseer, then, must be above reproach, the husband of one wife, temperate, prudent, respectable, hospitable, able to teach, [3]not addicted to wine or pugnacious, but gentle, peaceable, free from *the love of money*. . . . [6]and not a new convert, so that he will not become *conceited* and fall into the condemnation incurred by the devil. [7]And he must have a good reputation with those outside the church, so that he will not fall into reproach and the *snare* of the devil.

1 Timothy 4:8

For bodily discipline is only of little profit, but *godliness* is profitable for all things, since it holds promise for the present life and also for the life to come.

OTHER PAULINE PARALLELS

Romans 1:28–31

And just as they did not see fit to acknowledge God any longer, God gave them over to a *depraved mind*, to do those things which are not proper, [29]being filled with all unrighteousness, wickedness, greed, *evil*; full of *envy*, murder, *strife*, deceit, malice; they are gossips, [30]slanderers, haters of God, insolent, arrogant, boastful, inventors of evil, disobedient to parents, [31]without *understanding*, untrustworthy, unloving, unmerciful.

2 Corinthians 11:4

For if one comes and preaches another Jesus whom we have not preached, or you receive a *different* spirit which you have not received, or a different gospel which you have not accepted, you bear this beautifully.

Galatians 5:19–21

Now the deeds of the flesh are evident, which are: immorality, impurity, sensuality, [20]idolatry, sorcery, enmities, *strife*, jealousy, outbursts of anger, *disputes*, dissensions, factions, [21]*envying*, drunkenness, carousing, and things like these, of which I forewarn you, just as I have forewarned you, that those who practice such things will not inherit the kingdom of God.

Philippians 4:11–12

Not that I speak from want, for I have learned to be *content* in whatever circumstances I am. [12]I know how to get along with humble means, and I also know how to live in prosperity; in any and every circumstance I have learned the secret of being filled and going hungry, both of having abundance and suffering need.

Colossians 3:5, 8

Therefore consider the members of your earthly body as dead to immorality, impurity, passion, evil *desire*, and greed, which amounts to idolatry. . . . [8]But now you also, put them all aside: anger, wrath, malice, slander, and *abusive* speech from your mouth.

2 Timothy 2:14, 23
Remind them of these things, and solemnly charge them in the presence of God not to wrangle about *words*, which is useless and leads to the *ruin* of the hearers. . . . [23]But refuse foolish and ignorant speculations, knowing that they produce quarrels.

2 Timothy 3:8
Just as Jannes and Jambres opposed Moses, so these men also oppose the *truth, men of depraved mind*, rejected in regard to the *faith*.

Titus 1:10–11
For there are many rebellious men, empty talkers and deceivers, especially those of the circumcision, [11]who must be silenced because they are upsetting whole families, teaching things they should not teach for the sake of sordid *gain*.

Titus 3:9–11
But avoid foolish *controversies* and genealogies and *strife* and *disputes* about the Law, for they are unprofitable and worthless. [10]Reject a factious man after a first and second warning, [11]knowing that such a man is perverted and is sinning, being self-condemned.

OTHER BIBLICAL PARALLELS

Proverbs 30:8
Keep deception and lies far from me, Give me neither poverty nor *riches*; Feed me with the *food* that is my portion.

Ecclesiastes 5:15
As he had come naked from his mother's womb, so will he return as he came. He will *take nothing* from the fruit of his labor that he can carry in his hand.

Matthew 6:25
"For this reason I say to you, do not be worried about your life, as to what you will eat or what you will drink; nor for your body, as to what you will put on. Is not life more than *food*, and the body more than clothing?"

2 Peter 2:1–3
But false prophets also arose among the people, just as there will also be false teachers among you, who will secretly introduce destructive heresies, even denying the Master who bought them, bringing swift *destruction* upon themselves. [2]Many will follow their sensuality, and because of them the way of *the truth* will be maligned; [3]and in their greed they will exploit you with false words; their judgment from long ago is not idle, and their destruction is not asleep.

NONCANONICAL PARALLELS

Pseudo-Phocylides, Sentences *42–47*
The love of money is the mother of every *evil*. [43]Gold and silver are always a delusion for people. [44]Gold, you source of evils, life-destroyer, crushing everything, [45]would that you were not to mortals such a desirable disaster! [46]On your account there are fights and robberies and murders, [47]and children are enemies to their parents, and brothers to their kinfolk.

1 Timothy 6:11–16

But flee from these things, you man of God, and pursue righteousness, godliness, faith, love, perseverance and gentleness. [12]Fight the good fight of faith; take hold of the eternal life to which you were called, and you made the good confession in the presence of many witnesses. [13]I charge you in the presence of God, who gives life to all things, and of Christ Jesus, who testified the good confession before Pontius Pilate, [14]that you keep the commandment without stain or reproach until the appearing of our Lord Jesus Christ, [15]which He will bring about at the proper time—He who is the blessed and only Sovereign, the King of kings and Lord of lords, [16]who alone possesses immortality and dwells in unapproachable light, whom no man has seen or can see. To Him be honor and eternal dominion! Amen.

1 TIMOTHY PARALLELS

1 Timothy 1:1
Paul, an apostle of Christ Jesus according to *the commandment* of God our Savior, and of Christ Jesus, who is our hope . . .

1 Timothy 1:17–19

Now to *the King* eternal, *immortal*, invisible, the only God, *be honor* and glory forever and ever. *Amen.* [18]This command I entrust to you, Timothy, my son, in accordance with the prophecies previously made concerning you, that by them you *fight the good fight,* [19]keeping *faith* and a good conscience, which some have rejected and suffered shipwreck in regard to their faith.

1 Timothy 2:5–6

. . . the man Christ Jesus, [6]who gave Himself as a ransom for all, the testimony given *at the proper time.*

1 Timothy 5:21

I solemnly *charge you in the presence of God and of Christ Jesus* and of His chosen angels, to maintain these principles without bias, doing nothing in a spirit of partiality.

OTHER PAULINE PARALLELS

2 Corinthians 9:13

Because of the proof given by this ministry, they will glorify God for your obedience to your *confession* of the gospel of Christ and for the liberality of your contribution to them and to all.

Galatians 5:22–23

But the fruit of the Spirit is *love,* joy, peace, patience, kindness, goodness, *faithfulness,* [23]*gentleness,* self-control; against such things there is no law.

Philippians 3:11–12

. . . in order that I may attain to the resurrection from the dead. [12]Not that I have already obtained it or have already become perfect, but I press on so that I may lay *hold* of that for which also I was laid hold of by Christ Jesus.

2 Timothy 1:9

. . . who has saved us and *called* us with a holy calling, not according to our works, but according to His own purpose and grace which was granted us in Christ Jesus from all eternity.

2 Timothy 2:2

The things which you have heard from me *in the presence of many witnesses,* entrust these to faithful men who will be able to teach others also.

2 Timothy 2:22

Now *flee* from youthful lusts and *pursue righteousness, faith, love* and peace, with those who call on the Lord from a pure heart.

2 Timothy 3:10

Now you followed my teaching, conduct, purpose, *faith,* patience, *love, perseverance.*

2 Timothy 4:1–2

I solemnly *charge you in the presence of God and of Christ Jesus,* who is to judge the living and the dead, and by His *appearing* and His kingdom: [2]preach the word; be ready in season and out of season; reprove, rebuke, exhort, with great patience and instruction.

2 Timothy 4:7–8

I have *fought the good fight,* I have finished the course, I have kept the *faith;* [8]in the future there is laid up for me the crown of *righteousness,* which the Lord, the righteous Judge, will award to me on that day; and not only to me, but also to all who have loved His *appearing.*

Titus 2:11–13

For the grace of God has appeared, bringing salvation to all men, [12]instructing us to deny ungodliness and worldly desires and to live sensibly, *righteously* and *godly* in the present age, [13]looking for the blessed hope and the *appearing* of the glory of our great God and Savior, Christ Jesus.

OTHER BIBLICAL PARALLELS

Exodus 33:20

But He said, "You cannot see My face, for *no man can see* Me and live!"

Deuteronomy 10:17

"For the LORD your God is the God of gods and the *Lord of lords,* the great, the mighty, and the awesome God who does not show partiality nor take a bribe."

Deuteronomy 33:1

Now this is the blessing with which Moses the *man of God* blessed the sons of Israel before his death.

Psalm 104:1–2

Bless the LORD, O my soul! O LORD my God, You are very great; You are clothed with splendor and majesty, ²Covering Yourself with *light* as with a cloak, Stretching out heaven like a tent curtain.

John 18:37

Therefore *Pilate* said to Him, "So You are a king?" Jesus answered, "You say correctly that I am a king. For this I have been born, and for this I have come into the world, to testify to the truth. Everyone who is of the truth hears My voice."

Revelation 17:14

These will wage war against the Lamb, and the Lamb will overcome them, because He is *Lord of lords* and *King of kings*, and those who are with Him are the *called* and chosen and faithful.

NONCANONICAL PARALLELS

4QLiturgical Work *(4Q392) 1.7–8*

With Him there is a *light* which cannot be inspected nor can it be known, . . . for it doubles all the deeds of God. We ⁸are flesh, which does not understand these things.

Philo, On the Special Laws *1.18*

Just as the mind that is inside us, even though it is extremely small and invisible, is the ruler of our sense organs, the mind of the universe, that which is great and most perfect, is *King of kings*, kings who are seen by Him though He is not *seen* by them.

1 Timothy 6:17–21

Instruct those who are rich in this present world not to be conceited or to fix their hope on the uncertainty of riches, but on God, who richly supplies us with all things to enjoy. ¹⁸Instruct them to do good, to be rich in good works, to be generous and ready to share, ¹⁹storing up for themselves the treasure of a good foundation for the future, so that they may take hold of that which is life indeed. ²⁰O Timothy, guard what has been entrusted to you, avoiding worldly and empty chatter and the opposing arguments of what is falsely called "knowledge"— ²¹which some have professed and thus gone astray from the faith. Grace be with you.

1 Timothy 1:6–7

For some men, *straying* from these things, have turned aside to fruitless discussion, ⁷wanting to be teachers of the Law, even though they do not understand either what they are saying or the matters about which they make confident assertions.

1 Timothy 1:18–19

This command I *entrust to you, Timothy,* my son, in accordance with the prophecies previously made concerning you, that by them you fight the good fight, ¹⁹keeping faith and a good conscience, which some have rejected and suffered shipwreck in regard to their *faith.*

1 Timothy 2:3–4

This is good and acceptable in the sight of God our Savior, ⁴who desires all men to be saved and to come to the *knowledge* of the truth.

1 Timothy 2:9–10

Likewise, I want women to adorn themselves with proper clothing, modestly and discreetly, not with braided hair and gold or pearls or costly garments, ¹⁰but rather by means of *good works*, as is proper for women making a claim to godliness.

1 Timothy 3:2–3, 6

An overseer, then, must be above reproach, the husband of one wife, temperate, prudent, respectable, hospitable, able to teach, ³not addicted to wine or pugnacious, but gentle, peaceable, free from the love of money, . . . ⁶and not a new convert, so that he will not become *conceited* and fall into the condemnation incurred by the devil.

1 Timothy 4:10

For it is for this we labor and strive, because we have *fixed* our *hope* on the living God, who is the Savior of all men, especially of believers.

1 Timothy 6:8–10

If we have food and covering, with these we shall be content. ⁹But those who want to get *rich* fall into temptation and a snare and many foolish and harmful desires which plunge men into ruin and destruction. ¹⁰For the love of money is a root of all sorts of evil, and some by longing for it have wandered away from the *faith* and pierced themselves with many griefs.

Colossians 4:18
I, Paul, write this greeting with my own hand. Remember my imprisonment. *Grace be with you.*

2 Timothy 1:13–14
Retain the standard of sound words which you have heard from me, in the *faith* and love which are in Christ Jesus. [14]*Guard*, through the Holy Spirit who dwells in us, the treasure which has been *entrusted to you.*

2 Timothy 2:16–18
But *avoid worldly and empty chatter*, for it will lead to further ungodliness, [17]and their talk will spread like gangrene. Among them are Hymenaeus and Philetus, [18]men who have *gone astray* from the truth saying that the resurrection has already taken place, and they upset the *faith* of some.

2 Timothy 2:24–25
The Lord's bond-servant must not be quarrelsome, but be kind to all, able to teach, patient when wronged, [25]with gentleness correcting those who are in opposition, if perhaps God may grant them repentance leading to the *knowledge* of the truth.

2 Timothy 3:6–7
For among them are those who enter into households and captivate weak women weighed down with sins, led on by various impulses, [7]always learning and never able to come to the *knowledge* of the truth.

Job 36:19
"Will your *riches* keep you from distress, Or all the forces of your strength?"

Psalm 62:10
Do not trust in oppression And do not vainly hope in robbery; If *riches* increase, do not set your heart upon them.

Proverbs 11:28
He who trusts in his *riches* will fall, But the righteous will flourish like the green leaf.

Matthew 6:20
"But *store up* for yourselves *treasures* in heaven, where neither moth nor rust destroys, and where thieves do not break in or steal."

Acts 14:16–17
"In the generations gone by He permitted all the nations to go their own ways; [17]and yet He did not leave Himself without witness, in that He did good and gave you rains from heaven and fruitful seasons, satisfying your hearts with food and gladness."

James 1:10
The *rich* man is to glory in his humiliation, because like flowering grass he will pass away.

James 1:17
Every good thing given and every perfect gift is from above, coming down from the Father of lights, with whom there is no variation or shifting shadow.

2 Timothy

2 Timothy 1:1–7

Paul, an apostle of Christ Jesus by the will of God, according to the promise of life in Christ Jesus, ²To Timothy, my beloved son: Grace, mercy and peace from God the Father and Christ Jesus our Lord. ³I thank God, whom I serve with a clear conscience the way my forefathers did, as I constantly remember you in my prayers night and day, ⁴longing to see you, even as I recall your tears, so that I may be filled with joy. ⁵For I am mindful of the sincere faith within you, which first dwelt in your grandmother Lois and your mother Eunice, and I am sure that it is in you as well. ⁶For this reason I remind you to kindle afresh the gift of God which is in you through the laying on of my hands. ⁷For God has not given us a spirit of timidity, but of power and love and discipline.

2 TIMOTHY PARALLELS

2 Timothy 2:1

You therefore, *my son*, be strong in the *grace* that is in Christ Jesus.

2 Timothy 3:14–15

You, however, continue in the things you have learned and become convinced of, knowing from whom you have learned them, ¹⁵and that from childhood you have known the sacred writings which are able to give you the wisdom that leads to salvation through *faith* which is in Christ Jesus.

2 Timothy 4:9

Make every effort to come to me soon.

OTHER PAULINE PARALLELS

Romans 1:9–10

For *God, whom I serve* in my spirit in the preaching of the gospel of His Son, is my witness as to how unceasingly I make mention of you, ¹⁰always in my *prayers* making request, if perhaps now at last by the will of God I may succeed in coming to you.

Romans 8:15

For you have not received a *spirit* of slavery leading to fear again, but you have received a spirit of adoption as sons by which we cry out, "Abba! Father!"

1 Corinthians 2:3–4

I was with you in weakness and in fear and in much trembling, ⁴and my message and my preaching were not in persuasive words of wisdom, but in demonstration of the Spirit and of *power*.

1 Corinthians 4:17

For this reason I have sent to you *Timothy*, who is *my beloved* and faithful child in the Lord, and he will remind you of my ways which are in Christ, just as I teach everywhere in every church.

2 Corinthians 1:1–2

Paul, an apostle of Christ Jesus by the will of God, and *Timothy* our brother, To the church of God which is at Corinth with all the saints who are throughout Achaia: ²*Grace* to you and *peace from God* our *Father* and the *Lord Jesus Christ.*

Ephesians 1:1–2

Paul, an apostle of Christ Jesus by the will of God, To the saints who are at Ephesus and who are faithful in Christ Jesus: ²*Grace* to you and *peace from God* our *Father* and the Lord Jesus Christ.

Philippians 1:3–4

I thank my *God* in all my *remembrance* of you, ⁴always offering *prayer* with *joy* in my every prayer for you all.

1 Thessalonians 1:2–3

We give *thanks* to *God* always for all of you, making mention of you in our *prayers*; ³*constantly* bearing in mind your work of faith and labor of *love* and steadfastness of hope.

1 Timothy 1:1–2

Paul, an apostle of Christ Jesus according to the commandment of God our Savior, and of Christ Jesus, who is our hope, ²*To Timothy*, my true child in the faith: *Grace, mercy and peace from God the Father and Christ Jesus our Lord.*

1 Timothy 1:5

But the goal of our instruction is *love* from a pure heart and a good *conscience* and a *sincere faith*.

1 Timothy 4:7

But have nothing to do with worldly fables fit only for old women. On the other hand, *discipline* yourself for the purpose of godliness.

1 Timothy 4:14

Do not neglect the spiritual *gift* within you, which was bestowed on you through prophetic utterance with *the laying on of hands* by the presbytery.

OTHER BIBLICAL PARALLELS

Numbers 27:18–20

So the LORD said to Moses, "Take Joshua the son of Nun, a man in whom is the Spirit, and *lay* your *hand on* him; ¹⁹and have him stand before Eleazar the priest and before all the congregation, and commission him in their sight. ²⁰You shall put some of your authority on him, in order that all the congregation of the sons of Israel may obey him."

Acts 13:2–3

While they were ministering to the Lord and fasting, the Holy Spirit said, "Set apart for Me Barnabas and Saul for the work to which I have called them." ³Then, when they had fasted and prayed and *laid* their *hands on* them, they sent them away.

Acts 16:1–3

Paul came also to Derbe and to Lystra. And a disciple was there, named *Timothy*, the son of a Jewish woman who was a believer, but his father was a Greek, ²and he was well spoken of by the brethren who were in Lystra and Iconium. ³Paul wanted this man to go with him; and he took him and circumcised him because of the Jews who were in those parts, for they all knew that his father was a Greek.

Acts 20:17, 36–38

From Miletus he sent to Ephesus and called to him the elders of the church. . . . ³⁶When he had said these things, he knelt down and prayed with them all. ³⁷And they began to weep aloud and embraced *Paul*, and repeatedly kissed him, ³⁸grieving especially over the word which he had spoken, that they would not see his face again. And they were accompanying him to the ship.

Acts 24:14–16

"But this I admit to you, that according to the Way which they call a sect *I* do *serve* the *God* of our fathers, believing everything that is in accordance with the Law and that is written in the Prophets; ¹⁵having a hope in God, which these men cherish themselves, that there shall certainly be a resurrection of both the righteous and the wicked. ¹⁶In view of this, I also do my best to maintain always a blameless *conscience* both before God and before men."

1 John 2:25

This is the *promise* which He Himself made to us: eternal *life*.

2 Timothy 1:8–14

Therefore do not be ashamed of the testimony of our Lord or of me His prisoner, but join with me in suffering for the gospel according to the power of God, ⁹who has saved us and called us

with a holy calling, not according to our works, but according to His own purpose and grace which was granted us in Christ Jesus from all eternity, ¹⁰but now has been revealed by the appearing of our Savior Christ Jesus, who abolished death and brought life and immortality to light through the gospel, ¹¹for which I was appointed a preacher and an apostle and a teacher. ¹²For this reason I also suffer these things, but I am not ashamed; for I know whom I have believed and I am convinced that He is able to guard what I have entrusted to Him until that day. ¹³Retain the standard of sound words which you have heard from me, in the faith and love which are in Christ Jesus. ¹⁴Guard, through the Holy Spirit who dwells in us, the treasure which has been entrusted to you.

2 TIMOTHY PARALLELS

2 Timothy 2:2–3

The things *which you have heard from me* in the presence of many witnesses, *entrust* these to faithful men who will be able to teach others also. ³*Suffer* hardship with me, as a good soldier of Christ Jesus.

2 Timothy 2:8–9, 15

Remember Jesus Christ, risen from the dead, descendant of David, according to my *gospel*, ⁹for which I *suffer* hardship even to *imprisonment* as a criminal; but the word of God is not imprisoned. . . . ¹⁵Be diligent to present yourself approved to God as a workman who does not need to be *ashamed*, accurately handling the word of truth.

2 Timothy 4:8

In the future there is laid up for me the crown of righteousness, which the Lord, the righteous Judge, will award to me on *that day*; and not only to me, but also to all who have loved His *appearing*.

OTHER PAULINE PARALLELS

Romans 1:16

For *I am not ashamed* of *the gospel*, for it is *the power of God* for salvation to everyone who believes, to the Jew first and also to the Greek.

Romans 8:9

However, you are not in the flesh but in the Spirit, if indeed *the Spirit* of God *dwells* in

you. But if anyone does not have the Spirit of Christ, he does not belong to Him.

Romans 8:28

And we know that God causes all things to work together for good to those who love God, to those who are *called according to His purpose*.

1 Corinthians 15:26, 53

The last enemy that will be *abolished* is *death*. . . . ⁵³For this perishable must put on the imperishable, and this mortal must put on *immortality*.

Ephesians 2:8–9

For by *grace* you have been *saved* through *faith*; and that not of yourselves, it is the gift of God; ⁹not as a result of *works*, so that no one may boast.

Ephesians 3:1–2

For this reason I, Paul, the *prisoner* of Christ Jesus for the sake of you Gentiles— ²if indeed you have heard of the stewardship of God's *grace* which was given to me for you.

Philippians 1:7

For it is only right for me to feel this way about you all, because I have you in my heart, since both in my *imprisonment* and in the defense and confirmation of *the gospel*, you all are partakers of *grace* with me.

Philippians 3:20

For our citizenship is in heaven, from which also we eagerly wait for a *Savior*, the Lord *Jesus Christ*.

1 Timothy 1:1

Paul, *an apostle* of Christ Jesus according to the commandment of God *our Savior*, and of Christ Jesus, who is our hope . . .

1 Timothy 1:13–14

Yet I was shown mercy because I acted ignorantly in unbelief; ¹⁴and the *grace* of our Lord was more than abundant, with *the faith and love which are* found *in Christ Jesus*.

1 Timothy 2:7

For this *I was appointed a preacher and an apostle* (I am telling the truth, I am not lying) as *a teacher* of the Gentiles in faith and truth.

1 Timothy 3:16

By common confession, great is the mystery of godliness: He who was *revealed* in the flesh, Was vindicated in *the Spirit,* Seen by angels, Proclaimed among the nations, Believed on in the world, Taken up in glory.

1 Timothy 6:3

If anyone advocates a different doctrine and does not agree with *sound words,* those of our Lord Jesus Christ, and with the doctrine conforming to godliness . . .

1 Timothy 6:20

O Timothy, *guard* what *has been entrusted to you,* avoiding worldly and empty chatter and the opposing arguments of what is falsely called "knowledge."

Titus 2:11–13

For the *grace* of God has appeared, bringing salvation to all men, [12]instructing us to deny ungodliness and worldly desires and to live sensibly, righteously and godly in the present age, [13]looking for the blessed hope and *the appearing* of the glory of our great God and *Savior, Christ Jesus.*

Titus 3:5–6

He *saved us,* not on the basis of deeds which we have done in righteousness, but according to His mercy, by the washing of regeneration and renewing by *the Holy Spirit,* [6]whom He poured out upon us richly through *Jesus Christ our Savior.*

OTHER BIBLICAL PARALLELS

Mark 8:38

"For whoever is *ashamed* of Me and My words in this adulterous and sinful generation, the Son of Man will also be ashamed of him when He comes in the glory of His Father with the holy angels."

1 Peter 4:16

If anyone *suffers* as a Christian, he is not to be *ashamed,* but is to glorify God in this name.

2 Peter 1:10–11

Therefore, brethren, be all the more diligent to make certain about His *calling* and choosing you; for as long as you practice these things, you will never stumble; [11]for in this way the entrance into the eternal king- dom of our Lord and *Savior Jesus Christ* will be abundantly supplied to you.

2 Timothy 1:15–18

You are aware of the fact that all who are in Asia turned away from me, among whom are Phygelus and Hermogenes. [16]The Lord grant mercy to the house of Onesiphorus, for he often refreshed me and was not ashamed of my chains; [17]but when he was in Rome, he eagerly searched for me and found me— [18]the Lord grant to him to find mercy from the Lord on that day—and you know very well what services he rendered at Ephesus.

2 TIMOTHY PARALLELS

2 Timothy 4:7–12

I have fought the good fight, I have finished the course, I have kept the faith; [8]in the future there is laid up for me the crown of righteousness, which the Lord, the righteous Judge, will award to me on *that day;* and not only to me, but also to all who have loved His appearing. [9]Make every effort to come to me soon; [10]for Demas, having loved this present world, has deserted me and gone to Thessalonica; Crescens has gone to Galatia, Titus to Dalmatia. [11]Only Luke is with me. Pick up Mark and bring him with you, for he is useful to me for *service.* [12]But Tychicus I have sent to *Ephesus.*

2 Timothy 4:16

At my first defense no one supported me, but all deserted me; may it not be counted against them.

2 Timothy 4:19

Greet Prisca and Aquila, and *the household of Onesiphorus.*

OTHER PAULINE PARALLELS

Ephesians 6:19–20

Pray on my behalf, that utterance may be given to me in the opening of my mouth, to make known with boldness the mystery of the gospel, [20]for which I am an ambassador in *chains;* that in proclaiming it I may speak boldly, as I ought to speak.

Philippians 1:7

For it is only right for me to feel this way about you all, because I have you in my heart, since both in my imprisonment and in the defense and confirmation of the gospel, you all are partakers of grace with me.

Philippians 2:25, 30

But I thought it necessary to send to you Epaphroditus, my brother and fellow worker and fellow soldier, who is also your messenger and minister to my need, . . . [30]because he came close to death for the work of Christ, risking his life to complete what was deficient in your *service* to me.

1 Timothy 1:3

As I urged you upon my departure for Macedonia, remain on at *Ephesus* so that you may instruct certain men not to teach strange doctrines.

OTHER BIBLICAL PARALLELS

Acts 19:1, 22

It happened that while Apollos was at Corinth, Paul passed through the upper country and came to *Ephesus*, and found some disciples. . . . [22]And having sent into Macedonia two of those who ministered to him, Timothy and Erastus, he himself stayed in *Asia* for a while.

Acts 28:14–16, 30

There we found some brethren, and were invited to stay with them for seven days; and thus we came to *Rome*. [15]And the brethren, when they heard about us, came from there as far as the Market of Appius and Three Inns to meet us; and when Paul saw them, he thanked God and took courage. [16]When we entered Rome, Paul was allowed to stay by himself, with the soldier who was guarding him. . . . [30]And he stayed two full years in his own rented quarters and was welcoming all who came to him.

Jude 21

Keep yourselves in the love of God, waiting anxiously for the *mercy* of our Lord Jesus Christ to eternal life.

NONCANONICAL PARALLELS

The Acts of Paul and Thecla 1

As Paul was going to Iconium after his flight from Antioch, his fellow-travelers were Demas and *Hermogenes*, the coppersmith, who were full of hypocrisy and flattered Paul as if they loved him.

The Acts of Paul and Thecla 2, 5

And a certain man, by name Onesiphorus, hearing that Paul was to come to Iconium, went out to meet him with his children Simmias and Zeno and his wife Lectra, in order that he might entertain him. Titus had informed him what Paul looked like. . . . [5]And after Paul had gone into *the house of Onesiphorus* there was great joy and bowing of knees and breaking of bread and the word of God about abstinence and the resurrection.

2 Timothy 2:1–7

You therefore, my son, be strong in the grace that is in Christ Jesus. [2]The things which you have heard from me in the presence of many witnesses, entrust these to faithful men who will be able to teach others also. [3]Suffer hardship with me, as a good soldier of Christ Jesus. [4]No soldier in active service entangles himself in the affairs of everyday life, so that he may please the one who enlisted him as a soldier. [5]Also if anyone competes as an athlete, he does not win the prize unless he competes according to the rules. [6]The hard-working farmer ought to be the first to receive his share of the crops. [7]Consider what I say, for the Lord will give you understanding in everything.

2 TIMOTHY PARALLELS

2 Timothy 1:8

Therefore do not be ashamed of the testimony of our Lord or of me His prisoner, but join with me in *suffering* for the gospel according to the power of God.

2 Timothy 1:13–14

Retain the standard of sound words which you have *heard* from me, in the faith and love which are in Christ Jesus. [14]Guard, through the Holy Spirit who dwells in us, the treasure which has been *entrusted* to you.

2 Timothy 4:5

But you, be sober in all things, endure *hardship*, do the work of an evangelist, fulfill your ministry.

OTHER PAULINE PARALLELS

1 Corinthians 4:17

For this reason I have sent to you Timothy, who is my beloved and *faithful* child in the Lord, and he will remind you of my ways which are in Christ, just as I *teach* everywhere in every church.

1 Corinthians 9:7, 10

Who at any time serves as a *soldier* at his own expense? Who plants a vineyard and does not eat the fruit of it? Or who tends a flock and does not use the milk of the flock? . . . [10]Or is He speaking altogether for our sake? Yes, for our sake it was written, because the plowman ought to plow in hope, and the thresher to thresh in hope of *sharing the crops*.

1 Corinthians 9:24

Do you not know that those who run in a race all run, but only one receives *the prize*? Run in such a way that you may *win*.

2 Corinthians 11:27

I have been in labor and *hardship*, through many sleepless nights, in hunger and thirst, often without food, in cold and exposure.

Ephesians 6:10

Finally, *be strong* in the Lord and in the strength of His might.

Philippians 4:9

The things you have learned and received and *heard* and seen in me, practice these things, and the God of peace will be with you.

Colossians 1:9–10

For this reason also, since the day we heard of it, we have not ceased to pray for you and to ask that you may be filled with the knowledge of His will in all spiritual wisdom and *understanding*, [10]so that you will walk in a manner worthy of the Lord, to *please* Him in all respects, bearing fruit in every good work and increasing in the knowledge of God.

1 Timothy 6:12

Fight the good fight of faith; take hold of the eternal life to which you were called, and you made the good confession *in the presence of many witnesses*.

1 Timothy 6:20–21

O Timothy, guard what has been *entrusted* to you, avoiding worldly and empty chatter and the opposing arguments of what is falsely called "knowledge"— [21]which some have professed and thus gone astray from the faith.

OTHER BIBLICAL PARALLELS

Proverbs 2:6

For the LORD gives wisdom; From His mouth come knowledge and *understanding*.

James 5:7

Therefore be patient, brethren, until the coming of the Lord. The *farmer* waits for the precious produce of the soil, being patient about it, until it gets the early and late rains.

2 Peter 2:20

For if, after they have escaped the defilements of the world by the knowledge of the Lord and Savior Jesus Christ, they are again *entangled* in them and are overcome, the last state has become worse for them than the first.

NONCANONICAL PARALLELS

Epictetus, Discourses *3.24.34, 36*

Life for each of us is a kind of campaign, a long and difficult one. You must observe the responsibilities of a *soldier* and carry out each duty at the general's command. . . . [36] . . . Such a person can pay only little attention to his own household.

2 Timothy 2:8–13

Remember Jesus Christ, risen from the dead, descendant of David, according to my gospel, [9]for which I suffer hardship even to imprisonment as a criminal; but the word of God is not imprisoned. [10]For this reason I endure all things for the sake of those who are chosen, so that they also may obtain the salvation which is in Christ Jesus and with it eternal glory. [11]It is a trustworthy statement: For if we died with Him, we will also live with Him; [12]If we endure, we will also reign with Him; If we deny Him, He also will deny us; [13]If we are faithless, He remains faithful, for He cannot deny Himself.

2 TIMOTHY PARALLELS

2 Timothy 1:8

Therefore do not be ashamed of the testimony of our Lord or of me His *prisoner*, but join with me in *suffering* for the *gospel* according to the power of God.

2 Timothy 3:15

From childhood you have known the sacred writings which are able to give you the wisdom that leads to *salvation* through faith which is in Christ Jesus.

2 Timothy 4:17

But the Lord stood with me and strengthened me, so that through me the proclamation might be fully accomplished, and that all the Gentiles might hear; and I was rescued out of the lion's mouth.

OTHER PAULINE PARALLELS

Romans 1:1, 3

Paul, a bond-servant of Christ Jesus, called as an apostle, set apart for the *gospel* of God . . . [3]concerning His Son, who was born of a *descendant of David* according to the flesh . . .

Romans 3:3

What then? If some did not believe, their unbelief will not nullify the *faithfulness* of God, will it?

Romans 5:17

For if by the transgression of the one, death reigned through the one, much more those who receive the abundance of grace and of the gift of righteousness will *reign* in life through the One, Jesus Christ.

Romans 6:8–9

Now if we have *died* with Christ, we believe that we shall also *live* with Him, [9]knowing that Christ, having been *raised from the dead*, is never to die again.

1 Corinthians 10:13

No temptation has overtaken you but such as is common to man; and *God is faithful*, who will not allow you to be tempted beyond what you are able, but with the temptation will provide the way of escape also, so that you will be able to *endure* it.

Ephesians 3:13

Therefore I ask you not to lose heart at my tribulations on your behalf, for they are your *glory*.

Philippians 1:7

For it is only right for me to feel this way about you all, because I have you in my heart, since both in my *imprisonment* and in the defense and confirmation of the *gospel*, you all are partakers of grace with me.

Colossians 1:24

Now I rejoice in my *sufferings* for your sake, and in my flesh I do my share on behalf of His body, which is the church, in filling up what is lacking in Christ's afflictions.

1 Thessalonians 5:9–10

For God has not destined us for wrath, but for obtaining *salvation* through our Lord Jesus Christ, [10]who died for us, so that whether we are awake or asleep, we will *live* together with Him.

2 Thessalonians 2:13

But we should always give thanks to God for you, brethren beloved by the Lord, because God has *chosen* you from the beginning for *salvation* through sanctification by the Spirit and faith in the truth.

1 Timothy 1:15

It is a trustworthy statement, deserving full acceptance, that Christ Jesus came into the world to save sinners, among whom I am foremost of all.

Titus 1:1–2

Paul, a bond-servant of God and an apostle of Jesus Christ, for the faith of those *chosen* of God and the knowledge of the truth which is according to godliness, [2]in the hope of eternal life, which God, who cannot lie, promised long ages ago . . .

Titus 1:15–16

To the pure, all things are pure; but to those who are defiled and unbelieving, nothing is pure, but both their mind and their conscience are defiled. [16]They profess to know

God, but by their deeds they *deny* Him, being detestable and disobedient and worthless for any good deed.

OTHER BIBLICAL PARALLELS

Numbers 23:19
"God is not a man, that He should lie, Nor a son of man, that He should repent; Has He said, and will He not do it? Or has He spoken, and will He not make it good?"

Matthew 1:1
The record of the genealogy of Jesus the Messiah, the son of *David*, the son of Abraham . . .

Matthew 10:22
"You will be hated by all because of My name, but it is the one who has *endured* to the end who will be saved."

Matthew 10:33
"But whoever *denies* Me before men, I will also *deny* him before My Father who is in heaven."

Matthew 19:28
"Truly I say to you, that you who have followed Me, in the regeneration when the Son of Man will sit on His glorious throne, you also shall sit upon twelve thrones, judging the twelve tribes of Israel."

1 Peter 5:10
After you have *suffered* for a little while, the God of all grace, who called you to His *eternal glory* in Christ, will Himself perfect, confirm, strengthen and establish you.

2 Timothy 2:14–19

Remind them of these things, and solemnly charge them in the presence of God not to wrangle about words, which is useless and leads to the ruin of the hearers. ¹⁵Be diligent to present yourself approved to God as a workman who does not need to be ashamed, accurately handling the word of truth. ¹⁶But avoid worldly and empty chatter, for it will lead to further ungodliness, ¹⁷and their talk will spread like gangrene. Among them are Hymenaeus and Philetus, ¹⁸men who have gone astray from the truth saying that the resurrection has already taken place, and they upset the faith of some. ¹⁹Nevertheless, the firm foundation of God stands, having this seal, "The Lord knows those who are His," and, "Everyone who names the name of the Lord is to abstain from wickedness."

2 TIMOTHY PARALLELS

2 Timothy 1:8
Therefore do not be *ashamed* of the testimony of our Lord or of me His prisoner, but join with me in suffering for the gospel according to the power of God.

2 Timothy 4:1–2
I *solemnly charge* you *in the presence of God* and of Christ Jesus, who is to judge the living and the dead, and by His appearing and His kingdom: ²*preach the word*; be ready in season and out of season; reprove, rebuke, exhort, with great patience and instruction.

OTHER PAULINE PARALLELS

1 Corinth1ians 3:10
According to the grace of God which was given to me, like a wise master builder I laid a *foundation*, and another is building on it. But each man must be careful how he builds on it.

1 Corinthians 4:17
For this reason I have sent to you Timothy, who is my beloved and faithful child in the Lord, and he will *remind* you of my ways which are in Christ, just as I teach everywhere in every church.

1 Corinthians 8:3
If anyone loves God, he is *known* by Him.

1 Corinthians 15:12
Now if Christ is preached, that He has been raised from the dead, how do some among you say that there is no *resurrection* of the dead?

1 Timothy 1:6–7
For some men, *straying* from these things, have turned aside to fruitless discussion, ⁷wanting to be teachers of the Law, even though they do not understand either what they are saying or the matters about which they make confident assertions.

. . . keeping *faith* and a good conscience, which some have rejected and suffered shipwreck in regard to their faith. [20]Among these are *Hymenaeus* and Alexander, whom I have handed over to Satan, so that they will be taught not to blaspheme.

1 Timothy 5:21

I *solemnly charge* you *in the presence of God* and of Christ Jesus and of His chosen angels, to maintain these principles without bias, doing nothing in a spirit of partiality.

1 Timothy 6:3–4, 20

If anyone advocates a different doctrine and does not agree with sound words, those of our Lord Jesus Christ, and with the doctrine conforming to godliness, [4]he is conceited and understands nothing; but he has a morbid interest in controversial questions and disputes about *words*, out of which arise envy, strife, abusive language, evil suspicions. . . . [20]O Timothy, guard what has been entrusted to you, *avoiding worldly and empty chatter* and the opposing arguments of what is falsely called "knowledge."

Titus 1:10–11

For there are many rebellious men, *empty* talkers and deceivers, especially those of the circumcision, [11]who must be silenced because they are upsetting whole families, teaching things they should not teach for the sake of sordid gain.

Titus 2:11–12

For the grace of God has appeared, bringing salvation to all men, [12]instructing us to deny *ungodliness* and *worldly* desires and to live sensibly, righteously and godly in the present age.

Titus 3:9

But *avoid* foolish controversies and genealogies and strife and disputes about the Law, for they are unprofitable and worthless.

OTHER BIBLICAL PARALLELS

Numbers 16:5

He spoke to Korah and all his company, saying, "Tomorrow morning *the* L ORD will show *who is His*, and who is holy, and will bring him near to Himself; even the one

whom He will choose, He will bring near to Himself."

Job 36:10

"He opens their ear to instruction, And commands that they return from evil."

Isaiah 26:13

O L ORD our God, other masters besides You have ruled us; But through You alone we confess Your *name.*

Isaiah 28:16

"Behold, I am laying in Zion a stone, a tested stone, A costly cornerstone for the *foundation, firmly* placed. He who believes in it will not be disturbed."

John 3:33

"He who has received His testimony has set his *seal* to this, that God is true."

John 10:14

"I am the good shepherd, and I *know* My own and My own know Me."

NONCANONICAL PARALLELS

The Acts of Paul and Thecla *14*

And Demas and Hermogenes said, . . . "And we shall teach you about *the resurrection* which he [Paul] says is to come, that it *has already taken place* in the children and that we rise again, after having come to the knowledge of the true God."

The Treatise on the Resurrection *49.9–24*

Therefore, do not [10]think in part, O Rheginos, nor live in conformity with this flesh for the sake of unanimity, but flee from the divisions and the [15]fetters, and *already* you have *the resurrection.* For if he who will die knows about himself that he will die—even if he spends many [20]years in this life, he is brought to this—why not consider yourself as risen and [already] brought to this?

2 Timothy 2:20–26

Now in a large house there are not only gold and silver vessels, but also vessels of wood and of earthenware, and some to honor and some to dishonor. [21]Therefore, if anyone cleanses himself from these things, he will be a vessel for honor, sanctified, useful to the Master, prepared for every good work. ²²Now flee from youthful lusts and pursue righteousness, faith, love and peace, with those who call on the Lord from a pure heart. ²³But refuse foolish and ignorant speculations, knowing that they produce quarrels. ²⁴The Lord's bond-servant must not be quarrelsome, but be kind to all, able to teach, patient when wronged, ²⁵with gentleness correcting those who are in opposition, if perhaps God may grant them repentance leading to the knowledge of the truth, ²⁶and they may come to their senses and escape from the snare of the devil, having been held captive by him to do his will.

2 TIMOTHY PARALLELS

2 Timothy 3:16–17

All Scripture is inspired by God and profitable for *teaching*, for reproof, for *correction*, for training in *righteousness*; ¹⁷so that the man of God may be adequate, equipped for *every good work*.

OTHER PAULINE PARALLELS

Romans 2:4

Or do you think lightly of the riches of His kindness and tolerance and patience, not knowing that the kindness of God leads you to *repentance*?

Romans 9:21

Or does not the potter have a right over the clay, to make from the same lump one *vessel* for *honorable* use and another for common use?

2 Corinthians 4:7

But we have this treasure in earthen *vessels*, so that the surpassing greatness of the power will be of God and not from ourselves.

Galatians 5:22

But the fruit of the Spirit is *love*, joy, *peace*, *patience*, *kindness*, goodness, *faithfulness*.

Galatians 6:1

Brethren, even if anyone is caught in any trespass, you who are spiritual, restore such a one in a spirit of *gentleness*; each one looking to yourself, so that you too will not be tempted.

Ephesians 2:10

For we are His workmanship, created in Christ Jesus for *good works*, which God *prepared* beforehand so that we would walk in them.

1 Timothy 1:4–5

. . . nor to pay attention to myths and endless genealogies, which give rise to mere *speculation* rather than furthering the administration of God which is by *faith*. ⁵But the goal of our instruction is *love* from a *pure heart* and a good conscience and a sincere faith.

1 Timothy 3:2–3, 6–7

An overseer, then, must be above reproach, the husband of one wife, temperate, prudent, respectable, hospitable, *able to teach*, ³not addicted to wine or pugnacious, but *gentle, peaceable*, free from the love of money, . . . ⁶and not a new convert, so that he will not become conceited and fall into the condemnation incurred by the devil. ⁷And he must have a good reputation with those outside the church, so that he will not fall into reproach and *the snare of the devil*.

1 Timothy 3:15

In case I am delayed, I write so that you will know how one ought to conduct himself in the *household* of God, which is the church of the living God, the pillar and support of *the truth*.

1 Timothy 6:3–5

If anyone advocates a different doctrine and does not agree with sound words, those of our Lord Jesus Christ, and with the doctrine conforming to godliness, ⁴he is conceited and understands nothing; but he has a morbid interest in controversial questions and disputes about words, out of which arise envy, strife, abusive language, evil suspicions, ⁵and constant friction between men of depraved mind and deprived of *the truth*, who suppose that godliness is a means of gain.

1 Timothy 6:11

But *flee* from these things, you man of God, and *pursue righteousness*, godliness, *faith*, *love*, perseverance and *gentleness*.

Titus 1:1

Paul, a *bond-servant* of God and an apostle of Jesus Christ, for the faith of those chosen of God and *the knowledge of the truth* which is according to godliness . . .

Titus 3:9–11

But avoid *foolish* controversies and genealogies and strife and disputes about the Law, for they are unprofitable and worthless. [10]Reject a factious man after a first and second warning, [11]knowing that such a man is perverted and is sinning, being self-condemned.

OTHER BIBLICAL PARALLELS

Luke 17:3

"Be on your guard! If your brother sins, rebuke him; and if he *repents*, forgive him."

Acts 8:22

"Therefore *repent* of this wickedness of yours, and pray the Lord that, if possible, the intention of your *heart* may be forgiven you."

Acts 11:18

When they heard this, they quieted down and glorified God, saying, "Well then, *God has granted* to the Gentiles also the *repentance* that leads to life."

James 4:1–2

What is the source of *quarrels* and conflicts among you? Is not the source your pleasures that wage war in your members? [2]You *lust* and do not have; so you commit murder. You are envious and cannot obtain; so you fight and quarrel. You do not have because you do not ask.

NONCANONICAL PARALLELS

Wisdom of Solomon 15:7

A potter kneads the soft earth and laboriously molds each vessel for our service, fashioning out of the same clay both the *vessels* that serve clean uses and those for contrary uses, making all alike; but which shall be the use of each of them the worker in clay decides.

2 Timothy 3:1–9

But realize this, that in the last days difficult times will come. [2]For men will be lovers of self, lovers of money, boastful, arrogant, revilers, disobedient to parents, ungrateful, unholy, [3]unloving, irreconcilable, malicious gossips, without self-control, brutal, haters of good, [4]treacherous, reckless, conceited, lovers of pleasure rather than lovers of God, [5]holding to a form of godliness, although they have denied its power; Avoid such men as these. [6]For among them are those who enter into households and captivate weak women weighed down with sins, led on by various impulses, [7]always learning and never able to come to the knowledge of the truth. [8]Just as Jannes and Jambres opposed Moses, so these men also oppose the truth, men of depraved mind, rejected in regard to the faith. [9]But they will not make further progress; for their folly will be obvious to all, just as Jannes's and Jambres's folly was also.

2 TIMOTHY PARALLELS

2 Timothy 2:12

If we endure, we will also reign with Him; If we *deny* Him, He also will deny us.

2 Timothy 4:3

For the *time will come* when they will not endure sound doctrine; but wanting to have their ears tickled, they will accumulate for themselves teachers in accordance to their own desires.

OTHER PAULINE PARALLELS

Romans 1:28–31

And just as they did not see fit to acknowledge God any longer, God gave them over to a *depraved mind,* to do those things which are not proper, [29]being filled with all unrighteousness, wickedness, greed, evil; full of envy, murder, strife, deceit, malice; they are *gossips,* [30]slanderers, haters of God, insolent, *arrogant, boastful,* inventors of evil, *disobedient to parents,* [31]without understanding, untrustworthy, *unloving,* unmerciful.

2 Thessalonians 3:6

Now we command you, brethren, in the name of our Lord Jesus Christ, that you keep away from every brother who leads an unruly life and not according to the tradition which you received from us.

1 Timothy 1:9–10

Law is not made for a righteous person, but for those who are lawless and rebellious, for the ungodly and *sinners,* for the *unholy* and profane, for those who kill their fathers or mothers, for murderers [10]and immoral men and homosexuals and kidnappers and liars and perjurers, and whatever else is contrary to sound teaching.

1 Timothy 4:1

But the Spirit explicitly says that in later *times* some will fall away from the *faith*, paying attention to deceitful spirits and doctrines of demons.

1 Timothy 4:7

But have nothing to do with worldly fables fit only for old *women*. On the other hand, discipline yourself for the purpose of *godliness*.

1 Timothy 5:6

But she who gives herself to wanton *pleasure* is dead even while she lives.

1 Timothy 6:3–5

If anyone advocates a different doctrine and does not agree with sound words, those of our Lord Jesus Christ, and with the doctrine conforming to *godliness*, [4]he is *conceited* and understands nothing; but he has a morbid interest in controversial questions and disputes about words, out of which arise envy, strife, abusive language, evil suspicions, [5]and constant friction between *men of depraved mind* and deprived of *the truth*, who suppose that godliness is a means of gain.

1 Timothy 6:10

For the *love of money* is a root of all sorts of evil, and some by longing for it have wandered away from *the faith* and pierced themselves with many griefs.

Titus 1:1

Paul, a bond-servant of God and an apostle of Jesus Christ, for *the faith* of those chosen of God and *the knowledge of the truth* which is according to *godliness* . . .

Titus 1:10–11, 16

For there are many rebellious men, empty talkers and deceivers, especially those of the circumcision, [11]who must be silenced because they are upsetting whole families, teaching things they should not teach for the sake of sordid gain. . . . [16]They profess to know God, but by their deeds they *deny*

Him, being detestable and *disobedient* and worthless for any good deed.

Titus 3:3

For we also once were foolish ourselves, *disobedient*, deceived, enslaved to various lusts and *pleasures*, spending our life in malice and envy, hateful, hating one another.

OTHER BIBLICAL PARALLELS

Exodus 7:10–12

So *Moses* and Aaron came to Pharaoh, and thus they did just as the LORD had commanded; and Aaron threw his staff down before Pharaoh and his servants, and it became a serpent. [11]Then Pharaoh also called for the wise men and the sorcerers, and they also, the magicians of Egypt, did the same with their secret arts. [12]For each one threw down his staff and they turned into serpents. But Aaron's staff swallowed up their staffs.

Exodus 8:18

The magicians tried with their secret arts to bring forth gnats, but they could not; so there were gnats on man and beast.

Exodus 9:11

The magicians could not stand before *Moses* because of the boils, for the boils were on the magicians as well as on all the Egyptians.

Jude 4

For certain persons have crept in unnoticed, those who were long beforehand marked out for this condemnation, ungodly persons who turn the grace of our God into licentiousness and *deny* our only Master and Lord, Jesus Christ.

Jude 18

"*In the last* time there will be mockers, following after their own ungodly lusts."

NONCANONICAL PARALLELS

The Damascus Document *(CD)* 5.17–19

For in ancient times there arose [18]*Moses* and Aaron, by the hand of the prince of lights and Belial, with his cunning, raised up *Jannes* and [19]his brother during the first deliverance of Israel.

2 Timothy 3:10–17

Now you followed my teaching, conduct, purpose, faith, patience, love, perseverance, [11]persecutions, and sufferings, such as happened to me at Antioch, at Iconium and at Lystra; what persecutions I endured, and out of them all the Lord rescued me! [12]Indeed, all who desire to live godly in Christ Jesus will be persecuted. [13]But evil men and impostors will proceed from bad to worse, deceiving and being deceived. [14]You, however, continue in the things you have learned and become convinced of, knowing from whom you have learned them, [15]and that from childhood you have known the sacred writings which are able to give you the wisdom that leads to salvation through faith which is in Christ Jesus. [16]All Scripture is inspired by God and profitable for teaching, for reproof, for correction, for training in righteousness; [17]so that the man of God may be adequate, equipped for every good work.

2 TIMOTHY PARALLELS

2 Timothy 1:5, 13

For I am mindful of the sincere *faith* within you, which first dwelt in your grandmother Lois and your mother Eunice, and I am sure that it is in you as well. . . . [13]Retain the standard of sound words which you have heard from me, in the faith and *love* which are in Christ Jesus.

2 Timothy 2:2

The things which you have heard from me in the presence of many witnesses, entrust these to faithful men who will be able to *teach* others also.

2 Timothy 2:10

For this reason I *endure* all things for the sake of those who are chosen, so that they also may obtain the *salvation* which is in Christ Jesus and with it eternal glory.

2 Timothy 2:21

Therefore, if anyone cleanses himself from these things, he will be a vessel for honor, sanctified, useful to the Master, prepared for *every good work.*

2 Timothy 4:18

The Lord will rescue me from every evil deed, and will bring me safely to His heavenly kingdom; to Him be the glory forever and ever. Amen.

OTHER PAULINE PARALLELS

Romans 15:4

For whatever was written in earlier times was written for our instruction, so that through *perseverance* and the encouragement of the *Scriptures* we might have hope.

1 Corinthians 10:11

Now these things happened to them as an example, and they were written for our instruction, upon whom the ends of the ages have come.

2 Corinthians 6:3–6

. . . giving no cause for offense in anything, so that the ministry will not be discredited, [4]but in everything commending ourselves as servants of God, in much *endurance*, in afflictions, in hardships, in distresses, [5]in beatings, in imprisonments, in tumults, in labors, in sleeplessness, in hunger, [6]in purity, in knowledge, in *patience*, in kindness, in the Holy Spirit, in genuine *love*.

2 Corinthians 12:10

Therefore I am well content with weaknesses, with insults, with distresses, with *persecutions*, with difficulties, for Christ's sake; for when I am weak, then I am strong.

Philippians 4:9

The things you have *learned* and received and heard and seen in me, practice these things, and the God of peace will be with you.

1 Timothy 4:12–13

Let no one look down on your youthfulness, but rather in speech, *conduct, love, faith* and purity, show yourself an example of those who believe. [13]Until I come, give attention to the public reading of *Scripture*, to exhortation and *teaching.*

1 Timothy 6:11

But flee from these things, you *man of God*, and pursue *righteousness, godliness, faith, love, perseverance* and gentleness.

Titus 1:9

. . . holding fast the faithful word which is in accordance with the *teaching*, so that he will be able both to exhort in sound doctrine and to refute those who contradict.

OTHER BIBLICAL PARALLELS

Matthew 24:5, 11

"For many will come in My name, saying, 'I am the Christ,' and will mislead many. . . . [11]Many false prophets will arise and will mislead many."

John 15:20

"Remember the word that I said to you, 'A slave is not greater than his master.' If they *persecuted* Me, they will also persecute you; if they kept My word, they will keep yours also."

Acts 13:14, 50

But going on from Perga, they arrived at Pisidian *Antioch*, and on the Sabbath day they went into the synagogue and sat down. . . . [50]But the Jews incited the devout women of prominence and the leading men of the city, and instigated a *persecution* against Paul and Barnabas, and drove them out of their district.

Acts 14:1, 5–6

In *Iconium* they entered the synagogue of the Jews together, and spoke in such a manner that a large number of people believed, both of Jews and of Greeks. . . . [5]And when an attempt was made by both the Gentiles and the Jews with their rulers, to mistreat and to stone them, [6]they became aware of it and fled to the cities of Lycaonia, *Lystra* and Derbe, and the surrounding region.

Acts 14:19

But Jews came from *Antioch* and *Iconium*, and having won over the crowds, they stoned Paul and dragged him out of the city, supposing him to be dead.

Acts 16:1

Paul came also to Derbe and to *Lystra*. And a disciple was there, named Timothy, the son of a Jewish woman who was a believer, but his father was a Greek.

2 Peter 1:20–21

But know this first of all, that no prophecy of *Scripture* is a matter of one's own interpretation, [21]for no prophecy was ever made by an act of human will, but men moved by the Holy Spirit spoke from God.

2 Timothy 4:1–5

I solemnly charge you in the presence of God and of Christ Jesus, who is to judge the living and the dead, and by His appearing and His kingdom: [2]preach the word; be ready in season and out of season; reprove, rebuke, exhort, with great patience and instruction. [3]For the time will come when they will not endure sound doctrine; but wanting to have their ears tickled, they will accumulate for themselves teachers in accordance to their own desires, [4]and will turn away their ears from the truth and will turn aside to myths. [5]But you, be sober in all things, endure hardship, do the work of an evangelist, fulfill your ministry.

2 TIMOTHY PARALLELS

2 Timothy 1:10

. . . but now has been revealed by the *appearing* of our Savior Christ Jesus, who abolished death and brought life and immortality to light through the gospel.

2 Timothy 1:13

Retain the standard of *sound* words which you have heard from me, in the faith and love which are in Christ Jesus.

2 Timothy 2:3

Suffer *hardship* with me, as a good soldier of Christ Jesus.

2 Timothy 2:14

Remind them of these things, and *solemnly charge* them *in the presence of God* not to wrangle about words, which is useless and leads to the ruin of the hearers.

2 Timothy 2:24

The Lord's bond-servant must not be quarrelsome, but be kind to all, able to teach, *patient* when wronged.

2 Timothy 3:1–2, 4, 7

But realize this, that in the last days difficult *times will come.* [2]For men will be lovers of self, lovers of money, boastful, arrogant, revilers, disobedient to parents, ungrateful, unholy, . . . [4]treacherous, reckless, conceited, lovers of pleasure rather than lovers of God, . . . [7]always learning and never able to come to the knowledge of *the truth.*

OTHER PAULINE PARALLELS

Ephesians 4:11–12

And He gave some as apostles, and some as prophets, and some as *evangelists,* and some as pastors and *teachers,* [12]for the equipping of the saints for the work of service, to the building up of the body of Christ.

Colossians 4:17

Say to Archippus, "Take heed to the *ministry* which you have received in the Lord, that you may *fulfill* it."

1 Thessalonians 2:10–12

You are witnesses, and so is God, how devoutly and uprightly and blamelessly we behaved toward you believers; [11]just as you know how we were *exhorting* and encouraging and imploring each one of you as a father would his own children, [12]so that you would walk in a manner worthy of the God who calls you into His own *kingdom* and glory.

1 Thessalonians 5:14

We urge you, brethren, admonish the unruly, encourage the fainthearted, help the weak, be *patient* with everyone.

1 Timothy 1:3–4, 6–7

As I urged you upon my departure for Macedonia, remain on at Ephesus so that you may *instruct* certain men not to teach strange *doctrines,* [4]nor to pay attention to *myths* and endless genealogies, which give rise to mere speculation rather than furthering the administration of God which is by faith. . . . [6]For some men, straying from these things, have *turned aside* to fruitless discussion, [7]wanting to be *teachers* of the Law, even though they do not understand either what they are saying or the matters about which they make confident assertions.

1 Timothy 4:1

But the Spirit explicitly says that in later times some will fall away from the faith, paying attention to deceitful spirits and *doctrines* of demons.

1 Timothy 5:1

Do not sharply *rebuke* an older man, but rather appeal to him as a father, to the younger men as brothers.

1 Timothy 5:20–21

Those who continue in sin, *rebuke* in the presence of all, so that the rest also will be fearful of sinning. [21]*I solemnly charge you in the presence of God and of Christ Jesus* and of His chosen angels, to maintain these principles without bias, doing nothing in a spirit of partiality.

1 Timothy 6:13–14

I charge you in the presence of God, who gives life to all things, *and of Christ Jesus,* who testified the good confession before Pontius Pilate, [14]that you keep the commandment without stain or reproach until the *appearing* of our Lord Jesus Christ.

Titus 1:13–14

For this reason *reprove* them severely so that they may be *sound* in the faith, [14]not paying attention to Jewish *myths* and commandments of men who *turn away from the truth.*

Titus 2:13–15

. . . looking for the blessed hope and the *appearing* of the glory of our great God and Savior, Christ Jesus, [14]who gave Himself for us to redeem us from every lawless deed, and to purify for Himself a people for His own possession, zealous for good deeds. [15]These things speak and *exhort* and *reprove* with all authority. Let no one disregard you.

OTHER BIBLICAL PARALLELS

Acts 10:42

"And He ordered us to *preach* to the people, and solemnly to testify that this is the One who has been appointed by God as *Judge of the living and the dead.*"

Acts 21:8

On the next day we left and came to Caesarea, and entering the house of Philip the *evangelist,* who was one of the seven, we stayed with him.

1 Peter 1:13

Therefore, prepare your minds for action, keep *sober* in spirit, fix your hope completely on the grace to be brought to you at the revelation of Jesus Christ.

2 Timothy 4:6–8

For I am already being poured out as a drink offering, and the time of my departure has come. ⁷I have fought the good fight, I have finished the course, I have kept the faith; ⁸in the future there is laid up for me the crown of righteousness, which the Lord, the righteous Judge, will award to me on that day; and not only to me, but also to all who have loved His appearing.

2 TIMOTHY PARALLELS

2 Timothy 1:10
. . . but now has been revealed by the *appearing* of our Savior Christ Jesus, who abolished death and brought life and immortality to light through the gospel.

2 Timothy 1:12
For this reason I also suffer these things, but I am not ashamed; for I know whom I have believed and I am convinced that He is able to guard what I have entrusted to Him until *that day.*

2 Timothy 2:5
Also if anyone competes as an athlete, he does not win the prize unless he competes according to the rules.

OTHER PAULINE PARALLELS

1 Corinthians 9:24–26
Do you not know that those who run in a race all run, but only one receives the prize? Run in such a way that you may win. ²⁵Everyone who competes in the games exercises self-control in all things. They then do it to receive a perishable wreath, but we an imperishable. ²⁶Therefore I run in such a way, as not without aim; I box in such a way, as not beating the air.

Philippians 1:23–24
But I am hard-pressed from both directions, having the desire to *depart* and be with Christ, for that is very much better; ²⁴yet to remain on in the flesh is more necessary for your sake.

Philippians 2:14–18
Do all things without grumbling or disputing; ¹⁵so that you will prove yourselves to be blameless and innocent, children of God above reproach in the midst of a crooked and perverse generation, among whom you appear as lights in the world, ¹⁶holding fast the word of life, so that in the *day* of Christ I will have reason to glory because I did not run in vain nor toil in vain. ¹⁷But even if *I am being poured out as a drink offering* upon the sacrifice and service of your *faith,* I rejoice and share my joy with you all. ¹⁸You too, I urge you, rejoice in the same way and share your joy with me.

1 Timothy 1:18–19
This command I entrust to you, Timothy, my son, in accordance with the prophecies previously made concerning you, that by them you *fight the good fight,* ¹⁹*keeping faith* and a good conscience, which some have rejected and suffered shipwreck in regard to their faith.

1 Timothy 6:12–15
Fight the good fight of *faith*; take hold of the eternal life to which you were called, and you made the good confession in the presence of many witnesses. ¹³I charge you in the presence of God, who gives life to all things, and of Christ Jesus, who testified the good confession before Pontius Pilate, ¹⁴that you keep the commandment without stain or reproach until the *appearing* of our Lord Jesus Christ, ¹⁵which He will bring about at the proper time.

OTHER BIBLICAL PARALLELS

Numbers 28:3, 7
"This is the offering by fire which you shall offer to the Lord: two male lambs one year old without defect as a continual burnt offering every day. . . . ⁷Then the drink offering with it shall be a fourth of a hin for each lamb, in the holy place you shall *pour out a drink offering* of strong drink to the Lord."

Psalm 7:11
God is a *righteous judge,* And a God who has indignation every day.

Acts 20:24
But I do not consider my life of any account as dear to myself, so that I may *finish* my

course and the ministry which I received from the Lord Jesus, to testify solemnly of the gospel of the grace of God.

Hebrews 12:1–2

Therefore, since we have so great a cloud of witnesses surrounding us, let us also lay aside every encumbrance and the sin which so easily entangles us, and let us run with endurance the race that is set before us, [2]fixing our eyes on Jesus, the author and perfecter of _faith_, who for the joy set before Him endured the cross, despising the shame, and has sat down at the right hand of the throne of God.

James 1:12

Blessed is a man who perseveres under trial; for once he has been approved, he will receive the _crown_ of life which the Lord has promised to those who _love_ Him.

NONCANONICAL PARALLELS

Wisdom of Solomon 5:15–16

But the _righteous_ live forever, and their reward is with the Lord; the Most High takes care of them. [16]Therefore they will receive a glorious _crown_ and a beautiful diadem from the hand of the Lord, because with his right hand he will cover them, and with his arm he will shield them.

4 Maccabees 17:11–15

Truly the contest in which they were engaged was divine, [12]for on that day virtue gave the awards and tested them for their endurance. The prize was immortality in endless life. [13]Eleazar was the first contestant, the mother of the seven sons entered the competition, and the brothers contended. [14]The tyrant was the antagonist, and the world and the human race were the spectators. [15]Reverence for God was victor and gave the _crown_ to its own athletes.

2 Timothy 4:9–15

Make every effort to come to me soon; [10]for Demas, having loved this present world, has deserted me and gone to Thessalonica; Crescens has gone to Galatia, Titus to Dalmatia. [11]Only Luke is with me. Pick up Mark and bring him with you, for he is useful to me for service. [12]But Tychicus I have sent to Ephesus. [13]When you come bring the cloak which I left at Troas with Carpus, and the books, especially the parchments. [14]Alexander the coppersmith did me much harm; the Lord will repay him according to his deeds. [15]Be on guard against him yourself, for he vigorously opposed our teaching.

2 TIMOTHY PARALLELS

2 Timothy 1:3–4

I thank God, whom I serve with a clear conscience the way my forefathers did, as I constantly remember you in my prayers night and day, [4]longing to see you, even as I recall your tears, so that I may be filled with joy.

2 Timothy 1:15–18

You are aware of the fact that all who are in Asia turned away from me, among whom are Phygelus and Hermogenes. [16]The Lord grant mercy to the house of Onesiphorus, for he often refreshed me and was not ashamed of my chains; [17]but when he was in Rome, he eagerly searched for me and found me— [18]the Lord grant to him to find mercy from the Lord on that day—and you know very well what _services_ he rendered at Ephesus.

2 Timothy 2:24–26

The Lord's bond-servant must not be quarrelsome, but be kind to all, able to teach, patient when wronged, [25]with gentleness correcting those who are in _opposition_, if perhaps God may grant them repentance leading to the knowledge of the truth, [26]and they may come to their senses and escape from the snare of the devil, having been held captive by him to do his will.

OTHER PAULINE PARALLELS

2 Corinthians 2:12

Now when I came to _Troas_ for the gospel of Christ and when a door was opened for me in the Lord . . .

2 Corinthians 8:23

As for _Titus_, he is my partner and fellow worker among you; as for our brethren, they are messengers of the churches, a glory to Christ.

Galatians 2:3

But not even *Titus*, who was with me, though he was a Greek, was compelled to be circumcised.

Ephesians 6:21–22

But that you also may know about my circumstances, how I am doing, *Tychicus*, the beloved brother and faithful minister in the Lord, will make everything known to you. *22I have sent* him to you for this very purpose, so that you may know about us, and that he may comfort your hearts.

Colossians 4:7, 10, 14

As to all my affairs, *Tychicus*, our beloved brother and faithful servant and fellow bond-servant in the Lord, will bring you information. . . . *10Aristarchus*, my fellow prisoner, sends you his greetings; and also Barnabas's cousin *Mark* (about whom you received instructions; if he comes to you, welcome him). . . . *14Luke*, the beloved physician, sends you his greetings, and also *Demas*.

1 Timothy 1:20

Among these are Hymenaeus and *Alexander*, whom I have handed over to Satan, so that they will be taught not to blaspheme.

1 Timothy 6:17

Instruct those who are rich in *this present world* not to be conceited or to fix their hope on the uncertainty of riches, but on God, who richly supplies us with all things to enjoy.

Titus 1:4

To *Titus*, my true child in a common faith: Grace and peace from God the Father and Christ Jesus our Savior.

Titus 3:12

When I send Artemas or *Tychicus* to you, *make every effort to come to me* at Nicopolis, for I have decided to spend the winter there.

Philemon 23–24

Epaphras, my fellow prisoner in Christ Jesus, greets you, *24as do Mark*, Aristarchus, *Demas, Luke*, my fellow workers.

Acts 12:12

And when he realized this, he went to the house of Mary, the mother of John who was also called *Mark*, where many were gathered together and were praying.

Acts 12:25

And Barnabas and Saul returned from Jerusalem when they had fulfilled their mission, taking along with them John, who was also called *Mark*.

Acts 15:37–39

Barnabas wanted to take John, called *Mark*, along with them also. *38But Paul kept insisting that they should not take him along who had deserted them in Pamphylia and had not gone with them to the work. *39And there occurred such a sharp disagreement that they separated from one another, and Barnabas took Mark with him and sailed away to Cyprus.

Acts 16:1, 8

Paul came also to Derbe and to Lystra. And a disciple was there, named Timothy, the son of a Jewish woman who was a believer, but his father was a Greek. . . . *8And passing by Mysia, they came down to *Troas*.

Acts 19:33–34

Some of the crowd concluded it was *Alexander*, since the Jews had put him forward; and having motioned with his hand, Alexander was intending to make a defense to the assembly. *34But when they recognized that he was a Jew, a single outcry arose from them all as they shouted for about two hours, "Great is Artemis of the Ephesians!"

Acts 20:4–6

And he was accompanied by Sopater of Berea, the son of Pyrrhus, and by Aristarchus and Secundus of the Thessalonians, and Gaius of Derbe, and Timothy, and *Tychicus* and Trophimus of Asia. *5But these had gone on ahead and were waiting for us at *Troas*. *6We sailed from Philippi after the days of Unleavened Bread, and came to them at Troas within five days; and there we stayed seven days.

The Acts of Paul and Thecla *1*

As Paul was going to Iconium after his flight from Antioch, his fellow-travelers were *Demas* and Hermogenes, the coppersmith, who were full of hypocrisy and flattered Paul as if they loved him.

2 Timothy 4:16–22

At my first defense no one supported me, but all deserted me; may it not be counted against them. [17]But the Lord stood with me and strengthened me, so that through me the proclamation might be fully accomplished, and that all the Gentiles might hear; and I was rescued out of the lion's mouth. [18]The Lord will rescue me from every evil deed, and will bring me safely to His heavenly kingdom; to Him be the glory forever and ever. Amen. [19]Greet Prisca and Aquila, and the household of Onesiphorus. [20]Erastus remained at Corinth, but Trophimus I left sick at Miletus. [21]Make every effort to come before winter. Eubulus greets you, also Pudens and Linus and Claudia and all the brethren. [22]The Lord be with your spirit. Grace be with you.

2 TIMOTHY PARALLELS

2 Timothy 1:15–16

You are aware of the fact that all who are in Asia turned away from me, among whom are Phygelus and Hermogenes. [16]The Lord grant mercy to *the house of Onesiphorus*, for he often refreshed me and was not ashamed of my chains.

2 Timothy 3:10–11

Now you followed my teaching, conduct, purpose, faith, patience, love, perseverance, [11]persecutions, and sufferings, such as happened to me at Antioch, at Iconium and at Lystra; what persecutions I endured, and out of them all *the Lord rescued me*!

OTHER PAULINE PARALLELS

Romans 1:4–5

. . . Jesus Christ our Lord, [5]through whom we have received grace and apostleship to bring about the obedience of faith among *all the Gentiles* for His name's sake.

Romans 16:3, 23, 27

Greet Prisca and Aquila, my fellow workers in Christ Jesus . . . [23]Gaius, host to me and to the whole church, greets you. *Erastus*, the city treasurer greets you, and Quartus, the brother. . . . [27]To the only wise God, through Jesus Christ, *be the glory forever. Amen.*

1 Corinthians 15:32

If from human motives I fought with wild beasts at Ephesus, what does it profit me? If the dead are not raised, LET US EAT AND DRINK, FOR TOMORROW WE DIE.

1 Corinthians 16:19

The churches of Asia *greet you. Aquila* and *Prisca* greet you heartily in the Lord, with the church that is in their house.

Philippians 1:12–14

Now I want you to know, brethren, that my circumstances have turned out for the greater progress of the gospel, [13]so that my imprisonment in the cause of Christ has become well known throughout the whole praetorian guard and to everyone else, [14]and that most of the brethren, trusting in the Lord because of my imprisonment, have far more courage to speak the word of God without fear.

Philippians 4:23

The *grace* of the Lord Jesus Christ *be with your spirit.*

Colossians 4:18

I, Paul, write this greeting with my own hand. Remember my imprisonment. *Grace be with you.*

1 Timothy 1:12

I thank Christ Jesus our Lord, who has *strengthened* me, because He considered me faithful, putting me into service.

1 Timothy 2:7

For this I was appointed a preacher and an apostle (I am telling the truth, I am not lying) as a teacher of *the Gentiles* in faith and truth.

Titus 1:2–3

. . . in the hope of eternal life, which God, who cannot lie, promised long ages ago, [3]but at the proper time manifested, even His word, in the *proclamation* with which I was entrusted according to the commandment of God our Savior.

Titus 3:12

When I send Artemas or Tychicus to you, *make every effort to come* to me at Nicopolis, for I have decided to spend the *winter* there.

OTHER BIBLICAL PARALLELS

Psalm 22:21

Save me from *the lion's mouth*; From the horns of the wild oxen You answer me.

Daniel 6:22

"My God sent His angel and shut *the lions' mouths* and they have not harmed me, inasmuch as I was found innocent before Him; and also toward you, O king, I have committed no crime."

Matthew 26:55–56

At that time Jesus said to the crowds, "Have you come out with swords and clubs to arrest Me as you would against a robber? Every day I used to sit in the temple teaching and you did not seize Me. [56]But all this has taken place to fulfill the Scriptures of the prophets." Then all the disciples left Him and fled.

Acts 7:59–60

They went on stoning Stephen as he called on the Lord and said, "Lord Jesus, receive my spirit!" [60]Then falling on his knees, he cried out with a loud voice, "Lord, do *not* hold this sin *against them*!" Having said this, he fell asleep.

Acts 18:2

And he found a Jew named *Aquila*, a native of Pontus, having recently come from Italy with his wife *Priscilla*, because Claudius had commanded all the Jews to leave Rome.

Acts 19:22

And having sent into Macedonia two of those who ministered to him, Timothy and *Erastus*, he himself stayed in Asia for a while.

Acts 20:4

And he was accompanied by Sopater of Berea, the son of Pyrrhus, and by Aristarchus and Secundus of the Thessalonians, and Gaius of Derbe, and Timothy, and Tychicus and *Trophimus* of Asia.

Acts 21:29

For they had previously seen *Trophimus* the Ephesian in the city with him, and they supposed that Paul had brought him into the temple.

NONCANONICAL PARALLELS

The Acts of Paul and Thecla *2, 5*

And a certain man, by name Onesiphorus, hearing that Paul was to come to Iconium, went out to meet him with his children Simmias and Zeno and his wife Lectra, in order that he might entertain him. Titus had informed him what Paul looked like. . . . [5]And after Paul had gone into *the house of Onesiphorus* there was great joy and bowing of knees and breaking of bread and the word of God about abstinence and the resurrection.

Titus

Titus 1:1–4

Paul, a bond-servant of God and an apostle of Jesus Christ, for the faith of those chosen of God and the knowledge of the truth which is according to godliness, ²in the hope of eternal life, which God, who cannot lie, promised long ages ago, ³but at the proper time manifested, even His word, in the proclamation with which I was entrusted according to the commandment of God our Savior, ⁴To Titus, my true child in a common faith: Grace and peace from God the Father and Christ Jesus our Savior.

TITUS PARALLELS

Titus 3:4–7

But when the kindness of *God our Savior* and His love for mankind appeared, ⁵He saved us, not on the basis of deeds which we have done in righteousness, but according to His mercy, by the washing of regeneration and renewing by the Holy Spirit, ⁶whom He poured out upon us richly through *Jesus Christ our Savior*, ⁷so that being justified by His grace we would be made heirs according to *the hope of eternal life.*

OTHER PAULINE PARALLELS

Romans 1:1–2, 7

Paul, a bond-servant of Christ Jesus, called as *an apostle*, set apart for the gospel of God, ²which He *promised* beforehand through His prophets in the holy Scriptures, . . . ⁷to all who are beloved of God in Rome, called as saints: *Grace* to you and *peace from God* our *Father* and the Lord *Jesus Christ.*

Romans 16:25–26

Now to Him who is able to establish you according to my gospel and the preaching of

Jesus Christ, according to the revelation of the mystery which has been kept secret for *long ages* past, ²⁶but now is *manifested*, and by the Scriptures of the prophets, *according to the commandment of* the eternal *God*, has been made known to all the nations, leading to obedience of *faith.*

2 Corinthians 8:23

As for *Titus*, he is my partner and fellow worker among you; as for our brethren, they are messengers of the churches, a glory to Christ.

Colossians 1:25–26

Of this church I was made a minister according to the stewardship from God bestowed on me for your benefit, so that I might fully carry out the preaching of the *word* of God, ²⁶that is, the mystery which has been hidden from the past *ages* and generations, but has now been *manifested* to His saints.

1 Timothy 1:1–2, 11

Paul, an apostle of Christ Jesus *according to the commandment of God our Savior*, and of Christ Jesus, who is our *hope*, ²To Timothy, *my true child in* the *faith*: Grace, mercy and peace from God the Father and Christ Jesus our Lord. . . . ¹¹according to the glorious gospel of the blessed God, with which I have been *entrusted.*

1 Timothy 2:2–6

. . . so that we may lead a tranquil and quiet life in all *godliness* and dignity. ³This is good and acceptable in the sight of *God our Savior*, ⁴who desires all men to be saved and to come to *the knowledge of the truth.* ⁵For there is one God, and one mediator also between God and men, the man Christ

Jesus, [6]who gave Himself as a ransom for all, the testimony given *at the proper time.*

1 Timothy 6:3–4
If anyone advocates a different doctrine and does not agree with sound words, those of our Lord Jesus Christ, and with the doctrine conforming to *godliness,* [4]he is conceited and understands nothing.

2 Timothy 1:1–2
Paul, an apostle of Christ Jesus by the will of God, according to the *promise* of *life* in Christ Jesus, [2]To Timothy, my beloved son: *Grace,* mercy and *peace from God the Father and Christ Jesus* our Lord.

2 Timothy 1:9–10
. . . who has saved us and called us with a holy calling, not according to our works, but according to His own purpose and grace which was granted us in Christ Jesus from all eternity, [10]but now has been revealed by the appearing of *our Savior Christ Jesus,* who abolished death and brought *life* and immortality to light through the gospel.

2 Timothy 2:13
If we are faithless, He remains faithful, for He cannot deny Himself.

2 Timothy 4:10
Demas, having loved this present world, has deserted me and gone to Thessalonica; Crescens has gone to Galatia, *Titus* to Dalmatia.

2 Timothy 4:17
But the Lord stood with me and strengthened me, so that through me the *proclamation* might be fully accomplished, and that all the Gentiles might hear; and I was rescued out of the lion's mouth.

OTHER BIBLICAL PARALLELS

Numbers 23:19
"*God* is not a man, that He should *lie,* Nor a son of man, that He should repent; Has He said, and will He not do it? Or has He spoken, and will He not make it good?"

Isaiah 45:15
Truly, You are a God who hides Himself, O God of Israel, *Savior!*

Luke 1:47
And my spirit has rejoiced in *God* my *Savior.*

Hebrews 6:18
. . . so that by two unchangeable things in which it is impossible for *God* to *lie,* we who have taken refuge would have strong encouragement to take hold of the *hope* set before us.

James 1:1
James, *a bond-servant of God* and of the Lord Jesus Christ, To the twelve tribes who are dispersed abroad: Greetings.

2 Peter 1:1–2
Simon Peter, *a bond-servant* and *apostle of Jesus Christ,* To those who have received a *faith* of the same kind as ours, by the righteousness of *our God* and *Savior, Jesus Christ:* [2]*Grace and peace* be multiplied to you in *the knowledge* of God and of Jesus our Lord.

NONCANONICAL PARALLELS

Dio Chrysostom, Orations *1.84*
And this is what made him [Heracles] *Savior* of the earth and of humankind, not that he protected them from wild beasts, . . . but that he punished savage and wicked men and crushed and destroyed the power of arrogant tyrants.

Titus 1:5–9

For this reason I left you in Crete, that you would set in order what remains and appoint elders in every city as I directed you, [6]namely, if any man is above reproach, the husband of one wife, having children who believe, not accused of dissipation or rebellion. [7]For the overseer must be above reproach as God's steward, not self-willed, not quick-tempered, not addicted to wine, not pugnacious, not fond of sordid gain, [8]but hospitable, loving what is good, sensible, just, devout, self-controlled, [9]holding fast the faithful word which is in accordance with the teaching, so that he will be able both to exhort in sound doctrine and to refute those who contradict.

Titus 2:1–4

But as for you, speak the things which are fitting for *sound doctrine*. [2]Older men are to be temperate, dignified, *sensible*, sound in faith, in love, in perseverance. [3]Older women likewise are to be reverent in their behavior, not malicious gossips nor enslaved to much *wine*, teaching *what is good*, [4]so that they may encourage the young women to love their *husbands*, to love their *children*.

OTHER PAULINE PARALLELS

1 Corinthians 4:1–2

Let a man regard us in this manner, as servants of Christ and *stewards* of the mysteries of God. [2]In this case, moreover, it is required of stewards that one be found trustworthy.

Ephesians 5:18

And do not get drunk with *wine*, for that is *dissipation*, but be filled with the Spirit.

Philippians 1:1

Paul and Timothy, bond-servants of Christ Jesus, To all the saints in Christ Jesus who are in Philippi, including the *overseers* and deacons . . .

2 Thessalonians 2:15

So then, brethren, stand firm and *hold* to the traditions which you were taught, whether by word of mouth or by letter from us.

1 Timothy 3:1–4

It is a trustworthy statement: if any man aspires to the office of *overseer*, it is a fine work he desires to do. [2]An overseer, then, must be *above reproach, the husband of one wife*, temperate, prudent, respectable, *hospitable*, able to teach, [3]*not addicted to wine* or *pugnacious*, but gentle, peaceable, free from the love of money. [4]He must be one who manages his own household well, keeping his *children* under control with all dignity.

1 Timothy 3:8, 10, 12

Deacons likewise must be men of dignity, not double-tongued, or *addicted to much wine* or *fond of sordid gain*. . . . [10]These men must also first be tested; then let them serve as deacons if they are beyond *reproach*. . . . [12]Deacons must be *husbands of* only *one wife*, and good managers of their *children* and their own households.

1 Timothy 4:6

In pointing out these things to the brethren, you will be a good servant of Christ Jesus, constantly nourished on the words of the faith and of the *sound doctrine* which you have been following.

1 Timothy 5:17–20

The *elders* who rule well are to be considered worthy of double honor, especially those who work hard at preaching and *teaching*. [18]For the Scripture says, "YOU SHALL NOT MUZZLE THE OX WHILE HE IS THRESHING," and "The laborer is worthy of his wages." [19]Do not receive an accusation against an elder except on the basis of two or three witnesses. [20]Those who continue in sin, rebuke in the presence of all, so that the rest also will be fearful of sinning.

2 Timothy 4:3–4

For the time will come when they will not endure *sound doctrine*; but wanting to have their ears tickled, they will accumulate for themselves teachers in accordance to their own desires, [4]and will turn away their ears from the truth and will turn aside to myths.

OTHER BIBLICAL PARALLELS

Numbers 11:16–17

The LORD therefore said to Moses, "Gather for Me seventy men from the *elders* of Israel, whom you know to be the elders of the people and their officers and bring them to the tent of meeting, and let them take their stand there with you. [17]Then I will come down and speak with you there, and I will take of the Spirit who is upon you, and will put Him upon them; and they shall bear the burden of the people with you, so that you will not bear it all alone."

Acts 14:20–23

The next day he went away with Barnabas to Derbe. [21]After they had preached the gospel to that city and had made many disciples, they returned to Lystra and to Iconium and to Antioch, [22]strengthening the souls of the disciples, encouraging them to continue in the faith, and saying, "Through many tribulations we must enter the kingdom of God." ²³When they had *appointed elders* for them in every church, having prayed with fasting, they commended them to the Lord in whom they had *believed.*

Acts 20:28

"Be on guard for yourselves and for all the flock, among which the Holy Spirit has made you *overseers,* to shepherd the church of God which He purchased with His own blood."

Acts 27:7–8

When we had sailed slowly for a good many days, and with difficulty had arrived off Cnidus, since the wind did not permit us to go farther, we sailed under the shelter of *Crete,* off Salmone; ⁸and with difficulty sailing past it we came to a place called Fair Havens, near which was the city of Lasea.

1 Peter 5:1–2

Therefore, I exhort the *elders* among you, as your fellow elder and witness of the sufferings of Christ, and a partaker also of the glory that is to be revealed, ²shepherd the flock of God among you, exercising oversight not under compulsion, but voluntarily, according to the will of God; and not for *sordid gain,* but with eagerness.

NONCANONICAL PARALLELS

Testament of Judah *16:1*

"Take care to be temperate with *wine,* my children; for there are in it four evil spirits: desire, heated passion, debauchery, and *sordid* greed."

Titus 1:10–16

For there are many rebellious men, empty talkers and deceivers, especially those of the circumcision, ¹¹who must be silenced because they are upsetting whole families, teaching things they should not teach for the sake of sordid gain. ¹²One of themselves, a prophet of their own, said, "Cretans are always liars, evil beasts, lazy gluttons." ¹³This testimony is true. For this reason reprove them severely so that they may be sound in the faith, ¹⁴not paying attention to Jewish myths and commandments of men who turn away from the truth. ¹⁵To the pure, all things are pure; but to those who are defiled and unbelieving, nothing is pure, but both their mind and their conscience are defiled. ¹⁶They profess to know God, but by their deeds they deny Him, being detestable and disobedient and worthless for any good deed.

TITUS PARALLELS

Titus 2:15

These things speak and exhort and *reprove* with all authority. Let no one disregard you.

Titus 3:3

For we also once were foolish ourselves, *disobedient, deceived,* enslaved to various lusts and pleasures, spending our life in malice and envy, hateful, hating one another.

OTHER PAULINE PARALLELS

Romans 14:14, 20

I know and am convinced in the Lord Jesus that nothing is unclean in itself; but to him who thinks anything to be unclean, to him it is unclean. . . . ²⁰Do not tear down the work of God for the sake of food. All things indeed are clean, but they are evil for the man who eats and gives offense.

Romans 16:18

For such men are slaves, not of our Lord Christ but of their own appetites; and by their smooth and flattering speech they *deceive* the hearts of the unsuspecting.

2 Corinthians 11:13

For such men are false apostles, *deceitful* workers, disguising themselves as apostles of Christ.

Galatians 2:11–12

But when Cephas came to Antioch, I opposed him to his face, because he stood condemned. ¹²For prior to the coming of certain men from James, he used to eat with the Gentiles; but when they came, he began to withdraw and hold himself aloof, fearing the party of *the circumcision.*

Philippians 3:2

Beware of the dogs, beware of the evil workers, beware of *the* false *circumcision.*

Colossians 2:20–22

If you have died with Christ to the elementary principles of the world, why, as if you were living in the world, do you submit yourself to decrees, such as, [21]"Do not handle, do not taste, do not touch!" [22](which all refer to things destined to perish with use)—in accordance with the *commandments* and teachings *of men*?

1 Timothy 1:3–9

As I urged you upon my departure for Macedonia, remain on at Ephesus so that you may instruct certain men not to *teach* strange doctrines, [4]nor to *pay attention to myths* and endless genealogies, which give rise to mere speculation rather than furthering the administration of God which is by *faith*. [5]But the goal of our instruction is love from a pure heart and a good *conscience* and a sincere faith. [6]For some men, straying from these things, have turned aside to fruitless discussion, [7]wanting to be *teachers* of the Law, even though they do not understand either what they are saying or the matters about which they make confident assertions. [8]But we know that the Law is good, if one uses it lawfully, [9]realizing the fact that law is not made for a righteous person, but for those who are lawless and *rebellious*, for the ungodly and sinners, for the unholy and profane.

1 Timothy 4:4–5

For everything created by God is good, and nothing is to be rejected if it is received with gratitude; [5]for it is sanctified by means of the word of God and prayer.

1 Timothy 6:3–5

If anyone advocates a different doctrine and does not agree with *sound* words, those of our Lord Jesus Christ, and with the doctrine conforming to godliness, [4]he is conceited and understands nothing; but he has a morbid interest in controversial questions and disputes about words, out of which arise envy, strife, abusive language, evil suspicions, [5]and constant friction between men of depraved mind and deprived of *the truth*, who suppose that godliness is a means of *gain*.

1 Timothy 6:20–21

O Timothy, guard what has been entrusted to you, avoiding worldly and *empty* chatter and the opposing arguments of what is falsely called "knowledge"— [21]which some have *professed* and thus gone astray from *the faith*.

2 Timothy 3:6

For among them are those who enter into households and captivate weak women weighed down with sins, led on by various impulses.

2 Timothy 4:2–4

Preach the word; be ready in season and out of season; *reprove*, rebuke, exhort, with great patience and instruction. [3]For the time will come when they will not endure *sound* doctrine; but wanting to have their ears tickled, they will accumulate for themselves *teachers* in accordance to their own desires, [4]and will *turn away* their ears from *the truth* and will turn aside to *myths*.

OTHER BIBLICAL PARALLELS

Luke 11:39–41

But the Lord said to him, "Now you Pharisees clean the outside of the cup and of the platter; but inside of you, you are full of robbery and wickedness. [40]You foolish ones, did not He who made the outside make the inside also? [41]But give that which is within as charity, and then all things are clean for you."

Acts 10:14–15

But Peter said, "By no means, Lord, for I have never eaten anything unholy and unclean." [15]Again a voice came to him a second time, "What God has cleansed, no longer consider unholy."

1 John 2:4

The one who says, "I have come *to know* Him," and does not keep His commandments, is a *liar*, and the truth is not in him.

NONCANONICAL PARALLELS

Clement of Alexandria, Stromata *1.59.2–3*

. . . Epimenides of Crete, whom the apostle Paul mentions in his letter to Titus, saying as follows: "*One of themselves, a prophet, said* as follows, '*Cretans are always liars, evil beasts, lazy gluttons.*' [3]And *this testimony is true*." Do you see how he grants a measure of truth to the prophets of Greece as well and is not ashamed, in a discussion designed to build them up and direct them to self-examination, to use Greek poems?

Polybius, Histories 6.47.5
Except in a few extreme cases can one find personal conduct more guileful and public policy more unjust than in *Crete*.

Titus 2:1–10

But as for you, speak the things which are fitting for sound doctrine. ²Older men are to be temperate, dignified, sensible, sound in faith, in love, in perseverance. ³Older women likewise are to be reverent in their behavior, not malicious gossips nor enslaved to much wine, teaching what is good, ⁴so that they may encourage the young women to love their husbands, to love their children, ⁵to be sensible, pure, workers at home, kind, being subject to their own husbands, so that the word of God will not be dishonored. ⁶Likewise urge the young men to be sensible; ⁷in all things show yourself to be an example of good deeds, with purity in doctrine, dignified, ⁸sound in speech which is beyond reproach, so that the opponent will be put to shame, having nothing bad to say about us. ⁹Urge bondslaves to be subject to their own masters in everything, to be well-pleasing, not argumentative, ¹⁰not pilfering, but showing all good faith so that they will adorn the doctrine of God our Savior in every respect.

TITUS PARALLELS

Titus 1:3
. . . but at the proper time manifested, even His word, in the proclamation with which I was entrusted according to the commandment of *God our Savior*.

Titus 1:7–9
For the overseer must be above *reproach* as God's steward, not self-willed, not quick-tempered, not addicted to *wine*, not pugnacious, not fond of sordid gain, ⁸but hospitable, loving *what is good, sensible*, just, devout, self-controlled, ⁹holding fast the faithful word which is in accordance with the *teaching*, so that he will be able both to exhort in *sound doctrine* and to refute those who contradict.

OTHER PAULINE PARALLELS

1 Corinthians 14:34
The *women* are to keep silent in the churches; for they are not permitted to speak, but are to *subject* themselves, just as the Law also says.

Ephesians 5:22
Wives, be *subject* to your own *husbands*, as to the Lord.

Ephesians 6:5–8
Slaves, be obedient to those who are your *masters* according to the flesh, with fear and trembling, in the sincerity of your heart, as to Christ; ⁶not by way of eyeservice, as men-pleasers, but as slaves of Christ, doing the will of God from the heart. ⁷With good will render service, as to the Lord, and not to men, ⁸knowing that whatever good thing each one does, this he will receive back from the Lord, whether slave or free.

Philippians 3:17
Brethren, join in following my *example*, and observe those who walk according to the pattern you have in us.

Colossians 3:22–24
Slaves, in all things obey those who are your *masters* on earth, not with external service, as those who merely please men, but with sincerity of heart, fearing the Lord. ²³Whatever you do, do your work heartily, as for the Lord rather than for men, ²⁴knowing that from the Lord you will receive the reward of the inheritance. It is the Lord Christ whom you serve.

1 Timothy 2:11, 15
A woman must quietly receive instruction with entire submissiveness. . . . ¹⁵But *women* will be preserved through the bearing of *children* if they continue in *faith* and *love* and sanctity with self-restraint.

1 Timothy 3:2–4, 7–8
An overseer, then, must be above *reproach*, the husband of one wife, *temperate*, prudent, respectable, hospitable, able to *teach*, ³not addicted to *wine* or pugnacious, but gentle, peaceable, free from the love of money. ⁴He must be one who manages his own household well, keeping his *children* under control with all *dignity*. . . . ⁷And he must have a good reputation with those out-

side the church, so that he will not fall into reproach and the snare of the devil. [8]Deacons likewise must be men of dignity, not double-tongued, or addicted to much wine or fond of sordid gain.

1 Timothy 3:11
Women must likewise be *dignified, not malicious gossips*, but *temperate*, faithful in all things.

1 Timothy 4:12
Let no one look down on your youthfulness, but rather in *speech*, conduct, *love, faith* and *purity, show yourself an example* of those who believe.

1 Timothy 5:1–2
Do not sharply rebuke an *older man*, but rather appeal to him as a father, to the *younger men* as brothers, [2]the *older women* as mothers, and the *younger women* as sisters, in all *purity*.

1 Timothy 5:13–14
At the same time they also learn to be idle, as they go around from house to house; and not merely idle, but also *gossips* and busybodies, talking about things not proper to mention. [14]Therefore, I want younger widows to get married, bear *children*, keep house, and give the enemy no occasion for *reproach*.

1 Timothy 6:1–2
All who are under the yoke as *slaves* are to regard their own *masters* as worthy of all honor so that the name of God and our *doctrine* will not be spoken against. [2]Those who have believers as their masters must not be disrespectful to them because they are brethren, but must serve them all the more, because those who partake of the benefit are believers and beloved.

OTHER BIBLICAL PARALLELS

Matthew 24:45
"Who then is the faithful and *sensible slave* whom his master put in charge of his household to give them their food at the proper time?"

1 Peter 2:12
Keep your behavior excellent among the Gentiles, so that in the thing in which they

slander you as evildoers, they may because of your *good deeds*, as they observe them, glorify God in the day of visitation.

1 Peter 2:18
Servants, be submissive to your *masters* with all respect, not only to those who are good and gentle, but also to those who are unreasonable.

NONCANONICAL PARALLELS

Xenophon, Memorabilia *2.1.16*
Let us consider this as well, how *masters* treat such *slaves*. Do they not discipline them with hunger so there is no desire in them? Do they not prevent them from stealing by locking up anything that might be taken? Do they not stop them from escaping with chains? Do they not force the laziness out of them with blows?

Titus 2:11–15

For the grace of God has appeared, bringing salvation to all men, [12]instructing us to deny ungodliness and worldly desires and to live sensibly, righteously and godly in the present age, [13]looking for the blessed hope and the appearing of the glory of our great God and Savior, Christ Jesus, [14]who gave Himself for us to redeem us from every lawless deed, and to purify for Himself a people for His own possession, zealous for good deeds. [15]These things speak and exhort and reprove with all authority. Let no one disregard you.

TITUS PARALLELS

Titus 1:1, 4
Paul, a bond-servant of God and an apostle of Jesus Christ, for the faith of those chosen of God and the knowledge of the truth which is according to *godliness*, . . . [4]To Titus, my true child in a common faith: *Grace* and peace from God the Father and *Christ Jesus our Savior*.

OTHER PAULINE PARALLELS

Galatians 1:3–4
. . . the Lord Jesus Christ, [4]*who gave Himself* for our sins so that He might rescue us from

this *present* evil *age*, according to the will of our God and Father.

Philippians 3:20–21

For our citizenship is in heaven, from which also we eagerly wait for a *Savior*, the Lord *Jesus Christ*; [21]who will transform the body of our humble state into conformity with the body of His *glory*.

1 Timothy 2:3–6

This is good and acceptable in the sight of *God our Savior*, [4]who desires *all men* to be saved and to come to the knowledge of the truth. [5]For there is one God, and one mediator also between God and men, the man Christ Jesus, [6]*who gave Himself* as a ransom for all, the testimony given at the proper time.

1 Timothy 4:10–13

For it is for this we labor and strive, because we have fixed our *hope* on the living God, who is the *Savior* of *all men*, especially of believers. [11]Prescribe and teach these things. [12]Let no one look down on your youthfulness, but rather in speech, conduct, love, faith and purity, show yourself an example of those who believe. [13]Until I come, give attention to the public reading of Scripture, to *exhortation* and teaching.

1 Timothy 6:13–14

I charge you in the presence of God, who gives life to all things, and of Christ Jesus, who testified the good confession before Pontius Pilate, [14]that you keep the commandment without stain or reproach until *the appearing of* our Lord *Jesus Christ*.

2 Timothy 1:8–10

. . . God, [9]who has saved us and called us with a holy calling, not according to our works, but according to His own purpose and *grace* which was granted us in Christ Jesus from all eternity, [10]but now has been revealed by *the appearing* of *our Savior Christ Jesus*, who abolished death and brought life and immortality to light through the gospel.

2 Timothy 2:21

Therefore, if anyone cleanses himself from these things, he will be a vessel for honor, sanctified, useful to the Master, prepared for every *good* work.

2 Timothy 3:12

Indeed, all who desire to live *godly* in Christ Jesus will be persecuted.

2 Timothy 4:2

Preach the word; be ready in season and out of season; *reprove*, rebuke, *exhort*, with great patience and instruction.

OTHER BIBLICAL PARALLELS

Deuteronomy 7:6

"For you are a holy people to the Lord your God; the Lord your God has chosen you to be *a people for His own possession* out of all the peoples who are on the face of the earth."

Psalm 130:8

And He will *redeem* Israel From all his iniquities.

Ezekiel 36:25, 31

"Then I will sprinkle clean water on you, and you will be clean; I will cleanse you from all your filthiness and from all your idols. . . . [31]Then you will remember your evil ways and your *deeds* that were not good, and you will loathe yourselves in your own sight for your iniquities and your abominations."

1 Peter 1:18–19

. . . knowing that you were not *redeemed* with perishable things like silver or gold from your futile way of life inherited from your forefathers, [19]but with precious blood, as of a lamb unblemished and spotless, the blood of Christ.

1 Peter 3:13

Who is there to harm you if you prove *zealous for* what is *good*?

2 Peter 1:1

Simon Peter, a bond-servant and apostle of Jesus Christ, To those who have received a faith of the same kind as ours, by the righteousness of *our God and Savior, Jesus Christ* . . .

NONCANONICAL PARALLELS

2 Maccabees 3:30

And the temple, which a little while before was full of fear and disturbance, was filled with joy and gladness, now that the Almighty Lord had *appeared.*

Plato, *Gorgias* 507C

The *sensible* man, because he is *righteous* and brave and pious, is, as we have seen, a completely good man, and the good man does well and admirably whatever he does.

Ephesus: Inscription (SIG 3.760)

The cities that are in Asia and the [districts] and the tribes: (in honor of) Gaius Julius, son of Gaius, Caesar, Pontifex Maximus, Imperator and consul for the second time, descended from Ares and Aphrodite, the *god* who has *appeared* and *savior* of human life everywhere.

Titus 3:1–8

Remind them to be subject to rulers, to authorities, to be obedient, to be ready for every good deed, ²to malign no one, to be peaceable, gentle, showing every consideration for all men. ³For we also once were foolish ourselves, disobedient, deceived, enslaved to various lusts and pleasures, spending our life in malice and envy, hateful, hating one another. ⁴But when the kindness of God our Savior and His love for mankind appeared, ⁵He saved us, not on the basis of deeds which we have done in righteousness, but according to His mercy, by the washing of regeneration and renewing by the Holy Spirit, ⁶whom He poured out upon us richly through Jesus Christ our Savior, ⁷so that being justified by His grace we would be made heirs according to the hope of eternal life. ⁸This is a trustworthy statement; and concerning these things I want you to speak confidently, so that those who have believed God will be careful to engage in good deeds. These things are good and profitable for men.

TITUS PARALLELS

Titus 1:1–4

Paul, a bond-servant of God and an apostle of Jesus Christ, for the faith of those chosen of God and the knowledge of the truth which is according to godliness, ²in *the hope of eternal life*, which God, who cannot lie, promised long ages ago, ³but at the proper time manifested, even His word, in the proclamation with which I was entrusted according to the commandment of *God our Savior*, ⁴To Titus, my true child in a common faith: Grace and peace from God the Father and *Christ Jesus our Savior.*

Titus 1:16

They profess to know God, but by their deeds they deny Him, being detestable and *disobedient* and worthless for any *good deed.*

OTHER PAULINE PARALLELS

Romans 1:29–30

. . . being filled with all unrighteousness, wickedness, greed, evil; full of *envy*, murder, strife, deceit, *malice*; they are gossips, ³⁰slanderers, haters of God, insolent, arrogant, boastful, inventors of evil, *disobedient* to parents.

Romans 3:23–24, 28

For all have sinned and fall short of the glory of God, ²⁴being *justified* as a gift *by His grace* through the redemption which is in Christ Jesus; . . . ²⁸For we maintain that a man is justified by faith apart from works of the Law.

Romans 5:5

Hope does not disappoint, because the *love* of God has been *poured out* within our hearts through *the Holy Spirit* who was given to us.

Romans 8:16–17

The Spirit Himself testifies with our spirit that we are children of God, ¹⁷and if children, *heirs* also, heirs of God and fellow heirs with Christ, if indeed we suffer with Him so that we may also be glorified with Him.

Romans 12:2

And do not be conformed to this world, but be transformed by the *renewing* of your mind, so that you may prove what the will of God is, that which is *good* and acceptable and perfect.

Romans 13:1

Every person is to be in *subjection* to the governing *authorities*. For there is no authority except from God, and those which exist are established by God.

Ephesians 2:4–5, 7–9

But God, being rich in *mercy*, because of His great *love* with which He loved us, ⁵even when we were dead in our transgressions, made us alive together with Christ (by *grace* you have been *saved*), . . . [7]so that in the ages to come He might show the surpassing riches of His grace in *kindness* toward us in Christ Jesus. [8]For by grace you have been saved through faith; and that not of yourselves, it is the gift of God; [9]not as a result of works, so that no one may boast.

1 Timothy 2:1–4

First of all, then, I urge that entreaties and prayers, petitions and thanksgivings, be made on behalf of *all men,* [2]for kings and all who are in *authority,* so that we may lead a tranquil and quiet life in all godliness and dignity. [3]This is good and acceptable in the sight of *God our Savior,* [4]who desires all men to be *saved* and to come to the knowledge of the truth.

2 Timothy 1:8–10

. . . God, [9]who has *saved us* and called us with a holy calling, not according to our works, but according to His own purpose and *grace* which was granted us in Christ Jesus from all eternity, [10]but now has been revealed by the appearing of *our Savior Christ Jesus,* who abolished death and brought *life* and immortality to light through the gospel.

2 Timothy 3:2–4, 13

For men will be lovers of self, lovers of money, boastful, arrogant, revilers, *disobedient* to parents, ungrateful, unholy, [3]unloving, irreconcilable, malicious gossips, without self-control, brutal, haters of good, [4]treacherous, reckless, conceited, lovers of *pleasure* rather than lovers of God. . . . [13]But evil men and impostors will proceed from bad to worse, deceiving and being *deceived.*

Matthew 19:28–29

"Truly I say to you, that you who have followed Me, in the *regeneration* when the Son of Man will sit on His glorious throne, you also shall sit upon twelve thrones, judging the twelve tribes of Israel. [29]And everyone who has left houses or brothers or sisters or father or mother or children or farms for My name's sake, will receive many times as much, and will inherit *eternal life.*"

Acts 10:45

All the circumcised believers who came with Peter were amazed, because the gift of *the Holy Spirit* had been *poured out* on the Gentiles also.

1 Peter 2:13–14

Submit yourselves for the Lord's sake to every human institution, whether to a king as the one in *authority,* [14]or to governors as sent by him for the punishment of evildoers and the praise of those who do right.

Baruch 4:22

For I have put my *hope* in the Everlasting to *save* you, and joy has come to me from the Holy One, because of the *mercy* that will soon come to you from your everlasting *savior.*

Philo, On the Cherubim *99*

If we are going to welcome [mortal] kings, we brighten and prepare our homes. . . . What sort of house shall be prepared for God the King of kings and Ruler of all, who in his *mercy* and *love for mankind* has deigned to visit creation and descend from the heights of heaven to the ends of the earth to show his goodness to humanity?

Philo, On the Cherubim *114*

What becomes of it [the soul] after death? At that time those of us who are an embodied compound of substances will hasten to a *regeneration,* to join those who are unbodied, having no compound or substance.

Titus 3:9–15

But avoid foolish controversies and genealogies and strife and disputes about the Law, for they are unprofitable and worthless. [10]Reject a factious man after a first and second warning, [11]knowing that such a man is perverted and is sinning, being self-condemned. [12]When I send Artemas or Tychicus to you, make every effort to come to me at Nicopolis, for I have decided to spend the winter there. [13]Diligently help Zenas the lawyer and Apollos on their way so that nothing is lacking for them. [14]Our people must also learn to engage in good deeds to meet pressing needs, so that they will not be unfruitful. [15]All who are with me greet you. Greet those who love us in the faith. Grace be with you all.

Titus 1:13–14, 16

This testimony is true. For this reason reprove them severely so that they may be sound in the faith, [14]not paying attention to Jewish myths and commandments of men who turn away from the truth. . . . [16]They profess to know God, but by their deeds they deny Him, being detestable and disobedient and *worthless* for any *good deed.*

OTHER PAULINE PARALLELS

Romans 16:17

Now I urge you, brethren, keep your eye on those who cause dissensions and hindrances contrary to the teaching which you learned, and turn away from them.

1 Corinthians 16:6, 12, 20

Perhaps I will stay with you, or even *spend the winter,* so that you may send me on my way wherever I may go. . . . [12]But concerning *Apollos* our brother, I encouraged him greatly to come to you with the brethren; and it was not at all his desire to come now, but he will come when he has opportunity. . . . [20]*All* the brethren *greet you. Greet* one another with a holy kiss.

Ephesians 6:21–24

But that you also may know about my circumstances, how I am doing, *Tychicus,* the beloved brother and faithful minister in the Lord, will make everything known to you. [22]*I* have *sent* him *to you* for this very purpose, so that you may know about us, and that he may comfort your hearts. [23]Peace be to the brethren, and love with *faith,* from God the Father and the Lord Jesus Christ. [24]*Grace be with all* those who *love* our Lord Jesus Christ with incorruptible love.

Philippians 4:21

Greet every saint in Christ Jesus. The brethren *who are with me greet you.*

Colossians 4:7–8

As to all my affairs, *Tychicus,* our beloved brother and faithful servant and fellow bond-servant in the Lord, will bring you

information. [8]For *I* have *sent* him *to you* for this very purpose, that you may know about our circumstances and that he may encourage your hearts.

Colossians 4:18

I, Paul, write this greeting with my own hand. Remember my imprisonment. *Grace be with you.*

2 Thessalonians 3:18

The *grace* of our Lord Jesus Christ *be with you all.*

1 Timothy 1:3–7

As I urged you upon my departure for Macedonia, remain on at Ephesus so that you may instruct certain men not to teach strange doctrines, [4]nor to pay attention to myths and endless *genealogies,* which give rise to mere speculation rather than furthering the administration of God which is by faith. [5]But the goal of our instruction is *love* from a pure heart and a good conscience and a sincere *faith.* [6]For some men, straying from these things, have turned aside to fruitless discussion, [7]wanting to be teachers of *the Law,* even though they do not understand either what they are saying or the matters about which they make confident assertions.

1 Timothy 6:3–5

If anyone advocates a different doctrine and does not agree with sound words, those of our Lord Jesus Christ, and with the doctrine conforming to godliness, [4]he is conceited and understands nothing; but he has a morbid interest in *controversial* questions and *disputes* about words, out of which arise envy, *strife,* abusive language, evil suspicions, [5]and constant friction between men of depraved mind and deprived of the truth, who suppose that godliness is a means of gain.

2 Timothy 2:14, 16, 23

Remind them of these things, and solemnly charge them in the presence of God not to wrangle about words, which is useless and leads to the ruin of the hearers. . . . [16]But *avoid* worldly and empty chatter, for it will lead to further ungodliness. . . . [23]But refuse *foolish* and ignorant speculations, knowing that they produce quarrels.

2 Timothy 4:9–12

Make every effort to come to me soon; [10]for Demas, having loved this present world, has deserted me and gone to Thessalonica; Crescens has gone to Galatia, Titus to Dalmatia. [11]Only Luke is with me. Pick up Mark and bring him with you, for he is useful to me for service. [12]But *Tychicus I* have *sent* to Ephesus.

2 Timothy 4:21–22

Make every effort to come before *winter.* Eubulus *greets you,* also Pudens and Linus and Claudia and *all* the brethren. [22]The Lord be with your spirit. *Grace be with you.*

OTHER BIBLICAL PARALLELS

Matthew 18:15–17

"If your brother *sins,* go and show him his fault in private; if he listens to you, you have won your brother. [16]But if he does not listen to you, take one or two more with you, so that BY THE MOUTH OF TWO OR THREE WITNESSES EVERY FACT MAY BE CONFIRMED. [17]If he refuses to listen to them, tell it to the church; and if he refuses to listen even to the church, let him be to you as a Gentile and a tax collector."

Acts 18:24

Now a Jew named *Apollos,* an Alexandrian by birth, an eloquent man, came to Ephesus; and he was mighty in the Scriptures.

Acts 20:4

And he was accompanied by Sopater of Berea, the son of Pyrrhus, and by Aristarchus and Secundus of the Thessalonians, and Gaius of Derbe, and Timothy, and *Tychicus* and Trophimus of Asia.

NONCANONICAL PARALLELS

Philo, On Moses 2.45–47

The most holy books . . . [46]have a historical part as well as a second part, which is concerned with commands and prohibitions. . . . [47]The historical part is then further divided into the account of the world's creation and the *genealogies,* which concern both the punishment of the impious and the honoring of the righteous.

Philemon

Philemon 1–9

Paul, a prisoner of Christ Jesus, and Timothy our brother, To Philemon our beloved brother and fellow worker, ²and to Apphia our sister, and to Archippus our fellow soldier, and to the church in your house: ³Grace to you and peace from God our Father and the Lord Jesus Christ. ⁴I thank my God always, making mention of you in my prayers, ⁵because I hear of your love and of the faith which you have toward the Lord Jesus and toward all the saints; ⁶and I pray that the fellowship of your faith may become effective through the knowledge of every good thing which is in you for Christ's sake. ⁷For I have come to have much joy and comfort in your love, because the hearts of the saints have been refreshed through you, brother. ⁸Therefore, though I have enough confidence in Christ to order you to do what is proper, ⁹yet for love's sake I rather appeal to you—since I am such a person as Paul, the aged, and now also a prisoner of Christ Jesus.

PHILEMON PARALLELS

Philemon 20–21
  Yes, brother, let me benefit from you in the Lord; *refresh* my *heart* in Christ. ²¹Having *confidence* in your obedience, I write to you, since I know that you will do even more than what I say.

OTHER PAULINE PARALLELS

Romans 1:8–10
  First, *I thank my God* through Jesus Christ for you all, because your *faith* is being proclaimed throughout the whole world. ⁹For God, whom I serve in my spirit in the

preaching of the gospel of His Son, is my witness as to how unceasingly I *make mention of you*, ¹⁰always *in my prayers* making request, if perhaps now at last by the will of God I may succeed in coming to you.

1 Corinthians 16:17–18
  I rejoice over the coming of Stephanas and Fortunatus and Achaicus, because they have supplied what was lacking on your part. ¹⁸For they have *refreshed* my spirit and yours. Therefore acknowledge such men.

2 Corinthians 1:1–2
  Paul, an apostle of Christ Jesus by the will of God, and *Timothy our brother*, To *the church* of God which is at Corinth with all *the saints* who are throughout Achaia: ²*Grace to you and peace from God our Father and the Lord Jesus Christ.*

2 Corinthians 7:4, 13
  I am filled with *comfort*; I am overflowing with *joy* in all our affliction. . . . ¹³And besides our comfort, we rejoiced even much more for the joy of Titus, because his spirit has been *refreshed* by you all.

Ephesians 1:15–17
  For this reason I too, having *heard* of the *faith* in the Lord Jesus which exists among you and your *love* for *all the saints*, ¹⁶do not cease giving *thanks* for you, while *making mention of you in my prayers*; ¹⁷that the God of our Lord Jesus Christ, the Father of glory, may give to you a spirit of wisdom and of revelation in the *knowledge* of Him.

Ephesians 3:1
  For this reason I, *Paul*, the *prisoner* of Christ Jesus for the sake of you Gentiles . . .

Philippians 1:1–4, 7, 9–10

Paul and *Timothy*, bond-servants of Christ Jesus, To all the saints in Christ Jesus who are in Philippi, including the overseers and deacons: [2]*Grace to you and peace from God our Father and the Lord Jesus Christ.* [3]*I thank my God* in all my remembrance of you, [4]always offering prayer with *joy* in my every *prayer* for you all. . . . [7]For it is only right for me to feel this way about you all, because I have you in my heart, since both in my *imprisonment* and in the defense and confirmation of the gospel, you all are partakers of grace with me. . . . [9]And this I pray, that your *love* may abound still more and more in real *knowledge* and all discernment, [10]so that you may approve the things that are excellent, in order to be sincere and blameless until the day of Christ.

Philippians 2:25

But I thought it necessary to send to you Epaphroditus, my *brother* and *fellow worker* and *fellow soldier*, who is also your messenger and minister to my need.

Colossians 1:1–4

Paul, an apostle of Jesus Christ by the will of God, and *Timothy our brother*, [2]To the saints and faithful brethren in Christ who are at Colossae: *Grace to you and peace from God our Father.* [3]We give *thanks* to *God*, the Father of our Lord Jesus Christ, *praying always* for you, [4]since we *heard* of your *faith* in Christ Jesus and the *love* which you have for *all the saints.*

Colossians 4:15–17

Greet the brethren who are in Laodicea and also Nympha and the church that is in her house. [16]When this letter is read among you, have it also read in the church of the Laodiceans; and you, for your part read my letter that is coming from Laodicea. [17]Say to *Archippus*, "Take heed to the ministry which you have received in the Lord, that you may fulfill it."

1 Thessalonians 1:2–3

We give *thanks* to *God always* for all of you, *making mention of you in* our *prayers*; [3]constantly bearing in mind your work of *faith* and labor of *love* and steadfastness of hope in our Lord Jesus Christ in the presence of our God and Father.

1 Thessalonians 2:5–6

For we never came with flattering speech, as you know, nor with a pretext for greed— God is witness— [6]nor did we seek glory from men, either from you or from others, even though as apostles of Christ we might have asserted our authority.

2 Timothy 1:8

Therefore do not be ashamed of the testimony of our Lord or of me His *prisoner*, but join with me in suffering for the gospel according to the power of God.

2 Timothy 2:3–4

Suffer hardship with me, as a good *soldier* of Christ Jesus. [4]No soldier in active service entangles himself in the affairs of everyday life, so that he may please the one who enlisted him as a soldier.

OTHER BIBLICAL PARALLELS

Leviticus 19:32

"You shall rise up before the grayheaded and honor *the aged*, and you shall revere your God; I am the LORD."

Acts 16:1

Paul came also to Derbe and to Lystra. And a disciple was there, named *Timothy*, the son of a Jewish woman who was a believer, but his father was a Greek.

Philemon 10–16

I appeal to you for my child Onesimus, whom I have begotten in my imprisonment, [11]who formerly was useless to you, but now is useful both to you and to me. [12]I have sent him back to you in person, that is, sending my very heart, [13]whom I wished to keep with me, so that on your behalf he might minister to me in my imprisonment for the gospel; [14]but without your consent I did not want to do anything, so that your goodness would not be, in effect, by compulsion but of your own free will. [15]For perhaps he was for this reason separated from you for a while, that you would have him back forever, [16]no longer as a slave, but more than a slave, a beloved brother, especially to me, but how much more to you, both in the flesh and in the Lord.

1 Corinthians 4:14–15

I do not write these things to shame you, but to admonish you as *my* beloved *children.* [15]For if you were to have countless tutors in Christ, yet you would not have many fathers, for in Christ Jesus I became your father through *the gospel.*

1 Corinthians 7:21–24

Were you called while *a slave*? Do not worry about it; but if you are able also to become free, rather do that. [22]For he who was called in the Lord while a slave, is the Lord's freedman; likewise he who was called while free, is Christ's slave. [23]You were bought with a price; do not become slaves of men. [24]Brethren, each one is to remain with God in that condition in which he was called.

2 Corinthians 9:7

Each one must do just as he has purposed in his heart, not grudgingly or under *compulsion,* for God loves a cheerful giver.

Galatians 3:28

There is neither Jew nor Greek, there is neither *slave* nor free man, there is neither male nor female; for you are all one in Christ Jesus.

Galatians 4:19

My children, with whom I am again in labor until Christ is formed in you . . .

Ephesians 6:5

Slaves, be obedient to those who are your masters according to *the flesh,* with fear and trembling, in the sincerity of your heart, as to Christ.

Philippians 1:7

For it is only right for me to feel this way about you all, because I have you in my *heart,* since both in *my imprisonment* and in the defense and confirmation of *the gospel,* you all are partakers of grace with me.

Philippians 2:25, 29

But *I* thought it necessary to *send to you* Epaphroditus, my brother and fellow worker and fellow soldier, who is also your messenger and *minister* to my need. . . .

[29]Receive him then in the Lord with all joy, and hold men like him in high regard.

Colossians 4:7–9

As to all my affairs, Tychicus, our beloved brother and faithful servant and fellow bond-servant in the Lord, will bring you information. [8]For *I have sent him to you* for this very purpose, that you may know about our circumstances and that he may encourage your hearts; [9]and with him *Onesimus,* our faithful and *beloved brother,* who is one of your number. They will inform you about the whole situation here.

Colossians 4:18

I, Paul, write this greeting with my own hand. Remember *my imprisonment.*

1 Timothy 6:2

Those who have believers as their masters must not be disrespectful to them because they are brethren, but must serve them all the more, because those who partake of the benefit are believers and *beloved.* Teach and preach these principles.

2 Timothy 2:8–9

Remember Jesus Christ, risen from the dead, descendant of David, according to my *gospel,* [9]for which I suffer hardship even to *imprisonment* as a criminal; but the word of God is not imprisoned.

2 Timothy 4:11

Only Luke is with me. Pick up Mark and bring him with you, for he is *useful* to me for service.

Deuteronomy 23:15–16

"You shall not hand over to his master *a slave* who has escaped from his master to you. [16]He shall live with you in your midst, in the place which he shall choose in one of your towns where it pleases him; you shall not mistreat him."

1 Peter 5:1–2

Therefore, I exhort the elders among you, as your fellow elder and witness of the sufferings of Christ, and a partaker also of the glory that is to be revealed, [2]shepherd the flock of God among you, exercising oversight not under *compulsion,* but voluntarily, according to the will of God; and not for sordid gain, but with eagerness.

Xenophon, Memorabilia *2.1.16*

Let us consider this as well, how masters treat such *slaves.* Do they not discipline them with hunger so there is no desire in them? Do they not prevent them from stealing by locking up anything that might be taken? Do they not stop them from escaping with chains? Do they not force the laziness out of them with blows?

Pliny the Younger, Epistles *9.21*

Your freedman with whom you said you were angry has been with me; he threw himself at my feet and clung to me as if I were you. He begged me . . . to intercede for him; in short, he convinced me of his sincere repentance. . . . Let me prevail with you to pardon him. . . . I am afraid that if I add my prayers to his I would seem to be using *compulsion* rather than persuasion in asking you to pardon him.

Letter to Stotoetis (BGU 37)

I have sent you my Blastus for forked sticks for my olive gardens. See that you do not *keep* him; for you know how I need him every moment.

Philemon 17–25

If then you regard me a partner, accept him as you would me. ¹⁸But if he has wronged you in any way or owes you anything, charge that to my account; ¹⁹I, Paul, am writing this with my own hand, I will repay it (not to mention to you that you owe to me even your own self as well). ²⁰Yes, brother, let me benefit from you in the Lord; refresh my heart in Christ. ²¹Having confidence in your obedience, I write to you, since I know that you will do even more than what I say. ²²At the same time also prepare me a lodging, for I hope that through your prayers I will be given to you. ²³Epaphras, my fellow prisoner in Christ Jesus, greets you, ²⁴as do Mark, Aristarchus, Demas, Luke, my fellow workers. ²⁵The grace of the Lord Jesus Christ be with your spirit.

Philemon 1

Paul, a *prisoner* of Christ Jesus, and Timothy our brother, To Philemon our beloved brother and *fellow worker* . . .

Philemon 7–8

For I have come to have much joy and comfort in your love, because the *hearts* of the saints have been *refreshed* through you, brother. ⁸Therefore, though I have enough *confidence* in Christ to order you to do what is proper . . .

Romans 15:7

Therefore, *accept* one another, just as Christ also accepted us to the glory of God.

Romans 15:30, 32

Now I urge you, brethren, by our Lord Jesus Christ and by the love of the Spirit, to strive together with me in *your prayers* to God for me, . . . ³²so that I may come to you in joy by the will of God and find *refreshing* rest in your company.

1 Corinthians 16:21

The greeting is in *my own hand—Paul.*

2 Corinthians 1:9–11

Indeed, we had the sentence of death within ourselves so that we would not trust in ourselves, but in God who raises the dead; ¹⁰who delivered us from so great a peril of death, and will deliver us, He on whom we have set our hope. And He will yet deliver us, ¹¹you also joining in helping us *through your prayers*, so that thanks may be given by many persons on our behalf for the favor bestowed on us through the prayers of many.

2 Corinthians 2:3

This is the very thing I wrote you, so that when I came, I would not have sorrow from those who ought to make me rejoice; having *confidence* in you all that my joy would be the joy of you all.

Galatians 6:11, 18

See with what large letters *I am writing* to you *with my own hand.* . . . ¹⁸*The grace of* our

Lord Jesus Christ be with your spirit, brethren. Amen.

Philippians 2:23–24

Therefore I hope to send him [Timothy] immediately, as soon as I see how things go with me; [24]and I trust in the Lord that I myself also will be coming shortly.

Colossians 1:7–8

. . . just as you learned it from *Epaphras,* our beloved fellow bond-servant, who is a faithful servant of Christ on our behalf, [8]and he also informed us of your love in the Spirit.

Colossians 4:10, 12–14

Aristarchus, my fellow prisoner, sends you his greetings; and also Barnabas's cousin *Mark* (about whom you received instructions; if he comes to you, welcome him); . . . [12]*Epaphras,* who is one of your number, a bondslave of Jesus Christ, sends you his greetings, always laboring earnestly for you in his prayers, that you may stand perfect and fully assured in all the will of God. [13]For I testify for him that he has a deep concern for you and for those who are in Laodicea and Hierapolis. [14]*Luke,* the beloved physician, sends you his greetings, and also *Demas.*

2 Thessalonians 3:17

I, *Paul, write* this greeting *with my own hand,* and this is a distinguishing mark in every letter; this is the way I write.

1 Timothy 3:14

I am writing these things to you, hoping to come to you before long.

2 Timothy 4:9–11

Make every effort to come to me soon; [10]for *Demas,* having loved this present world, has deserted me and gone to Thessalonica; Crescens has gone to Galatia, Titus to Dalmatia. [11]Only *Luke* is with me. Pick up *Mark* and bring him with you, for he is useful to me for service.

2 Timothy 4:22

The Lord *be with your spirit. Grace* be with you.

OTHER BIBLICAL PARALLELS

Acts 15:37–39

Barnabas wanted to take John, called *Mark,* along with them also. [38]But Paul kept insisting that they should not take him along who had deserted them in Pamphylia and had not gone with them to the work. [39]And there occurred such a sharp disagreement that they separated from one another, and Barnabas took Mark with him and sailed away to Cyprus.

Acts 19:29

The city was filled with the confusion, and they rushed with one accord into the theater, dragging along Gaius and *Aristarchus,* Paul's traveling companions from Macedonia.

Acts 27:2

And embarking in an Adramyttian ship, which was about to sail to the regions along the coast of Asia, we put out to sea accompanied by *Aristarchus,* a Macedonian of Thessalonica.

Hebrews 13:18–19

Pray for us, for we are sure that we have a good conscience, desiring to conduct ourselves honorably in all things. [19]And I urge you all the more to do this, so that I may be restored to you the sooner.